The Tate Gallery 1982–84

The Tate Gallery 1982–84

ILLUSTRATED CATALOGUE OF ACQUISITIONS

Contents

cover illustration
Raoul Dufy, **Cornfield** 1929   ©DACS
T 03564

ISBN 0 946590 49 4
Published by order of the Trustees 1986
Copyright © 1986 The Tate Gallery
Designed and published by Tate Gallery Publications
Millbank, London SWIP 4RG
Printed and bound in Great Britain by
Butler & Tanner Limited, Frome and London

Foreword

This volume catalogues all the acquisitions made through purchase, gift and bequest by the Trustees of the Tate Gallery between April 1982 and March 1984. A total of 1136 works are catalogued – 104 for the Historic British Collection (that is, artists born before 1860) and 400 for the Modern Collection, together with 632 for the Print Department. This is an exceptionally large number; indeed never before have so many works entered the Gallery in a two year period.

This may help to explain why, on this occasion, there are some omissions in the notes on the modern works acquired. A choice had to be made between accepting that some entries would be missing, or delaying publication, and despite the misgivings of the curatorial staff I have decided that we must go ahead. Some of the notes of the works are now major, almost essay-length studies, containing invaluable original material often supplied by the artists themselves, and it is not sensible to continue to print such contributions only in the Biennial catalogues. Our first priority is now the multi-volume series of catalogues that will shortly begin to appear. The names of the Tate Gallery curators who have written the catalogue entries appear on page 6; they have been generously helped by many artists, collectors, scholars, dealers, museum officials and others to whom we owe our sincere thanks.

The pages that follow will make plain the enormous debt which is owed by the Tate Gallery to our many benefactors. Once again we are grateful to the National Heritage Memorial Fund, the National Art-Collections Fund, the Contemporary Art Society, and of course, the Friends of the Tate Gallery, together with their new affiliate, the Patrons of New Art. Of particular importance in the two years under review have been the bequest from Mrs Kessler of her choice post-impressionist collection, the gift of fifty-seven sculptures by Lipchitz from the Jacques and Yulla Lipchitz Foundation, and the anonymous donation in memory of Terence Rattigan of a remarkable collection of works ranging from Thomas Churchyard to William Johnstone, centred on a group of turn of the century oil sketches. To them and to all our friends and benefactors the Tate Gallery remains profoundly indebted.

Alan Bowness *Director*

Entries in the British Collection have been written by
Martin Butlin, Leslie Parris, Elizabeth Einberg, Judy Egerton,
Robin Hamlyn

Entries in the Modern Collection have been written by
Ronald Alley, Richard Morphet, David Fraser Jenkins, Richard Francis,
Catherine Lacey, Richard Calvocoressi, Judith Collins, Jeremy Lewison,
Ann Jones, Paul Moorhouse, Rosemary Harris, Krzysztof Cieszkowski,
Jane Savidge, Caroline da Costa, Pat Turner, Susan Liddell,
Sarah Tinsley, Julia von Meijer, Helen Sloan

Entries in the Print Collection have been written by
Elizabeth Knowles, Jeremy Lewison, Paul Moorhouse

The British Collection

Henry Anderton c.1630–1665

T 03543 Mountain Landscape with Dancing Shepherd c.1650–60

Oil on canvas 18 × 23½ (457 × 597)
Inscribed 'Anderton Fecit' on rock, centre
foreground
Bequeathed by Hugh Paget CBE 1982
Prov: ...; ? Marchioness of Bath (old label on
frame); ...; acquired by the donor in
Mexico
Exh: *English Pictures from Suffolk Houses*,
Agnew, February–March 1980(1)
Lit: B. Buckeridge, 'An Essay towards an
English School' in De Piles, *The Art of
Painting*, 1754, p.355; M.H. Grant, *The
Old English Landscape Painters*, I, 1957,
p.60, pl.17, fig.36

This is the only known signed work by a painter who
according to Buckeridge's 'Essay' (written in 1706) was
a pupil of the Serjeant Painter Robert Streeter (1625–
79). He started as a landscape and still-life painter, but
later, after he 'fell to face Painting', he is said to have
rivalled Lely in portraiture. His most famous painting
was a half-length of the Duchess of Richmond which,
according to Mrs Beale's *Diary* (Vertue IV, *Walpole
Society*, XXIV, 1936, p.173) was in 1677 in the collection
of Baptist May, Keeper of the Privy Purse to Charles
II. Virtually nothing else is known about him, except
that 'he studied some years after the antique' in Rome.
   This painting strongly reflects the influence of the

Dutch Romanist school of landscape painting which
Anderton would have studied during his stay in Italy,
and was probably painted after his return home from
abroad.

James Barry 1741–1806

T 03784 –03788 Five engravings from the series after 'The Progress of Human Culture and Knowledge' first published 1792–5

Etching and engraving on hand-made
paper, various sizes, each cut close to
plate-mark
Purchased (Grant-in-Aid) 1983
Prov: ...; Christopher Mendez, from whom bt
by the Tate Gallery
Exh: James Barry, *An Account of the Series of
Pictures in the Great Room of the Society
of Arts, Manufacturers and Commerce at
the Adelphi*, 1783, reprinted in [ed. Dr
Edward Fryer], *The Works of James Barry,
Esq....*, II, 1809, pp.301–415 (also
abridged in [ed. D.G.C. Allan], *The
Progress of Human Knowledge: A Brief
Description of the Paintings by James Barry
in the ... Great Room of the Royal Society
of Arts*, 1974 and later eds.); James Barry,
*A Letter to the ... President, Vice
Presidents and the Rest of the Noblemen and
Gentlemen of the Society ... of Arts*, 1793,
reprinted in *Works ...*, II, 1809, pp.417–
74; D.G.C. Allan, 'The Progress of
Human Knowledge and Culture; James
Barry's Paintings for the Royal Society of
Arts ... 1777–1801', part i, *Connoisseur*,
CLXXXVI, 1974, pp.100–109, part ii,
Connoisseur, CLXXXVIII, 1975, pp.98–107;
William L. Pressly, *The Life and Art of
James Barry*, 1981, pp.86–122, 127–32,
'Catalogue of Prints', pp.263, 272–9

The Society of Arts, Manufacturers and Commerce,
founded in 1754, moved in 1772 into a house designed
by Robert and James Adam, behind the Strand and
opposite the Adelphi, in a street now called John Adam
Street (where the Society still thrives). The Society then

invited nine artists including Barry to paint pictures for its new Great Room; this invitation was declined. In 1777 Barry proposed to the Society that he should undertake the entire decoration of the Great Room without fee (the Society providing him with canvases, paints and models); this offer was accepted. Barry painted a series of six large canvases, each twelve feet high and of varying widths, which were installed as murals in the Great Room, his decorative sequence being interrupted (to his displeasure) only by portraits of the Society's first President by Gainsborough and the second President by Reynolds.

In Barry's words, the unifying purpose of his paintings for the Society of Arts was to illustrate 'one great maxim or moral truth, viz. that the obtaining of happiness, as well individual and public, depends upon cultivating the human faculties. We begin with man in a savage state ... and we follow him through several gradations of culture and happiness, which, after our probationary state here, are finally attended with beatitude or misery' (*Account*, 1783, reprinted in *Works*, p.322). He gave the six subjects individual titles; these titles, in order of the paintings' narrative sequence and their arrangement round the room, are 'Orpheus', 'A Grecian Harvest-Home', 'Crowning the Victors at Olympia', 'Commerce, or the Triumph of the Thames', 'The Distribution of Premiums in the Society of Arts' and 'Elysium, or the State of Final Retribution'. Though neither Barry nor the Society gave the paintings or Barry's prints after them a collective title, such a title evolved as 'The Progress of Human Culture and Knowledge', by which both paintings and prints are now generally known.

In 1783, when his paintings for the Great Room were virtually finished, Barry published a pamphlet inviting subscriptions to a series of six prints, one after each painting. He first published these six 'large' prints in 1792. Between 1793 and c.1802, he engraved and published six further 'small' prints of details from the paintings. One of these, 'The Diagorides Victors' (T 03788), was taken from 'The Crowning of the Victors at Olympia'; the other five were of different groups of figures in 'Elysium'. Barry also engraved a double plate of 'King George and Queen Charlotte', whose portraits he had hoped to paint as 'the two Grand Centres' of his scheme for the Great Room. The six 'large' and six 'small' and the double royal portrait were republished after Barry's death as a volume, with letterpress, entitled *A Series of Etchings by James Barry, Esq from his Original and Justly Celebrated Paintings in the ... Society of Arts*, 1808.

Barry had discussed the subject-matter of his paintings for the Great Room in his *Account* of 1783. He discussed his engravings of them in his *Letter* of February 1793. In this he pointed out firstly, that his account of the paintings would be 'misleading' to a student of the prints, as he had made many 'alterations'

in them necessitated by reducing the scale from the 'natural heroic size' of his paintings (twelve feet high) to a height of seventeen inches, a size governed by the size of paper and glass available rather than by the proportions of the paintings. Barry's prints of the subjects are certainly by no means purely reproductive, as their composition and details show many alterations. Secondly, he explained (*Letter* 1793, reprinted *Works*, p.421) that he had intended to publish the large prints and his account of them simultaneously; but as he had met with 'disappointment' from the printers, he had been obliged to print the engravings himself. This delayed their publication by a year (the 'large' prints bear the publication date 1791, but were not in fact issued until May 1792), and 'this labour so fatigued me that I let the prints go out without any writing to notify the alterations'. Characteristically, Barry suspected a conspiracy which 'tampered with' his printers; he refers to a 'dark and dirty influence' and to a 'long steadily continued Machiavellian industry, which has followed this work, and endeavoured to quash and interrupt it in every stage of its progress'.

Barry continued to add or alter details both in the paintings and in the prints. The numbering of the various states of the prints is established in Pressly 1981 ('Catalogue of Prints', pp.263–81) and followed here. Pressly (p.131) quotes a bill, said to be in Barry's handwriting, but undated, which includes '3 sets of "Human Culture" ... £18 18 0', indicating that Barry had begun to use the short title 'Human Culture' for his Society of Arts paintings and that he charged six guineas for each set of the prints.

One detail of Barry's fifth picture, 'The Distribution of Premiums in the Society of Arts', is of special relevance to Barry's print-making. In his *Account* of 1783 Barry describes his inclusion of various items for which the Society had awarded premiums and bounties; these include 'large paper of a loose and spongy quality, proper for copperplate printing, which is, and has long been a very great desideratum, as our engravers (whose works are now a considerable article of commerce) are for the most part obliged to make use of French grand aigle and colombiez, at six times the price of what paper of the same quality might be manufactured for in England' (p.348). Evidently Barry used 'paper of a loose and spongy quality' for making his Society of Arts prints.

T 03784 **A Grecian Harvest Home** first published 1792

Etching and engraving 16¼ × 19⅞ (413 × 505) on paper 18½ × 24⅝ (470 × 625) Etched inscription below subject 'A Grecian Harvest Home' upper centre; 'Vos, o Clarissima' and 'Ye Deities who Fields and Plains protect | who rule the Seasons and the Year direct' l.; 'Bacchus and Fostring Ceres Pow'rs Divine | who gave us Corn for Mast for Water Wine. Dryden's Virgil' centre; '3d' far r.; 'Painted Engraved & Publish'd by Jamˢ Barry R.A. Professor of Painting to the Royal Academy May 1ˢᵗ 1791' ('7' reversed) from b.l. to bottom centre

Lit: Pressly 1981, pp. 272–3, no.18, second state of four

Barry discusses this print in his *Letter* of 1793 (*Works*, II, p.422). He notes that 'the print and its picture are circumstantially the same', except that the figures dancing round the double terminal figure of Faunus and Sylvanus are 'removed a little to the right' (in fact, to the left) to make room for the seated figures of the elderly master of the feast and his wife at the far right. There are other alterations in the actions and poses of the youths near the ladder and upon the haystack in the background, upper right.

T 03785 **The Thames, or the Triumph of Navigation** first published 1792

Etching and engraving 16⁷⁄₁₆ × 20¹⁄₁₆ (418 × 510) on paper 18 × 22⅛ (457 × 562) Etched inscription below subject 'The Thames, or the Triumph of Navigation'

upper centre; 'Nor are his blessings to his banks confin'd | But free and common as the Sea or Wind' l.; 'So that to us, nothing no place is strange | While his fair bosom is the world's exchange. Denham' r.; '5ᵗʰ' far r.; 'Painted, engraved & publish'd by James Barry, R.A. Professor of Painting to the Royal Academy. May 1. 1791' lower centre

Lit: Pressly 1981, p.273, no.20, second state of six

Barry discusses this print in his *Letter* of 1793 (*Works*, II, p.424). The most significant alteration from the painted subject is that the figure of 'Mercury, or Commerce' now flies much lower over the personification of the Thames, since the subject has undergone horizontal compression. The naval pillar or tower which, in response to a competition of *c.*1801 to design a monument to England's naval victories, Barry added in 1801 to his painting of this subject, was also added to the third state of Barry's copperplate, and appears in all the later states.

T 03786 **The Distribution of Premiums in the Society of Arts** first published 1792

Etching and engraving 16½ × 20¹⁄₁₆ (420 × 510) on paper 16¹⁵⁄₁₆ × 20¾ (430 × 528) Etched inscription below subject 'The Society for the Encouragement of ARTS &c in the Distribution of their Annual Premiums' across upper centre; 'Painted, Engraved & Published by James Barry R.A. Professor of Painting to the Royal Academy May 1. 1791.' across lower

centre; crest of the Prince of Wales inscribed 'ICH DIEN' centre, in middle of inscription; '7th' far r.

Lit: Pressly 1981, pp.273–4, no.21, third state of four

Barry discusses this print in his *Letter* of 1793 (*Works*, II, pp.424–5). He points out that 'there is no difference of arrangement between the print and the picture'; but because this crowded composition has had to be compressed, some heads and figures of comparatively minor importance have been omitted, notably in the group which portrays Dr Samuel Johnson between the Duchesses of Rutland and Devonshire. The print does not include the silver tea kettle which was later added to other items of British design and manufacture in the lower right corner in the painting.

Barry's copperplate of this subject, 421 × 511mm, impressed on the back 'B. WHITTON | NO.44 SHOE LANE | LONDON', is in the collection of the Royal Society of Arts.

T 03787 **Elysium and Tartarus** first published 1792

Etching and engraving on paper $20\frac{5}{8} \times 36\frac{3}{8}$ (524 × 925)
Etched inscription within burnished-out box at middle of lower centre of subject 'Elysium and Tartarus or the State of FINAL RETRIBUTION – | – All now are vanish'd! Virtue sole survives, Imortal never failing friend of man, His guide to happiness on high. Thomson | Painted, Engraved & Publish'd by James Barry R.A. Professor of Painting to the Royal Academy. May 1. 1791. Laus Deo O.M.' centre; 'This Picture & the Victors at

Olympia on the opposite wall are each | 42 English feet in length' r. and '8th' far r.

Lit: Pressly 1981, p.274, no.22

Barry discusses this print in his *Letter* of 1793 (*Works*, II, pp.425–36). He notes that some alterations have been made in Elysium, 'for the most part confined to the space between William Penn, and the termination where the view of Tartarus commences', and itemizes the figures which have had to be left out in the print.

T 03788 **Detail of the Diagorides Victors** published 1795

Etching and engraving $28\frac{7}{8} \times 18\frac{1}{2}$ (733 × 470) on paper $30\frac{5}{16} \times 20$ (770 × 508)
Etched inscription 'The laws of Olympia requiring that these Contested Strenuous Exertions should be accompanied with | the conservation of Integrity as the only becoming & the True Victory, this Group &c' in the burnished-out area within bottom of subject, left, continuing

'Questo Gruppo di Diagoras e i suoi Figlioli preso dal Quadro dei Vittori Olympici comme un picolo mazzo di fiori ed intestimonio dal piu profondo e affectionatissimo Veneratione e gratituaine e gettato per | ornare il Corso Esemplare & Triumphante del Governo Papale di Roma, Madre e graziosa Prottetrice delle Arti Laudabile e Ingenosi per Giacomo Barry R.A. Professor of Painting to the Royal Academy & Member of the Clemen–|–tine Academy of Bologna Painted En.d & Publ.d May 1. 1795 by J.B.' below subject across bottom

Lit: Pressly 1981, p.277, no.28, fourth state of four

Whereas T03784–7 are engravings of complete paintings, T03788 is of a detail from the painting 'The Crowning of the Victors at Olympia'; it shows Diagoras of Rhodes, a former victor in the Olympic Games, carried in triumph on the shoulders of his two victorious sons. Barry discusses this print in his *Letter* of 1793 (*Works*, II, pp.422–3), explaining that 'in order to obtain a greater magnitude in the figures', some 'minor alterations' have been made. The background introduces a terraced stadium with additional figures.

Thomas Churchyard 1798–1865

T03618   **Windmills**

Oil on panel $6\frac{7}{16} \times 4\frac{13}{16}$ (164 × 122)
Inscribed 'January 25. 18 [...] Between 10 & 11 [...]' on the back

Presented anonymously in memory of Terence Rattigan 1983
Prov: ...; Roland, Browse & Delbanco 1959; ...; Spink & Son Ltd, from whom bt by the donor 1966
Exh: *Christmas Present Exhibition*, Roland, Browse & Delbanco, November–December 1959 (75)

This sketch is painted on a cigar box lid, a type of support frequently used by Churchyard. As very little of Churchyard's work is datable, it is difficult to suggest what the missing digits in the faint pencil inscription are. The scene is probably at Woodbridge and the tower that of St Mary's church.

T03619   **A House by a River**

Oil on panel $5\frac{9}{16} \times 7\frac{7}{8}$ (142 × 200)
Inscribed on the back 'T.C.' and 'Harriet Churchyard'
Presented anonymously in memory of Terence Rattigan 1983
Prov: Harriet Churchyard (1836–1927), the artist's daughter; ...; Spink & Son Ltd, from whom bt by the donor 1966

A small watercolour by Churchyard of the same subject was included in Philip Goodman's exhibition *Cotman to Seago*, King Street Galleries 1984 (16, repr.). The scene was said to be traditionally identified as Rackham's Mill, Wickham Market, Suffolk. Like many of Churchyard's works, T03619 is inscribed on the back with the name of the daughter who inherited it.

T 03620 **The Garden Tent**

Oil on oak panel $7\frac{1}{16} \times 6\frac{7}{16}$ (180 × 164)
Inscribed on the back 'T.C' and 'Bessy'
Presented anonymously in memory of
Terence Rattigan 1983

Prov: Elizabeth ('Bessy') Churchyard (1834–
1913), the artist's daughter; ...; bt by the
donor from the Simon Carter Gallery,
Woodbridge 1967

Exh: *Oils & Watercolours by Thomas
Churchyard*, Simon Carter Gallery,
Woodbridge, December 1967 (6)

The scene is probably in the garden of Churchyard's
house in Cumberland Street, Woodbridge and the figures in the tent may be two of his daughters. The oak
panel on which the work is painted appears to have been
taken from wall panelling or from a piece of furniture.

This painting is the subject of Kevin Crossley-
Holland's poem 'In "The Garden Tent"', published
in *With a Poet's Eye, A Tate Gallery Anthology*, ed. Pat
Adams, Tate Gallery 1986, p.52 (repr. in col. p.53).

T 03621 **Aldeburgh Beach**

Oil on board $4\frac{3}{4} \times 6\frac{1}{16}$ (120 × 154)
Inscribed on the back 'Emma –' and
'Harriett.'
Presented anonymously in memory of
Terence Rattigan 1983

Prov: The artist's daughters Emma (1828–78)
and Harriet Churchyard (1836–1927); bt
at the latter's sale, Arnott & Everett,
Woodbridge, 11 April 1927 (lot not
identified) by Wilfred G. Watsham who

sold it to the Revd Eric C. Charlesworth
1963; sold by him to the Simon Carter
Gallery, Woodbridge, from whom bt by
the donor 1967

Exh: *Oils & Watercolours by Thomas
Churchyard*, Simon Carter Gallery,
Woodbridge, December 1967 (9)

The exhibition mentioned above also included six drawings or watercolours by Churchyard of Aldeburgh
beach and an oil sketch of the beach by his daughter
Ellen. Numerous other watercolours of Aldeburgh subjects were included in the Churchyard exhibition held
at Gainsborough's House, Sudbury in 1973.

Sir George Clausen 1852–1944

T 03666 **Winter Work** 1883–4

Oil on canvas $30\frac{1}{2} \times 36\frac{1}{4}$ (775 × 920)
Inscribed 'G CLAUSEN 1883–4. |
CHILDWICK' b.l. and 'WINTER

WORK.│G. CLAUSEN.│1883.' on the back
Purchased (Grant-in-Aid) with assistance
from the Friends of the Tate Gallery 1983

Prov: ...; anon. sale, Sotheby's 3 November
1982 (37, repr. in col.) £34,100 bt Fine
Art Society Ltd, from whom bt by the Tate
Gallery

Exh: Grosvenor Gallery 1883 (152)

Lit: Kenneth McConkey, *Sir George Clausen,
R.A., 1852–1944*, exhibition catalogue,
Bradford, RA, Bristol, Newcastle, 1980,
under nos.32–3; Kenneth McConkey,
'Figures in a field – *Winter work* by Sir
George Clausen, RA', *Art at Auction, The
year at Sotheby's 1982–83*, 1983, pp.72–7,
fig.7 (col.); Malcolm Warner, 'Victorian
Paintings at the Tate Gallery, Recent
Acquisitions', *Apollo*, CXXIII, 1986, p.263,
fig.9

This is one of the earliest and most impressive of Clausen's essays in 'rustic naturalism', a style of painting which he adopted after seeing Bastien-Lepage's pictures of French rural labour, especially 'Les Foins' when it was shown at the Grosvenor Gallery in 1880. The example of John Robertson Reid's 'Toil and Pleasure' (1879, Tate Gallery) also helped point Clausen in this new direction, away from his earlier Whistlerian manner.

'Winter Work' was painted at Childwick Green, near St Albans, where the artist settled with his wife in 1881. Clausen, who previously lived at Hampstead, later wrote of the move as 'a liberation': 'We went because it was cheaper to live, and there were better opportunities of working. One saw people doing simple things under good conditions of lighting: and there was always landscape. And nothing was made easy for you: you had to dig out what you wanted' ('Autobiographical Notes', *Artwork*, VII, 1931, p.19). The subject Clausen chose in this case was labourers topping and tailing mangolds for sheep fodder. Pencil studies of the principal man and woman show the latter in a different pose, facing left, from the one finally used in the painting (RA; McConkey 1983, figs.3–4). This earlier version of the woman's pose is more or less repeated in a photograph by Clausen (Royal Photographic Society, Bath; ibid. fig.5) and in an oil sketch of the whole subject, known as 'December' (Private Coll.; ibid. fig.6). The latter includes neither the figure of the girl in the foreground nor that of the boy in the background of 'Winter Work'. A small drawing presumably made by Clausen for *Grosvenor Notes* on the occasion of the first exhibition of 'Winter Work' (but not published) suggests that the girl was in fact added after the exhibition, no doubt in 1884, the latest date given in the inscription on the front of the picture (RA; McConkey 1980, no.33, repr.).

Although 'December' is regarded here as a preliminary to 'Winter Work', Kenneth McConkey has raised the possibility of it having been painted after the larger work (McConkey 1983, p.77, n.5).

A watercolour of 1883, 'Hoeing Turnips', is related in composition (exh. *Rural and Urban Images*, Pyms Gallery 1984, no.14, repr.) and, like other works by Clausen of this period, uses the same model for the woman.

John Constable 1776–1837

T 03607 **Study of a Girl in a Cloak and Bonnet** 1810

Oil on millboard $12\frac{7}{16} \times 6\frac{7}{8}$ (316 × 175)
Inscribed 'E Bergholt 1810–' b.l. and
'Minna. Dc^r 27th 47' in a later hand on the back
Purchased (Grant-in-Aid) 1983

Prov: Allocated to the artist's daughter Maria
Louisa ('Minna') in a division of the
family collection 27 December 1847 (see
inscription); inherited on her death in
1885 by her brother Lionel and sister
Isabel and on Lionel's death in 1887 by
Isabel alone; she died 1888; said (see
below) to have been included in one of the
sales of her collection (Christie's 28 May
1891, 17 June 1892) and to have been bt
by Thomas J. Barratt; ...; Kojiro
Matsukata, sold *c*.1930 to another
Japanese collector, from whom bt 1954 by
Tokuzo Mizushima and offered for sale,

Sotheby's 2 March 1983 (75, repr. in col.), bt in and sold privately to the Tate Gallery

Lit: Leslie Parris, 'Some recently discovered oil sketches by John Constable', *Burlington Magazine*, CXXV, 1983, p.223, fig.40

Constable spent the late summer and autumn of 1810 in his native Suffolk, going down to East Bergholt sometime in August and returning to London by 11 November (R.B.Beckett, *John Constable's Correspondence*, Ipswich, I, 1962, pp.49–50, IV, 1966, p.19). One or two dated works from this visit are known, including oil sketches made at Flatford and Bergholt on 27 and 30 September respectively (Johnson Collection, Philadelphia; exh. *Constable*, Tate Gallery 1976, nos.92–3) but the bulk of the work Constable did during his stay is less directly identifiable. Almost certainly he was making some of the oil sketches later used for 'Flatford Lock and Mill', exhibited in 1812 as 'A Watermill' (currently on anon. loan to the Corcoran Gallery, Washington) and – a more immediate concern – preparing for his first major exhibition picture, the 'Dedham Vale: Morning' shown in 1811 (Private Coll., exh. *Constable*, Tate Gallery 1976, no.100). Although not on a large scale, the figures of country people walking along a lane or resting beside it play an important part in the latter picture and in the several oil studies connected with it. Without being related to the composition, T 03607 also illustrates Constable's interest at this time in figures seen in the open. Earlier in 1810 he had exhibited 'The Church Porch, East Bergholt' (Tate Gallery), which includes a similar figure of a seated girl.

Very few figure studies in oil by Constable are known and T 03607 appears to be the only dated example. The others include 'Mary Constable in a Red Cloak' (R. Hoozee, *L'opera completa di Constable*, Milan 1979, no.106), 'Study of a Seated Man' (ibid. no.107), 'A Girl in a Bonnet' (ibid. no.520) and 'A Girl in a White Bonnet' (Sotheby's 2 March 1983 lot 76, and 16 November 1983 lot 94).

The history of T 03607 after Isabel Constable's death is a little uncertain. A label on the back is inscribed 'By John Constable R.A. | Bought at his daughter's | sale (Isabella Constable)' followed in a different hand by a nearly illegible signature. The most likely reading of the latter seems to be 'Thomas Barratt', i.e. Thomas J. Barratt of the firm of A. & F. Pears, who is known to have owned works by or attributed to Constable. However, it has not been possible to identify the work in either of Isabel Constable's sales or in records of Barratt's collection. Similar labels occur on five other works by John or Lionel Constable offered for sale with T 03607 at Sotheby's on 2 March 1983, including the 'Girl in a White Bonnet' mentioned above. All six were at one time in the collection of the Japanese industrialist

Kojiro Matsukata (1865–1950), whose French paintings formed the basis of the National Museum of Western Art in Tokyo.

Thomas Cook ?1744–1818 after William Hogarth 1697–1764

T 03827 Dr Benjamin Hoadly, Bishop of Winchester *c.*1800

Engraving 12⅝ × 10⅜ (321 × 259) on paper 22⁹⁄₁₆ × 17⅞ (573 × 442); plate-mark 16¹¹⁄₁₆ × 11½ (424 × 292)
Writing-engraving '*Painted by Wᵐ· Hogarth* | *Engraved by T. Cook.* | *The Right Reverend Father in God* | Dᴿ· BENJAMIN HOADLY, LORD BISHOP OF WINCHESTER | *Prelate of the Most Noble Order of the Garter.* | *London: Published by G. & L. Robinson, Paternoster Row, & F. Cook, Nº· 38, Tavistock Street, Covent Garden*' and the Bishop's seal within the Garter ribbon in the centre
Transferred from the reference collection 1984

Prov: Unknown

Hogarth's original painting of his friend is in the Tate Gallery (N 02736). An engraving after it (facing in the same direction as the painting) by Bernard Baron was published in July 1743 (R. Paulson, *Hogarth's Graphic Works*, 1970, no.226, pl.266) and led to the erroneous assumption that this was also the date of the original, which, however, is signed and dated 1741 (see J. Ingamells, *The English Episcopal Portrait 1559–1835*, 1981, p.224). Cook's engraving appears to be closer to Baron's print than to the original painting and was probably copied from the former. Although it is undated, it probably pre-dates Cook's much simplified, reduced and reversed version of it published in 1809 by Longman, Hurst & Rees and used as an illustration to J. Nichols & G. Steevens, *The Genuine Works of William Hogarth* (II, 1810, facing p.164).

Abraham Cooper 1787–1868

T 03422 **The Day Family** 1838

Oil on canvas 38⅛ × 50⅛ (968 × 1273)
Inscribed 'A C [monogram] 1838' b.l. and below figures from b.l. to b.r. 'Mrs: Anne Day', 'Mrs. Day' | 'John Day Jun!', 'John Day', 'Venison ridden by Sam¹ Day' and 'Chapeau d'Espagne ridden by Willm Day'
Bequeathed by Mrs F. Ambrose Clark from the collection of the late F. Ambrose Clark through the British Sporting Art Trust 1982

Prov: Commissioned by John Barham Day; ...; Partridge, from whom purchased by Agnew and sold to Daniel H. Farr 1920; Hermann Kinnicutt; E.J. Rousuck, from whom purchased by F. Ambrose Clark by 1958; his widow, Mrs F. Ambrose Clark

Exh: ?this picture, or the version noted below, RA 1838 (309, as 'The Day family, viz. grandmother and Mrs Day in the mule carriage, John Day the father with his son John standing on the right, with his two sons; the late Sam mounted on Venison in the distance'); Tate Gallery, August–September 1982, and York City Art Gallery, March–September 1984, with other paintings from Mrs F. Ambrose Clark's Bequest (no catalogue); National Horseracing Museum, Newmarket, March–December 1985 (no catalogue); *Paintings exhibited by the British Sporting Art Trust*, Vestey Gallery, National Horseracing Museum, Newmarket, April–December 1986 (unnumbered, repr.)

Lit: [E.J. Rousuck], *The F. Ambrose Clark Collection of Sporting Paintings*, privately printed, New York 1958, p.62, repr. pp.56 (in col.) and 100

An apparently identical version, similarly signed, dated and inscribed with the sitters' names, is in the South African National Gallery (unseen by the compilers; catalogued in *British Sporting Paintings and Drawings in the Sir Abe Bailey Collection*, SANG, Cape Town 1970, pp.9–10, repr.).

Three generations of the Day family are depicted here. The most senior is Anne Day, widow of John Day I, who had been a racing adviser to the Prince Regent; she, the 'grandmother' of the 1838 RA title, stands waiting to alight from the mule carriage. Her son John Barham Day (John Day II), having driven the mule carriage in to the scene, now stands beside it with a whip in his left hand; his wife Harriet Day is seated within the carriage. Three of their sons appear in this group. The eldest, John Day III, stands at the head of the carriage, leaning on its shafts; his younger brothers, Samuel and William, each in Jockey's silks, ride horses from the Day stables, Samuel (in the centre of the group) riding Venison, and William on Chapeau d'Espagne on the right.

This is a family of jockeys and racing trainers. John Barham Day (1794–1860) established the Day racing stables at Danebury, near Stockbridge, on the Hampshire Downs. He had begun his career at Newmarket as apprentice to Smallman, the Prince Regent's trainer. As a jockey, he won the Oaks four times and the St Leger twice, the last of these Classic victories being at the age of 46 when he rode Crucifix to victory in the Oaks of 1840 two years after Cooper's portrait: as a trainer, he trained the Derby winners of 1846, 1847 and 1854. John Barham Day was given to punctilious religious observances (he used to read Blair's sermons to the stable lads on Sundays), but his nickname of 'Honest John Day' was ironic. The Day stables became the centre of heavy and fraudulent betting. The Day family's successes continued, though under warnings from the Jockey Club and in the teeth of considerable unpopularity. John Barham Day died at Woodyates, Dorset, on 21 March 1860. The kindest judgment of him was given by 'The Druid' (H.H. Dixon, *Scott and*

Sebright, 1862; 1895 ed., p.40): 'Perhaps he was greatest as a jockey in his earliest days, when he had not so much training and betting on his mind'.

John Barham Day married Harriet Goddard; they had (as well as two daughters) five sons who were jockeys and trainers. Each of the three portrayed here is identified by an inscription on the painting itself as well as in the RA exhibition catalogue. John Day III (baptized 9 August 1815, died 1882) was a successful jockey, and succeeded to the management of the Day stables. Samuel Goddard (baptized 9 August 1818, buried 18 March 1838, and described in the 1838 title as 'the late Sam.') and William Henry (baptized 9 September 1823, died 1908), later trainer at Woodyates, Dorset, and author of *The Racehorse in Training* (1880), *Reminiscences of the Turf* (1886) and *The Horse: How to Breed and Rear him* (1888), were both jockeys in the 1830s.

Assuming that the Day children were baptized soon after their births, John would have been aged 24 in this portrait dated 1838, Samuel 19 and William 14: ages which, in the case of the two younger boys, seem too old for them. Had it not been for the artist's inscription, one might have supposed that the younger boy might have been Henry (baptized 1827) or Alfred (born 1830) rather than William but had it been in error, it is unlikely that the inscription, in both versions of the picture, would have remained uncorrected, and the full RA title of the picture refers to William as 'little Will'.

The Tate's collection includes a portrait by Harry Hall of John Barham Day with his son John and another man, dated 1841 (T01887). Individual members of the Day family were portrayed by Ben Marshall, Abraham Cooper, John Ferneley and John Frederick Herring (examples in the collections of Brodick Castle, National Trust for Scotland; Mr Paul Mellon KBE and Richard Green). Vignette portraits of John Barham Day and his sons John and Alfred and his brother Samuel are given in Frederic Boase, *Modern English Biography*, and a notice of William in *DNB*, 2nd Supplement.

Francis Danby 1793–1861

T03667 **Children by a Brook** *c.*1822

Oil on canvas 13$\frac{9}{16}$ × 18$\frac{1}{8}$ (345 × 460)
Purchased (Grant-in-Aid) 1983
Prov: ...; anon. sale, Sotheby's 7 July 1982 (47, repr. in col.) £16,500 bt Spink and Son Ltd from whom bt by the Tate Gallery

This is one of several small poetic landscapes with figures which Danby painted during his last years in Bristol. By 1824, when he settled in London, he was

painting more spectacular subjects and had given up the close attention to natural detail seen here.

A larger, upright version of the subject, measuring 29$\frac{1}{2}$ × 24$\frac{1}{2}$in, is in the Paul Mellon Collection at the Yale Center for British Art (Eric Adams, *Francis Danby*, 1973, no.14, fig.23). The figures of the girl and the two boys at her feet are very similar in both works, as is the central part of the landscape with its effect of sunlight filtered through foliage. However, the Yale Center picture includes an additional boy standing on a rock facing the other two and lacks the bridge seen at the left of T03667. There are other variations occasioned by the differences of format.

The Bristol Art Gallery's 'Boy Sailing a Little Boat' (Adams 1973, no.15, fig.24), which is related in subject to the two versions of 'Children by a Brook', carries an inscription on the back identifying the location of the scene as Stapleton near Bristol, and Adams takes the setting of the Yale Center 'Children by a Brook' (the Tate version was unknown when he wrote in 1973) to be 'an idealized rendering of the River Frome at Stapleton'.

The dating of T03667 to *c.*1822 is suggested by comparison with Danby's 'View of the Avon Gorge' (Bristol; Adams no.8, fig.16), which is dated that year, and with Richard Redgrave's description of Danby's 'Clearing up after a Shower' exhibited at the RA in 1822 (unlocated; Adams no.157).

Peter de Wint 1784–1849

T03669 **Study of Burdock and Other Plants**

Oil on board laid on panel 10$\frac{3}{8}$ × 13$\frac{1}{4}$ (262 × 335)
Purchased (Grant-in-Aid) 1983

Prov: As one of a group of four oil studies of
plants: Harriet de Wint, the artist's
widow; by descent to her grand-daughter
Miss H.H. Tatlock, by whom bequeathed
to her companion Miss G.M. Bostock, by
whom given or sold by 1937 to Geoffrey
Harmsworth. Three of the four, including
T 03669, were sold by him *c.*1977 to
R.R.M. Prior, from whom purchased by
Andrew Wyld 1978; purchased from him
by the Tate Gallery

Exh: *Peter de Wint Centenary Exhibition*, Vokins
1884; *The Works of Peter de Wint*, Usher
Art Gallery, Lincoln 1937 (84, as 'Study
of Foliage'); *Peter de Wint*, Andrew Wyld,
September–October 1979 (7); *The
Discovery of the Lake District*, Victoria
and Albert Museum, September 1984–
January 1985 (173)

Lit: David Scrase, *Drawings and Watercolours
by Peter de Wint*, exhibition catalogue,
Fitzwilliam Museum, Cambridge 1979,
p.13

This is one of a group of four small oil studies of wild
plants which stayed together until *c.*1977 (see *Prov:*);
all four were included in the de Wint exhibitions of
1884 and 1937, each as 'Study of Foliage' (in the 1937
exhibition the other three were nos.83, 86 and 87). One
of the four passed after Sir Geoffrey Harmsworth's
death in 1980 to a beneficiary of his will. Of the three
(including T 03669) acquired in 1978 by Andrew Wyld,
who identified the various plants, 'Sorrell and Cow
Parsley' (no.8 in his 1979 exhibition) is now in a private
Californian collection; another, slighter, study is in the
collection of the Huntington Library, San Marino, California. Writing of the group of four in the catalogue of
the Fitzwilliam Museum's exhibition of watercolours
and drawings by de Wint, David Scrase considers that

each of them 'shows De Wint's manner in oil at its very
best'. None of the four oil studies is dated, and it is
difficult to suggest a date for T 03669. De Wint made
many watercolour studies of docks and reeds, and some
more detailed studies of flowers; some of the best examples are in the collection of the Usher Art Gallery,
Lincoln.

Dr Bernard Vedcourt, Herbarium and Library, Royal
Botanic Gardens, Kew, confirms that the big leaves in
T 03669 are probably one of the burdocks (*Arctium*); the
other plants and reeds are not identifiable.

In the Victoria and Albert Museum's *Lake District*
exhibition of 1984–5, this study was juxtaposed with
'Derwentwater' (no.172), a watercolour by de Wint in
the collection of the Lady Lever Art Gallery, Port Sunlight, the catalogue suggesting (p.75) that this oil study
contributed to that finished watercolour. Whether the
two works are directly related is arguable, especially as
similar plants occur in the foreground of many of de
Wint's Lincolnshire watercolours.

William Charles Thomas Dobson 1817–1898

T 03448 **The Child Jesus Going Down
with his Parents to
Nazareth** 1856

Oil on arched canvas $46\frac{7}{8} \times 35\frac{3}{8}$
(1090 × 900)
Inscribed 'WCTD 1856' (in monogram)
b.l.
Purchased (Grant-in-Aid) 1982

Prov: Perhaps bought from the artist by
Baroness Burdett Coutts (d. 1906); the Rt
Hon. W. Burdett Coutts MP, sold
Christie's 4/5 May 1922 (177) 8 gns bt
Sampson; New Gallery, Brown's
Buildings, Liverpool *c.*1924; . . .; ? Hinson
Fine Paintings, Sheffield *c.*1975; . . .; anon.
sale, Sotheby's Belgravia 25 October 1977
(137, repr. in col.) £1,700 bt ?Colnaghi;
. . .; Fine Art Society by 1979; . . .; anon.
sale, Sotheby's 10 November 1981 (8, repr.
in col.) bt in; Fine Art Society from whom
bt by the Tate Gallery

Exh: RA 1857 (556)

Engr: Mezzotint by W.J. Edwards, 'Arrival at
Nazareth', pub. Henry Graves & Co. 29
January 1867

Lit: Malcolm Warner, 'Victorian Paintings at
the Tate Gallery, Recent Acquisitions',
Apollo, CXXIII, 1986, p.260, fig.1

Dobson's picture depicts the twelve year old Jesus being
carried back to Nazareth after Joseph and Mary had
returned to Jerusalem and found him with the elders in
the Temple. The artist used Chapter 2 of the Gospel
according to St Luke as his source for this incident in
the life of Christ.

Much of Dobson's output betrays the time he spent
as a pupil of Sir Charles Eastlake and the period he
passed in Italy and Germany during the 1840s and 50s –
at which time he came into contact with the work of
the Nazarenes. Whilst some aspects of Germanism in
British Art were to prove controversial at this time,
as, indeed, were Pre-Raphaelite treatments of religious
subjects (as, for example in the case of Millais's 'Christ
in the House of His Parents', 1850, now Tate Gallery
N 03584), Dobson's pictures fared rather better with
the general public. His cooler palette – which owes
something to Nazarene influence – allied to that fairly
rigorous handling of gesture and design inherited from
the same source, and which he has in common with
Eastlake and the Pre-Raphaelites, probably proved
more acceptable because his characterization was
diluted by a certain degree of sentimentalization.

Despite this, the reception which the critics gave
'The Child Jesus' at the time it was exhibited was not
particularly enthusiastic. A writer in the *Athenaeum*
stated that 'Mr Dobson grows tiresome with his clean-
painted saints, with no expression but a sort of pious
and vacant stare' and described the work as 'ugly and
too large and heavy' (16 May 1857, p.633). John Ruskin
in his *Academy Notes* thought the picture 'very tender
in expression, but common-place; and in general idea
more or less false or improbable' (E.T. Cook and A.
Wedderburn, eds., *The Library Edition of the Works of
John Ruskin*, XIV, 1904, p.114).

When the picture was unframed for conservation
treatment the bottom and right-hand edges of the canvas were found to be marked-up for the grid which the
engraver used to copy the image onto his metal plate.
The preliminary marks for the grid had been made in
pencil, at centres of $2\frac{1}{8}$in (52mm) along both edges. Pins
(the pin holes only now remain) were then pushed into
the canvas a fraction of an inch in from the edges and
the grid of vertical and horizontal threads was then
stretched over the surface of the canvas. In the area of
the picture where more precision was needed in copying – the heads of the holy family – the size of the grid
was reduced to $1\frac{1}{16} \times 1\frac{1}{16}$in (26 × 26mm).

John Ferneley I 1782–1860

T 03423 **John Burgess of Clipstone,
Nottinghamshire, on a
Favourite Horse, with his
Harriers** 1838

Oil on canvas $37\frac{3}{4} \times 55$ (959 × 1398)
Inscribed 'J. Ferneley|Melton
Mowbray|1838' bottom centre
Bequeathed by Mrs F. Ambrose Clark
from the collection of the late F. Ambrose
Clark through the British Sporting Art
Trust 1982

Prov: Commissioned by a committee of
gentlemen for presentation to John
Burgess; by descent to R.S. Burgess, sold
Christie's 12 December 1930 (140) bt
W.M. Sabin, from whom purchased by F.
Ambrose Clark by 1958; his widow Mrs
F. Ambrose Clark

Exh: Tate Gallery, August-September 1982,
and York City Art Gallery, March–
September 1984, with other paintings

from Mrs F. Ambrose Clark's Bequest (no catalogue)

Lit: Guy Paget, *The Melton Mowbray of John Ferneley*, Leicester 1931, Account Books p.145, no.456; [E.J. Rousuck], *The F. Ambrose Clark Collection of Sporting Paintings*, privately printed, New York 1958, p.101, repr. pp.83 (in col.), 100

This picture is recorded in the artist's Account Books as 'Portrait of John Burgess Esq., on a Favourite Horse, with his Harriers, etc.', commissioned in 1838 by 'The Gentlemen of the Committ[ee] Presenting J. Burgess, Esq., with a Portrait of Himself'.

John Burgess (?1791–1842) was a gentleman farmer of Clipston-on-the Wolds, a hamlet about six miles south east of Nottingham, where he was a tenant of Earl Manvers. Clipston-on-the Wolds is on the fringe of the Quorn country. John Burgess hunted with the Quorn, but here he is portrayed with his own pack of harriers, to which he acted as huntsman as well as Master. The 'Gentlemen of the Committee' who commissioned this portrait presumably hunted with John Burgess, who had himself earlier (in 1823) commissioned Ferneley to paint a 'Portrait of his Son on Horseback' (Paget, p.131, no.151). In T 03423 the setting is probably the Wolds and the Vale of Belvoir.

There is a brief mention of 'Mr. Burgess of Clipstone, Notts., who hunted his own harriers when he was not out with the Quorn', presiding at a dinner given to Mr. Rowland Errington on undertaking the Mastership of the Quorn in 1835 (W.C.A. Blew, *The Quorn Hunt*, 1899, p.163). 'John Burgess Esq. of Clipstone' is recorded in the burial register of Holme Pierrepont (a village near Clipston) as having been buried on 30 April 1842, aged 51 (information kindly communicated by Adrian Henstock, Principal Archivist, Nottinghamshire Record Office).

T 03424 Sir Robert Leighton after Coursing, with a Groom and a Couple of Greyhounds 1816

Oil on canvas $41\frac{3}{8} \times 55$ (1050 × 1397)
Inscribed 'J. Ferneley | Melton Mowbray | 1816' b.r.
Bequeathed by Mrs F. Ambrose Clark from the collection of the late F. Ambrose Clark through the British Sporting Art Trust 1982

Prov: Commissioned by Sir Robert Leighton; ...; Sir Jonathan North (d.1939); ...; E.J. Rousuck, from whom purchased by F. Ambrose Clark by 1958; his widow Mrs F. Ambrose Clark

Exh: Tate Gallery, August–September 1982, and York City Art Gallery, March–September 1984, with other paintings from Mrs F. Ambrose Clark's Bequest (no catalogue); *Paintings exhibited by the British Sporting Art Trust*, Vestey Gallery, National Horseracing Museum, Newmarket, April–December 1986 (unnumbered, repr.)

Lit: Guy Paget, *The Melton Mowbray of John Ferneley*, Leicester 1931, Account Books p.128, no.59; [E.J. Rousuck], *The F. Ambrose Clark Collection of Sporting Paintings*, privately printed, New York 1958, p.106, repr. p.107

Ferneley's Account Books (transcribed by Paget) record that he charged £26.5.0. for this picture, Sir Robert Leighton paying him £10 on account in 1816 and settling the account on 3 June 1817.

Sir Robert Leighton, 5th Bart., of Loton Park, Shropshire, was the younger son of Sir Charlton Leighton, 3rd Bart., by his second wife Emma, daughter of Sir Robert March. On his elder brother's death in 1784, he succeeded to the baronetcy. He was sheriff of Shropshire, 1786–7. He died unmarried on 21 February 1819, in his sixty-sixth year, and was succeeded by his first cousin, Major-General Baldwin Leighton (*Gentleman's Magazine*, 1819, i, p.280; George Edward Cokayne, *Complete Baronetage*, IV, 1904, p.160).

T 03425 **Mr Powell and his Son, with Norton, a Grey Hunter** 1819

Oil on canvas $33\frac{7}{8} \times 42\frac{3}{8}$ (860 × 1076)
Inscribed 'J. Ferneley | Melton
Mowbray | 1816' b.l. on mounting-block
Bequeathed by Mrs F. Ambrose Clark
from the collection of the late F. Ambrose
Clark through the British Sporting Art
Trust 1982

Prov: Commissioned by Mr Power; . . .; Lt. Col.
Sir Jonathan North (d.1939); E.J.
Rousuck, from whom purchased by F.
Ambrose Clark by 1958; his widow Mrs
F. Ambrose Clark

Exh: Tate Gallery, August–September 1982,
and York City Art Gallery, March–
September 1984, with other paintings
from Mrs F. Ambrose Clark's Bequest (no
catalogue)

Lit: Guy Paget, *The Melton Mowbray of John
Ferneley*, Leicester 1931, Account Books
p.134, no.224; [E.J. Rousuck], *The F.
Ambrose Clark Collection of Sporting
Paintings*, privately printed, New York
1958, p.109, repr. p.108 (as 'The Power
Gentlemen, with Norton their Hunter')

Ferneley's Account Books (published by Paget, 1931)
record the payment in June 1820 of £7.7.0 by 'Mr
Powell' for 'Portrait of "Norton" | Mr Powell and Son'.
The sitters have not been further identified. The church
in the background appears to be the parish church of
Melton Mowbray.

T 03426 **Defiance, a Brood Mare, with
Reveller, a Foal** 1833

Oil on canvas 28 × 37 (712 × 940)
Inscribed 'J Ferneley | Melton

Mowbray | 1833' bottom centre and
'Reveller' b.l.
Bequeathed by Mrs F. Ambrose Clark
from the collection of the late F. Ambrose
Clark through the British Sporting Art
Trust 1982

Prov: Commissioned by Isaac Sadler 1833; . . .;
Sir Walter Gilbey, sold by his executors,
Christie's 11 June 1915 (321) bt Banks;
Tresham Gilbey, sold by his executors,
Christie's 30 May 1947 (67) bt Stevens &
Brown; E.J. Rousuck, by whom sold to F.
Ambrose Clark by 1958; his widow Mrs F.
Ambrose Clark

Exh: Tate Gallery, August–September 1982,
and York City Art Gallery, March–
September 1984, with other paintings
from Mrs F. Ambrose Clark's Bequest (no
catalogue); *Paintings exhibited by the
British Sporting Art Trust*, Vestey
Gallery, National Horseracing Museum,
Newmarket, April–December 1986
(unnumbered, repr.)

Lit: Guy Paget, *The Melton Mowbray of John
Ferneley*, Leicester 1931, Account Books
p.141, no.371; [E.J. Rousuck], *The F.
Ambrose Clark Collection of Sporting
Paintings*, privately printed, New York
1958, p.90, repr. p.91

Defiance was a chestnut filly by Rubens. As a three-
year-old she was owned by Isaac Sadler; she raced in
his colours during 1819–20, winning the Duke of York's
Plate at Ascot, a sweepstake at Bath and the St Leger
Stakes at Warwick in 1819, and a Handicap sweepstakes
at Cheltenham in 1820. After that year she appears to
have retired as a brood mare.

T 03439 Major Healey, Wearing Raby Hunt Uniform, Riding with the Sedgefield Hunt c.1833

Oil on canvas 30⅛ × 38³⁄₁₆ (764 × 970)
Inscribed 'John Ferneley | Melton Mowbray' bottom centre and 'To Major Healey | with Mʳ Ferneley | of Melton Mowbrays | Compliments' on stretcher
Presented by Violet N. Cross through the British Sporting Art Trust 1982

Prov: Presented by the artist to the sitter; his widow, Anna Mildred Healey, by whom given or bequeathed to her great-niece Isabel Wintour, by whom offered at Sotheby's 25 April 1934 (136), bt in and later bequeathed to her niece Violet N. Cross

Lit: Guy Paget, *The Melton Mowbray of John Ferneley*, Leicester 1931, pp.31–3

The portrait of Major Healey on a chestnut hunter is taken from Ferneley's large painting 'Portraits of the Gentlemen of the Sedgefield Hunt' (repr. Paget, facing p.32), in which Major Healey appears in the foreground on the left, riding after a fox well ahead of the field (including the hounds: see below). That picture, painted for J. Bell of Thirsk Hall, Yorkshire (? and still in his descendants' collection), is recorded in Ferneley's Account Books (Paget, p.141, no.362): 'Jan. 1833. J. Bell Esq. A large Scurry, with Portraits of Gentlemen and Horses. £115.10.0'. When it was exhibited at the Society of British Artists in 1833 (469), the *New Sporting Magazine*'s reviewer (quoted by Paget, pp.31–3) stressed the fact that 'this picture was designed more with a view of obtaining portraits of certain gentlemen and horses' rather than as a realistic reflection of the 'confusion' of a hunt scurry: this, he suggested, accounted for 'one or two points which the hypercritical

connoisseur might cavil at – such as one gentleman riding after the fox before the body of the hounds are out of cover'.

Major Healey is portrayed both in the big 'Sedgefield Hunt' picture and in T 03439 wearing the Raby Hunt uniform: scarlet coat and black collar embroidered in gold with a fox. Sotheby's sale catalogue of 1934 described Major Healey as 'of Morris Grange, Richmond, Yorkshire, a hard rider who hunted with the Zetland, Raby, Bedale, Hurworth and Sedgefield packs and who was a well-known figure in the hunting-field'. Presumably he was a friend of Ferneley. Preserved with the picture are an old photograph (?c.1870) inscribed 'Colonel Healey in old age', recognizably the same individual as Ferneley's sitter, a photograph of his wife and two photographs of Morris Grange, Yorkshire.

Major Healey has not been further identified. He may be the John Healey who appears in Army Lists from at least 1815 to 1868–9, attaining the rank of Lieutenant in the 7th Regiment of Foot on 8 September 1815, promoted Captain in the same regiment on 26 June 1823, transferring the next year to the 39th Regiment of Foot and continuing to be listed there on half pay from 15 January 1824. His styling as 'Major' is presumably an honorary rank after his retirement from active service.

John Ferneley II *c.*1815–1862

T 03427 Hunt Scurry 1832

Oil on canvas 17 × 35 (432 × 889)
Inscribed 'J. Ferneley Jr. | 1832' b.r.
Bequeathed by Mrs F. Ambrose Clark from the collection of the late F. Ambrose Clark through the British Sporting Art Trust 1982

Prov: ...; Lord Kinnaird; F. Ambrose Clark by 1958; his widow Mrs F. Ambrose Clark

Exh: Tate Gallery, August–September 1982, and York City Art Gallery, March–September 1984, with other paintings from Mrs F. Ambrose Clark's Bequest (no catalogue)

Lit: [E.J. Rousuck], *The F. Ambrose Clark Collection of Sporting Paintings*, privately printed, New York 1958, p.93, repr. p.92 (as 'Hounds Entering Billesdon Coplow' by John Ferneley)

Catalogued by Rousuck as by John Ferneley Senior, and of a famous stretch of Leicestershire hunting country; but the work is not up to the standard of the elder Ferneley, the younger Ferneley's signature is clearly visible, and the landscape appears not to be precisely identifiable.

Marcus Gheeraedts II *c.*1561–1636

T 03456   **Portrait of a Woman in Red** 1620

Oil on oak panel $44\frac{15}{16} \times 35\frac{1}{2}$ (1142 × 902)
Inscribed '1620' above the sitter's left arm
Purchased (Grant-in-Aid) 1982

Prov: ...; Duke of Norfolk; passed to an English private collection after 1973; sold to Oscar and Peter Johnson Ltd, from whom bt by the Tate Gallery

Exh: *The Age of Charles I*, Tate Gallery, November 1972–January 1973 (24)

This portrait of a young woman, clearly in an advanced state of pregnancy, is traditionally thought to represent a lady of the Constable family, who were ancestors of the Dukes of Norfolk in the Herries line. If this were so, she could be Anne, daughter of Sir William Roper.

She married Sir Philip Constable Bt, of Everingham, Yorkshire, and is known to have borne several children between 1618 and 1630. Although the details are difficult to make out, the elaborate pendant jewel on her forehead appears to incorporate an 'R' (? for Roper).

As Sir Oliver Millar points out in *The Age of Charles I* catalogue, T 03456 'with its tender mood, delicate handling and sensitive colour, can be confidently attributed to the last phase of Gheeraedts's career'. The painting is a harmony of various shades of red, which would have been even richer when the colours, now a little faded with time, were pristine. Although the pose is a standard one for the period, the soft modelling of the face, elegant hands, and a sense of impeccable balance between shapes (for example, the way in which the curtain unobtrusively follows the outline of the figure) are Gheeraedts's own.

Gheeraedts's ability to respond to the iconic grandeur required of portraiture in the later years of Queen Elizabeth's reign made him the most fashionable painter of the 1590s. He was well able to adapt to the still rather stiffly formal style of the Jacobean court, and became the favourite painter of the new Queen, Anne of Denmark. After her death in 1619, however, court patronage began to look towards the more progressive and flamboyant styles of the continent, and by 1620, when this portrait was painted, Gheeraedts's work was looking old-fashioned and provincial beside that of newcomers like Daniel Mytens. His gentle and rather two-dimensional style still found patrons among scholars and the gentry for a while, but his last known dated work is of 1629, and he probably retired from painting round about 1630.

T 03466   **Portrait of a Man in Masque Dress, probably Philip Herbert, 4th Earl of Pembroke** *c.*1610

Oil on octagonal oak panel $21\frac{7}{8} \times 17\frac{9}{16}$ (556 × 446)
Purchased (Grant-in-Aid) 1982

Prov: ...; R. Gilbertson, sold Christie's 7 July 1967 (8 as 'Gentleman said to be Robert Carr, Earl of Somerset') bt Agnew; ...; anonymous sale, Christie's 20 November 1981 (89, repr.) bt in, and offered again at Christie's 30 July 1982 (4, repr.) bt Leggatt for Tate Gallery

Exh: *Dictionary of National Biography*, 1908, for Herbert, Montgomery and Dormer; R. Strong, *The English Icon*, 1969, p.300, fig.306; *The Tate Gallery 1982–84, Illusrated Biennial Report*, p.26, repr.

The attribution to Gheeraedts was first made by Sir Oliver Millar when the painting appeared on the art market in 1967 as a putative portrait of Robert Carr, Earl of Somerset, an identification that cannot be sustained on comparison with known portraits of Somerset. The Gheeraedts attribution has been fully accepted by all subsequent writers, and the high quality of the work revealed during its recent restoration further reinforces the view that the painting is an unusual and fine example of the atist's middle period, after the flat and two-dimensional images of the Elizabethan era had begun to yield to the still formal but more shadowed and substantial style of the Jacobean period.

On grounds of likeness it can now be argued that the sitter is Philip Herbert, Earl of Montgomery and 4th Earl of Pembroke (1584–1650), whose passion for hunting endeared him to James I, as did his craggy good looks, whose salient features an unfriendly Oxford lampoonist described graphically in 1648:

His nose was notch'd like country garden pales
His brow and chin more mountainous than Wales . . .

(quoted in A.J. Finberg, 'Two Anonymous Portraits of Cornelius Johnson', *Walpole Society*, IV, 1918, p.12). Many authenticated portraits of the 4th Earl exist, among which this would be the earliest. Conveniently, all show the head from the same angle, and the distinctive tawny colouring, long bumpy nose, hooded eyes under light, arched eyebrows and bulging forehead are discernible in all. They are more elegantly rendered in Van Dyck's portrait of him in his maturity, c.1634 (National Gallery of Victoria, Melbourne), and flatteringly evened out in the magnificent full-length of the Earl in peer's robes, c.1615, by William Larkin at Audley End (The Hon. R.C. Neville; Strong 1969,

p.316, fig.327 in col.). The most compelling similarity, however, is with the three-quarter length of c.1628 at Hatfield, now firmly attributed to Daniel Mytens (E. Auerbach and C. Kingsley Adams, *Paintings and Sculpture at Hatfield House*, 1971, pl.VIII in col.).

What is clearly a companion to the Tate picture is in the collection of the Stanford University Museum of Art, California (21 × 17in, 533 × 433mm, Mortimer C. Leventritt Fund 77.181, bt from Hazlitt, Gooden and Fox 1977, ex coll. Lord Kinnaird). It shows a dark-haired man in a similar false oval on an octagonal panel, against the same blue background and wearing identical dress, but facing the other way. This could well represent Philip's elder brother William Herbert, 3rd Earl of Pembroke (1580–1630), although so far it has not been possible to ascertain if both paintings originally came from the same collection; they are differently framed, the Stanford portrait, unlike the Tate picture, being in a modern frame. Comparisons of likeness are less straightforward, as there are fewer portraits of William, and those that are known show him bearded and after he had become heavy in middle age. It is clear however that, unlike his brother, he was dark, and the structure of the face and characteristic hairline correspond well with that in the earliest known portrait of him by Paul van Somer, signed and dated 1617, in the Royal Collection (O. Millar, 'A Little-known Portrait by Paul van Somer', *Burlington Magazine*, XCII, 1950, p.294, fig.22). He is always shown wearing an annulet in his ear, as is the man in the Stanford picture.

Annulets, like the fleurs-de-lys embroidered on the tunics of both men in these two ovals, are part of the Montgomery coat-of-arms. Although it was the 3rd Earl's brother Philip who was created Earl of Montgomery in 1605, Montgomery Castle in Wales had been in the possession of the Herbert family for generations, and was a bone of contention between Edward Herbert, 1st Baron Herbert of Cherbury (1583–1648) and his kinsman Earl Philip throughout the years 1607–13. Significantly, a not dissimilar medallion portrait of Lord Herbert of Cherbury at Charlcote Park, datable to c.1609–10 and fairly convincingly attributed to William Larkin, shows him wrapped in a cloak covered with the five-pointed stars also found on the Montgomery arms (oil on copper, 22 × 18in, Strong 1969, p.315, fig.325). These heraldic elements are found today only on the arms of the Montgomeries of Scotland (e.g. the Earls of Eglinton) who, however, trace their descent from the legendary vassal of William the Conqueror, Roger de Montgomery, later Earl of Shrewsbury (died c.1093), the original builder of Montgomery Castle. Roger was celebrated by early historians as being 'literally foremost among the conquerors of England' (see E.A. Freeman, *History of the Norman Conquest*, 1867–79, II, p.194), endowed with all the attributes of a classic hero, justice, wisdom, moderation and lavish patronage of various religious institutions: in other words, a truly noble adversary of the English as represented in legend by the Arthurian Knights.

The Welsh wizard Merlin, King Arthur and an assortment of legendary knights figured in *Prince Henry's Barriers*, a military entertainment with speeches by Ben Jonson, staged on 6 January 1610 at the Banqueting House in Whitehall to celebrate Prince Henry's first bearing of arms (for a full account see S. Orgel and R. Strong, *Inigo Jones, The Theatre of the Stuart Court*, 1973, I, pp.158–76). Against a setting of Roman ruins to represent the Fallen House of Chivalry, the ancient Briton Meliadus (Prince Henry) and six chosen companions restore Chivalry to her former glory by successfully challenging fifty-six defendants 'consisting of Earles, Barons, Knights and Esquiers' dressed in a variety of exotic and mythological costumes. Only a few of the participants are known by name, but among them was the Earl of Montgomery, who acquitted himself so well as a defendant, that he was adjudged a prize. It is likely that William, assiduous courtier that he was, also participated in this glittering state occasion, and that these portraits could be a memento of it. It is not known what costume Montgomery wore, but the production had a strong classical bias, with the costume thought to be for Merlin, for instance, apparently based on the figure of Homer in Raphael's 'Parnassus'. Both portraits have a strong affinity with Isaac Oliver's celebrated miniature of Prince Henry *à l'antique*, posed in Roman dress, in profile against a classical shell niche, and also dated to *c*.1610 (Fitzwilliam Museum, Cambridge).

Although very different in character, both Herbert brothers shone at court, in the tiltyard and at masques. William, who suffered from migraines and was described as a melancholy young man, though 'immoderately given up to women' (he had a scandalous affair with Mary Fitton) had pleasing manners and was a favourite of Queen Anne of Denmark. Philip, on the other hand, was ill-tempered and notoriously foul-mouthed, a man who, according to a contemporary, 'pretended to no other gratifications than to understand dogs and horses very well', but was held in high favour by the King (see T. Lever, *The Herberts of Wilton*, 1967, pp. 72–96). The brothers often appeared together at tournaments and other state occasions, and among the many dedications of books that they accepted as lavish patrons of the arts is the famous dedication to them of the First Folio of Shakespeare (1623) as 'The Incomparable Pair of Brethren'. Their appearance in identical costumes on some occasion would not, therefore, seem out of character.

It may be relevant to note that the collection at Rousham has a portrait of Sir Charles Cotterell (1615–1702) by William Dobson (octagonal canvas 20½ × 17½in, repr. in catalogue of Dobson exhibition, National Portrait Gallery 1983, no.33) very similar in shape and size,

and in an identical late seventeenth-century frame to T03466. He is shown wearing conventional armour, with a red cloak tied on his shoulder in a very similar manner as here. He is said to have spent his early years at Wilton, attending on the Earl of Pembroke, becoming Groom-Porter to James I and later Master of Ceremonies to Charles I. It is not inconceivable, though at present unprovable, that some chivalric notion connected this small group of nobles, and that in the late seventeenth century, especially as the Herberts and Cotterell-Dormers were distantly related by that time, these paintings formed part of a set of portraits or a decorative scheme of some sort.

Samuel Hieronymus Grimm 1733–1794

T03603 The Glacier of Simmenthal 1774

Watercolour on hand-made laid paper
11⅝ × 14⅝ (295 × 371)
Inscribed 'S.H. Grimm 1774' b.r.;
inscribed on the back 'The Glaciere of Simmenthal. | The borders of the distanz consist of a row of towering masses of pure Ice, a Glaciere extends itself from it on all sides, & evacuates its | Superfluities between two high Rocks into the Valley. On the left side of the picture the River Simmen tackes its origin & gives | the name to the valley'
Purchased (Grant-in-Aid) 1983

Prov: ...; Edward Basil Jupp (d.1877); Thomas William Waller; Elizabeth Stauffer Moore, by descent to Elizabeth

Richardson Simmons, by whom sold
Christie's 12 November 1968 (74) bt
Agnew; purchased from Agnew by Walter
Beck, bequeathed to his niece Margot
Beck, by whom re-sold to Agnew, from
whom bt by Tate Gallery

Exh: *110th Annual Exhibition of Watercolours
and Drawings*, Agnew 1983 (27)

Grimm exhibited 'A Glaciere in Switzerland' at the RA
in 1774 (113) and 'A View in the Alps, Switzerland; a
stained drawing' at the RA in 1775 (143). A native of
Switzerland, Grimm frequently portrayed its glaciers,
making it difficult to identify the two drawings exhibited
at the RA. He designed some of the views of glaciers
which illustrated G.S. Gruner, *Die Eisgebirge des
Schweizerlandes*, 2 vols., 1760 (republished in French,
1770); but the view of Simmenthal included in the
first volume of Gruner was engraved after Koch, not
Grimm. Grimm also drew 'Seven capital Views of Switzerland' (mainly glaciers) for James Tobin; these are
discussed by Rotha Mary Clay, *Samuel Hieronymus
Grimm*, 1941, pp.5–10. Some of Grimm's drawings of
glaciers are reproduced in Clay, pls.6, 8, 9 and 10
(between pp.8 and 9).

The glacier of Simmenthal is a fall of the Simme river
which rises in the Bernese Alps and joins the Kander
river, near Thun, in south-west central Switzerland.

This drawing was one of several hundred drawings by
various artists bound in one of the two extra-illustrated
series of volumes containing a complete collection of
the exhibition catalogues of the Society of Artists of
Great Britain and the Free Society of Artists, compiled
by Edward Basil Jupp in 1871. The volumes were
broken up for Christie's sale of 12 November 1968.

Atkinson Grimshaw 1836–1893

T 03683 **Bowder Stone,
Borrowdale** *c.*1863–8

Oil on canvas $15\frac{3}{4} \times 21\frac{1}{8}$ (400 × 536)
Inscribed 'Atkinson Grimshaw|
[?Borro'dale]' b.r.
Purchased (Grant-in-Aid) with assistance
from the Friends of the Tate Gallery 1983

Prov: ...; said to have been in a private collection
from *c.*1900 until sold anonymously,
Sotheby's 21 June 1983 (40, repr. in col.)
£28,600 bt Lady Abdy for the Tate
Gallery

Lit: *The Tate Gallery 1982–84, Illustrated
Biennial Report*, 1984, p.36, repr. in col.

Paintings of Lake District subjects by Grimshaw bearing the dates 1863, 1864, 1865 and 1868 survive (exh.
Atkinson Grimshaw, Leeds, Southampton, Liverpool
1979–80, nos.3, 7, 17–18, 21; see also Sotheby's 21 June
1983 lot 41). It is not known, however, how many visits
he paid to the Lakes or to what extent he relied in his
paintings on the photographs he collected of the region.
Twelve such photographs survive in an album of Grimshaw's now in Leeds City Art Gallery, including two
that relate to his paintings of 'Windermere', 1863, and
'Nab Scar', 1864 (Alexander Robertson, 'Atkinson
Grimshaw: Some New Acquisitions', *Leeds Art Calendar*, no.94, 1984, pp.13–14).

Not enough is yet known about the chronology of
Grimshaw's early work for a precise date to be ascribed
to T 03683 but it undoubtedly belongs to the same period as his other Lake District paintings and is accordingly dated *c.*1863–8 here. Like these other works, it
reveals the influence of Pre-Raphaelite painting, examples of which Grimshaw might have seen in his native
Leeds in the collections of Ellen Heaton and Thomas
Plint. By the late 1860s Grimshaw was already moving
in a different direction, painting the first of the moonlight scenes which were to make his reputation. His
early work was subsequently forgotten; the existence of
'Bowder Stone, Borrowdale' was unsuspected before its
reappearance at auction in 1983.

Sir James Guthrie 1859–1930

T 03446 The Wash 1882–3

> Oil on canvas 37 × 28$\frac{15}{16}$ (940 × 735)
> Inscribed 'J. Guthrie | – 83 –' b.l.
> Purchased (Grant-in-Aid) 1982
>
> *Prov:* The artist's cousin Frederick (later Sir
> Frederick) Gardiner, Glasgow; on his
> death in 1937 given by his widow either to
> his sister Eliza Jane Troup or to the latter's
> son William Annandale Troup;
> bequeathed by the latter in 1966 to his own
> son Judge A. Troup, from whom bt by the
> Tate Gallery through the Fine Art Society
> Ltd
>
> *Exh:* *Guthrie and the Scottish Realists*, Fine Art
> Society Ltd, Glasgow, November–
> December 1981, London, December
> 1981–January 1982 (9, repr.)
>
> *Lit:* Sir James Caw, *Sir James Guthrie*, 1932,
> pp.18, 213; Roger Billcliffe, *The Glasgow
> Boys*, 1985, pp.56–7, pl.46

Guthrie and two other Glasgow artists, E.A. Walton
and Joseph Crawhall, spent the summer of 1882 painting at Crowland in Lincolnshire. Roger Billcliffe suggests in his recent book that they may have chosen
this part of the country because it allowed them to
concentrate on their rustic figure subjects without the
distraction of grand scenery and the presence of other
artists and because it offered a more consistent light than
Scotland, where they had painted together in previous
years.

Guthrie presumably began 'The Wash' at Crowland
but did not finish and date it until the following winter
when he was working in the studio he had borrowed at
Helensburgh from the amateur artist John G. Whyte.
Billcliffe reasonably argues that most of it was painted
during the early part of Guthrie's stay at Crowland. It
shares the sombre tonality of 'A Funeral Service in the
Highlands' (Glasgow Art Gallery), painted in 1881–
2, rather than the brighter palette of Guthrie's other
Crowland paintings, for example the aptly named 'To
Pastures New' (1882–3, Aberdeen Art Gallery). The
change in Guthrie's colour and also in his handling may
be explained, Billcliffe suggests, by his discovery of the
work of Bastien-Lepage during a visit to London from
Lincolnshire that summer. The visit is not documented
but Guthrie would almost certainly have gone down to
see his own 'Funeral Service' hanging in that year's
Royal Academy exhibition. Four of Bastien-Lepage's
paintings were on view in London and Guthrie would
also have seen works by British artists who had already
come under the spell of this remarkably influential
Frenchman: Stanhope Forbes's 'A Street in Brittany'
(Walker Art Gallery, Liverpool), for example, was on
view at the RA.

'The Wash' originally belonged to Guthrie's cousin
Frederick Gardiner, who with his brothers James and
William had founded a successful shipping company.
During the 1880s they were major patrons of Guthrie
and other Glasgow artists.

Gavin Hamilton 1723–1798

**T 03365 Agrippina Landing at
Brindisium with the Ashes of
Germanicus** 1765–72

> Oil on canvas, painted area approx.
> 71$\frac{3}{4}$ × 100$\frac{3}{4}$ (1825 × 2560), stretcher
> 71$\frac{3}{4}$ × 101$\frac{1}{4}$ (1825 × 2575)
> Purchased (Grant-in-Aid) 1982
>
> *Prov:* Commissioned by John, 1st Earl Spencer
> 1765; by descent to George, 8th Earl
> Spencer, sold 1981 to P. & D. Colnaghi
> Ltd, from whom purchased by the Tate
> Gallery
>
> *Exh:* RA 1772 (109); *Bicentenary Exhibition*, RA
> December 1968–March 1969 (682); *Zwei
> Jahrhunderte Englische Malerei*, British
> Council, Haus der Kunst, Munich,
> November 1979–January 1980 (128, repr.)
>
> *Lit:* Algernon Graves, *The Royal Academy of
> Arts*, III, 1905, p.365; Ellis K.

in his catalogue, 'Dull and livid, like all his works'. The picture is a typical example of Hamilton's neo-classicism, based on the classical tradition as transmitted by Raphael, Poussin and the seventeenth-century Bolognese school.

Waterhouse, 'The British Contribution to the Neo-Classical Style in Painting', *Proceedings of the British Academy*, XL, 1954, pp.72–3, pl.11; David Irwin, 'Gavin Hamilton: Archaeologist, Painter, and Dealer', *Art Bulletin*, XLIV, 1962, p.96, fig.12; David Irwin, *English Neoclassical Art*, 1966, p.50, pl.39; David and Francina Irwin, *Scottish Painters at Home and Abroad 1700–1900*, 1975, p.104; Kenneth Garlick, 'A Catalogue of Pictures at Althorp', *Walpole Society*, XLV, 1976, p.35, no.261; Helmut von Erffa and Allen Staley, *The Paintings of Benjamin West*, 1986, pp.44–6, repr.

Germanicus Julius Caesar was born on 24 May 15 B C and adopted by his uncle, later the Emperor, Tiberius in A D 4; this placed him in the direct line of succession. He served as Consul, Proconsul and Commander in Chief in the Gallic and German provinces until he was recalled by Tiberius in A D 17 and sent to take up a new command in the eastern provinces. In A D 19 he fell mysteriously ill and died at Antioch on 10 October, convinced that he had been poisoned by Gnaeus Piso who had been appointed Governor of Syria by Tiberius to watch Germanicus's activities. His death caused grief and suspicion in Rome and Agrippina's return with his ashes in an urn, and her progress by foot with her children from Brindisi where she landed to Rome, was upheld as an example of wifely devotion. Ten years later she was banished by Tiberius and died from starvation in 33 A D.

No. T 03365 is one of a series of large canvases of classical subjects painted by Gavin Hamilton in Rome from the early 1760s onwards. It was commissioned in 1765 by the first Earl Spencer, for whom Hamilton was acting in the purchase of works by Italian seventeenth-century painters including Guercino. The painting was completed and in England in time to be exhibited at the Royal Academy in 1772, when Horace Walpole wrote

James Turpin Hart 1835–1899

T 03396   A Rustic Timepiece 1856

Oil on canvas 21 × 17 (533 × 432)
Inscribed 'Jas. T. Hart | 1856' b.r. and
'The Rustic Time- | Piece | J.T.
Hart | Upper Talbot St | Notting Hill' on
the back of the canvas
Purchased (Grant-in-Aid) 1982

Prov: ...; anon. sale, Phillips 26 April 1982 (146, repr.) £2,000 bt for the Tate Gallery

Exh: RA 1856 (1219)

J.T. Hart was born in Nottingham where he also received his initial artistic training before enrolling in the Schools of the RA. 'A Rustic Timepiece' was his first Academy exhibit and the first of a number of rustic genre scenes which constitute the most significant part of his output. His use of children in such scenes suggests the influence of more established painters like F.D. Hardy (1826–99) and W.H. Knight (1823–63). The landscape background of T 03396 has obvious links with Pre-Raphaelite landscape; the presence of ears of corn found between the back of the canvas and the stretcher during conservation work possibly indicates that he painted this part of the composition on the spot. The painting seems to have gone unnoticed by the critics at the time it was exhibited. The compiler is grateful to Heather Williams for supplying details of Hart's background and career.

William Havell 1782–1857

T 03393 **The Thames near Moulsford** 1807

Oil on board laid on panel 19 × 24½ (482 × 623)
Inscribed 'WHAVELL 1807' b.r.
Purchased (Grant-in-Aid) 1982

Prov: ...; anon. sale, Christie's 22 March 1968 (128) £178.50 bt Barclay; ...; Antique Hypermarket, Kensington, where bt c.1971 by Martyn Gregory and sold 1972 to Felicity Owen, from whom bt through Spink & Son Ltd by the Tate Gallery

Exh: *Landscape in Britain c.1750–1850*, Tate Gallery, November 1973–February 1974 (251, repr.); *William Havell 1782–1857*, Spink & Son Ltd, November–December 1981, Reading Museum & Art Gallery, January–February 1982, Abbot Hall Art Gallery, Kendal, March–April 1982 (51, repr.)

The view is identified in the catalogue of the 1981–2 Havell exhibition as looking downstream near Moulsford, close to the old Havell family home of Sowbury. Moulsford lies north-west of Reading, between Goring and Wallingford. Havell was a native of Reading but does not appear to have been especially active as a painter in the Thames Valley until about 1805: tours of Wales in 1802 and 1803 had supplied him with much of the material for his earlier work. The Tate Gallery oil sketch of 'Caversham Bridge', dated 1805, is one of

his first Thames works. During the following years he exhibited numerous watercolours of the area at the newly founded Society of Painters in Water Colours and in 1807 an oil painting of Reading Abbey at the Royal Academy (Reading Museum & Art Gallery). T 03393 was presumably painted later the same year.

Both 'Reading Abbey' and 'The Thames near Moulsford' owe something to the example of J.M.W. Turner, whom Havell greatly admired at this time. The former painting is reminiscent in particular of Turner's 'Windsor Castle from the Thames' of c.1805 (T 03870 below), of which a watercolour copy by Havell exists. Havell was doubtless influenced in his choice and treatment of subjects by Turner's work on the Thames but other artists were also active there in the early years of the century and Havell's friend William Delamotte was painting comparable river scenes on the Isis in 1805–6 (see Louis Hawes, *Presences of Nature*, New Haven 1982, pls.58, 61).

T 03394 **Windsor Castle** c.1807

Oil on card 4⁹⁄₁₆ × 8⅝ (116 × 219)
Inscribed 'Windsor –|31|Windsor Castle| in the distance|WHavell' on back of card
Purchased (Grant-in-Aid) 1982

Prov: ...; anon. sale, Phillips 19 May 1981 (part of 53, repr.) £550 bt Anthony Reed, from whom bt by Spink & Son Ltd 1981 and sold by them to the Tate Gallery

Exh: *William Havell 1782–1857*, Spink & Son Ltd, November–December 1981, Reading Museum & Art Gallery, January–February 1982, Abbot Hall Art Gallery, Kendal, March–April 1982 (54)

This sketch was dated to 1807 in the catalogue of the 1981–2 Havell exhibition on the supposition that it was a pair to 'On the Kennet, Reading', no.53 in the same exhibition (now Yale Center for British Art) and that the latter was probably painted about the time of the

'Reading Abbey' which Havell exhibited at the Royal Academy in 1807 (Reading Museum & Art Gallery). However, the two sketches are only a pair in the sense of being painted in a similar technique on the same size cards and there seems no particular reason to associate them with the May 1807 exhibit, a summer scene presumably at least begun in 1806. Havell did, nevertheless, exhibit watercolours of Windsor Castle at the Society of Painters in Water Colours in 1806, 1807 and 1808 and T 03394 may well date from this period.

Joseph Haynes 1760–1829 after William Hogarth 1697–1764

T 03828 The Stay-Maker 1782

Etching $10\frac{7}{16} \times 13\frac{7}{8}$ (265 × 352) on paper $13\frac{7}{8} \times 15\frac{7}{8}$ (378 × 404); plate-mark $12\frac{1}{2} \times 15\frac{1}{8}$ (317 × 384) cut at top margin
Writing-engraving '*The Stay-Maker | From an Original Sketch in Oil by Hogarth in the Possession of M.ʳ Sam.ˡ Ireland | Etch'd by Jos. Haynes Pupil to the late M.ʳ Mortimer | Publish'd as the Act directs Feb.ʸ 1 1782 at N.ᵒ 3 Clements Inn*'
Transferred from the reference collection 1984
Prov: Unknown
Lit: J. Nichols, *Biographical Anecdotes of William Hogarth*, 1782, p.324; A. Dobson, *William Hogarth*, 1907, p.267

This etching is the earliest record of the original oil sketch of the same title which is now in the Tate Gallery (N 05359). The painting derives its title from the print, and is thought to be one of the several unfinished canvases of 'The Happy Marriage' series on which Hogarth

was working in about 1745, but never completed. The print is also of interest in that it records Joseph Haynes as a pupil of the painter John Hamilton Mortimer (1740–79).

Charles Cooper Henderson 1803–1877

T 03428 Sportsman in Scottish Dress Driving to the Moors *c*.1845

Oil on canvas $13 \times 25\frac{1}{8}$ (331 × 612)
Inscribed 'CH' on case at back of cart
Bequeathed by Mrs F. Ambrose Clark from the collection of the late F. Ambrose Clark through the British Sporting Art Trust 1982
Prov: . . .; E.J. Rousuck, from whom purchased by 1958 by F. Ambrose Clark; his widow, Mrs F. Ambrose Clark
Exh: Tate Gallery, August–September 1982, and York City Art Gallery, March–September 1984, with other paintings from Mrs F. Ambrose Clark's Bequest (no catalogue); *Paintings exhibited by the British Sporting Art Trust*, Vestey Gallery, National Horseracing Museum, Newmarket, April–December 1986 (unnumbered, repr.)
Lit: [E.J. Rousuck], *The F. Ambrose Clark Collection of Sporting Paintings*, privately printed, New York 1958, p.118 (as 'August Twelfth. The Day of St. Grouse'), repr. p.119

The four sportsmen, similarly dressed in plaids, two of them wearing tam-o'shanters and the other two Glengarry bonnets, are described by Rousuck as 'two masters and the gillies', perhaps because the barrels of only two guns are visible; but the cheerful manner in which they are crowded into a small spring-cart, laden with game bags, a retriever, a flask and a hamper, suggests that they are friends, of equal social standing, driving in unpretentious style to share a day's shooting.

Marylian Watney draws attention (in correspondence) to the very unusual fact that the cart is drawn not only by a horse within the shafts but also by a pony which has been hitched beside the horse, but outside the shafts: she suggests that the pony was probably hired for part of the trip 'in order to help pull the heavy load of four stalwart gentlemen up the Scottish hills'.

Colonel Charles Lane suggests (in correspondence) a date of c.1845 for T03428 because it has much in common with Cooper Henderson's 'Going to the Moors', which with its companion 'Going to Cover' was engraved in aquatint in 1847, published by Fores.

T03429 Mail Coach in a Snowstorm c.1835–40

Oil on canvas 17⅞ × 30⅛ (331 × 612)
Inscribed 'CH' on mail-bag to right of coach-top
Bequeathed by Mrs F. Ambrose Clark from the collection of the late F. Ambrose Clark through the British Sporting Art Trust 1982

Prov: ...; E.J. Rousuck; F. Ambrose Clark by 1941; his widow Mrs F. Ambrose Clark

Exh: *Outdoor England*, Century Club, New York, February–April 1941 (5); Tate Gallery, August–September 1982, and York City Art Gallery, March–September 1984, with other paintings from Mrs F. Ambrose Clark's Bequest (no catalogue); *Paintings exhibited by the British Sporting Art Trust*, Vestey Gallery, National Horseracing Museum, Newmarket, April–December 1986 (unnumbered, repr.)

Lit: [E.J. Rousuck], *The F. Ambrose Clark Collection of Sporting Paintings*, privately printed, New York 1958, p.121, repr. p.120

Snow has obliterated the lettering on the coach, leaving its destination vague and only its royal coat of arms visible. A date of circa 1835–40 or earlier is suggested (in correspondence) by Colonel Charles Lane, who notes that 'the great snowstorm of 1836' seems to have prompted Pollard early in 1837, and Cooper Henderson about the same time, to paint snow-bound coaching scenes.

John Frederick Herring 1795–1865

T03430 The Hunting Stud 1845

Oil on canvas 17⅞ × 27⅞ (455 × 708)
Inscribed 'J.F. Herring. Senʳ 1845' b.r.
Bequeathed by Mrs F. Ambrose Clark from the collection of the late F. Ambrose Clark through the British Sporting Art Trust 1982

Prov: ...; N.C. Bechman, sold Christie's 19 December 1919 (133) bt Fores; ...; F. Ambrose Clark by 1941; his widow Mrs F. Ambrose Clark

Exh: *Outdoor England*, Century Club, New York, February–April 1941; Tate Gallery, August–September 1982, and York City Art Gallery, March–September 1984, with other paintings from Mrs F. Ambrose Clark's Bequest (no catalogue)

Engr: Aquatint, ? by J. Harris, pub. Messrs Fores, London 10 February 1846 and Goupil & Vibert, Paris

Lit: [E.J. Rousuck], *The F. Ambrose Clark Collection of Sporting Paintings*, privately printed, New York 1958, p.170, repr. p.171

This is one of a set of four paintings which were engraved and published as 'Stable Scenes'. The other three subjects are 'The Mail Change', 'The Team' and 'Thoroughbreds'. Herring's painting of 'The Team' was sold at Christie's 26 April 1985 (19, repr.).

John Hill *c.*1780–1841

T 03668 **Interior of the Carpenter's Shop at Forty Hill, Enfield**
? exh. 1813

Oil on canvas 18½ × 27⅞ (578 × 794)
Inscribed (? *c.*1900) on label pasted to back of original canvas (now separately preserved) 'Interior of the Carpenter's Shop at Forty Hill Enfield painted|by John Hill of Forty Hill about|1800 his first finished picture|he was entirely self taught|exhibited at Somerset House' Presented by the Friends of the Tate Gallery 1983

Prov: ? Given by the artist to Nancy Hill (? his niece, d. 1899, having married Henry Want); Henry Want; Mrs M. Want (old storage label in her name formerly on back); ...; anon. sale Christie's South Kensington, 10 November 1982 (112) bt Anthony Reed, from whom purchased for the Tate Gallery 1983

Exh: ? RA 1813 (333, as 'Interior of a Carpenter's Shop'); *Spring Medley*, Anthony Reed, March 1983 (14, detail repr.)

Lit: Jack Warans, 'Inside Two "Carpenters' Shops"', *The Tate Gallery 1982–84, Illustrated Biennial Report*, 1984, pp.22–5, repr. in col. p.22

This is almost certainly the picture exhibited at the RA in 1813 and, again almost certainly, depicts John Hill's own workshop or that of his father Thomas Hill (d.1814), also a carpenter.

Five other paintings by John Hill depicting landscape in and around Forty Hill were included in Christie's 1982 sale, all bought by Anthony Reed and (with T 03668) exhibited by him in 1983 (nos.14–19). Each painting had an old label pasted on the verso; from transcripts made by Anthony Reed, and from information supplied to him by G. Dalling, Borough Librarian, Enfield (all kindly given by Anthony Reed to the Tate's archives), various facts relating to Hill emerge. In the 1841 Census for Enfield, Hill's occupation is given as 'builder'; he lived at the junction of Forty Hill and Goat Lane, almost certainly in a house called Worcester Lodge (the subject of one of his paintings, no.18 in Reed's 1983 exhibition). In the Enfield section of Pigot's *Directory*, 1839, John Hill is listed as a carpenter, and his address is given simply as Forty Hill. John Hill died on 21 November 1841, leaving no issue; he must have been born between 1779 and 1783, for the 1841 Census Returns (which rounded ages up or down to the nearest five years) give his age that year as sixty.

The interior depicted in T 03668 is that of a small joinery shop, flagstoned and largely timber-built, with a view of the countryside seen through an open window at the back of the shop. It is at this vantage point that the master carpenter (distinguished from his assistants by his moleskin hat and dark jacket) is portrayed at work, planing timber. His two assistants are in shirt-sleeves; each wears the traditional carpenter's cap made of stout white paper folded into a box-like shape (also worn by the Carpenter in Tenniel's illustrations to *Alice: Through the Looking-Glass*). John Hill may here portray himself as the master, unless the master is his father Thomas Hill (d.1814) and he himself is one of the assistants.

A detailed description of the tools and equipment in the workshop is given by Warans. These include a sash-cramp (for use in making sash windows), an adze, a gauge, a bow-saw and a coffin-maker's saw, a metal-working vice, various templates for objects used in house-building, such as staircase balusters, a picture-frame (perhaps an allusion to Hill's own pictures) and a carved eagle, perhaps the prototype of a carving for a church pulpit. Such details convey abundant information about the different sorts of work carried out in this shop.

Warans notes (pp.22–3) that 'None of these details are picturesque props; all of them are painted from first-hand knowledge of the carpenter's trade. The three men at work in this interior are not posing for the artist. Each of them is absorbed in his work and in command of the task to which he is putting his skills'. He notes that each of the three men is evidently a fully-qualified carpenter, for each has beside him his carpenter's tool box, usually elaborately constructed and inlaid, which he would have made during his apprenticeship. Warans adds (p.23) that the only unrealistic note is the axe lying unprotected on the flagstones in the foreground ('no carpenter would leave an axe on the floor like that'); otherwise he compares the realism of this picture to the unrealistic symbolism in the details of Millais's 'Christ in the House of His Parents (The Carpenter's Shop)', N03584 in the Tate's collections, repr. Warans p.24.

Celina Fox, Museum of London, notes (in correspondence) that representations of craftsmen at work are rare in British art of this period, and suggests that this work is most closely related to Thomas Baxter's depiction of his father's china-painting workshop (Victoria & Albert Museum; exhibited at the RA in 1811, two years earlier than Hill's picture); possibly Baxter's picture inspired Hill to do something comparable. Hill also exhibited 'A Carpenter's Yard, Enfield' at the RA in 1820 (333).

William Hogarth 1697–1764

T03613   **The Dance (The Happy Marriage ?VI: The Country Dance)** *c.*1745

Oil on canvas 26$\frac{7}{8}$ × 35$\frac{1}{8}$ (683 × 892)
Purchased (Grant-in-Aid) with assistance from the National Heritage Memorial Fund 1983

Prov: In Hogarth's studio until his death; bt from Mrs Hogarth by Samuel Ireland before 1782; his sale, Sotheby's May 1801 (460 as 'The First Sketch of the Dance to the Analysis of Beauty') £3.13.6 bt Vernon; ...; W.B. Tiffin, print and book seller in the Strand, by 1833; ...; Charles Meigh of Grove House, Shelton, Staffs, sold Christie's 21 June 1850 (105 as 'The

Happy Wedding. The Ball.') bt Hoare; ...; William Carpenter of Forest Hill by 1875 when lent to RA; bequeathed by him to the South London Art Gallery 1899; sold by the London Borough of Southwark to the Tate Gallery

Exh: RA Winter 1875 (35 as 'Sketch for a Country Dance at the Wanstead Assembly, Essex'); *British Art*, Whitechapel Art Gallery 1911 (68); *Peinture Anglaise*, Musée Moderne, Brussels 1929 (86); *English Conversation Pieces*, 25 Park Lane 1930 (123, pl.32 in souvenir catalogue); *British Art*, RA, Winter 1934 (232; no.67, pl.XXVIII in souvenir catalogue); *Masterpieces of British Painting*, British Council tour, Chicago, New York, Toronto 1946–7 (5, repr.); *British Painting 1730–1850*, British Council tour, Lisbon, Madrid 1949 (21); *British Painting from Hogarth to Turner*, British Council tour, Hamburg, Oslo, Stockholm, Copenhagen 1949–50 (61); *William Hogarth 1697–1764*, Tate Gallery, June–July 1951 (63); *European Masters of the Eighteenth Century*, RA, November 1954–January 1955 (28); *Hogarth the Londoner*, Guildhall Art Gallery 1957 (26); *British Painting in the Eighteenth Century*, British Council tour, Museum of Fine Art, Montreal, National Gallery of Canada, Ottawa, Art Gallery, Toronto, Museum of Art, Toledo (Ohio) 1957–8 (35, repr.); *Painting in Great Britain 1700–1960*, British Council tour, Pushkin Museum, Moscow, Hermitage, Leningrad 1960 (7); *British Painting 1700–1960*, British Council tour, Cologne, Zurich, Rome (7, repr.), Warsaw (29, repr.) 1966–7; on loan to Tate Gallery 1968–83; *Hogarth*, Tate Gallery, December 1971–February 1972 (148, repr. in col.)

Engr: Adapted and engraved by William Hogarth as Plate II for *The Analysis of Beauty*, 1753; etching by T. Ryder for Ireland II, 1799, as Plate IV of 'The Happy Marriage'

Lit: J. Nichols, *Biographical Anecdotes of William Hogarth*, 1782, pp.39–42, 258–62, 1785 edition, pp.46–9, 115, 327–31; S. Ireland, *Graphic Illustrations of Hogarth*, II, 1799, pp.129–31, engr. facing p.130; J. Nichols and G. Steevens, *The Genuine Works of William Hogarth*, I, 1808, p.128 n., II, 1810, pp.198–9 (quoting Nichols

1782), repr. as T. Cook's engr. after *Analysis of Beauty* facing p.198, III, 1817, pp.207, 258; J.B. Nichols, *Anecdotes of William Hogarth*, 1833, pp.356–7; A. Dobson, *William Hogarth*, 1907, pp.196, 206, 310; R.B. Beckett, *Hogarth*, 1949, pp.67–8, pl.168; F. Antal, *Hogarth and his Place in European Art*, 1962, pp.28, 30, 51, 105, 113–16, 163, 183, 199, 204, 209, 217, 231 n.101, 237 n.1, 238 n.26, 251 n.52, pl.94a; G. Mandel and G. Baldini, *L'Opera Completa di Hogarth*, Milan 1967, p.110, no.163, pl.XLVII (col.); R. Paulson, *Hogarth*, New Haven and London 1971, II, pp.15, 18–19, 174, pl.197; J. Lindsay, *Hogarth: His Art and His World*, 1977, pp.130–1, repr. facing p.182; M. Webster, *Hogarth*, 1979, pp.115–18, 186, no.147, repr. p.122; D. Bindman, *Hogarth*, 1981, pp.160–2, figs.127, 128 (col. detail)

Nichols, writing in 1781–2, was the first to point out that 'The Dance' is one of six scenes for the 'Happy Marriage', planned by Hogarth as a counterpart to his 'Marriage A-la-Mode' series painted in 1743. It was to contrast a virtuous country marriage with the evils and hypocrisies of the doomed London marriage of the earlier set. Three of the sketches ascribed to it by S. Ireland and engraved for his *Graphic Illustrations* 1799 (repr. Beckett 1949, figs.163, 166, 167) are lost, so that little comment can be made as to their authenticity. Of the three surviving sketches, this is certainly the most finished, and is arguably one of the most brilliant studies of figures in action in early 18th-century painting. In addition a case can be made out for the inclusion of 'The Staymaker' in this series (Tate Gallery N 05359).

The scene is a country dance in the hall of an old-fashioned Jacobean country mansion (this can be surmised from the open sky and the outlines of the village church seen through the window). The participants represent a gamut of individual types, from the elegant couple on the right, to the country bumpkins further down the line. One perspiring reveller has removed his wig to mop his bald pate in the cool night breeze at the open window. The silvery moonlight contrasts with the warm light of the brilliantly painted chandelier in the centre of the room, – significantly, it is these two different sources of light that are the most finished part of the painting. The action of the dance is framed by a dark foreground of which the main feature is a minstrels' gallery in the upper left corner, below which a shadowy group of people, including a lady and a clergyman, appear to be settling down to a quiet game of cards. The figure on the floor in the centre is probably the boot-boy whose task it would be to look after the pile of visitors' hats on the floor beside him. Hogarth is said to have intended to paint each hat in such a way that the viewer could identify its owner in the crowd: he did this with considerable success in the later engraving, though such detail would have been difficult to achieve in dark oil paint. The dark strip down the right hand margin is an afterthought, and was painted by Hogarth over the original window surround, which continues underneath, as an effective contrast to the colourful action beyond.

From the late nineteenth century until recently, this scene has been frequently called 'The Wanstead Assembly' due to a confusion with Hogarth's group portrait of the Child family in the great hall of their mansion at Wanstead, now in the Philadelphia Museum of Art. At the root of it is probably the radically altered Palladian setting of the scene for the print of 1753, which, according to John Ireland (*Hogarth Illustrated*, 1793, I, p.lxxvi) was said to represent Wanstead House. Since Samuel Ireland's account of 1799 it has also been usual to call it 'The Wedding Dance', on the assumption that the scene represents the ball after the wedding. The fact remains, however, that Hogarth's intended narrative is not known. We do know, however, that one scene represented the actual wedding in church. This painting was cut up some time before 1833 (possibly by 1782, when Nichols gave the opinion that 'there is little reason to lament the loss of it'), and the fragment from it in the collection of the Marquess of Exeter (Beckett 1949, fig.164) of a parson's head looks quite genuine. We have some inkling of what the scene looked like from Nichols's complaint (1782, p.42) that 'An artist, who representing the marriage ceremony in a chapel, renders the clerk, who lays the hassocks, the principal figure in it, may at least be taxed with want of judgment.' This has the ring of authentic, irreverent Hogarthian invention, of the kind that easily upset Nichols's somewhat narrow sense of decorum and at times misled him into regarding Hogarth as an uncouth primitive. Recent X-rays of the much earlier 'Beckingham Wedding' (Metropolitan Museum, New York) show that just such a detail had been painted out in the left foreground of this otherwise very formal group. This raises the intriguing possibility that Hogarth, frustrated on this issue in an early commissioned work, subsequently made a point of including such a feature in wedding scenes where he had only himself to please, i.e. 'The Happy Marriage', and the wedding scene in 'The Rake'.

The second surviving scene is of 'The Wedding Banquet', now in the Royal Institution of Cornwall, Truro, and formerly in the possession of Mrs Garrick. It is, as Nichols rightly noted, set in the same Jacobean mansion as the Tate painting, and the principal figure in it is the old squire who raises a toast to the young couple, while the musicians (not confined to the gallery as in this picture) strike up a tune in the background.

Both Nichols and Ireland assume that the narrative culminates in the wedding itself, but this is to ignore the time scale of 'Marriage A-la-Mode' to which this was to be a parallel. This assumption also fails to leave room for 'The Staymaker', which stylistically belongs to this series and appears to show the young couple surrounded by children. If one were to interpret 'The Staymaker' as a scene showing the fitting of the ballgown for the ball to follow, then one could see 'The Country Dance' as a *grande finale* of the series, the first assembly given by the young squire for his tenants and neighbours after coming into his inheritance on the death of his father – after, naturally, a decent period of mourning, perhaps represented by one of the lost scenes engraved for Ireland in 1799, e.g. Plate III, 'Relieving the Indigent' (repr. Beckett 1949, pl.166), which has a tomb-like structure in the background. This would explain the absence here of the father so prominent in the 'Banquet', and the rather isolated female figure in the shadows at the card table on the left, who could be the widow, for whom it would be indecorous to join in the dancing. A further pointer is given indirectly by Nichols, who pillories Hogarth for his ignorance of etiquette in allowing the bride and groom to dance with each other at their wedding (Nichols's knowledge of correct behaviour in such matters may well have been better than Ireland's, who dismisses the criticism in 1799). From what we now know of Hogarth, it is highly unlikely that he would have made a mistake of this sort, and fitting the series into the suggested time scale would solve the problem. It would also be relevant in the sense that, as the earlier series began its descent into tragedy with the disintegration of a once-great estate, it would be fitting for the contrasting series to take as its conclusion the felicitous transfer of a well-run estate from one generation to the next, since inheritance and the management of property often forms the mainspring of Hogarth's moral tales.

The painting remained in Hogarth's studio until his death, and his own high estimation of it is shown by the fact that he adapted the design for Plate II of his *Analysis of Beauty*, published in 1753. This changes the Jacobean setting to a very different Palladian one, and transforms the leading couple into aristocratic personages, in some editions even into the Prince and Princess of Wales. This design is no longer part of a narrative, but a purely didactic work to illustrate his theory that the serpentine 'Line of Grace of Beauty' lies at the basis of all that is inherently pleasing to the eye, in this instance in the weaving lines of a country dance and the graceful deportment of the leading couple. That he was deeply involved with this theory by 1745, the presumed date of this picture, can be seen from the fact that he gave the 'Line' a prominent place in his 'Self-Portrait with a Pug Dog' of that year (Tate Gallery N00112). It is therefore quite possible that he planned from the outset that his 'happy' series should illustrate his theories of true harmony not only on a moral plane, but also on the level of design, albeit in a much more spontaneous and less didactic fashion than in the later print.

William Hogarth, Prints after: see Cook, Haynes

Thomas Jones 1742–1803

T 03367 **In the Road to Santa Maria de' Monti, near Naples: Morning** 1781

Pencil and watercolour on hand-made laid paper $8\frac{5}{16} \times 10\frac{15}{16}$ (211 × 278)
Inscribed 'In the Road to Sᵃ Mᵃ de' Monti by Naples| 10th May 1781–' (the date corrected from '[?] Oct 1780') in pencil upper centre; 'morng' (i.e. morning) and again more faintly 'morng', with a sketch of the sun's rays, in pencil t.r. and 'wallnut' in pencil within branches of a tree on the left; 'Mrs Adams' on the back
Purchased (Grant-in-Aid) 1982

Prov: ? by collateral descent from the artist until 1978; sold, as 'The Property of a Lady', Christie's 14 March 1978 (101, repr.) £3,200 bt Morton Morris & Co. Ltd, from whom purchased by the Tate Gallery
Exh: *English Watercolour Drawings*, Spink 1979 (5, repr.)
Lit: [ed. A.P. Oppé], 'Memoirs of Thomas Jones', *Walpole Society*, XXXII, 1951, pp.102–4

Santa Maria de' Monti, not yet identified, appears to have been a church or convent (? no longer extant) in the Naples countryside, within easy walking distance of the city, in the direction (presumably) of Capo di Monte.

In his 'Memoirs' Jones does not mention any of the numerous drawings which he made during 1781 of the road to Santa Maria de' Monti, though he does describe something of the appeal which 'this romantick place' had for him. On 2 June 1781 he made a long and partly retrospective entry which begins with an account of walking from his lodgings in Naples to meet his fellow-artist William Pars, who had lodgings at Capo di Monte, 'at an Osteria in the road to S'a M'a de Monti' Jones continues, 'In this *hollow* Way is a most beautiful Series of picturesque Objects, which I discovered by Accident in one of my perambulations – Here may visibly be traced the Scenery that Salvator Rosa formed himself upon – Only taking away the Pinetrees, which were, perhaps, planted since his time, and which indicate a State of Cultivation not suited to his gloomy mind, with the addition of Water & a few Banditti – And every hundred yards presents you with a new and perfect Composition of that Master –'.

Jones continues, 'When Towne was in Naples, I took him with me to see this romantick place, with which he seemed much delighted'. Earlier entries record that Francis Towne arrived in Naples on 8 March 1781, returning to Rome on 3 April 1781, and that during that time Jones offered Towne his services as *cicerone*, and was able to conduct him to 'many picturesque Scenes of my Own discovery, entirely out of the common road of occasional visitors'. Evidently Jones's fascination with the road to Santa Maria de' Monti lay at least partly in the fact that it was of his 'own discovery'.

Under 2 June 1781 Jones recounts a 'whimsical incident' which he and Towne had encountered during their walk along this road: 'Proceeding up the valley whose boundaries contracted more and more as we advanced, increasing in proportion the Gloominess of the Scene; We arrived at a spot, which might very properly have been termed *the Land of Darkness & the Shadow of Death* – This sequestered place was environed on all Sides, with hanging rocks here and there protruding themselves from behind dark masses of a variety of wild Shrubs, and overshadowed by branching Trees – Here, says I, Mr Towne, is Salvator Rosa in perfection we only want Banditti to compleat the picture – I had scarcely uttered the words, when turning round a Projection of the Rocks, we all-at once pop'd upon three ugly-looking fellows dressed in the fantastic garb of the *Sbirri di Campagna*, with long knives, cutting up a dead jackAss ... *Towne* started back as if struck by an Electric Shock – ... "I'll go no farther" says he, with a most solemn face, adding with a forced smile that however he might admire such Scenes in a Picture – he did not relish them in Nature, – So we wheeled about and returned to the more cultivated environs of the City –'.

Jones adds 'I have many a time since that Period, taken a solitary walk up this romantick Dingle, and seen the bleached and scattered bones of the poor animal, but I thank God, never met with Robbers or assassins there or anywhere else in the Country –'.

Jones made at least thirteen studies, mostly in water-colour (some in pencil only), of different stretches of the winding road to Santa Maria de' Monti. Ten of these were shown in the *Thomas Jones* exhibition, Marble Hill House, Twickenham and National Museum of Wales, Cardiff, June–September 1970 (49–55, 57: the 1970 exhibition numbers are used below to distinguish versions), lent from private collections except for no.57, lent by the Whitworth Art Gallery. T 03367 was not exhibited in 1970; nor was a watercolour version in the collection of the Yale Center for British Art (B 1977.14.5299). These drawings (except for no.51b, which is undated) are almost all dated between 2 April and 10 May 1781; no.57 is dated 6 October 1781. Like T 03367, nos.51a, 54 and 55 are dated 10 May 1781; like T 03367, no.51a is a view made in the morning.

The different studies are all made from different points along the road, and (apparently) at different times of day. Walnut trees, clumps of umbrella pines and rocky banks overhung with plants and shrubs are common to all of them. In T 03367, Jones shows the rays of the morning sun shining from the top right of his picture, which must be the east; the view must therefore be looking northwards, presumably to Capo di Monte, with the city of Naples behind him. The sun in T 03367 appears to be just striking the right of the trees and shrubs, indicating that it is still some hours before midday, and the colouring is fresh and light-toned. Some of the other studies have heavily shadowed foregrounds and are more sombre in colouring, but none of them is 'gloomy' in the Salvator-esque sense. The drawings express Jones's recurring private pleasure in the scene; the 'Memoirs', characteristically, give rein to an extrovert sense of humour, partly at the expense of his more timid fellow-artist Francis Towne.

The tall several-storeyed building in the background of T 03367, which has a square tower surmounted by a cupola, has not been identified; it cannot be Santa Maria de' Monti, which Jones shows in some of the other studies as a fairly squat (?) two-storeyed building with a low dome at one point on its otherwise flat roof.

An oil sketch of the road, inscribed 'Near Capo di Monte Naples' ($13\frac{1}{2} \times 19$in) is in the collection of John Appleby.

Jones recorded in his 'Memoirs' under 5 July 1777, 'Went with Tresham to see the Antique Rooms just discovered, by digging for antient Bricks, in the Villa Negroni – The painted Ornaments much in the Chinese taste – figures of Cupids bathing &c and painted in *fresco* on the Stucco of the Walls – The Reds, purples, Blues & Yellows very bright – but had a dark & heavy effect – NB Tresham made a purchase of these paintings for 50 Crowns, to be taken off the walls at his Own Expence –'.

There seems every reason to suppose that Jones painted this scene (or at least made the crayon under-drawing of it) on or shortly after 5 July 1777, the date recorded in his 'Memoirs' for his visit to the newly-discovered site. In his inscription on the back of T 03544 however Jones dates the discovery to 'ye Year 1779'. The '1779' is written with a sharper pencil than the rest of the inscription, and may have been added later, Jones relying on his memory (in this case at fault) rather than on his 'Memoirs'.

In her catalogue of the 1974 exhibition *British Artists in Rome*, Lindsay Stainton observed that 'Considering the number of excavations that were made in Rome in the eighteenth century it is surprising that there are so few visual records of any'. Writing before the inscription on the back of T 03544 established the site of this scene, Stainton correctly supposed that the scene corresponded with Jones's description of his visit to the grounds of the Villa Negroni with Henry Tresham on 5 July 1777, and suggested that the building to the left in the background was the convent of S. Eusebio seen from the north-east. She also suggested that Jones gained admittance to the excavation through the influence of the dealer Thomas Jenkins, who had been a friend of Jones's teacher Richard Wilson in Rome in the 1750s. She notes that Henry Tresham's purchase of wall-paintings, recorded by Jones, proved a good investment, being later sold to the Earl-Bishop of Derry, and that Thomas Hardwick, another friend of Jones, made a ground-plan of the 'antique Rooms' and recorded the wall-paintings in a cross-section drawing (both in the RIBA collection).

Jones seldom introduces figures into his scenes. The presence here of several spectators, as well as labourers on the site, perhaps testifies to the interest aroused by the excavation, at least among English visitors.

John Dale married Thomas Jones's younger daughter Elizabetha

Exh: *Thomas Jones*, Marble Hill House, Twickenham, and National Museum of Wales, Cardiff, June–September 1970 (62); *Painting from Nature*, Arts Council, Fitzwilliam Museum, Cambridge and RA, November 1980–March 1981 (21, repr.); *På Klassick Mark*, Nationalmuseum, Stockholm, September–December 1982 (187)

Lit: [ed. A.P. Oppé], 'Memoirs of Thomas Jones', *Walpole Society*, XXXII, 1951, pp.110–11; Lawrence Gowing, *The Originality of Thomas Jones*, 1985, pp.44–5, pl.39. *Also repr: The Tate Gallery 1982–84, Illustrated Biennial Report*, 1984, p.29 in col.

Dated on the back 'May 1782', this must have been painted between 9 May and the end of that month. Jones records in his 'Memoirs' under 3 May 1782 that as well as moving to new sleeping quarters at 'Mr Thomas Francis, the English Taylor's, without the porta di Chaja', he also acquired – for a few weeks only, as it turned out – a new painting-room within the Borgo of the Chiaja, on the ground floor of a small convent called the Capella Vecchia and overlooking the convent of the Capella Nuova, taking possession of this on 9 May. Under 12 May 1782, Jones relates that 'The Room which I was in possession of at the Convent, was large and commodious for such a place, and as it was on the ground floor and vaulted above, very cool and pleasant at this Season of the Year – The only window it had, looked into a Small Garden, and over a part of the Suburbs, particularly the *Capella nuova*, another Convent, the Porta di Chaja, Palace of Villa Franca, and part of the Hill of Pusilippo, with the Castle of S. Elmo

& convent of S. Martini &c all of which Objects, I did not omit making finished Studies of in Oil upon primed paper –'.

T 03546 **A Scene in the Colosseum, Rome** ?1777

Oil on hand-made laid paper $17 \times 11\frac{3}{8}$ (432×289), irregularly cut on all four sides
Inscribed 'N°7 | A Scene in the Collosseo at Rome | T Jones' in pencil on back
Presented by Canon J.H. Adams 1982

Prov: By descent from the artist to Canon J.H. Adams, whose great-grandfather Captain John Dale married Thomas Jones's younger daughter Elizabetha

Exh: *Thomas Jones*, Marble Hill House, Twickenham and National Museum of Wales, Cardiff, June–September 1970 (32); *Painting from Nature*, Arts Council, Fitzwilliam Museum, Cambridge and RA, November 1980–March 1981 (20, repr.); *På Klassick Mark*, Nationalmuseum, Stockholm, September–December 1982 (124)

A date of 1777 is suggested for this because a wider view of the Colosseum inscribed 'View in the Colosseo | 9 April 1777' is included in the artist's sketchbook, 'bought at Rome 17 February 1777', in the collection of the British Museum (Department of Prints and Drawings, 1981–5–16–18 f.20). Alternatively, T 03546 may have been painted during Jones's first few weeks in Rome; his 'Memoirs' (p.53, fully cited under

T 03544/5) relate that he spent the time between 27 November and 12 December 1776 'in visiting the Ruins, Churches and palaces – sometimes in Company and sometimes alone, for I could not always persuade my Country men to attend me to see Sights with which they had already been glutted'.

A work in oil on paper approximately the same size, inscribed 'No.6' and 'A Scene in the Collosseo at Rome' was presumably executed at the same time as T 03456; then in the collection of W.A. Brandt, it was also included in the 1970 Thomas Jones exhibition (31).

Charles Samuel Keene 1823–1891

T 03840   **Two Artists Working by Lamplight in a Studio** *c.*1860

Pen and brown ink on grey-cream thin wove paper $7\frac{3}{8} \times 5$ (187 × 127), the left edge torn (? from a sketch-book)
Inscribed on the back 'Hayes & Rossiter' in ink top centre and 'C K' in monogram in pencil b.l.
Purchased (Grant-in-Aid) 1984

Prov: 'The artist's sale, Hammersmith' (? a house sale after Keene's death in 1891; not in Lugt, and not yet traced), bt 'Mr Cockerell, the builder', by whom given to Edith Holman-Hunt, William Holman Hunt's second wife (see below); . . .; anon. sale Christie's 19 June 1979 (193, repr. facing p.39) bt Fine Art Society, from whom purchased by the Tate Gallery

Exh: *Paintings and Drawings of the 1860 Period*, Tate Gallery, April–July 1923 (315, as 'W. Holman-Hunt instructing Dante Gabriel Rossetti in his Cleveland Street studio . . . 1847', lent by Mrs Holman-Hunt)

Even without the monogram 'C K' on the back (or even if this were still invisible; see below), there can be no doubt stylistically that this drawing is by Charles Keene; it corresponds in style with other works of *c.*1860.

According to Christie's 1979 catalogue, there was a label (apparently now lost) attached to the backboard 'signed and inscribed by Mrs. M.E. [sic] Holman Hunt, the artist's second wife' (in fact Edith, née Waugh, whom he married in 1876) which read 'Drawing by Sandys ? of Holman Hunt in his Cleveland Street studio where D.G. Rossetti came to him as a pupil. D.G.R.'s head is seen sitting behind W.H.H. The gas-stand shown beside W.H.H. I sold when I gave up the studio 1919 – My builder Mr. Cockerell bought the drawing at Charles Keene's sale in Hammersmith & gave it to me'. As the drawing was formerly stuck to another sheet of paper, Charles Keene's monogram and the inscription 'Hayes & Rossiter' may not have been seen by her, though it is possible that the name 'Rossiter' was mis-reported to her or mis-read by her as that of Rossetti. Mrs Holman-Hunt's comments on the drawing were presumably invited by the compiler of the 1923 exhibition; she evidently supposed that the drawing was by 'Sandys' (presumably Frederick Sandys, 1829–1904) and that it portrayed William Holman Hunt and Rossetti in about 1847, a period in Holman Hunt's life of which she can have had no first-hand knowledge. The 1923 catalogue correctly attributed the drawing to Keene; it added a reference presumably supplied by Mrs Holman-Hunt to William Holman Hunt's *Pre-Raphaelitism and the Pre-Raphaelite Brotherhood*, 2nd ed., 1913, I, p.78, a passage in which Hunt recalled that in about 1847 he decided to live in his studio (in Cleveland Street), whereupon Rossetti 'again broached the project of working under me for my hourly super-intendence and instruction in painting' and of sharing Hunt's studio. Mrs Holman-Hunt's belief that the drawing depicts such a scene probably accounts for the date of '1847' attached to the drawing in the 1923 exhibition catalogue.

The inscription 'Hayes & Rossiter' on the back of T 03840, apparently in Keene's hand, and in a prominent place, suggests that 'Hayes' and 'Rossiter' may be the two artists portrayed here; but they have not been identified. 'Hayes' could be one of several artists of that name; 'Rossiter' could be the Charles Rossiter mentioned by H.L. Mallalieu as an art teacher who married the artist Frances Rossiter in 1860 (*Dictionary of Watercolour Artists up to 1920*, 1976, p.225), or possibly the William

Rossiter, follower of F.D. Maurice, founder of the Working Men's College, who himself began a South London equivalent in 1868.

Or does Charles Keene in fact include a self-portrait here? The face of the foremost figure – bearded, moustached, with thin features and tousled hair – seems to bear a distinct resemblance to that of Keene as he portrayed himself, both at work, in a series of sketches repr. Derek Hudson, *Charles Keene*, 1947, pl.1, and in a small pen and ink self-portrait, seated, in the Tate's collection (T 02088).

Tilly Kettle 1734 or 5–1786

T 03373 **Mrs Yates as Mandane in 'The Orphan of China'** exh. 1765

Oil on canvas $75\frac{3}{4} \times 51$ (1924 × 1295)
Inscribed 'Mrs Yates' b.l. in yellow paint
Purchased (Grant-in-Aid) with assistance from the Friends of the Tate Gallery 1982
Prov: ...; Marquess of Hastings, Donington Park, Leicestershire, by 1847; Hastings sale, Phillips 25–26 February 1869 (106 as by Zoffany) 17 gns bt Noseda; ...; Sir Hugh Lane by 1910 when lent to the Whitechapel Art Gallery, but left collection, according to Manners and Williamson (1920), before Lane's death in 1915; ...; Sir Edmund Davis JP, sold anonymously Christie's 11 July 1930 (97 as by Liotard) 150 gns bt in ('Wells'); ...; bt by Gavin Graham on art market in

Nice, France, 1981, sold by him and Anthony Dallas & Sons to the Tate Gallery
Exh: SA 1765 (64 as 'Portrait of a lady; whole length); *Shakespeare Memorial Exhibition*, Whitechapel Art Gallery, October–November 1910 (7 as by Zoffany)
Lit: Arthur Murphy, *Life of Garrick*, Dublin 1801, pp.213–20; *Dictionary of National Biography*, 1909, for Yates and Murphy; Lady Victoria Manners and G.C. Williamson, *Johann Zoffany RA*, 1920, p.213; J.D. Milner, 'Tilly Kettle 1735–1786', *Walpole Society*, XV, 1927, pp.60, 61, 85

The portrait represents the actress Mary Ann Yates (1728–87) in the part of the Chinese princess Mandane in Arthur Murphy's tragedy 'The Orphan of China'. This was an adaptation of Voltaire's 'L'Orphelin de la Chine' of 1755, and was first produced at Drury Lane on 21 April 1759. The part of Mandane first raised Mrs Yates to eminence as a tragic actress, and she played the role many times from its initial performance until 4 February 1767, including twice (28 April 1759 and 16 February 1760) by command of the Prince of Wales. In 1759 she spoke a cheering Epilogue to the play (printed in *Gentleman's Magazine*, XXIX, 1759, p.227; the play's long and complex plot is described on pp.217–20), but on 2 April 1764 she delivered a new Prologue, written especially for her, and it is possible that the painting shows her doing this. Murphy, who was a family friend and as a fellow-actor is said to have coached her towards her success on the stage, wrote that in the play 'her exertions were such, that she astonished all the performers' and caused Garrick to predict her ascendancy over Mrs Cibber (Murphy 1801).

Born Mary Ann Graham into a humble but respectable family (her father was a captain's steward), she began her acting career in Dublin in 1752, but moved to London the following year. In 1756 she married the comedy actor Richard Yates (?1706–96), and they lived in comfortable circumstances in their houses at Richmond and Stafford Row, Pimlico, entertaining elegantly a wide circle of theatrical and literary friends, including Murphy and Garrick. Mrs Yates died on 3 May 1787 and was buried with her parents in Richmond church. Acclaimed as the best tragic actress before Mrs Siddons, she was admired for her noble manner and majestic deportment, and is said to have courted a likeness to the solemn composure of an antique statue.

Something of this demeanour is captured in Kettle's portrait, which was his first exhibited work in the grand manner modelled on Reynolds, whom he greatly admired. While using the exotic pink, black and gold costume to great effect, its country of origin suggested only by a discreet Chinese Chippendale dado on the wall behind, he has adapted the outfit to accord more with the lines of fashionable dress (true stage costumes tended to have more extravagantly exaggerated proportions), so that, despite its outlandishness, Mrs Yates presents a figure of statuesque, almost classical, dignity. Even so, the portrait was not considered very flattering, and an anonymous review in *The Public Advertiser* on 10 May 1765 opined that '... Mr. Kettle has by no Means done Justice to the Beauty of Mrs. Yates. – This *Kettle* is just the Opposite to the *Kettle* of Medea which renewed Youth, for the Copy appears twenty Years older than the Original'. A reply printed the following day, also anonymous, points out that the portrait did the sitter full justice as an actress, since she was meant to represent the 'Distres'd Mother of a Son grown up to Manhood'. It also complains that the picture was hung in 'the darkest Corner of the Room' – a reflection maybe of the hanging committee's response to what must have struck eighteenth-century sensibilities as an uncommonly bold colour scheme. The following year Kettle again tried to capture attention by showing a full-length of an actress in character, Mrs Anne Elliot as Juno (lost), but clearly the results were disappointing, for by mid-1768 he had laid his plans to go to India.

In spite of being one of Kettle's most spectacular works, it seems to have lost its attribution quite early. The earliest reference to it after the 1765 exhibition is found so far in the Donington Park inventory, compiled for probate in November 1847 (Leicestershire Record Office, DG30 Hastings/Donington MS, DE362 Box 4091/11), where it is listed in the 'Rural Simplicity Bed Chamber' as 'Mrs. Yates in an Indian Costume', valued at 20 gns and unattributed to any painter. As it cannot be traced in any of the earlier Donington Park inventories of *c.*1794 – after 1813 among the Hastings papers now in the Huntington Library, San Marino, California, it may have been acquired for the collection in the early nineteenth century because her costume was thought to be Indian: the 1st Marquess of Hastings (1754–1826) had served in India as, among other things, Governor of Bengal and Commander-in-Chief of the Army 1812–23. This supposed Indian connection would have then suggested the attribution to Zoffany (who worked in India 1783–89) under which it appeared in the Hastings sale of 1869, and where it can be identified from George Scharf's detailed notes in the National Portrait Gallery's copy of the sale catalogue.

The compilers are grateful to Geoffrey Ashton for information on Mrs Yates's theatrical career.

Sir Edwin Landseer 1803–1874

T 03395   **The Harper** 1821–2

Oil on canvas 35⅞ × 28 (912 × 710)
Inscribed 'EL' on top of the harp
Purchased (Grant-in-Aid) 1982

Prov: ...; Thomas Landseer, the artist's elder brother, sold Christie's 14 April 1880 (280, as 'A Welsh Bard') 17 gns bt Permain; ...; R. Durant, sold Christie's 12 June 1886 (127, as 'The Bard') 24 gns bt Nathan; ...; purchased *c.*1950 at a saleroom in Tunbridge Wells by Mr and Mrs R. Beling who in 1970 gave it to their daughter from whom bt by the Tate Gallery

Exh: BI 1822 (284)

Lit: *New Monthly Magazine*, VI, 1822, p.159

'The Harper' was first shown at the British Institution when Landseer was just entering his twentieth year and it was unusual in being the first of his exhibited pictures (having established his reputation as an *animalier* after his debut at the Royal Academy in 1815) to deal solely with the human figure.

The subject of the Bard had been treated by a number of British artists before this date – most notably by Thomas Jones (in 1774), Benjamin West (in 1778, see Tate Gallery T 01900), Henry Fuseli (in 1780), William Blake (in ?1809, see Tate Gallery N 03551) and John Martin (in 1817). Landseer's picture is a re-working of the proto-romantic image of the heroic poet described in Thomas Gray's pindaric ode *The Bard* (published in 1757) which had provided the inspiration for these earlier paintings; however, in Landseer's case, there might well be a more specific debt to Walter Scott's poem *The Lay of the Last Minstrel*, first published in 1805, which was widely read during the early years of the nineteenth century.

This particular picture betrays an academic pre-occupation both with the handling of chiaroscuro and the disposition of drapery – all clearly based on the study of a model in the studio – as well as with the need to set the figure in an appropriate landscape – in this case a wild and stormy one. A study of this sort at this particular moment in Landseer's career inevitably recalls that period between 1815 and 1818 when the young artist was working simultaneously in the studio of the history painter B.R. Haydon and studying in the Royal Academy Schools. Such an interest in the conventions of academic art which 'The Harper' betrays, seems to suggest that, rather than merely glancing backwards, Landseer was consciously looking forward with an awareness that the most likely way to professional eminence and respectability was through the more familiar interpretation of historical subject-matter – employing the human figure – rather than through those depictions of the brute creation on which his remarkable rise to fame was founded. It was, indeed, a large canvas in which human figures played an important part, 'The Battle of Chevy Chase' (RA 1826, Birmingham City Art Gallery) which finally ensured Landseer's election as an ARA in November 1826, and, in a sense, therefore, 'The Harper' anticipates this later work.

When it was exhibited 'The Harper' was only noticed by the critic of the *New Monthly Magazine*, who described it as a work in 'a quiet and subdued style, which is not without promise in another line of the art than that in which Landseer is unquestionably destined to reach the most distinguished excellence'. The latter prediction accurately foretells Landseer's great success as an animal painter; if there is one feature of this picture which clearly links it with the greater part of Landseer's output it is the beard of the Harper himself – a remarkable *tour de force* of brushwork in which seemingly every hair is accounted for.

Henry Herbert La Thangue 1859–1929

T 03413 **The Return of the Reapers** 1886

Oil on canvas $46\frac{7}{8} \times 27\frac{3}{8}$ (1190 × 695)
Inscribed 'H·H·LATHANGUE' b.l.
Purchased (Grant-in-Aid) 1982

Prov: Probably acquired from the artist by Herbert Mitchell; still his in 1933 when lent to RA; ...; acquired from Cooling Galleries by the Fine Art Society Ltd 1968 and sold by them to Arthur Grogan 1972; bt from him by the Tate Gallery

Exh: *Commemorative Exhibition of Works by Late Members*, RA, January–March 1933 (212); *Channel Packet*, Fine Art Society Ltd, March–April 1969 (67, repr.); *A Painter's Harvest, works by Henry Herbert La Thangue*, Oldham Art Gallery, November–December 1978 (5, repr.); *Post-Impressionism*, RA, November 1979–March 1980 (316, repr.)

Lit: *The Tate Gallery 1982–84, Illustrated Biennial Report*, 1984, p.37, repr. in col; Malcolm Warner, 'Victorian Paintings at the Tate Gallery, Recent Acquisitions', *Apollo*, CXXIII, 1986, p.263, fig.10

The catalogues of the last three exhibitions listed above state that 'The Return of the Reapers' is initialled and dated 1886 on the back. No such inscription could be found when the work was acquired by the Tate Gallery but there seems little reason to doubt that it was once there, perhaps on a label which later became detached.

T 03413 was presumably painted in Norfolk, where La Thangue went to live on his return from France in 1884. It was while in France, studying in Paris and painting in Brittany and the Rhone Valley with Stanhope Forbes and Harvard Thomas, that La Thangue adopted the 'square brush' technique used with striking effect in this picture. 'The Return of the Reapers' also shows La Thangue's characteristic device of placing figures against a high horizon, thereby flattening the picture space. In both this and his use of large square brushes, La Thangue (like other British artists of his generation) was following the example of the French painter Jules Bastien-Lepage.

In his catalogue of the 1978 Oldham exhibition, Kenneth McConkey describes La Thangue's 'A Portrait' in the Towner Gallery, Eastbourne (exh. 1978, no.6, repr.) as probably a study of the female reaper in T 03413. Although not otherwise connected with the latter, this small portrait does seem to be of the same person. McConkey also points out that 'The Return of the Reapers' was apparently not exhibited by La Thangue and that it was probably purchased directly from the artist by its first known owner, La Thangue's friend Herbert Mitchell, son of the Bradford textile manufacturer Abraham Mitchell. The Mitchells are portrayed in La Thangue's painting 'The Connoisseur' of 1887 (Bradford Art Gallery; exh. Oldham 1978, no.7, repr.).

Charles Robert Leslie 1794–1859

T 03789   **The Carved Room, Petworth House, Sussex** c.1826

Verso: Sketch of a Seated Male Figure in Van Dyck Costume 1844
Oil on millboard 14 × 12 (352 × 300)
Inscribed on verso '*N*' and 'Dec 4th|1844'
Purchased (Grant-in-Aid) 1983

Prov: The artist's wife, Harriet, probably until her death in 1885; ? the artist's youngest son, George Dunlop Leslie RA (1835–1921); his eldest son, David Leslie and then by descent to his daughter Barbara (died c.1960); purchased from the administrators of her estate by her cousin Thomas Leslie Twidell from whom bt by the Tate Gallery

Exh: RA Winter 1870 (199 as 'Carved Drawing-Room at Petworth')

Petworth House at Petworth in Sussex was the country seat of George O'Brien, the 3rd Earl of Egremont (1751–1837). As one of the most enlightened and generous of all patrons of living British painters and sculptors during the nineteenth century – he owned works by, for example, Beechey, Blake, Flaxman, Jones, Northcote, Opie and Turner – he frequently invited artists to be his guests at Petworth. Here they had the freedom of the house and its grounds and there are a number of recorded instances where Egremont set aside rooms which his artist-guests could use as studios.

C.R. Leslie's first contact with Lord Egremont came in May 1823 when, at the suggestion of Thomas Phillips RA (Egremont's 'official' portraitist), he was asked to make a portrait of one of his grandchildren who was dying. Soon afterwards Egremont commissioned a more substantial picture from Leslie – the subject to be chosen by the artist – and in response he painted a scene from Cervantes's *Don Quixote*, 'Sancho Panza in the Apartment of the Duchess'; a small preliminary study in oils for this picture is in the Tate Gallery (N 01798). The finished canvas, which is now at Petworth House, was exhibited at the Royal Academy in 1824 and its success not only led Egremont to predict, with some accuracy, that Leslie would become 'the Hogarth of Elegant life' (Egremont to Lord Holland, 6 May 1824; Holland House MSS. British Museum Add. MSS 51725, ff 59–60) but also produced an immediate commission from his patron for a companion work – with the proviso that should the artist in the meantime receive other commissions then he should give them priority over Egremont's. In fact, after the 'Sancho Panza', Leslie painted five more pictures for Egremont: portraits of two of his daughters (1830), 'A scene from the *Taming of the Shrew*' (1830–1; RA 1832); 'Gulliver's Introduction to the Queen of Brobdinag' (1834–5; RA 1835), and 'Charles II and the Lady Bellenden' (RA 1837).

With the possible exception of J.M.W. Turner, Leslie appears to have had a stronger attachment to Petworth and its owner than had any of his other colleagues who were visitors to the house. The most obvious reason for this was that Egremont's commissions for 'Sancho

Panza' and its companion came at an important moment in Leslie's career and enabled him to consolidate his position as one of the leaders among contemporary painters of literary *genre*. In addition to this, however, in the end Leslie's association with Petworth was inextricably bound up with his own family life in a way that no other artist experienced. A striking instance of this is found in the fact that when his second son was born in 1835 he was named George, after Lord Egremont.

Leslie's first visit to Petworth was made in 1826 with his wife (C.R. Leslie, *Autobiographical Recollections*, 1860, I, p.102) and then subsequently during the Earl's lifetime he made further visits – invariably with his wife and children – in 1827 (when Leslie's eldest son sat for a zephyr in Beechey's portrait of Egremont's niece, 'Mrs Hasler as Flora': C.R. Leslie to Ann Leslie, 2 January 1828; private coll.), 1828, 1829(?), 1831 (when he finished 'A Scene from the *Taming of the Shrew*'), 1832, 1833, 1834 (twice; on the second occasion he commenced work on 'Gulliver'), 1835 (when he worked on 'Autolycus', a commission for another patron, John Sheepshanks); 1836 and 1837 (twice; on the second occasion he was attending Lord Egremont's funeral). After Egremont's death we know that Leslie went to stay in Petworth, and almost certainly visited the house, in 1848, 1853, 1856, 1857 and 1859. On the last four occasions he stayed with his friend the engraver J.H. Robinson RA and in the latter year he was to die very shortly after returning home to London from his visit.

Whilst guests at Petworth, Leslie and his family were given a large sitting room and a suite of bedrooms (Robert C. Leslie, 'With Charles Robert Leslie, RA', *Temple Bar*, CVI, 1896, p.356). During his visits the artist himself would, in the words of one of Egremont's grand-daughters, 'go about the rooms making sketches in his little sketchbook of the ... old china vases and Venetian mirrors' ('Painter and Patron. Glimpses of Turner and other artists at Petworth', *Times*, 9 December 1959, p.14). Leslie's studio sale (Foster's, 25–28 April 1860) contained about two dozen such sketches, along with a few landscape studies of the environs of the house, a few of which can be identified as the sources for accessories in some of Leslie's finished pictures. Another aspect of the use to which he put his time at Petworth is seen in the copies which he made, for his own pleasure and instruction as well as for the benefit of his friends, from paintings by the old and modern masters which hung in the house. Three of these were in Leslie's studio sale, but there were others: in 1830 he sent sketches taken from van Dyck's portrait of Ann Carr, Countess of Bedford, and Reynolds's 'Death of Cardinal Beaufort', to his former instructor in Philadelphia, Thomas Sully (C.R. Leslie to Sully, 12 January 1830; coll. Boston Public Library), and in 1832 he made a slight copy of a landscape by Thomas Gainsborough which he gave to his close friend John

Constable (C.R. Leslie, *Memoirs of the Life of John Constable*, 1845, p.222).

Of all the works by C.R. Leslie which owe their inspiration to Egremont and Petworth T 03789 is unique in being an exact record of one of the rooms in the house. It also appears to be, apart from the large group of watercolours showing views of Petworth which Turner made in about 1828–9 (now Turner Bequest, nos. CCXLIII and CCXLIV), the only instance of one of Egremont's artist visitors setting out specifically to make a record of the inside of the great house. Turner, as it happens, also made a sketch of the Carved Room when in use as a dining room (TB CCXLIV–36) but Leslie's rendering of the scene, unlike any of Turner's very much more spontaneous sketches, has a documentary precision which reflects his concern, when in the right surroundings, for noting appropriate background material which could be turned to good account in his own subject pictures.

T 03789 shows the north-west end of the Carved Room, which takes its name from the carved wall panels which were completed by Grinling Gibbons in 1692. With its exquisitely wrought carvings, in wood, of trophies, *putti*, flowers, fruit and animals the room, which is the largest in the house, is the most splendid apartment in Petworth and Gibbons's work in it certainly ranks among the finest examples of his art (for the best concise account of the Carved Room see Christopher Hussey, 'Petworth House II' *Country Life*, LVIII, 5 December 1925, pp.862–71). So exact is Leslie's treatment of his subject that it is possible to identify the actual items of furniture and works of art in the room; all of them are still at Petworth. The table nearest the viewer on the left is a Louis XIV porphyry topped table which dates from the end of the seventeenth century (for an illustration see 'Furniture at Petworth', *Country Life*, LIX, 13 February 1926, pl.13) and the pier table between the two windows can be identified as one of a pair of Italian gilt-wood and marble tables with additions of *c*.1760 (see Gervase Jackson-Stops, 'Furniture at Petworth', *Apollo*, CV, 1977, p.364, pl.21). Amongst the pieces of classical sculpture in the room, all of which were purchased in Rome for the 2nd Earl of Egremont in the 1750s and 60s, the bust on the nearest table might be the idealized head of a woman, at one time known as 'Sabina' and 'Artemis', which is a Roman work dating from the 2nd Century AD, and the bust on the bracket on the wall is probably the portrait head of the Emperor Hadrian, which is carved out of Parian marble and which is set into a Renaissance bust of coloured marble (see Margaret Wyndham, *Catalogue of Greek and Roman Antiquities in the Possession of Lord Leconfield*, 1915, nos.28 and 78 respectively). The two portraits on the far wall are (over the fireplace), Frances Prinne, Lady Seymour of Trowbridge, now attributed to William Larkin (active 1610–

20) but at one time given to P. van Somer (see *Petworth House*, National Trust Guide, 1978, p.20 and C.H. Collins Baker, *Catalogue of the Petworth Collection of Pictures in the Possession of Lord Leconfield*, 1920, p.129) and (over the door), Elizabeth Howard, Countess of Northumberland, by Sir Peter Lely (1618–80). This latter picture is still in the same position today but the portrait of Frances Prinne was replaced, at an unknown date, by a portrait of Charles I on horseback after van Dyck. The view through the open door into what was in Leslie's day called the Red Room shows an arrangement of paintings and furniture which is identical to that depicted in a watercolour sketch of the Red Room by Turner (TB CCXLIV–21). The painting of which part appears beyond the top left hand corner of the doorway is probably van Dyck's portrait of Sir Robert Shirley for, in a note dealing with Turner's picture, Violet, Lady Leconfield, identifies this as the work which hangs on the left hand side of the door on the north wall of the Red Room (notes added to the copy of A.J. Finberg's *Complete Inventory of the Drawings of the Turner Bequest*, 1909, in the Department of Prints and Drawings, British Museum). In or about 1869, the Red Room was devoted completely to the works of Turner and renamed the 'Turner Room'.

Leslie's view of the Carved Room can be dated to the time of his earliest visits to Petworth, most probably those of 1826 or 1827, for a number of reasons. In the first place the room does not appear to have the extensive wood carvings which were added to Gibbons's original scheme by Jonathan Ritson (c.1780–1846) between about 1827 and 1846 (the compiler is grateful to Alison McCann of West Sussex Record Office for supplying these dates from the Petworth House Archives). Most of these additional carvings, which covered much of the wall area and some of the ceiling, were eventually removed after the 2nd Lord Leconfield succeeded to the title in 1869 at which time the white paint which covered the original seventeeth-century panelling, and which is so evident in Leslie's painting, was also stripped off (see Hussey, op.cit.). At the same time, it should also be noted, four paintings by Turner which had been installed in c.1829 on the east wall of the room, almost as predellas to the full-length portraits which hung there, were removed and placed in the Turner Room (see Turner T 03883–6 below, and *Petworth House*, National Trust Guide, 1978, p.21). Secondly, in a small picture which Leslie painted for the 1st Earl of Mulgrave (1755–1831) in c.1829–30, 'Laura Introducing Gil Blas to Arsenia', (now coll. Marquess of Lansdowne), there are elements of the composition, particularly a marble topped and giltwood table and the arrangement of a group of paintings hung on a wall seen through an open door, which are clearly borrowed directly from T 03789. Thirdly, T 03789 clearly dates from that period of Leslie's career – the 1820s – when

the influence of the seventeenth-century Dutch masters of genre on his own painting was at its strongest. In 1821 he wrote to his friend Washington Irving that 'the more I see of the Dutch School, the more I venerate them and the more hopeless appears the chance of coming near them' (C.R. Leslie, ed. T. Taylor, *Autobiographical Recollections*, 1860, II, p.112). In expressing such sentiments Leslie was reflecting the widespread public taste at that time for Dutch and Flemish paintings. But he was also indicating the more particular interest among contemporary artists in the technical virtuosity and skilful handling of subject matter which these painters possessed and the lessons which artists like himself felt such works held for the creators of modern cabinet pictures. Like David Wilkie, who had, earlier on, looked at the examples of David Teniers (1610–90) and Jan Steen (1626–79) when he was treating subjects from Scottish peasant life, Leslie, in looking for examples of how he could treat the more subtle dramas of domestic life which appealed to him, had lighted upon the work of Pieter de Hooch (1629–after 1684) and Gerard Ter Borch (1617–81).

As early as 1817, on his first visit to Paris, Leslie had made a sketch of one of the de Hoochs in the Louvre (Leslie 1860, I, p.41, II, p.291) but a more telling experience of art of this period came at the time of the exhibition of the whole of George IV's collection of Dutch paintings which was held at the British Institution during the summer of 1826. There can be little doubt that Leslie went to this exhibition and here was one work by de Hooch, 'The Card Players', which held his attention. It is a characteristic work by the artist: it shows a group of figures in an interior, lit from a large window which is partly covered by a thin curtain and with a view through an open door into a brightly lit courtyard beyond. In later life Leslie, who thought the picture 'the finest work of de Hooch with which I am acquainted', described it in the following terms:

> It represents an interior, with a few figures drinking, smoking, and playing at cards. Its largest masses are gray, but as this serves for a foil to warm lights, the tone is delicious, and is exactly that of the finest summer weather. In the lights, there is a predominance of the most refined red and yellow, and though there is one large mass of blue drapery, yet it is of the deepest dye. There is no sunshine in this picture, but something even more beautiful, the reflection of sunshine on an open door, from some object outside, but not seen . . .
>
> (C.R. Leslie, *A Hand-Book for Young Painters*, 1855, p.194)

'The Carved Room' contains no figures and it is a literal representation of the room. In one respect, therefore, it has close affinities with a tradition, of which Leslie would have been well-aware, of interior view-taking established by Charles Wild and James Stephan-off in their illustrations for W.H. Pyne's *The History of the Royal Residences* (3 vols. 1819). Nevertheless, Leslie's artistry, his sense of what, in technical and historical terms, is appropriate to the subject in hand, raises his view of this interior at Petworth above the level of a mere architectural record. The conscious debt to de Hooch is obvious in the view-point which he has adopted and in the preoccupation with the luminous quality of daylight, tinted by colour (in this case, the red of the curtains); in the manner the adjoining spaces are suffused with light and in the delicacy with which the paint itself is applied in order to achieve this effect.

Although in these respects 'The Carved Room' stands apart from the sort of sketching by Leslie which Egremont's granddaughter mentioned – when he noted likely 'props' for his subjects – nonetheless, the artist did turn to the work for such a purpose on at least two occasions. The first has already been mentioned. More interestingly, however, in another painting, entitled 'The Heiress', which he exhibited at the Royal Academy in 1845 (no.131; oil on canvas 34 × 26¼, 813 × 654; private collection; repr. *Exhibition of English Paintings*, Leger Galleries, 1968, no.29). Here Leslie recreated the Carved Room, with a number of variations, as the setting for a slight domestic incident in which the young heiress, with her servants, is receiving and discarding the proposals which have been written to her by hopeful suitors. The costumes and many of the background details are unmistakeably Victorian: the work is, in fact, Leslie's most successful attempt at reinterpreting the seventeenth-century Dutch models which were so dear to him, in nineteenth-century terms.

The date on the verso of T03789 would seem to be associated with the period of Leslie's work on 'The Heiress' but the study of the figure in van Dyck dress does not relate to any finished picture by the artist.

As a postscript to this discussion of T03789 and C.R. Leslie at Petworth, a seventh and final commission which the artist commenced for Lord Egremont should perhaps be mentioned. The subject of the painting was an incident from the Earl's own family history, 'Lucy Percy, Countess of Carlisle, bringing the pardon to her Father' and it was a work in which Egremont took a close interest. The artist records that the Earl even went up to the top rooms in the house in order to retrieve an old globe which was to be introduced into the foreground of the picture (Leslie 1860, 11, p.242) but in fact Egremont died before the painting had progressed very far and was put aside. It was eventually re-commenced at the end of 1845, at the request of Egremont's son and heir, Colonel George Wyndham (later 1st Lord Leconfield), and finished in September 1846.

For Leslie, the course of this particular commission undoubtedly marked a painful conclusion to much that was dear to him about Petworth. Not only was it inter-rupted by Egremont's death, but also Colonel Wynd-ham obviously conducted his affairs with artists in a manner totally different to that of his father. Known, rather wryly, by Harriet Leslie as 'the fox-hunter' – he was famous throughout southern England for his devotion, above all else, to the chase – Wyndham appears to have been both inept and insensitive towards Leslie. It is obvious from a letter written by Harriet that the Colonel at one point pleaded shortage of money as an excuse for not forwarding payment to the artist (Harriet Leslie to C.R. Leslie, n.d.; private coll.) and right at the last moment when the picture was finished he wrote to Leslie to say that if any of the painter's friends wanted the work he would be 'very glad to relinquish all claims to it'. The artist's comment 'bless his dear heart! he's as shabby as ever' referred as much to his sense of being let down over a very practical matter as to the fact that he was now, in the circumstances, unlikely to take the picture down to Petworth House as he had hoped (C.R. Leslie to Harriet Leslie, 26 September 1846; private coll.).

A few days earlier Harriet had herself articulated her husband's feelings and hopes about the picture – and about Petworth as he remembered it: her tone is curiously redolent of the sentiment which informs J.M.W. Turner's picture 'Interior at Petworth', painted just after Egremont's death (Martin Butlin and Evelyn Joll, op.cit., no.449), and an apt reminder of how powerful an influence, for the good of all those who lived under his roof, Egremont had been during his lifetime:

When you take it home, as I hope you will to dearest Petworth, do not forget to point out all its nice little points. Remember such people [i.e. Wyndham] *don't see very often*, & unless *dear* Lord Egremont rises one moonlight night & takes a peep at your picture, it may be, will never be valued or looked at as it ought to be, but I flatter myself the dearest Lord will look upon it ere the moon be on its wane; nothing of yours can go to Petworth without his knowledge . . .

(Harriet Leslie to C.R. Leslie, 24 September 1846; private coll.)

William Marlow 1740–1813

T 03602 **A Post-House near Florence** *c.*1770

Inscribed 'W Marlow' bottom centre
Watercolour over traces of pencil on hand-made wove paper 10 × 14 (252 × 356)
Purchased (Grant-in-Aid) 1983

Prov: . . .; (?) Sant Angelo; J.W. Giles, by whom acquired as a gift 1959 and sold Sotheby's 11 November 1982 (65, repr.) bt Agnew, from whom bt by the Tate Gallery

Exh: *110th Annual Exhibition of Watercolours and Drawings*, Agnew, January–February 1983 (22)

There is a smaller watercolour version (7 × 5½in) in the Henry R. Huntington Library and Art Gallery (ex. coll. Gilbert Davis, exh. *Watercolours and Drawings*, Colnaghi, April–May 1955, no.61). A date of *c.*1770 is suggested by Michael Liversidge, who considers (in correspondence) that both drawings were made after Marlow's return to London from his continental tour of 1765–6; he notes that apart from sketches and pencil outline drawings which served as a models for later painted or finished watercolour compositions, no oil or watercolour painting was actually executed abroad by Marlow.

Ben Marshall 1768–1835

T 03431 **James Belcher, Bare-knuckle Champion of England** ?1803

Oil on canvas 35⅝ × 27⅝ (906 × 702)
Bequeathed by Mrs F. Ambrose Clark from the collection of the late F. Ambrose Clark through the British Sporting Art Trust 1982

Prov: Commissioned by Charles Slingsby Duncombe; by descent to Richard Slingsby Peirse Duncombe, by whom sold Christie's 18 December 1953 (37), bt Agnew, from whom purchased by E.J. Rousuck of Wildenstein, New York; F. Ambrose Clark by 1958; his widow Mrs F. Ambrose Clark

Exh: Tate Gallery, August–September 1982, and York City Art Gallery, March–September 1984, with other paintings from Mrs F. Ambrose Clark's Bequest (no catalogue)

Lit: [E.J. Rousuck], *The F. Ambrose Clark Collection of Sporting Paintings*, privately printed, New York 1958, p.162, repr. pp.6 (in col.) and 163; Aubrey Noakes, *Ben Marshall*, Leigh-on-Sea 1978, p.35, no.59.

James ('Jem') Belcher, bare-knuckle champion of England from 1800 to 1803, was 'as well-known to his own generation as Pitt or Wellington' (anon., quoted in DNB, Supplement, XXII, 1909, p.165). He was born in Bristol on 15 April 1781; his maternal grandfather was the noted pugilist Jack Slack (d.1778). Apparently self-taught as a boxer, Belcher came to London in 1798 and sparred with Bill Warr of Covent Garden, a veteran boxer. Belcher's first important prize-fight was on 12 April 1799, a few days before his eighteenth birthday, when he beat Tom Jones of Paddington at Wormwood Scrubs; the following year he beat Jack Batholomew on Finchley Common. There were in this period no permanent or officially-controlled prize rings. Fights were staged wherever their backers could arrange them, and were fought with bare knuckles; since a round ended when one or other pugilist fell to the ground, fights sometimes went into seventy or eighty rounds. The first acknowledged bare-knuckle champion was John Figg, in 1719, the succession thereafter going to the next successful contender for the title.

On 22 December 1800, near Abershaw's gibbet on Wimbledon Common, Belcher won the championship by defeating Andrew Gamble in five rounds. He defended it successfully over the next three years. In July 1803 Belcher lost an eye in an accident when playing at rackets, and went into semi-retirement keeping the Jolly Brewers tavern in Wardour Street, the championship being assumed by his pupil Hen Pearce ('the Bristol game-chicken'). Despite Belcher's handicap, he continued to fight, displaying all his old courage, but not his old skill or form. He challenged Hen Pearce for the championship on Barnby Moor, on 16 December 1805, but was defeated after eighteen rounds. The championship passed on Pearce's death to John Gully, and then to Tom Cribb, whom Belcher twice unsuccessfully challenged, in two heroic fights, the first of forty-one rounds on 8 April 1807, and the second – Belcher's last fight – of thirty-one rounds on 1 February 1807.

According to Pierce Egan, his contemporary, Belcher was about five feet eleven and a half inches in height; he weighed just under twelve stone. Marshall's portrait bears out Egan's description of Belcher as having 'a prepossessing appearance, genteel, and remarkably placid in his behaviour. There was nothing about his person that indicated bodily strength; yet, when stripped, his form was muscular and elegant'. His style in the ring was 'completely intuitive', his manner 'good natured in the extreme, and modest and unassuming to a degree bordering upon bashfulness'. Egan concludes that 'Belcher's *bottom*, judgment and activity have never been surpassed' (*Boxiana*, I, 1812, pp.120–2, with a head and shoulders portrait facing p.120).

After his last fight, however, Belcher became morose, and was deserted by his old backers. In the words of the *Gentleman's Magazine* (1811, ii, p.194), he 'fell a martyr to his indiscretions', presumably drink. By this time he owned the Coach and Horses tavern in Frith Street, Soho; he died there on 30 July 1811, in his thirty-first year. He is commemorated in the English language by the word 'belcher', used to denote a neckerchief such as he wears in Marshall's portrait, with large white spots on a blue ground and a dark blue spot or eye in the centre (OED, sometimes applied to any particoloured handkerchief worn round the neck).

Several facts suggest a date between July and September 1803 for this portrait. According to Christie's 1953 sale catalogue, the portrait was commissioned 'when the Artist lived in Beaumont Street'; as Honorary Exhibitor to the RA, Marshall gave his address as Beaumont Street between 1801 and 1810. Since Belcher's

left eye appears to be sightless, the portrait was probably painted after the loss of his eye in July 1803; Charles Slingsby Duncombe who commissioned it died on 11 September 1803. Finally, the dog portrayed with Belcher is almost certainly Trusty, a celebrated bull-terrier given to Belcher by his patron Thomas Pitt, 2nd Lord Camelford, before the latter's death in March 1804, Camelford having reputedly observed that 'two conquerors ought to reside together'.

Marshall painted 'gentlemanly' portraits of at least two other famous pugilists, John Gully and John Jackson; both portraits were engraved in mezzotint by Charles Turner (repr. W. Shaw Sparrow, *George Stubbs and Ben Marshall*, 1929, following p.64).

T 03432   Interior of a Barn with a Milkmaid and Farm Labourer *c.*1820

Oil on canvas $34\frac{9}{16} \times 41$ (877 × 1041)
Inscribed 'MAR' and 'SHALL' upside down on two feed bags t.l.
Bequeathed by Mrs F. Ambrose Clark from the collection of the late F. Ambrose Clark through the British Sporting Art Trust 1982

Prov: . . .; D. Lewis, sold anonymously Christie's 2 July 1928 (76) bt Hugh Blaker; E.J. Rousuck, from whom purchased by F. Ambrose Clark by 1958; his widow Mrs F. Ambrose Clark

Exh: Tate Gallery, August–September 1982, and York City Art Gallery, March–September 1984, with other paintings from Mrs F. Ambrose Clark's Bequest (no catalogue)

Lit: [E.J. Rousuck], *The F. Ambrose Clark Collection of Sporting Paintings*, privately printed, New York 1958, p.170 (as 'Rural Courtship'), repr. p.171; Aubrey Noakes, *Ben Marshall*, Leigh-on-Sea 1978, p.59, no.272

Some unevenness in this work has prompted suggestions that it is partly or even wholly the work of the artist's son, Lambert Marshall. The compiler believes it to be wholly by Ben Marshall, possibly painted during the period when he was recovering from serious injuries sustained in a mail-coach accident in 1819.

T 03433   **Portraits of Cattle of the Improved Short-Horned Breed, the Property of J. Wilkinson, Esq. of Lenton, near Nottingham** 1816

Oil on canvas 40 × 50 (1015 × 1271)
Inscribed 'B. Marshall 1816' bottom centre
Bequeathed by Mrs F. Ambrose Clark from the collection of the late F. Ambrose Clark through the British Sporting Art Trust 1982

Prov: ...; S.C. Yeomans, sold anonymously Christie's 9 May 1930 (116) bt Ellis & Smith, from whom purchased by F. Ambrose Clark

Exh: RA 1818 (225); *Outdoor England*, Century Club, New York, February–April 1941 (15); Tate Gallery, August–September 1982, and York City Art Gallery, March–September 1984, with other paintings from Mrs F. Ambrose Clark's Bequest (no catalogue)

Engr: Etching and aquatint by R. Woodman, pub. R. Woodman 20 March 1818, commonly known as 'The Celebrated Bull Alexander' from its writing-engraving: 'This print of the celebrated bull Alexander & the rest of the cattle, the property of Mr. J. Wilkinson of Lenton, near Nottingham, is respectfully inscribed to Genl. The Honble. Francis Needham' (D.A. Boalch, *Prints and Paintings of British Farm Livestock 1780–1910: A Record of the Rothamsted Collection*, Harpenden 1958, p.17, no.44, pl.XXII)

Lit: W. Shaw Sparrow, *A Book of Sporting Painters*, 1931, pp.87–8, repr. facing p.88; [E.J. Rousuck], *The F. Ambrose Clark Collection of Sporting Paintings*, privately printed, New York 1958, p.173, repr. p.172; Aubrey Noakes, *Ben Marshall*, Leigh-on-Sea 1978, p.144, no.135

John Wilkinson of Lenton (active *c.*1807–52) was one of the pioneers in breeding Shorthorn cattle. He was a tenant farmer at Grove Cottage farm in the village of Lenton, about a mile and a half from the centre of Nottingham (now part of the city suburbs). In T 03433 Marshall depicts one of his Shorthorn bulls, identified in Woodman's engraving as 'The Celebrated Bull Alexander', with three cows and a calf, grazing in Nottingham Park, with a view of Nottingham Castle in the background on the left. Shaw Sparrow comments on Marshall's representation of the celebrated bull Alexander that 'his head is too small to be in scale with his body, and he looks almost as mild as a henpecked Sultan'.

After a visit to Wilkinson's herd in 1852, the Scottish Shorthorn breeder Amos Cruikshank declared that it was 'the finest herd of Shorthorns I ever beheld' (H. Robinson, *Features of Nottinghamshire Agriculture*, Nottingham, reprinted from the *Journal of the Royal Agricultural Society of England*, LXXXVIII, 1927, p.11). On 20 April 1854, the sale of 'the principal stock of a superior breed of prime shorthorn cattle, bred by the late M. John Wilkinson' was conducted by Mr Strafford, auctioneer; it was attended by the most eminent cattle breeders in England, Ireland and America. 'Fifty cows and heifers, and fifteen bulls, were sold, the average price realised by the former being £57.0.0d., and by the latter, exclusive of one or two calves, £47. The aggregate of the sale exceeded £2,900. Bull calves from this stock, shortly after the sale, were sold for 150 guineas' (J.J. Godfrey, *The History of the Parish and Priory of Lenton*, 1884, p.147. We are indebted to Adrian Henstock, Principal Archivist, Nottinghamshire Record Office, for this information). Later accounts of the Wilkinson herd are included in the *Livestock Journal*, 20 August 1886 and 17 July 1891.

Nottingham Castle and Park were owned by the Duke of Newcastle in Wilkinson's day, but the Castle was largely uninhabited or partly let, and the Park was let out as grazing land. General Francis Needham, the dedicatee of the engraving of Marshall's painting, was almost certainly a member of the wealthy Nottingham family of Needham who lived at Lenton House.

James Pollard 1792–1867

T 03434   Coursers Taking the Field at Hatfield Park, Herts., the Seat of the Marquess of Salisbury exh.1824

Oil on canvas 41 × 56$\frac{15}{16}$ (1042 × 1472)
Inscribed 'J Pollard' (initials in monogram) b.l.
Bequeathed by Mrs F. Ambrose Clark from the collection of the late F. Ambrose Clark through the British Sporting Art Trust 1982

Prov: ...; anon. sale, Christie's 27 April 1917 (131) bt Ellis & Smith; F. Ambrose Clark by 1941; his widow Mrs F. Ambrose Clark

Exh: BI 1824 (360); *Outdoor England*, Century Club, New York, February–April 1941 (19); Tate Gallery, August–September 1982, and York City Art Gallery, March–September 1984, with other paintings from Mrs F. Ambrose Clark's Bequest (no catalogue)

Engr: Aquatint by the artist, coloured by hand, pub. R. Pollard & Sons 6 November 1824 (Selway 1972, p.58, no.833, as pair to no.832)

Lit: Ed. William Page, *Victoria County History, Hertfordshire*, I, 1902; [E.J. Rousuck], *The F. Ambrose Clark Collection of Sporting Paintings*, privately printed,

New York 1958, p.210, repr. p.211; N.C. Selway, *The Golden Age of Coaching and Sport*, 1972, p.43, no.385

This scene provided Pollard with one of the subjects for a pair of engravings published in February 1824, the other being entitled 'Coursing in Hatfield Park'.

In the forefront of the field is the Dowager Marchioness of Salisbury, wearing the livery of the Hatfield Hunt, sky blue with black collar and cuffs and silver buttons. She had been born in 1750, as Lady Emily Mary Hill, daughter of the Irish Earl of Downshire; in 1773 she married James Cecil, 21st Earl and later 1st Marquess of Salisbury, who died in 1823. The Marchioness was 'an enthusiastic sportswoman who delighted in archery, in riding, above all in hunting. She took over the Mastership of the local hunt when her husband got bored with it and directed the chase with zest'. Contemporary gossip is full of anecdotes about 'Dow. Sal' or 'Old Sarum' (Lord David Cecil, *The Cecils of Hatfield House*, 1973, p.191). Her enthusiasm for sport continued into old age. Pollard's painting, probably painted in 1823, the year before it was exhibited, depicts her at the age of 73, an eyeglass affixed to the top of her whip her only concession to old age. She died in a fire which destroyed the west wing of Hatfield House on 27 November 1835, aged 85.

The Marchioness of Salisbury, who loved entertaining on a large scale, held a three-day coursing meeting in Hatfield Park every year; the first two days were reserved for matches between her own greyhounds and those of her friends, but on the third day the meetings were open to spectators and the general public. Pollard's painting evidently depicts the third day of such a meeting. His preliminary pencil drawing of the subject, squared for the purpose of engraving, is inscribed at the top 'Coursing in Hatfield Park|Engraved by J. Pollard' and, along the bottom, 'Large Picture Painted by J. Pollard and Exhibited at British|Institution Pall Mall' (9 × 15in, in an album of drawings by Pollard, British Museum 1933–10–14–133).

A painting by J.F. Sartorius showing the 1st Marquess and the Marchioness of Salisbury coursing in Hatfield Park, dated 1805 and exhibited at the RA in 1806, is in the collection of the present Marquess of Salisbury.

T 03435   The 'Tally-Ho' London–Birmingham Stage Coach Passing Whittington College, Highgate 1836

Oil on canvas 14$\frac{1}{2}$ × 18 (369 × 457)
Inscribed 'J Pollard 1836' b.r. and 'JP' on a trunk at rear of coach; the coach is variously lettered (see below)

evidence firmly identifies this coach as the 'Tally-Ho' London–Birmingham stage coach, which departed from 'The Saracen's Head' inn on Snow Hill in the City of London at 7.45 a.m., arriving eleven hours later at the Swan Hotel in Birmingham, from which passengers could travel by other stages to Manchester, Liverpool etc.

A detailed study of the coach itself, in pen and ink over pencil, is in an album of Pollard drawings in the British Museum ($4\frac{7}{8} \times 7\frac{1}{8}$in; 1933–10–14–172). This drawing carries the same lettering as the painting (and is inscribed with colour notes and with 'Sarison's Head' for its point of departure and 'Swan Hotel Birmingham' for its terminus), and the same clearly numbered licence plate, '3462'. *The Directory of Stage Coach Services 1836*, compiled by Alan Bates, 1968, p.5, records '3466 and '3501' as licence numbers for the 'Tally Ho' London–Birmingham coach, and '3462' for its competitor, the 'Greyhound' London–Birmingham coach. Pollard's clear evidence is to be preferred on this point.

The background depicts Whittington College, a two-storied row of almshouses built by the Mercers' Company from 1823 to replace almshouses at St Michael's Paternoster established by the Mercers executing the Will of Sir Richard Whittington ('Dick' Whittington, thrice Lord Mayor of London, d.1423). Whittington College, Highgate, contained flats for almswomen who were widows and spinsters and aged over 55; as Pollard shows, there was a chapel in the middle of the central block and two houses (for the Chaplain and Matron) at the end of each wing. The road in the foreground was built by the Highgate Archway Company as a commercial venture, to bypass the steep Highgate Hill. An Act of Parliament in 1809 authorized the Company to build a road and to levy tolls on vehicles, animals and pedestrians; the charges were 6d. for a horse-drawn cart or carriage, 3d. for a horse and rider, 2d. for a donkey and 1d. for a pedestrian. This toll-gate and its keeper can be seen on the right in Pollard's painting. In 1966 Whittington College was demolished to make way for the Archway Road Improvement Scheme, and rebuilt at Felbridge in Sussex (information kindly provided by Joan Davies, Jim Connell and Arthur Drage).

Bequeathed by Mrs F. Ambrose Clark from the collection of the late F. Ambrose Clark through the British Sporting Art Trust 1982

Prov: ...; 'Christie's 1914' (according to Selway 1972, but sale untraced); F. Ambrose Clark by 1937; his widow Mrs F. Ambrose Clark

Exh: *Sporting Prints and Paintings*, Metropolitan Museum of Art, New York, March–April 1937 (32); Tate Gallery, August–September 1982, and York City Art Gallery, March–September 1984, with other paintings from Mrs F. Ambrose Clark's Bequest (no catalogue)

Lit: Hugh McCausland, *The English Carriage*, 1948, p.117, repr. facing p.120; [E.J. Rousuck], *The F. Ambrose Clark Collection of Sporting Paintings*, privately printed, New York 1958, p.217, repr. p.216; N.C. Selway, *The Golden Age of Coaching and Sport*, 1972, p.30, no.103

The painting has hitherto been exhibited and described as 'The Manchester–Liverpool Mail Coach...'; but the meticulous detail with which Pollard records the embellishment of the vehicle firmly establishes this as the 'Tally-Ho' London–Birmingham Stage Coach, licence number 3462 (Pollard depicts the number plate affixed to the door panel of the coach behind its headlamp). 'BIRMINGHAM' and LONDON' are lettered on the lower part of the door, with the picture of a turbaned head between them; above them are lettered the coach proprietors' names, 'W. CHAPLIN & CO.| TH. WADDELL| S.A. MOUNTAIN & CO.'. 'MANCHESTER' and 'LIVERPOOL' are lettered on the bodywork to the left of the coach door, and '[...]VEN[...]' (Coventry) to its right. A tubular holder for the guard's horn hanging from the roof of the coach is lettered 'TALLY-HO' and also carries the image of a turbaned head. All this

T 03436 Fly Fishing in the River Lea near the Ferry Boat Inn 1831

Oil on canvas $14 \times 17\frac{9}{16}$ (356 × 446)
Inscribed 'J. Pollard 1831' b.l.
Bequeathed by Mrs F. Ambrose Clark from the collection of the late F. Ambrose Clark through the British Sporting Art Trust 1982

I.G. Murray, Archivist of the Bruce Castle Museum, London N.17, for establishing the location of this scene.)

Prov: ...; Arthur N. Gilbey, sold by his executors Christie's 25 April 1940 (110, as 'Fly Fishing at Tottenham Mills') bt C. Dunlop, New York; F. Ambrose Clark after 1958; his widow Mrs F. Ambrose Clark

Exh: *Loan Exhibition of Sporting Paintings,* Viscount Allendale's, 144 Piccadilly, 1931 (75); Tate Gallery, March–September 1984, with other paintings from Mrs F. Ambrose Clark's Bequest (no catalogue); *Paintings exhibited by the British Sporting Art Trust,* Vestey Gallery, National Horseracing Museum, Newmarket, April–December 1986 (unnumbered, repr.)

Engr: Aquatint by G. Hunt, 'Fly Fishing', pair to 'Trolling for Pike', pub. J. Moore 1831 (Selway 1972, p.58, no.813)

Lit: Sir Walter Gilbey, *Animal Painters,* II, 1900, p.101, repr. facing p.102; Walter Shaw Sparrow, *Angling in British Art,* 1923, p.103; N.C. Selway, *The Golden Age of Coaching and Sport,* 1972, p.41, no.356

Pair to T03437 (q.v.). Nine other angling paintings by Pollard were included in the sale of Arthur N. Gilbey's collection of angling pictures in 1940. Angling was Pollard's own favourite recreation, and his angling scenes, usually involving only a day's excursion from the centre of London, have the lively and informal air of personal enjoyment. Here the background is the Ferry Boat Inn, which still stands; the bridge on the left is the Ferry Bridge which carried Ferry Lane across the River Lee to Tottenham Mills. T03436 was formerly known as 'Fly Fishing at Tottenham Mills', but those mills, out of sight here, stood on a mill stream some way to the west. In Pollard's day, this area was within the county of Essex; since 1965 it has been part of the London Borough of Waltham Forest. (We are grateful to Mr

T03437 Trolling for Pike in the River Lea 1831

Oil on canvas $14 \times 17\frac{9}{16}$ (356 × 446)
Inscribed 'J. Pollard 1831' b.r.
Bequeathed by Mrs F. Ambrose Clark from the collection of the late F. Ambrose Clark through the British Sporting Art Trust 1982

Prov: ...; Arthur N. Gilbey, sold by his executors, Christie's 25 April 1940 (111, repr.) bt C. Dunlop, New York; F. Ambrose Clark after 1958; his widow Mrs F. Ambrose Clark

Exh: *Loan Exhibition of Sporting Paintings,* Viscount Allendale's, 144 Piccadilly, 1931 (74); Tate Gallery, August–September 1982, and York City Art Gallery, March–September 1984, with other paintings from Mrs F. Ambrose Clark's Bequest (no catalogue); *Paintings exhibited by the British Sporting Art Trust,* Vestey Gallery, National Horseracing Museum, Newmarket, April–December 1986 (unnumbered, repr.)

Engr: Aquatint by G. Hunt, pair to 'Fly Fishing', pub. J. Moore 1831 (Selway 1972, p.58, no.814)

Lit: Sir Walter Gilbey, *Animal Painters,* II, 1900, p.101; Walter Shaw Sparrow, *Angling in British Art,* 1923, p.103, repr. facing p.100; N.C. Selway, *The Golden Age of Coaching and Sport,* 1972, p.41, no.357

Pair to T 03436 (q.v.). To 'troll' in angling is to fish with a running line. The 1940 sale catalogue of Arthur N. Gilbey's collection of angling pictures gives the following description of this scene: 'Three anglers on the bank of a stream below a weir; one, standing, has hooked a Jack, whilst a second kneels by him with a gaff, and the third stands by with a rod over his shoulder and a creel in his hand, a live-bait can, rod covers, a fishing-seat and a creel on the ground beside them'.

A small sketch in pen and ink over pencil (5 × 7¼in) of this stretch of the river, without figures, is included in an album of Pollard's drawings in the British Museum (1933–10–14–278).

George Romney 1734–1802

T 03547 **John Howard Visiting a Lazaretto** c.1791–2

Pen and iron gall ink and wash over pencil on hand-made laid paper 13½ × 19¼ (343 × 490), edges uneven
Purchased (Grant-in-Aid) 1982

Prov: ...; private collection, Paris, from which purchased through Stephen Somerville by Christopher Powney, from whom purchased by the Tate Gallery

John Howard, philanthropist and self-appointed inspector of prisons from c.1773 until his death in 1790, travelled widely in England and abroad visiting prisons, hospitals, lazarettos and workhouses. His *State of The Prisons in England and Wales* was first published in 1777, and his *Account of the Principal Lazarettos in Europe* in 1789. Among the many objects of his concern was the high incidence of plague, smallpox and fever in prisons and lazarettos.

For Romney's meditations, over several years, on the 'scenes of human wretchedness' reported in Howard's surveys, see Patricia Jaffé, *Drawings by George Romney from the Fitzwilliam Museum, Cambridge*, the catalogue of an exhibition shown at the Fitzwilliam Museum in 1977 (and at Kenwood and various centres outside London in 1978). Romney evidently intended to paint at least one oil painting of Howard visiting a lazaretto, but did not do so; Mrs Jaffé (pp.58–9) quotes the artist's son Revd John Romney as writing, in 1818, of 'two or three large pictures, wch. Mr R. intended to have painted', modifying this in 1830 to 'one or two large pictures which Mr Romney intended to have painted'.

Romney made numerous sketches and studies of the subject. Mrs Jaffé considers that 'the compositions probably do not illustrate particular incidents, but are generalized pictures of the miseries of pestilence ridden lazarettos' (p.58). The Fitzwilliam Museum's 1977 exhibition included 'Figures in a Lazaretto' (no.94), described by Mrs Jaffé as an early version on the theme, and seven drawings, each called 'Howard visiting a lazaretto' (nos.95–100b, most of them repr. pls.43–6). Nine of the Fitzwilliam Museum's 'Howard drawings' were included in the bound volume of his father's drawings presented by the Revd John Romney in 1818. Others were included in the large group of Romney drawings purchased by the Museum in 1874; Mrs Jaffé notes (p.60) that some of these appear to have come from sketch-books and that two pages, probably from the same sketch-book, were on the London art market in 1968.

Mrs Jaffé notes (p.60) that 'it would be a long job to list all comparable drawings from sketch-books', but records two particular sources for 'Howard drawings': 'a sketch-book, broken up, probably, in the 1920s, by F.R. Meatyard' (p.58) and a sketch-book dated 'August 1792' on the front cover, 'formerly in the collection of Kenneth Garlick (sold Sotheby's and subsequently broken up in the summer of 1963)' (pp.59–60). The Fitzwilliam Museum's 'Howard drawings' are of various sizes; no.98 in the 1977 exhibition (14⅛ × 19½in), from the group purchased in 1874, some of which had evidently come from sketch-books, most nearly corresponds to the size of T 03547, whose early provenance is unknown, but which may also have come from a sketch-book. Elizabeth Romney's sale at Christie's, 24–25 May 1894, which included numerous lots of unspecified drawings, should also perhaps be considered as a possible (but unverifiable) source for T 03547. (We are indebted to Mrs Jaffé for discussing this drawing, and for suggesting its dating as c.1791–2.)

Dante Gabriel Rossetti 1828–1882

T03817 Sketch of Angels' Heads ?c.1875

White chalk $17\frac{7}{16} \times 19\frac{11}{16}$ (443 × 500) on canvas $20\frac{5}{16} \times 22\frac{5}{16}$ (515 × 567), the drawing over a reddish-brown ground, the rest of the canvas only primed
Presented by W. Graham Robertson (as part of N05064) 1940

Prov: N05064 was painted for F.R. Leyland, at whose sale, Christie's 28 May 1892 (48), it was bt by W. Graham Robertson, but it is not known at what point T03817 became attached to the painting

This chalk sketch is on a fragment of canvas taken from the bottom left corner of a larger canvas; the original tacking edges remain at the left and bottom. The fragment was found attached to the back of Rossetti's 'Proserpine', N05064, when W. Graham Robertson presented the painting in 1940, but was only separately registered by the Gallery in 1984. The canvas was pinned to a board with the drawing facing the back of 'Proserpine', the whole being 'Nailed on lower half of stretcher at back and papered down' according to a note made on 7 August 1940 by D.C. Fincham, then an Assistant at the Gallery.

The heads, one complete, the other cut by the edge of the canvas, bear some relation to those of the angels in Rossetti's 'The Blessed Damozel' of 1875–8 (Fogg Art Museum, Harvard University; Virginia Surtees, *The Paintings and Drawings of Dante Gabriel Rossetti*, Oxford 1971, no.244, pl.355). T03817 might be a fragment from an abandoned canvas of the subject. It is not known how or when the fragment came to be attached to the back of 'Proserpine', or whether any significance should be given to the fact that the latter was painted in 1874 when Rossetti was making preparations for 'The Blessed Damozel'.

Alexander Runciman 1736–1785

T03604 Fingal Encounters Carbon Carglass first printed c.1773

Etching $5\frac{7}{8} \times 9\frac{5}{8}$ (149 × 245) on hand-made wove paper $6\frac{3}{8} \times 10$ (158 × 254)
Etched inscription 'AR. fecit' (initials in monogram) within plate lower left
Purchased (Grant-in-Aid) 1983

Prov: ...; Christopher Mendez, from whom bt by the Tate Gallery

Lit: J.M. Gray, 'Notes on the Art Treasures at Penicuik House', 1889, typescript copy in Department of Prints & Drawings, British Museum; Susan Booth, 'The Early Career of Alexander Runciman and his Relations with Sir James Clerk of Penicuik', *Journal of the Warburg and Courtauld Institutes*, XXXII, 1969, pp.332–43; *William Blake in the Art of his Time*, exhibition catalogue, Santa Barbara 1969, pp.64–5; David and Francina Irwin, *Scottish Painters At Home and Abroad 1700–1900*, 1975, pp.107–9

This subject was one of twelve scenes from Ossian which Runciman painted in 1772–3, in oil on plaster, on the ceiling of the Great Room in Sir James Clark of Eldin's new Palladian house at Penicuik, Midlothian. As these paintings were destroyed by fire in 1899, an account of Runciman's work there must rely on surviving descriptions and a small number of drawings and etchings (mainly in the collection of the National Gallery of Scotland).

Booth points out (pp.334–5) that Runciman's commission to paint decorative schemes for Penicuik not only made possible his visit to Italy, 1776–70, but also 'coloured Runciman's attitude to his studies in Rome and gave him the necessary incentive to experiment with new tendencies at work there' among such artists as James Barry, Johann Tobias Sergell, Henry Fuseli and Runciman's own fellow-Scots Gavin Hamilton and John Brown. These influences, particularly Hamilton's, encouraged Runciman to devise epic and classical themes and a Neo-classical style for the Penicuik decorations.

For the ceiling of the Great Room, Runciman drew his subjects from the recently-published epics which purported to be translations from the ancient Scottish bard Ossian but which in fact proved to be the inventions of Runciman's contemporary James Macpherson. Of these, *Erse Fragments* was published in 1760, *Fingal* in 1762 and *Temora* in 1763; though later the subject of controversy, all were greeted with the enthusiasm born of rising Scottish patriotism after the defeat of 1745. Booth notes (p.339) that Runciman was the first artist to illustrate Ossian's work on a large scale; she also observes that Runciman 'concentrated on those stories where strangeness, tragedy and melancholy are the dominant traits'.

Gray makes the point (p.6) that Runciman, 'in the manner afterwards adopted by Barry in the case of his illustrations of "Human Progress"' (see T 03784–8 in this catalogue), evidently wished to preserve a record of his work at Penicuik by himself making etchings (on a reduced scale) of his work there.

The subject of T 03604 is taken from Ossian's *Fingal*. Carbon Carglass, daughter of Torcul Tormo, is held prisoner by King Starno, her father's murderer and Fingal's deadly enemy. Fingal finds her by moonlight.

> Fingal rushed in all his arms, wide-bounding over Truthor's stream, that sent its sullen roar, by night, through Gormal's misty vale. A moonbeam glittered on a rock; in the midst stood a stately form; a form with floating locks like Lochlin's white-bosomed maids. Unequal are her steps and short, she throws a broken song on wind. At times she tosses her white arms, for grief is dwelling in her soul.

She calls on the spirit of her father. '"Who art thou?" said Fingal "Voice of Night?" She trembling turned away. "Who art thou, in thy darkness?" She shrank into the cave. The King loosed the thongs from her hands.' (quoted by Booth, p.341).

Probably this (rather than the small, upright version; see T 03605 below) was the design painted on the ceiling of the Great Room at Penicuik, but there seems no certainty over this.

Runciman's loose and free etched line is very individual. Booth (p.341) considers this etching of 'Fingal Encounters Carbon Carglass' to be 'the most satisfactory' of Runciman's etchings. It is not clear whether these etchings were published or privately printed. T 03604–6 are printed on wove paper, which came into common use in England in the 1770s; these impressions could be first printings, though the appearance of the paper makes it unlikely.

T 03605   **Fingal Encounters Carbon Carglass (upright version)** first printed *c.*1773

Etching $5\frac{3}{4} \times 3\frac{3}{8}$ (145 × 106) on hand-made wove paper $6 \times 4\frac{7}{8}$ (152 × 123)
Etched inscription 'A Runciman [?inv]' below subject and within plate lower left
Purchased (Grant-in-Aid) 1983
Prov: As for T 03604
Lit: As for T 03604

In this etching the figure of Carbon Carglass is virtually the same as in T 03604, but reversed and placed on the left of the composition; Fingal approaches from behind her on the right, without his shield and with a less billowing cloak. In the Santa Barbara exhibition catalogue of 1969 (p.64, fig.g), a reproduction of a late pull from this plate, bound with nine other Runciman prints in a volume lent by Robert N. Essick, is entitled 'Catholda', which is probably a mistake; Gray describes 'Catholda' as 'a nymph drawing a bow', and it is anyway unlikely that Runciman would have used a virtually identical figure for two different Ossianic characters. Perhaps this image was designed before T 03604, which is larger and considerably more dramatic.

T 03606 **Agrippina with the Ashes of Germanicus** ? first printed

*c.*1773

Etching $5\frac{5}{8} \times 4\frac{3}{16}$ (144 × 106) on hand-made
wove paper $6\frac{3}{8} \times 4\frac{7}{8}$ (161 × 123)
Etched inscription 'AR [?inv]' (initials in
monogram) below subject and within
plate lower left, and '[G]ERMANICUS'
round urn of ashes
Purchased (Grant-in-Aid) 1983

Prov: As for T 03604
Lit: As for T 03604

Runciman's choice of this subject (which derives from
Tacitus) may well have been influenced by Gavin Hamilton and by the latter's admiration for Poussin which
he encouraged Runciman to share. Poussin had painted
'The Death of Germanicus' (Anthony Blunt, *The Paintings of Nicolas Poussin: A Critical Catalogue*, 1969,
pp.112–13, no.156). Hamilton's painting 'Agrippina
Landing at Brindisium with the Ashes of Germanicus'
was exhibited at the RA in 1772, and is now in the
Tate's collection (T 03365, q.v. in this catalogue, with a
summary of Agrippina's story); Runciman's pen and
ink drawing of 'Agrippina's Landing at Brindisium with
the Ashes of Germanicus' was exhibited at the RA in
1781 (374) and is now in the collection of the National
Gallery of Scotland.

T 03606 does not appear to be related to Runciman's
decorative schemes at Penicuik, except perhaps
indirectly. As well as painting the ceiling of the Great
Room at Penicuik, Runciman was commissioned to
paint six large panels for the cupolas surmounting
Penicuik's two staircases, and chose to paint scenes from

the life of St Margaret of Scotland there. He seems to
have been interested in other subjects depicting women
in stress behaving nobly.

Sir William Segar active 1580 or 5– 1633, attributed to

T 03576 **Portrait of a Man in a Slashed Black Doublet** *c.*1605

Oil on oak panel $39\frac{3}{8} \times 31\frac{1}{4}$ (924 × 806)
Purchased (Grant-in-Aid) 1983

Prov: …; ? at Clearwell Court, Gloucestershire,
by the nineteenth century, and by descent
to the Earl and Countess of Dunraven,
Adare Manor, Limerick; Dunraven sale,
Christie's 9 June 1982 (78, repr., as by
unknown follower of Custodis) bt Wilkins
and Wilkins, from whom bt by the Tate
Gallery

The sitter in this unusually well-preserved and
strongly-drawn portrait remains unknown. The tall hat,
narrow sleeves and open double collar of his costume
can be dated to the first decade of the seventeenth
century; the focal point is a finely embroidered sword
belt and an additional dagger or short sword at his right
side, partly covered by a blue tassel. Attached to the
back of the panel is a nineteenth-century label stating
that the 'Unknown' sitter comes 'From Clearwell
Court'. If correct, this would suggest that the painting
was once at Clearwell Court or Castle in Gloucester-

shire, one of the properties of the Wyndham family. The already distantly related Wyndham and Dunraven families merged when Caroline, only daughter and heir of Thomas Wyndham of Clearwell, married Windham Henry, 2nd Earl of Dunraven, in 1810.

Although Segar's heraldic career is fairly well charted, from his appointment as Portcullis Pursuivant in 1585, to Garter King of Arms in 1603 and the granting of a Knighthood in 1617, his *oeuvre* as a painter of life-size portraits has to be reconstructed from a few contemporary references and one documented work, the portrait of Robert Devereux, 2nd Earl of Essex, 1590, now in the National Gallery of Ireland, Dublin (repr. Roy Strong, *The English Icon*, 1969, fig. 175). The attribution of this painting to Segar or his circle has been suggested by Strong on grounds of a similarity of style which it shares with a group of slightly earlier portraits seen as related to the Dublin portrait.

Joseph Severn 1793–1879

T 03357 **The Infant of the Apocalypse saved from the Dragon** c.1827–31/1843

Oil on canvas, painted area (arched top) approx. 88 × 50 (2235 × 1270), stretcher 89⅛ × 50½ (2260 × 1285)
Purchased (Grant-in-Aid) 1982

Prov: Promised as a gift by the artist to Cardinal Thomas Weld, who however died in 1837; sold 1843 to W.E. Gladstone, sold Christie's 26 June 1875 (627, as 'The

Vision of St John in Patmos') bt Cox; ...; J. Stuart Castle; his executors, sold Phillips 9 April 1979 (118) bt Julian Hartnoll, sold anonymously Sotheby's 17 March 1982 (83, repr.) bt Tate Gallery

Exh: RA 1838 (35); *Victorian Art, Sacred and Secular*, Julian Hartnoll at Burlington Fine Art Fair, RA, September–October 1979 (1, repr.)

Lit: 'Foreign Correspondence: Rome, March 1834', *Athenaeum*, 5 April 1834, p.257; 'Fine Arts: Royal Academy', *Athenaeum*, 19 May 1838, p.363; Mrs [Sarah] Uwins, *Memoir of Thomas Uwins, R.A.*, 1858, II, pp.216, 274–5; William Sharp, *Life and Letters of Joseph Severn*, 1892, pp.292–3; M.R.D. Foot, *The Gladstone Diaries*, 1968, I, p.474, II, pp.527–8, 548; Marcia Pointon, 'W.E. Gladstone as an Art Patron and Collector', *Victorian Studies*, XIX, 1975, p.94; Barbara Coffey and Julian Hartnoll in *Victorian Art, Sacred and Secular*, exhibition catalogue, RA 1979, no.1, repr.; William Vaughan, *German Romanticism and English Art*, 1979, pp.180, 283, n.13

When this picture was exhibited at the Royal Academy in 1838 the catalogue included a reference to Revelation XII, and continued, 'A study for a large altarpiece, presented by the late Cardinald [sic] Weld to the Church of St. Paul at Rome'. In Chapter XII of 'The Revelation of St. John the Divine', who is shown writing down his account of his vision on the Island of Patmos, the 'woman clothed with the sun' gives birth to 'a man child, who was to rule all nations with a rod of iron' while the 'great red dragon, having seven heads and ten horns, and seven crowns upon his heads' waits 'to devour her child as soon as it was born'. The chapter also mentions the war in heaven in which Michael and his angels fight against the dragon; Michael's host is suggested in the sky at the left. However, the chaining of the dragon does not take place until Chapter XX. The eagle at St John's feet is his traditional symbol.

The story of Severn's altarpiece filled much of his first stay in Rome, from his arrival with John Keats in 1820 until he returned and took up residence in London in 1841. The project is first mentioned in a letter from Severn to Thomas Uwins of 10 November 1827: 'you must be content with also hearing that my not twenty but fifteen feet of the Revelations is making, and I am employed at night in making a large drawing of it; so, please my stars, I shall soon begin'. It is not clear whether by this 'drawing' Severn meant an actual drawing or the laying in of the *modello* now in the Tate. Severn's own account, printed by William Sharp, gives the next stage in the story. The newly created Cardinal Weld (his creation took place in March 1830) helped Severn over a law suit and while doing so 'had seen the sketch several times and greatly admired it, and he had known my intention of doing it on the large scale, indeed of having actually begun it'. He then commissioned a full-scale version, apparently already with the intention of placing it in the Church of San Paolo fuori le Mure, though an account in the *Athenaeum* reporting events in Rome in March 1834 suggests another destination: 'I have seen the *abozzo* of Severn's altarpiece. Did I tell you Cardinal Weld has given the commission, and that the picture may be enshrined in no lesser place than the Pantheon?' (The report goes on to praise the upper part of the composition while criticising the lower: 'conception feeble – arrangement monotonous'.) No price was mentioned which caused trouble later on as Cardinal Weld died before Severn succeeded in placing his altarpiece in San Paolo. As a foreigner and a non-Catholic Severn encountered every form of opposition, above all from the Roman painter Baron Cammucini. Finally, with the help of the architect in charge of the rebuilding of the church, still not complete, after the devastating fire of 1823, Severn succeeded in 1840 in hanging the altarpiece in a bricked-up archway. Although he realised that this was only a temporary solution he returned to England with his family the following year. When the church was consecrated in 1854, Severn's altarpiece was said to be awaiting a new site in one of the side chapels of the nave, but when Krzysztof Cieszkowski of the Tate Gallery library visited the church in 1983 he was told that the altarpiece was rolled up in an outbuilding. (The full text of Severn's own account of his problems, a separate chapter in his manuscript 'Incidents of my Life', is given as an appendix in William Sharp's *Life and Letters*, pp.293–301.)

Severn had planned to give the half-size modello as a thank-offering to Cardinal Weld but this was prevented by the Cardinal's death in 1837. The young W.E. Gladstone had admired the unfinished altarpiece or the *modello* in Severn's studio sometime during April 1832, noting in his diary, 'a very large picture "the chaining of the dragon from the Revelations"'. In 1838 Gladstone was again in Rome and again saw the altarpiece in Severn's studio, noting in his diary that 'the Chaining of the Dragon is a great object of interest: a bold effort, a new subject, finely conceived and executed ... The picture has caused much jealousy, as it is to go to a Chapel in San Paolo, a present from Cardinal Weld to the Pope'. The modello was already in England having been shown at the Summer Exhibition at the Royal Academy. In 1843 Severn, back in England, offered Gladstone 'the large study of the Roman Altarpiece'. Gladstone sent Severn an advance of £50 and left him the choice of the work, provided that Cardinal Weld's heirs did not claim it which they did not. On 12 April 1843 Severn said that he would like to do more to the picture as 'In this way I feel sure I can make it a finished work and more worthy of the esteem you are pleased to honour it with'. On 22 June, after Gladstone had bought the picture for a total of £80, Severn wrote that 'I have got the traced drawing of the large picture and will bring it to judge of the Angel's arm and correct it', which suggests that he did do some further work on the *modello* at this time. However, the picture remains thinly painted in many places, with the pencil under-drawing showing through. (This entry is largely based on that in the *Victorian Art* catalogue of 1979 by Barbara Coffey and Julian Hartnoll.)

William Henry Simmons
1811–1882
after **Abraham Solomon**
1823–1862

T03616 **Waiting for the Verdict** 1866

Mezzotint $21\frac{13}{16} \times 27\frac{1}{2}$ (555 × 700) on India paper laid on wove paper $25\frac{3}{4} \times 31\frac{3}{16}$ (655 × 792); plate-mark $25\frac{5}{16} \times 29\frac{7}{8}$ (644 × 786)
Engraved inscription 'ASolomon 1857·' (initials in monogram) b.l. of image; etched inscription '*London Published Novr 1st 1862, by Henry Graves & Co. the Proprietors Publishers to the Queen, 6 Pall Mall*' above image t.r.
Presented anonymously by the former owner of T03614–15, 1982

T03617 **The Acquittal** 1866

> Mezzotint $21\frac{11}{16} \times 27\frac{9}{16}$ (552 × 720) on wove
> paper $27\frac{1}{16} \times 32$ (686 × 812); plate-mark
> $26\frac{1}{8} \times 31$ (665 × 781)
> Writing-engraving 'PAINTED BY A.
> SOLOMON|London, Published Jany 1st
> 1866, by Henry Graves & Co the
> Proprietors, Publishers to the Queen 6
> Pall Mall|ENGRAVED BY W.H.
> SIMMONS|THE ACQUITTAL.|*Engraved
> from the original Picture in the Collection of
> Charles Lucas Esqre of Sister House
> Clapham Common*' below image
> Presented anonymously by the former
> owner of T03614-15, 1982

For discussion of the subjects of T03616–17, see the
entries on the original paintings by Abraham Solomon,
T03614–15 below.

Despite the inscription on T03616 it seems clear that
these prints were both published together on 1 January
1866. According to the declaration made by the
publisher, Henry Graves, to the Printsellers' Association on 15 January of that year, they were issued in the
following quantities: 200 Artist's Proofs, priced at 8
guineas each; 25 Presentation Proofs 100 Proofs before
Letters at 6 guineas each and 100 Proofs; with Letters
at 4 guineas each. Ordinary prints, run off according to
demand, were priced at 2 guineas each (*An Alphabetical
List of Engravings Declared at the Office of the Printsellers' Association, London, 1847–1891*, 1892). Simmons
exhibited copies of both engravings at the Royal Academy in 1866 (831, 832) and such was the popularity of
'Waiting for the Verdict' that, in the words of one writer
in 1919, copies of the print could, even at that late
date, 'still be seen in cottage homes and inns' (G.C.
Williamson, *Murray Marks and his Friends*, 1919,
p.156).

Francesco Sleter 1685–1775

T03465 **A Representation of the
Liberal Arts: Ceiling Design
for the State Dining Room at
Grimsthorpe Castle** *c.*1724

> Oil on canvas $24\frac{1}{8} \times 30$ (613 × 762)
> Purchased (Grant-in-Aid) 1982
> *Prov:* ...; sold Sotheby's 19 February 1975 (91
> as by Amiconi) bt Lawrence Riolfo of
> Venice, sold by him to Sarawood Antiques,
> bt R.I.H. Paul, by whom sold through
> Harari & Johns to the Tate Gallery
> *Lit:* H.A. Tipping & C. Hussey, *The Work of
> Sir John Vanburgh and his School*, 1928,
> p.317, fig.463 (as by Thornhill); E. Croft-
> Murray, *Decorative Painting in England
> 1537–1837*, II, 1970, pp.277–8, fig.24; J.
> Lees-Milne, *English Country Houses:
> Baroque 1685–1715*, 1970, pp.190–2,
> figs.313–14

Vanbrugh completed Grimsthorpe Castle for Peregrine
Bertie, 2nd Duke of Ancaster, in 1724, which is presumably when work on the interior decorations of the
State Rooms was begun. These have been previously
attributed to Sir James Thornhill and to Antonio
Bellucci, but this seems unlikely both on stylistic
grounds and in view of the fact that Bellucci is now
known to have left England in 1722. Croft-Murray,
who recognized the true nature of this sketch at the
1975 sale, attributes the Staircase and the State Dining
room ceilings to Sleter on grounds of style.

The final version of this composition as executed
at Grimsthorpe (repr. Croft-Murray 1970 and Lees-
Milne 1970) is somewhat different from this sketch,
having been made into a broader design, with more

figures and with some of the groups differently disposed in relation to each other. For instance, the scholar writing in front of the figure holding up a light, probably emblematic of Knowledge, is transposed from the lower right here to the lower left corner of the finished version, with Knowledge now holding up the light with her other arm, making it more the focal point of the entire composition. She is flanked there by the additional winged figure of Time, who further emphasizes the light by pointing up towards it. Also in the final painting the composition is made yet wider by the addition of two extruded semicircular ends, while the architectural surround, shown in the sketch here, is abandoned.

Abraham Solomon 1823–1862

T 03614 **Waiting for the Verdict** 1857

Oil on canvas 40⅛ × 50⅛ (1020 × 1273)
Inscribed 'A Solomon 57' b.l.
Purchased (Grant-in-Aid) with assistance from the National Art-Collections Fund and the Sue Hammerson Charitable Trust 1982

Prov: Perhaps bt from the artist by Charles Thomas Lucas (d.1895) and with him by 1862 when lent to International Exhibition; . . .; C.J. Lucas in 1896 when lent to Victorian Era Exhibition; for sale, along with its companion T 03615, at that exhibition but still with C.J. Lucas in 1909; . . .; Cotching & Son, Horsham by 1958; . . .; anon. sale, Sotheby's Belgravia 9 April 1974 (104, repr. in col.) £2,700 bt R. Dell; . . .; a private collector from whom bt by the Tate Gallery through Albion Fine Art

Exh: RA 1857 (562); Liverpool Academy 1857 (193); International Exhibition, South Kensington 1862 (720); *Victorian Era*

Exhibition, Earls Court 1897 (316); *Great Victorian Pictures*, AC tour, Leeds City Art Gallery, January–March 1978, Leicestershire Museum and Art Gallery, March–May 1978, Bristol City Art Gallery, May–July 1978, RA, July–September 1978 (51, repr.); *Solomon. A Family of Painters*, Geffrye Museum, November–December 1985, Birmingham Museum and Art Gallery, January–March 1986 (17, repr.)

Engr: Mezzotint by W.H. Simmons, pub. Henry Graves & Co. 1 January 1866 (see T 03616 above)

Lit: *Daily News*, 5 May 1857, p.2; *Illustrated London News*, XXX, 9 May 1857, p.444; *Critic*, 15 May 1857, p.233; *Athenaeum*, 16 May 1857, p.633; *Literary Gazette*, 16 May 1857, p.476; *Punch*, 16 May 1857, p.200; *Times*, 18 May 1857, p.9; *Critic*, 1 June 1857, p.255; *Art Journal*, III, 1 June 1857, p.174; John Ruskin, *Academy Notes*, 1857 (E.T. Cook and A. Wedderburn, eds., *The Library Edition of the Works of John Ruskin*, XIV, 1904, p.114); *Illustrated London News*, XXX, 20 June 1857, p.613, repr. p.614 in wood engraving by H.O. Smith; *Art Journal*, VI, 1 February 1862, pp.74–5; *Athenaeum*, 27 December 1862, p.848; *Art Journal*, VII, 1 January 1863, p.29; J.G. Millais, *The Life and Letters of Sir John Everett Millais*, 1899, I, p.240; *Dictionary of National Biography*, XVIII, 1909, p.625; G.C. Williamson, *Murray Marks and his Friends*, 1919, p.156; Mary Bennett, 'The Pre-Raphaelites and the Liverpool Prize', *Apollo*, LXXVI, 1962, p.749; Lionel Lambourne, 'Abraham Solomon, Painter of Fashion, and Simeon Solomon, Decadent Artist', *Transactions*, Jewish Historical Society of England, XXI, 1968, pp.276–7; Rosemary Treble, *Great Victorian Pictures: their paths to fame*, exhibition catalogue, Arts Council, 1978, pp.74–5; Malcolm Warner, 'Victorian Paintings at the Tate Gallery, Recent Acquisitions', *Apollo*, CXXIII, 1986, pp.259–60, fig.2.

T 03615 **Not Guilty (The Acquittal)**

Oil on canvas 40 × 50 (1016 × 1270)
Inscribed on a label (now removed) on the stretcher 'No 1 | "Not Guilty." | companion picture to "Waiting for the | Verdict," exhibited in 1857. | A Solomon | 18 Gower Street | Bedford Square'

[59]

p.137; Malcolm Warner, 'Victorian Paintings at the Tate Gallery, Recent Acquisitions', *Apollo*, CXXIII, 1986, pp.259–60, fig.3; see also *Lit* for T 03614

Until Abraham Solomon exhibited 'Waiting for the Verdict' at the Royal Academy in 1857 his reputation rested chiefly upon his output of literary and domestic *genre* scenes which were frequently inspired by eighteenth-century sources. However, like his slightly older contemporary W.P. Frith (1819–1909), who by 1851 had grown 'weary of costume painting' and 'determined to try [his] hand on modern life, with all its drawbacks of unpicturesque dress' (W.P. Frith, *My Autobiography*, 1887, I, p.243), Solomon, from 1854 onwards, showed a greater concern for contemporary subject matter, beginning with a pair of paintings, 'First Class – the meeting' (National Gallery of Canada, Ottawa) and 'Second Class – the parting' (Australian National Gallery, Canberra), which he exhibited at the Academy that year. Of these the first, which showed an encounter in a railway carriage between a handsome young man and an attractive young woman (whose father or guardian is asleep beside her), is very much a modern-dress treatment of the kind of imminent flirtation which was customarily dealt with by genre painters of the day by putting the characters in 'period' costume. The sequel, 'Second Class', which showed a widowed mother accompanying her young son on a train journey down to a sea port to join his ship, demonstrates rather better Solomon's ability to deploy contemporary subject matter to some effect.

With the painting 'A Contrast' of 1855 (private collection), which depicts a scene on the sands at Boulogne where a rich and pretty English lady, confined to her wheelchair, is the object of the curiosity and pity and, ultimately, the indifference of a pair of passing rosy-cheeked fishergirls, Solomon again showed his interest in aspects of contemporary life and the morals which might be drawn from them. But it was 'Waiting for the Verdict' of 1857 that established Solomon as a more substantial painter than hitherto had been thought the case. It was immediately identified by the critic in the *Athenaeum* as 'much more refined and with much more purpose' than the artist's previous works and in its truth to nature was linked, by the writer in the *Critic*, to the work of the Pre-Raphaelites. Even so, the same writer expressed the opinion, not uncommon at this time when subjects of a similar nature were under review but somewhat surprising to present-day audiences, that 'the principal objection to the picture is, that it is far too painful to be often looked at. So tragical a moment as this is hardly fit to be perpetuated in all its terrible features'.

Possibly the latter reason might explain why the picture was still unsold at the end of the Academy exhi-

Purchased (Grant-in-Aid) with assistance from the National Art-Collections Fund and the Sue Hammerson Charitable Trust 1982

Prov: Perhaps commissioned by Charles Thomas Lucas (d.1895) as a companion to T 03614; then as for T 03614 but Sotheby's Belgravia 9 April 1974 (105, repr. in col.) £2,900 bt R. Dell; ...; a private collector from whom bt by the Tate Gallery through Albion Fine Art

Exh: RA 1859 (557); International Exhibition, South Kensington 1862 (734); *Victorian Era Exhibition*, Earls Court 1897 (323); *Great Victorian Pictures*, AC tour, Leeds City Art Gallery, January-March 1978, Leicestershire Museum and Art Gallery, March–May 1978, Bristol City Art Gallery, May–July 1978, RA, July–September 1978 (52, repr.); *Solomon. A Family of Painters*, Geffrye Museum, November–December 1985, Birmingham Museum and Art Gallery, January-March 1986 (18, repr.)

Engr: Mezzotint by W.H. Simmons, 'The Acquittal', pub. Henry Graves & Co. 1 January 1866 (see T 03617 above)

Lit: *Athenaeum*, 30 April 1859, p.586; *Daily News*, 30 April 1859, p.2; *Critic*, 7 May 1859, p.447; *Literary Gazette*, 14 May 1859, p.594; *Gazette des Beaux Arts*, 15 May 1859, p.243; *Times*, 18 May 1859, p.12; *Illustrated London News*, 21 May 1859, p.498; *Morning Star*, 23 May 1859, p.2; *Spectator*, 23 May 1859, p.550; *Critic*, 28 May 1859, p.520; *Art Journal*, v, 1859, p.170; *Universal Review*, I, 1859, p.581; *Blackwood's Magazine*, August 1859,

bition. When it was exhibited in Liverpool later in the year it was still on sale at 500 guineas. A slightly better indication of how widely Solomon's picture was appreciated is found in the fact that when, at that exhibition, Millais's 'The Blind Girl' (Birmingham Museum and Art Gallery) was awarded the £50 prize given by Liverpool Academy of Arts to the best work by a non-Liverpool artist, the decision was only reached by a casting vote against another painting by Millais and Solomon's 'Waiting for the Verdict'.

With its heightened atmosphere of pathos and carefully sustained air of uncertainty Solomon contrived to make his audience speculate about the outcome of the trial which is the subject of the painting. He produced a sequel, 'Not Guilty', which appeared at the Royal Academy in 1859. It was hung badly: the writer in the *Critic* described it as being 'so far above the line as to obscure a large portion of its merits [and] placed immediately over an abominable work which seems to have been designedly selected to kill all its good effects'. By general consent, the sequel was disappointing and even though there is some invitation to the spectator to continue trying to puzzle out the circumstances of the trial – there is a hint that the acquitted man might have been either wrongly accused or the victim of a malicious charge – the element of suspense, so crucial in the earlier work, has now evaporated. The *Daily News* adopted a rather higher moral tone in its strictures:

> what is far more startling is that this acquittal deprives the former picture of all its ethical value and meaning. It certainly was not so evident in the first work as it should have been that the verdict must inevitably be guilty; but it was only this assumption that reconciled us to what, if not being indicative of the consequences of crime, was otherwise a most gratuitous exhibition of the sufferings of a poor family. All our fancied insight into the artist's moral purpose is now, however, overturned, that we will not venture to elucidate the rapture of this same 'Not Guilty' ...

A few years later, when the two pictures were exhibited at the International Exhibition, F.T. Palgrave described, more succinctly, the inherent weakness of Solomon's concept when he termed them 'spirited melodrama' (F.T. Palgrave, *Descriptive Handbook to the Fine Art Collections in the International Exhibition*, 2nd ed., 1862, p.61). The paintings later gained a much wider popularity through Simmons's engravings, for which see T 3616–17 above.

Other versions of T 03614 and T 03615 exist: (1) a pair of reduced replicas signed and dated 1859 (oil on canvas 24 × 29; 610 × 735) last on the London art market at Christie's, 30 November 1984 (31, repr.); (2) a pair of reduced replicas (oil on panel 14 × 16; 355 × 406), Tunbridge Wells Museum and Art Gallery; (3) a pair

of reduced replicas lent by R.R. Hyatt to St Judes, Whitechapel in 1884 (98, 99) when they were referred to as 'copies of larger pictures in the South Kensington Museum'. This might indicate that they were copies made by another artist at the time the originals were exhibited in the International Exhibition at South Kensington in 1862.

Various studies for T 03614–15 were included in Solomon's studio sale held at Christie's, 14 March 1863: lot 1, described as 'Waiting for the Verdict – 50in. by 40in.' in chalk, bt £3.10.0 Gilbert; 2, 'a study for "The Acquittal"' in chalk, bt 16s. Noseda; 46, '"The Acquittal" – 40in. by 50in.', described as a 'Cartoon', bt £4.5.0 Smart; and 66, 'A first Study for "The Acquittal" – 18in. by 24in.', probably painted in oil, bt 4 gns G. Earl.

Simeon Solomon 1840–1905

T 03702 **A Youth Relating Tales to Ladies** 1870

Oil on canvas 14 × 21 (355 × 534)
Inscribed 'SS|1870' at right (initials in monogram)
Presented by the Kretschmer family in accordance with the wishes of William Kretchmer 1983

Prov: ...; Victor Coverley Price, from whom bt by the Fine Art Society Ltd 1963 and sold to William Kretchmer 1968
Exh: RA 1870 (77)

The type of frieze-like arrangement of figures in a shallow space which is seen in this picture occurs in a number of Solomon's works of the 1865–70 period and may owe something to the example of Albert Moore. Rather than classical drapes, however, Solomon clothes his figures in vaguely Regency style or in fancy dress of his own invention. As in the work of Moore, Whistler and other 'Aesthetic' artists of the 1860s and 1870s, narrative is at a discount. The 'youth' in Solomon's painting seems hardly to have the energy for even the slight activity demanded of him by the title. One reviewer of the 1870 RA exhibition found the work 'alarmingly lackadaisical' and concluded that 'these "tales" could not have sparkled with wit' (*Art Journal*, 1870, p.163). Another was, perhaps surprisingly, reminded of Stothard (*Athenaeum*, 28 May 1870, pp.713–14).

Sidney Starr 1857–1925

T 03643   **A Study** *c*.1887

Oil on canvas 18 × 14 (455 × 355)
Inscribed on reverse of canvas 'A STUDY|Sidney Starr|38 Abercorn Place|Abbey Road,|N.W.'
Presented anonymously in memory of Terence Rattigan 1983

Prov: ...; Walter Sickert by 1889, given to Miss Florence Pash, later Mrs Humphrey Holland, sold to Rex Nan Kivell of the Redfern Gallery; ...; ?Roland, Browse and Delbanco, sold August 1954 to H.E. Bates; H.E. Bates, sold March 1960 to Roland, Browse and Delbanco, sold April 1960 to the donor

Exh: ?Royal Society of British Artists, winter 1887–8 (368, as 'A Study'); *London Impressionists*, Goupil Gallery, December 1889 (5, as 'Portrait Sketch', and as lent by Brandon Thomas); *Sidney Starr Memorial Exhibition*, Goupil Gallery, June 1926 (22, as 'Portrait Sketch'); *The Early Years of the New English Art Club*, City Museum and Art Gallery, Birmingham, July–August 1952 (92, as 'A Woman in a Basket Chair', and as lent by John Russell); *Plaisirs de L'Epoque*, Redfern Gallery, December 1954–January 1955 (49, as 'Le Repos')

The inscription on the back of the canvas gives some clue as to when this picture was first exhibited. Starr lived at Abercorn Place 1883–9. Works exhibited as 'A Study' during this period are: RA 1884 (217, the address mistakenly being given as 'Aberdeen Place'); Royal Society of British Artists (RBA) 1884 (58, £8.8s); RBA winter 1884–5 (245, £10.10s); and RBA winter 1887–8 (368, £21). The general similarity of this picture to the pastel 'The Pink Shawl' in the Graves Art Gallery, Sheffield (also known as 'The Convalescent'), which is signed and dated 1887, suggests the last possibility. Besides the stylistic similarity both works seem to show the same winged arm-chair. This painting also belonged to Sickert; he gave it to Florence Pash and she to Rex Nan Kivell (letter of 16 April 1974).

The painting's provenance is confused. Brandon Thomas is given as lender of the work to the *London Impressionists* exhibition in 1889 but apparently, according to Mrs Marchant, this was only because he took the picture into the Goupil Gallery in the absence of Sickert in the South of France. Both the 1952 Birmingham catalogue and the records of Roland, Browse and Delbanco (now Browse and Darby) state that John Russell owned the painting but this is denied by John Russell in a letter of 10 August 1982, although he did own two other works by Starr. Lillian Browse, in a letter of 19 December 1978, suggests that John Russell had bought the picture from Rex Nan Kivell and states that Roland, Browse and Delbanco purchased it from John Russell in May 1954 and sold it to H.E. Bates in August 1954. However, H.E. Bates had another picture called 'Le Repos', the same title as that under which T 03643 was known at the time, and the sales may be confused; this smaller work, in oil on panel, 10 × 6 in, was also lent to the *Plaisirs de L'Epoque* exhibition of 1954–5 (127), for which, incidentally, H.E. Bates wrote the foreword. (The provenance given here is based on the research of the donor, in itself based on letters from H.E. Bates of 25 April 1978 (and also from his son), Rex Nan Kivell of 16 April 1974, and Lillian Browse of 19 December 1978.)

The donor suspects that the sitter may have been the person who was the cause of Starr's departure for the United States in 1892. A letter from the artist Whistler to his brother William of 14 April 1892 (in the Library, University of Glasgow), repeating information apparently given him by Sickert, states that Starr ran off with the wife of a patron who had given him both a commission and a studio. The lady's relatives stopped them and Whistler says that the lady turned out to be mad. (Letter from Margaret MacDonald of 24 October 1973, now at the Tate Gallery.)

'Reapers' and its companion 'Hay-Makers', at 'Two Pounds Ten Shillings the Pair', in a printed prospectus dated 24 September 1788 (repr. Judy Egerton, *George Stubbs*, 1984, p.225), in which he also advertised prints he had already published.

George Stubbs 1724–1806

T 03778 **Reapers** published 1791

Engraving, mixed method, image and plate $18\frac{15}{16} \times 26\frac{15}{16}$ (482 × 685) on hand-made laid paper $20\frac{3}{8} \times 27\frac{3}{4}$ (517 × 705); watermark: a dovecote; variation on Heawood 1234, an Auvergne paper used in England *c*.1784
Writing-engraving within the image bottom centre 'REAPERS.|Painted, Engraved & Published by Geo: Stubbs, 1 Jan.ᵞ 1791. N.º 24 Somerset Street, Portman Square, London. – '; on the back, stamped twice by the British Museum (i) on accession, with no.1865–1–14–906; (ii) on transfer, as 'British Museum Duplicate', endorsed 'JKR' in ink (initials of John K. Rowlands, Keeper of Prints and Drawings, British Museum)
Transferred by the Trustees of the British Museum 1983

Prov: . . .; purchased by the British Museum from Mr Daniell (from whom sixteen other Stubbs prints were purchased at the same time: presumably the print dealer F.B. Daniell) 1865; transferred to the Tate as a duplicate 1983

Lit: Basil Taylor, *The Prints of George Stubbs*, 1969, no.16, repr. p.49; Richard Godfrey, 'George Stubbs as a Printmaker', *Print Collector's Newsletter*, XIII, no.4, 1982, p.116

Engraved in reverse direction after the oil painting of 1785 now in the Tate Gallery, T 02257. In the engraving Stubbs has brought the figures of the central girl and the man on horseback into more prominence by bringing them forward and enlarging them in proportion to the other figures.

Stubbs invited subscriptions for the publication of

T 03779 **Labourers** published 1789

Engraving, mixed method, image and plate $20\frac{7}{8} \times 27\frac{7}{8}$ (530 × 707) on hand-made wove paper closely trimmed to plate-mark (lower right edge cut within image)
Writing-engraving within image bottom centre 'LABOURERS.|Painted, Engraved & Published by Geo. Stubbs, 1 Jan.ᵞ 1789, N.º 24, Somerset Street, Portman Sq. London.'; on the back, stamped twice by the British Museum (i) on accession, with no. 1865–1–14–905; (ii) on transfer, like T 03778
Transferred by the Trustees of the British Museum 1983

Prov: . . .; purchased by the British Museum from Mr Daniell (see T 03778) 1865; transferred to the Tate as a duplicate 1983

Lit: Basil Taylor, *The Prints of George Stubbs*, 1969, no.15, repr. p.47 from another impression; Richard Godfrey, 'George Stubbs as a Printmaker', *Print Collector's Newsetter*, XIII, no.4, 1982, p.116; Judy Egerton, *George Stubbs*, 1984, p.47

Probably engraved after the oil painting of 1779 (National Trust, Upton House, Lord Bearsted Collection), in reverse direction, centering the group of labourers, cart and dog and omitting part of the background, including the view of the lodge and park at Southill. In Stubbs's print prospectus of 1788 (see T 03778), 'Labourers' was advertised as a companion to 'Farmer's Wife and Raven', price £1. 6s. 0d. each.

Godfrey draws attention to 'one small but significant detail, indicative of his [Stubbs's] concern with the smallest facet of his prints: even the inscription spaces, planted at the center base of the designs, contribute to their careful balance, and indeed in the "Labourers" ... the inscription block takes on a physical role as a support for a brick that presses down its corner'.

An engraving of the subject by Amos Green, published in 1790, was made from Stubbs's first painted version of 1767, commissioned by Lord Torrington and in his sale in 1778 (now in the Philadelphia Museum of Art), after Amos Green had substantially repainted the background, depicting a generalized woodland scene in place of the lodge and park at Southill.

T 03780 **A Foxhound** published 1788

Engraving, mixed method, $3\frac{9}{16} \times 4\frac{1}{2}$ (92 × 115) on hand-made thick-textured paper $6\frac{5}{8} \times 8\frac{1}{8}$ (169 × 206); plate-mark $4\frac{1}{8} \times \frac{15}{16}$ (105 × 127)
Writing-engraving below image 'Publish'd by Geo Stubbs 1 May 1788'; on the back, stamped twice by the British Museum (i) on accession, with no. 1865–1–14–921; (ii) on transfer, like T 03778
Transferred by the Trustees of the British Museum 1983

Prov: ...; purchased by the British Museum from Mr Daniell (see T 03778) 1865; transferred to the Tate as a duplicate 1983

Lit: Basil Taylor, *The Prints of George Stubbs*, 1969, no.12, repr. p.41 from another impression; Richard Godfrey, 'George Stubbs as a Printmaker', *Print Collector's Newsletter*, XIII, no.4, 1982, p.115

This is one of four prints of foxhounds made by Stubbs; the others are 'A Foxhound Viewed from Behind' (Taylor 11, of which T 03781 below is an impression),

'A Foxhound on the Scent' (Taylor 10, repr. p.39) and 'Two Foxhounds in a Landscape' (Taylor 13, repr. p.43). These were advertised in Stubbs's print prospectus (see T 03778) as 'Three Prints of Single Dogs', price 1s. 6d. each, and 'two Dogs', price 2s. 6d.

Godfrey includes the foxhound prints among prints which reveal 'the full richness of his [Stubbs's] mature technique' and notes that in them 'Stubbs seems to have made original and delightful use of soft-ground etching'.

Each of the foxhound prints is related (in reverse direction) to portraits of individual hounds which occur among the pack of foxhounds in Stubbs's large canvas 'The 3rd Duke of Richmond with the Charlton Hunt', one of three large canvases painted for the Duke c.1759–60, and still at Goodwood House (repr. Judy Egerton, *George Stubbs*, 1984, p.52). For 'A Foxhound on the Scent' a highly sensitive and finished pencil study survives (Paul Mellon Collection, Upperville, Virginia, repr. Taylor p.39, beside the print); Taylor notes this as 'the only specific evidence to support a belief that the prints were based upon drawings even in those cases in which there was also a painted version'.

More uncertainly related is a group of small studies of details from the Goodwood hunting picture painted (in the same direction, ? by Stubbs) in oil on paper which is then stuck down to make a small picture to which a generalized landscape setting is added; examples of these include 'Huntsman with a Grey Hunter and two Foxhounds' (a group which includes the 'Foxhound Viewed from Behind', Paul Mellon Collection, Upperville, Virginia, repr. Basil Taylor, *Stubbs*, 1971, pl.9) and two small pictures of foxhounds, one the subject of T 03781, the other the 'Foxhound on the Scent' (sold Sotheby's 12 March 1985, lots 114–15, repr., bt Spink).

T 03781 **A Foxhound Viewed from Behind** published 1788

Engraving, mixed method, $3\frac{5}{16} \times 4\frac{3}{16}$ (84 × 107) on hand-made wove paper $7\frac{1}{8} \times 10\frac{1}{4}$ (180 × 260); plate-mark $4\frac{1}{8} \times 4\frac{15}{16}$ (106 × 127)
Writing-engraving below image 'Publish'd by Geo Stubbs 1 May 1788'; on the back, stamped twice by the British Museum (i) on accession, with no. 1872–10–12–3698; (ii) on transfer, like T 03778
Transferred by the Trustees of the British Museum 1983

Prov: ...; purchased by the British Museum from Mr Daniell (see T 03778) 1872; transferred to the Tate as a duplicate 1983

Lit: Basil Taylor, *The Prints of George Stubbs*,
1969, no.11, repr. p.41 from another
impression; Richard Godfrey, 'George
Stubbs as a Printmaker', *Print Collector's
Newsletter*, XIII, no.4, 1982, p.115

See note to T 03780 above

T 03843   A Horse Attacked by a Lion (A Lion Devouring a Horse)
published 1788

Engraving, mixed method, $9\frac{13}{16} \times 13\frac{3}{16}$
(250×335) on hand-made wove paper
$11\frac{3}{16} \times 15$ (284×380); plate-mark
$10\frac{7}{8} \times 13\frac{15}{16}$ (277×355)
Writing-engraving below image 'Painted,
Engrav'd & Publish'd by Geo. Stubbs,
1788, Nº 24 Somerset Str. Portman Sq.
London.'; on the back, stamped twice by
the British Museum (i) on accession, with
no.1931–12–24–3; (ii) on transfer, like
T 03778
Transferred by the Trustees of the British
Museum 1984

Prov: ...; presented to the British Museum by
C.H. Sykes 1931; transferred to the Tate
as a duplicate 1984

Lit: Basil Taylor, 'George Stubbs: "The Lion
and Horse" Theme', *Burlington
Magazine*, CVII, 1965, pp.81–6, Appendix
p.86, no.14; Basil Taylor, *The Prints of
George Stubbs*, 1969, no.4, repr. p.28 from
another impression; Richard Godfrey,
'George Stubbs as a Printmaker', *Print
Collector's Newsletter*, XIII, no.4, 1982,
p.115, repr.

In Stubbs's print prospectus of 1788 (see T 03778), this
print was advertised as 'A Lion devouring a Horse',
price 5s. 0d. (In the hope of avoiding confusion between
Stubbs's various treatments of the 'Lion and Horse'
theme', in which four different episodes can be distinguished, the Tate's painted version of this subject
(T 01192, discussed below) is so far known as 'Horse
Attacked by a Lion', the phrase 'devouring' or
'devoured by' being reserved for Stubbs's one known
version of the final episode (also in the Tate, T 02058)
in which the horse is forced to the ground; but the titles
need further sorting-out to be consistent with Stubbs's
own usage).

After Stubbs's death, this print was reproduced as a
line engraving by William Nicholls for publication in
the *Sporting Magazine*, July 1808, facing the title-page;
the Editor noted (p.115) that the engraving was 'from
a fine enamel picture in possession of Mr Stubbs's
executrix' (Mary Spencer). No enamel to which
Stubbs's print exactly corresponds is now known; since
Stubbs is usually faithful to all or most details in trans-
lating his paintings into prints, it seems reasonable to
hope that one may be discovered. The poses of the horse
and lion in the print are almost identical to those in one
of Stubbs's earliest versions of the theme, the very large
'Horse Attacked by a Lion' of *c.*1762, painted for the
Marquess of Rockingham and now in the Yale Center
for British Art, Paul Mellon Collection (repr. Godfrey,
p.115, above his illustration of the print), though the
angle of the lion's upflung tail and the landscape foreground and background are different. The Tate's
enamel painting of 'Lion Attacking a Horse' of 1769
(T 01192) is octagonal in shape; the horse is in the same
pose as in the print, but there are differences in the
position of the lion's paws, its tail is curled behind
it, and the landscape foreground and background are
different.

T 03844   A Lion Resting on a Rock
published 1788

Engraving, mixed method, $8\frac{7}{8} \times 12\frac{3}{8}$
(227×314) on hand-made wove paper

$9\frac{7}{8} \times 12\frac{7}{8}$ (252 × 326)

Writing-engraving below image 'Painted Engravd & Published by Geo Stubbs 1 May 1788 N° 24 Somerset Str Portman Sq London'; on the back, stamped twice by the British Museum (i) on accession, with no.1874–5–9–170; (ii) on transfer, like T03778

Transferred by the Trustees of the British Museum 1984

Prov: ...; purchased by the British Museum from Mr Francis 1874; transferred to the Tate as a duplicate 1984

Lit: Basil Taylor, *The Prints of George Stubbs*, 1969, no.7, repr. p.35 from another impression; Richard Godfrey, 'George Stubbs as a Printmaker', *Print Collector's Newsletter*, XIII, no.4, 1982, pp.114–15; Judy Egerton, 'George Stubbs: Two rediscovered enamel paintings', *Burlington Magazine*, CXXVIII, 1986, pp.24–7

Engraved after the enamel painting of 1775, now in a private collection, Switzerland (repr. Egerton, p.26, fig.31). This is the print entitled 'a Lion' in Stubbs's print prospectus of 1778 (see T03778), for which the price was 5s. 0d.

Godfrey considers that 'Lion Resting on a Rock' and 'Recumbent Leopard by a Tree' (Taylor 6, repr. p.33) 'represent the transitional stage' in Stubbs's printmaking 'between the two early linear prints' ('Horse Frightened by a Lion', Taylor 1, repr. p.23, and 'Leopards at Play', Taylor 2, repr. p.25; a 1974 printing of the latter is no. T01986 in the Tate's collection, together with the copperplate, T01985) 'and the later more elaborately worked-up tonal engravings. The forms are described by minute perambulation of line, but Stubbs was also beginning to realize the value of tools such as roulettes and mezzotint rockers for working up textural effects. He gives the impression of an artist stooped over a

copper plate with a small battery of tools beside him, the function of each being diverted to original and unexpected use as it came to hand'.

J.M.W. Turner 1775–1851

The ownership of the following oil-paintings was transferred from H.M. Treasury to the Tate Gallery in 1984; they will however remain at Petworth House in Sussex as part of the Egremont Collection administered by the National Trust. All were fully catalogued by Evelyn Joll in *The Paintings of J.M.W. Turner* by himself and Martin Butlin, published for the Paul Mellon Centre for Studies in British Art and the Tate Gallery by Yale University Press in 1977 with a revised edition in 1984. The entries below are largely abbreviated from Evelyn Joll's, though physical examination of certain of the pictures has resulted in minor modifications to dimensions and, in one case, past exhibitions; in one further case the dating of the picture has been modified. However, for full information about all exhibitions (apart from those in Turner's lifetime which are given in the entries below) and for full references to the literature the reader is referred to Butlin and Joll 1984 under the pages and catalogue numbers given; these catalogue numbers are further abbreviated in the general texts of the entries to the form 'BJ ... '. Roman numerals, e.g. LXXXI, refer to A.J. Finberg's *Complete Inventory of the Drawings of the Turner Bequest*, 1909 (these works have recently been transferred from the Department of Prints and Drawings at the British Museum to the Clore Gallery at the Tate).

T03868 **Ships bearing up for Anchorage ('The Egremont Seapiece')** exh.1802

Oil on canvas 48 × 72$\frac{1}{8}$ (1120 × 1830)
Inscribed 'JMW Turner pinx' b.r.

Prov: Bought from Turner by George, third Earl of Egremont (1751–1837) possibly in 1802 at the RA but in any case he owned it by 1805 (see below); by descent to the third Lord Leconfield who in 1947 conveyed Petworth to the National Trust; in 1957 the contents of the State Rooms were accepted by the Treasury in part payment of death duties; transferred to the Tate Gallery 1984

Exh: RA 1802 (227)

Engr: Mezzotint by Charles Turner, 'Ships in a Breeze', pub. 20 February 1808 in the *Liber Studiorum*. There are considerable

differences from the original, which no doubt account for the alteration in the title as the ships are no longer 'bearing up for anchorage' in the print, the composition of which is a good deal more concentrated. There is a drawing for the print in the Turner Bequest CXVI-M

Lit: Butlin and Joll 1984, p.17, no.18, pl.14 (col.)

This is the earliest Turner in the Petworth collection though it is not certain whether the third Earl of Egremont bought it at the Royal Academy Exhibition of 1802 or later; he certainly owned it by 1805 when Turner went through his 'Calais Pier' sketchbook (LXXXI) annotating some of the related drawings 'Ld. Egremont's Picture' (a number of other drawings in the sketchbook are inscribed 'Study not painted 1805'). The most finished study for the painting occurs on pp.72–3 of the 'Calais Pier' sketchbook (repr. inside front covers of Gerald Wilkinson, *Turner's Early Sketchbooks 1789–1802*, 1972); there are other drawings on pp.74–5, 76–7, 88–9, 112–13 and 115. Further sketches occur on pp.114, 115 and 118 of the 'Dolbadarn' sketchbook (XLVI) and there are some much slighter studies in the 'Studies for Pictures' sketchbook (LXIX, pp.29–32, 40 verso–41 and 91). Professor Bachrach pointed out, in conversation with Evelyn Joll, the similarity between the ship at anchor and one of the ship models owned by Turner and now in the Tate Gallery.

T 03869   Narcissus and Echo   exh.1804

Oil on canvas 34 × 46 (865 × 1170)

Prov: Bought from Turner by the third Earl of Egremont after 1810 but before 1819 (see below); by descent to the third Lord Leconfield who in 1947 conveyed Petworth to the National Trust; in 1957 the contents of the State Rooms were accepted by the Treasury in part payment of death duties; transferred to the Tate Gallery 1984

Exh: RA 1804 (207); BI 1806 (258)
Engr: Soft-ground etching by Turner himself for the *Liber Studiorum* but unpublished
Lit: Butlin and Joll 1984, pp.41–3, no.53, pl.63

This was exhibited by Turner at the Royal Academy with the following verses from Addison's translation of Ovid's *Metamorphoses* (Book iii, ll.601–12):

> So melts the youth, and languishes away;
> His beauty withers, and his limbs decay;
> And none of those attractive charms remain
> To which the slighted Echo sued in vain.
> She saw him in his present misery,
> Whom, spite of all her wrongs, she griev'd to see:
> She answer'd sadly to the lover's moan,
> Sigh'd back his sighs, and groan'd to every groan:
> 'Ah! youth beloved in vain!' Narcissus cries;
> 'Ah! youth beloved in vain!' the nymph replies.
> 'Farewell!' says he. The parting sound scarce fell
> From his faint lips, but she reply'd 'Farewell!'

Echo was a daughter of the Air and Tellus, one of Juno's attendants, and became the confidante of Jupiter's amours. However, her loquacity displeased Jupiter and she was punished by Juno by only being able to speak in the form of answers to questions put to her. She subsequently fell in love with Narcissus and, scorned by him, pined away and was changed into a stone; this still however retained the power of voice.

Although exhibited in 1804 the picture still seems to have been in Turner's possession in about 1810. It is listed on p.36 of the 'Finance' sketchbook (CXXII) coupled with three other pictures with the price £200 against them, suggesting that the pictures were all unsold (and indeed the other three remained in the Turner Bequest). The list faces a note giving a date in November 1809 but includes works that were exhibited in both 1809 and 1810. Evelyn Joll suggests that the four pictures had been valued down to £50 each for stock-taking purposes and that this tempted Egremont to buy the picture. Alternatively, the four pictures could have been grouped as being of the kind for which Turner usually charged £200.

The picture seems however to have belonged to Lord Egremont by the beginning of 1819 though the evidence is pretty tenuous. On p.2a of the 'Farnley' sketchbook (CLIII) there is a list of *Liber Studiorum* plates to be published on 1 January 1819 that includes 'Egremont's Picture' and it has been assumed that this is the 'Narcissus and Echo', although only an unfinished, unpublished soft-ground etching of this subject prepared by Turner for the *Liber Studiorum* exists.

Turner may have been attracted to the subject by seeing Claude's picture of the same subject of 1644 (National Gallery) that hung in Sir George Beaumont's house in London until he moved to the country in 1808. John Gage has suggested that another source may have been George Field's idea that reflection in colour might be compared to echo in sound (this was later published in Field's 'Aesthetics, or the Analogy of the Sensible Sciences Indicated', *The Pamphleteer*, XVII, 1820, pp.212–13).

T 03870   **Windsor Castle from the Thames** *c.*1805

Oil on canvas 35¾ × 48 (910 × 1220)
Inscribed 'IMW Turner RA ISLEWORTH' b.r.

Prov: Bought from Turner by the third Earl of Egremont; by descent to the third Lord Leconfield, who in 1947 conveyed Petworth to the National Trust; in 1957 the contents of the State Rooms were accepted by the Treasury in part payment of death duties; transferred to the Tate Gallery 1984

Exh: Society of British Artists 1834 (15, lent by Lord Egremont)
Lit: Butlin and Joll 1984, p.113, no.149, pl.156 (col.)

The reference to Isleworth in the inscription almost certainly means that the painting dates from the period when Turner was living at Sion Ferry House, Isleworth where he was first listed as rate payer on 23 May 1805; he was similarly listed on 2 November 1805 and 15 May 1806 but had left by 30 October 1806. The address also occurs in the inside cover of the 'Studies for Pictures; Isleworth' sketchbook (XC) on p.29 verso of which there is a watercolour study for the painting (repr. Gerald Wilkinson, *The Sketches of Turner, R.A. 1802–20*, 1974, p.108). A slight pencil sketch on p.2 of the 'Windsor and Eton' sketchbook (XCVII) may also be connected, and there is a related drawing among a group of sketches for *Liber Studiorum* subjects (CXVIII-e) which is also related to the painting, particularly in the group of figures and sheep in the foreground on the right.

T 03871   **The Thames near Windsor** ?exh.1807

Oil on canvas 35 × 47 (890 × 1195)
Prov: Bought by the third Earl of Egremont, possibly in 1807; by descent to the third Lord Leconfield, who in 1947 conveyed Petworth to the National Trust; in 1957 the contents of the State Rooms were accepted by the Treasury in part payment of death duties; transferred to the Tate Gallery 1984
Exh: ?Turner's gallery 1807
Lit: Butlin and Joll 1984, pp.50–51, no.64, pl.74

It was suggested by Finberg that this was one of the Thames views shown at Turner's gallery in 1807; Benjamin West told Farington that the pictures he saw there were 'Views on the Thames, crude blotches, nothing could be more vicious', and the review by John Landseer(?) of Turner's 1808 exhibition says that the 1808 exhibition included 'the pictures of Thames scenery which Mr Turner has formerly exhibited'. A date of c.1807 is supported by the style of the picture. There is a sketch for the composition on p.30 of the 'Hesperides (1)' sketchbook (XCIII) which includes drawings related to pictures exhibited in 1806, 1807 and 1808 as well as later years.

T 03872 The Thames at Weybridge
c.1805–6

Oil on canvas 35 × 47 (890 × 1195)

Prov: Bought by the third Earl of Egremont, possibly from Turner's gallery c.1807 but in any case by 1819 (see below); by descent to the third Lord Leconfield who in 1947 conveyed Petworth to the National Trust; in 1957 the contents of the State Rooms were accepted by the Treasury in part payment of death duties; transferred to the Tate Gallery 1984

Engr: Mezzotint by W. Say, 'Isis', pub. 1 January 1819 in the *Liber Studiorum* ('Picture in the Possession of the Earl of Egremont')

Lit: Butlin and Joll 1984, p.126, no.204, pl.201 (col.)

The present title was used by Dr Waagen (*Treasures of Art in Great Britain*, 1854, III, p.39) and the 1856 Petworth inventory but Edward Croft-Murray suggested that the picture might show a view along the river from Isleworth with the battlemented corner of Syon House seen in the break between the trees on the left. The large piece of classical entablature in the foreground suggests, to follow an idea of Evelyn Joll's, that the view may be to some extent a 'capriccio'. This, and the very formal nature of the composition with its strong classical feeling, suggest a rather earlier date than the c.1807–10 proposed by Evelyn Joll. Like 'Windsor Castle from the Thames' (T 03870 above) it is based on drawings in the 'Studies for Pictures; Isleworth' sketchbook (XC, pp.6, 9, 29 and 31; see also pp.28 verso and 29). This sketchbook seems to have been used while Turner was staying at Sion Ferry House in 1805–6 and there seems no good reason to date this oil painting any later. It certainly seems to precede the more atmospheric landscapes that followed Turner's campaigns of sketching from a boat on the Thames of 1806–7, campaigns reflected in the two groups of oil sketches in the Turner Bequest (BJ 160-73 and 177-94).

T 03873 The Thames at Eton exh.1808

Oil on canvas 23½ × 35½ (595 × 900)

Prov: Bought by the third Earl of Egremont perhaps from the exhibition in Turner's gallery in 1808; by descent to the third Lord Leconfield, who in 1947 conveyed Petworth to the National Trust; in 1957 the contents of the State Rooms were accepted by the Treasury in part payment of death duties; transferred to the Tate Gallery 1984

Exh: Turner's gallery 1808

Lit: Butlin and Joll 1984, p.55, no.71, pl.81

Turner's exhibits in his own gallery in 1808 were the subject of a long review in the *Review of Publications of Art* for June 1808, almost certainly by John Landseer. This is the second picture described, under the title 'Eton College'. No printed catalogue of this exhibition is known. Whether Lord Egremont bought this picture during the exhibition is unknown.

T 03874   **The Confluence of the Thames and the Medway** exh.1808

Oil on canvas 35⅞ × 48 (910 × 1220)
Inscribed 'J M W Turner RA fe[?cit]' b.r.

Prov: Bought by the third Earl of Egremont probably from Turner's gallery in 1808; by descent to the third Lord Leconfield who in 1947 conveyed Petworth to the National Trust; in 1957 the contents of the State Rooms were accepted by the Treasury in part payment of death duties; transferred to the Tate Gallery 1984

Exh: Turner's gallery 1808

Lit: Butlin and Joll 1984, pp.57–8, no.75, pl.85 (col.)

This picture was described by John Landseer(?) in his long review of the 1808 exhibition in Turner's own gallery under the above title although it was inventoried in 1837 as 'Sheerness'. It has also been confused with 'The Junction of the Thames and the Medway' now in the National Gallery of Art, Washington (BJ 62) but the identification is now secure.

A watercolour on p.41 of the 'Hesperides (1)' sketchbook (XCIII) shows the hoy crossing and partly masking the man-of-war as shown on the right of this picture. A drawing of fishing boats on p.32 of the 'River and Margate' sketchbook (XCIX) may also be connected.

T 03875   **The Forest of Bere** exh.1808

Oil on canvas 35 × 47 (890 × 1195)
Inscribed '[...] Turner RA' at bottom, right of centre

Prov: Bought by the third Earl of Egremont from Turner's gallery in 1808; by descent to the third Lord Leconfield who in 1947 conveyed Petworth to the National Trust; in 1957 the contents of the State Rooms

were accepted by the Treasury in part payment of death duties; transferred to the Tate Gallery 1984.

Exh: Turner's gallery 1808

Lit: Butlin and Joll 1984, pp.58–9, no.77, pl.87 (col.)

Lord Egremont's estates included the Forest of Bere which lies a few miles north of Havant. Turner had passed through the Forest on his way to Portsmouth in October 1807 to sketch the arrival of Stanhope's squadron after the surrender of the Danish fleet at Copenhagen, the subject of 'Spithead: Boat's Crew recovering an Anchor', also exhibited in Turner's gallery in 1808 and now part of the Turner Bequest at the Tate Gallery. The picture shows figures engaged in barking chestnut branches for caulking and tanning, activities practised on Lord Egremont's estates, and it may well have been, as Evelyn Joll suggests, that Turner was deliberately seeking Lord Egremont's patronage. He succeeded in that it is reported, in the *Examiner* of 8 May 1808, that Lord Egremont had bought the picture from Turner's exhibition. The identity of this picture is confirmed by the detailed description by John Landseer(?) in the *Review of Publications of Art* for June 1808.

T 03876   **Margate** exh.1808

Oil on canvas 35½ × 47½ (900 × 1205)

Prov: Bought by the third Earl of Egremont perhaps from Turner's gallery in 1808; by descent to the third Lord Leconfield who in 1947 conveyed Petworth to the National Trust; in 1957 the contents of the State Rooms were accepted by the Treasury in part payment of death duties; transferred to the Tate Gallery 1984

Exh: Turner's gallery 1808

Lit: Butlin and Joll 1984, pp.59–60, no.78, pl.88

That this picture was exhibited in Turner's gallery in 1808 is confirmed by the description of John Landseer (?) in the *Review of Publications of Art*, June 1808. In the 1856 Petworth inventory it was listed as 'Seapiece' and later it was twice misidentified as showing Whitby or Hastings, the last on account of the inscription on the stern of the fishing smack on the left. The same view occurs in the watercolour of Margate painted *c*.1822 for *Picturesque Views on the Southern Coast of England* in the Yale Center for British Art, Paul Mellon Collection. The Turner Bequest includes what seems to be a more or less contemporary oil sketch, possibly done on the spot, showing the same view but from a nearer vantage point (N 02700; BJ 174).

descent to the third Lord Leconfield, who in 1947 conveyed Petworth to the National Trust; in 1957 the contents of the State Rooms were accepted by the Treasury in part payment of death duties; transferred to the Tate Gallery 1984

Exh: Turner's gallery 1809 (8)
Lit: Butlin and Joll 1984, pp.65–6, no.88, pl.98

This was included in Turner's exhibition of 1809, a catalogue of which has been traced, unlike that for 1808. It includes, under this title, the following lines from Gray:

> Say, Father Thames, for thou hast seen
> Full many a sprightly race,
> Disporting on thy margin green,
> The paths of pleasure trace,
> Who foremost now delight to cleave
> With pliant arms thy glassy wave.

In a letter of 26 April 1809, two days after the opening of Turner's exhibition, Sir Thomas Lawrence wrote to a Mr Penrice of Yarmouth recommending the purchase of this work: 'The subject is "A scene near Windsor", with young Etonians introduced ... If the expression can apply to landscape it is full of sentiment, and certainly of genius ... It is in his [Turner's] own peculiar manner, but *that* at its best; no Flemish finishing, but having in it fine principles of art, the essentials of beauty, and (as far as the subject admits it) even of grandeur'. However, the picture went to Lord Egremont, though it is not certain whether he bought it directly from Turner's exhibition.

T 03877 Near the Thames' Lock, Windsor exh.1809

Oil on canvas 35 × 46½ (890 × 1180)
Inscribed 'JMW Turner RA' b.r.
Prov: Bought by the third Earl of Egremont perhaps from Turner's gallery in 1809; by

T 03878 Tabley, Cheshire, the Seat of Sir J.F. Leicester, Bart.: Calm Morning exh.1809

Oil on canvas $35\frac{7}{8} \times 47\frac{3}{4}$ (910 × 1215)
Inscribed 'JMW Turner RA' b.r.

Prov: Painted for Sir John Leicester, later Lord
de Tabley, together with BJ 98, in 1808;
sale conducted by Christie's in Lord de
Tabley's house in London, 24 Hill Street,
7 July 1827 (34) bt third Earl of Egremont;
by descent to the third Lord Leconfield
who in 1947 conveyed Petworth to the
National Trust; in 1957 the contents of
the State Rooms were accepted by the
Treasury in part payment of death duties;
transferred to the Tate Gallery 1984

Exh: RA 1809 (146); Liverpool Academy 1811
(9, this may refer to the companion picture
BJ 98)

Lit: Butlin and Joll 1984, pp.70–71, no.99,
pl.107 (col.)

This is a companion to 'Tabley, the Seat of Sir J.F.
Leicester, Bart.: Windy Day'. Both were painted for Sir
John Leicester in 1808 following a visit to his seat,
Tabley House near Knutsford, Cheshire. Both were
exhibited at the Royal Academy in 1809, the companion
picture as no.105; despite the gap between the two
exhibition numbers the pictures were probably close
together in the very crowded hanging of the Royal
Academy in those days. Sir John Leicester was created
Lord de Tabley in 1826 and died the following year
and, unlike its companion, the Petworth picture was
sold in the subsequent sale and was then bought by
Lord Egremont. The other painting remained at Tabley
until it passed to the Victoria University of Manchester;
it is now on long loan to the Whitworth Art Gallery,
Manchester (BJ 98).

There are a number of sketches for these two paintings in the 'Tabley No.1' (CIII, pp.15 verso, 16 and 17)
and 'Tabley No.3' (CV, pp.7 and 17) sketchbooks. There
is also a small oil sketch for the Petworth painting that
originally formed part of the 'Tabley No.1' sketchbook
and which has been folded into four, presumably for
despatch to Sir John Leicester to gain his approval
(BJ 208). This sketch omits the large, uncompromising
water tower that Turner, however, included in both the
finished oil paintings.

There are labels on the back of the picture for the
Royal Academy winter exhibitions of 1871 (giving the
title 'A Landscape with the White Horse') and 1888.
The only possible candidates seem to be, for 1871,
no.235, 'Landscape, with Cattle', and, for 1888, no.7,
'Evening'. It has hitherto been thought that it was 'The
Forest of Bere' (No. T03875) that was the work in these
two exhibitions; the identification is understandable in
view of the fact that that painting, like others at
Petworth, seems to have lost its original title early on
and become known as 'Evening: the Drinking Pool'. It
seems from the labels however that it was in fact
'Tabley' that was the work exhibited.

T03879   **Cockermouth Castle** exh.1810

Oil on canvas $23\frac{3}{4} \times 35\frac{1}{2}$ (605 × 900)

Prov: Painted for the third Earl of Egremont; by
descent to the third Lord Leconfield who
in 1947 conveyed Petworth to the National
Trust; in 1957 the contents of the State
Rooms were accepted by the Treasury in
part payment of death duties; transferred
to the Tate Gallery 1984

Exh: Turner's gallery 1810 (13); Society of
British Artists 1834 (122)

Lit: Butlin and Joll 1984, p.77, no.108, pl.115
(col.)

Following the success of his views of Tabley, Turner
painted a number of other views of country houses,
presumably on commission. Cockermouth Castle, originally in the possession of the Earls of Northumberland,
went in 1750 with the Egremont title and Petworth to
Sir Charles Wyndham, nephew of the 7th Duke of
Somerset and the father of Turner's patron. Cockermouth, which lies north-east of Egremont in Cum-
bria, was one of the places visited by Turner in the
summer of 1809 and there are sketches in the 'Petworth'
(CIX, pp.14, 24) and 'Cockermouth' (CX, pp.16, 17, 21)
sketchbooks.

T03880   **Petworth, Sussex, the Seat of
the Earl of Egremont: Dewy
Morning** exh.1810

Oil on canvas $36 \times 47\frac{1}{2}$ (915 × 1205)
Inscribed 'JMW Turner RA 1810' b.l.

Prov: Painted for the third Earl of Egremont in
1810; by descent to the third Lord
Leconfield who in 1947 conveyed
Petworth to the National Trust; in 1957
the contents of the State Rooms were
accepted by the Treasury in part payment
of death duties; transferred to the Tate
Gallery 1984

Exh: RA 1810 (158)
Lit: Butlin and Joll 1984, pp.79–80, no.113,
pl.120 (col.)

This view of the house in which the painting still hangs
is based on a pencil sketch on p.4 of the 'Petworth'
sketchbook (CIX; repr. Gerald Wilkinson, *The Sketches
of Turner R.A., 1802–20*, 1974, p.98). This sketchbook
was in use in the summer of 1809. The statement by
A.J. Finberg (*Life of J.M.W. Turner, R.A.*, 2nd ed.
1961, p.171) that Turner was paid 200 guineas for this
paintings and 100 guineas for 'Cockermouth Castle'
(T 03879 above) seems to be based on supposition rather
than hard fact. Turner annotated the purchase of stock
on 14 June 1810 for £428.11.5 with the name Egremont,
suggesting that Lord Egremont was the source of the
money but that seems to be all the evidence there is
(Finberg's transcript as given in 1961 differs from that
in his *Complete Inventory of the Drawings of the Turner
Bequest*, 1909, I, p.299 where, among other things, the
date is given as 15 June 1810; Evelyn Joll mistakenly
states that this account is in Turner's 'Finance' sketchbook (CXXII) rather than, as he correctly states under
'Cockermouth Castle', the 'Hastings' sketchbook
(CXI)).

T 03881   Hulks on the Tamar   ?exh.1812

Oil on canvas 35½ × 47½ (900 × 1205)
Inscribed 'JMW Turner RA' b.r.

Prov: Bought by the third Earl of Egremont,
perhaps from Turner's gallery in 1812 (see
below); by descent to the third Lord
Leconfield who in 1947 conveyed
Petworth to the National Trust; in 1957
the contents of the State Rooms were
accepted by the Treasury in part payment
of death duties; transferred to the Tate
Gallery 1984
Exh: ?Turner's gallery 1812
Lit: Butlin and Joll 1984, pp.84–5, no.119,
pl.126

There are traces of what may have been a date following
the signature but these are now indecipherable. A.J.
Finberg (*Life of J.M.W. Turner*, 1961, p.191) suggests
that this was the picture exhibited in Turner's gallery
in 1812 as 'The River Plym', which was one of seven
new landscapes mentioned in the review of the exhibition in the *Sun* for 9 June, and is otherwise untraced
since 1812. There are drawings of similar scenes, though
not directly related, on pp.6 and 7 of the 'Ivy Bridge to
Penzance' sketchbook (CXXV) that Turner used in the
summer of 1811, and drawings of hulks on a river in
the 'Devon Rivers' sketchbook (CXXXIII), apparently
used from 1812–15; that on p.28 verso of the latter is
closest to the painting. Again only related by subject is
a watercolour in the Turner Bequest, CXCVI-E (repr.
Gerald Wilkinson, *The Sketches of Turner, R.A., 1802–
20*, 1974, p.135).

T 03882   Teignmouth   exh. 1812

Oil on canvas 35½ × 47½ (900 × 1205)
Inscribed 'JMW Turn[...]' b.l.

Prov: Bought by the third Earl of Egremont
probably from Turner's gallery in 1812;

by descent to the third Lord Leconfield who in 1947 conveyed Petworth to the National Trust; in 1957 the contents of the State Rooms were accepted by the Treasury in part payment of death duties; transferred to the Tate Gallery 1984

Exh: Turner's gallery 1812

Lit: Butlin and Joll 1984, p.85, no.120, pl.127 (col.)

C.H. Collins Baker (*Catalogue of the Petworth Collection of Pictures in the Possession of Lord Leconfield*, 1920, p.126, no.658) transcribed the signature as complete with the date 1812 but this is no longer legible, the picture, like T03881 above, having suffered considerably. In this case however the picture can be securely identified as one of the pictures exhibited in Turner's gallery in 1812 on the basis of the review in the *Sun* for 9 June 1812. Similar in theme to 'Hulks on the Tamar' it perhaps helps to establish that that work too was in the same exhibition.

There is a sketch for the painting on pp.36–7 of the 'Corfe to Dartmouth' sketchbook (CXXIV) which Turner used in the summer of 1811. Another drawing on p.35 shows a different view of the same scene. A watercolour of 'Teignmouth' in the Yale Center for British Art, Paul Mellon Collection, is similar in composition though differing in detail; it was engraved by W.B. Cooke in 1815 for *Picturesque Views of the Southern Coast* and again in aquatint in 1828 for *A Selection of Facsimiles of Watercolour Drawings by British Artists.*

T03883   **The Lake, Petworth: Sunset, Fighting Bucks** *c.*1829

Oil on canvas 24½ × 57½ (620 × 1460)

Prov: Painted for the third Earl of Egremont for the dining-room at Petworth; by descent to the third Lord Leconfield who in 1947 conveyed Petworth to the National Trust; in 1957 the contents of the State Rooms were accepted by the Treasury in part payment of death duties; transferred to the Tate Gallery 1984

Exh: Line engraving by J. Cousen, 'Petworth Park', first pub. James S. Virtue in *The Turner Gallery* 1859–61

Lit: Butlin and Joll 1984, pp.164–5, 167, no.288, pl.290 (col.)

This painting and the next three items were originally inset into the Grinling Gibbons panelling of the dining-room at Petworth, below full-length seventeenth-century portraits. They are closely related to five sketches more or less the same size in the Tate Gallery, four being of much the same subjects, and indeed one if not two of these less finished pictures were seen by Thomas Creevey when he visited Petworth on 16–17 August 1828 actually hanging in what must have been the same 'compartments' in the dining room. Although certain details were changed as between the two versions of the same compositions it seems more likely that Lord Egremont objected to the lack of finish in the paintings that reverted to Turner's own possession. Following a long gap in his patronage of Turner's works he may well have been uneasy over Turner's greatly different style; indeed, he seems to have preferred the relatively traditional 'Jessica' (T03887 below) to the 'Palestrina' that Turner seems to have painted for him when he was in Rome in the winter of 1828–9 (BJ 295; now in the Tate Gallery).

It is possible that Turner and Lord Egremont renewed their friendship, possibly strained by the affair of 'Apullia in Search of Appullus' in 1814 (see Butlin and Joll 1984, pp.91–2, no.128), at the de Tabley sale conducted by Christie's in Lord de Tabley's house in London on 7 July 1827, when Egremont bought 'Tabley, Cheshire, the seat of Sir J.F. Leicester, Bart.: Calm Morning' (see T03878 above). In any case, Turner was staying at Petworth in August 1827 and it may have been then that he began to work on these long landscapes of local scenes. Some if not all of these may have been painted in the studio specially provided for Turner at Petworth. George Jones, in his manuscript 'Recollections of Sir Francis Chantry', written in 1849, gives the story of how, 'When Turner painted a series of landscapes at Petworth, for the dining-room, he worked with his door locked against everybody but the master of the house. Chantrey was there at the time, and determined to see what Turner was doing; he imitated Lord Egremont's peculiar step, and the two distinct raps on the door by which his lordship was accustomed to announce himself: and the key being immediately turned, he slipped into the room before the artist could shut him out, which joke was mutually enjoyed by the two attached friends'.

This picture is closely related to 'Petworth Park: Tillington Church in the Distance' in the Tate Gallery (N00559; BJ 283). In the Petworth picture the charming vignette of the nine dogs rushing out of the house apparently to greet their master has been replaced by a cricket match. There are more deer and Turner has introduced the black sheep which are still a feature of Petworth today.

There are also a number of views of the lake at sunset among the 'Petworth Watercolours', or rather gouaches on blue paper (CCXLIV, pp.3, 4, 6, 7, 14 and 18). For a view of the Carved Room at Petworth see Leslie T 03789 above.

T 03884   The Lake, Petworth: Sunset, a Stag drinking *c.*1829

Oil on canvas 25 × 52 (635 × 1320)

Prov: Painted for the third Earl of Egremont for the dining-room at Petworth; by descent to the third Lord Leconfield who in 1947 conveyed Petworth to the National Trust; in 1957 the contents of the State Rooms were accepted by the Treasury in part payment of death duties; transferred to the Tate Gallery 1984

Lit: Butlin and Joll 1984, pp.164–5, 167–8, no.289, pl.291 (col.)

See T 03883 above. This landscape is closest to 'The Lake, Petworth, Sunset' in the Tate Gallery (N 02701; BJ 284). The lake is seen from somewhat further away and the viewpoint may be rather different: the large clump of trees just to the left of centre of the Tate Gallery picture is absent. There is more detail including deer, swans and ducks. The small figure who seems to be attracting the attention of the dogs in the Tate Gallery's 'Petworth Park, Tillington Church in the Distance' appears to have been reintroduced into this picture, on the far side of the lake just to the right of the centre. The most striking element, the setting sun, is a feature of both versions of the composition.

T 03885   Chichester Canal *c.*1829

Oil on canvas 25 × 52 (635 × 1320)

Prov: Painted for the third Earl of Egremont for the dining-room at Petworth; by descent to the third Lord Leconfield who in 1947 conveyed Petworth to the National Trust; in 1957 the contents of the State Rooms

were accepted by the Treasury in part payment of death duties; transferred to the Tate Gallery 1984

Lit: Butlin and Joll 1984, pp.164–5, 168, no.290, pl.292 (col.)

See T 03883 above. This is related to the picture of the same title in the Tate Gallery (N 00560; BJ 285) which in its turn seems to be derived from the slightly earlier 'Evening Landscape, probably Chichester Canal' also in the Tate Gallery (N 05563; BJ 282) though in this last there is no sign of the Cathedral that breaks the horizon on the right and the hills in the centre distance have distinct peaks.

Lord Egremont had a financial interest in Chichester Canal as he did in Brighton Pier, the subject of T 03886 below. The canal was opened in 1822 but Lord Egremont withdrew his money from the company in 1826 which suggests that this picture, and indeed the whole group, may have been planned as early as that year. Indeed, Evelyn Joll suggests that the fifth landscape in similar format in the Tate Gallery, 'A Ship Aground' (N 02065; BJ 287) might originally have been painted as a replacement for 'Chichester Canal'.

T 03886   Brighton from the Sea *c.*1829

Oil on canvas 25 × 52 (635 × 1320)

Prov: Painted for the third Earl of Egremont for the dining-room at Petworth; by descent to the third Lord Leconfield who in 1947 conveyed Petworth to the National Trust; in 1957 the contents of the State Rooms were accepted by the Treasury in part payment of death duties; transferred to the Tate Gallery 1984

Engr: Line engraving by R. Wallis, 'The Chain
Pier, Brighton', first pub. James S. Virtue
in *The Turner Gallery* 1859–61
Lit: Butlin and Joll 1984, pp.184–5, 188–9,
no.291, pl.293 (col.)

See T 03883 above. As in the case of 'Chichester Canal',
the differences between this version of the composition
and that still in the Tate Gallery (N 02064; BJ 286) are
largely questions of detail and greater finish. There are
various drawings of the Chain Pier together with distant
views of the town in the 'Arundel and Shoreham'
sketchbook (CCXLV, pp.18, 20, 23, 30 and 68).

The Chain Pier, which was opened in 1823, was
another enterprise in which Lord Egremont had a
financial interest. Turner may also have been spurred
on to paint this subject by Constable's 'Chain Pier,
Brighton', exhibited at the RA in 1827 and now in the
Tate Gallery (N 05957).

Evelyn Joll has had the satisfaction of proving the
artist G.P. Boyce (1826–97) wrong in his anecdote concerning what he heard on a visit to Petworth in 1857:
'He introduced in the foreground of it [the Petworth
'Brighton from the Sea'] a broken basket with some
floating turnips, carrots etc. and as the old butler told
me (who was in the house at the time and didn't relish
the painter's uncouth manners) was savage when at
Lord E's suggestion as to their specific gravity, he asked
for a tub of water and some of the identical vegetables
and found that the latter all sank'. A practical experiment has demonstrated that carrots and similar vegetables do in fact float, and would be all the more likely
to do so in sea-water.

T 03887 Jessica exh.1830

Oil on canvas 48 × 36 (1220 × 915)
Prov: Bought from Turner by the Third Earl of
Egremont; by descent to the third Lord
Leconfield who in 1947 conveyed
Petworth to the National Trust; in 1957
the contents of the State Rooms were
accepted by the Treasury in part payment
of death duties; transferred to the Tate
Gallery 1984
Exh: RA 1830 (226)
Lit: Butlin and Joll 1984, pp.186–7, no.333,
pl.333 (col.)

Turner exhibited this picture at the Royal Academy in
1830 with the following quotation:

> '*Shylock* – Jessica, shut the window, I say.' –
> *Merchant of Venice.*

These words do not in fact occur in *The Merchant of
Venice* though Turner may have had in mind the scene
outside Shylock's house (Act II, scene v) when Shylock
instructs Jessica to:

> Lock up my doors ...
> But stop my house's ears, I mean my casements.

In the event, however, Jessica follows Launcelot's
different advice:

> Mistress, look out at window, for all this;
> There will come a Christian by,
> Will be worth a Jewess' eye.

Jerrold Ziff (review of Butlin and Joll, first edition,
1977, in *Art Bulletin*, LXII, 1980, p.170) suggests that
Turner may also have intended, as well as an allusion
to Shakespeare, one to the poem *Italy* by his friend
Samuel Rogers:

> ... Now a Jessica
> Sung to her lute, her signal as she sate
> At her half-open window ...

The Library of the Fine Arts for April 1831 reported
that 'It is also said that his lordship [Lord Egremont]
has purchased Mr Turner's picture of *Jessica*'. This
seems to have been a replacement or in compensation for
his failure to purchase 'Palestrina', the large landscape
begun for him '*con amore* as a companion picture to his
beautiful Claude', the first canvas Turner touched after
he arrived in Rome in August 1828 (Tate Gallery
N 06283; BJ 295); this was also exhibited at the Royal
Academy in 1830.

An article in *The Times* for 9 December 1959 by an
anonymous writer whose mother was Lord Egremont's
grand-daughter claimed that Turner painted this picture in answer to the challenge that 'A yellow background is all very well in landscapes, but would not be

possible in our kind of pictures'. Turner is said to have replied, addressing Lord Egremont, 'subject pictures are not my style but I will undertake to paint a picture of a woman's head with a yellow background if Lord Egremont will give it a place in his gallery'. That Lord Egremont did not in fact purchase the picture until nearly a year after it was exhibited suggests that this account cannot be entirely accurate but it may contain part of the genesis of the picture.

Lord Egremont may in part have been reconciled to the novelty of Turner's style at this period by the painting's dependence on Rembrandt. A number of portraits have been suggested as models (see Butlin and Joll 1984, p.187), as has Rembrandt's 'Lucretia', in the Wombwell collection by 1854 but perhaps in England considerably earlier and now in Minneapolis; the 'Jewish Bride', in London in the hands of the dealer John Smith from 1825 until 1836 and now in the Rijksmuseum Museum, Amsterdam, has also been suggested as an influence.

This was perhaps the most violently abused of all Turner's exhibited works and came to be called the 'mustard pot'.

John Vanderbank 1694–1739

T 03539 A Youth of the Lee Family, probably William Lee of Totteridge Park 1738

Oil on canvas 66⅛ × 421/16 (1679 × 1068)
Inscribed 'Jnᵒ Vanderbank Fecit 1738·' b.l.
Purchased (Grant-in-Aid) 1982
Prov: ...; by descent to Mrs Benedict Eyre (née

Lee) of Hartwell House, sold Sotheby's 26 April 1938 (27c) bt M. Harris; ...; The Duke of Kent by February 1939; by descent to the Duchess of Kent, sold Christie's 14 March 1947 (58) bt Middleton; ...; Lord Hesketh, sold Sotheby's 21 November 1979 (104, repr.); ...; Sotheby's 10 November 1982 (18, repr.) bt Leggatt for Tate Gallery

Lit: W.H. Smyth, *Aedes Hartwelhanae*, 1851, p.96; J. Kerslake, *National Portrait Gallery: Early Georgian Portraits*, 1977, I, p.166

At the Hartwell House sale in 1938 this was thought to represent William Lee Antonie of Colworth MP (1756–1815), but this is evidently impossible in view of the date of the painting. The subject is more likely to be the father of the foregoing, William Lee of Totteridge Park (1726–78) who would have been around 12 or 13 at the time this portrait was painted. His father was Sir William Lee of Hartwell (1688–1754), Lord Chief Justice and Privy Councillor from 1737, in which year he was also knighted. It may be significant that he was also painted by Vanderbank in 1738; the original of several copies was in the Hartwell sale of 1938, lot 49, and was also bought by M. Harris (a copy is reproduced in Kerslake 1977, II, figs.458, 489). William was his only son by his first wife Anne Goodwin (died 1729) and he succeeded to the manor of Totteridge, near Barnet, which Lee had purchased in 1748. From 1827, after the male Lee line became extinct, both Hartwell and Totteridge Park were vested in the female line of the Chief Justice's descendants.

It is also possible that the painting could represent one of the sons of the Lord Chief Justice's brother, Sir Thomas Lee, Bart. (1687–1749), either Thomas (1722–*d.s.p.* 1740) or Sir William, 4th Bart. (1726–99).

William Lee of Totteridge Park married Philadelphia, daughter of Sir Thomas Dyke, Bart., of Lullingstone Castle, and died on 13 August 1778, aged 52. Both he and his wife are buried in Hartwell Church.

The painting is in a dramatic white and gold frame of *c*.1750, decorated with carved swags of drapery and flowers, topped with an eagle, that was *en suite* with other frames and furniture original to Hartwell.

Vanderbank, who consciously affected the manner of Rubens and Van Dyck, appears to have based this composition on Van Dyck's well-known portrait of Philippe le Roy, Seigneur de Ravels (Wallace Collection, London).

James Ward 1769–1859

T 03440 **The Moment** 1831

Oil on panel 14 × 18⅝ (367 × 466)
Inscribed 'J WARD [in monogram] RA.
1831' b.r.
Purchased (Grant-in-Aid) 1982

Prov: ...; anon. sale, Christie's 24 June 1977 (114
as 'Marengo and the Serpent', repr.)
£6,000 bt anon.; ...; Mrs E. Riley Smith,
sold Sotheby's 7 July 1982 (125 as
'Marengo and the Serpent', repr. in col.)
£8,800 bt for the Tate Gallery

Exh: RA 1833 (150)

Lit: Edward J. Nygren, *The Art of James Ward,
R.A., 1769–1854,* unpublished
dissertation, Yale University, 1976, pp.28–
34, 79–84

Although this picture has most recently been known as
'Marengo and the Serpent' there seems little doubt that
it can be identified as 'The Moment' – a painting which
was exhibited at the Royal Academy and which was
described by one critic as representing 'a huge snake on
the point of attacking a white horse, whose attitude
exhibits the fear so formidable an adversary might be
supposed to inspire' (*New Sporting Magazine,* V, no.
26, 1833, p.134; the compiler is grateful to Edward J.
Nygren for supplying this reference).

The former, incorrect, title was undoubtedly given
to the work because there are obvious similarities
between it and Ward's portrait of the grey Arab 'Marengo' (the charger ridden by Napoleon at Waterloo) which
was painted in 1824 and which is now in the collection
of the Duke of Northumberland; the picture is best
known through a lithograph published by Ackermann
but Ward also repeated the subject in a painting of 1829
(London art market 1965).

John Wainwright active 1859–1869

T 03378 **Flower-piece** 1867

Oil on canvas 26⅟₁₆ × 22 (662 × 559)
Inscribed 'John Wainwright 1867' on
stone ledge towards b.l.
Bequeathed by Mrs Bessie Gornall 1982

Prov: ...; Mrs Bessie Gornall

Very little is known about John Wainwright. He exhibited flower pictures and other still life subjects at the
British Institution and the Society of British Artists in
1861, giving his address as 6 Hemmings Row, London.
A picture of 'Partridges' was submitted to the British
Institution from an address in Teignmouth in 1865 and
a flower-piece to the Society of British Artists from
Skerton, Lancaster in 1869. Paintings by him seen on
the market in recent years have all been flower-pieces
similar in character to T 03378, bearing dates between
1859 and 1869. Otherwise his life and work appear to
be unrecorded.

The central urn in T 03378 with its bacchic figures
reappears in a flower-piece by Wainwright dated 1869,
the pair to which, also dated 1869, includes a figurated
urn similar to the one seen at the top left of T 03378 (the
pair: sold Sotheby's New York 20 April 1983 lot 71).
Another version of the second of these 1869 pictures,
also dated that year and called 'Summer', was with Frost
and Reed, Bristol in 1979 together with its companion
'Winter'. Wainwright seems to have played many variations on the same theme, itself derived from the
eighteenth-century Dutch still-life masters.

However, unlike 'Marengo', 'The Moment' depicts a terrifying confrontation between a horse and a snake and it is thus clearly related to a number of other paintings by Ward which treat the same subject and which use, as a model for the horse, 'Adonis', the charger which belonged to King George III (1738–1820) and not Napoleon's 'Marengo'. The first of these was the life-size 'Liboya Serpent Seizing its Prey' exhibited at the Royal Academy in 1803 (now lost but a large study was formerly in the collection of the Dowager Duchess of Sutherland) and then Ward returned to the theme in 1822, but this time identifying the horse (which is the same as that in the 1803 picture) in a so-called 'study for a large picture' entitled 'The Boa Serpent seizing a horse, portrait of "Adonis", the favourite charger of his late Majesty, George the Third' (whereabouts unknown). A drawing of 'Adonis' by Ward of c.1803, now in the British Museum, Department of Prints and Drawings, can, in conjunction with an inscription on the back of the mount and a statement made in a letter of 11 November 1843 which Ward wrote to Thomas Garle (also British Museum, Department of Prints and Drawings, 167, a.41), be identified as the original sketch on which the artist based the horses in the pictures of both 1803 and 1822 as well as that in T 03440.

Although compositionally far less complicated than either 'The Liboya Serpent' or, as far as one can deduce, 'The Boa Serpent seizing a horse', 'The Moment' does nevertheless still possess the iconographic complexity which characterizes these works. The image of a serpent or snake, traditionally associated with, among other things, evil and tyranny, about to strike a white horse has immediately obvious connotations. In the case of 'The Liboya Serpent' Nygren has convincingly suggested that the work is an allegory against the slave trade. Given Ward's consistent use of allegory in his animal paintings it is difficult not to see in 'The Moment', which returns to a theme which in its previous treatments had powerful nationalistic and historical overtones, some sort of commentary by the artist on contemporary events. In 1831, the date on the painting, such a commentary could probably only refer to the agitation in the country which accompanied the debates on the first two Reform Bills in the House of Commons. For the conservatively inclined Ward, as for many others, the prospect of a reform, sustained by vehement, popular support, which changed the character of Parliament and extended the franchise, was to have the very constitution threatened and most likely destroyed by the tyranny of radicalism and revolution. It is quite conceivable that 'The Moment', with the serpent poised for the kill before 'Adonis', by now associated in Ward's mind with the monarchy and all it stands for, is an allegory of these events. The First Reform Act was eventually passed by the Lords on 4 June 1832 – George III's birthday.

T 03577   **First Compositional Study for 'Gordale Scar'** 1811

Pencil on cream paper $10\frac{3}{4} \times 14\frac{1}{4}$ (273 × 364)
Inscribed 'Malham water | Aug! 15th 1811' in pencil lower left with 'JWD. [in monogram] RA' added in pencil below that, at a later date, and 'Gordale' also added in pencil, at a later date, bottom left of centre
Purchased (Grant-in-Aid) 1983

Prov: By descent from the artist to Professor Robert Werner and thence to his daughter Mme E. Arnold, from whom purchased by the Tate Gallery

Exh: *James Ward's Gordale Scar – An Essay in the Sublime*, Tate Gallery, November 1982–January 1983 (2, repr. p.36)

This is one of the earliest studies for the very large (131 × 166in) painting generally known as 'Gordale Scar', on which Ward worked from 1811 to 1815, and which he exhibited at the RA in 1815 (225) with the title 'A View of Gordale, in the manor of East Malham in Craven, Yorkshire, the property of Lord Ribblesdale'; the painting is in the Tate's collection (N 01043).

Edward J. Nygren's note on this drawing in the *Gordale Scar* exhibition catalogue (pp.36–7) is as follows: 'The first overall dated compositional study for the painting, this perspective drawing of the Scar treats the view in terms of mass and planes. By this time, Ward must have visited most of the sites in the area since his view is less an accurate transcription of the Scar itself than a synthesis of visual impression of the geological features of the area, including nearby Malham Cove. There are faint line drawings of the bull on the right and cattle on the left.'

Three studies for 'Gordale Scar' already in the Tate's

collection were included in the *Gordale Scar* exhibition of 1982–3: a panoramic view (5, repr., N 03703), a view of the falls of water (12, repr., N 02142) and a preliminary study of fighting stags (27, repr., N 05161). For another study acquired with T 03577, see T 03578 below.

Thomas Weaver 1774 or 5–1843

T 03578 Study for 'Gordale Scar': Details of Rocks near Waterfall 1811

Pencil on cream paper 11 × 15½ (280 × 394)
Inscribed 'Gordale|Augt 19.th 1811' in pencil bottom right of centre, with 'JWD [in monogram] RA' added beside 'Gordale' in pencil at a later date
Purchased (Grant-in-Aid) 1983
Prov: As for T 03577 above
Exh: As for T 03577 above (8, repr. p.39)

Acquired with T 03577 above. Edward J. Nygren's note on this drawing in the *Gordale Scar* exhibition catalogue (pp.39–40) is as follows: 'The exact formations which inspired these sketches have not been positively identified; however, it is possible that the left-hand area is the left side of the fall at the point where the cataract divides to make its final plunge ... The void in the centre of the sheet would then be the water; the details on the right, the boulder and rocks of the corresponding bank. The sketch separated from the rest in the upper right-hand corner of the sheet could be the indentation in the cavern wall on the right above the falls. In view of the lack of a firm geological context, the identification must remain conjectural.'

Nygren adds 'With their dramatic use of line to create precise, discreet forms of a strange unearthly character, the sketches on this page bear an interesting resemblance to drawings by Leonardo da Vinci in the Royal Collection, which Ward could have known'.

T 03438 Ram-Letting from Robert Bakewell's Breed at Dishley, near Loughborough, Leicestershire 1810

Oil on canvas 40$\frac{7}{16}$ × 50$\frac{11}{16}$ (1028 × 1286)
Inscribed 'T. Weaver Pinx^t 1810' b.r.
Bequeathed by Mrs F. Ambrose Clark from the collection of the late F. Ambrose Clark through the British Sporting Art Trust 1982
Prov: ...; (Rousuck gives 'The Earl of Yarborough' at this point, and it was presumably Rousuck who added a plaque (now removed) to the frame lettered 'from the Collection of the Earl of Yarborough'; this must however be in error, since the present Lord Yarborough has no knowledge that this painting was ever in his family's collection and it is not in the record of pictures made in 1906 after the fire at Brocklesby); William S. Martin, Vermont, U.S.A. (? the American collector whose purchase of the picture in 1929, for £500, was recalled by Lord Balerno in 1971, in correspondence with the Editor of *Farmer's Weekly*: see *Lit.* below); E.J. Rousuck; F. Ambrose Clark by 1958; his widow Mrs F. Ambrose Clark
Exh: International Livestock Show, Chicago 1937 (no catalogue traced); *Sporting Paintings*, Museum of Modern Art Gallery, Washington D.C., December 1937–January 1938 (pictures not individually listed in catalogue); Tate

Gallery, August–September 1982, and York City Art Gallery, March–September 1984, with other paintings from Mrs F. Ambrose Clark's Bequest (no catalogue)

Lit: [E.J. Rousuck], *The F. Ambrose Clark Collection of Sporting Paintings*, privately printed, New York 1958, p.268, repr. p.269; 'Who has this great farming picture?', 'Editor's Diary', *Farmer's Weekly*, 18 June 1971, p.34; 'The Bakewell picture that went to America', 'Editor's Diary', *Farmer's Weekly*, 19 November 1971, p.30 (background correspondence not preserved)

Robert Bakewell (1725–95) was a pioneer in breeding improved breeds of sheep and cattle to supply a steadily increasing demand for meat and (in his day) for fat. He was a tenant farmer at Dishley Grange near Loughborough, Leicestershire, where he pioneered irrigation and the cultivation of select fodder crops for grazing. As a stock-breeder, Bakewell was particularly successful with the 'New Leicester' or 'Dishley' breed of sheep which Weaver portrays here; they were finer-boned than the old Leicester breed and had far greater potential for producing meat and fat. W. Pitt in 1809 described the New Leicester sheep thus: 'Their backs are broad and strait, their breasts are full, bellies tucked up, heads small, necks short, legs thin, pelts light and wool fine of its kind. They are quiet in temper and disposition, and capable of being fattened in a short time, on a small proportion of food, and to a great weight, in proportion to their size' (*General View of Agriculture in Count Leicestershire*, quoted by Squire de Lisle, 'Robert Bakewell', *Journal of the Royal Agricultural Society*, cxxxvi, 1975, pp.55–62; for Bakewell's stockbreeding, see also Helen Harris, 'Pioneer of Britain's Livestock', *Country Life*, 26 June 1975, pp.1709–10).

Other contemporaries noted that within half a century, Bakewell's sheep 'spread themselves over every part of the United Kingdom and to Europe and America' and that thanks to Bakewell, England 'has 2 lbs. of mutton where there was only 1 lb. before' (quoted in *DNB*, I, 1908, p.942). Bakewell also produced new breeds of Dishley Longhorn cattle and of black draught-horses. The Dishley Society, already formed in Bakewell's lifetime, aimed to perpetuate the purity of his breeds.

T 03438 was formerly called 'Robert Bakewell's Ram-Letting'. The setting is reputedly the great barn at Dishley where Bakewell held regular displays of livestock and where he conducted, for high fees, the business of ram-letting, the first to do so on a large scale; though Bakewell's own farmhouse and farm buildings have not survived, it seems credible that Weaver has here portrayed the great barn at Dishley. But Robert

Bakewell himself died in 1795, without issue, and Weaver's picture is dated 1810, fifteen years later; Bakewell himself cannot be portrayed here, or not from life. Was his ram-letting business carried on by the successor to his farm and livestock or, conceivably, by members of the Dishley Society? Some records of the Dishley Society are preserved in the University of Nottingham Library, but none are extant for c.1810, and earlier records throw no light on the subject of this picture (information kindly communicated by Mrs L. Shaw, Assistant Keeper of the Manuscripts).

Rousuck prints a so-called 'key' to the portraits in T 03438, consisting of a list of sixteen names, numbered 1–16; but more than sixteen gentlemen are portrayed in the picture, and if a diagrammatic key once existed it cannot now be traced (and no engraving of the picture has been found). Rousuck's list is mostly of names of eminent agriculturists and scientists, and is as follows:

1 Thomas Bate
2 Mr. Davy, celebrated chemist
3 Sir Joseph Banks
4 Captain Barclay of Ury
5 H. Stafford
6 John Richardson (J.M. Richardson's paternal grandfather)
7 Sir John Sinclair
8 Arthur Young, Secretary to the Board of Agriculture
9 William Wetherill
10 Thomas Booth
11 Thomas William Coke, M.P.
12 Sir Charles Knightly
13 Charles Colling
14 Robert Colling
15 Mr. Waters of Durham
16 John Maynard of Eryholme, Darlington

Another list of seventeen names allegedly relating to this picture (a typescript, signed Edward N. Wentworth) is in the archives of the Institute of Agricultural History and Museum of English Rural Life, Reading; this list adds the name of Bakewell himself, and is differently ordered.

Efforts have been made to compare the portraits in T 03438 with painted or engraved portraits of at least the more eminent of those whose names are listed by Rousuck and Wentworth, with no success; not even in the case of Thomas William Coke of Holkham, twice portrayed elsewhere by Weaver (in a portrait signed and dated 1809, in the Government Art Collection, and in the painting 'Thomas Coke and his Sheep', in the collection of the Earl of Leicester) can a likeness to any of the gentlemen portrayed in T 03438 be found. Though Weaver is not a distinguished portraitist, this seems odd, and must reinforce doubts as to whether either list in fact relates to this picture. Such doubts have been expressed independently (in correspondence) by Keith Robinson, to whom the Keeper of the Museum of English Rural Life referred the Tate's queries, and L.M. Waud, formerly of the Ministry of Agriculture. Both Mr Robinson and Mr Waud point out that Rousuck's and Wentworth's lists are chiefly of men particularly interested in breeding dairy Shorthorn cattle, whereas T03438 depicts sheep, and Bakewell's Dishley breed of cattle were Longhorns. Mr Waud also doubts whether a ram-letting, which was evidently more like a cattle fair, would have been attended by such a small group of visitors. But even if Weaver's gentlemen are unidentifiable, the picture offers a lively idea of how a display of prize livestock was conducted in 1810 and of the sort of gentlemen who attended it.

Sir David Wilkie 1785–1841

T03821   Recto: **Five preliminary studies for figures in 'The Village Holiday'**
         Verso: **Two preliminary studies for parts of figures in 'The Village Holiday' 1809–10**

Black chalk on laid paper, originally a letter sent to the artist, 7¼ × 11 (184 × 278)
Inscribed, recto, in ink in the hand of John Inigo Richards RA, 'Mr D. Wilkie', and in another hand 'no 1' b.r., and verso, in the same hand, 'no 2' t.r.
Purchased (Grant-in-Aid) 1984

Prov: ...; said to have been purchased at Phillips in Edinburgh or Glasgow c.1980; acquired shortly afterwards from the purchaser at that sale by Mr R. Easson from whom bt by the Tate Gallery

The studies on T03821 were drawn by Wilkie on a letter which was written by J.I. Richards RA, Secretary to

the Royal Academy, to Wilkie on 29 November 1809 requesting him to meet the President and Council on 1 December, so he could receive his Diploma which admitted him as an Associate of the Royal Academy. Wilkie records the receipt of this letter in his journal for 30 November 1809: 'Had a note from Mr Richards, requesting my attendance at the Royal Academy to receive my diploma and sign my obligations' (A. Cunningham, *The Life of Sir David Wilkie*, 1843, I, pp.265–6). The letter itself survives on the verso of T03821 and is a printed form, taken from an engraved plate, the blank spaces of which have been filled in as necessary by Richards in his own hand.

Wilkie's picture of 'The Village Holiday' which is now in the Tate Gallery (N00122) was commenced in September 1809, though the idea of such a subject had first occurred to him in August 1808. The finished picture was first shown in public at an exhibition of his own work which Wilkie organized in Pall Mall in 1812. In accordance with his usual practice, Wilkie both worked and reworked his ideas on the canvas and also in small sketches on paper as he thought through aspects of the composition in more detail. T03821 is one of a number of such sketches which survive from the time Wilkie was working on 'The Village Holiday' and according to his journal, which is published by Cunningham, the period of his most intense activity on the picture ended in June 1810. Other related drawings include one in the Tate Gallery (N01187), three small studies in pencil in the National Gallery of Scotland (D4296), four small studies, again in pencil, in the Witt Collection (2295A and B), and a pen and sepia sketch in the Dyce Collection at the Victoria and Albert Museum (940). A small study in ink was sold at Christie's, 12 May 1970 (118). A series of eight larger, more finished watercolour sketches was, in 1972, in the collection of the late Earl and Countess of Swinton.

The studies on the recto of T03821 relate to the following figures in the finished picture: (i) the seated man drinking out of a glass by the inn door at the left-hand side (b.l.); (ii) the group of people leaning over the balcony over the porch at the left (centre left); (iii) the men pulling the drunkard in the principal group (r.); (iv) the figures leaning out of the window behind the pot girl at the centre of the composition (centre right) and the man seated at the table and holding a bottle in his left hand, b.l. (t.r.). The two slight studies on the verso are not readily identifiable with any parts of the finished painting.

T03821 would seem to date from about the same period as the small studies in the National Gallery of Scotland. The study of the people leaning over the balcony shows the building behind them with a dormer window in the roof. This feature appears in one of the drawings in Scotland but not in the finished canvas.

Richard Wilson 1713 or 14–1782

T 03665 **Westminster Bridge Under Construction** 1744

Oil on canvas 28½ × 57½ (725 × 1460)
Inscribed 'R Wilson | 1744' very faintly b.l.
on tablet in wall
Purchased (Grant-in-Aid and Miss M.
Deakin Bequest) with assistance from the
National Heritage Memorial Fund 1983

Prov: ...; F.A. Durell, by descent to his great-grand-daughter Joan Durell-Stables of Offord Hill House, Huntingdon; bequeathed 1980 to a relative by whom sold to Spink & Son, from whom bt by the Tate Gallery

Exh: *Richard Wilson*, Tate Gallery, November 1982–January 1983, National Museum of Wales, Cardiff, January–March 1983, Yale Center for British Art, New Haven, April–June 1983 (5, repr.)

Lit: W.G. Constable, *Wilson*, 1953, p.180, pl.44a (Philadelphia version); H. Preston, *London and the Thames*, exhibition catalogue, Somerset House, July–October 1977, no.31; R.J.B. Walker, *Old Westminster Bridge*, 1979, pp.151–65, 282–5; *The Tate Gallery 1982–84, Illustrated Biennial Report*, p.27, repr. in col.

The view shows Westminster Bridge as seen from Parliament Stairs, more or less as it must have appeared sometime in September 1744. Charles Labelye, its designer and chief engineer, had reported to the Works Committee on 5 September 1744 that the centering on the western 72-foot arch (the one to the left of the middle arch, which was the first to be built) could be struck 'immediately' (Walker 1979, p.155). In the painting workmen are shown dismantling it, lowering timbers from the top of the centering. Work on the two arches immediately to the east of the middle arch had begun that summer, and James Vauloué's tall pile-driving engine (repr. Walker 1979, fig.10) is shown at work

on the tenth pier, counting from the Westminster side. On the far side of the river is the nearly completed 25-foot arch of the Lambeth abutment near Stangate, the centering for which had been ordered in January 1744. The last of the centerings of the three cleared arches on the left had been removed by 6 June that year; the centerings supporting the two visible arches next to the Westminster bank (the final abutment arch is hidden from view) were struck in January and February the following year.

Wilson has allowed himself or was asked to use some artistic licence as far as the middle arch is concerned, as the balustrade over it, though contracted for with Jelfe and Tufnell in March 1744, was not completed until August 1745, and the baroque statues of river gods, representing the Thames and the Isis, though initially planned, were never set up at all. It is not known when exactly this part of the design was abandoned, and no drawings or designs for them are known. Canaletto, in his view of the completed bridge with the Lord Mayor's Day procession of 23 November 1746 (Yale Center for British Art, New Haven) also includes them as the focal point of view, so that perhaps until that date at least some hopes of erecting the statues may have remained, before they fell victim to the usual mounting costs and the engineering difficulties that beset the structure after the fifth pier (fourth from the left in this picture) sank 16 inches in 1747 and had to be rebuilt. As far as one can make out, neither Canaletto's nor Wilson's centrepiece resembles the design published in *The Gentleman's Magazine* in February 1754, and it is possible that they used a lost drawing, or perhaps Labelye's model of the bridge, now also lost, which was known to be one of his most prized possessions. (For the best and fullest account of all aspects of the construction of the bridge, see Walker 1979, on which most of the information given here is based.)

Wilson seeks to give the impression of a hot afternoon in late summer, judging from the near-cloudless sky and the naked urchins bathing on the mud flats at low tide in front of the wall of Cotton and Speaker's Gardens on the left. Behind the trees are the twin turrets of St Stephen's Chapel (demolished in the nineteenth century), then in use as the House of Commons, with the roof of Westminster Hall just visible on the extreme left. The dome of St Paul's dominates the skyline on the right, and the white double pillars of Somerset House Stairs are just visible through the largest of the cleared arches, with parts of the Old Savoy framed by the arch to the left of it. On the far bank are the Lambeth timber yards and the barge houses of the Archbishop, the City Companies, and the nobles who had their houses on the Westminster side.

Begun in 1738, the bridge was one of the major civic projects of the century. It was not finally opened until 1750, and during that period it was painted many times at almost all stages of its construction by most view-painters then working in London, notably Griffier, Joli, Canaletto and Samuel Scott (see T01193). The recent re-emergence of this painting makes Wilson a distinguished member of this group.

Although it is known that Wilson was painting London views as early as 1737 (see N02984), until his departure for Italy in 1750 he practised chiefly as a fairly conventional portrait painter. Yet the handful of English views of the 1740s attributable to him show an accomplished landscape painter who had assimilated all that the British school of landscape painting had to offer at that period. This view, though somewhat dry and old-fashioned in technique compared to Wilson's more impastoed mature style, stands apart from other contemporary paintings of this type in that it treats what is essentially an urban view as an open landscape, placing much greater emphasis on the interaction of natural elements like light and shade, water and the nature of the river banks at low tide, rather than on the delineation of buildings and other topographical details, which are treated in a summary though apparently accurate manner.

A smaller and rather damaged version of this painting, signed and dated 1745, is in the Philadelphia Museum of Art (repr. Preston 1977, no.31 and Constable 1953, pl.44a). It shows the bridge with an additional arch completed and has a similar elegant couple going down the landing stage in the foreground, but the ferry boat seems to have been painted out, probably because it bulked too large in the narrower composition.

It is not known if Wilson painted these views as commissions or as a speculative venture, though the long and narrow overmantel shape of the Tate version suggests that it was meant for a specific location. The building of the bridge involved many notable and reasonably wealthy people who may have wished to own a souvenir of this sort. The view-point of this picture, for example, is taken from close to the spot where Andrew Jelfe, property speculator and chief masonry-contractor throughout the building of the bridge, had his earlier house and one of his stone wharves: he might have enjoyed seeing his masonry blocks stacked on the causeway of the uncompleted bridge, as shown here. His son-in-law Captain Griffen Ransom owned a timber yard at Stangate which he offered freely, 'with kindness and civility', to the Bridge Committee when the foundations of the Lambeth abutment were laid – a site noticeably prominent in this painting. Wilson may have hoped that the subject would attract higher patronage, and it is worth noting, in view of the important commission received by Wilson in the late 1750s to paint Wilton House for the 10th Earl of Pembroke, that the latter's father, the 9th Earl, had been the chief promoter of the Westminster Bridge project from its inception in the 1730s, until his death in 1750.

The figures which animate the foreground have, as David Solkin rightly notes in his catalogue of the 1982–3 Wilson exhibition, something of the Frenchified rococo elegance disseminated in the 1730s and 40s by the drawing master Hubert Gravelot (1699–1773) at the St Martin's Lane Academy, which Wilson is said to have attended, although this compiler would dispute that the couple must necessarily be patrician, or that the waterman's stance is in any way noticeably subservient. The notoriously independent and surly fraternity of Thames watermen, said to have numbered some 30,000 at this period, was closely linked with the bridge in the public mind, not least through its members' vociferous and sometimes violent resistance to a project which they rightly saw as a threat to their livelihood. Many would have sympathised with their cause, and a certain amount of nostalgia would have attached to their more leisurely and smooth mode of transport (bearing in mind that coaches were still poorly sprung), in which case this juxtaposition of an impeccably turned out ferry-boat, with its correctly and neatly uniformed waterman, and the bridge beyond, could be seen as a poignant contrast between the old and the new ways of crossing the river.

Richard Wilson 1713 or 14–1782 and John Hamilton Mortimer 1740–1779

T03366 Meleager and Atalanta c.1770

Oil on canvas $41\frac{1}{8} \times 51$ (1045 × 1295)
Purchased (Grant-in-Aid) 1982

Prov: ...; probably the version owned by Robert Sayer 1771, and passed to his relative James Sayer by 1794; ...; acquired by Samuel Rogers c.1802, but not in his sale 1856; ...; Sir Frederick Cook by 1903 and until 1949 when lent to Birmingham and the Tate Gallery; . . .; ?Mrs Drey; . . .; Boyd Alexander, on whose death in 1980 it passed to his stepson Jonathan Alexander, sold through Agnew to the Tate Gallery

Exh: RA Winter 1903 (28); *Richard Wilson and his Circle*, City Museum and Art Gallery, Birmingham, November 1948–January 1949 (13), Tate Gallery, January 1949 (12)

Engr: Mezzotint by Richard Earlom, as from an original picture in the possession of 'Mr. Sayer', pub. Robert Sayer, September 1771; engraving by Woollett and Pouncey, lettered 'Landskip painted by R. Wilson|figures by Mr. Mortimer', pub. R. Sayer and J. Bennett 1 December 1779; engraving by Woollett and Pouncey, as from 'the Original Picture in the Possession of James Sayer Esq.', pub. Laurie and Whittle 1794

Lit: T. Wright, *Life of Richard Wilson*, 1824, p.21; *Catalogue of Pictures at Doughty House*, 1915, III, no.401, repr.; W.G. Constable, *Wilson*, 1953, pp.116–18, 166–7, pl.25(b); R. Simon, 'New Light on Richard Wilson', *Burlington Magazine*, CXXI, 1979, pp.437–9, fig.66; R.Simon, 'Richard Wilson's "Meleager and Atalanta"', *Burlington Magazine*, CXXIII, 1981, pp.414–17, figs.28, 29 (detail); K. Cave (ed.), *The Diary of Joseph Farington*, New Haven and London, VII, 1982, pp.2796–7

The subject is taken from Ovid's *Metamorphoses*, Book VIII, which describes the slaying of the Calydonian boar by the lovers Meleager and Atalanta and their hunting companions. The monstrous beast had been sent by the goddess Diana to devastate the countryside of Calydon, whose king had offended her. A quarrel over the trophies of the hunt was to precipitate further devastation and the eventual death of the hero. Wilson's savage and doom-laden landscape echoes the brutality of the action, and represents a development from his earlier attempts to depict mood and passion through landscape in the manner of Salvator Rosa's 'banditti' subjects, for example in 'The Murder', 1752, now in the National Gallery of Wales, Cardiff (repr. Constable 1953, pl.12b).

That Wilson was at pains to get the balance of human and natural drama exactly right is shown by his disapproval of the fact that Robert Sayer, who owned the painting in 1771, had the figures of the main group (the group with Atalanta on the left appears untouched) repainted by John Hamilton Mortimer (1740–79), who was known for his 'banditti' subjects. Presumably

Sayer's motive was to strengthen the human element in order to conform more closely to conventional ideas of what a 'history painting' should look like; as a print-seller and publisher he may have felt that this would increase sales of the engraving after it. A marginal note by Faithfull Christopher Pack (1759–1840) in a copy of Wright's *Life of Richard Wilson*, now in the Nottingham University Library, records that he remembered seeing 'the picture of Meleager at Mr. Mortimer's, who told him that "... Wilson has been here he heard that I had been employed to paint other Figures in the *place* of *His* in the picture of Meleager I said I have done so and showed him the Picture and he seemed much displeased and said your Figures are good but you have not put them in the right places and have broken the unity of effect that I had left"' (this passage is fully discussed by Robin Simon 1979 and 1981).

Despite Wilson's understandable resentment, Mortimer's alterations appear respectful of the original, leaving the figure at the rear of the group almost untouched except for the changed angle of the spear. They are most noticeable in the recumbent figure, and in the altered stance of the two huntsmen on the right, around whom numerous pentimenti of Wilson's original group are discernible. Sayer's aim had obviously been to replace Wilson's highly individual, softly handled figures with a more high-lighted and sculptural group, that showed up better in an engraving and was more reminiscent of the antique.

It would appear that 'Meleager' had as a pendant Wilson's 'Apollo and the Seasons', presumably the version in the Viscount Allendale collection (repr. Constable 1953, pl.26a). Like the Tate painting, with which it is identical in size, it also has figures by Mortimer and was published as a print several times, including in 1779 a companion to the 'Meleager' print, from a painting also in the possession of James Sayer. The paintings were still together in 1806, when Farington remarked in his diary on 26 June 1806 that 'The two pictures which Rogers has painted by Wilson, formerly belonged to Sayer, the Print seller. – Rogers gave about 160 guineas for the pair'. It appears that Rogers noted their purchase *c.*1802 in his commonplace book (information kindly supplied by Gillian Malpass, who is working on the Rogers collection).

A pen and wash drawing of the part of the painting which includes the Mortimer figure group is in the Bolton Museum and Art Gallery (repr. Simon 1981, fig.30). It is on French blue rag paper of the 1760s, but cannot be ascribed to either Wilson or Mortimer. The style is closer to Joseph Farington, who was Wilson's pupil 1763–7 (the attribution was first made by Judy Egerton). Simon suggests that it may have been executed by Farington as a specific record of an alternation to the work of an acknowledged master, especially as the alteration seems to have been sufficiently well publicised for Wilson to come to inspect it.

A drawing of the altar in the foreground, bearing the inscriptions 'GENIO HVIC DEO|SACRUM' and 'Villa Madama', is in the Victoria and Albert Museum (Dyce 661).

Peter de Wint: see under 'de'

The Modern Collection

Ivor Abrahams b.1935

T 03369 Lady in Niche 1973

Green flock, polystyrene, fibreglass,
household paint and plywood
$82\frac{1}{2} \times 62 \times 30$ (2095 × 1575 × 762)
Not inscribed
Purchased from Mayor Gallery (Grant-in-
Aid) 1982

Prov: Purchased from the artist by Mayor
Gallery

Exh: *Ivor Abrahams*, Kölnischer Kunstverein,
Cologne, June–August 1973, Lijnbaan
Centrum, Rotterdam, August–September
1973 (not catalogued); *Ivor Abrahams,
Sculptures and Works on Paper*, City
Museum and Art Gallery, Portsmouth,
March–April 1979, Ferens Art Gallery,
Hull, June–July 1979, Art Gallery,
Middlesbrough, July–September 1979,
City Museum and Art Gallery, Stoke-on-
Trent, October–November 1979, St
Enoch's Gallery, Glasgow, December
1979–January 1980 (1, repr.); *British
Sculpture in the 20th Century*, part 2,
Whitechapel Art Gallery, November
1981–January 1982 (110); *Ivor Abrahams,
Sculptures 1972–1982*, Warwick Arts

Trust, November–December 1982
(3, repr. in col.)

Lit: R.J. Rees, 'Ivor Abrahams's Sculptures',
Studio International, CLXXXXIII, June
1972, pp.263–5
Also repr: Ivor Abrahams, Yorkshire
Sculpture Park, exhibition catalogue,
1984, p.11

Abrahams's 'Lady in Niche' is one of a group of large
sculptures he made in the early 1970s of garden subjects,
in this case a decorative sculpture in a niche, in which
foliage is represented by green flock. This commercial
technique, usually used for example on model toys or
wallpaper, was first used by Abrahams as a surface for
sculpture in 1970, and was an elaboration of the setting
of his 'Nude Statue on Lawn' (1966–8) which was
placed on a carpet of rayon flock. The origin of much
of his later sculpture in this work is described by the
artist in a conversation with R.J. Rees published in the
exhibition catalogue *Ivor Abrahams*, Kölnischer Kunstverein, 1973, pp.16–18, and the technique is described
in an article by R.J. Rees (*Studio International*, loc.cit.).

A version of this sculpture 26 in. high was made and
exhibited in the previous year, 1972 (Kölnischer Kunstverein, op.cit., repr. p.41). In this the flock surrounds
the figure, covering the 'niche', and it is a single piece
(unlike the Tate Gallery's sculpture in which the flocked
part is separate). This smaller work was reproduced
in ceramic in 1972, in conjunction with the Ceramic
Workshop, Edinburgh. An etching of this subject was
made in 1976, part of a series titled 'Works Past'.

Several preceding sculptures and reliefs by Abrahams
similarly depict a more or less classical statue covered
with foliage (such as the relief 'Distant View', 1971)
and photographs of some of his earliest sculptures show
them set in a landscape in a comparable way, particularly 'Figure Fragment' of 1956 (repr. Kölnischer
Kunstverein, op.cit., p.10).

Roger Ackling b.1947

T 03562 Five Sunsets in One Hour 1978

Burnt lines and Letraset on card mounted
on paper-covered card 22 × $14\frac{1}{2}$
(559 × 368)
Letraset inscription 'A COUNTRY
SKETCH/CHILLERTON DOWN ISLE OF

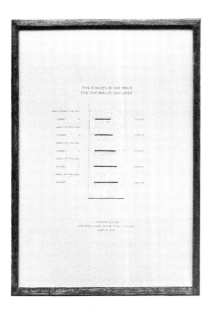

WIGHT ENGLAND/JUNE 24 1978' b.c.
Presented by the Contemporary Art
Society 1983

Prov: Purchased from the Lisson Gallery by the
Contemporary Art Society, October 1979

Exh: *Roger Ackling – Drawings*, Lisson Gallery,
September–October 1979 (no catalogue,
40 on typed sheet); *Contemporary Choice*,
Serpentine Gallery, October–November
1982 (*Art and Artists* special issue no.143,
2, p.42)

Lit: Fenella Crichton, 'London' (exhibition
review), *Art and Artists*, XIV, November
1979, pp.44–5; artist's statement in *Aspects
of British Art Today*, exhibition
catalogue, Metropolitan Art Museum,
Tokyo, 1982, p.54

The support for this work consists of a sheet of paper-
covered card. On this has been mounted a smaller rectangle of coarse brown woodpulp board measuring
200 × 73 and about 1mm thick. This smaller board
carries five short horizontal parallel lines which the
artist has burned into it by concentrating the sun's rays
through a hand-held magnifying glass. Beneath the
scorched lines Ackling has recorded that the work was
made at Chillerton Down on the Isle of Wight in June
1978 and above the lines, that the work consists of 'Five
Sunsets in One Hour/Five one minute sun lines'. He
has marked each 'sun line' with the exact time at which
it was made (6.50pm, 7.07pm, 7.15pm, 7.36pm and
7.50pm).

To the left of the lines, and positioned between them,
the printed legend 'Walk up the Hill' is repeated at five
intervals, indicating the artist's ascent of Chillerton

Down. Above the top scorched line, he has printed
'Walk down the Hill'.

The following notes are based on a conversation with
the artist (5 March 1986).

Chillerton Down, a hill on the Isle of Wight, is well
known to Ackling because it is situated directly behind
the house where his parents have lived for the past
twelve years and is accessible from their garden. He
visits the Isle of Wight at least once a year and makes a
work on each trip. (For the past few years he has also
been making a private cumulative fixed work near the
top of Chillerton Down, which he adds to on each visit.)

To obtain the scorched 'sun lines' for T03562,
Ackling stopped at given intervals during his walk up
Chillerton Down and sat with his back to the setting
sun, holding up a magnifying glass at an angle, so as to
deflect the rays on to his board. He described these five
stages as 'sunsets' in the work because each time the
sun sank below his immediate horizon line, he had to
climb higher to catch sight of it again and to 'catch' it
in his glass. Thus his ascent paralleled the sun's descent.
It seemed to him that the sun set five times as it sank
from view and he felt as though he was resurrecting it
each time he climbed further up the hill.

During the period when he made T03562, Ackling
based all his work on the time scale either of one minute
or of one hour. Here he used (as he still does) an ordinary
magnifying glass which he trained against a special
coarse pulp board for exactly one minute at each stop-
ping point. As he climbed higher and the sun sank, its
rays naturally became weaker and, in consequence, the
lines become shorter towards the top of the card. The
progressive shortening of the lines creates a curve which
relates formally but also actually to the curve of the
Down; Ackling has also compared it to the curve of the
earth's surface, which finally obscures the setting sun.

He has said that for him such works are very specific,
having to do with particular times, days, seasons and
specific locations, whether made in Great Britain or
abroad (he frequently travels abroad to work). In
T03562 and other works on card, the card remains the
constant factor and it is the combination of hand and
lens which determines the length and strength of the
lines recorded.

Ackling points out that T03562 also records the wind
conditions on the day it was made. The degree and
angle of the smudging around each line indicates that
the wind was stronger at 6.50pm but had weakened and
changed direction by 7.15pm.

Nowadays Ackling works with wood and although
his engraving process remains the same he gives precedence to images in the newer pieces and does not
supply written information on the works themselves.
However, as with all his work, he sees T03562 as part
of a total experience of landscape and has pointed out
that by harnessing the sun he is channelling energy

but also releasing it back into the atmosphere through burning. He also remains aware of the scale of man within a universal scale ('the grid inside oneself is the same grid that the earth is composed of').

Ackling called T 03562 a 'Country Sketch' because it was made in the landscape and he wished to invest it with the immediacy and informality of a more traditional landscape sketch in situ.

On the same visit to the Isle of Wight in 1978 Ackling made one other work which he has compared to 'Five Sunsets in One Hour'. It was also exhibited at the Lisson Gallery in September–October 1979 ('The Sun Over My Right Shoulder, September '78', 33, on typed sheet), and was made at Barndown, a site near Chillerton Down.

This entry has been approved by the artist.

Eileen Agar b.1904

T 03809   Angel of Anarchy 1936–40

Fabric over plaster and mixed media
$20\frac{1}{2} \times 12\frac{1}{2} \times 13\frac{1}{4}$ (520 × 317 × 336)
Inscribed 'AGAR/ANGEL OF ANARCHY' on back of neck
Presented by the Friends of the Tate Gallery 1983

Prov: Purchased from the artist by the Friends of the Tate Gallery 1983

Exh: Eileen Agar, Retrospective Exhibition, Commonwealth Art Gallery, September–October 1971 (18); Dada and Surrealism Reviewed, Hayward Gallery, January–March 1978 (14.3, repr.); Weich und Plastich, Soft-Art, Kunsthaus, Zurich, November 1979–February 1980 (repr. p.77); British Sculpture in the Twentieth Century, part 1, Whitechapel Art Gallery, September–November 1981 (177, repr.); The Women's Art Show, 1550–1970, Castle Museum, Nottingham, May–August 1982 (83, repr. in col.); Milestones in Modern British Sculpture, Mappin Art Gallery, Sheffield, October–November 1982 (10); La planète affolée. Surréalisme, dispersion et influences, 1938–1947, Centre de la Vieille Charité, Marseilles, April–June 1986 (1, repr. in col. p.170)

Lit: Paul Nash, 'Artists and their work – 4. Surrealism: Objects and Pictures', BBC television, 21 January 1938; Anna Gruetzner, 'The Surrealist Object and Surrealist Sculpture', British Sculpture of the Twentieth Century, Whitechapel Art Gallery, 1981, pp.113–23 (repr. p.115); Penny McGuire, 'Surreal Life Legend', Observer Magazine, 20 November 1983, pp.20–5 (repr. p.21); Frances Spalding, British Art Since 1900, 1986, p.117 (repr. p.119).
Also repr: Du, 1983, 1, p.53

This head is a second and quite different version of a sculpture of the same title which was made by Eileen Agar in 1934–6 and lost shortly afterwards, never being returned from an exhibition in Amsterdam in June 1938.

The lost first version was reproduced on the cover of the exhibition catalogue Surrealist Objects and Poems, London Gallery, November 1937 (photographed by the artist) where it was first exhibited. It is listed there in the section titled 'Surrealist Objects' as 'Angel of Anarchy', along with three other works by Agar. It is a plaster head of a man, with coloured paper and paper doilies, green feathers and black Astrakhan fur attached to it, not painted except on the lips. This head Agar made in the first place in clay, at her studio in Earl's Court, as a portrait of Joseph Bard (her future husband). Bard, a Hungarian and a poet, had been editor of the art magazine The Island (1931–2), which was financed by Agar and organised by pupils of Leon Underwood at his school in Brook Green, which both she and Bard attended for drawing. Underwood had already modelled a portrait head of Bard, and Agar felt that she could improve on it. Her sculpture was made from sittings with the model, and is severely geometrical.

Agar sent her clay to be cast in plaster, and received two copies, one of which she then covered with 'whatever came to hand' (conversation of 18 May 1984), in part in order to hide its whiteness. This was the first sculpture she had made, although she had been in contact with modern sculptors since visiting Brancusi's studio in Paris in 1930, and she had bought a carving by Henry Moore in about 1932. She did not know Surrealist artists personally before the *International Surrealist Exhibition* in London in June 1936, and was invited to show in this by Herbert Read. She exhibited there three paintings and five 'objects', the latter now only known by title. Following this exhibition she made both the first version of 'Angel of Anarchy' and another dressed up head 'Rococo Cocotte' (repr. Anna Greutzner, op.cit., p.117), although in this the head itself was not made by the artist. At the *Exposition Internationale du Surréalisme*, Galerie Robert, Amsterdam (June 1938) the former was listed as 'L'ange de l'anarchie (1934–1936)'.

The first version retained its character as a portrait of Joseph Bard, but was associated by Agar in its title with Herbert Read, the critic who had been one of the organisers of both the 1936 and 1937 Surrealist exhibitions in London:

> ... the title was suggested by the fact that Herbert Read was known to the Surrealists as a benign anarchist, so that is how I thought of the title 'Angel of Anarchy', for anarchy was in the air in the late thirties (note from the artist, 18 May 1984).

The title was invented after the work was made, and partly by chance, as Agar recalled hearing some builders in the studio mentioning the wood 'Archangel pine', while she was thinking what to call it.

At the start of the war it was evident that the sculpture would not be returned from Amsterdam:

> so in 1940 I started covering the second plaster head (now in the Tate). This one I decided should be totally different, more astonishing, powerful (and forgetting about a portrait) more malign. Although the same base it has ostrich feathers for the hair, a Chinese silk blindfold, a piece of bark cloth round the neck and African beads at the back of the head, as well as occasional osprey feathers and a diamanté nose (note of 18 May 1986).

The African tapa cloth and the bead fringe were bought for this purpose in antique shops, and most of the other materials were supplied from Agar's mother's wardrobe.

The head was stored by the artist and not retrieved until William Seitz, the curator of 'The Art of Assemblage' exhibition at the Museum of Modern Art, New York (1961) enquired for her pre-war sculpture and collages.

Boris Anrep 1883–1969

T 03538　Nude and Ruins 1944

Gouache on board $23\frac{1}{4} \times 14\frac{5}{8}$ (604 × 370)
Inscribed 'BORIS ANREP/1944' on reverse and BORIS ANREP/NUDE & RUINS./PAINTED 1944' on label on reverse
Bequeathed by Mrs M.J.A. Russell (d.1981); accepted 1982

Prov:　Believed to have been acquired by Mrs Russell from the artist

Justin Vulliamy, who assisted Boris Anrep in his work in mosaic, writes of this work (letter, 23 February 1986):

> I would say that Boris painted it while at his Heath Studio NW3, when working as Russian monitor at Reuters, at about the time when his friendship with Maud Russell was formed, and I have a feeling that it may have been made as a gift for her, with an esoteric meaning ... Boris could be an accomplished painter, but his work in this medium is rare ... I agree that the picture was probably meant as a tribute to Maud Russell.

The figure in the Tate's picture is without question based on the image of a particular bronze by Maillol. Anrep's own copy of Maurice Denis, *A. Maillol*, Paris, Editions des 'Cahiers d'Aujourd'hui', 1925, which Anrep gave to Justin Vulliamy, reproduces this work seen from two different angles. The right hand image in plate 30 shows it from an angle of view virtually identical to that in the Tate's picture in which, however, Anrep has substituted fragments of masonry for Maillol's integral base. The 1925 monograph contains no captions for the illustrations, no list of work and no index. It is therefore not known in what way Anrep may have interpreted the iconography of the Maillol, a work of 1899 reproduced elsewhere as 'Eve à la Pomme'. In Justin Vulliamy's view, Anrep 'may not have known, or cared, for an Eve connotation of the figure, which might equally well have been, in a classical context, a Judgement of Paris (or Pomona)'.

Dr Igor Anrep, the artist's son, told the compiler that his father was interested in classical art in general, in theories about the classical in art, and in classical ruins. But Justin Vulliamy adds that 'as for classical antiquity Boris had rather slight regard for stylistic purity; he was of course a Byzantinist (tending to modified mosaical forms) and with knowledge of the Russian ikon (Roublev etc.). Without doubt he had the latter in mind while doing the background of the "Nude".'

Recalling that Anrep's mosaics often had double meanings, Ivor Anrep thinks it possible that 'Nude and Ruins' might have been intended to signify the collapse of European civilisation. There is also an obvious possible link with Anrep's experience of the Blitz in the London of 1944, in which the volume on Maillol in which the related image appears suffered damage from exposure to the elements, as a result of bomb damage to Anrep's studio.

Anrep is known to have made two portraits of the testator, Mrs Gilbert Russell (1891–1981). One, believed to be a watercolour, was also made in the early 1940s, represents her standing by a spring, and contains zodiacal and astrological imagery (private information). The other, bearing the legend 'FOLLY', forms part of 'The Modern Virtues', the fourth and final sequence (located in the North Vestibule) of Anrep's mosaic floors in the National Gallery, London. It is reproduced on the back cover of Angelina Morhange, *Boris Anrep: The National Gallery Mosaics*, 1979. The commission for 'The Modern Virtues' was offered to the National Gallery by Mrs Russell in March 1945 and the work was opened to the public in November 1952. Mrs Russell also bequeathed to the Tate an imaginary portrait of Anrep by Pierre Roy, of 1949 (T 03537).

Mrs Russell owned a pencil drawing by Maillol of a standing female nude ('Etude de Nu', $13\frac{1}{4} \times 8\frac{1}{2}$ in, sold Sotheby's 1 December 1982 (131, repr.) with other works from her collection). The pose is related only very indirectly to that in the Tate's painting.

Arman b.1928

T 03380 **Venus of the Shaving Brushes** 1969

Shaving brushes embedded in polyester
$32\frac{7}{8} \times 11\frac{3}{8} \times 12\frac{1}{2}$ (835 × 290 × 320)
Not inscribed
Purchased from Galerie Reckermann, Cologne (Grant-in-Aid) 1982

Prov: Private collection, Nice
Exh: *Nice – Milano – Paris – Düsseldorf: École de Nice/Nouveau Réalisme/Zéro: ... Arman* [et. al.], Galerie Reckermann, Cologne, May–September 1981 (not numbered, repr.); *Forty Years of Modern Art 1945–1985*, Tate Gallery, February–April 1986 (not numbered, repr. in col p. 73)
Lit: Henry Martin, *Arman*, New York 1973, pp.29–35; Jan van der Marck, *Arman*, New York, 1984, pp.63–72 (repr. in col. on dustjacket)

T 03381 **Condition of Woman I** 1960

Bathroom rubbish in glass case on ornamental wooden plinth $75\frac{1}{2} \times 18\frac{1}{4} \times 12\frac{5}{8}$ (1920 × 462 × 320)
Not inscribed
Purchased from Galerie Tarica, Paris (Grant-in-Aid) 1982

Exh: *Arman*, Stedelijk Museum, Amsterdam, September–November 1964 (15);

Arman, Museum Haus Lange, Krefeld, April–May 1965 (16); *Forty Years of Modern Art 1945–1985*, Tate Gallery, February–April 1986 (not numbered)

Lit: Henry Martin, *Arman*, New York 1973, pp.29–56 (repr. pl.51 in col.); Jan van der Marck, *Arman*, New York 1984, pp.59–63

Kenneth Armitage b.1916

T 03708   **Seated Woman with Square Head (Version B)** 1955

Bronze 23½ × 10 × 12¼ (600 × 250 × 310)

Inscribed 'Susse Fondeur Paris' at back of base

Transferred from the Victoria and Albert Museum 1983

Prov: Purchased from the artist by Department of Circulation, Victoria and Albert Museum 1960 (Circ. 182–1960)

Exh: ?*Recent Sculpture by Kenneth Armitage*, Gimpel Fils, October–November 1957 (12, repr., unspecified cast); ? *29 Biennale Internazionale d'Arte*, Venice, June–October 1958 (71, unspecified cast); ? *5e Biennale voor Beeldhouwkunst Middelheimpark*, Antwerp, May–September 1959 (unspecified cast); ? *11 Documenta*, Kassel, July–October 1959 (repr., unspecified cast); ? *A retrospective exhibition of sculpture and drawings based on the XXIX Venice Biennale of 1958*, initially organised by the British Council, Whitechapel Art Gallery, July–August 1959 (24, repr., unspecified cast)

Lit: Roland Penrose, *Kenneth Armitage*, 1960, p.12 and pl.16; Norbert Lynton, *Kenneth Armitage*, 1962, n.p.

The sculpture was modelled in clay in London, shortly after Armitage's return there from Leeds, where he had been Gregory Fellow (1953–5). It was the last of a group of four small sculptures of seated women:

1. 'Seated Figure' 1954. Modelled at Leeds and cast in Corsham in June 1954. 17½" high, with both hands on knees and elbows bent inwards to touch.
2. 'Seated Woman with Square Head' 1954. Modelled at Leeds and cast in Corsham in November 1954. 14" high, and similar to the Tate Gallery bronze but with long legs extended forward from the body.

Both these bronzes are unique, and were bought by Joseph Hirshhorn soon after they were cast and now belong to the Hirshhorn Museum, Washington.

The Tate Gallery figure was made in two versions, the later of which was more extreme and was cast first:

3. 'Seated Woman with Square Head' 1955 (Version A). 24" high, cast for the first time in 1984. This differs from T 03708 chiefly in the position of the head, which is off centre towards the figure's left and tilted towards her right. It has a horizontal ridge on the head, representing eyes.
4. The Tate work (Version B) was made immediately after 3. These bronzes were cast by Susse in Paris in 1957 in an edition of six, one of which still belongs to the artist. The vertical line cut into the torso of the figure emphasises its more geometric and block-like appearance, in contrast to the less formal earlier version.

The artist possesses at least one drawing made in preparation for numbers 3 and 4, a chalk sketch of two views of the same figure, dated 1954.

The monumental character of the Tate Gallery bronze looks forward to the five foot high bronze of two seated figures 'Diarchy' of 1957 (T01268).

Gallery, Birmingham, 1983, pp.13–16; *Art and Language*, Los Angeles Institute of Contemporary Art, Los Angeles, 1983, p.24; Sanda Miller, 'Art and Language: Extracts from a conversation with Sanda Miller', *Artscribe*, no.47, July–August 1984, p.18

Art and Language (Michael Baldwin b.1945 and Mel Ramsden b.1944)

T03453 Courbet's Burial at Ornans ... 1981

Black ink, wash and wax crayon on paper, mounted on canvas; three panels each $127\frac{5}{8} \times 91\frac{3}{4}$ (3240 × 2330); overall dimensions $127\frac{5}{8} \times 275\frac{1}{4}$ (3240 × 6990)
Comprising
a) The left-hand third of Courbet's 'Burial at Ornans' Expressing a Sensuous Affection ...
b) The centre third of Courbet's 'Burial at Ornans' Expressing a Vibrant Erotic Vision ...
c) The right-hand third of Courbet's 'Burial at Ornans' Expressing States of Mind that are Obsessive and Compelling ...

Not inscribed
Purchased from Galerie Eric Fabre, Paris (Grant-in-Aid) 1982
Exh: *'Gustave Courbet's Burial at Ornans Expressing ...'*, Galerie Eric Fabre, Paris, June–July 1981 (no catalogue); *New Art at the Tate Gallery*, Tate Gallery, September–October 1983 (no catalogue number)
Lit: Charles Harrison and Fred Orton, *A Provisional History of Art and Language*, Paris, 1982, pp.72–4; Charles Harrison, 'The Orders of Discourse: The Artist's Studio', in *Art and Language*, Ikon

T03800 Index: The Studio at 3 Wesley Place, in the Dark (VI), showing the Position of 'Embarrassments' in (IV) 1982

Photograph, black ink, wax crayon and metallic pencil on sandwich of paper and plastic foam, $31\frac{1}{2} \times 66\frac{1}{4}$ (797 × 1680)
Not inscribed
Presented by Art & Language and the Lisson Gallery 1983
Exh: *Art and Language*, Lisson Gallery, March–April 1983 (1)
Repr: *Art and Language*, Ikon Gallery, Birmingham, 1983 (as 'Index: The Studio at 3 Wesley Place in the Dark, showing the Position of 'Embarrassments' in (III)'), no.26; *Art and Language*, Institute of Contemporary Art, Los Angeles, 1983 (as 'Index: The Studio at 3 Wesley Place in the Dark, showing the Position of 'Embarrassments' in (III)'), no.25

T03801 Index: The Studio at 3 Wesley Place, in the Dark (IV), and illuminated by an Explosion nearby (VI) 1982

Photograph, pencil, watercolour and acrylic on tracing paper mounted on paper mounted on sandwich of paper and plastic foam, $30\frac{7}{8} \times 64\frac{1}{8}$ (784 × 1627)
Not inscribed
Presented by Art & Language and the Lisson Gallery 1983

Exh: As above, Lisson Gallery (2)
Repr: *Art and Language*, Ikon Gallery,
Birmingham, 1983 (as 'The Studio at 3
Wesley Place in the Dark (III), and
illuminated by an Explosion nearby (VI)')
no.24; *Art and Language*, Institute of
Contemporary Art, Los Angeles, 1983 (as
'The Studio at 3 Wesley Place in the Dark
(III), and illuminated by an Explosion
nearby (VI)'), no.23

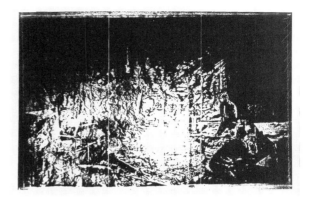

Not inscribed
Presented by Art & Language and the
Lisson Gallery 1983
Exh: As above, Lisson Gallery (6)
Repr: *Art and Language*, Ikon Gallery,
Birmingham 1983 (as 'The Studio at 3
Wesley Place (VI), illuminated by an
Explosion nearby (V)'), no.28; *Art and
Language*, Institute of Contemporary Art,
Los Angeles, 1983 (as 'The Studio at 3
Wesley Place (VI), illuminated by an
Explosion nearby (V)'), no.27

**T 03802   Index: The Studio at 3 Wesley
Place, executed by mouth
(II)** 1982

Pencil and carbon paper tracings on paper
mounted on sandwich of paper and plastic
foam, $38\frac{3}{8} \times 82\frac{3}{4}$ (975 × 2100)
Not inscribed
Presented by Art & Language and the
Lisson Gallery 1983
Exh: As above, Lisson Gallery (4)
Repr: *Art and Language*, Ikon Gallery,
Birmingham, 1983, no.25; *Art and
Language*, Institute of Contemporary Art,
Los Angeles, 1983, no.24

**T 03803   Index: The Studio at 3 Wesley
Place (VI), illuminated by an
Explosion nearby** 1982

Photograph mounted on sandwich of
paper and plastic foam, $42 \times 63\frac{1}{8}$
(1067 × 1603)

**T 03804   Index: The Studio at 3 Wesley
Place** 1981–2

Photograph, pencil, pen and ink,
watercolour, black washes and collage on
paper mounted on sandwich of paper and
plastic foam, 30×64 (762 × 1623)
Not inscribed
Purchased from the Lisson Gallery
(Grant-in-Aid) 1983
Exh: As above, Lisson Gallery (3)
Repr: *Art and Language*, Ikon Gallery,
Birmingham 1983, no.19

The following is part of the text of a leaflet written by
Charles Harrison and published by the Tate Gallery,
to accompany the display of these and three other draw-

ings by Art and Language at the Tate Gallery in September–October 1985 (works not listed individually):

The first maquette for Art & Language's 'Studio – Drawing (i)' – could be seen as fulfilling two requirements. It serves to establish the nature of a composition; it also assembles and lists a set of objects and references. It is both a 'study' and an 'index'. As an index 'Drawing (i)' describes or represents the practice of Art & Language in terms of certain persons and activities, certain products of that practice and of other practices associated with it, certain resources, certain interests and so on. The picture is retrospective – in the sense, for instance, that both early works and early reading are represented. It also serves to map out a current position.

As a consequence of its being an adequate index 'Drawing (i)' is inadequate as a 'compositional study' for an ambitious modern painting; i.e. it seems to presuppose a somewhat conservative (literal, descriptive, unexpressive) end result. Modernism in painting has conventionally been identified with the precedence of (expressive) composing over (descriptive) listing. 'Drawing (ii)', in a private collection, provides a less literally descriptive and apparently more expressive version of the Studio picture. It was drawn from 'Drawing (i)' with a pencil held in the mouth. For the painting 'Index: The Studio at 3 Wesley Place Painted by Mouth (I)' and accidents and distortions generated by the by-mouth process were copied exactly, by hand, onto the full-sized paper, $12\frac{1}{2} \times 25$ft (3750×7500mm). This was coloured in by hand and then painted over by mouth, in black ink, by reference to 'Drawing (i)', in order to generate an 'expressive' surface. For the painting 'Index ... (II), Drawing (ii)' was copied on to full-sized paper by mouth, with brushes and ink and without squaring up. The levels and scale of distortion were thus increased while the legibility of descriptive detail decreased.

The third painting, 'Index: The Studio at 3 Wesley Place in the Dark (III)' was based on 'Drawing (iii)', an imaginary representation of the subject-matter of 'Drawing (i)' seen as if under different and more dramatic lighting conditions, and 'Drawing (iv)', a second by-mouth copy of 'Drawing (i)' produced without initial squaring-up (thus generating a larger scale of distortion than 'Drawing (ii)'. In the finished painting, in acrylic on canvas $12\frac{1}{2} \times 25$ft (3750×7500mm), the great majority of the detail has become indecipherable in the darkness of the surface. Across this surface are stencilled representations of Art & Language's own 'failures', works edited-out in compiling the list which 'Drawing (i)' represents. The positioning of these 'embarrassments' was worked out in 'Drawing (v)'.

As the by-mouth process calls into question the authenticity of the expressive qualities it appears to produce, so the self-conscious and embarrassing failures call into question the authenticity of the original descriptive list.

All the drawings are *working* drawings. The 'Studio' paintings were envisaged as a series, and the series was originally defined in terms of a system. The system broke down and the series developed through seven large images in ways which could not have been envisaged at the outset. The drawings reflect this breakdown and also allow some order of development to be perceived in retrospect. 'Drawing (v)', for instance, was produced mid-way through work on the third 'Studio' painting, when it became clear that something had to be *done* to it. The requirements of practice are critiques of planning.

What happened to the details, the autobiographical, artistic and intellectual references assembled in 'Drawing (i)'? With hindsight it can be seen that though they were necessary to the project as a whole, and though they continued at some level to determine the appearance of the 'Studio' paintings, it was increasingly unnecessary that they be discernible as imagery. Indeed, for the purposes of going on painting, it seems to have been necessary that they be obliterated or otherwise stripped of significance. This may say something about painting.

In 'Drawing (vi)' the details and references are as it were sealed in by the superimposition of another representational level. Here the picture of the studio is itself represented as a surface – the reflecting surface of part of 'Drawing (iii)' – on which light falls from an event in another world and time, on another representational level. The all revealing light within the first 'Studio' is now remote. No firm perceptual line divides the fragmentary illumination of depicted people and things from accidental features of an actual illuminated surface. From the series as a whole a kind of theoretical and critical assertion might be derived: what is described and expressed in art is always indirectly described and expressed; there is no simple truth-value in description or expression; to be plausible now, painting must live with the ironies involved.

T 03800–T 03804 were made at 3 Wesley Place, Chacombe near Banbury, Oxon, where Charles Harrison lived in 1982.

Richard Artschwager b.1923

T 03793 Table and Chair 1963–4

> Melamine laminate over wood; table
> $29\frac{3}{4} \times 52 \times 37\frac{1}{2}$
> $(755 \times 1320 \times 952)$; chair $45 \times 17\frac{1}{4} \times 21$
> $(1143 \times 438 \times 533)$
> Not inscribed
> Purchased from Leo Castelli Gallery
> (Grant-in-Aid) 1983
>
> *Exh:* *Pop Art*, Hayward Gallery, July–
> September 1969 (4); *Richard
> Artschwager's Themes*, Buffalo, Albright-
> Knox Art Gallery, July–August 1979 and
> travelling (no catalogue no., repr.);
> *Richard Artschwager*, Daniel Weinberg
> Gallery, San Francisco, May 1980; *Castelli
> and his artists, twenty-five years*, La Jolla
> Museum of Contemporary Art, April–
> June 1982 and travelling (5, repr.); *Day
> in/day out, ordinary life as a source for art*,
> Freedman Gallery, Reading (PA), March–
> April 1983 (6); *New Art at the Tate Gallery
> 1983*, September–October 1983 (no
> catalogue no., repr.)
>
> *Lit:* Michael Compton, *New Art at the Tate
> Gallery 1983*, exhibition catalogue, Tate
> Gallery, 1983, p.40, repr. p.45; Michael
> McNay, 'Refresher course in yesterday's
> news', *The Guardian*, 16 September 1983;
> *Also repr: Richard Artschwager's Themes*,
> exhibition catalogue, Albright–Knox Art
> Gallery, Buffalo, 1979, repr. p.26

Gillian Ayres b.1930

T 03458 Antony and Cleopatra 1982

> Oil on canvas $114\frac{1}{4} \times 113\frac{5}{16}$ (2893×2872)
> Inscribed 'Gillian Ayres' b.r.
> Purchased from Knoedler Gallery (Grant-
> in-Aid) 1982
>
> *Exh:* *Gillian Ayres*, Knoedler Gallery, April–
> May 1982 (20, as 'Anthony and Cleopatra');
> *Gillian Ayres*, Serpentine Gallery,
> November 1983–January 1984 (17, as
> 'Anthony and Cleopatra')
>
> *Lit:* Tim Hilton, introduction to *Gillian Ayres*,
> exhibition catalogue, Serpentine Gallery,
> November 1983–January 1984, p.16 as
> 'Anthony and Cleopatra'

The following entry is based upon a conversation between the compiler and the artist held on 8 April 1986 and has been approved by the artist.

The title of T 03458, like all those of Ayres's recent works, was conceived after the painting was completed. The titles of her paintings are thought up by a group of four people, sometimes individually and sometimes in combinations, namely Gareth Williams, Tim Hilton, John Kasmin and the artist herself. The title of T 03458 was suggested by Tim Hilton while the work was being hung at the Knoedler Gallery in April 1982. In all cases any title suggested must be approved by the artist before it is allocated. Ayres considers the naming of a work to be 'like a christening. I like the titles and I care about them but they do not describe the paintings.' The titles have a resonance and refer to things to which Ayres warms.

T03458 was painted in the artist's studio at Llaniestyn, North Wales during the winter of 1981–2. Ayres had moved to Wales that winter having given up her post as Head of Painting at Winchester School of Art. She felt liberated by this action and elated at the prospect of being able to paint every day. She was also excited at the openness and the light of the Welsh landscape. The painting does not refer to landscape, however. She stated that 'Antony and Cleopatra' has a greater openness than previous paintings and that she wanted to achieve a sense of the sublime through the scale of markings. She felt, at the time, that 'Antony and Cleopatra' was an important painting but she now considers it to have a character all of its own within her oeuvre. Unlike other paintings of this period, it has a yellow ochre ground, the reason being that she had no white lead at the time and was unable to purchase any because she was snowed in for a number of days.

T03458 is executed in oil paint, a medium Ayres has used consistently since renouncing the use of acrylic paint in 1977. Her first oil paintings of this period were thickly impastoed, the paint being built up to a great density and being heavily worked. Many of the paintings made between 1978 and 1980 had an iridescent quality. Since 1981, however, she has produced both thickly and thinly painted works and T03458 falls into the latter category. It was directly preceded by 'Ariadne on Naxos' 1981 (repr. *Gillian Ayres: Paintings*, exhibition catalogue, Museum of Modern Art, Oxford, October–November 1981, p.8), a thinly painted work which introduced lines and enclosed shapes into Ayres's vocabulary. In T03458 these take the form of broad sweeps of colour juxtaposed with short and sharply accented curves. In addition, the frieze-like markings at the top of 'Ariadne on Naxos' are repeated along the top and bottom of T03458.

T03458 was painted on canvas fixed to the wall and was stretched only on completion. It is larger than a number of Ayres's previous works, the reason being that her studio in North Wales is larger than the studio she left behind in London. It was the first painting she began and completed after her move to North Wales.

Michael Ayrton 1921–1975

T03611 **The Temptation of St Anthony** 1942–3

Oil on panel 22⅞ × 29⅝ (581 × 752)
Inscribed 'michael ayrton f./1942–1943' t.r.
Purchased from Christopher Hull Gallery (Grant-in-Aid) 1983

Prov: Richard Gorer, 1943; Michael Ayrton,

mid-1960s; Elizabeth Ayrton, 1975; Christopher Hull Gallery, 1982

Exh: *Basil Jonzen, Michael Ayrton, Hugo Dachinger, also French paintings*, Redfern Gallery, July 1943 (71); *Michael Ayrton, Humphrey Spender: paintings*, Redfern Gallery, March–April 1947 (19); *Michael Ayrton*, Wakefield City Art Gallery, August–September 1949 (travelling to Harrogate, Halifax and Hull) (20, repr.); *The compulsive image: sculpture and paintings by Michael Ayrton*, Birmingham City Art Gallery, January–February 1977 (6); *Michael Ayrton, 1921–1975: sculpture, paintings and graphics*, Christopher Hull Gallery, September–October 1982 (ex-catalogue)

Lit: Robert Melville, 'Michael Ayrton: The Temptation of St. Anthony', exhibition catalogue *Basil Jonzen, Michael Ayrton, [etc.]*, Redfern Gallery, 1943, p.4; 'Perspex' [= ? Herbert Furst], 'Art Notes' (review of exhibition *Basil Jonzen, Michael Ayrton, [etc.]*, Redfern Gallery, July 1943), *Apollo*, XXXVIII, 1943, pp.45, 55; James Laver, *Paintings by Michael Ayrton*, 1949, pp.6, 11, repr. pl.7 (dated 1946); Peter Cannon-Brookes, *Michael Ayrton: An Illustrated Commentary*, Birmingham, 1978, pp.11, 15, repr. pl.18

In his *Apollo* review of Ayrton's 1943 exhibition, 'Perspex' quotes extensively from a letter from the artist, explaining his engagement with the legend of St Anthony; Ayrton writes:

The subject was originally conceived in Vienna shortly after the Dolfuss putsch, partly out of admiration for the Flemish and German XVth and XVIth century painters, in particular Bosch, Grünewald, Schongauer ... and partly from a feeling

[97]

that St Anthony himself was possessed of Promethean qualities, which in his trials symbolized the state of man as much to-day as in A.D. 360. I felt very intensely about the philosophical problem involved and very much drawn to work at my own version of the subject in relation to my own life and the world as I felt it to be.

Ayrton stayed with relatives in Vienna in 1934–5. Again, in autobiographical notes for the catalogue of the exhibition *Word and Image I & II: Wyndham Lewis, Michael Ayrton* (National Book League, 1971), Ayrton writes:

> ... in the early 'forties he had conceived a series of paintings and drawings on the theme of 'The Temptation of St Anthony' which drew its inspiration from Grünewald and other German and Flemish 16th Century masters and in a considerable degree from Flaubert's novel, but it did not occur to him at the time to relate his own words to his images ...

(Gustave Flaubert's *La Tentation de Saint Antoine* was published in 1874.)

St Anthony the Great (? 251–356) retired into the Egyptian desert as a hermit, and was regarded as one of the founders of Western monasticism; his asceticism resulted in vivid hallucinations or visions, which involved assault by demons in the form of wild animals or monsters that tore at his flesh (hence his patronage of those afflicted with erysipelas or St Anthony's Fire), and temptations of a more erotic nature. The subject had particularly attracted Northern artists, combining as it did the erotic with the monstrous, and in post-Christian art it continued to exercise a fascination.

According to Cannon-Brookes:

> 'The Temptation of St. Anthony' was begun in 1942 [...] and Michael Ayrton painted his own arms and legs to shadow the muscles and emphasize the veins before executing, with the use of mirrors, the figure of St Anthony from himself. This was exceptional, marking his deep emotional relationship with St Anthony, since Michael Ayrton very rarely worked from posed models.

Elizabeth Ayrton writes:

> Michael never used models, but positioned his own shoulders, or a leg, or hand, as he wanted it in whatever he was painting; observed it in a tall mirror (a cheval glass, in point of fact) and drew it in a pocket sketchbook, as one might make a note for a story one was writing. Unless it was a hand he would draw as he stood. He usually made such sketches as he was undressing for bed, but he never drew himself as a whole unless he was making a self-portrait.

I'm not sure how much he identified with St Anthony. Of course he did in some degree, but he also stood back from him, both in terms of a subject for solving certain problems in paint, and as a fascinating philosophical and psychological study. (Letter to the cataloguer, 28 April 1986.)

Ayrton worked on the painting in his studio at 67 Belsize Park Gardens, and completed it after moving to a larger studio in 4 All Souls Place. Although the work was exhibited in 1943, he continued to explore the theme until 1946; a second interpretation of the subject (in oil, 45 × 36 (1240 × 912), location unknown), depicting the isolated figure of the saint and dated 'Autumn/Winter '45/46' by the artist, was exhibited at the Redfern Gallery in March–April 1947 (no.19).

The present painting was exhibited at the Redfern Gallery in July 1943, together with 14 preliminary studies, including a compositional sketch in gouache; Robert Melville contributed a short introductory essay to the catalogue, which traces the development of the composition through the preliminary studies, and remains the most cogent account of Ayrton's interpretation of the subject:

> Michael Ayrton's 'Temptation of St Anthony' recapitulates several aspects of the history of the theme. Schongauer & Grünewald depicted St Anthony receiving a terrible beating from a group of demons: they illustrated the notion that man is defenceless against the forces of temptation and is dependent upon divine intervention. The direct assault on the hermit in Michael Ayrton's version has something in common with the German illustrations, but the hermit has not given up the struggle. The demons are not zoomorphic inventions as in the work of Bosch, but macabre studies of the human figure, and if they are less horrific than the zoomorphs they are more sinister. The demon on the left is a debased and putrefying conjurer, performing with fire. The degenerate child holds out a cross to the hermit in imitation of an act of succour. In their use of miracle and holy emblem, and their open conniving with the bird which threatens the hermit's sight they powerfully demonstrate the forces of confusion.
>
> The preliminary studies assembled for exhibition with the 'Temptation' reveal the many changes, formal and psychological, which have occurred during the process of elucidating the action. The charming female nude in one of the gouaches has become, in the final work, a demented harlot. The change in the placing of this figure was a brilliant move. In the gouache the woman is in the group of demons, but in the oil she has been set apart from the action, and the adjustment allows the figures closing in on the hermit to become personifications

of his own impulses and associates the segregated female figure with the fissure in the rock, which in itself carries a sexual significance together with the inference that it is the mouth of hell.

Three of the preliminary studies ('St Anthony No. xxi', 'Study for St Anthony' and 'Study for the Child in Temptation of St Anthony', all dated 1942), in the collection of Birmingham Museums and Art Gallery, are reproduced in Cannon-Brookes (op.cit., illus. 14–16, p.14), and another study appears in the *Apollo* review by 'Perspex'. Six preliminary pencil-drawings were presented by Elizabeth Ayrton to the Tate Gallery and are deposited in the Archive; a further 13 sketches and drawings related to the painting, in gouache, pen and pencil, remain in the possession of Mrs Ayrton, and another 24 related studies are in other private collections.

Shortly after Ayrton had painted his interpretation of the subject, 'The Temptation of St Anthony' was the theme of a competition associated with the Loew-Lewin film 'The Private Affairs of Bel Ami' (United Artists, 1947), with Marcel Duchamp, Alfred H. Barr, Jr, and Sidney Janis as jurors. Entries were invited from twelve American and European artists, including Ivan Albright, Salvador Dali, Paul Delvaux, Max Ernst, Leonor Fini, Stanley Spencer and Dorothea Tanning. The resulting works were exhibited in 1946–7 by the American Federation of Arts, Washington, touring the United States and Britain, and Max Ernst's painting (now in the Wilhelm-Lehmbruck-Museum, Duisburg), which had won the $2500 prize, was featured in the film itself.

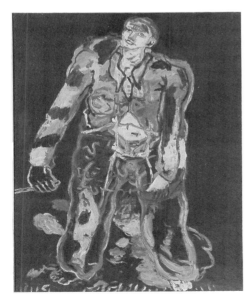

T 03442

Georg Baselitz b.1938

T 03442 **Rebel** 1965

Oil on canvas $64\frac{1}{16} \times 51\frac{1}{4}$ (1627 × 1302)
Inscribed 'G. Baselitz/Rebell' on back of canvas
Purchased from Galerie Michael Werner, Cologne (Grant-in-Aid) 1982

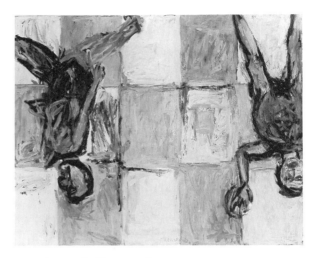

T 03672 **Adieu** 1982

Oil on canvas $98\frac{1}{2} \times 118\frac{1}{4}$ (2052 × 3004)
Inscribed '17.111.82 G. Baselitz' b. centre
Purchased from Xavier Fourcade Inc., New York (Grant-in-Aid) 1983

Joseph Beuys 1921–1986

T 03594 **Four Blackboards** 1972

Chalk on four blackboards, each $47\frac{7}{8} \times 36 \times \frac{3}{4}$ (1216 × 914 × 18)
Not signed: numerous expository inscriptions on blackboard
Transferred from the Archive 1983

T 03825 **Untitled (Vitrine)** 1983

Mixed media in glass, plywood and wood cabinet on steel framework $81\frac{1}{8} \times 86\frac{5}{8} \times 19\frac{3}{4}$ (2060 × 2200 × 500)
Not inscribed
Purchased from Anthony d'Offay Ltd (Grant-in-Aid) 1984

T 03594

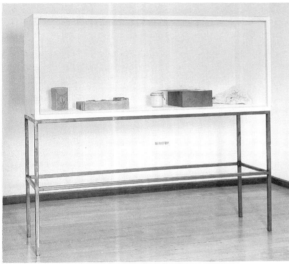

T 03825

T 03825

Exh: *Joseph Beuys vitrines: Forms from the
Sixties*, Anthony d'Offay, September–
October 1983 (as 'Fat'); *Forty Years of
Modern Art 1945–1985*, Tate Gallery,
February–April 1986 (not numbered)

T 03826 Untitled (Vitrine) 1983

Mixed media in glass, plywood and wood
cabinet on steel framework $81\frac{1}{8} \times 86\frac{5}{8} \times 19\frac{3}{4}$
($2060 \times 2200 \times 500$)
Not inscribed
Purchased from Anthony d'Offay Ltd
(Grant-in-Aid) 1984

Exh: *Joseph Beuys vitrines: Forms from the
Sixties*, Anthony d'Offay, September–
October 1983 (as 'Rail'); *Forty Years of
Modern Art 1945–1985*, Tate Gallery,
February–April 1986 (not numbered, repr.
in col. p.112)

Peter Blake b.1932

T 03419 The First Real Target 1961

Household gloss enamel on canvas and
collage on hardboard $21\frac{3}{8} \times 19\frac{7}{16}$
(537×493)
Inscribed 'Peter Blake, "THE FIRST REAL
TARGET"/June 1961' on stretcher
Purchased from Waddington Galleries
(Grant-in-Aid) 1982

Prov: Arthur Tooth and Sons 1962; E.J. Power
1962; Waddington Galleries 1972; private
collection, London 1972; Waddington
Galleries 1982

Exh: *British painting and sculpture today and
yesterday*, Arthur Tooth and Sons, April
1962 (12, repr.); *Peter Blake*, Robert
Fraser Gallery, October–November 1965;
Peter Blake, City Art Gallery, Bristol,

THE FIRST REAL TARGET?

Johns, but in the ironical question with which he addresses his viewer.

The text is separated from the actual target it refers to by a batten, painted green. The small squares of wood with paper attached and letters printed on them are from Victorian word games. Blake, who has always been interested in lettering, collected and used such letters in his series of Wrestlers and Strippers. Here, the lettering is undamaged and easy to read, helping to give the statement greater impact. Furthermore the use of these toy letters ensures that the question remains light hearted. Blake maintains a strong appreciation for the work of Johns.

Blake has always publicly discussed art, using the medium of his exhibitions and the press to initiate debate. For his Tate retrospective exhibition in 1983 he published a booklet to accompany the catalogue including thoughts on his exhibition, as well as good and bad reviews. 'The First Real Target' is intended similarly to provoke comment.

This entry is based on a conversation with the artist on 2 May 1986, and is approved by him.

November–December 1969 (40, repr.); *Peter Blake: Souvenirs and Samples*, Waddington and Tooth Galleries, April–May 1977 (78, repr.); *Peter Blake*, Tate Gallery, February–March 1983 (33, repr.); *Peter Blake*, Kestner Gesellschaft, Hannover, April–June 1983 (25, repr.)

Lit: Mario Amaya, *Pop as Art: A survey of the new super realism*, 1965, p.34; Lawrence Alloway, 'The Development of British Pop', in Lucy Lippard, *Pop Art*, 1966, p.53, illus.32, p.46; Roger Coleman, 'Peter Blake's Nostalgia', *Art and Artists*, IV, January 1970, p.31; Michael Compton, *Pop Art*, 1970, p.61, repr. p.65; Michael Compton, 'Peter Blake', *Peter Blake* exhibition catalogue, Tate Gallery, 1983, p.26, repr. p.83; Marina Vaizey, *Peter Blake*, 1986, p.24, pl.16

Painted during Peter Blake's period as a teacher at St Martin's School of Art (1960–2), 'The First Real Target' comments on the art of the time, and in particular on Jasper Johns's series of 'Target' Paintings, begun in the 1950s. Where Johns paints his target on to the canvas in a very 'painterly' way with visible brushstrokes loosely applied, Blake purchases his original Slazenger archery target from a sports shop. The surface of Blake's canvas is treated in such a way, without any obvious brushmarks, that it becomes less of a painting and more of a physical 3D object. Blake comments that his target is not therefore a 'fine art' piece as with Johns's, and his direct question asks that perhaps this makes it the 'real' one in art historical terms?

Blake involves his viewer not only through the joint knowledge they both share in the references to Jasper

T03790 **'The Meeting' or 'Have a Nice Day, Mr Hockney'** 1981–3

Oil on canvas 39 × 49 (992 × 1244)
Not inscribed
Presented by the Friends of the Tate Gallery (purchased out of funds bequeathed by Miss Helen Arbuthnot) 1983

Prov: Purchased from Waddington Galleries, by the Friends of the Tate Gallery

Exh: *Peter Blake*, Tate Gallery, February–March 1983 (105, repr., also repr. in earlier state, p.2 of loose supplement inserted in catalogue); *Peter Blake*, Kestner Gesellschaft, Hannover, April–

June 1983 (cat.80, repr. in col. in earlier state); *The Hard-Won Image*, Tate Gallery, July–September 1984 (25, repr.); *Forty Years of Modern Art*, Tate Gallery, February–April 1986 (works not listed)

Lit: Carl Haenlein, 'Über Peter Blake und Pop Art', *Peter Blake* exhibition catalogue, Kestner Gesellschaft, Hannover, 1983, pp.9, 16, repr. in col p.17; *The Tate Gallery Illustrated Biennial Report 1982–84*, 1984, p.63, repr. in col.; Marina Vaizey, *Peter Blake*, 1986, p.40, pl.31

This painting records a visit made by the artist and Howard Hodgkin to David Hockney in Venice, California, in 1979. At the end of this trip Peter Blake and Howard Hodgkin each decided to commemorate their journey with a series of three 'souvenir' works to be painted on their return to England. Blake's companion pieces to this painting are 'A Remembered Moment in Venice, Cal' and 'Montgomery Clift was a Twin'. Both works were exhibited at Peter Blake's retrospective exhibition at the Tate Gallery, 1983, as 'works in progress' (cat.2 and 5, of supplement to exhibition, both repr.). The artist still hopes to exhibit these alongside Howard Hodgkin's works as a completed project. The works by Hodgkin are 'David's Swimming Pool' 1982, 24½ × 31¼″ (62.2 × 31.2), mixed media on paper; 'David Hockney in Hollywood' 1982, 42½ × 51½″ (108 × 130.8); 'Déjà Vous' 1982, 35 × 51″ (88.9 × 129.5) (they all belong to the artist).

Peter Blake has based the Tate's painting on Courbet's 'The Meeting' or 'Bonjour Monsieur Courbet' 1854 (Musée Fabre, Montpellier). The two visiting painters in Blake's work take the place of Monsieur Bruyas (Blake) and his manservant (Hodgkin) in the original, as they greet Courbet (Hockney). Each painting is a documentary account of an event in its artist's life. In the Courbet the artist has just been left at the roadside, and the carriage which brought him on this first visit to his patron, near Montpellier, can be seen disappearing into the distance. Blake refers to this by imitating the horse and carriage in graffiti on the back wall of his painting (between the two tree trunks on the right). Courbet places a dog in the centre of his painting as does Blake, although Blake bases his foxhound on a painting by Stubbs in the Tate ('A Hound and a Bitch in a Landscape' (1792), T01705, oil on canvas, 40 × 50″ (101.6 × 127)).

If Blake had continued with the painting he would have included more people involved in what he sees as the self obsessiveness of making themselves more 'beautiful', with body builders and joggers jostling in the confined space and California sun. The figure of his daughter Liberty is seen skating off to the right – a manifestation of healthy living. Blake intended originally to place her between the figures of himself and

Hockney, literally weaving in and out of the three static 'and rather dowdy Englishmen'. Their incongruity is further emphasised by the typically English dog, after Stubbs.

Blake used photographs of skaters taken in Battersea Park as reference for the figures in his painting. There are no working drawings, only preliminary sketches and notes. Photographs were also taken for the three central characters and they helped Blake to establish poses consistent with those in Courbet's painting. When asked to stand as the figure for Courbet, Hockney could not find a pole similar to the staff in the original painting; he did however have to hand the large brush depicted (which had been used in advertising a paint brush company). Blake used this impromptu joke in the final painting.

Blake is fascinated by the inconsistent fall of shadows in Courbet's work and intended to emulate this feature in his own painting. However only Hodgkin's and his own shadows are completed. Courbet's painting was influenced by a popular print of the period, 'The Wandering Jew', and Courbet placed himself in the position of the Jew to suggest his isolation on this visit to the countryside. In similarly portraying Hockney in this 'isolated' position, Blake intended to emphasise his detachment from England.

For this series of works Blake chose three similar frames which are intended to echo the heavy gilded frames of the nineteenth century Salons. In this way Blake both recalls Courbet by using his type of frame and provides a distinct contrast to the wide painted frames in the works of Howard Hodgkin, to which Blake's own in this series are expected to be hung in close proximity. The frame on the Tate's picture was bought by Peter Blake from a local junk shop, and is meant to be exhibited in its damaged state. It is an instance of Blake's interest in 'found objects' and his affection for objects with past associations. The frame therefore plays a specific role in the overall understanding of this painting.

The entry is based on a conversation with the artist on 2 May 1986, and is approved by him.

Charles Henry Blaymires 1908–c.1970s

T 03709 **Inscription 'To be afraid'**
c.1925

Portland stone 15 × 26⅜ × 3½
(380 × 670 × 90)
Inscribed 'To be afraid and behave as if you/weren't afraid – *That is courage*/To be ashamed and behave as if you/weren't

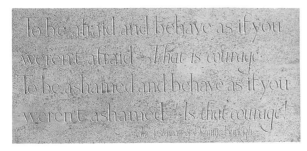

Verso

ashamed – *Is that courage!*/The Testament of Dominic Burleigh'
Transferred from the Victoria and Albert Museum 1983

Prov: Purchased from B.J. Fletcher, Director of the Central School of Arts and Crafts, Birmingham, by the Department of Circulation, Victoria and Albert Museum, 1927 (Circ. 175–1927)

Lit: Travelling exhibitions of Department of Circulation, Victoria and Albert Museum

Blaymires was a student at the Central School of Arts and Crafts, Birmingham from 1921 to 1933. This inscription was one of several which were 'cut some time ago and happen to be in the school now' and which were offered for sale to the Victoria and Albert Museum in 1926 (letter from B.J. Fletcher to the Museum, 22 December 1926).

Recto

David Bomberg 1890–1957 and Richard Michelmore b.1928

T 03600   Recto: **Messiah** 1953
           Verso: **Messiah** 1953

Oil on board 24 × 36⅜ (715 × 1080)
Recto inscribed 'Bomberg 53/Michelmore' b.l.; verso also inscribed 'Bomberg 53/Michelmore' b.l.
Presented by Richard Michelmore 1983

Exh: *Exhibition of Paintings and Drawings by The Borough Bottega and L. Marr and D. Scott*, Berkeley Galleries, November–December 1953 (6 in typed handlist available in gallery; works not listed in catalogue); Borough Bottega exhibition, Black Hall, Oxford, January–February 1954 (title of exhibition not known; no catalogue traced); *David Bomberg paintings and drawings 1915–1953, The Borough Bottega paintings and drawings by members*, Heffer Gallery, Cambridge, May–June 1954 (29)

Both sides of this painting were begun and completed during a single evening's session in one of the life classes taught by Bomberg at the Borough Polytechnic. In both pictures the view is from the same position downwards towards the same female model, who is lying on a mattress, with a sheet at lower left.

Richard Michelmore became a student at the Bartlett School of Architecture, University College, London, in September 1945. At that time Bomberg had just been engaged by the Bartlett to take a class in freehand drawing on Saturday mornings. As there were 120 students in the first year, they attended these classes in groups of twenty, each group going every sixth Saturday. The earliest of these classes of Bomberg's that Michelmore attended were held in the Cast Courts at the Victoria and Albert Museum. He owns drawings executed jointly by Bomberg and himself of the Temple, Temple Church, Westminster Bridge and the interior of Westminster Abbey. In 1949, after leaving the Bartlett, Michelmore began to attend Bomberg's life classes held in the evenings at the Borough Polytechnic. He continued to attend them regularly until Bomberg left for Ronda in 1954. From 1953 to 1955 he studied at Kingston Polytechnic where he qualified as an architect.

Michelmore found Bomberg (who always called him 'Micklemore') enormously encouraging. Bomberg believed in allowing a student to take a painting quite far according to the student's own conception. On occasion, however, he would take over a student's brushes and work on the painting himself. He did this on both sides of the present work. On the recto (the side in which the parting in the model's hair is the more clearly defined) Bomberg painted the hair, explaining that while local colour was not of concern in itself it could help to identify the image. Bomberg also painted the start of the edging of the white sheet, which he told Michelmore to complete. On the verso, Bomberg drew into the paint with the tip of the brush handle, to outline the form of the figure.

At the end of a painting session, Bomberg would sometimes recommend that a student clean his brushes on unpainted areas of the background in order to give the picture more of the look of a finished work; this partly explains the marks at top right of the recto of the present work. It was not Michelmore's custom to sign his paintings, but at Bomberg's insistence both sides of this work were signed by both artists; Michelmore cannot recall another instance of this happening. Both sides were signed in the life studio on the evening they were painted; Bomberg had to show Michelmore how to paint his signature. Bomberg felt the work should be exhibited, and himself painted the old frame, which Michelmore obtained and which still surrounds the work. Michelmore and other students could not afford artists' materials. In the present work paint powder bought by Michelmore in packets from a builder's ironmonger on Euston Road was mixed, on the palette, with linseed oil.

T 03600 has been identified by Bomberg's stepdaughter Mrs Dinora Davies-Rees (letter, 28 June 1986) as being the work exhibited as 'Messiah' in 1953 and 1954. In the 1953 exhibition, 'Messiah' was listed in the typed handlist as being by both Bomberg and Michelmore, a point which Michelmore confirms makes the identification of T 03600 as 'Messiah' conclusive. In that list it was priced at 150 guineas. The only two other works so priced, Bomberg's 'Antigone' and 'They Came to a City', are of similar dimensions. In the catalogue of the 1954 exhibition in Cambridge 'Messiah' was listed as being by Bomberg alone. Mrs Davies-Rees writes (ibid.):

why it was listed as being by Bomberg alone at Heffer in 1954 eludes me – an oversight I should have noticed at the time. I can only assume that David chose the title . . . he was unlikely to have let anyone title a work of his, even in this unique case . . . I am sure that the title 'Messiah' applied to both sides.

The inclusion of 'Messiah' in the 1954 exhibition in Oxford is attested by a reference to a painting of this title by Bomberg and Michelmore in a review of the exhibition in the *Oxford Mail*, 27 January 1954.

Roy Oxlade, another Borough Polytechnic student of Bomberg's, and who owns a drawing by himself of the same model completed by Bomberg, was the first to identify T 03600 to the Tate as 'Messiah'. He wrote (letter, 1 April 1985):

'Messiah' is an unusual title I agree, but I'm not sure how much significance should be attached to it. The slumped figure does recall a pieta Christ and Bomberg did occasionally suggest mythological or scriptural titles *after* paintings were completed.

It is not at present known which side of 'Messiah' was exhibited at any of the exhibitions cited above. Dinora Davies-Rees cannot remember, but agrees with Richard Michelmore in attaching significance to the fact that when the work was returned to Michelmore by Lilian Bomberg in about 1974 the side visible in the frame was that now described as the recto, even though this was after the painting had been removed from the frame for cleaning. On the other hand Roy Oxlade is sure that the work exhibited at the exhibition in Cambridge in 1954 was that now described as the verso; while he recalls that side from the 1954 exhibition, he does not think he had ever seen the recto until he saw the work unfitted at the time of its cleaning in 1974.

This entry has been approved by Richard Michelmore.

James Boswell 1906–1971

T 03459   **Le Sphinx** 1937

Black ink on paper $12\frac{5}{8} \times 18\frac{1}{8}$ (320 × 460)
Not inscribed
Presented by Ruth Boswell 1982

Exh: *James Boswell 1906–71 Drawings, Illustrations and Paintings*, Nottingham University Art Gallery, November–December 1976 (66); *Le Sphinx*, The Workshop Gallery, October 1977 (no catalogue); *James Boswell 1906–1971*, Royal College of Art, January 1978;

[?] *Paintings, drawings and prints by James Boswell Satirist, painter and illustrator 1906–1971*, The Portico Library Gallery, Manchester, October–November 1978 (14–17, T03461 and three other [unspecified] drawings from the series were shown)

T03460   Le Sphinx 1937

Black ink on paper $13\frac{1}{2} \times 19\frac{7}{8}$ (342 × 506)
Not inscribed
Presented by Ruth Boswell 1982

Exh: *James Boswell 1906–71 Drawings, Illustrations and Paintings*, Nottingham University Art Gallery, November–December 1976 (66); *Le Sphinx*, The Workshop Gallery, October 1977 (no catalogue); Display to promote publication of portfolio of reproductions [see Repr. below], Liberty's, October–December 1977 (no catalogue); *James Boswell 1906–1971*, Royal College of Art, January 1978; [?] *Paintings, drawings and prints by James Boswell Satirist, painter and illustrator 1906–1971*, The Portico Library Gallery, Manchester, October–November 1978 (14–17, T03461 and three other [unspecified] drawings from the series were shown)

Repr: T03460, together with T03461 and three other drawings from the series [not in the Tate's collection], published by The Workshop, London, as a portfolio of lithographic reproductions in an edition of 500, 1977

T03461   Recto: Le Sphinx 4am 1937

Black ink on paper $13\frac{1}{2} \times 19\frac{7}{8}$ (341 × 505)
Inscribed 'Le Sphinx 4AM' b.r.
Verso: **Three figure drawings** *c.*1937
Pink and black inks on paper
Not inscribed

Presented by Ruth Boswell 1982

Exh: *James Boswell 1906–71 Drawings, Illustrations and Paintings*, Nottingham University Art Gallery, November–December 1976 (66); *Le Sphinx*, The Workshop Gallery, October 1977 (no catalogue); Display to promote publication of portfolio of reproductions [see Repr. below], Liberty's, October–December 1977 (no catalogue); *James Boswell 1906–1971*, Royal College of Art, January 1978; *Paintings, drawings and prints by James Boswell Satirist, painter and illustrator 1906–1971*, The Portico Library Gallery, Manchester, October–November 1978 (14–17, T03461 and three other [unspecified] drawings from the series were shown)

Repr: [Recto only] T03461, together with T03460 and three other drawings from the series [not in the Tate's collection], published by The Workshop, London, as a portfolio of lithographic reproductions in an edition of 500, 1977; *James Boswell 1906–1971*, Royal College of Art, 1978, on the exhibition poster; *Paintings, drawings and prints by James Boswell Satirist, painter and illustrator 1906–1971*, The Portico Library Gallery, Manchester, 1978, on the cover of the exhibition catalogue

The following entry is based on a letter received from Sally Shuel on 19 June 1986, containing answers to the compiler's questions put to Betty Boswell on his behalf, on a letter from Ruth Boswell dated 30 April 1986, and on conversations with Sally Shuel and Ruth Boswell on 19 June 1986 and 26 June 1986 respectively.

   These three works are part of a series of nine 'Le Sphinx' drawings which Boswell made in the summer of 1937. Le Sphinx was a celebrated Parisian brothel, located at 31 Boulevard Edgar Quinet in Montparnasse, which Brassai describes in *The Secret Paris of the 30's* (London, 1976). It flourished during the 1930s and was a favourite haunt of artists. Giacometti was a regular visitor and regarded it as 'a place more marvellous than any other' (quoted in James Lord, *Giacometti*, New York, 1985, p.78). His bronze sculpture, 'Quatre Figurines sur Bas' 1950 and 1965, represents 'Several nude women seen at the "Sphinx"' (letter from Giacometti to Pierre Matisse); there is a cast in the Tate's collection (T 00773). Boswell visited Le Sphinx in the early part of 1937 and this experience directly inspired the drawings which were executed shortly after, in the artist's home at Charlbert Court, St John's Wood, London.

Exhibitions of the drawings have wrongly dated the works as having been completed in 1939. The evidence for the earlier date of 1937 and for their not having been made in situ, as previously thought, is as follows. From August 1936 until the time of his conscription into the army in January 1941, Boswell was Art Director for the publicity department of Asiatic Petroleum, later Shell (he also occupied the post for a brief period immediately after the war). His widow, Betty, recalls that Boswell visited Le Sphinx while on a short business trip to Paris. He was accompanied by a colleague who wanted to spend a night with a girl from Le Sphinx and they were both taken to the brothel by Boswell's opposite number in Paris. The approximate date of the trip can be established because Betty Boswell recalls that she was unable to accompany her husband as this would have involved bringing along their infant daughter, Sally, who had been born in July 1936 and was at that time only about eight months old. The visit must therefore have occurred around March 1937. Betty Boswell is certain that the drawings were made at Charlbert Court and the family had moved from their address at Haverstock Hill, Belsize Park, London, to Charlbert Court by May 1937 because there is a photograph of the Boswells' daughter, which is now in her possession, with this new address in the background; the photograph is annotated with this date. She vividly recollects the circumstance in which the drawings were made because 'the occasion ... was so absurd'. Boswell required a model and Betty, of whom Boswell produced numerous drawings in the sketchbooks, remembers that she 'sat, naked on a chair, feeding [Sally] mashed banana as [Sally] sat in a high chair, while Jim drew ...' Betty Boswell also remembers that, although she disliked the drawings because she 'did not like his slight obsession with dwarfs' (a dwarf who was a permanent inmate of Le Sphinx can be seen in two of the drawings not in the Tate's collection), she did not mind posing nude because the weather was warm on that occasion. This suggests that the time of year was summer. The results of this sitting are evident in T 03459. Betty Boswell has identified herself as the dark haired female seated on the extreme right and also recognises her waist, hips, and legs in the light haired girl seated on a stool at the bar. In addition, in a 'Le Sphinx' drawing belonging to Ruth Boswell which

depicts three prostitutes and a dwarf, Betty Boswell was the model for the girl on the left of the picture. The inscription on T 03461: 'Le Sphinx 4AM' refers, therefore, to a drawing which is intended to evoke the scene as it might have appeared at that time. It is not a record of the moment when the drawing was completed.

That Boswell did not produce the drawings while actually at Le Sphinx is suggested further by the fact that it was not until after the war that he adopted the practice of transporting larger sheets to make drawings out of the studio. Sally Shuel, Boswell's daughter, has stated that it was 'not until very much later in life [that her father] had access to a car [and] used to draw on Ingres, on sheets about 12 × 16 [inches] or so which he would carry in a small portfolio which doubled as a drawing board – this was when we went on holiday – it all had to fit into the suitcase'. She remembers, however, that it was Boswell's invariable habit to carry a small sketchbook with him. It is possible, therefore, that Boswell could have made some smaller sketches during his visit to Le Sphinx but, if these exist, their whereabouts is not known. Three small 'Le Sphinx' drawings do exist in a sketchbook (Tate Gallery Archive, 8224.9, pp.24, 25, 26) but a sketch of Sally, aged about three years, in the same book indicates that these drawings must have been made around 1939 (Sally Shuel has stated that Boswell would normally have kept only one sketchbook in use at any one time and these would not therefore be filled with work from different periods). As it is known that Boswell made another visit to Paris in 1939, this would account for the sketchbook material and also a small ($10\frac{1}{2} \times 16\frac{7}{8}$) 'Le Sphinx' drawing of two prostitutes and a dwarf on pink paper, now in the possession of Ruth Boswell. The style of these drawings is characterised by a feathery line technique and differs from the larger drawings which have been drawn with a broad tipped reed and are bolder in execution. The drawing on pink paper is the only 'Le Sphinx' drawing to be signed and dated 1939 and has been thought, incorrectly, to have been completed at the same time as the series to which the Tate's three drawings belong.

There is a drawing on the verso of T 03461 of what appears to be one girl in three different stages of undress. The largest figure is completely nude. Sally Shuel has suggested that this side of the paper was used in the first instance, and the other side used on a subsequent occasion for 'Le Sphinx 4am', because of shortage of materials at that time; realising the success of this second drawing, Boswell went on to complete the other eight drawings in the series. A standing nude in a sketchbook 1939–40 (Tate Gallery Archive, 8224.11, p.10), closely resembles the nude on the verso of T 03461 but Boswell made numerous drawings of this type and there is no evidence of any connection with Le Sphinx.

Le Sphinx opened around 1930. Brassaï described the opening as follows:

Hundreds of artists had been invited, and the champagne flowed like water. The main salon was like a café, but in the background, under a waterfall, was a glittering statue of a golden sphinx – the only luxury in the bordello. For this house broke with the usual tradition: heavy curtains, red velvet sofas, walls covered with fabrics ... At the Sphinx, everything was enamelled, waxed, white, clean, functional, hygienic. It was like an operating room. There was another innovation: the men could bring their wives and children. Going to the Sphinx was like a family outing. The little boys would stare wide-eyed at the Sylphs offering their charms, weaving stark naked in and out among the tables. A foretaste of the sex education of the future. For these children, the mystery had gone out of the huge numerals, the closed shutters. Woman, before they reached puberty. There were other bordellos that welcomed couples, who came out of curiosity and didn't go upstairs. And sometimes drinks at these houses were more profitable than tricks (*The Secret Paris of the 30's*, London, 1976, n.p.)

Drawing on client's reminiscences, Ruth Boswell records that:

It attracted a wide public – artists, writers and businessmen. For students it acted as a kind of initiation rite.

People often dropped in for only a drink and a chat. A girl might sit down on a neighbouring stool, asking permission first, but she soon moved away if told 'J'attends ma régulière'. Indeed so discreet were they that it was not unusual for men to bring their wives. The standard procedure then was for a girl to ask: 'May I speak to your husband?' Permission granted, the couple went upstairs to the bedroom on the next floor, in a lift that was considered a great luxury.

The decor was respectable, like that of a good provincial hotel, the atmosphere one of genteel respectability. One client describes 'Le Sphinx' as being more like a Lyons tea-house than a brothel, with the girls good-natured, wholesome and exceedingly pretty.

The dwarf in the drawings was a permanent inmate who would fetch and carry for the girls, and amuse them when business was slack. They, in turn, treated him as a pet.

One visitor from 1936 remembers seeing purses being suspended over private parts, which seems wonderfully appropriate, another mentions light cloaks over bare breasts (text accompanying portfolio of five lithographs, 1977).

'Le Sphinx' closed in 1946.

T 03462   **Punch and Judy** *c.*1945

Inks and gouache on paper $6\frac{3}{4} \times 10\frac{15}{16}$
(170×277)
Not inscribed
Presented by Ruth Boswell 1982

The following entry is based on a letter received from Sally Shuel on 19 June 1986, containing answers to the compiler's questions put to Betty Boswell on his behalf, on a letter from Ruth Boswell dated 30 April 1986, and on conversations with Sally Shuel and Ruth Boswell on 19 June 1986 and 26 June 1986 respectively.

'Punch and Judy' relates to the series of drawings which Boswell began to make on this theme from around 1936. Betty Boswell remembers that the first works of this type were executed at their home in Haverstock Hill, Belsize Park, London, which they left between 1936–7, and most of the Punch and Judy drawings were completed before the war. There are also a number of small drawings of 'Punch and Judy' and related sketches in which a Punch-type character figures, in a sketchbook 1939–40 (Tate Gallery Archive, 8224.11, pp.37, 38, 39, 64) as well as six loose 'Punch and Judy' illustrations on small scraps of paper, including the reverse side of a letter which has been torn in two halves and is dated 1944. It was Boswell's custom to carry around and draw on small fragments of paper in this way and he referred to these as his 'thumbnails'.

His daughter, Sally, has noted that the Tate's 'Punch and Judy' is smaller in format than those made during the thirties and much less 'coarse' in content. The earlier drawings are also more violent. In addition, she has stated her opinion that some areas of the drawing, notably the treatment of the sky, are similar to a style which Boswell developed after the thirties. For this reason, she believes that the work is a later example of its type or else it includes additions which Boswell made subsequently. Comparison of the decoration on the curtain or stage-surround, which appears in some of the 'Punch and Judy' works, may assist in dating this work. The motif used in the stage-surround of a 'Punch and Judy' related drawing in a sketchbook (Tate Gallery

Archive, 8224.11, p.39) is characterised by 'S' shapes and contrasts sharply with the overlapping squares and rectangles which distinguish the decorative pattern used in T 03462. The sketchbook drawing must have been made between 1939–41 because the book also includes pencil sketches which Boswell has annotated as having been made on the set of the film 'Thunder Rock'. This was released in 1942 and Betty Boswell recalls that Herbert Marshall, a close friend of the artist, arranged for him to visit the set during shooting in 1940. On the other hand, the curtain decoration of T 03462 bears a distinct resemblance to that used in a 'Punch and Judy' drawing contained in another, later sketchbook (Tate Gallery Archive, 8224.20). There is firm evidence for the date of this work also, in that the sketchbook also contains three studies for 'Café, Kentish Town', T 03463 (see below), which is in turn related to work which Boswell was producing for a poster for the film 'It Always Rains On Sundays' during 1947. It seems likely, therefore, that T 03462 was produced after 1945 or contains additions which were made around this time.

Neither Boswell's widow nor his daughter remembers him expressing any particular interest in 'Punch and Judy' shows and Sally recalls that, even when in 1946–7 there was a regular 'Punch and Judy' stand close to their address at 28 Parliament Hill, Hampstead, Boswell was never sufficiently interested to accompany her to watch. Nevertheless, Betty believes that Boswell was attracted to the violence involved in 'Punch and Judy' and that he found in its characters and action a means of expressing and having fun with his interest in the erotic. Referring to Boswell's general interests, Betty Boswell has stated that 'as a colonial [Boswell was born in New Zealand], Jim found all sorts of traditional things fascinating' and, while his interest in 'Punch and Judy' is a part of this, Boswell also enjoyed circuses (Ruth Boswell has a number of drawings of clowns) and events such as the Hampstead Fair. More specifically, Boswell was a great admirer of the Commedia dell'Arte. Some of the so-called 'Punch and Judy' drawings, for example in the sketchbook (Tate Gallery Archive, 8224.11, p.39), although including 'Punch' characters, are more reminiscent of the Commedia dell'Arte, which is a related, but quite different, theatrical genre.

T 03463   Café, Kentish Town 1947

Inks and gouache on paper $15\frac{1}{8} \times 20\frac{7}{8}$
(396 × 530)
Not inscribed
Presented by Ruth Boswell 1982

The following entry is based on a letter received from Sally Shuel on 19 June 1986, containing answers to the compiler's questions put to Betty Boswell on his behalf,

and on conversations with Sally Shuel and Betty Boswell on 19 June 1986 and 26 June 1986 respectively.

This work was made in connection with the poster which Boswell produced for the film 'It Always Rains on Sundays' (repr. in col., *Projecting Britain*, BFI, 1982, p.19), released in 1947. The Tate's drawing was executed either in 1947 or shortly before. It was the first of a series of commissions from Ealing Studios which included posters for 'The Blue Lamp', 1950, 'Pool of London', 1951, and 'The Gentle Gunman', 1952 (repr. in col., *Projecting Britain*, pp.20–2). Whether S. John Woods, who was in charge of the Ealing Studios advertising department 1943–59, approached Boswell as a result of drawings of Camden Town street scenes which Boswell was then making, or whether they sprang from an interest which was initiated by the commission, is not known. Whatever the reason, Boswell produced many similar drawings.

The work was titled 'Café, Kentish Town' only after Boswell's death and, although it is not drawn from life and is not of any actual place in particular, it is composed of impressions of neighbouring Camden Town which were assembled to form the work. From 1947 to its demise in 1959 Boswell was art director of the pocket-sized satirical magazine *Lilliput*, which began publication in 1937. Four smaller drawings, entitled 'Little Gold Mine', 'Private Enterprise', 'Saturday Night' and 'Spring Fever' which are connected with 'Café, Kentish Town' and which resemble particular areas and characters within the Tate's work, were reproduced in *Lilliput*, XX, April 1947, pp.321–4, with the general title 'Portrait of a Neighbourhood'. The accompanying commentary for the pictures was by Eric Hobsbawm and stated: 'Camden Town, [is] the subject of the four pictures James Boswell has painted for *Lilliput* ...' According to the artist's daughter, Boswell loved Camden Town and 'was fascinated by the tarts' who frequented its streets. She has described how Boswell would collate impressions, imaginary elements and details with private significance, in order to produce street scenes of this type. With regard to the latter, a favourite device, for instance, was to incorporate friends' names into the signs which appear over the shop fronts depicted in some scenes (see Sketchbooks: 1938–39 Vol.1 [Street scenes and caricatures], 1938–9 Vol.2 [Street scenes and caricatures], 1939 [Essays, London], Tate Gallery Archive, 8224.8, 8224.9, 8224.10). The girl in the foreground of the drawing was drawn from imagination and is typical of the stereotype which Boswell evolved and drew repeatedly. She closely resembles the tallest of the two girls in the poster for 'It Always Rains on Sundays' and the image is based on the girls Boswell had seen around the Camden Town area. The blond hairstyle worn high on the head is an example of the prevailing fashion at the time when the drawing was made but also manifests Boswell's own fascination with this particular 'look'. There are three studies for T 03463 which show Boswell developing the composition and aspects of detail, in the sketchbook 1945–9 (Tate Gallery Archive, 8824.20).

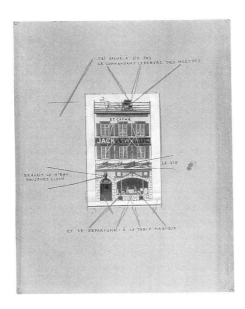

André Breton 1896–1966

T 03807 **I saluted at six paces Commander Lefebvre des Noëttes (poem object)** 1942

Collage of printed colour postcard, black paper, silver paint, silk thread, silver sequins $13\frac{1}{2} \times 9\frac{3}{4}$ (340 × 250)
Inscribed 'J'AI SALUÉ À SIX PAS/LE COMMANDANT LEFEBVRE DES NOËTTES' t.r., 'ET CACHÉ' t.centre, 'JACK L'ÉVENTREUR' centre, 'BRAVAIT LE HIBOU/TOUJOURS CLOUÉ' lower l., 'LA VIE' lower r., and 'ET SE REPARFUMAIT À LA TABLE MAGIQUE' across bottom
Purchased from John Armbruster (Grant-in-Aid) 1983
Prov: Mrs Jacqueline Lamba Breton; John Armbruster
Lit: *Dada and Surrealism Reviewed*, exhibition catalogue, Hayward Gallery, 1978, p.388

This poem object is one of an edition of about twenty (although originally advertised as fifty) published by the New York Surrealist magazine VVV where Breton acted as joint literary adviser with Max Ernst.

The poem object was sold as part of a portfolio of eleven original works; etchings, frottage and objects by André Breton, Alexander Calder, Leonora Carrington, Marc Chagall, Max Ernst, David Hare, André Masson, Matta, Robert Motherwell, Kurt Seligmann and Yves Tanguy. The portfolio was intended to raise money for further numbers of VVV.

According to a letter to the Tate from John Armbruster, the previous owner, each one of the poem objects was individually assembled by Breton who used different coloured papers and slightly varied the composition. The Tate's version is inscribed on the back by André Breton's second wife, Jacqueline Lamba Breton:

Poème objet d'André Breton créé à partir d'une carte postale Trouvée à New York en 1942 et donnée à Jacqueline LAMBA Breton dans le même temps.

There is another version of 'I saluted at six paces Commander Lefebvre des Noëttes' in the Musée National d'Art Moderne, Paris, and a plan for the work, dated 1943, is illustrated in André Breton's *What is Surrealism?*, Selected Writings, ed. Franklin Rosemont, 1978, p.302. André Breton began making poem objects in 1929 and in the same year defined the procedure as:

Combining the resources of poetry and sculpture and in speculating on their reciprocal powers of exaltation (Jose Pierre (ed.), *Dictionary of Surrealism*, 1974).

Breton explains his method of composition for a poem object in an essay of 1942 included in André Breton, *Surrealism and Painting*, London, 1972, pp.284–5.

Alan Bridgwater 1903–1962

T 03710 **Inscription 'Remember Jane Snowfield'** 1927

Portland stone, the letters painted $10\frac{5}{8} \times 21\frac{1}{4} \times 2\frac{3}{4}$ (270 × 540 × 70)

REMEMBER JANE SNOWFIELD 1854÷1927

Inscribed 'Remember/Jane Snowfield/1854 ÷ 1927'
Transferred from the Victoria and Albert Museum 1983

Prov: Purchased from B.J. Fletcher, Director of the Central School of Arts & Crafts, Birmingham, by the Department of Circulation, Victoria and Albert Museum, 1927 (Circ. 636–1927)

Exh: Travelling exhibitions of Department of Circulation, Victoria and Albert Museum

Bridgwater was a student at the Central School of Arts & Crafts, Birmingham, from 1923–1933. The text of this inscription was one of several suggested by B.J. Fletcher, the Director of the School, in a letter of 30 March 1927 to the Circulation Department of the Victoria and Albert Museum. There is no information in this letter about Jane Snowfield. Shortly afterwards the Museum chose this text, and received the inscription itself in October of the same year, paying the school for it.

The letters of the name are painted red, and the rest black. The letter forms resemble the style of Eric Gill, and are comparable to his 'Roman Capitals ... and Arabic numerals' published as plate 16 of Edward Johnston's *Manuscript and Inscription letters* (1909, and many later editions). The letters at the start of each line are exaggerated, as Gill's often are, and the numbers are very similar, particularly in the characteristic placing of the 4 on the line.

This inscription is not typical of Bridgwater's work as it is a student piece, to a set text, and he subsequently became a figure sculptor. Another and more elaborate inscription, made in the early 1930s, belongs to his widow.

Marcel Broodthaers 1924–1976

T 03696 Paintings 1973

Letterpress on nine unstretched primed canvases each $31\frac{1}{2} \times 39\frac{1}{2}$ (800 × 1003), overall dimensions variable between approximately $102\frac{3}{8} \times 126\frac{3}{8}$ (2600 × 3209) and 104 × 128 (2840 × 3449)

Not inscribed (though the entire imagery consists of printed inscriptions)
Purchased from Galerie Michael Werner, Cologne (Grant-in-Aid) 1983

Prov: Wide White Space Gallery, Antwerp; Galerie Michael Werner, Cologne

The Gallery has a photocopy of Broodthaers's certificate for this work, written by hand on two sheets of paper, numbered 'I' and 'II'. Each sheet is headed by the inscription "PEINTURES". On sheet I this is followed by a drawn plan indicating both the arrangement (three rows of three) and the sequence in which the canvases should be hung. The numbers, from 1 to 9, given to each rectangle in the plan are allocated horizontally in the normal order, starting with the canvas at top left. The remainder of the certificate reads as follows:

1. la perspective – prix → noir
   autres mots → violet – pression plus légère

2. le prix – pinceau → noir
   autres mots → jaune

3. le sujet – l'image et les autres mots → noir

4. le sujet – figures → noir. forte pression
   autres mots → noir – pression légère

5. les figures – le style → noir
   les chiffres dans ttes les couleurs

6. le pinceau – la brosse → noir
   autres mots → violet – bleu

7. le sujet – l'image → noir
   autres mots → rouge

8. le prix – la valeur → noir
   autres mots → jaune

9. le sujet – figures → noir forte pression
   autres mots → vert

"PEINTURES" : ensemble formé de 9 pièces (chacune de format 100 × 85 cms) de toile imprimées typographiquement.

L'ensemble est traité en cinq versions différenciées l'une de l'autre par l'usage des couleurs, la pression de la machine, la disposition des pièces ou le changement des mots.

Celui auquel le présent certificat fait allusion a été réalisé en août 73.

Cologne, septembre 73

M. Broodthaers

Rmq [remarque]: Ce certificat a pour but secondaire d'éviter une signature sur chaque pièce afin d'empêcher la dispersion de l'ensemble.

All nine canvases have white painted grounds, on to which are printed a number of words. The only canvas also to bear numerals is the central one of the ensemble (5), on which are painted all the numerals from 1 to 9. The words and numerals are printed in various colours in either oil inks or thinned oil paint. The words which appear in 'Paintings' are as follows (words in brackets are English translations where appropriate):

Appearing 11 times:	figures
Appearing 9 times:	prix (price)
Appearing 8 times:	chassis (stretcher) pinceau (brushwork) chevalet (easel) sujet (subject) couleur (colour)
Appearing 7 times:	image (picture)
Appearing 6 times:	style (style)
Appearing 5 times:	brosse (brush)
Appearing 4 times:	clous (nails)
Appearing 3 times:	perspective (perspective) valeur (value)
Appearing twice:	composition (composition) dessin (drawing)
Appearing once:	apprêt (ground)

The word 'prix' appears twice on canvas 1 and the word 'figures' appears twice on canvas 4 and twice on canvas

9. Nine of the sixteen words appear sometimes with and sometimes without the definite article; the other seven are always without it.

The artist's widow, Maria Gilissen (who has approved this entry), provided the following information in 1986. T03936 is one of a series of five nine-canvas works by Broodthaers with the general title 'Peintures', all made in 1973. Of these five works, three are believed to belong to dealers on the continent and a fourth belongs to Maria Gilissen. 'Peintures' is the word which appears at the top of the certificate of another work in the series, while in the same place on the certificate of a third work in the same series is the title 'Série l'Art et les Mots'.

The series 'Peintures' is one of eight series of nine-canvas works which Broodthaers made. These are:

'Série en Langue française' 1972 (also known as 'Série de neuf Peintures sur un Sujet littéraire')

'Peintures' 1973

'Série anglaise' 1973

'Pierre Paul Rubens' 1973 (also known as 'Petrus Paulus Rubens')

'Série des Figures' 1973

'Série allemande' 1973 (also known as 'Die Welt')

'Les Poissons' 1975

'Puzzle' 1975 (also known as 'Energie')

All but one of these series of nine-canvas works consist of five works. The exception is 'Série en Langue française', which consists of *six* nine-canvas works. Broodthaers's intention was to complete the suite of series of five nine-canvas works by making a ninth series, but he did not live to do this. In this final series he would have repeated each of the eight existing series on a single canvas of each nine-canvas work, but it is not known what he would have printed on the ninth canvas.

In addition to the eight complete series which he did make, Broodthaers began but decided to discontinue two further series of nine-canvas works, 'Culture Internationale' (in which he made three works) and 'Le Chien' (in which he made one). He also made some individual nine-canvas works which were not intended to become part of a series. These include 'La Souris écrit rat' and 'Un Chateaubriand bien saignant pour deux'. Printed in several of the series other than 'Peintures' are the names and dates of famous people, among whom writers, painters, poets, composers and philosophers are prominent.

Examples from some of Broodthaers's series of nine-canvas works are in museum collections, as follows: 'Série en Langue française', van Abbemuseum, Eindhoven; 'Pierre Paul Rubens', Museum voor Hedendaagse Kunst, Gent, Museum Boymans-van Beuningen, Rotterdam, Musée National d'Art Moderne,

Paris; 'Les Poissons', Museum of Modern Art, New York.

All of Broodthaers's nine-canvas works were printed in Brussels at the Imprimerie Laconti (which closed in the late 1970s). They were printed from metal blocks, the styles of script used being chosen by Broodthaers. The works were sometimes printed in Broodthaers's absence (though on his detailed instructions) but mostly in his presence. In all cases he maintained close supervision. He always decided the colours to be used (and especially whether an impression should be light or heavy) at the printing works, usually during the actual printing sessions.

In all the nine-canvas works, the canvases are unstretched. Broodthaers intended that they should be displayed pinned directly to the wall, but in many of the works (including the Tate's) the canvases have been glazed and backed by boards which provide a means of attachment. This is in order to protect and preserve the works, and has been approved by Maria Gilissen, who confirms that the width of the gaps between the canvases should be ± 10 to 12 cms. Most of Broodthaers's nine-canvas works are intended to be displayed in three rows of three. Broodthaers occasionally displayed examples of 'Série en Langue française' in a straight line. His 'Série Anglaise' 'English Poets' was displayed in the exhibition *Falls the Shadow* (Hayward Gallery, April–June 1986) in two horizontal rows of four with a ninth canvas alone in the centre of the third and lowest row.

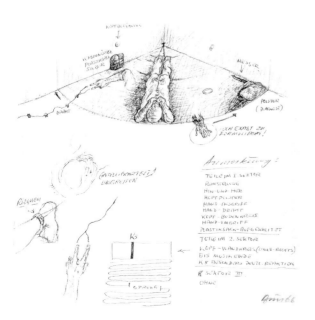

Günter Brus b.1938

T 03695 **Run-through of an Action** 1966

Pencil and blue ball-point pen on paper, each $7\frac{7}{8} \times 8\frac{1}{4}$ (200 × 209) or $8\frac{1}{4} \times 7\frac{7}{8}$ (209 × 200)
Seventeen sheets of drawing, diagram and text, most inscribed 'Brus' or 'Brus 66' b.r.
Purchased from Galerie Heike Curtze, Düsseldorf (Grant-in-Aid) 1983

Exh: *Westkunst: Zeitgenössische Kunst seit 1939,* Museen der Stadt Köln, Cologne, May–August 1981 (759, repr.); *Brus-Muehl-Nitsch-Schwarzkogler: Photos, Zeichnungen, Partituren, Bilder 1960–1970,* Galerie Heike Curtze, Düsseldorf, November 1982–January 1983 (137, six sheets repr. p.14)

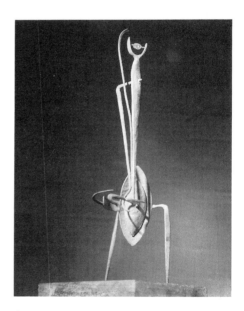

Reg Butler 1931–1981

T 03392 **Maquette for 'Woman'** 1949

Forged and welded iron $12\frac{1}{2} \times 4\frac{1}{4} \times 4\frac{1}{8}$ (317 × 109 × 107) including brick base
Not inscribed
Purchased from Maxwell Davidson (Grant-in-Aid) 1982

Exh: *Reg Butler,* Tate Gallery, November 1983–January 1984 (16, repr.)

T 03703 **Musée Imaginaire** 1963

Bronze, in wooden display cabinet
$31\frac{1}{2} \times 48\frac{1}{2} \times 4\frac{3}{4}$ (800 × 1231 × 120)
Thirty-nine figures of various heights,
each stamped 'RB' and '$\frac{2}{8}$'
Purchased from Galería Freites, Caracas
(Grant-in-Aid) 1983

Exh: *Reg Butler*, Tate Gallery, November
1983–January 1984 (63, repr.)

T 03711 **Crouching Woman I** 1948

Forged and welded iron, $7\frac{1}{2} \times 4 \times 2$
(190 × 100 × 50)
Not inscribed
Transferred from the Victoria and Albert
Museum 1983

Richard Carline 1896–1980

T 03597 **Sea Shore** 1920

Oil on canvas $37 \times 22\frac{1}{8}$ (940 × 562)
Inscribed 'Richard Carline 1920.' b.r. and
'sea shore/Richard Carline/14A
Downshire Hill/Hampstead' on top
turnover of canvas
Presented by the artist's widow, Mrs
Nancy Carline 1983

Exh: *New English Art Club 62nd Exhibition*,
RWS Galleries, June–July 1920 (51); *The
Spencers and Carlines in Hampstead in the
1920s*, Odney Club, Cookham, May–June
1973 (Richard Carline 3, as 'The jetty at
Seaford'); *Paintings 1914–24*, South
London Art Gallery, May–June 1974 (21);
Spencers and Carlines, New Metropole
Arts Centre, Folkestone, October–
November 1980, City Art Gallery, York,
December 1980–January 1981 (123, as
'The Breakwater, Seaford'); *Richard
Carline 1896–1980*, Camden Arts Centre,
June–July 1983 (10, repr. as 'The jetty,
Seaford')

In April 1920, Richard Carline, his parents, brother
Sydney, sister Hilda and Stanley and Gilbert Spencer
stayed at Seaford, on the Sussex coast between
Newhaven and Eastbourne. A letter from Stanley Spencer to William Rothenstein dated 23 April 1920, written
from Seaford and published in Rothenstein's *Men and
Memories 1900–1922*, II, 1931, pp. 348–9, describes a
painting expedition by the whole party on the nearby
Downs.

The entry on the Tate's picture in the catalogue of the exhibition at Cookham in 1973 states, almost certainly on information from the artist, that it was painted from memory. However, Mrs Nancy Carline owns a watercolour sketch for the painting, $22\frac{1}{2} \times 14$ (571 × 355), inscribed by the artist on the reverse to the effect that the watercolour was painted at Seaford.

Mrs Nancy Carline writes (letter, 20 March 1986) that 'the sketch in particular reminds me of some of his war time aerial sketches and paintings, in which the skyline is very high and one looks down on the sea and breakwater almost as if viewed from an aeroplane, and I always think that this aspect of his early work can't be stressed too strongly – in fact there are very few of his compositions which have a low horizon'. As an official war artist, Richard Carline made sketches from the air of battle grounds in France in 1918, and in 1919, with his brother Sydney (also an official war artist), made many aerial views of war zones in the Middle East.

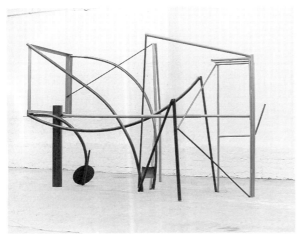

Anthony Caro b.1924

T 03455 **Emma Dipper** 1977

Steel rusted and painted grey
84 × 67 × 126 (2130 × 1700 × 3200)
Not inscribed
Presented by the artist 1982

Exh: *Anthony Caro Emma Lake Sculptures*, André Emmerich Gallery, New York, October–November 1978 (works not numbered, repr.); *Anthony Caro Sculpture 1969–1984*, Serpentine Gallery, April–May 1984 (15, repr. in two views), Whitworth Art Gallery, Manchester, June–July 1984, Leeds City Art Gallery, August–September 1984, and then British Council tour to Ordrupgaard Samlingen, Copenhagen, October–November 1984

(19, repr. in colour in two views on catalogue covers), Kunstmuseum, Dusseldorf, January–March 1985, Fundacio Joan Miro, Barcelona, March–May 1985

Lit: Dieter Blume, *Anthony Caro, Catalogue Raisonné*, Vol. III, Galerie Wentzel, Cologne (1173); Diane Waldman, *Anthony Caro*, 1982, pl.231

Emma Lake is a summer arts workshop run by the University of Saskatchewan, situated 200 miles north of Saskatoon, Canada. Caro spent the month of August 1977 there as an invited guest artist, and began work on fifteen sculptures, all of which bear the word Emma in their titles (Nos. 1171–85, Vol. III, *Anthony Caro, Catalogue Raisonné*, Galerie Wentzel, Cologne). The Emma series of sculptures were 'made of light material – much of it tube, rod and thin angle ... because we were working 200 miles north of Saskatoon on a gravel area with only a crane lift from the back of a truck. It was impossible to use heavy material. We were also a long way from the scrapyard. Douglas Bentham, who was helping me, went back after one or two days to fetch some more material' (letter from the artist to the compiler, 25 March 1986). Caro worked on more than one sculpture at the same time and had the assistance of Douglas Bentham, 'a local sculptor, living in Saskatoon, an excellent artist and craftsman, he came to Emma Lake with his wife, and helped me make my sculptures. He welded the pieces and I worked in close contact with him as I always do with my assistants – seeking responses and suggestions. He fabricated the pieces.' When asked if the title Emma Dipper refers to any configuration of the formal elements, the artist replied that 'The name Dipper comes from a Bar-/Restaurant that we all went to one night whilst at the workshop.'

After his spell at the workshop in the summer of 1977, Caro returned to London while

the works went to Saskatoon, all taken there by Doug Bentham, and they stayed on his farm until some months later Sheila [Girling, the artist's wife and a painter] and I went to Saskatoon. I looked at the sculptures then and made changes to them; they subsequently were all taken to New York City prior to the show at André Emmerich's and here I made more changes. One of the series in fact I finished last year. I think it was at this time (in New York City before the Emmerich show) that I fixed on the colours for them. Sheila chose the colours for the sculpture.

When asked if 'Emma Dipper' was originally painted the colours it is now, the artist replied 'it was never painted differently to what it is now (painted various greys, normal American household paints) as far as I can remember. I have no record of the exact shades used.'

The compiler asked if there was any relationship between polychrome tubular works like 'Emma Dipper' and those of the early 1960s which employed painted tubes such as 'Month of May'. Caro replied, 'I am not particularly conscious of these criteria and relationships. The colour is pragmatic in almost every case. I would say that both "Emma Dipper" and "Month of May" are concerned with a kind of internal activation of space.'

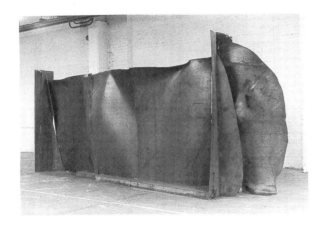

T 03457 Tundra 1975

Steel 105 × 228 × 52 (2720 × 5790 × 1320)
Not inscribed
Purchased from T.M. and P.M. Caro
(Grant-in-Aid) 1982

Exh: *Aspects of British Art Today*, British Council tour of Japan, Tokyo Metropolitan Art Museum, February–April 1982, Tochigi Prejectural Museum of Fine Arts, April–May 1982, The National Museum of Art, Osaka, June–July 1982, Fukuoaka Art Museum, August 1982, Hokkaido Museum of Modern Art, September–October 1982 (4, repr. in colour)

Repr: Dieter Blume, *Anthony Caro, Catalogue Raisonné*, Vol. III, Galerie Wentzel, Cologne (1114); Diane Waldman, *Anthony Caro*, 1982, pl.170 (colour)

In 1972 Caro found a supply of soft ends of steel rollings in a scrapyard in Milan and the discovery of this material led to his Veduggio series of sculptures. In 1973, in Britain, he discovered similar ends of soft-edged rolled steel at the steel mills of Consett in County Durham. 'Tundra' is a work made of steel from Consett. The artist wrote to the compiler about the metal, 'when steel is rolled it sometimes doesn't come out flat and we bought about 11 tons of these "cobbles" which are the pieces in the rolling system which get twisted and are normally thrown away' (letter to the compiler, 25 March 1986). T 03457 was made in the artist's studio in Camden Town. The rusted steel surfaces of 'Tundra' have been treated with paint and wax applications. The artist writes, 'it is a surface finish that I liked very much and I regard as an important integral part of the work. It is definitely an indoor piece, particularly because of its surface finish. But also because its scale, though large, is more in keeping with internal contained space' (letter of 24 June 1986).

The compiler asked the artist if 'Tundra', as a work, stood alone or was part of a series: 'The piece is not completely on its own without similar pieces. There is a sculpture called 'Monsoon Drift' [1975], which is in the Hirshhorn Museum Collection [Washington] and 'Footprint' [1975], all of which have a feel of a screen, albeit a soft one. They are also closely related to the York series which I made earlier in Toronto [1974].'

'Tundra' is one of the artist's 'largest pieces with a solid appearance'.

T 03455 and T 03457 have been approved by the artist.

Eugène Carrière 1849–1906

T 03638 Head of a Child (Jean-René Carrière?) c.1891

Oil on cardboard 9¾ × 6¾ (247 × 171)
Inscribed 'EUGENE CARRIERE' b.centre

Presented anonymously in memory of
Terence Rattigan 1983

Prov: Roland, Browse and Delbanco (bought at
a sale at the Hôtel Drouot, Paris, in
December 1954); the donor 1955

Exh: *French Paintings and Drawings of the 19th
and 20th Century*, Roland, Browse and
Delbanco, April–May 1955 (17)

This painting, which appears to represent a boy, is
almost certainly a portrait of one of the artist's own
children. The most likely subject would be his second
son, Jean-René Carrière, who was born in 1888, as his
first son Eugène Léon was born as early as 1881 and his
third son Arsène as late as 1899; dates which seem too
early and too late on stylistic grounds. If it is Jean-
René, and he is aged about two and a half, the picture
must have been painted *c*.1891.

Jesse Dale Cast 1900–1976

T 03598 'The Windmill', Clapham Common 1934

Oil on canvas 17 × 21½ (432 × 546)
Inscribed 'J. Dale Cast 1934' b.r. and
'"The Windmill" £300.' on stretcher and
'Jesse Dale Cast/73B Southside/Clapham
Common SW4' on reverse of frame
Presented by David Cast, the artist's son
1983

Exh: RA 1934 (551); *Jesse Dale Cast*, South
London Art Gallery, October–November
1980 (24, repr.)

The Windmill public house is on Clapham Common;
the artist's studio at Clapham Common South Side was
opposite. A pencil and wash drawing for this painting,

also dated 1934, was included in the artist's retrospective exhibition at the South London Art Gallery,
and is reproduced in the catalogue (82). It is less detailed
than the painting, and shows exactly the same view and
is squared for transfer.

T 03599 Self Portrait 1934

Pastel on paper 15¾ × 11½ (400 × 290)
Inscribed 'JDC 34' b.r.
Presented by David Cast, the artist's son
1983

Exh: *Jesse Dale Cast*, South London Art
Gallery, October–November 1980 (84)

The catalogue of the artist's exhibition in 1980 listed
two further self portrait drawings of 1930 and 1935, and
a small oil painting of 1923. A self portrait was included
in a group portrait of 1924 ('Figure Composition (Margaret and Others with Self Portrait)', 4, repr.). No other
works were listed in pastels.

Lynn Chadwick b.1914

T 03712 Conjunction 1953

Wrought iron and composition
16½ × 11¾ × 8 (420 × 300 × 200)
Not inscribed
Transferred from the Victoria and Albert
Museum 1983

Prov: Purchased from the artist by the
Department of Circulation, Victoria and
Albert Museum 1954 (Circ. 37–1954)

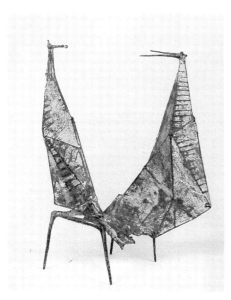

pages 12/13

Marc Camille Chaimowicz b.1947

T 03384 **Le Désert ...** 1981

Photographs, silkscreen, Xerox, acetate, and type on grey Rivco paper, elephant hide paper, cream laid on paper and Xerox paper mounted on card, 13 framed panels, $14\frac{5}{8} \times 11\frac{3}{8}$ (370 × 290); $14\frac{5}{8} \times 20\frac{1}{2}$ (370 × 520); 11 remaining panels, $14\frac{5}{8} \times 22\frac{7}{8}$ (370 × 580)

Inscribed 'Marc C.C. 81' on each panel with date and page number and 'Marc C.C. Spring 81' on last panel

Purchased from Nigel Greenwood Inc. Ltd (Grant-in-Aid) 1982

Exh: *Maquettes ...* , Nigel Greenwood Inc. Ltd., December 1981–January 1982 (no catalogue); *Prints and Works on Paper from the Modern Collection*, Tate Gallery, August–November 1982 (7, as 'Le Désert (A chapter for a book)', detail repr. in leaflet)

Lit: Sarah Kent, exhibition review, *Time Out*, January 8–14 1982, p.76 (detail repr.); Jean Fisher and Stuart Morgan, *Past Imperfect: Marc Camille Chaimowicz 1972–1982*, Liverpool, Londonderry, Southampton, Leeds, 1983, book accompanying exhibition travelling to Bluecoat Gallery, Liverpool, Orchard Gallery, Londonderry, John Hansard Gallery, Southampton 1983–4, pp.47–50 and 60–3 (detail repr. in col. pp.48–9); Marc Camille Chaimowicz, *Café du Rêve*, Paris and London, 1985 (repr. in col. pp.9–33)

While it functions as a complete statement, 'Le Désert ... ' is also the original artwork for the first chapter of a book, *Café du Rêve*, consisting of texts by the artist, designs, drawings and photographs, which was published in Paris on 9 May 1985, by the Galerie de France

Exh: *London Group*, New Burlington Galleries, November 1953 (219); travelling exhibitions of the Department of Circulation, Victoria and Albert Museum; *London Group, 1914–64 Jubilee Exhibition*, Tate Gallery, July–August 1964, National Museum of Wales, Cardiff, August–September 1964, Museum and Art Gallery, Doncaster, October 1964 (131, repr.)

Lit: A. Bowness, *Lynn Chadwick*, 1962, n.p. *Also repr*: J.P. Hodin, *Lynn Chadwick*, 1961, pl.12

Chadwick's first exhibited sculptures were mobiles, such as the Tate Gallery's 'Dragonfly' (1951, N 06035). During 1953 he made static sculptures in a new technique, in which he filled a cage of welded together iron rods with a material called 'stolit', which was a mixture of plaster and powdered iron. Excess material which protruded beyond the shape of the rods was filed away. The powdered iron on the surface has since rusted, as intended, and gives the sculpture its colour. Alan Bowness wrote (op.cit.) that 'Conjunction' was one of the first sculptures made in this new technique. The mobiles were of animal subjects, and 'Conjunction' is also one of his first sculptures of a human couple.

Chadwick subsequently made a series of 'Conjunctions', the next in 1954 (private collection, Chicago, reproduced in Herbert Read, *Lynn Chadwick*, 1958, no.9, $17\frac{1}{2}$ ins. high).

and Editions du Regard. It was exhibited at the Galerie de France (9 May–15 June 1985) with some of the original artwork, but not T03384. A second edition of the book was published by Thames and Hudson and launched by the Nigel Greenwood Gallery in London in September 1985. Both editions have English texts.

Café du Rêve contains seven chapters, a biography and a bibliography, the density of text and image – and therefore the relationship between them – varying from chapter to chapter. According to Jean Fisher (in *Past Imperfect*, op.cit., p.47) 'Le Désert' was the first chapter to be completed although at the time of its completion the artist was also working on 'Partial Eclipse' (Chapter 4, which contains the only preoriginated material in the book and records Chaimowicz's performance of the same name), 'North Africa Song' (Chapter 3) and 'Le Parc' (Chapter 2). In the early stages of the project T03384 was conceived as the fifth chapter but in the final publication, the sequence is as follows:

1. 'le Désert ... '
2. 'le Parc ... '
3. 'North Africa Song'
4. 'Partial Eclipse, a performance'
5. 'Chorus, a letter from Vienna'
6. 'Liaison'
7. 'le Select ... '

As the original for a chapter, T03384 was always intended for reproduction. It consists of a range of different paper grounds on which the artist has drawn in pencil and Indian ink, silkscreened, painted with watercolour and collaged photographs. When acquired by the Gallery, it consisted of 18 single and one double sheet of card, supporting photographs collaged on to decorative backgrounds of the artist's own design, and in places accompanied by short texts. After acquisition, all but the title page were framed in pairs, on the instruction of the artist. At five intervals throughout the sequence, a collaged sheet has been paired with a blank sheet.

A motif repeated eight times throughout the chapter, in each case in a slightly modified form, is a reproduction of an old postcard, showing a photograph of Saharan date palms, bearing the legend '6222 Scènes et types – Paysage Saharien – Palmiers Dattiers – LL'.

The framed pages are displayed in the following sequence:

1. The title page, bearing the title 'le désert' set on printer's film which had been laid on a background decorated in watercolour covered with a small pen or brush design (the trim lines are clearly visible); the title is placed within a rectangle of dotted lines corresponding in dimensions to the postcard image referred to above.

2/3. A double frame containing two pages each silkscreened with a bold rippling design in grey and white; the left-hand page carries the dedication 'For Angelo B' surmounted by a reproduction of the back of a French postcard, complete with the address of its manufacturer in Paris; a reproduction of the date palm postcard already described is collaged to the right-hand page.

4/5. A double frame with, on the left, a blank area, facing another empty rectangular dotted outline but surrounded by cut-up fragments of the postcard image.

6/7. Again a double panel; here set against a plain grey ground is a postcard of the church of San Ambrogio in Milan, facing the date palm card. Beneath the desert image is a statement made by Cardinal Hume on Thames Television in 1981: 'I understand the need to frequent the market place ... but miss the chances of going into the desert.' Chaimowicz gives a footnote, in the final panel of T03384, explaining Cardinal Hume's appointment to Westminster in 1976 which he describes as a 'radical' appointment.

8/9. Pages 8/9 are similar in layout to 6/7 but with a more open background pattern which runs across both panels; the image on the left is titled '157 TUNIS Mosquée rue des Tanneurs -LL'; the date palm image is repeated on the right.

10/11. On the left, against a dark background, is a simple outline drawing in black ink of a desert scene showing an American-looking cactus and a pyramid. Facing it, beneath a darkened image of date palms and laid over a decorated ground again with cactus drawings, are four verses of 'Berlin', a song about urban despair by Lou Reed (1973) which starts 'How do you think it feels/When you're speeding and lonely/'.

12/13. Against a brightly coloured red, green and white background, a hand-coloured postcard, with the title '1186 PAYSAGE DU SUD – DANS L'OASIS' faces another reproduction of the 'Paysage Saharien' above the following excerpt from *The Immoralist*, by André Gide, Penguin 1960 edition, p.107:
Oh Michael! Every joy is always awaiting us, but it must always be the only one; It insists on finding the bed empty and demands from us a widower's welcome.
Oh Michael! Every joy is like the manner of the desert which corrupts from one day to the next; It is like the fountain of Ameles, whose waters, says Plato, could never be kept in any vase ... (The Penguin edition retains the French spelling, Michel)

14/15. A vertical format postcard of 'TUNIS – Souk-et-Blat' against the same silkscreened background as panels 2 and 3 and beneath, again from Gide:

Tunis! The quality of the light here is not strength but abundance. The shade is still full of it. The air itself is like a luminous fluid in which everything is steeped; One bathes, one swims in it. This land of pleasure satisfies desire without appeasing it, and desire is sharpened by satisfaction. (André Gide, op.cit., p.148)

Opposite is a paler print of the date palm postcard and the quotation:

Poverty is a slave-driver; in return for food, men give their grudging labour; all work that is not joyous is wretched, I thought, and I paid many of them to rest. 'Don't work', I said, 'you hate it.' In imagination, I bestowed on each of them that leisure without which nothing can blossom. (André Gide, op.cit., p.146)

16/17. A blank page, facing a one decorated in shades of grey on which is pasted a small reproduction of two seated naked boys; at the foot of the page Chaimowicz gives the following information 'Wilhelm Von Gloeden, Taormina, 1902–1003 (detail).' [Taormina in Sicily, where many of von Gloeden's photographs were taken, was also visited by Michel, the narrator in Gide's novel *The Immoralist*]

18/19. Again a blank page, facing a bright ground with a differently coloured version of the card used for panel 12.

20/21. A blank page faces a silkscreened ground (the design is also used as background in panels, 2, 3, 7, 14 and 19) on which is collaged a small slightly out-of-focus photograph showing a transparent crucifix and the outline of a pyramid shape with, underneath, the caption, 'Approach Road, London 1977' (detail) (this image, which also appears in 'Partial Eclipse' relates to a flat Chaimowicz used to occupy. Iconography related to this flat has been used in a number of his works).

22/23. A blank sheet, this time facing a photocopy of the ubiquitous date palms which Chaimowicz had modified by drawing over them with images of American cacti.

24/25. The final pages. Although the right-hand page carries a very pale image of the palms, these pages chiefly consist of text by the artist beneath the heading 'The Desert ... '

This concludes:

he reconsidered the desert ...
as magnet to those who seek truth, mirror of serenity,
as image of openness and context for privacy,
mirage and oasis, cacti and hyena,
as quiet illusion of sullen staticity ...
as cruel wasteland , fierce desolation, unforgiving and extreme ...
The black tents of the nomads echoing a deep silence, both of wonder and fearful ...
wanton and sensual as in French literature,
a colonization, body to the Parisian mind ...
as sublime in appearance yet shifty as any urban drifter ...
sanctuary to the spirit, haven of amorality ...
he remembered the Cardinal
reconnected the telephone, glanced at his
correspondence ... dressed and was last seen
walking, well and lightly, towards a land of
discourse and of dance, of intoxication and
gaiety ...

Marc Chaimowicz published his first illustrated book, *Dream, an Anecdote* in London in 1977 but *Café du Rêve* was his most ambitious published project at the time of publication and a number of his catalogues between 1982 and 1984 contain preliminary ideas for it, for example, the illustrated pamphlet, *Marc Camille Chaimowicz Humanic Artist in Residence, Vienna, Spring 1982*, which anticipates chapters 3 and 5 and refers briefly to chapter 2.

In her introduction to *Past Imperfect* (cited above, p.5), Jean Fisher compares Chaimowicz's work to a journey or quest ' ... a ... tender exploration of the microcosmic world of everyday experience'. Despite the multifarious nature of his art, she points to:

a cohesion ... an interlocking of recurrent images and motifs. A content that expands into the public area of the performance may become transferred and represented through the intimate pages of a book.

In an unpublished interview with a member of the Tate Gallery staff (8 January 1983), Chaimowicz discussed how he began working on *Café du Rêve*:

I suspect I remember a kind of frustration with certain forms of work ... one of which was performance ... the performances I did were invariably very introspective. I was intellectually and philosophically drawn to the need [to work] in that kind of a direct manner but I would tend to retreat into myself by working obliquely and time and space seemed more appropriately translated into the physicality of the book ... the actual activity of turning even a page, the privacy of the book, the form of the book fascinates me ...

I think there are a number of roads that led to the book ... one was to do, oddly enough, with some screens ... I did a show for Nigel [Greenwood] at the end of '79. I did three screens, in the most overt sense manifested with ambiguity, screens being something which both reveal and conceal ... which have a back and a front ... which can be stored away easily enough or brought out ... I found books, a logical extension of screens in a formal sense.

I see this book as very musical, in terms of how I order the relationship of text to image and of rhythm, the quiet parts and of busy parts and of climaxes and ... it seems to me ..., loosely symphonic. It seems to offer an accessibility as well as a complexity and a richness which I've not found in any other media. I have looked into other means, like working with video-tape or film, or sound-tape and these are logically 20th Century media that are easily reproducible and easily marketed and easily played back and yet they don't seem to offer the richness and variety of interpretation ...

In the interview, the artist also commented on the individual chapters in *Café du Rêve*:

It's difficult for me to be explicit. I suppose if one were to use a contemporary metaphor I would in a way see it not unlike the memorable albums by groups, by rock groups for example, that I have high regard for ..., each group I've liked has produced one or two albums, one or two have perhaps produced more, which are so good that each track has the potential of being a successful single.

Of his choice of images of the French North African desert as a central theme, he said:

I think mythically that was the strongest single image, and it therefore becomes the leit motif in that particular chapter. I've equally alluded to other definitions of the desert. There's a song from Lou Reed which seemed to me the epitome of a certain kind of urban alienation, a very New York kind of sensibility which is in contrast to the French colonialist image. There's also the references to Cardinal Hume. I think the impossibility of using a loaded image such as the desert is that one has to resort to mythical interpretations because the desert no longer exists other than through loaded references, and that, in a way, became the premise of the work.

Chaimowicz's first book, *Dream, an Anecdote*, has been described by Jean Fisher (above, p.30) as creating a serene quiet mood 'which allows the image to act as a screen onto which can be projected the fantasy and drama of the other scene, relayed by the text'. What Fisher describes as 'a strategy of interlocution between two textural spaces' is, she suggests, fully realised in *Café du Rêve*. She describes the latter (op.cit., p.47) as a travelogue, 'a record of a journey through the time and space of memory and experience which nurture

creative life' ... like a performance, 'the book is a spatio temporal structure: we turn the leaves, and through the interrelationship between image, text and design. We move through the literal space of the paper and the figural space of its contents.' Fisher compares the narrative structure to a musical score ... 'with passages of melody or rhythm, sounds and silences'.

She describes 'Le Désert' as 'a journey within a journey' and the repeated image of date palms as 'a "place" which embodies the relationship between text and image – the mirage that contains all the personal and collective fantasies evoked by the word "desert", from the urban wasteland of Lou Reed to the exotic body of France'. As the first chapter, 'Le Désert' acts as a preface, it has less text than later chapters and the emphasis is on visual build-up before the final two pages of text.

'Le Désert' is a predominantly pictorial and ultimately cyclical meditation on the possibility of arriving at what Chaimowicz has described elsewhere as 'a temporary truce between the ideal and the real'. Here this search for balance is represented as a journey into an imaginary desert which, at the outset, suggests the possibility of an escape to solitude, a respite from worldly distractions. However, as the piece unfolds, Chaimowicz increasingly emphasises the impossible nature of the quest by showing that while the idea of escape into a virgin wilderness appears desirable, 'the desert' is no longer intact, having been 'colonized' or invaded by its many different interpretations in art and literature. We are eventually led back to the artist's starting point, towards an essentially optimistic acceptance of the imperfection of 'real' life.

Less obvious when T 03384 is displayed on the wall is the chapter's carefully orchestrated structure. The recurring image of date palms acts as a central theme against which pictures and texts are introduced in counterpoint. As the piece gradually builds up to its finale, colours and patterns become more intense and blank pages appear more frequently, like points of punctuation, or rests in a musical score. However, Stuart Morgan has written (op.cit.) that:

to suggest that escape is proposed as an ideal would falsify the complexity of Chaimowicz's position. At the same time as he recognizes that the extremes of isolation necessary for self-analysis are alien to his nature, his 'self' must be preserved from too much perfection and the consequent engulfment. The dilemma is explored in 'Le Désert' with a title borrowed from Albert Camus. Exotic yet arid, it is a wilderness in which the choice between boredom and temptation must be made. In contrast to 'le Parc', in which a specific urban setting offers the protagonist consolation, the desert is less a physical space than a mental construct. To emphasize its boredom and sterility the same photograph, a found postcard of the Sahara, printed hard or soft, is used again and again, each time in the same position in the layout. Though it is associated with spiritual retirement it also provides an opportunity for what Chaimowicz calls 'wantonness'. Oscillation between the two states of mind distinguishes this chapter of the book.

The following articles deal generally with *Café du Rêve*:

Alan Parker, Café du Rêve, *Performance Magazine*, no.37, October–November 1985, pp.22–3 (repr., detail of panel 4); Cathy Courtney, 'Artist's Books', *Art Monthly*, no.91, November 1985, p.30; Book News, *Artline*, II, no.10, Winter 1985, pp.13–14.

This entry has been approved by the artist.

William Chappell b.1907

T 03654 **Young Man Playing a Guitar** 1926

Oil on papier mâché tray $11\frac{1}{4} \times 8\frac{1}{2} \times \frac{3}{4}$ (285 × 215 × 18)
Inscribed 'chappell./1926' b.r. Reverse bears pencil drawing of a head in profile and three other pencil marks.
Presented anonymously in memory of Terence Rattigan 1983

Prov: Given by the artist to Michael Salaman; the artist, by whom given to Sir Terence Rattigan (d.1977); the donor

The reverse of the tray bears the manufacturer's impressed monogram, and is stamped with the number $6202\frac{1}{2}$.

The artist is the distinguished dancer, designer and producer. He is also the editor of *Edward Burra, A Painter Remembered by His Friends*, 1982, and of *Well, Dearie! The Letters of Edward Burra* 1985. He and Burra met as art students at Chelsea Polytechnic in 1921. The artist wrote of the Tate's work (letter 18 September 1983):

There was no sitter. He was an imagined figure as *I* imagined all young men should look in the 20's corpse like and faintly (?) decadent. He is playing a *ukelele* an instrument that made a very nasty plonking noise and was the in thing to pretend to play amongst the young of that day. There was a singer (78 rpm) called Cliff Edwards but also known as Ukelele Ike who was very popular. It should be called – if you are going to dignify it by a title –

Young man playing a guitar. The depicted interior was like most of my friends lived in (not Edward Burra who had a very comfortable 1850s Victorian home outside Rye). The sparseness was due to no-one being rich, except perhaps [...] Everyone lived in bare studios and apartments faintly like the room depicted ... I still have some drawings of the same period and in the same style. I don't think it had any influence on my future development (as a stage designer) but I do think it is very typical of my outlook at the time, and my group of friends. We went from being extremely arty into becoming worshippers of elegance and 'chic'.

In a later letter the artist added that a private collector owns another painting by him on a tray, in the same style and painted around the same time.

Sandro Chia b.1946

T 03469 **Water Bearer** 1981

Oil and pastel on canvas $81\frac{1}{2} \times 67$ (2065 × 1700)
Inscribed 'Sandro CHIA 1981' on reverse with an outline of a fish
Purchased from Anthony d'Offay Ltd. (Grant-in-Aid) 1982

Exh: *Sandro Chia*, Anthony d'Offay Gallery, December 1981 – January 1982 (no catalogue); *Italian Art Now: An American*

Perspective, Solomon R. Guggenheim Museum, New York, April–June 1982 (17, repr.); *Sandro Chia*, Stedelijk Museum, Amsterdam, April–May 1983 (20, repr. in col.); *New Art at the Tate Gallery*, Tate Gallery, September–October 1983 (repr. in col. p.35); *Sandro Chia*, Bilder 1976–1983. Kestner-Gesellschaft, Hannover, December 1983–January 1984 (31, repr. in col.); *Forty Years of Modern Art 1945–1985*, Tate Gallery, February–April 1986 (works not listed, repr. in col. p.114)

Lit: Anne Seymour, *The Draught of Dr Jekyll, An Essay on the Work of Sandro Chia*, 1981; Carter Ratcliff, 'On Iconography and Some Italians', *Art in America*, LXX, September 1982, pp.152–9 and repr. cover; Jules B. Farber, 'Holland Focus: 2 High C's From Italy', *International Herald Tribune*, 7–8 May 1983, p.7 (repr. in reverse)

Chia's paintings at the time of the 'Water Bearer' were almost all of figures, usually engaged in some startling action. He had several times before depicted men with fish, notably in the etching, 'Self Portrait with Fish', 1978, in which a large fish lies along the bare feet of the standing figure. The artist said in conversation (17 April 1986) that the origin of the 'Water Bearer' was his chance sight of an illustration of a classical sculpture of the same subject. He made several preparatory drawings, including a complete study in coloured chalks (24 × 11", signed and dated 1981, Josh Baer Gallery, New York); the colours in this are less bright, notably lacking the strong red of the fish's tail. The subject, he said, was its title, and both were invented together: since the fish lives in water the man, by association, is a water bearer.

Chia's subjects are often men or boys travelling, and usually also enacting some role. An essay by Anne Seymour based on conversations with the artist was published by the d'Offay and Sperone Galleries for the London exhibition of 1981 which included the 'Water Bearer'. She describes the metaphorical character of these subjects:

This perhaps gives substance to the feeling one has, that the male figures in Chia's pictures are searching for something, or perhaps that they are pilgrims of a sort, for they often seem bound on some unidentified mission. They are, the artist points out, figures born of painting and thus possessed of a strong code of morals and justice, for the rules of painting are strict and the responsibilities heavy. He sees them as having something in common with heroes and with monks, and their moment of action in his painting as being their moment of ecstasy. Embodying thus the moral lessons of painting they become part of man's great pursuit of the absolute and their existence a physical step towards mystery.

The boy carrying a fish recalls the story of Tobias in the Apocrypha (Tobit 6, vv. 2–3), who was told by an angel to take a large fish with him on his journey to find a bride. The story was often painted during the Italian Renaissance, although not in the same way. There is no specific connection to Chia's painting, but he confirmed that the subject was relevant to it, as part of the same family of images.

The painting is signed and dated on the reverse of the canvas with an outline of a fish saying, in a balloon, 'Sandro Chia 1981'. An etching of the subject, in reverse, was published in 1983 (*Sandro Chia Prints 1973–1984*, Metropolitan Museum of Art, New York, repr. p.46).

Geoffrey Clarke b.1924

T03713 **Head** 1952

> Forged iron on integral stone base
> $7\frac{1}{8} \times 3\frac{1}{2} \times 4\frac{3}{4}$ (180 × 90 × 110)
> Not inscribed
> Transferred from the Victoria and Albert Museum 1983
>
> Prov: Purchased from the artist by the Department of Circulation, Victoria and Albert Museum 1953 (Circ. 3–1953)
> Exh: *Annual review of works by artists of gallery Gimpel Fils*, Gimpel Fils, summer 1952 (repr. p.13); travelling exhibitions of the

Department of Circulation, Victoria and Albert Museum

Geoffrey Clarke made a large number of small forged iron sculptures between 1951 and 1955 in a studio near the Royal College of Art, where he had been a pupil. Many of these were 'heads' or 'masks', although they were not usually set into a stone base. In some the head was horizontal, as if a stand with objects on it. This design was also printed, as in the Tate Gallery's aquatint 'Woman and Child', 1953 (P01010).

Robert Clatworthy b.1928

T03714 **Bull** 1956

> Bronze $7\frac{1}{8} \times 14\frac{7}{8} \times 5\frac{7}{8}$ (180 × 380 × 150)
> Not inscribed
> Transferred from the Victoria and Albert Museum 1983
>
> Prov: Purchased from the Hanover Gallery, 1957, by the Department of Circulation, Victoria and Albert Museum (Circ. 636–1957)
> Exh: Robert Clatworthy, Hanover Gallery, September 1957 (4, repr.); travelling exhibitions of Department of Circulation, Victoria and Albert Museum

This and T00265 (purchased in 1959) are both studies for a life size sculpture of a bull, which was exhibited, as a plaster, at the London County Council open air exhibition *Sculpture 1850 and 1950* in Holland Park in the summer of 1957.

The starting point was the sight of a bull in a field next to the artist's studio in Sussex. Clatworthy remembers making about fifteen studies of this size and two larger ones, about 36 ins. across, all made directly in plaster. They were not completed as a sequence, and sometimes altered after others had been begun. About eight were cast in bronze. It is possible that T03714 was the first study with a rectangular piece of plaster, separately cast, added to the shoulder, serving as a formal device to stress the vertical and horizontal beside the twisting body. The white dust in the crevices of the bronze are remnants of the mould, deliberately not removed.

The large sculpture was admired at Holland Park by the architect (for the London County Council) of the Alton Estate in Roehampton (built 1952–8), who commissioned the bronze cast that is there.

Francesco Clemente b.1952

T03551 **Midnight Sun II 1982**

Oil on canvas 79 × 98½ (2010 × 2507)
Not inscribed
Purchased from Anthony d'Offay Ltd.
(Grant-in-Aid) 1983

Exh: *Francesco Clemente, The Midnight Sun,* Anthony d'Offay Gallery, January–February 1983

Lit: Mark Francis, 'Pagan Mysteries', *Francesco Clemente: The Fourteen Stations,* exhibition calatogue, Whitechapel Art Gallery, January 1983; Giancarlo Politi, 'Francesco Clemente', *Flash Art,* No.117, April–May 1984, pp.12–21; *Francesco Clemente, Pastelle 1973–1983,* Munich, 1984; Michael Auping, *Francesco Clemente,* exhibition catalogue, The John and Mable Ringling Museum of Art, Sarasota, Florida, October 1985, repr. in col. pl.18

In January 1983, two major series of paintings by Clemente were exhibited in London. The Whitechapel Art Gallery showed 'The Fourteen Stations' (in fact, a cycle of twelve paintings, supplemented for the exhibition by three other closely related works) painted in New York in late 1981 and early 1982. At the same time, a slightly later series, also consisting of twelve works and also completed in New York, 'The Midnight Sun' I–XII, was exhibited at the Anthony d'Offay Gallery.

For six years before taking a studio in New York late in 1981, Clemente had spent part of each year in Italy and part in Madras in India and had worked with a range of media, his choice being based on the particular cultural context in which he happened to be working but also being influenced by specific imagery (see Mark Francis in 'Pagan Mysteries' cited above, p.37). In New York he began to work on a large scale in oil paint for the first time, finding this medium appropriate to the city; in an interview with Edit deAk (*Interview* XII, pp.69–70) he said of the earlier and more sombre of the two series:

> ... I wanted to get something new going and to do that I needed to do something that I didn't know, and that was to paint large oil paintings. I added the light, the light of the night, which I knew very well from the paintings I lived with when I was a little boy in Naples.

In another interview (*Flash Art,* cited above), he discussed the two New York series first shown in London:

> ..., I've always worked in what I call collections rather then cycles, always on this idea of starting from the beginning and working my way through a technique or a process, say of creating a frame and working inside this frame to try all its possibilities, and even go beyond. I've always wished that these collections would be scattered round the world, and that everyone would see just a fragment. I've always been interested in the idea of a collection on one hand, and in that of a fragment on the other – the idea that the work always refers to another work that can't be seen but exists or will exist ... I drew quite a lot between 1971 and 1978. I did thousands of drawings, very dry and severe, each of which was tied to an idea. From that time on my energy has gone into executing these works that aren't just born like that ...

In a brief conversation with a Tate curator (at the time of his London exhibitions, January 1983) Clemente confirmed that those being shown at the Whitechapel Art Gallery were painted in the winter of 1981/2 and said that he had originally intended the second series ('The Midnight Sun') to be a repeat. However it had developed independently and he had worked on each painting in sequence rather than on several at one time. He referred to a narrative thread running throughout the group but said that this was personal and not important in a wider context.

In a lecture on T03551, given at the Tate Gallery in September 1983, Mark Francis said that despite the Northern inference of the title the work was started on Capri and completed in Clemente's New York studio in October/November 1982. The 12 paintings within the series are only very loosely related to each other, unlike 'The Fourteen Stations' (now coll. Charles and Doris Saatchi) which constitute a more formal set. He also referred to T03551 as a 'summer' painting, contrasting it with 'Station XI' ('the thousand eyes of the night look down on the lovers clinging together', Whitechapel catalogue, p.41, repr. p.27, op.cit) and said it was related to a sequence of drawings reproduced at the end of the catalogue. Mark Francis suggested that there was an iconographic connection with the Hindu legend of the God Indra who was punished for a sexual indiscretion by having his body covered in a thousand marks of the 'yoni' or vagina; to ease his shame, these were eventually changed into eyes.

'Midnight Sun II' shows three figures, one female the other two androgynous, one being blindfold; their bodies are intertwined in what might almost be a swastika configuration, against a honeycomb ground which is 'pierced' by numerous eyes, with, in most cases, clearly painted pupils; however, the eyes are ambiguous images as they also appear to be boats, having in some cases painted sides and all being rigged with lateen sails – suggesting the Mediterranean and giving the impression of both looking through the canvas and resting upon it. Clemente has used a similar image in 'Station X' (repr. *Francesco Clemente: The Fourteen Stations*, p.25) where a female figure holds up a small rounded boat with mast but no sail.

Michael Auping writes (in *Francesco Clemente*, cited above, p.11):

One should not be surprised if it takes time to 'understand' Clemente's pivoting spray of images. The connections and cross references between his autobiographical analysis, mutating self-portraits, erotic fantasies and fears, and odd anatomical expressions combined with his fascination for metaphysical systems (Christianity, alchemy astrology, mythology, the Tarot) all overlayed with his reinterpretation of various artistic sources (ancient, Renaissance, Surrealist, Hindu, Expressionist), create a labyrinthine field that is not easily deciphered by normal codes of logic.

The artist has said of the complex repertoire of images in his paintings:

I'm always interested in building up my paintings as though they were force fields, like those diagrams in the crossword section of the paper where you have to connect the dots. In another sense they are born as ideograms. After the severity of ideograms they go on to a more theatrical state. I've always seen my paintings as ideograms in costume, clothed or disguised. They have the ideogram's capability to express, to make references ... they are a field of relations that makes reference to another field of relations without resorting to direct allusion. At that stage, if I think like that, I have no need for reality. I have to think, then afterwards I need reality to do away with the grotesque. And I need reality as a commonplace. I always have to lead the painting back to a commonplace appearance [in *Flash Art*, op.cit.]

The postures and gestures of the trinity in T03551 suggest some sort of ritualised sexual activity and a connection with Tantric imagery. The eye has numerous traditional symbolic associations – the all seeing eye of God, the sun, the eyes of the sky gods (or stars), the oval female sign surrounding the male circle (suggesting androgyny), and the third eye of Shiva, or wisdom, in Hindu philosophy. Ships, too, may be interpreted as representing the female principle and Fortune. The goddess of antiquity is associated with ships; as mistress of the sea, she is sometimes depicted blindfold and holding a ship or in a ship (see the figure on the left in T03551 and the central figure in 'Station X').

The arrangement of the figures suggests a spoked wheel. The eye motif also relates to Clemente's interest in depicting the orifices of the body, as discussed by Michael Auping (op.cit.) and Francesco Pellizzi (p.153 in the same catalogue). The following works illustrated in the catalogue also relate to T03551: pl.28, 'Everything I Know', 1983 – a pastel drawing which includes a reclining figure whose body is covered in blue eyes; pl.63, 'Midnight Sun III'; pl.29, 'Midnight Sun IV'; pl.30, 'Midnight Sun V'. In addition, the ship/eye motif appears between plates 24 and 25.

This entry has been approved by the artist.

Prunella Clough b.1919

T03450 **Yellow Mesh** 1981

Oil on canvas 48 × 75¼ (1227 × 1912)
Inscribed '↑Clough' on reverse
Purchased from the New Art Centre
(Knapping Fund) 1982

See entry on T03451. 'Yellow Mesh' is painted on the reverse of a primed canvas, and a different painting, evidently abandoned by the artist, is on the other side.

T03451 **Wire and Demolition** 1982

Oil on canvas 60 × 65¾ (1520 × 1670)
Inscribed '↑Clough' on reverse

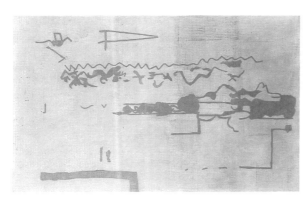

T 03450

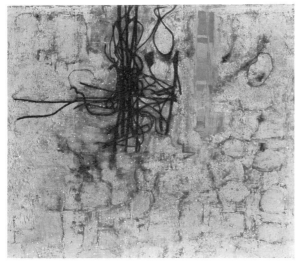

T 03451

'Yellow Mesh' includes particles of dust (identified by the artist as either ash or silver sand) mixed with the paint.

The canvas is partly painted on the reverse.

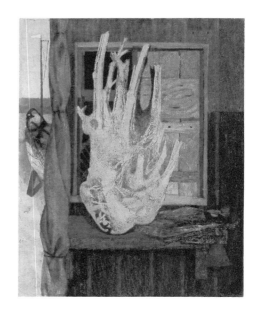

Purchased from the artist (Grant-in-Aid) 1982

Exh: *Prunella Clough, New Paintings, 1979–82*, Warwick Arts Trust, April–May 1982 (62, repr.); *Prunella Clough*, Fitzwilliam Museum, Cambridge, May–July 1982 (no catalogue)

The artist's interview (1982) with Bryan Robertson was printed as the introduction to the Warwick Arts Trust catalogue. In this she describes her work in terms of urban landscape, particularly the light industrial estates of London. Subjects are not sketched on the spot, and any reference to real places is from memory. Four of the artist's photographs of such areas, of gates, a door and a wall, were published in this catalogue, not for any direct connection with particular paintings, but as a demonstration of a way of looking at such scenes in the terms of her abstract paintings.

The titles of Clough's paintings of 1980–1 often refer to gates, fences, wire mesh and wire. The surface of

T 03810   The White Root 1946

Oil on board $19\frac{3}{4} \times 16$ (505 × 395)
Inscribed 'Clough' and illegible date b.r. and on reverse '↑' and 'Mr Bowas....' (illegible)
Purchased from Fischer Fine Art Ltd. (Grant-in-Aid) 1982

Prov: Purchased from the artist by Fischer Fine Art Ltd.

Exh: *Recent Paintings by Prunella Clough and Walter H. Nessler*, The Leger Galleries, March-April 1947 (8); *The British Neo-Romantics 1935–1950*, Fischer Fine Art, July-August 1983, National Museum of Wales, Cardiff, August–September 1983 (102)

Prunella Clough returned to painting in 1945, having left art school immediately before the war, and the earliest works in her retrospective exhibition at the Whitechapel Art Gallery in 1960 were of this date. She visited the Suffolk coast from her home in London, and many of her paintings of these years have coastal subjects. The artist has confirmed that these scenes were neither discovered nor arranged in this way, but were deliberate reconstructions.

Sir William Coldstream b.1908

T 03704   Seated Nude 1951–2

Oil on canvas 42 × 27⅞ (1067 × 707)
Inscribed 'William Coldstream. Painted
for Adrian Stokes' on canvas turnover, top
centre
Purchased from Mrs Ann Stokes Angus
(Grant-in-Aid) 1983

Prov: Adrian Stokes (purchased from the artist
between 1952 and 1954); Mrs Ann Stokes
(later Mrs Ann Stokes Angus)

Exh: *Critic's Choice*, Arthur Tooth & Sons Ltd.,
July 1958 (2, repr. as 'Portrait of a model');
William Coldstream, AC tour, South
London Art Gallery, April–May 1962,
The University, Leeds, June 1962, City
Art Gallery, Bristol, July 1962, Glynn
Vivian Art Gallery, Swansea, August 1962,
Southampton Art Gallery, September
1962, City Museum and Art Gallery,
Birmingham, September–October 1962
(50, repr.); *From Life*, Camden Arts
Centre, January 1968 (31, repr. as 'Sitting
Woman'); *Eight figurative painters*, Yale
Center for British Art, New Haven,
Connecticut, October 1981–January 1982,
Santa Barbara Museum of Art, Santa
Barbara, California, January–March 1982
(24, repr.)

Lit: Alan Clutton-Brock, 'Round the London
Galleries', *The Listener*, LX, 10 July 1958,
pp.60–1 repr.; Claude Rogers, 'William
Coldstream, Painter', *The Studio*,

CLXIII, May 1962, pp.166–71 repr. in col.
as 'Seated Nude Miss Hoyer'

The following entry is based on conversations held with
the artist on 16 April, 12 May and 14 May 1986 and on
information supplied by Peter Rumley and Ann Stokes
Angus. It has been approved by the artist.

'Seated Nude' was painted in the artist's studio at the
Slade School of Fine Art between autumn 1951 and
summer 1952. Coldstream recalls that not less than
thirty sittings were required, each sitting lasting about
two hours. The artist has stated that, in painting from
the model, it was his occasional practice to make preliminary pencil sketches but these would not either be
squared up onto the canvas or used for reference while
actually painting. He does not recall making any preliminary studies for 'Seated Nude'. It was the first
painting to be completed following his appointment
as Slade Professor in 1949 and the first nude which
Coldstream had undertaken since 'Standing Nude'
1938, painted in the studios of the School of Drawing
and Painting in the original location at Fitzroy Street.

The work was a result of a commission from the
artist's friend, Adrian Stokes (1902–73), who had
known Coldstream since 1937. Ann Stokes Angus has
stated that her late husband 'had an unbounded belief
[in] and admiration for his friend'. Stokes was concerned that Coldstream, since his appointment as Professor, was spending too much time on administrative
matters at the Slade and was not painting. Coldstream
has confirmed that he was indeed deeply involved with
his responsibilities at the Slade. This is suggested further by the fact that progress had slowed on portraits
of Bernard Hallward, Headmaster of Clifton College,
Bristol, and Lord Jowitt, First Earl of Stevenage, for
the Middle Temple, although Coldstream attributes
this also to difficulty in obtaining frequent and regular
sittings. The commission was designed to redress the
balance by once more involving him in 'serious painting'. Stokes also commissioned a portrait of Dr Melanie
Klein, the eminent child psychoanalyst, which Coldstream worked on at the same time as the 'Seated Nude'.
This portrait was unfinished and is now lost.

When the Tate's picture was reproduced in Claude
Rogers's article of 1962 (loc.cit.) it was incorrectly titled
'Seated Nude Miss Hoyer'. Miss Hoyer was in fact the
model for Coldstream's 'Seated Nude' 1960 (repr. *Eight
figurative painters*, op.cit., 27), which like his 'Seated
Nude' 1971–3 (repr. *Apollo*, CIV, November 1976,
fig.5, p.412) echoes the pose of the model in the Tate's
picture. The model for the Tate's picture was a Miss
Mond, whom Coldstream believes to have been possibly
a Slade model. This is the only time he painted her. Her
pose was determined more by concern for the model's
comfort and the ease with which it could be recreated
over a long period of sittings than by any overriding

aesthetic aim. This embodies Coldstream's idea of 'straight painting' which seeks to achieve an accurate transcription of what is seen and eschews striving for particular artistic effects. The artist's position in relation to the model was similarly influenced by practical considerations. Coldstream has described how he set up the easel 8 or 9 feet away from and to the right of the model and with the light striking the surface of the canvas from the left so that he did not stand in his own light. The backdrop to the painting is a studio screen which Coldstream frequently used. Here it is treated in a very generalised and painterly manner and contrasts with the carefully observed figure. The screen was also used to reposition the model exactly for each sitting by reference to small coloured markers on its surface. As is his usual practice the artist permitted himself the use of a single brush only: a size 9 Winsor and Newton sable.

Coldstream has observed that 'once I start painting I am occupied mainly with putting things in the right place' (William Coldstream, 'How I Paint', *The Listener*, XVIII, no.453, 15 September 1937, p.572). 'Seated Nude' exemplifies this aim. Characteristically the surface of the model's skin exhibits the small coloured dots which are the result of a long and painstaking process of measuring and relating the points on the body using plumbline and brush-handle. Although Claude Rogers commented on this work that it 'is not exactly the nakedness of a particular young girl which the method used might reasonably lead one to expect' (William Coldstream Painter', op.cit.), Coldstream's own estimation of it is that it is 'very literal'.

Constant b.1920

T 03705 Après Nous la Liberté 1949

Oil on canvas 55 × 42 (1395 × 1066)
Inscribed 'Constant/1949' centre and 'Constant 57 rue Pigalle 1x' on stretcher
Purchased from Galerie van de Loo, Munich (Grant-in-Aid) 1983

Exh: *Westkunst: Zeitgenössische Kunst seit 1939*, Museen der Stadt Köln, Cologne, May–August 1981 (365, repr.); *COBRA 1948–51*, Kunstverein Hamburg, September–November 1982 (30, repr. in col. p.87)

James Cowie 1886–1956

T 03549 An Outdoor School of Painting 1938–41

Oil on canvas 34 × 65 (864 × 1651)
Inscribed 'J.Cowie' b.r.
Purchased from Dr Barbara Cowie (Grant-in-Aid) 1983

Exh: *James Cowie: the Artist at Work*, Scottish Arts Council, Collins Exhibition Hall, University of Strathclyde, Glasgow, April–May 1981 and tour to Dumfries, Inverness, Edinburgh, Stromness, Aberdeen and London (Fine Art Society), January–February 1982 (28)

Lit: Richard Calvocoressi, *James Cowie*, Edinburgh 1979, p.15 (repr. pl.34)

Stephen Cox b.1946

T 03794 Gethsemane 1982

Relief of 15 carved pieces of peperino stone, overall size 118 × 236 × 3½ (2297 × 5994 × 90)
Not inscribed

Purchased from Nigel Greenwood Inc.
Ltd. (Grant-in-Aid) 1983

Exh: *Stephen Cox*, Galleria La Salita, Rome,
May–June 1982 (not numbered); *Aperto
82*, XL Biennale Venice, June-September
1982 (not numbered, repr.); *New Art at
the Tate Gallery*, Tate Gallery,
September–October 1983 (not numbered,
repr.); *Forty Years of Modern Art 1945–
1985*, Tate Gallery, February–April 1986
(not numbered)

Lit: Filiberto Mena, 'La Biennale Arti Visive
'82: Arte Come Arte La Persisteriza
dell'Opera', *Harpers Gran Bazaar*,
September–October 1982 (Italian
edition); *The Tate Gallery Illustrated
Biennial Report 1982–84*, repr. p.64; R.J.
Rees, Sarah Kent, Andrea Schlieker,
*Stephen Cox, 'We Must Always Turn
South' Sculpture 1977–85*, exhibition
catalogue, Arnolfini, Bristol, 1985, pp.8,
33–5, 44, repr. in col.; Lewis Biggs,
'Stephen Cox', *The British Show*,
exhibition catalogue, British Council tour
of Australia, 1985, pp.33–6, repr. p.36;
Also repr: 'Venice: Artventure Alla
Biennale', *Domus*, September 1982
(Italian edition), p.90 in col.; *Stephen Cox*,
exhibition catalogue, San Giovanni
Valdarno, 1984

Stephen Cox first worked in Italy in 1979 and two years
later he returned to embark on a grand tour of centres
of Italian stone production, as referred to in Giorgio
Vasari's *parte teorica* (an introductory volume to the
complete text of *The Lives of The Artists*, 1568) which
deals with methods and materials. Also during this
period, he was reading Adrian Stokes, *Critical Writings
1930–7*, London, 1978.

T 03794 was made between December 1981 and
March 1982, at the American Academy in Rome where
the artist had taken a studio to work for the La Salita
exhibition. The first of a series of 'broken reliefs',
Gethsemane was made of peperino stone, a volcanic
material from Viterbo, a medieval city built of this stone
on Etruscan foundations. The material came from the
quarry of 'Anselmi Company' in Viterbo, for whom the
artist has continued to work. The artist worked directly
on the stone, having first executed a number of loose
drawings of a complete image, broken by dotted lines.
Individual elements, which the artist referred to as
'offshoots', were exhibited at Galleria La Salita in 1982.

The name 'Gethsemane' comes from the New Testament where in St Luke (22:39) it is referred to as 'the
mount of olives'. St Mark (14:32) and St Matthew
(26:36) both make direct reference to it. In an interview
with the compiler (23 July 1986) the artist commented:

Vasari *On Technique* mentions peperino and
although I had intended to work in 'travertino', I
discovered that peperino formed the foundations of
much Roman architecture. This was even better
because of its association with the antique. It was
one of the most productive periods I have had in
Italy. Gethsemane represented the jelling of lots of
ideas, particularly those I had been working on in
'Soglia' (threshold) (1981, private collection). I had
moved away from the 'minimal' work of the leaning
slabs, to the lunette and circular shapes as in 'Tondo:
We must Aways Turn South' (1981, Tate Gallery)
where you have a perspective projection of the circle,
which becomes an oval within the classical tondo
shape. In 'Soglia' you can see within the semicircular archway on the vertical wall, the half elipse,
which is the continuation of the foreshortened semicircular step which, it mirrors, which exists in true
space. I used this idea in 'Gethsemane' but did not
need the architectural step as there already existed
a threshold into the illusionistic space. I retained
the archway.

I was pushing further, populating the abstract
space of 'Soglia' with landscape. At the time I was
looking at Italian landscapes with olive groves,
making a sculpture featuring landscape seemed
unusual, while the green stone seemed reminiscent
of aspects of aridity in southern Italy.

Peperino is cut by using a toothless blade with
sand abrasive which oxidises the metal of the blade
and creates a discolouration of the stone. Carving
into this exposes a lighter under surface which
emphasises the drawing in the sculpture.

At this time there was a exhibition of the young
David in Rome at the Villa di Medici – I realised
the power of titles or narrative reference. Today our
vocabulary of narrative is limited, possibly only
relative to the New Testament. The use of the
narrative added another dimension. The use of
'Gethsemane' had a highly charged significance on

top of the classical, meditative, stillness. I was experimenting in how strongly a reference could be projected. My point was proved when one article referred to it as 'the wounded stone of Cox' (Fabrizio d'Amico, 'La pietra ferita di Cox', *La Repubblica*, Rome, February 1982). This referred also to the central stone where there is a red iron oxide stain.

The fragmentation in 'Gethsemane' is formed by solid, irregularly shaped elements fixed to a wall, which create irregularly shaped voids held within the orderly boundaries of the semi-circle. Each disparate element is a self-contained unit yet is an intrinsic part of the whole, creating 'a matrix of perspective'. While working on 'Gethsemane' the artist was consciously looking at his surroundings – the classical ruins and the dispersed remnants of Ancient Rome.

Stephen Cox's work is gallery-orientated and although works have been placed outside they are visualised for interior settings, particularly the contemporary context of the art gallery.

Tony Cragg b.1949

T 03791   **Axehead** 1982

Wood and mixed media, 48 elements, overall dimensions approximately $45 \times 154\frac{3}{4} \times 193$ ($1092 \times 3931 \times 4902$) Not inscribed
Purchased from Lisson Gallery (Grant-in-Aid) 1983

Exh: *Documenta 7*, Kassel, June–September 1982 (not numbered, as part of 'Still Life (Axehead-Boat-House)'); *Forty Years of Modern Art*, Tate Gallery, February–April 1986 (not in catalogue)

Lit: *Tony Cragg's Axehead*, Tate New Art/The Artist's View, 1984 (repr. on cover). *Also repr*: *Tony Cragg*, exhibition catalogue, Kunsthalle, Bern, 1983, p.78

Tony Cragg's 'Axehead' was first assembled at his studio in Wuppertal, Germany. It was made from mainly wooden furniture, small objects and scrap material that he had previously collected.

On the subject of 'Axehead', in a taped interview with the compiler of this entry in 1984, Cragg stated the following about his work process:

I have a store of objects already in my studio. Sometimes by just looking at one, or several that have been in the studio for a long time, I have a certain idea about what I want to make. At times it is something about the nature of the object, at others it's the material the objects are made from. Then there are times when I just have to go out and in the process of looking suddenly something occurs to me. I actually believe in useless activities. I mean, not aiming to make a work, just walking and looking for something and seeing whether it starts to make an interesting association; whether there is something that I can learn from that. I have to learn about something before I can do anything. I have to learn about the material or an object. There isn't one way or another. Both possibilities are there. Sometimes I just see an image, or an event happens, or a person says something. So there are different ways of starting. At times I know exactly what I want to make, at others I have no idea at all.

In Germany, exactly where I live, there is a very interesting combination of landscape and town. There are lots of industrial zones, so, I look through these areas, on wasteland (even on a factory site, if people will let me), or around river banks or roadsides, anywhere I will find things. It is not a religion that I should actually find the objects, though. If something is missing and I need it, then I will buy it. Finding things is a very useful way for me to start work because objects do provide very complicated associations. It's a sort of plastic process in a way. You have the chance of forming your ideas as you go along. It also offers a variety which you could not possibly sit down and write out like an order book or a shopping list. It's a very complicated process. Objects and ideas are suggested to me from the world I encounter. It is a very different kind of challenge to walk into a store. I have just made a couple of works and bought all the things. It is an incredible challenge to say 'Right I am going to buy all I need in this store.' Phenomenally difficult.

I always describe the parameters of my work in a very loose way. I think there are three aspects which are always working in a triangular relationship. There is the material, there is the object and there is the image. They are three very distinct aspects. Sometimes they are all equally dominant, at others one is much stronger than the other. I recently made a series of self-portraits which use the dimensions of myself. 'Britain seen from the North' is one of that genre. I just had an image and I really wanted to see it. On other occasions the process is a more complicated playing with forms and objects in the studio. It can be very exhausting just to change things continually; to build objects up, take them down again, or to dismantle until I arrive at a formal solution to the work.

The other kind of laying out, the filling in of a flat image on the wall with plastic pieces, I tend not to think about very much. I just stick things up very quickly. It is just a method of covering a surface as fast as I can, largely avoiding consideration of formal relations between one object's parts and another. The parts become homogenous rather then specific.

There are works where the materials are stacked up or they are piled upon each other or pushed up against each other. In the type of making used in 'Britain seen from the North' and 'Axehead' it is physically quite different. I want to retain a balance between an overall form of an image and the individual parts of that image. As soon as the objects overlap you start to get a very different perceptual understanding of the work. It looks very, very different. It is something which hasn't interested me so far.

It's the abuse, or lack of understanding, of how art can be useful rather than the uselessness that I am making reference to. Images and objects can actually provide insight into a person's life, into the way things function, into what it is to be a particular human being. I think the attitude that art objects should be things that basically give pleasure is a less interesting attitude. You see one prequalification for me to be interested in making a work is that it has to be visually interesting. After that other ways of thinking connected with the work's content do make complicated connections and implications but not in the sense of telling stories. One can use an object or an image in the way philosophy has used words to describe things, to express ideas. I think that is a function of art. When people feel discomfort, even aggression towards 'Axehead' perhaps they should look at it carefully, consider it, and notice the number of industrial techniques used to make those objects. Just note the great variety of woods there, and think about man's relationship to certain materials such as wood and stone, and to elements like fire and water. These relationships are very complicated.

It isn't just a physical relationship, it is also metaphysical. That means it has a depth and richness, a wealth of cultural connections and it started early in the evolutionary process for us. We now surround ourselves with so many new materials, plastic materials.

There isn't a literal content in this work I think. The form of the 'Axehead' has been decided not for an allegorical reason, but for a formal reason. It is the form that enabled me to make the work and vice versa and for me that is the validity of it. Although it is interesting to see what relations do come out of it, I am not trying to make them seem violent or to make a theatrical statement.

John Craxton b.1922

T03836 Dreamer in Landscape 1942

Black ink and white chalk on paper laid on board 21⅝ × 30 (548 × 762)
Inscribed '– Craxton 42 –' on lower edge near centre
Purchased from the artist through Christoper Hull (Grant-in-Aid) 1984

Exh: *John Craxton paintings and drawings 1941–1966*, Whitechapel Art Gallery, January–February 1967 (99, as 'Dreamer in a Landscape'); *British Drawings 1939–49*, Scottish National Gallery of Modern Art, Edinburgh, June 1969 (no catalogue); *John Craxton*, Hamet Gallery, September–October 1971 (18, repr. on cover); *John Craxton Drawing and Painting 1942–1972*, MacRobert Centre Art Gallery, University of Stirling, February 1972 (20); *Decade 40's*, AC tour, Whitechapel Art Gallery, November 1972, City Art Gallery, Southampton, December 1972–January 1973, Museum and Art Gallery, Carlisle, January–February 1973, Durham Light Infantry Museum and Arts Centre, Durham, February–March 1973,

City Art Gallery, Manchester, March–
April 1973, City Art Gallery, Bradford,
April–May 1973, Museum and Art
Gallery, Aberdeen, May–June 1973 (79,
as 'Dreamer in a Landscape'); *The British
Neo-Romantics 1935–1950*, Fischer Fine
Art, July–August 1983, National Museum
of Wales, Cardiff, August–September
1983 (63, as 'Dreamer in a Landscape',
detail repr.).
Also repr.: *Horizon*, v, March 1942, p.189,
as 1941; in col. in William Feaver,
'Wartime Romances', *The Sunday Times
Colour Magazine*, 20 May 1973, pp.74–85
(as 'Dreamer in a Landscape', repr. p.76)

In June 1986 Craxton told the Gallery that the correct
title of this work is as given here, without the indefinite
article.

In answer to a question from Bryan Robertson, in
'Dialogue with the Artist' in the catalogue of his
Whitechapel retrospective in 1967, Craxton explained
that:

In my formative years, travel was restricted because
of the war. When I began to paint and draw, even
at preparatory school, landscape was my first
preoccupation as well as figures in landscapes. Being
a Londoner, I needed landscape; at any rate there
was always a strong pull towards nature as a contrast
to town life and as a source of refreshment.

In an interview with Gerard Hastings published in
the catalogue of *John Craxton, An Exhibition of Paintings and Drawings 1980–1985*, Christopher Hull
Gallery, June–July 1985, pp.21–3, Craxton recounted
that Peter Watson (on whom see the entry on Craxton
T03838, below):

showed me proofs of some Palmer illustrations to be
published in Horizon Magazine. They were the first
Palmers I ever saw, and were not very good proofs
actually, but they were all I needed. And I had not
even heard of Palmer before that ... I think you have
to look at what I did, to see the influence; Palmer
took the essence of something and paraphrased it so
that one had a poetic image of it. It was a distillation
of nature, and I suppose that I wanted that clarity of
purpose. You might say that my work is 'escapist'
art and, somehow, it became an antidote to the war
in the same way that Palmer's was an antidote to his
times: he felt an impulse to draw the way he did
despite the contemporary scene.

In a letter to the compiler postmarked 26 April 1986,
Craxton wrote of 'Dreamer in Landscape':

I can't see much of Palmer in this work; it's very
much a winter scene in feeling touched with

childhood memories of North Wales but again it
would never have looked like it is without having
seen two Palmers in Horizon 'Valley Thick with
Corn' and 'Early Morning'. I'm sure too, that seeing
Picasso's Minotauromachy etching [1935] in Peter
Watson's flat plus a book on Marcantonio
[Raimondi, Italian engraver of Raphael and others,
c.1480–c.1534] helped.

The two works by Palmer, both of 1825 and both in
the collection of the Ashmolean Museum, Oxford, were
reproduced in *Horizon*, iv, November 1941, between
pp.318 and 319.
In the same letter Craxton also explained that if there
were preparatory drawings for 'Dreamer in Landscape'
they would probably have been very fleeting in character.

I very rarely *do* drawings or preparatory works. I
know that the dreamer was done with the idea in my
head quite clearly before I started. I was working in
a minute and cluttered room in Abbey Road
Mansions (our house had been bombed). A German
refugee boy staying with us posed for the figure. At
the time I had a deep nostalgia for mountains, rocks,
and such places. I probably used the convenient
house plants on my window sill as vegetation. The
moon trees are inspired by the strange pollarded
trees of St John's Wood that rose up behind the
garden walls gesticulating at the sky.

'Dreamer in Landscape' is close in both imagery and
feeling to two other works by Craxton of the same
period and dimensions, 'Poet in Landscape' 1941 and
'Poet and Birdcatcher in Landscape' 1942 (both reproduced in Geoffrey Grigson, *John Craxton Paintings and
Drawings*, 1948, plates 3 and 4). Prominent in all three
works is a figure with eyes lowered or almost closed,
an abundance of plant forms, and the same kind of
distinctive twisting and pointed tree branches. All three
works include a crescent moon. In the 1985 interview
quoted from above, Craxton also stated:

I suppose that the figures in some early landscapes
are myself. Between 1941 and 1945, before I went
to Greece, I drew and occasionally painted many
pictures of landscapes with shepherds or poets as
single figures. The landscapes were entirely
imaginary; the shepherds were also invented – I had
never seen a shepherd – but in addition to being
projections of myself they derived from Blake and
Palmer. They were my means of escape and a sort of
self-protection. A shepherd is a lone figure, and so
is a poet. I wanted to safeguard a world of private
mystery, and I was drawn to the idea of bucolic calm
as a kind of refuge.

T 03837　**Dark Landscape** 1944–5

Oil on board $21\frac{1}{2} \times 27\frac{3}{4}$ (546 × 705)
Inscribed 'Craxton '44' b.r.
Purchased from the artist through
Christopher Hull (Grant-in-Aid) 1984
Exh:　*John Craxton*, St George's Gallery,
summer 1945 (almost certainly in parts of
May and/or June; no catalogue); *John
Craxton paintings and drawings 1941–
1966*, Whitechapel Art Gallery, January–
February 1967 (13, dated 1945 but repr.
as 1944–45)
Repr:　In col. in Peter Watson, 'Note sur deux
peintres anglais', *La Littérature anglaise
depuis la Guerre: Enquête* 1945, pp.24–7
(special French-language issue of *Horizon*
magazine, published from London by
'Editions Horizon', July 1945), repr. opp.
p.25, dated 1945; in col. in Geoffrey
Grigson, *John Craxton Paintings and
Drawings* 1948, plate 2.

Craxton's own photographic record dates this work
autumn 1944–spring 1945 and he writes (letter, 3 May
1984):

The correct date for 'Dark Landscape' is 1944–45.
It's most probable that I felt it was finished in 1944,
but I continued to work on it into 1945 without
bothering to add the extra date. I remember Peter
Watson urging me to hurry up and deliver it to the
block makers.

In a letter to the compiler postmarked 26 April 1986,
Craxton wrote:

Preparatory drawings for 'Dark Landscape' as far as
I know don't exist. The place that is at the back of
it existed and that is the Mill, Alderholt [Dorset],
[near] Fordingbridge [Hampshire] – the footbridge
over the stream and the main bridge etc. I can't

explain the floppy hat! nor the dead tree shaped like
a moon cow's horns coming out of the bush nor the
young and alive tree coming out of another. If the
painting has mystery and enigma then that is what I
wanted it to have. Incidentally at that time Lucian
[Freud] and I were allowed to attend the Surrealist
dinners once a week at the Casa Pepé with Mesens,
Robert Melville and all. Lucian painted a marvellous
self portrait of himself holding a feather at about the
same time which may have a faint connection with
'Dark Landscape'.

The Freud painting is 'Man with a Feather (Self Portrait)' 1943 (oil on canvas 30 × 20 inches, repr. Lawrence Gowing, *Lucian Freud* 1982, p.18). There is a close
connection between 'Dark Landscape' and Craxton's
'Reaper with a Mushroom' 1944–5 (conté crayon on
blue paper, 17 × 24 inches, repr. in catalogue of Craxton's 1967 Whitechapel Gallery retrospective, cited
above). In both works a single figure wearing a hat with
a wide, curved brim stands in front of a tree, the trunk
of which culminates at the top in a spike, and extends
a mushroom in one hand. Like 'Dark Landscape', the
drawing 'Painter's Landscape' 1944 (repr. in catalogue
of same Whitechapel exhibition) gives prominence to a
crescent moon (the form of which is echoed by the sickle
held by the reaper in 'Reaper with a Mushroom'), and
also to spiked trees. The horned form in the centre of
'Dark Landscape' is echoed by the horns of the bull
which enters at the left of the picture in 'Painter's
Landscape' (in the middle distance of 'Reaper with a
Mushroom' prances a fierce animal of indeterminate
species). Other works reproduced in 1945 in the same
article as 'Dark Landscape' were Craxton's 'Welsh
Farmyard' 1944, in which the twin prongs of the
implement held by the single figure echo the horns
in 'Dark Landscape'; Graham Sutherland's 'Horned
Forms' 1944 (Tate Gallery, T 00834); and Sutherland's
'The Intruding Bull' 1944. In his interview with Gerard
Hastings in the catalogue of *John Craxton, An Exhibition
of Paintings and Drawings 1908–1985*, Christopher Hull
Gallery, June–July 1985, Craxton stated:

Peter Watson introduced me to Sutherland, whom I
already admired. When he saw my picture 'Poet in
Landscape' (1941) in Watson's flat he said 'I wish I
had been able to paint something like that when I
was your age'. I went to Pembrokeshire with him for
the first time in 1943 and learnt a lot.

In *The Poet's Eye* 1944, an anthology chosen by
Geoffrey Grigson with sixteen lithographs by Craxton,
the images facing pp.38 and 42 are reminiscent in several
ways of 'Dark Landscape'. Both are printed in various
blues and black, as is the image facing p.31, which also
includes a crescent moon in white. Craxton points out
(letter postmarked 16 June 1986) that the image facing

p.102, which is printed in greens and black, 'is the same landscape from a different view over the watermeadows' and that the black and white image on p.9, which relates to the right hand form in T03837, 'is growling bush with sapling'.

T03838   Pastoral for P.W. 1948

Oil on canvas 78½ × 103⅜ (2045 × 2626)
Inscribed 'to-P-W. Craxton 48' b.l. in oval.
Purchased from the artist through Christopher Hull (Grant-in-Aid) 1984

Exh: *Work from 1947 to 1949 by John Craxton*, The London Gallery, June–July 1949 (1, as 'Pastoral, to P.W.'); *John Craxton paintings and drawings 1941–1966*, Whitechapel Art Gallery, January–February 1967 (34, as 'Pastoral' and with incorrect dimensions); *John Craxton Drawing and Painting 1942–1972*, MacRobert Centre Art Gallery, University of Stirling, February 1972 (9, as 'Pastoral'); *Decade 40's*, AC tour, Whitechapel Art Gallery, November 1972, City Art Gallery, Southampton, December 1972–January 1973, Museum and Art Gallery, Carlisle, January–February 1973, Durham Light Infantry Museum and Arts Centre, Durham, February–March 1973, City Art Gallery, Manchester, March–April 1973, City Art Gallery, Bradford, April–May 1973, Museum and Art Gallery, Aberdeen, May–June 1973 (82, as 'Pastoral')

Lit: [Robert Melville], 'Exhibitions: Current and Recent', in 'Marginalia', *The Architectural Review*, CVI, August 1949,

pp.129–30 (repr. fig.1, p.130, as 'Pastoral, to P.W.')
Also repr.: In col. in Geoffrey Grigson, *John Craxton Paintings and Drawings* 1948, plate 1, as 'Pastoral' (incorrect dimensions given)

In a letter to the Tate Gallery of March 1984, the artist wrote:

I painted 'Pastoral' as a homage to Peter Watson, its title was originally 'Pastoral for P.W.' ... Peter took the dedication off the title when it was reproduced in the Horizon monograph [by Grigson, cited above] as he had preferred to keep a low profile. I would like to have the correct title put back if possible.

Victor William Watson (1908–56), known as Peter, was a co-founder both of the magazine *Horizon* (in 1939, first issue published January 1940) and of the Institute of Contemporary Arts (in 1948). His obituary in *The Times*, 5 May 1956, recorded that:

he was ... an animator who lent his encouragement and gave his support wherever he saw genius or talent. He was one of those very rare people whose faith is in the creative genius of others. [He was] one of the very few people who bring to work and to other people the passion of personal choice – and have the time and means endlessly to encourage artists.

Adam magazine, nos.385–90, 1974–5 (a single issue) contains articles on Peter Watson by Alan Pryce-Jones, Roland Penrose, Priaulx Rainier, Michael Wishart and David Mellor, on pp.91–101.

In a letter postmarked 16 June 1986 Craxton recalled:

My friendship with Peter Watson really began in 1941. Due to the war he had been forced to leave his flat in Paris with its collection of paintings, and had installed himself in a flat in 10 Palace Gate, London. I remember when I called there Colquhoun and MacBryde were temporarily in residence, on the walls were 'Entrance to a Lane' and 'Gorse on a Sea Wall' by Sutherland, a marvellous Christopher Wood, Picasso's 'Minotauromachy' to name but a few. Lucian and I were often there, going through old Cahiers d'Art, Minotaur, and Verve. Peter's records were also a revelation to me. I could listen to Stravinsky, Berg, Bartok, Hindemith and Jean Francaix for the first time. In 1942 he encouraged me to find a studio and send him the bill. Lucian joined me in sharing a maisonette in St. Johns Wood.

In a letter to the compiler postmarked 26 April 1986, Craxton stated:

It's sad that so few people know today of the extraordinary influence Peter Watson had on the

artistic life in England from 1940 till his death ...
Just to list his interests doesn't really do him justice,
because he was above all a marvellously intelligent
friend to so many poets, sculptors, musicians,
writers, painters etc. He was certainly the most
perceptive 'man of taste' I've ever known, with an
extraordinary 'nose'. His encouragement for the arts
was not only verbal but practical. Personal
encouragement is quite different from that doled out
by committees and such like ... At the time he was
alive he and Roland Penrose shone out like beacons.

A major theme of 'Pastoral for P.W.' is Craxton's
response to Greece, which he first visited in 1946, and
where he eventually settled and still lives. In answer to
a question from Bryan Robertson in 'Dialogue with
the Artist' in the catalogue of his exhibition at the
Whitechapel Art Gallery in 1967, Craxton recounted
that:

I went to St David's Head, in Pembrokeshire, with
Peter Watson and Graham Sutherland, in 1943.
There were cloudless days and the land was reduced
to basic elements of life; rocks, fig trees, gorse, the
nearness of sea on all sides, a brilliantly clear light.
Everything was stripped away – all the verbiage, that
is – to the essential sources of existence. Sitting and
talking there one day with Peter Watson, I was told
that the landscape was like Greece, and this was
possibly the crystallisation of my desire to travel to
Greece ... In 1946, through a fortuitously happy
series of coincidences, I was invited to go to Greece
by Peter Norton [Lady Norton, on whom see below].
I don't consider that there is any radical break
between what I was painting before visiting Greece
and work done subsequently: I had always been
drawn towards certain features of landscape, and a
human identity in it, an inhabited landscape if you
like, which were like tokens for Greece. But I only
understood this after I arrived in Greece. At the
back of all this is the fact that through the war years
I was very conscious of Poussin, as well as the North
African journal of Delacroix, and bearing in mind
my concern for people living in a landscape, and the
obvious need for sun and light after the war years, I
also wanted to reorientate myself and get away from
the possible limitations of the English tradition – at
any rate, the circumscribed area as it was during the
war years. Above all I wanted to get direct first-hand
experience of what I knew I needed from life, and a
real place and people, rather than through art. I felt
that only a drastic uprooting would give me the
stimulus I needed.
    Greece was more than everything that I had
imagined and far more than I had expected. As my
first contact with the Mediterranean and the
discovery of the actions of light and shadow, the way

the light behaves, the arrival in Greece was
astonishing. In all other ways, it seemed like a
homecoming. Perhaps the other central discovery
though, was the salutary one, for a painter, that life
is more important than art.

At the time 'Pastoral for P.W.' was painted, Peter Watson's flat was small. 'He was at one moment very serious
about buying Matisse's "Red Studio" in 1943 which he
could have bought for £700 from the Redfern. I was
going to house it in my studio till Peter found space for
it' (letter of April 1986). 'Pastoral for P.W.' is larger
than Matisse's 'Red Studio'. Craxton records about it
that:

the idea I had of doing it as a gift for Peter Watson
was a sly joke as he lived in a minute flat choc full
of wonderful books, paintings, furniture, sculpture,
etc., hardly room to swing a mouse. No-one wanted
large paintings so it was an act of Joie de Vivre ['a
gesture against confined space' (letter, March
1984)]. I bought the largest piece of canvas available
and nailed it to the largest wall of my room [in
London] ... [It] was done with the actual size of the
canvas dictating the composition from the start. I
have somewhere a very slight sketch for it all but it's
an absurd scribble (ibid.).

While 'Pastoral for P.W.' was in progress, Felix Man
took a photograph of Craxton standing in front of it
(repr. as frontispiece in Grigson, 1948, op.cit., and
slightly more fully in William Feaver, 'Wartime
Romances', *The Sunday Times Colour Magazine*, 20
May 1973, pp.74–85, repr. p.76). Part of the painting
can be seen. 'I was ill with pleurisy at the time and I
think I looked it!' (letter, April 1986).
'Pastoral for P.W.':

was a celebration of the power of music. My sister
[the distinguished oboist Janet Craxton] was
learning the oboe on the same floor at the time and
the house was full of her scales and exercises coupled
with my discovery that goats, which seem to be
daemonic, wilful and undisciplined, are held in
thrall by the sound of a flute, or have I gone a step
further and frozen them into my geometry with a
paint brush? (ibid.)

In his letter postmarked 16 June 1986, Craxton added:

I suppose the flautist was in origin myself but a very
emblematic me. It was good that this painting marks
the end of all those ubiquitous self portraits. It was
in 1948 that I discovered Crete and made a large
number of objective portraits of Cretan shepherds,
real ones!

For several decades goats have been one of the principal
subjects of Craxton's painting. Although Craxton
emphasises that 'Pastoral for P.W.' 'hasn't any more

need of programme notes than has Stravinsky's Symphony in 3 Movements that I was incidentally playing over and over again at the same time when I first started the painting' (letter, 3 May 1984), the goats in this picture have more than purely animal origins:

I had, on the commencement of the painting, the idea of making it a kind of 'Enigma Variation' with all the goats being 'capricious' portraits of my friends (Lady Norton acquired a private name from the charmingly wicked Sir Steven Runciman from this painting – she was *very* fond of rock climbing!). As I progressed I dropped the idea. I feel it still remains an area where the geometry of order and the forces of disruption are at play (ibid.). Peter Watson was the goat on the right, Lady Norton at the bottom and so on. The tall tree in the middle was completed after a weekend at Geoffrey Grigson's. I spent some time with a prismatic lens ['The tree in the middle was finished as a result of looking at branches through a crystal' (letter, March 1984)] (letter, April 1986).

I had at least painted a celebration that came from the heart, knowing of course that no-one could house it or want it. It hung for years in my father's studio ... Later it joined up with the large Giacometti chandelier that Peter Watson had commissioned for the *Horizon* offices in Bedford Square, an amusing link-up (letter, March 1984).

This chandelier, which Craxton bought after it had been in store for years after Peter Watson's death, was 'commissioned from Alberto and Diego in or about 1948'. A portrait of Peter Watson by Alberto Giacometti, dated 1954, belongs to the Alberto Giacometti Stiftung.

One of the originally-intended goat-portraits was to have been of Lucian Freud. Lady Norton (d.1972), who is mentioned above as the subject of another, was a founding supporter of the Institute of Contemporary Arts. In a letter postmarked 16 June 1986, Craxton recalls that she:

was married to Sir Clifford Norton who, before the war, was British Minister in Warsaw. In 1940 they escaped and reached Switzerland where he headed the Legation in Bern during the war years ... Lady Norton (Peter to her friends) was instrumental in taking me to Greece for the first time in May–June 1946. She was a very remarkable person and to call her an original is not nearly enough. Her enthusiasms were backed up by acts. She was always helping artists and moving heaven to help them. I remember Peter Watson writing to me from Switzerland when he first met her, describing her as 'Art mad, even madder than I am'! Her deepest passion was for abstract art, but before the war [she]

had run the London Gallery in Cork Street with Edward Mesens, exhibiting now well known painters from abroad for the first time ... I remember in Athens [where Sir Clifford Norton was British Ambassador 1946–51] she transformed the Embassy into something unique with her modern paintings on the walls.

Peter Watson 'was always sparing in comments ... He never said much when he *liked* something, but I remember he liked the 'dislocated rhythms' of 'Pastoral' and the gas flame blue of 'Dark Landscape'. The fact that he reproduced them was comment enough' (letter, 26 April 1986). Craxton's 'Elegiac Figure (in memory of Peter Watson)' 1959 is reproduced in the catalogue of his Whitechapel Art Gallery retrospective of 1967.

'Pastoral for P.W.' is close in style to the following four paintings, each of which, like the Tate's picture, represents one or more people and one or more goats, and includes similar semi-abstract triangular subdivisions of the composition and sharply-delineated trees or foliage: 'Greek Farm' (repr. *Penguin New Writing*, 32, 1947 (n.p.)); 'Shepherds near Knossos' 1947 (approx. 914 × 1220 mm, repr. Grigson, op.cit., plate 20 and 1967 Whitechapel catalogue); 'Galatas' 1947 (oil on canvas, 760 × 1015 mm, collection The British Council, repr. Grigson op.cit., plate 21); and 'Farm Yard' 1947–8 (oil on canvas, 1047 × 1346 mm, repr. 1967 Whitechapel catalogue). The Tate Gallery owns Craxton's first Greek landscape, 'Hotel by the Sea' 1946 (T 00117), of which Peter Watson owned a small version.

Carlos Cruz-Diez b.1923

T 03715   **Physichromie No.123** 1964

Construction of perspex, paper and board, painted $15\frac{3}{4} \times 9\frac{1}{8} \times 1\frac{5}{8}$ (400 × 230 × 40)
Not inscribed
Transferred from the Victoria and Albert Museum 1983

Prov: Purchased by the Department of Circulation, Victoria and Albert Museum, from Signals, 1966 (Circ.139–1966)

Exh: *2nd Pilot Show*, Centre for Advanced Creative Study, 1964; *A Decade of Physichromies*, Signals, September–October 1965 (repr. on cover); travelling exhibitions of the Department of Circulation, Victoria and Albert Museum

Lit: Carlos Cruz-Diez, 'Physichromies', *Signals*, 1, February-March 1965, p.10; Frank Popper, 'The Physichromies of Carlos Cruz-Diez', *Signals*, 1, August–October 1965, p.11

Also repr: *Signals*, 1, September 1964, p.2

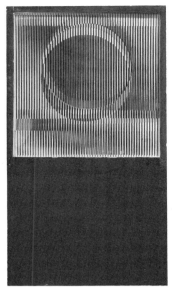

The title 'Physichromie' was invented by the artist from the words 'physical chromatism'. A larger construction 'Physichromie 113' (1963, reconstructed 1976) also belongs to the Tate Gallery (T02094).

Prov: Purchased by New Art Centre from the artist's estate
Exh: *Hubert Dalwood, Sculptures and Reliefs*, AC tour, Hayward Gallery, January–March 1979, Fruitmarket Gallery, Edinburgh, April–May 1979, University Gallery, Leeds, May–June 1979, Rochdale Art Gallery, June–July 1979, Newport Museum and Art Gallery, August–September 1979 (66); *Hubert Dalwood, 1924–1976*, Gimpel Fils and New Art Centre, February 1982 (18)
Repr: *British Sculptors '72*, RA, 1972 (17); *Arts Review*, XXIV, 15 January 1972, p.9

'Arbor' was a very large sculpture (180 × 192 × 192 ins.) made to be installed at the Royal Academy's *British Sculptors '72* exhibition in their Gallery VIII and later destroyed by the artist. This maquette was used as a model and was followed closely, except that the pieces on a large scale were in proportion thinner, and gave a more open appearance.

This maquette is 'opus 122' in the artist's own catalogue. It is listed there as unique but 'copy available in gesso and wood or aluminium or bronze', although no further copies were made in wood or plaster. 'Opus 125' is an aluminium cast of this, and was purchased by the Arts Council of Great Britain in 1975. Dalwood was seriously ill during the years 1971–4, and made few other sculptures.

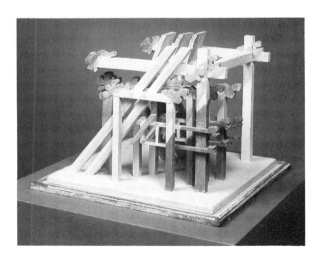

Hubert Dalwood 1924–1976

T03474   Maquette for 'Arbor' 1971

Painted plaster on wood 14 × 19 × 18 (335 × 485 × 457)
Not inscribed
Purchased from New Art Centre (Gytha Trust) 1982

T03475   O.A.S. Assassins 1962

Painted aluminium and ribbon
$30\frac{1}{8}$ × 20 × $13\frac{3}{8}$ (765 × 510 × 340)
Inscribed 'RF' on both sides of crest, one in reverse

Purchased from Gimpel Fils (Knapping Fund) 1982

Exh: ? *British Art Today*, San Francisco Museum of Art, November–December 1962 (108, repr., unspecified cast); ? *Englische Kunst der Gegenwart*, Stadtische Kunstgalerie, Bochum, April–June 1964 (37, unspecified cast); ? *Hubert Dalwood*, Gimpel Fils, September 1964 (1, repr., unspecified cast); ? *British Sculpture in the Sixties*, Contemporary Art Society, Tate Gallery, February–April 1965 (30, unspecified cast); ? *Society of Scottish Artists*, Royal Scottish Academy, Edinburgh, September–November 1965 (3, unspecified cast); *Hubert Dalwood, 1924–1976*, Gimpel Fils and New Art Centre, February 1982 (9, as 'O.A.S. assassin')

Lit: Norbert Lynton, 'Introduction', *Hubert Dalwood Sculpture and Reliefs*, exhibition catalogue, 1979, pp.5–39; *Also repr*: William Packer, *Out of Sight*, *Financial Times*, 9 February 1982, p.15

'O.A.S. Assassins' is 'opus 65' in the artist's own catalogue. The first cast is in the collection of the Ferens Art Gallery, Hull (exhibited at *Hubert Dalwood*, Gimpel Fils, September 1964 (1)), and the Tate Gallery's is the second cast of a projected edition of six. The correct title has 'Assassins' in the plural, as in the artist's record books and at Gimpel Fils in 1964, although this has been put in the singular in some later exhibitions. The cast at Hull was included in the artist's retrospective exhibition at the Hayward Gallery in 1979 (27, as 'O.A.S. Assassin').

The title refers to the Organisation de l'Armée Secrète, a right-wing group in France opposed to de Gaulle's policy in Algeria. Dalwood visited Paris in January 1962, coincidentally at a time when this group seemed about to cause a civil war: the 'RF' on the crest stands for République Française. Political subjects are extremely rare in Dalwood's work, except for a few sculptures of 1962–3. Norbert Lynton, in his introduction to the catalogue of the Hayward Gallery retrospective exhibition, discusses this sculpture and points out that Dalwood's attitude is ambiguous, although in other works the gay appearance – colours, ribbons – is ironic.

T03716 **Lucca** 1958

Painted aluminium 26 × 24¼ × 9½ (660 × 620 × 240)
Not inscribed
Transferred from the Victoria and Albert Museum 1983

Prov: Purchased by the Department of Circulation, Victoria and Albert Museum, from Gimpel Fils 1960 (Circ.243–1960)

Exh: *Recent Sculpture by Hubert Dalwood*, Gimpel Fils, January 1960 (10); *Hubert Dalwood, Sculptures and Reliefs*, AC tour, Hayward Gallery, January–March 1979, Fruitmarket Gallery, Edinburgh, April–May 1979, University Gallery, Leeds, May–June 1979, Rochdale Art Gallery, June–July 1979, Newport Museum and Art Gallery, August–September 1979 (10)

'Lucca' is 'opus 32' in the artist's own catalogue. Two other casts belong to private collections, out of a projected edition of six. The first title of the sculpture in the artist's record book was 'Tree', referring to its shape, but this was aleady changed to 'Lucca' by the time of its exhibition in 1960 (another sculpture had already been titled 'Tree' in 1957). Dalwood worked in Italy, and titled other sculptures also after Italian towns (eg. 'Bergamo (relief), 1958') for no particular reason.

Hanne Darboven b.1941

T03410 **Construction 19 × $\frac{42}{60}$ Part 2** 1975

Black ink and black offset printing ink on yellow lightweight paper and grey medium weight paper on white cartridge paper mounted on board, 10 framed panels, each 74 × 87 (1880 × 2210), each containing 60 sheets 11⅝ × 8¼ (294 × 210); framed index 37 × 86 (940 × 2185)
Inscribed 'Hanne Darboven, 1975' c. of index
Purchased from Sperone Westwater Fischer Inc., New York (Grant-in-Aid) 1982

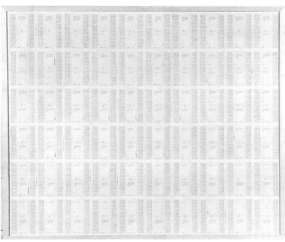

Panel no.10

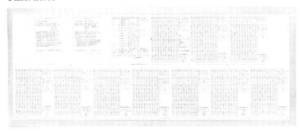

Index

Exh: *Hanne Darboven Part 2*, Sperone
Westwater Fischer, New York, April 1978
(no catalogue, detail of index repr. in
brochure);
Explorations in the '70s, Pittsburgh Plan
for Art, Pittsburgh, April–May 1980 (not
numbered, detail repr. pp.22–3)

Lit: Valentin Tatransky, 'Hanne Darboven',
exhibition review, *Arts Magazine*, LII,
June 1978, p.35, detail repr.; Madeleine
Burnside, 'Hanne Darboven', exhibition
review, *ARTnews*, LXXVII, Summer
1978, p.201; Edit DeAk, exhibition review,
Artforum, XVI, Summer 1978, pp.76–7,
detail repr. p.77; John Anthony Thwaites,
'Eight Artists, two generations, singular
preoccupations', *ARTnews*, LXXVII,
October 1978, statement by the artist p.71;
Thomas Lawson, 'Hanne Darboven at
Castelli and Sperone, Westwater, Fischer',
exhibition review, *Art in America*, LXVI,
September–October 1978, p.117

Honoré Daumier 1808–1879

T03593 **Serenade** c.1858

Oil on panel 12 × 15 9/16 (305 × 395)

Not inscribed
Bequeathed by Mrs A.F. Kessler 1983

Prov: E.J. van Wisselingh & Co., Amsterdam;
Sir Michael Sadler, Oxford (by 1924);
Reid and Lefevre; Mrs Kessler

Exh: *Loan Collection of Pictures*, Norwich
Castle Museum, October–November 1925
(43); *Paintings and Pastels by 19th and 20th
Century French Masters*, Independent
Gallery, June 1928 (10); *French Art 1200-
1900*, Royal Academy, January–March
1932 (383); *French Paintings of the
Nineteenth Century: Ingres to Cézanne*,
Lefevre Gallery, June–July 1933 (11);
Corot to Cézanne, Lefevre Gallery, June
1936 (14); *Nineteenth Century French
Paintings*, National Gallery, December
1942–January 1943 (7); *French Paintings
from the Kessler Collection*, York Art
Gallery, May 1948 (2); *The Kessler
Collection*, Wildenstein Gallery, October–
November 1948 (3, repr); *Daumier, Millet,
Courbet (from British Collections)*,
National Museum of Wales, Cardiff,
September 1957 and Glynn Vivian Art
Gallery, Swansea, October 1957 (7);
Daumier: Paintings and Drawings, Tate
Gallery, June–July 1961 (46, repr.);
*Géricault to Courbet: A New Look at the
Period*, Roland, Browse and Delbanco,
May–June 1965 (11, repr.); *The Kessler
Bequest*, Tate Gallery, February–April
1984 (not numbered, repr.)

Lit: Eduard Fuchs, *Der Maler Daumier*,
Munich, 1927, p.50 repr. p.116; Jean
Adhémar, *Honoré Daumier*, Paris, 1954,
p.127, repr. pl.143, dated c.1858-60; K.E.
Maison, *Honoré Daumier: Catalogue
Raisonné of the Paintings, Watercolours
and Drawings*, I, London, 1968, no.I–113,

p.111, repr. pl.55 (dated c.1858); Luigi Barzini and Gabriele Mandel, *L'Opera Pittorica Completa di Daumier*, Milan, 1971, no.144, p.100, repr. as 'Suonatrice Ambulante in un Ristorante all 'Aperto' *Also repr*: Michael Sadleir, *Daumier, The Man and the Artist*, 1924, repr. in col. pl.48 as 'La Sérénade', owned by Sir Michael Sadler; *Apollo*, VIII, 1928, p.50; Giovanni Scheiwiller, *Honoré Daumier*, Milan, 1936, frontispiece in col.

A partly unfinished picture. Although known since at least 1924 as 'Serenade' ('La Sérénade'), the subject is actually a 'chanteuse de la rue' singing in a garden restaurant. There is an earlier drawing of the same theme, differently composed, in the City Art Museum of St Louis, Missouri, USA.

Alan Davie b.1920

T03815   Village Myths No.36   1983

Oil on canvas 84 × 68 (2135 × 1730)
Inscribed 'Alan Davie/JUNE 83' and 'VILLAGE MYTHS NO 36/84' × 68"/OPUS 01019 JUNE 83' on back of canvas and '36 JUNE 83' on stretcher
Purchased from Gimpel Fils (Grant-in-Aid) 1983

Exh: *Alan Davie, Village Myths and Other Works*, Gimpel Fils, September–October 1983 (15)

Lit: Waldemar Januszczak, in *Alan Davie, Village Myths and Other Works*,

exhibition catalogue, Gimpel Fils, 1983; Dore Ashton, 'On Alan Davie', in *Alan Davie, Village Myths and Other Recent Paintings*, Gimpel & Weitzenhoffer, New York, March–April 1984

The following entry is based on a conversation with the artist on 29 April 1986 and a letter of 9 June 1986, and has been approved by him. The numbering and dates of the works were established by reference to records at Gimpel Fils gallery.

'Village Myths' is the overall title of a group of thirty gouaches (Nos. 1 to 30) and sixteen oil paintings (Nos. 31 to 46) produced by Alan Davie between November 1982 and August 1983.

The title is simply a way of naming the series and no reference to any particular myth is intended.

The oils were painted quickly: no.31, and probably nos.32 and 33, in May 1983; nos.34–6 in June; nos.37–40 in July, and nos. 41–6 in August. The Tate's painting is based on two gouaches, no.12 (January 1983) and particularly no.25 (February 1983), from which it differs in only a few details. Both gouaches are in the same private collection in Los Angeles.

The 'Village Myths' paintings are one of the groups of work which Davie produced in the following way. He works in cycles of twelve months, passing alternate six month periods at his studios in St Lucia and in Rush Green, Hertfordshire. He has had a studio in St Lucia for twelve years, and this is where each new body of work originates. Davie embarks upon a series of automatic drawings using black ink on paper, applied with a brush. At this stage there is no conscious control over the free flow of the images; he has no preconceptions about the paintings that will eventually be produced, and no idea or message to convey. Davie mentions Klee's well known recommendation of 'going for a walk with a line', and also compares the process to his improvisations as a musician:

> I can sit down at the piano and just play a few notes. Before I know it, I am entering a world of ideas which are presenting themselves to me out of the manipulation of sounds: with drawings ideas evolve out of just making marks on paper, and henceforth improvisations are evolving using these ideas and developing them into larger gouaches in colour and further developed eventually in large oils. Each medium dictates certain changes according to its own inherent qualities.

The drawings are produced over a period of about one month, and the gouaches are worked on throughout the remaining months in St Lucia. The 'Village Myths' gouaches were made between November 1982 and April 1983.

The oil paintings are executed at the artist's Rush Green studio, and are based on what he feels to be the most powerful 'magic' imagery from the gouaches. Davie confirms that he felt the horned figure in the Tate Gallery's painting to be a particularly potent and curious image. It is not based on an object he has seen. He also says that the text in the picture, in common with that in most of his work, is a nonsense language.

Asked about the influence of Indian art in the 'Village Myths' paintings, Davie agrees that there are Indian elements in them, but emphasises that such elements are used intuitively and that there is no symbolic meaning to them in his paintings. He is increasingly often asked about the symbolism or meaning of his work, where there is none. He has been interested in ancient cultures, especially Zen Buddhism and Tantric art, for many years. 'I feel free to steal ideas from other cultures.' He recalls seeing, two years ago (therefore after 'Village Myths' were painted), diagrams of the Jain (a Buddhist sect) cosmology at the Navin Kumar Gallery, New York. These, and the illustrations in the book *The Jain Cosmology* (1981), published by Ravi Kumar, have become what he describes as 'a new obsession'. His subsequent series of paintings, 'Meditations and Hallucinations' (1983-5), derives from it.

Reiterating that he is not trying to express anything specific in his art, Davie adds that the pictures 'are open to poetic interpretation, and should work as a magical experience'. When asked about a possible link between the clear and explicit way the imagery is presented in the painting, and the way one sees very clearly in dreams, he observes that his 'pictures are not like dreams, they are dreams'.

There are works from 'Village Myths' in private collections in the United Kingdom, USA, Venezuela and Morocco, and at the McLauren Art Gallery, Ayr.

Edgar Degas 1834-1917

T 03563 **Woman in a Tub** c.1883

Pastel on paper $27\frac{1}{2} \times 27\frac{1}{2}$ (700 × 700)
Inscribed 'Degas' t.r.
Bequeathed by Mrs A.F. Kessler 1983
Prov: Henri Lerolle, Paris; Arthur Tooth & Sons; Mrs Kessler 1938
Exh: *Degas*, Orangerie des Tuileries, Paris, March–April 1937 (119, as 'Femme au Tub' c.1883); *La Flèche d'Or*, Arthur Tooth & Sons, November 1938 (29); *The Kessler Collection*, Wildenstein Gallery, October–November 1948 (4); *Degas*, Royal Scottish Academy, Edinburgh, August–September 1952 (19); *Degas*, Tate Gallery, September–October 1952 (19); *Edgar Degas 1834–1917*, Lefevre Gallery, June–July 1970 (7, repr.); *Post-Impressionism: Cross-Currents in European Painting*, Royal Academy, November 1979–March 1980 (62, repr.); *The Kessler Bequest*, Tate Gallery, February–April 1984 (not numbered, repr. in col.)
Lit: P.A. Lemoisne, *Degas et son Oeuvre*, Paris, 1946, III, no.738, p.420, repr. p.421 as 'Femme au Tub' c.1883; Franco Russoli and Fiorella Minervino, *L'Opera Completa di Degas*, Milan, 1970, no.885, p.126, repr.

Degas's exhibits at the 8th Impressionist Exhibition of 1886 included ten pastels of female nudes 'bathing, washing, drying, wiping themselves, combing their hair or having it combed', and this became one of his favourite themes from then on. This picture, with its carefully modelled forms set in space and relatively great amount of detail, is one of the earliest. However Degas took up this particular pose again many years later, about 1898, in another pastel (Lemoisne no.1335) in which the woman is kneeling on a towel instead of in a tub and is executed in the much more summary, blurred and relief-like manner characteristic of his later style.

Paul Delvaux b.1897

T 03361 **Leda** 1948

Oil on blockboard $60\frac{1}{8} \times 37\frac{3}{8}$ (1527 × 950)
Inscribed 'P. DELVAUX/–48' b.l.
Purchased from the executors of Sir Robert Adeane through the Mayor Gallery (Grant-in-Aid) 1982

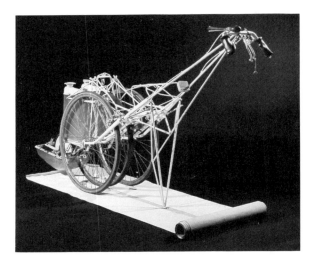

Gunther Demnig b.1947

T 03421 **Blood Trail (Kassel/London)** 1981

Line-making machine made from cycle parts $31\frac{1}{2} \times 19\frac{3}{4} \times 86$ (800 × 500 × 2185); blood on acrylic-primed canvas 223 × 24 (5620 × 600)
Inscribed 'Blutspur Demnig 81 Kassel-London Tate Gallery AM 23.9.81 Gunther Demnig' on canvas b.r.
Presented by the artist 1982

Lit: Jürgen Wilhelm, Harry Kramer, Georg Bussmann, *Duftmarken Cassel-Paris*, exhibition catalogue, Halle des Nordhaus, Kassel, April 1980; Gunther Demnig, *Blutspur Demnig 81*, Kassel 1981

This work, consisting of a three-wheeled machine adapted from a bicycle and a long strip of canvas, represents the surviving part of a documented walk Demnig made, 7–23 September 1981, from the Kunst-akademie in Kassel to the Tate Gallery in London, via the Kunstverein in Cologne, the Van Abbemuseum, Eindhoven and the Stedelijk Museum, Amsterdam. On the walk, Demnig pushed the machine, referred to by him as a 'Blutspurmachine' or blood tracing machine, which laid a continuous trail of pigs' blood (chosen as a readily available waste material). On his arrival at the front entrance of the Tate Gallery, Demnig continued the blood trail over a strip of canvas which he subsequently presented to the Gallery together with the tracing machine. His journey is documented with photographs and contemporary press reports in a fold-out book, *Blutspur Demnig 81*, cited above.

In 1980 Demnig made a similar journey from Kassel to the Musée National d'Art Moderne in Paris, also leaving a trail of blood.

Prov: Grosfils, Brussels; Govaert, Ostend; Harry Torczyner, New York; through Harold Diamond, New York; Barry Miller; Mayor Gallery; Sir Robert Adeane 1967

Exh: *Art from Belgium*, Finch College Museum of Art, New York, January–February 1965 (Delvaux 3, repr. as 'Le Songe'); Stamford Museum, Stamford, Conn., February 1965 (Delvaux 3, repr.); *A Loan Exhibition in Memory of Fred Hoyland Mayor*, Mayor Gallery, November–December 1973 (5, repr. as 'Leda et son Cygne')

Lit: Paul-Aloïse De Bock, *Paul Delvaux: L'Homme, Le Peintre, Psychologie d'un Art*, Brussels, 1967, no.93, p.295 as 'Léda', repr. pl.93 and detail p.164; Michel Butor, Jean Clair, Suzanne Houbart-Wilkin, *Delvaux*, Brussels, 1975, no.187, p.225, repr. as 'Léda'

The artist confirmed that the correct title of this picture is 'Léda' ('Leda') (and not 'The Dream' by which it has sometimes been known) and said that he painted it for his dentist in Brussels, M. Grosfils. It was later sold at auction in Brussels either by M. Grosfils himself or by his family. The background and the constructions are imaginary, while the swan harks back to the time, in 1920–4, when he did a lot of painting from nature at Rouge-Cloître, a place in the forest near Brussels, where there was a lake and some swans (information transmitted by Charles Van Deun, President of the Fondation Paul Delvaux, 13 November 1984).

which has been provided by Robert Stoppenbach, shows what appears to be the first state hanging on the wall: a very rigid, frontal study of a woman in a light-coloured (possibly white) dress, who occupies almost the full height of the picture, with her head right at the top, and her shoes protruding from beneath her dress at the very bottom. The painting has not yet been X-rayed, but the identification seems fairly certain.

André Derain 1880–1954

T 03368 Mme Derain in a White Shawl c.1919–20

Oil on canvas $76\frac{3}{4} \times 38\frac{3}{8}$ (1955 × 975)
Not inscribed
Purchased from the artist's son André Derain through Stoppenbach & Delestre Ltd. (Grant-in-Aid) 1982

Exh: *Cinquante Tableaux Importants de André Derain*, Galerie Charpentier, Paris, 1955 (19, repr.); *Derain*, Musée Cantini, Marseilles, June–September 1964 (44); *Derain 1880–1954*, Galerie Schmit, Paris, May–June 1976 (26, repr. in col.); *Derain*, Villa Medici, Rome, November 1976–January 1977 (26, repr.); *André Derain*, Grand Palais, Paris, February–April 1977 (30, repr.)

Lit: Denys Sutton, *André Derain*, 1959, p.158, repr. facing p.9; *The Tate Gallery Illustrated Biennial Report 1982–84*, 1984, p.43 in col.

A portrait of the artist's wife Alice, who told Denys Sutton that it was painted about 1919–20. It is the last of a small series of full-length portraits of a seated figure with an open window in the background which began with the group portrait 'Saturday' executed in 1911–12. The French title of this work is 'Madame Derain au Châle blanc'.

Various pentimenti show beyond any doubt that this picture was painted over an entirely different composition representing a full-length standing figure. An old photograph of Derain's studio taken about 1914,

François Desnoyer 1894–1972

T 03406 Large Port of Sète 1950

Oil on canvas $44\frac{7}{8} \times 63\frac{3}{4}$ (1140 × 1620)
Inscribed 'DESNOYER' b.r.
Presented by Mme Souza Desnoyer 1982

Exh: *F. Desnoyer*, Kunstmuseum, Lucerne, January–March 1951 (1); La Biennale Internazionale d'Arte Marinara, Palazzo dell' Accademia, Genoa, October–November 1951 (France 2, repr.); *François Desnoyer: Paintings and Drawings*, Marlborough Fine Art, October 1955 (25, repr.); Salon d'Automne, Paris, November–December 1960 (Desnoyer 49); *Desnoyer: 50 Ans de Peinture*, Musée Ingres, Montauban, June–September 1968 (51); *Desnoyer; Peintures à l'Huile et Aquarelles (1930-1972)*, Musée Municipal d'Art et d'Histoire, Saint-Denis, October–November 1972 (35, repr.); *François Desnoyer*, Chambre de Commerce, Chartres, June–September 1974 (5)

Repr: Souza Desnoyer, *Desnoyer: Sa Vie, son Oeuvre, ses Amis, ses Voyages*, Montfermeil, 1972, p.169 in col.

Desnoyer settled at Sète on the Mediterranean coast in 1945, after the Liberation, and painted many pictures of the port there. Although the port has several harbours, there is neither a 'large port' nor a 'small port'; the title simply refers to the size of the picture. In fact Desnoyer painted several other pictures of the same port, but all of them were smaller.

Pierre Fortassier, who supplied this information on behalf of the artist's widow, said that Desnoyer never painted canvases as large as this direct from nature. It must be an enlargement, made in the studio, of a small study painted on the spot on canvas or plywood; he thinks that he has seen the actual study for it but he has so far been unable to trace it again (letter of 26 March 1985).

T 03718   **Op Structure** 1967

Construction of coloured, opalescent and transparent perspex $26\frac{3}{4} \times 28\frac{3}{4} \times 18$ (680 × 730 × 460)
Not inscribed
Transferred from the Victoria and Albert Museum 1983

Prov: Purchased by the Department of Circulation, Victoria and Albert Museum, from the artist 1967 (Circ. 982–1967)

See entry for T 03717.

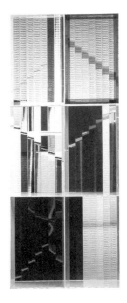

Michael Dillon

T 03717   **Op Structure** 1967

Construction of coloured, opalescent and transparent perspex $36 \times 14\frac{1}{2} \times 5\frac{1}{2}$ (910 × 360 × 136)
Not inscribed
Transferred from the Victoria and Albert Museum 1983

Prov: Purchased by the Department of Circulation, Victoria and Albert Museum, from the artist 1967 (Circ. 983–1967)

The two op art constructions (this and T 03718) with the same title by Michael Dillon were made while he was a student at the Royal College of Art.

Braco Dimitrijevic b.1948

T 03684   **The Casual Passer-By I met at 11.28 A.M. London, October** 1972

3 black and white photographs, each $11\frac{7}{8} \times 8\frac{7}{8}$ (303 × 226), and one text mounted on board $11\frac{7}{8} \times 8\frac{1}{2}$ (303 × 215), overall size $16\frac{1}{8} \times 40$ (409 × 1016)
Part printed and part handwritten

inscription 'THE CASUAL PASSER-BY I MET AT 11.28 A.M. P. M./London, Oct. 1972/Braco D./Braco Dimitrijevic 1969' Purchased from Waddington Galleries (Grant-in-Aid) 1983

Prov: Situation Gallery 1972; Robert Self Gallery 1976; with the artist 1976–9; Waddington Galleries ?1980

Exh: Situation Gallery, ? October 1972 (no catalogue); *Braco Dimitrijevic*, Galerija Suvremene Umjetnosti, Zagreb, 8–25 February 1973 (16, room no.5 and 6, detail repr.); *Braco Dimitrijevic Arbeiten/Works 1968–1978*, Badischer Kunstverein, Karlsruhe, March–May 1979 (not numbered, detail repr. figs. 15 and 67); *Braco Dimitrijevic*, Stedelijk van Abbemuseum, Eindhoven, May–June 1979 (not numbered, detail repr.); *Braco Dimitrijevic*, ICA, September–October 1979 (as 'The Casual Passer-By I met at 11.28 P.M.', detail repr.); According to Braco Dimitrijevic T 03684 is a unique work. However, in addition to the above exhibitions it also appears to have been shown in *European Dialogue 3rd Biennale*, Sydney, April–May 1979 (listed in catalogue)

Lit: Manfred Schmalriede, 'Remarks on the work of Braco Dimitrijevic', *Braco Dimitrijevic Arbeiten/Works 1968-1978*, exhibition catalogue, Badischer Kunstverein, Karlsruhe, 1979, pp.26–8; Adrian Morris, 'Biography', in *Braco Dimitrijevic 'Culturescapes' 1976–1984, Gemälde, Skulpturen, Fotografien*, exhibition catalogue, Museum Ludwig, Cologne, March 1983 (p.127, detail repr.); David Brown, *Braco Dimitrijevic, Triptychos Post Historicus*, exhibition leaflet, Tate Gallery, September 1985, n.p. *Also repr*: Braco Dimitrijevic *Tractatus Post Historicus*, Tübingen 1976 (detail, n.p.)

Braco Dimitrijevic began working on a series, to which he gave the title 'The Casual Passer-By', involving passers-by – people he had met by chance in the street – in Zagreb, in his native Yugoslavia, in 1968. The first such work used the name of a pensioner, Tihomir Simcicz (b.1905, retired 1960) – 'The Casual Passer-By I met at 11.40 A.M. Zagreb 1969'. Dimitrijevic's choice of subject depends on chance; he chooses the first person who accepts after the opportunity becomes available to make such a work. He sees the negotiations surrounding the organisation of his publicly sited works as part of the work itself (in one instance it took two years to gain

a city's acceptance for a work that was to be publicly sited out-of-doors).

According to the chronology section of *Braco Dimitrijevic 'Culturescapes'*, p.124 (1968–9), Dimitrijevic only arranges the initial situation:

while its development depends on chance, understanding and approval of other persons. When entering a gallery, a visitor is prepared to see a work of art. I have tried to choose people at random, without knowing whether they have any affinity for art, and make them not only the spectators but persons who co-operate with the 'arranger', i.e. create. They have thus been included into the act of creating, and the dividing line that formally existed between artist and non-artist has been removed.

In a note to David Brown (May 1985), Dimitrijevic gave the following brief history of 'The Casual Passer-By' series:

In 1968 I joined the Academy of Fine Art in Zagreb. In that year I made pieces from the series 'Accidental Sculpture' 'Accidental Drawings and Paintings' which lead up to the pieces about a casual passer-by. 'The Casual Passer-By' would touch or deal with [the] following problems; inner and outer perception. The context in which it was placed would lead one to think that it was [a] person from public life. Learning that it was a person selected at random one would in future reflect on the subject within a similar context. These pieces were rooted in [the] 'Flag of the World' piece from 1963 where [the] national flag on my boat was replaced with [a] cloth used for cleaning brushes. [See *Braco Dimitrijevic 'Culturescapes' 1976–1984*, p.123].

'Casual Passer-By' stands for the unrecognised creative potential or creative person whose ideas we have missed as they were too advanced. In 1969 I wrote a story, 'About two artists' [See *Braco Dimitrijevic 'Culturescapes 1976–1984*, p.125]. ['About two artists': Once upon a time, far from cities and towns there lived two painters. One day, the King, hunting nearby, lost his dog. He found him in the garden of one of the painters. He saw the works of that painter and took him to the castle. The name of that painter was Leonardo da Vinci. The name of the other disappeared forever from human memory.] So 'Passer-By' could also be an answer to that story. (For a chronology of events with 'Casual Passer-By' pieces see Cologne catalogue years 1968–71, pp. 125–7, op.cit.)

When I joined [the] advanced sculpture course at St Martin's [School of Art in London], the first pieces I ... realised were memorial plaques to Casual Passers-By. [Dimitrijevic produced memorial plaques inscribed with the names of people living in neighbouring buildings and he also made a 'portable monument' – a stone plaque bearing the inscription 'This could be a place of Historical Importance'.] London and its monuments have inspired me to add one more, 'Monument to Casual Passer-By' having tried to find the most appropriate contexts for my works. [This was a fibre glass bust of David Harper the 'Casual Passer-By I met at 1.10 p.m.' which was installed for one day in the gardens of Berkeley Square in April 1972, timed to coincide with an exhibition at Situation Gallery. Preview guests were gathered in the square before going to the gallery. Dimitrijevic made the bust at St Martin's.] Some words regarding the 'Piece with Bus' [T 03684]. London is a very large city and unlike some Mediterranean towns has no piazza that people would be passing every day. [The] Equivalent of a facade on [a] main piazza in a smaller town here is the poster board on the bus which crosses the town. This is how I came to use Bus No.14 so that I would have my show passing through the city via St Martin's every 20 minutes.

Dimitrijevic went to St Martin's in 1971 and it was while he was a student there that he made T 03684. In October 1972, he photographed a man, hitherto unknown to him, who happened to be passing, outside the main college building in the Charing Cross Road. He first related the story of the two artists (op.cit.) to the man who, he remembers, readily agreed to participate in the work. He had the photograph of the passer-by enlarged as a poster and through the Situation Gallery obtained permission from London Transport to have the posters displayed on certain No.14 buses for a limited period. As he has noted, the No.14 bus passes directly in front of St Martin's on its route North East towards King's Cross.

For presentation outside its original context (which had been the side of a bus in this case), Dimitrijevic always juxtaposes a photographic portrait of his passer-by subject with data about the origins of the work.

The Tate's work consists of three photographs and a certificate signed by the artist and is the second, documentary and exhibitable part of a work which existed in its original form for a limited duration. It consists of two photographs of the same bus (registration No. NML 613E). In one photograph, the bus passes St Martin's School of Art and in the other, it is shown heading south west, towards South Kensington. To the left of the photographs is a printed certificate, signed by the artist, giving the exact time of the meeting between Dimitrijevic and the 'passer-by'. This certificate bears the month and year of the meeting (October 1972) but also the year the series was formally initiated (1969). On the extreme left is a portrait photograph of the passer-by himself.

According to Dimitrijevic, the 'Casual Passer-By' series is open ended – he believes that he has made at least 25 in Britain. Apart from T 03684, the following have been documented in the catalogues cited in the exhibition and literature sections above:

Sarah Knipe, the casual passer-by I met at 2.52 pm, London 1971
Peter Martin, 'Cars I see from my window'. Film shot by a casual passer-by I met at 6.40 pm, London 1971
John Foster, the casual passer-by I met at 10.05 am, London 1972
Monument to David Harper, the casual passer-by I met at 1.10 pm, London 1972
Ann Sander, the casual passer-by I met at 7.15 pm, London 1974
Michael Davies, the casual passer-by I met at 1.19 pm, Coventry 1975
The casual passer-by I met at 4.57 pm, Edinburgh 1975
The casual passer-by I met at 1.14 pm, London 1978
John Fane, the casual passer-by I met at 6.14 pm, Henley-on-Thames 1978

All the works in the 'Casual Passer-by' series have used forms which generally denote public acceptability and imply that the subject is well-known, eg. photoportraits, posters, placards, memorial plaques, public sculptures.

After making T 03684, Dimitrijevic used the image of the 14 bus again, juxtaposing it with a photograph of a European bus, also covered with large photographic portraits – in the latter case, advertising posters. He subtitled the 'genuine' bus 'This could be a work of B.D.' (repr. in *Braco Dimitrijevic Arbeiten/Works 1968–75*, exhibition catalogue, op.cit., p.27). (The artist has confirmed that T 03684 is a unique work.)

T 03685 **Louvre ('J.M.W. Turner' 'Edward Rampton')** 1975–9

Two bronze busts, each on integral pedestal in green marble 'J.M.W. Turner 75⅝ × 13 × 13¾ (1870 × 330 × 350) and 'Edward Rampton' 73⅛ × 13 × 13¾ (1860 × 330 × 350)
'J.M.W. Turner' inscribed 'JMW/TURNER' on front of base and 'Edward Rampton' inscribed 'EDWARD/RAMPTON' in front of base
Purchased from Waddington Galleries (Grant-in-Aid) 1983

Exh: *Braco Dimitrijevic*, Van Abbemuseum, Eindhoven, May–June 1979 (not numbered, repr.); *Braco Dimitrijevic*,

Kunsthalle, Tübingen, 1–30 September 1979 (not numbered, repr.); *New Art at the Tate Gallery 1983*, September–October 1983 (listed p.67); *Forty Years of Modern Art 1945–1985*, Tate Gallery, February–April 1986 (not in catalogue)

Lit: Braco Dimitrijevic, *Tractatus Post Historicus*, Tübingen, 1976; David Brown, *Braco Dimitrijevic, Triptychos Post Historicus*, exhibition leaflet, Tate Gallery, September 1985 (n.p.)

See entry on Dimitrijevic T 03686

T 03686 Louvre ('Leonardo da Vinci' 'Albert Evans') 1975-82

Two bronze busts, each on integral pedestal in green marble
'Leonardo da Vinci' $72\frac{1}{2} \times 13 \times 13\frac{3}{4}$ ($1841 \times 330 \times 350$) and 'Albert Evans' $72 \times 13 \times 13\frac{3}{4}$ ($1830 \times 330 \times 350$)
'Leonardo da Vinci' inscribed 'LEONARDO/DA/VINCI' on front of base and 'Albert Evans' inscribed 'ALBERT/EVANS' on front of base
Purchased from Waddington Galleries (Grant-in-Aid) 1983

Exh: *Aspects of British Art Today*, Metropolitan Art Museum, Tokyo, February–April 1982, Tochigi Prefectural Museum of Fine Arts, Utsunomiya Tochigi, April–May 1982, National Museum of Art, Osaka, June–July 1982, Fukuoka Art Museum, Fukuoka, August 1982, Hokkaido Museum of Modern Art, Sapporo, September–October 1982 (60, repr.); *Sculpture*, Waddington Galleries, September–October 1982 (11, as 'Leonardo da Vinci: Painter, Scientist, Genius, John Evans: The Casual Passer-by I met, 1975–82', repr.); *New Art at the Tate Gallery 1983*, September–October 1983 (listed p.67); *Forty Years of Modern Art 1945–1985*, Tate Gallery, February–April 1986 (not in catalogue)

Lit: Braco Dimitrijevic, *Tractatus Post Historicus*, Tübingen, 1976; David Brown, *Braco Dimitrijevic, Triptychos Post Historicus*, exhibition leaflet, Tate Gallery, September 1985 (n.p.)

'Louvre ('J.M.W. Turner' 'Edward Rampton')' and 'Louvre ('Leonardo da Vinci' 'Albert Evans')' each consist of two paired bronze heads on marble pedestals. According to the artist, 'Turner' and 'Rampton' were first exhibited at the Van Abbemuseum, Eindhoven as part of a series of eight paired sculptures, collectively titled 'Louvre' 1975, a title chosen because it suggests the ultimate museum. The complete installation is reproduced in the catalogue for Dimitrijevic's exhibition at the Kunsthalle Tübingen in 1979 (n.p.). In the Eindhoven installation, the following pairs were exhibited with 'Turner and Rampton': 'Leonardo da Vinci and Gerhard Hecht' (now coll. Stadtisches Museum Abteiberg Möchengladbach), 'Albrecht Dürer and Dieter Koch' (private collection) and 'Rembrandt van Rijn and Frans van Dooren' (coll. Van Abbemuseum, Eindhoven). 'Leonardo da Vinci and Albert Evans' were cast later and apart from exhibitions in London, have not, according to the artist, been shown in Europe.

Each pair portrays a famous artist beside a bust of an unknown. The selection of the 'unknown' was undertaken in the same manner as the selection for participators in the 'Casual Passer-by' series – the individuals were picked at random by Dimitrijevic, who told them his story of the Two Artists (see entry for T 03684).

In her introduction to Dimitrijevic's exhibition at the ICA in 1979 (op.cit.), Sarah Kent wrote:

'Louvre' is a discourse on the importance of art and artists. Bronze busts on marble plinths carry the likenesses of acknowledged 'geniuses' such as Leonardo da Vinci, Rembrandt van Rijn, J.M.W. Turner and Albrecht Dürer, alternating with the unknown passers-by Gerhard Hecht, Frans van Dooren, Edward Rampton and Dieter Koch. Like Dimitrijevic's other work, the busts raise a number of complex and difficult issues. The juxtaposition of world famous men of the past with our anonymous contemporaries encourages a comparison between past and present artistic achievements. Like the masks of ancient Greek theatre these heads offer two sides of the same coin – fame and anonymity. Whether or not we have the opportunity to flourish, Dimitrijevic suggests, is largely beyond our control – a mixture of historical accident and chance occurrence.

The artist has written (note to David Brown, May 1985):

[The] *Bust* pieces – Leonardo – Evans, Turner – Rampton, deal with [the] problem of the end of formal evolution, because [the] bust as a form of art as well as [a] form of glorification and commemoration existed for centuries. Its innovation is in composing the blocks of meaning (linked with busts) in order to create a new, semantic structure.

The catalogue for Dimitrijevic's exhibition at the Badischer Kunstverein, Karlsruhe reproduces the majority of works by him using the commemorative bust form, pairing famous artists with 'unknowns'. These have been:

'David Harper, the Casual Passer-by I Met at 1.10 PM' (see catalogue entry for T 03684, repr. Karlsruhe fig. 10)
'Monument to Albert Vieri, the Casual Passer-by I met at 4.15 PM, Turin 1973' (repr. Karlsruhe figs 68–70)
'This could be a masterpiece' (1975) using a bronze bust of the painter Max Roeden from the collection of Stadtisches Museum, Mönchengladbach
'Michelangelo Buonarotti – Mario Orsini', plaster (Karlsruhe fig. 12)

'Leonardo da Vinci – Andelko Hundic' 1976 (fig. 84), coll. Museum Van Hedendaagse Kunst, Ghent
'Leonardo da Vinci – Julius Rehse' 1976, plaster (fig. 89)
'About Two Artists: Albert Dürer – Dieter Koch' 1976, plaster (fig. 91), private collection
'About Two Artists: Michelangelo Buonarotti – Franco Grassi' 1977, plaster (figs. 95–8)

Dimitrijevic modelled the heads of Albert Evans and Edward Rampton from photographs and based those of the two artists on self portraits. For the head of Turner, he used the self portrait in the Tate (c.1798, N 00458; see Martin Butlin and Evelyn Joll, *The Paintings of J.M.W. Turner*, revised edition, New Haven and London, 1984, no.25, repr. pl.19). As with the earlier works involving heads, each pair may be exhibited without the other. The artist has confirmed to the compiler that when T 03686 was exhibited in Japan it was accompanied by a small framed certificate measuring approximately 30 × 40 cm which had been signed by him and carried the 'About Two Artists' story and that this is the correct method of display for both T 03685 and T 03686. This juxtaposition of story and statues was one he had already used in earlier works in the series, sometimes subtitled 'Dialectical Chapels', for example, the work he exhibited in the Venice Biennale in 1976, 'About Two Artists: Leonardo da Vinci: painter, scientist, genius. Andelko Hundic: casual passer-by I met'.

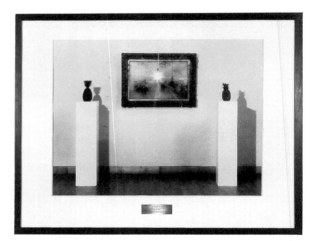

T 03687 **Triptychos Post Historicus or Entrance to the Palace of Light** 1982

Mounted coloured photograph in integral frame bearing brass title plate $44\frac{3}{4} \times 56\frac{3}{4}$ (1137 × 1441)
Engraved inscription on brass plate b.c. 'Braco Dimitrijevic/TRIPTYCHOS POST

HISTORICUS/or ENTRANCE TO THE
PALACE OF LIGHT/Tate Gallery
1982/Part One: St Benedetto, looking
towards Fusina J.M.W. Turner 1843/Part
Two: light bulb installed by Peter
Lockwood 1981/Part Three: pineapple'
Purchased from Waddington Galleries
(Grant-in-Aid) 1983

Exh: *Braco Dimitrijevic 'Culturescape' 1976–
1984, Gemälde, Skulpturen, Fotografien*,
Museum Ludwig, Cologne, March 1983–
May 1984, Kunsthalle Bern, June–August
1984 (not listed in catalogue, original
installation repr. in col. p.61)

Lit: David Brown, *Braco Dimitrijevic,
Triptychos Post Historicus*, exhibition
leaflet, Tate Gallery, September 1985
(n.p.)

Dimitrijevic began the extended series of three-dimensional still-lifes to which he has given the generic title
'Triptychos Post Historicus' in 1976. Each combines
an original work of art (an old or modern master, usually
borrowed from a museum collection), an everyday arte-
fact and an arrangement of fruit or vegetables. Dimitrijevic intends 'Post Historicus' to suggest a state which
might transcend the hierarchies and value systems of
recorded culture. In his book *Tractatus Post Historicus*
(Tübingen 1976, n.p.) he gives a clue to the series' title
when he describes his earlier 'Dialectical Chapel' works
(see entry for T 03685 and T 03686) as models for a 'post
historical' society. 'History was always created by the
power structure which selected only certain data (convenient to itself) to be recorded. By "post-historical" I
mean a situation which makes possible the co-existence
of different qualities.' In a note to David Brown (May
1985) the artist wrote that 'post history' ' . . . is the time
after history, time of multi-angular viewing, time of co-
existence of different qualities'.

The 'Triptychos' works generally exist in two forms,
as temporary installations in the gallery and in documentary form as photographs, as illustrated here.

The installations for T 03687 and T 03688 were made
in their original, three-dimensional form, and photographed by Dimitrijevic, at the Tate Gallery in 1982.
At the same time, he made two other installations. None
of these three-dimensional works went on public display
at that time but the three-dimensional versions of
T 03687 and T 03688 were remade for a special exhibition
of six of the artists' 'Triptychos' works, again based
around paintings already in the Tate, held in September–October 1985. The leaflet for this exhibition
lists these and contains an essay on the 'Triptychos'
works by David Brown, a chronology for the series
(noting that Dimitrijevic first made a work incorporating another work of art – a painting by his father –
in 1967) and an extensive bibliography.

Regarding the appropriation of the work of others
into his own works, Dimitrijevic has written (note to
David Brown, op.cit.):

If there are some people who might object to the fact
that I use other works to make mine, they should
have in mind that perhaps the stretched canvases
that Leonardo would paint on were sculptures by
an unrecognised minimal artist. At least in my case
there is the full appreciation of the other artist's
work with its complete socio-historical, spiritual and
material value incorporated.

According to the artist (same note), the 'Triptychos
Post Historicus' works:

are based on a similar principle [to] the bust pieces
[see entries for T 03685 and T 03686]. One element
belongs to high culture, art and history, [the] second
part is [an] object of everyday use and [the] third is
the element of nature. This is a piece about [the]
harmony of culture-nature, [a] portrait of our
planet-cosmos in small. All the elements presented
on [a] pedestal are like a micro version of what goes
on on Earth. It's also about perception and
measurement (colour shapes of prints and form and
colour in the printing . . .) when seen in two
dimensions. In a photographic version or in a
reproduction one immediately knows the size of the
painting in relation to common experience of the
apple size. It's also a measure for time; the eternity
of art – decay of nature.

The original installation, 'Triptychos Post Historicus:
Entrance to the Palace of Light', was subtitled:

Part One: 'St Benedetto, looking towards Fusina'
J.M.W. Turner (exh. 1843)
Part Two: Light Bulb Installed by Peter Lockwood
Part Three: Pineapples

In this installation, or three-dimensional still-life,
Turner's painting (Tate Gallery N 00534, see Martin
Butlin and Evelyn Joll, *The Paintings of J.M.W. Turner*,
revised edition, New Haven and London, 1984, no.406,
repr. pl.411) is surmounted by a bracket from which is
suspended a bare light bulb. This is hung, lit, directly
in front of the painting. On either side, two plinths
are surmounted by real pineapples. The artist told the
compiler that he chose the pineapples to represent
nature because of their colour and also because he
associates them with the Victorian era. The work juxtaposes science and art (the lightbulb 'illuminates' a
work by the master of painted light).

Dimitrijevic has written (note to David Brown,
op.cit.):

Long before science existed there was art as we call
it today. Art is about cognition of the world. Maybe

[149]

the walls of Altamira and Lascaux were the drawing boards of a man who was artist and scientist at the same time. As our civilisation 'progressed' the science of Altamira man, from today's point of view, became so simple and unsophisticated so that it became practically invisible. But one quality which is inherent in man, is creative thinking and performing. Apparently art has less to do with things on Earth than science, thus it is less practical and more free. Art deals often with questions that science would eventually prove later. It was not pure coincidence that Turner dealt with problems of light decades before Gebel and Edison.

[The] pineapple stands as a symbol of golden era of Queen Victoria's reign – Economy, commerce, India, travel, exotic fruits coming to England.

T 03688   **Triptychos Post Historicus or Artists' Hats Are High Above the Rainbow – Portrait of Barry** 1982

Mounted coloured photograph in integral frame bearing brass title plate, overall size 45 × 56½ (1140 × 1435)
Engraved inscription on brass plate b.c. 'Braco Dimitrijevic/TRIPTYCHOS POST HISTORICUS/PORTRAIT OF BARRY or ARTISTS' HATS ARE HIGH ABOVE THE RAINBOW/Tate Gallery 1982/Part One: 'Henri Matisse' Andre Derain 1905/Part Two: Barry Flanagan's coat and hat c.1970/Part Three: cucumber and apples'
Purchased from Waddington Galleries (Grant-in-Aid) 1983

Exh: *Braco Dimitrijevic 'Culturescapes' 1976–1984, Gemälde, Skulpturen, Fotografien*, Museum Ludwig, Cologne, March 1983– May 1984, Kunsthalle Bern, June–August

1984 (not listed in catalogue, original installation repr. in col. p.61)

Lit: David Brown, *Braco Dimitrijevic, Triptychos Post Historicus*, exhibition leaflet, Tate Gallery, September 1985 (n.p.)

When shown in the Tate in its original form, this work was subtitled:

Part One: 'Henri Matisse', André Derain, 1905
Part Two: Barry Flanagan's Coat and Hat, c.1970
Part Three: Apples and Cucumbers

The portrait of Matisse by Derain, described by Ronald Alley in *The Tate Gallery's Collection of Modern Art, other than works by British Artists*, 1981, p.167, was executed at Collioure in the summer of 1905 at the same time as a portrait of Derain by Matisse also in the Tate's collection (N 06241). When the work by Dimitrijevic is installed, a coat belonging to the sculptor, Barry Flanagan, is draped over one side of the portrait which is surmounted by an arc of (alternating) apples and cucumbers. Flanagan's hat is hung on the wall above the arc. Hitherto both coat and hat have been lent to the Gallery by Flanagan when the work has been installed.

Dimitrijevic has commented (note to David Brown, op.cit., see entry for T 03687):

I met Barry [Flanagan] in 1970. It was not only that I liked his work, but also his personality. He was the one who suggested and helped me to get to St Martin's. This piece is not only about friendship (like Matisse-Derain) but also about [the] reality of the poet. All his thoughts are under his hat which is high above the rainbow. [The] rainbow in my piece is made of curved vegetables i.e. cucumbers, apples; and apples with cucumbers cover the spectrum of rainbow colours.

Other works involving hats and coats are illustrated in *Braco Dimitrijevic 'Culturescapes'*, op.cit., pp.39 and 57.

The artist told the compiler that the gallery has the right to re-make the three-dimensional versions of T 03687 and T 03688 without seeking his permission on each occasion. Although he generally makes the photographic versions of his 'Tripychos' in editions of three, T 03687 and T 03688 are unique works.

In 1985 the artist presented a further 'Tripychos' to the Tate, but in its original three-dimensional form only. This is 'Triptychos Post Historicus: Repeated Secret' 1978-83 (T 04122, repr. in col. in the Tate Gallery Trustees' Biennial Report 1984–6).

Frank Dobson 1888-1963

T 03719 Charnaux Venus 1933-4

Composition and plywood in two pieces, painted
67 × 19¾ × 15¾ (1700 × 500 × 400)
Inscribed on base 'Charnaux' (twice)
Transferred from the Victoria and Albert Museum 1983

Prov: Commissioned from the artist by C. Douglas Stephenson on behalf of the Charnaux Patent Corset Co. Ltd., and given by him to the Victoria and Albert Museum, 1934 (A. 24–1934)

Exh: *Thirties, British Art and Design before the War*, Hayward Gallery, October 1979–January 1980 (21.9, repr., as 'Charnaux Corsets display figure')

Lit: P.Q., 'Art and Commerce – a New Departure', *Architectural Review*, LXXIII, May 1933, pp.210–11. *Also repr:* Eric G. Underwood, *A Short History of English Sculpture*, 1933 (plaster, repr. as frontispiece)

The firm of Charnaux Patent Corsets commissioned a 'Venus' from Dobson in 1933, and a photograph published in the same year shows him finishing the plaster (Eric G. Underwood, op.cit.). This plaster differs in pose only slightly from the Tate Gallery sculpture, although in the photograph the pedestal is not completed. It was later called the 'Manresa' Venus (after the street in Chelsea where Dobson lived), and was lent to his memorial exhibition in 1966 by C. Douglas Stephenson. Stephenson gave the version made in composition and plywood to the Bethnal Green Museum in

1934, where it was displayed in the costume section, before being transferred to the Tate Gallery.

The double page in the *Architectural Review* of 1933 cited above reproduces Dobson's plaster model and praises the Charnaux Company for asking a sculptor to design a lay figure 'to show off dresses, corsets and stockings'. Evidently this particular sculpture was not used commercially as it was immediately given to the Bethnal Green Museum, but there may have been other casts which were used in shop windows. The *Architectural Review* also reproduces four designs by Dobson for panels 'depicting types of elegance throughout the ages, which are to serve as its [the sculpture's] complement and setting ... from a charming Etruscan virgin ... to the voluptuous graces of a Boucher nymph'.

T 03720 Kneeling Figure 1935

Terracotta 8¼ × 5¼ × 5¾ (210 × 130 × 150)
Inscribed 'Dobson' on base
Transferred from the Victoria and Albert Museum 1983

Prov: Purchased from the artist by the Department of Circulation, Victoria and Albert Museum, 1938

Exh: *Frank Dobson*, Leicester Galleries, April–May 1935 (5); *Frank Dobson, Memorial Exhibition*, Arts Council Gallery, June–July 1966 (49); travelling exhibitions of the Department of Circulation, Victoria and Albert Museum

This terracotta is dated by the catalogue of Dobson's memorial exhibition in 1966, and was presumably made for his Leicester Galleries exhibition of 1935. It was purchased by the Victoria and Albert Museum together with a number of printed fabrics designed by Dobson.

T03721 Crouching Woman 1923

Bronze $4\frac{3}{8} \times 5\frac{3}{4} \times 3\frac{1}{4}$ (110 × 145 × 190)
Not inscribed
Transferred from the Victoria and Albert
Museum 1983

Prov: Given to the Victoria and Albert Museum by Dr Neville Goodman, 1971 (A. 32–1971)

Exh: Travelling exhibitions of the Department of Circulation, Victoria and Albert Museum; *True and Pure Sculpture, Frank Dobson*, Kettle's Yard, Cambridge, July–August 1981, Harris Museum and Art Gallery, Preston, September–October 1981, Ferens Art Gallery, Hull, October–November 1981, City Museum and Art Gallery, Birmingham, November 1981–January 1982 (35, repr.). *Also repr*: Raymond Mortimer, *Frank Dobson*, 1926, pl.5 (as 'Study. Bronze (1923)')

Dobson designed 'Cambria Receiving the Homage of Posterity' in 1923 as a Welsh National War Memorial for Cardiff. A bronze cast of the large maquette was first exhibited in the London Group in June 1925 (189), and consisted of a seated female nude with a very much smaller crouching nude beside her. This bronze was acquired by Manchester City Art Gallery in 1932. The Tate Gallery's 'Crouching Woman' is a cast of a study for this smaller figure, and differs from it by her not reaching so far forward.

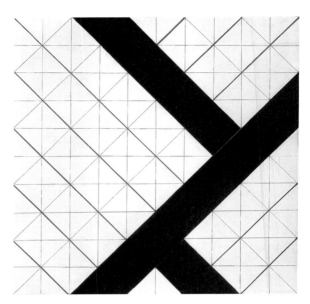

Theo van Doesburg 1883-1931

T03374 Counter-Composition VI 1925

Oil on canvas $19\frac{11}{16} \times 19\frac{11}{16}$ (500 × 500)
Inscribed 'HAUT' on top bar of stretcher and 'THEO VAN DOESBURG/1925' on back of canvas
Purchased from the estate of Frau Ilse E. Vordemberge-Leda through Juda Rowan Gallery (Grant-in-Aid) 1982

Prov: Friedrich Vordemberge-Gildewart, Hannover (from the artist, by exchange 1925); Frau Ilse E. Vordemberge-Leda, Rapperswil

Exh: *Theo Van Doesburg 1883–1931*, Stedelijk van Abbemuseum, Eindhoven, December 1968–January 1969 (A35); Gemeentemuseum, The Hague, February–March 1969 (A35); Kunsthalle, Nuremberg, April–June 1969 (A30); Kunsthalle, Basle, August–September 1969 (A30); *Vordemberge-Gildewart Remembered*, Annely Juda Fine Art, July–September 1974 (43, repr.); *Abstraction – Création 1931–1936*, Westfälisches Landesmuseum, Münster, April–June 1978 (Van Doesburg 1, repr.); *Line and Movement*, Annely Juda Fine Art, June–September 1979 (13, repr.); *The 1st Russian Show*, Annely Juda Fine Art, September–December 1983 (92, repr.)

Repr: *De Stijl*, VII, no.78, 1927, p.92 as 'Contre-Compositie' 1925; *The Tate Gallery Illustrated Biennial Report 1982–84*, 1984, p.44

Van Doesburg painted his first 'Counter-Composition' in 1924, the title denoting that the lines of the composition are at 45 degrees to the sides of the picture instead of being parallel to them, so that there is a dynamic interaction between the composition and the format of the canvas. The sketch for this particular work in an 'elementarist' sketchbook in the Van Doesburg archive at the Gemeentemuseum, The Hague, shows that it was originally conceived as a lozenge (that is to say hung obliquely by a corner), though the picture itself is inscribed 'HAUT' along the top bar of the stretcher, which indicates that it was meant to be hung in the conventional manner.

This picture belonged to the German abstract painter Friedrich Vordemberge-Gildewart, who joined the de Stijl group in 1924 and obtained it from Van Doesburg in Paris in 1925 in exchange for two of his own works.

The artist wrote (letter of 29 October 1984):

It is a unique cast from a wax original, and it was cast by Mr Reginald Davies, who, at the time, undertook a small amount of bronze casting and moulding having retired from the running of his foundry.

It was made in 1964 as a submission for a sculpture at Glossop Centre, Derbyshire. I was commissioned to do a full-scale work, about 5 ft. in height in a combination of resin and hard wood. I have no record of the work being exhibited ... It was bought by Mr Gates from me direct, subsequent to his acquisition of the drawings which related to it. The original idea for the piece was based on reference to the building where the full-scale work was to be sited. The vertical nature of the piece has an optional reference ... to the upward and growing nature of the educative process on to which are bound the horizontal element of the individual, or subjective opportunity represented by a squarish male and a receptive form that could be seen as female.

John Doubleday b.1947

T 03722 Maquette for 'Building Blocks' 1964

Bronze $10\frac{5}{8} \times 5\frac{1}{8} \times 2\frac{3}{4}$ (270 × 130 × 70)
Inscribed 'Doubleday 1967' on reverse
Transferred from the Victoria and Albert Museum 1983

Prov: Purchased from the artist by William Gates, who gave it to the Victoria and Albert Museum 1979 (A. 26–1979)

This is an early work by Doubleday, which is not characteristic of his later development, and was his first submission for a commissioned work.

Jean Dubuffet 1901-1985

T 03679 The Ups and Downs 1977

Acrylic on paper mounted on canvas
$82\frac{3}{4} \times 133\frac{1}{4}$ (2100 × 3390)
Inscribed 'J.D. 77' b.r. and 'n.42/Les vicissitudes' on reverse
Purchased from Pace Gallery, New York (Grant-in-Aid) 1983

Prov: Pace Gallery, New York (purchased from the artist)

Exh: *Dubuffet Retrospektive*, Akademie der Künste, Berlin, September–October 1980; Museum des 20. Jahrhunderts, Vienna, November 1980–January 1981; Joseph-Haubrich-Kunsthalle, Cologne,

February–March 1981 (334, repr. in black and white, and in col.)
Lit: *Catalogue des Travaux de Jean Dubuffet XXXII: Théâtres de Mémoire*, Paris, 1982, no.42, pp.46-7, repr. *Also repr: The Tate Gallery Illustrated Biennial Report 1982–84*, 1984, p.56 in col.

The French title of this work is 'Les Vicissitudes'. The particular series of nearly 100 assemblages to which this belongs grew out of making a large number of paintings on paper which were allowed to accumulate in disorder on the floor of the studio. Their chance arrangements and overlappings gave the artist the idea of cutting up the pieces and using them to make assemblages to which he gave the collective title 'Théâtres de Mémoire' (Theatres of memory) because of the way they combined evocations of a number of different places and scenes. This painting, which is one of the largest, was made on 21 January 1977 and incorporates as many as thirty-five pieces, some with Dubuffet's characteristic lively hobgoblin-like figures and some with contrasting patterns.

Raoul Dufy 1877-1953

T 03564　The Harvest 1929

Oil on canvas $51\frac{3}{16} \times 63\frac{3}{4}$ (1300 × 1620)
Inscribed 'Raoul Dufy' b.centre and again 'Raoul Dufy' b.r.
Bequeathed by Mrs A.F. Kessler 1983
Prov: Bernheim-Jeune, Paris; Marcel Bénard; Bénard sale, Drouot, Paris, 23–24 February 1931, lot 9, repr. as 'La Moisson'; bt Marcel Kapferer, 61,000 frs; Reid and Lefevre; Mrs Kessler
Exh: *Fransche Schilderkunst uit de Twintigste Eeuw: Ecole de Paris*, Stedelijk Museum, Amsterdam, April–May 1932 (76, as 'De Oogst' 1929); *Oeuvres Récentes de Raoul Dufy*, Galerie Max Kaganovitch, Paris, June 1936 (3, as 'Le Champ de Blé' 1928); *Oil Paintings and Watercolours 'The Châteaux of the Loire' by Raoul Dufy*, Lefevre Gallery, May 1938 (6); *French Paintings from the Kessler Collection*, York Art Gallery, May 1948 (3); *The Kessler Collection*, Wildenstein Gallery. October–November 1948 (8); *Raoul Dufy*, Tate Gallery, January–February 1954 (89); *Nineteenth and Twentieth Century French Paintings from English Private Collections*, Marlborough Fine Art, June–July 1965 (15, repr.); *The Kessler Bequest*, Tate Gallery, February–April 1984 (not numbered, repr. in col.)
Lit: Maurice Laffaille, *Raoul Dufy: Catalogue Raisonné de l'Oeuvre Peint*, Paris, 1976, III, no.1022, p.76, repr. as 'Champ de Blé' 1930. *Also repr*: Marcelle Berr de Turique, *Raoul Dufy*, Paris, 1930, p.186 as 'La Moisson' 1929; *Beaux-Arts*, VIII, March 1931, p.9; Maximilien Gauthier, *Raoul Dufy*, Paris, 1949, pl.XIV; Marcel Brion, *Raoul Dufy: Paintings and Watercolours*, 1959, pl.49, as 'The Harvest' 1930

This picture, which is widely regarded as one of Dufy's finest works, is one of nineteen oils of harvest scenes in Normandy painted at intervals over a period of some years. One of the others, made several years later, appears to show the same fields seen from a slightly different position and is known as 'Cornfield at Couliboeuf' (Laffaille 1024). Couliboeuf is a village to the east of Falaise. At least four of the other harvest scenes also appear to have been painted in this same area (Laffaille 1021, 1022 bis, 1023 and 1025).

Although usually known in recent years as 'Champ de Blé' (Cornfield), the original title of this work was 'La Moisson' (The Harvest).

T 03565　Open Window at Saint-Jeannet c.1926-7

Gouache on paper $25\frac{3}{4} \times 20$ (656 × 507)
Inscribed 'Raoul Dufy' b.r.
Bequeathed by Mrs A.F. Kessler 1983
Prov: Reid and Lefevre; Mrs Kessler
Exh: *The Kessler Collection*, Wildenstein Gallery, October–November 1948 (15, as 'The Open Window'); *The Kessler Bequest*, Tate Gallery, February–April 1984 (not numbered, repr.)

Lit: Fanny Guillon-Laffaille, *Raoul Dufy: Catalogue Raisonné des Aquarelles, Gouaches et Pastels*, Paris, 1982, II, no.1514, p.166, repr. as 'Fenêtre ouverte à Saint-Jeannet'

Saint-Jeannet is in the south of France, near Vence in the Alpes-Maritimes, and is situated half-way up a hillside. Dufy painted at least eleven oils of this village (including the Tate's 'The Baou de Saint-Jeannet' 1923) and about the same number of watercolours, all apparently on various short visits over the period 1920–7. This would clearly have been one of the later works and can be dated on style c. 1926–7.

He also painted a small number of other views through open windows from apartments in Vence, Cannes, Nice, Paris and elsewhere.

T 03566   The Kessler Family on Horseback 1931

Gouache on paper $19\frac{5}{8} \times 26\frac{3}{8}$ (500 × 669)
Not inscribed
Bequeathed by Mrs A.F. Kessler 1983

Prov: Mrs Kessler (purchased from the artist c.1931)

Exh: *The Kessler Collection*, Wildenstein Gallery, October–November 1948 (11, as 'Studies for an Equestrian Portrait'); *The Kessler Bequest*, Tate Gallery, February–April 1984 (not numbered, repr.)

Lit: Bernard Dorival, 'Raoul Dufy et le Portrait', *La Revue des Arts*, v, no.3, 1955, pp.175–80, repr. p.180; Fanny Guillon-Laffaille, *Raoul Dufy: Catalogue Raisonné*

des Aquarelles, Gouaches et Pastels, Paris, 1981, I, no.879, p.321, repr. as 'La Famille Kessler à Cheval' 1932; Bryan Robertson, 'An Introduction to Dufy', *Raoul Dufy 1877–1953*, exhibition catalogue, Hayward Gallery, 1983, p.54

A study for the whole composition, showing the figures as they appear in both the finished pictures. Mr and Mrs Kessler are in the centre, with their daughters Augusta and Anne in the foreground, to left and right, and behind them (again from left to right) Frances, Cornelia and Susan.

T 03567   Landscape study for 'The Kessler Family on Horseback' 1931

Gouache on paper $19\frac{3}{4} \times 26$ (503 × 660)
Not inscribed
Bequeathed by Mrs A.F. Kessler 1983

Prov: Mrs Kessler (purchased from the artist)

Exh: *The Kessler Collection*, Wildenstein Gallery, October–November 1948 (12, as

'Study of Trees'); *The Kessler Bequest*, Tate Gallery, February–April 1984 (not numbered, repr.)

Lit: Bernard Dorival, 'Raoul Dufy et le Portrait', *La Revue des Arts*, v, no.3, 1955, pp.175–80, repr. p.177; Fanny Guillon-Laffaille, *Raoul Dufy: Catalogue Raisonné des Aquarelles, Gouaches et Pastels*, Paris, 1981, 1, no.880, p.321, repr. as 'Etude du Paysage de "La Famille à Kessler Cheval"' 1932; Bryan Robertson, 'An Introduction to Dufy', *Raoul Dufy 1877–1953*, exhibition catalogue, Hayward Gallery, 1983, p.54

Mr J.B.A. Kessler had the idea in 1930 of commissioning a family portrait of himself, his wife and their five daughters on horseback (as they were all very keen on horses and riding); Mrs Kessler agreed provided she could choose the artist. On the advice of one of their French friends, Marcel Kapferer, who was the previous owner of Dufy's 'Harvest', she decided to ask Raoul Dufy, who was known for paintings of race-course scenes and had also made a few portraits of single figures.

Dufy, who had never painted a group portrait before or a portrait of someone he did not know already, came to England and stayed for three weeks at the Kesslers' country house, Gunthorpe, at Oakham in Rutland, both in order to get to know the family and to make preliminary studies. He executed a number of studies in watercolour and oil, and in the form of pen-and-ink drawings, of Mr and Mrs Kessler and their daughters both individually and as a group, posing on their horses under the trees, and of the horses in their stables. The gouache of the landscape setting and the one T03566 showing the whole composition were the most complete. Then in the autumn of 1931 he painted a large group portrait from these studies in his studio in Paris. However Mrs Kessler thought that the finished picture was too sketchy and that the group needed a little more space around it and in front of it, and a shade more detail in the face. Dufy therefore agreed to make another, and returned to London in 1932, staying at the Savoy Hotel, and painted a second, more finished and detailed version in this country.

The first version was presented by Mme Dufy to the Musée Nationale d'Art Moderne in Paris in 1954, the year after the artist's death. The second, which is the one acquired by Mrs Kessler, is also included in her gift to the Tate, but is still in the possession of one of her cousins, who has a life interest. They are both exceptionally large by Dufy's standards, measuring 213 × 260 cm. and 214 × 275 cm. respectively.

The first version, which now belongs to the Musée National d'Art Moderne, Centres Georges Pompidou, was included in the Dufy exhibition at the Hayward Gallery, which closed on 5 February 1984.

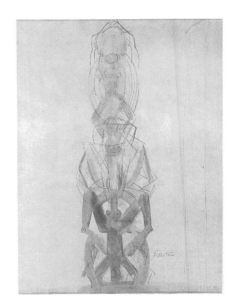

Sir Jacob Epstein 1880-1959

T03358 **Totem** c.1913

Pencil and watercolour on paper $22\frac{3}{4} \times 16\frac{1}{2}$ (580 × 415)
Inscribed 'Epstein' b.r.
Purchased from Anthony d'Offay Ltd. (Grant-in-Aid) 1982

Prov: Purchased by Anthony d'Offay from the artist's family; private collection, London; Anthony d'Offay

Exh: *?Drawings and Sculpture by Jacob Epstein*, Twenty-One Gallery, December 1913 – January 1914; *Jacob Epstein, the Rock Drill Period*, Anthony d'Offay Gallery, October–November 1973 (11, repr.); *Vorticism and its Allies*, Hayward Gallery, March–June 1974 (230); *Gauguin to Moore. Primitivism in Modern Sculpture*, Art Gallery of Ontario, Toronto, November 1981 – January 1982 (78, repr.); *British Drawings and Watercolours 1890-1940*, Anthony d'Offay Gallery, January–March 1982 (19); *'Primitivism' in 20th Century Art*, Museum of Modern Art, New York, September 1984 – January 1985 (repr. p.433)

Lit: Richard Cork, 'The Rock Drill Period', *Jacob Epstein, The Rock Drill Period*, exhibition catalogue, Anthony d'Offay, 1973, pp.5–15; Richard Cork, *Vorticism and Abstract Art in the First Machine Age*, 1976, p.474; Richard Cork, 'The Cave of the Golden Calf', *Artforum*, XXI, December 1982, pp.56–68, repr. p.64;

Alan G. Wilkinson, 'Paris and London. Modigliani, Lipchitz, Epstein and Gaudier-Brzeska', *'Primitivism' in 20th Century Art*, exhibition catalogue, Museum of Modern Art, New York, 1984, pp.431–43; Richard Cork, *Art Beyond the Gallery in Early 20th Century England*, 1985, pp.92–6, repr. p.97

Epstein was a precocious draughtsman, and included groups of drawings in many of his exhibitions and also exhibited drawings alone. The catalogue of his first one man exhibition, at the Twenty-One Gallery in December 1913, listed titles of eight drawings and stated also that 'other drawings will be added during the exhibition'. Epstein again included drawings in group exhibitions at Brighton in the same month and at the Goupil Gallery in March 1914, but drawings from this period were not again exhibited until the year after his death, 1960. At his memorial exhibition in Edinburgh in 1961 only four drawings of this period were included, all studies for the 'Rock Drill'.

It is reasonable to assume that the group of large Vorticist style drawings, including 'Totem', which were sold from his estate after his death were those that were drawn for the Twenty-One Gallery exhibition. There is no specific record that 'Totem' was included, and the original title of the drawing is unknown (the only drawing reproduced in a review is of the 'Rock Drill' seen from behind, in *New Age*, 25 December 1913, p.251) but its subject is comparable to those exhibited:

Mr. Epstein, at the Twenty-One Gallery in York Street, Adelphi, shows some sculpture and drawings. He seems to be obsessed by certain fundamental facts of life usually excluded from artistic representation, and we are not sure how far hieroglyphics based on the obvious physical aspect of these things can be considered to symbolise adequately their significance (*Athenaeum*, 6 December 1913).

'Totem' depicts, within a geometrical network, a nude man and woman making love, with the woman holding above her head a baby. She is painted light blue, and the man light red. The baby existed also as a plaster sculpture, painted red, exhibited at the London Group in March 1915 titled 'Cursed Be the Day Where-in I was Born' (repr. Bernard van Dieren, *Epstein*, 1920, pl.v and listed in the sale catalogue of the John Quinn collection, American Art Galleries, New York, 9–11 February 1927, 721). This sculpture appears to be a part of a larger work, since the shapes of the legs protrude below the feet which are painted onto them, although the other features are carved in detail. Richard Cork (opera cit.) compares 'Totem' to Epstein's plaster decoration of the columns of the 'Cave of the Golden Calf' club in London, which were completed for the opening in June 1912. Apart from the probable later date of the drawing, made after Epstein's contact with Brancusi and Modigliani in Paris in 1912, it is clear from the profile drawing at the right of the sheet that this totem did not reach to a ceiling, but was intended to stand in front of some support and to cap it, apparently with a separate piece.

'Totem' is similar to the watercolour now called 'Study for Man Woman' (British Museum). Alan Wilkinson (op.cit.) dates this to the 1920s on the grounds that Epstein acquired a similar primitive carving from Madagascar in 1923–4, but it is equally possible that he had seen such a carving earlier (the idea that Epstein made a sculpture called 'Man Woman' follows from a misreading of his wife's telegram to John Quinn of 25 June 1916 listing his unfinished works as 'Sungod Venus Man Woman Maternity and the Rockdrill', where each name seems rather to refer to a separate work). These two drawings are amongst the closest of Epstein's to primitive art, and Alan Wilkinson compares 'Totem' to sculpture both from New Guinea and West Africa. Although no source has been identified that Epstein could have seen, the similarities in design are striking, and Epstein often mentioned that his admiration of primitive art in the museums of London and Paris began long before he began to collect it himself.

A third drawing of a similar size, 'Study for Rock Drill' (repr. Richard Buckle, *Epstein Drawings*, 1962, pl.27), includes two sketches of abstracted figures making love in a similar upside down position seen from above as in 'Totem', but drawn in a different style of sharp angles and straight lines. This is in effect a reworking of 'Totem' in a more Vorticist style.

John Ernest b.1922

T03723 **Triangulated Relief** 1965

Construction of wood and formica, painted
$20\frac{7}{8} \times 27\frac{1}{2} \times 2\frac{3}{8}$ (530 × 700 × 60)

Not inscribed
Transferred from the Victoria and Albert
Museum 1983

Prov: Purchased from the Axiom Gallery by the
Department of Circulation, Victoria and
Albert Museum, 1968 (Circ. 835–1968)

Exh: *John Ernest, Robyn Denny*, Arnolfini
Gallery, Bristol, October 1966 (9); *Four
Artists, John Ernest, Anthony Hill,
Malcolm Hughes, Gillian Wise. Reliefs,
Constructions and Drawings*, Victoria and
Albert Museum touring exhibition, 1971
(1)

Max Ernst 1891–1976

T 03707 **Dadaville** c.1924

Painted plaster and cork mounted on
canvas
26¾ × 22 × 2½ (680 × 560 × 63)
Not inscribed
Purchased from the Trustees of Sir Roland
Penrose's Voluntary Settlement (Grant-
in-Aid) 1983

Prov: Paul Éluard, Paris (purchased from the
artist); Sir Roland Penrose, London, 1938

Exh: *Max Ernst*, London Gallery, December
1938 – January 1939 (23, as 'Forêt' 1924);
Max Ernst, Institute of Contemporary
Arts, December 1952 – January 1953 (10,
as 'Forest'); Retrospective Exhibition of
Paintings by Max Ernst, Matthiesen

Gallery, November–December 1965 (8, as
'Forest'); *Max Ernst*, Musée National
d'Art Moderne, Paris, November–
December 1959 (158, as 'Dadaville' 1923–
4); *Max Ernst*, Tate Gallery, September–
October 1961 (40); *Max Ernst: Oeuvre
Sculpté 1913–1961*, Le Point Cardinal,
Paris, November–December 1961 (3,
repr.); *Max Ernst: Målningar, Collage,
Frottage, Teckningar, Grafik, Böcker,
Skulpturer 1917–1969*, Moderna Museet,
Stockholm, September–November 1969
(14); *Dada and Surrealism Reviewed*,
Hayward Gallery, January–March 1978
(8.15, repr.)

Lit: Werner Spies, Sigrid and Günter Metken,
Max Ernst: Werke 1906–1925, Cologne,
1975, no.673, p.351, repr. as 'Dadaville'
c.1924
Also repr: Patrick Waldberg, *Max Ernst*,
Paris, 1958, p.140; Gaston Diehl, *Max
Ernst*, Paris, 1973, p.20 in col.

This painted relief, made mainly of cork, is unique in
Ernst's work and is one of his first experiments with
sculpture. The photograph reproduced by Patrick
Waldberg shows that it was originally more regular,
with four rows of button-like corks up the projecting
vertical strips; those up the left hand strip are now
missing and so is one from each of the two strips to the
right. The cork has crumbled away in places, particularly up the left-hand vertical strip and at the left-
hand side of the base, which originally extended further.

The relief has some affinity to the series of paintings
called 'Forest' which Ernst began making in 1925 and
was sold to Sir Roland Penrose by Paul Éluard in 1938
under this title; but the title was changed to 'Dadaville',
presumably at the artist's suggestion, at the time of his
exhibition at the Musée National d'Art Moderne in
Paris in 1959. 'Dadaville' can be translated as 'Dada
Town' implying a kind of fantastic Dada townscape.

Frederick Etchells 1886–1973

T 03724 **Inscription 'Let us now praise
famous men'** 1925

Hoptonwood stone, the letters painted
20⅛ × 35⅜ × 1 (510 × 910 × 25)
Inscribed 'LET US NOW
PRAISE/FAMOUS MEN & OUR
FATHERS/THAT BEGAT US + THE
LORD /HATH WROUGHT GREAT
GLORY/THROUGH THEM BY HIS
GREAT/POWER FROM THE
BEGINNING'

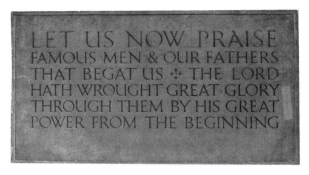

Transferred from the Victoria and Albert Museum 1983

Prov: ...; Department of Architecture and Sculpture, Victoria and Albert Museum, acquired 1934 (A. 47–1934)

Exh: ?*Art for the Slender Purse*, British Institute of Industrial Art, Victoria and Albert Museum, November–December 1929

There is no information at the Victoria and Albert Museum about the provenance of this inscription, but it seems likely that it was the one exhibited there in 1929. Etchells was a Vorticist painter and subsequently an architect, and is not otherwise known as a letter cutter.

The text is from Ecclesiasticus 44: 1–2. The first four words are painted gold, and the others black.

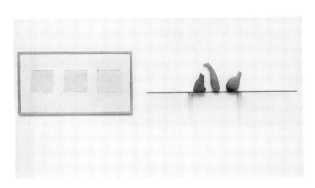

Joel Fisher b.1947

T 03445 Untitled 1981-2

Three cast wax sculptures and three pencil drawings on hand-made paper mounted on board, dimensions of sculptures $5\frac{1}{8} \times 3 \times 3\frac{1}{2}$ ($130 \times 75 \times 90$), $2\frac{1}{8} \times 2 \times 8\frac{3}{8}$ ($53 \times 51 \times 213$), $5\frac{1}{2} \times 3\frac{1}{2} \times 2\frac{3}{8}$ ($140 \times 90 \times 60$); dimensions of drawings $6\frac{1}{4} \times 6\frac{1}{16}$ (158×154), $6\frac{1}{4} \times 6\frac{1}{4}$ (160×160), $6\frac{1}{4} \times 6\frac{3}{8}$ (160×162); overall dimensions $17\frac{1}{8} \times 30\frac{1}{2}$ (435×775)
Not inscribed

Purchased from Nigel Greenwood Inc. Ltd. (Grant-in-Aid) 1982

Exh: *Joel Fisher, Sculptures, Watercolours, etchings*, Nigel Greenwood Inc., April–May 1982 (no catalogue)

Lit: Joel Fisher, 'Haddock's Eyes', *Joel Fisher, Between Two and Three Dimensions, Drawings and Objects since 1979*, exhibition catalogue, Kunstmuseum, Lucerne, May 1984, detail repr. p.35

Barry Flanagan b.1941

T 03608 Carving No.13 1981

Limestone $14 \times 55\frac{1}{2} \times 23$ ($355 \times 1410 \times 585$)
Not inscribed
Purchased from Waddington Galleries (Grant-in-Aid) 1983

Exh: *Barry Flanagan Stone and Bronze Sculptures*, British Pavilion, XL Biennale, Venice, June–September 1982, Museum Haus Esters, Krefeld, October–December 1982, Whitechapel Art Gallery, January–February 1983 (76, repr. in accompanying book, 15 in Venice leaflet only, 15 in Whitechapel leaflet only); *New Art at the Tate Gallery 1983*, Tate Gallery, September–October 1983 (not numbered in catalogue)

Lit: Michael Compton, 'A Developing Practice', *Barry Flanagan, Sculpture*, published to coincide with exhibition at British Pavilion, XL Biennale, Venice, London 1982, pp.25-6; Teresa Gleadowe, 'Stone and Bronze Sculptures', *Barry Flanagan, Stone and Bronze Sculptures*, exhibition leaflet, British Pavilion, XL Biennale, Venice 1982; Lynne Cooke, 'Paris Centre Georges Pompidou, Barry Flanagan', *The Burlington Magazine*, CXXV, July 1983, pp.47-8

Also repr: Barry Flanagan Sculptures, exhibition catalogue, Centre Georges Pompidou, Paris, March–May 1983, p.89; *Tema Celeste*, exhibition catalogue, Museo Civico d'Arte Contemporanea di Gibellina, Sicily, 1983, p.45

In conversation (16 October 1985) the artist said that the maquette for T 03608 was made by taking a piece of wet clay in one hand and squeezing it at one end, then turning it over and squeezing the other end with the same hand; the impressions of his fingers occur at either end but on opposite sides, diagonally across from each other. Michael Compton (in 'A Developing Practice', loc.cit., pp.25–6) refers to 'Carving No.13' as having an 'unnamable shape ... whose maquette appears to have been a lump of clay having no preconceived shape, only the imprint of squeezing and gently wringing hands and fingers' and points to the existence of another version (see reference to 'Carving No.8' in entry for T 03609) commenting:

> such resulting forms would be impossible for the craftsman to conceptualise geometrically or in any other terms other than their very own though lines formed in the model by the flattened overlapping of the pressed clay are interpreted in marble as incisions. The craftsman has formed a fossil fault, which happened to be in the stone, into its prototype in the clay. This piece at the moment represents the furthest extreme of Flanagan's device of extracting lively abstract form from the process of conducted scaling up and interpretation of a composition in one medium by the trained skills of another.

He goes on to mention a new set of carvings in process at the time of writing (in 1982) which included 'squeeze' pieces amongst others. Flanagan numbered his stone carvings from the beginning in two successive years; after the thirteen works of 1981, he made another set in 1982, which are numbered 1 to 6. Although the series of both 1981 and 1982 are abstract, the second set is much more obviously so and the earliest two works in the set (both, like T 03608, made in Travertine marble) are very closely related in shape ('Carving No.2' 1982 was included in Flanagan's exhibition at the Centre Pompidou in 1983 and is illustrated in the catalogue, op.cit., p.68). From the clay maquette (repr. p.95) small bronzes were made and one example is illustrated in the Paris catalogue, op. cit., p.63. There appear to be similarities between these later more abstract carvings and drawings of October/November 1979, reproduced in *Barry Flanagan, Sculpture*, fig.50, p.88 (see also entry for T 03609).

This entry has been approved by the artist.

T 03609 **Carving No.2** 1981

White Arni marble and Grey Imperial marble
$24\frac{1}{2} \times 24 \times 24$ (622 × 609 × 609)
Not inscribed
Purchased from Waddington Galleries (Grant-in-Aid) 1983

Exh: *Barry Flanagan, Sculptures in Bronze 1980-81*, Waddington Galleries, December 1981 (not in catalogue); *Barry Flanagan Stone and Bronze Sculptures*, British Pavilion, XL Biennale, Venice, June–September 1982, Museum Haus Esters, Krefeld, October–December 1982, Whitechapel Art Gallery, January–February 1983 (72, repr; also repr. fig.67, p.92, pp.52–3 in col. in accompanying book; 11 in Venice leaflet only, no.7 in Whitechapel leaflet only); *New Art at the Tate Gallery 1983*, Tate Gallery, September–October 1983 (not numbered in catalogue); *An International Survey of Recent Painting and Sculpture*, Museum of Modern Art, New York, May–August 1984 (listed in accompanying brochure, repr. in catalogue p.135); *Barry Flanagan Prints 1970–1983*, Tate Gallery, June–August 1986 (repr. p.11)

Lit: Michael Compton, 'A Developing Practice', *Barry Flanagan, Sculpture*, published to coincide with exhibition at British Pavilion, XL Biennale, Venice, London 1982, pp.25–6; Teresa Gleadowe, 'Stone and Bronze Sculptures', *Barry Flanagan, Stone and Bronze Sculptures*,

exhibition brochure, British Pavilion, XL Biennale, Venice 1982
Also repr: Barry Flanagan Sculptures, exhibition catalogue, Musée National d'art Moderne, Paris, March–May 1983, p.89

This sculpture and 'Carving No.13' (T03608) are from a series of thirteen closely related, abstract marble and stone carvings, produced in Italy in 1981 at the stone carving atelier of Sem Ghelardini, at Pietrasanta. The others in the series are:

'Carving No.1', Marble, $36\frac{1}{2} \times 26 \times 19\frac{1}{2}$ (927 × 660 × 490), Coll: Tochigi Prefectural Museum of Fine Arts, Utsunomiya, Japan;
'Carving No.3', marble, $14 \times 17 \times 16$ (356 × 432 × 406), coll: Artist;
'Carving Nos. 4, 5, 6' (3 separate elements), Travertine marble, each approx. $25 \times 14 \times 12$ (635 × 355 × 260), coll: Artist;
'Carving No.7', marble $12\frac{1}{2} \times 24 \times 9\frac{1}{2}$ (318 × 610 × 241), Waddington Galleries;
'Carving No.8', marble, $9 \times 30 \times 12$ (229 × 762 × 305), private collection, London;
'Carving No.9', marble, $11 \times 19 \times 15$ (279 × 483 × 380), coll: Tokyo Metropolitan Art Museum;
'Untitled' (Carving No.10), marble, $16\frac{1}{2} \times 26\frac{1}{4} \times 20\frac{1}{2}$ (419 × 667 × 520), Durand-Dessert, Paris;
'Travertino Toscana' (Carving No.11), marble, $16 \times 23 \times 14$ (406 × 584 × 355), private collection, Ackron, Ohio;
'Untitled' (Carving No.12), stone, $10\frac{1}{2} \times 26\frac{1}{4} \times 15$ (265 × 667 × 381), Waddington Galleries

For these sculptures, and a similar series in 1982 (see entry for T03608), Flanagan made small hand-sized maquettes in clay which were afterwards scaled up and re-interpreted in marble or other stone under his direction, by skilled craftsmen working at the atelier. This collaboration between artist and craftsmen extended to the choice of appropriate material to carve and as Michael Compton has pointed out ('A Developing Practice' in *Barry Flanagan, Sculpture*, op.cit., pp.24–5) the craftsman must translate from one medium into another combining in the resultant work's information given by the maquette and by the artist (who controls the production through word and gesture) with his own knowledge and technical skills. It is the craftsman who must translate models bearing all the flaws and immediacy of a pliable material that has been speedily shaped, into analogous but more monumental forms. Compton writes:

The scaling up is not mechanical. The forms have to be characterised, consciously or unconsciously, in the mind of the craftsman, so that he can recreate them in marble. He will do this partly by eliminating what is too detailed, like textures, fingerprints and sandy granules on the surface, partly by assimilating them to transformations of abstract stereotypes in the mind (triangle, spiral, etc.) as in 'Carving No.2' . . ., partly by relating them to analogous forms . . . and partly by his own educated sense of what is a good or pleasing form.

In an interview with Judith Bumpus (excerpts have been published in *Barry Flanagan, Sculpture*, in an updated Chronology for Flanagan's Paris exhibition in 1983 and in *Barry Flanagan prints 1970-1983*, all cited above) Flanagan discussed the sculptures he produced with the craftsmen at Pietrasanta:

they're produced from clay maquettes which are formed in the hand – rolled, coiled, twisted, squeezed, generally formed in and by the hand. Now these shapes have no geometric skeletal interiors. Form shaped by the cupping and squeezing together of both hands, of clay, will have a very delicate and exact form . . . this is a challenge, clearly, to any stone carver, to reproduce this form or even to appraise it. But of course the test is to produce another rather like it. Now, this challenge appeals to a good carver. One of these shapes, the size of a hand or formed in the hand, can easily go to stone four times its size. And the significance of four times the size is simply that the hand goes into the arm four times – approximately. Therefore, this gives the carver the continuity and the sense of the scaling up. There's a reason for how many times and there's a physical understanding immediately generated by the proximity of the maquette to the hand, the stone to the arm, which the carvers appreciate. You see, they must have an objective standard, which is perfectly understood, by which they achieve a carving. There are all sorts of mechanical aids which they bring to what's commonly known as 'scaling up'. However, when the work is interesting, far more can be brought to the production of the final piece through the authorship of the sculptor, through the hands and skills of a carver. And before I leave that subject, all I've got to say is that I've got to be the boss.

Now it's interesting to reflect that in the sculptor's . . . historically habitual working environment with the supportive facilities of bronze casting and carving, artisan and sculptor skills, supportive sculptor's skills, the place of the sculptor is actually recognised. And the authorship and interpretation and the entire environment, all these subjects are discussed and quickly come to be forming simply a part of what goes on in the studio. There are understandings which are reached. These understandings are traditional. They've always been available, if you go to the right places . . . it's very nice to remember that there *are* places where sculpture is actually made and mutual support and interest and skills, sculptor's skills are brought to bear by all individuals as among a group of musicians, all playing different parts but with the actual understanding and willingness to interpret the work in hand objectively and exclusively for the same purpose, to produce sculpture. It can lighten the load. It makes work a little more vital and a little more significant.

The carvers are in Italy near Pisa. There's Carrara itself and at the southern end of that district, just by the sea and below the Apuan Alps there's Pietrasanta. Well, of course, it's the stone mecca. They export everything from there from architectural facades, [and] cladding down to onyx jewellery.

In another interview (Kaleidoscope, BBC Radio 4, January 1982, excerpt reproduced in Chronology section, *Barry Flanagan, Sculpture*, p.92) the artist said:

I have been given the opportunity to find a place as author, related to other individuals who have special carving skills. So that from the maquettes that I've produced they are able to interpret in manners one carving to the next, even from the same maquette.

According to the Chronology (op.cit.), Flanagan first learned to carve in 1958, as a student at Birmingham College of Art and first visited Pietrasanta in 1973 (where he made stone carvings at Balderi's Yard). In 1975 he worked for a stone mason in Oxford for a short time and in 1978 was in contact with Pietrasanta again; the Chronology records that he ordered three ton of stone, selected by Sem Ghelardini (p.68).

In April 1980 Flanagan showed thirty-one sculptures – the earliest dating from 1973 – at the Waddington Galleries and Catherine Lampert noted (in 'Stone Sculptures', *Barry Flanagan, Sculptures in Stone 1973–1979*, exhibition catalogue, Waddington Galleries, April–May 1980) that the bulk of his work in the period covered by the exhibition had been made in stone. Among the works shown was 'Enlarged Marble Shape' 1978 (27), which has strong formal and procedural links with the series of 1981. Flanagan has sometimes made the conscious decision to delegate in part the production (or in the case of earlier works, arrangement) of his work to others. As its name suggests, 'Enlarged Marble Shape' is a scaled up version of a smaller marble carving, made by Flanagan. In this instance, the sculptor Peter Randall-Page produced the enlarged version, setting a precedent for Flanagan's collaborative venture at Pietrasanta in 1981. While this earlier sculpture differs from T 03608 in that the original model was itself marble, its smooth marble conch shape, measuring 16 × 26 × 16 (410 × 660 × 410) has both formal and textural similarities with the later work.

The final illustration in *Barry Flanagan, Sculpture* (op.cit., p.95) is a photograph of Sergio Benedetti and Sem Ghelardini holding two pale looking maquettes for the stone series of 1981. Because of similarities within the series, these maquettes relate in shape to all or part of all but three of the sculptures, although a number of small maquettes were made. The catalogue for Flanagan's exhibition held at the Musée National d'Art Moderne in Paris in 1983 illustrates a number of bronze casts taken from the maquettes. Ten of these relate directly to the thirteen larger works of 1981 (*Barry Flanagan, Sculptures*, March–May 1983, p.63). Three of the works in the large series consist of more than one element and taken as a whole, the thirteen works are all formed from variations of one or more of the following basic components or shapes: a) carved marble supports; b) discs; c) 'abstract' elements either supported on discs and legs or resting on the ground. In the case of Carvings Nos. '1', '4', '5' and '6' the supports have the appearance of rather roughly cut sectioned legs. T 03609 has as its supporting base, three marble 'cannon balls' which look like a truncated version of the longer legs of 'Carving No.1'. Flanagan was already working with similar stone shapes in the 'bub' and 'bollard' works of 1979 (illustrated in *Barry Flanagan, Sculpture*, pp. 46-7) which were worked from found objects (in this case, Cornish staddle stones, used for supporting and protecting hayricks), and 'Carving No.2' may also be compared with 'That Old Penny' 1978-80 (*Barry Flanagan*, p.42, 4464 × 610 × 559), a hollowed out stone disc resting on three stone balls. In conversation (16 October 1985) the artist told a Tate curator that the idea for the balls came from actual cannon balls which in the past were sometimes used for decorative arrangements. The chamfered disc of 'That Old Penny' is the inverted mushroom top of a staddle stone (used to prevent rats from reaching the ricks) and is the formal original of the supported and supporting disc in T 03609 and also in Carvings Nos. '1' and '3'. Also related is 'Marine Goddess' 1978 (*Barry Flanagan*, p.43, Hornton stone, 550 × 460 × 460) which with its spiral form (suggesting a large fossil) resting on stacked discs resembles Carvings Nos. '1' and '3'.

The third component, common to Carvings Nos. '1', '2', '3', '7', '9', '10' and '11' (and the only element present in the case of the latter four works but with slight variations in each case), is a strange organic looking shape, rather like a rolled up tongue. This was made in its small clay original by forming a cone of clay, rolling it with a spiral at one end and forming a point at the other. The combination of 'organic' form and dish is found in Nos. '1', '2', and '3' in the series. In 'Carving No.12', the spiral form appears in a flattened, gouged out version and in 'No.7' is rolled at either end to form an 'S'. This configuration also relates to a slightly earlier marble carving, not one of the series,

'Her Warm Tit Rolls' 1981. The final elements (Nos. '8' and '13') are abstract elongated shapes (see entry for T 03609).

The organic form in 'Carving No.2' and the other sculptures most closely related in the series is one which Compton suggests ('A Developing Practice', cited above p.25) is easy to project on to the sides of a block of stone. The particular shape is pre-figured in Flanagan's note books of 1978 (illustrated in *Barry Flanagan, Sculpture*, p.87, fig.38) where as Compton describes (p.25, op.cit.) it appears 'as a profile extended in parallel into the third dimension, and again sitting on a heap of objects to form an "Ubu" head. The interpretation is, for this reason, rather geometric and without something of the abstract dynamics (the theology or flow pattern) of the clay.' Flanagan's interest in Alfred Jarry's "Ubu" and the pseudo science of Pataphysics has been widely referred to and the spiral (perhaps the heraldic Pataphysical spiral) has recurred in his work in various forms; as cut out metal, in the sculptures of 1978, in a print of 1971 and in drawings, and cut into stone.

As already noted, Flanagan made maquettes in small editions for each of the thirteen sculptures and the Paris catalogue (op.cit., p.63) illustrates bronze versions of the following: 'No.1', 'No.2' (T 03609); Nos. '4', '5', '6' (each of these is a single 'leg' form but in the case of the original maquettes, these legs appear to support another form); No. '8'/'13' (see entry for T 03608); Nos. '9', '10', '11' (this group is also reproduced in *Barry Flanagan, Sculpture*, p.25, top illustration, as 'Maquettes for Stone Sculptures' 1981, each approx. 5 × 5 (128 × 128)) and No. '12'.

This entry has been approved by the artist.

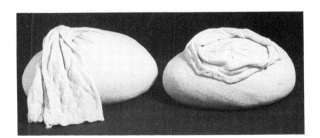

T 03725 **Sand Muslin 2** 1966

Two muslin bags filled with sand, dimensions variable, width about 12 (305)
Not inscribed
Transferred from the Victoria and Albert Museum 1983
Prov: Purchased by David Sylvester for the Contemporary Art Society; given by the Society to the Department of Circulation, Victoria and Albert Museum, 1972 (Circ. 38 and 38a–1972)

Exh: *Contemporary Art Society. An exhibition of works shortly to be presented to public art galleries in Great Britain and the Commonwealth*, Gulbenkian Hall, Royal College of Art, October 1971 (111); *Barry Flanagan*, Van Abbemuseum, Eindhoven, June–July 1977, Arnolfini Gallery, Bristol, July–August 1977, Serpentine Gallery, November 1978 – January 1979 (not numbered)
Lit: Catherine Lampert, 'Notes on Barry Flanagan', exhibition catalogue, *Barry Flanagan*, Van Abbemuseum, Eindhoven, 1977, n.p.

The sculpture 'Sand Muslin' belongs to the Arts Council of Great Britain, and was reproduced as the frontispiece in the Van Abbemuseum catalogue (1977).

Flanagan left St Martin's School of Art in 1966. The catalogue of his exhibition at the Rowan Gallery in August 1966 lists one work made of sand, 'ring n', a heap of sand with the top removed. Catherine Lampert (loc.cit.) associates his sand filled bags with the process of casting.

Lucio Fontana 1899-1968

T 03588 **Natura 13** 1959-60

Bronze 24 × 28¾ diameter (610 × 730)
Not inscribed
Purchased from Galerie Karsten Greve, Cologne (Grant-in-Aid) 1983

Prov: Mme Everaert, Brussels from 1961;
Galerie Karsten Greve, Cologne

Exh: *'Concetti Spaziali' de Fontana*, Galerie Iris
Clert, Paris, November 1961 (not
numbered, repr.); *L. Fontana*, Palais des
Beaux-Arts, Brussels, September–
November 1972 (50); *Lucio Fontana:
Plastiken und Bilder 1953–1962*, Galerie
Karsten Greve, Cologne, October 1980;
Lucio Fontana, Dia Art Foundation,
Cologne, March–May 1981 (87, 88, 89 or
90); *Westkunst*, Museen der Stadt,
Cologne, May–August 1981 (526, repr.);
El Espacio Come Exploraciòn, Palacio de
Velàzquez, Madrid, April–June 1982
(catalogue details and number not
ascertained); *Forty Years of Modern Art
1945–1985*, Tate Gallery, February–April
1986 (not numbered)

Lit: Enrico Crispolti, *Lucio Fontana*, Brussels,
1974, pp.104–5, repr. p.105

Edward Reginald Frampton

1872-1923

T 03414   Brittany: 1914 c.1920

Oil on canvas 30¼ × 36½ (768 × 926)
Inscribed 'E Reginald Frampton' b.r.
Purchased from a private collector through
Roy Miles Fine Paintings Ltd (Grant-in-
Aid) 1982

Prov: Fine Art Society 1920; Joseph Bibby,
Birkenhead 1924; Bibby family until 1979,
sold Sotheby's Belgravia, 2 October 1979
(260, repr. in col.); ...; Roy Miles Fine
Paintings Ltd 1981; ...

Exh: *RA Summer Exhibition* 1920 (62);
*Memorial Exhibition of Paintings and
Watercolours by the late E. Reginald
Frampton*, Fine Art Society, March 1924
(22); *Summer Show of Post-Impressionist
and Victorian Paintings*, Roy Miles Fine
Paintings, May–June 1981 (no catalogue
no., repr.)

This picture is probably unique in Frampton's oeuvre
on account of its subject matter. By 1910 Frampton had
gained recognition as a mural artist, fulfilling commissions for churches. He was also a regular contributor
to the RA summer exhibitions from 1910 to 1923, sub-
mitting easel paintings with a religious or symbolic
content. T 03414 has a prominently religious theme but
is allied to contemporary subject material, and this is
what makes it rare for Frampton; a young soldier and
his female companion kneel in prayer in front of a
wayside shrine before he goes off to war. This is made
clear by Frampton's inclusion of the date 1914 as part
of the painting's title.

During the period of his RA summer exhibition sub-
missions, 1910–23, Frampton lived at 1 Brook Green
Studios, Brook Green, London, but a letter of March
1913 in the archives of Cartwright Hall Art Gallery,
Bradford, reveals that Frampton spent some time in
1911 painting 'in a little fishing village in the extreme
north west corner of Finistère ... ' This letter was
written by Frampton when Cartwright Hall purchased
his 'A Madonna of Brittany' of 1911, a work which
bears similarities in terms of scenic background and
figure type to T 03414. The artist had tended to include a
landscape background in his earlier works for decorative
reasons, but his 'A Madonna of Brittany' includes two
sections of recognisable Breton scenery, 'part of the
Rade de Brest'. Increasingly after 1911 Frampton took
to painting landscapes which are true to fact and which
take a greater prominence in the picture composition.
Much of the composition of T 03414 is occupied with
the faithful rendering of a section of the Breton coastal
landscape, with the depiction of the harbour of Cama-
ret-sur-Mer, on the southern coastline of the Rade de
Brest. Situated near the end of the harbour wall is the
17th century chapel of Notre Dame de Rocamadour. St
Amadour was an early medieval saint who was believed
to have lived on an isolated hillside in what has now
become the village of Rocamadour in south west France,
and to have devoted his life to the Virgin Mary. The
young soldier and his female companion kneel and pray
in front of a wooden wayside shrine which bears a
painted wooden figure of the Virgin, dressed in blue
and white robes and adopting the crossed arm pose of
acceptance. The soldier wears the uniform of a private
in the French infantry, with his red kepi in his hands,
red trousers, dark blue overcoat crossed by webbing

holding his rifle, pack and blanket roll. This bright and nationalistic uniform was discontinued c.1915 when the French army chose an infantry uniform of duller hue, more in line with German and British uniforms. The girl wears a black cloak over a brown dress and a white cotton Breton coif. The girl's facial features are extremely close to a female figure depicted in two other Frampton paintings. One is 'A Madonna of Brittany' 1911, mentioned above, in which the girl faces left with her hands raised in prayer and wears a transparent voile coif over her plaited blond hair. The other is 'A Maid of Bruges' c.1919 (sold Sotheby's 21 June 1983, 101 repr. in col.). The girl faces right and wears a similar coif to that in T03414, only here, instead of being rolled back to form an edge, the two side flaps of the coif fall down either side of her face. T03414 has a scattering of pink flowers in the foreground; they are not botanically accurate but they look rather like pinks or carnations, and this flower iconographically stands as a symbol of betrothal. It is possible that Frampton intended these flowers, and the turned back coif of the girl (more revealing than the coif with flaps worn by a 'maid') to indicate that the girl and the soldier were betrothed.

The compiler is grateful to Philip New for information about the soldier's uniform.

Meredith Frampton 1894-1984

T03415 Marguerite Kelsey 1928

Oil on canvas $47\frac{1}{2} \times 55\frac{5}{8}$ (1208 × 1412)
Inscribed '19/ᴍꜰ/28' t.r. and 'MEREDITH FRAMPTON/90 CARLTON HILL. NW8./LONDON/TITLE: WOMAN RECLINING' on horizontal cross-bar of stretcher and '5 9½ tall/without shoes/New/frame 55 × 47/Sopha. Bl Black/Indian (+ L Red)/Silence' on reverse which also bears a drawing of a shoe with measurements and a drawing of a leg and shoe on a sofa with measurements, and also separate measurements
Presented by the Friends of the Tate Gallery 1982

Prov: Purchased from the artist by the Friends of the Tate Gallery 1982

Exh: RA 1928 (702, as 'Woman Reclining'); *Salon Triennial de la Société Royale d'Encouragement des Beaux-Arts*, Musée Royal des Beaux-Arts, Antwerp, November–December 1930 (126, as 'Femme se reposant'); *Meredith Frampton*, Tate Gallery, February–March 1982, Ferens Art Gallery, Hull, April–May 1982 (12, repr. p.48 and in col. on cover; also repr. in col. on poster)

Lit: 'A forgotten face' in 'Londoner's Diary', *The Standard*, 16 February 1982 (detail repr.); Waldemar Januszczak, 'Brightly through a microscope', *The Guardian*, 24 February 1982; 'Model return', *Daily Telegraph*, 29 March 1982; 'The girl in the portrait', *Mid-Sussex Times*, 9 April 1982 (photograph repr. of the sitter standing in front of the portrait on 3 March 1982); *Arts & Antiques*, 16 April 1982 (the same photograph repr.); *The Friends of the Tate Gallery Annual Report 1982–83*, 1983; p.13 (repr.)
Also repr: Royal Academy Illustrated, 1928, p.106, as 'Woman Reclining'; *The Times*, 5 May 1928, p.28, as 'Woman Reclining'; Gordon Burn, 'Meredith Frampton's late, late show', *Sunday Times Magazine*, 21 February 1982, pp. 36–41, repr. in col. p.36; Frances Spalding, *British Art since 1900*, 1986, pl.67, p.82, in col.)

Painted in the artist's St John's Wood studio. In conversation in 1981 he told the compiler that the magnolias, obtained from the Richmond home of the actor-manager Sir John Martin-Harvey, had to be painted extremely fast as they did not long retain their form. He still owned the sofa at the time of his death. On the Tate's acquisition of this painting he wrote to the Director that it 'was proposed as a Chantrey Purchase by Sir Walter Russell without success in 1928 when it was shown at the R.A. It is interesting that his hoped-for result has been achieved by other means over 50 years later'. The artist changed the title of this painting definitively to 'Marguerite Kelsey' during preparation of his Tate Gallery retrospective.

The sitter, a professional model, was in her late teens in 1928. When Meredith Frampton's retrospective opened at the Tate Gallery in 1982 she was the only still-living sitter represented in the exhibition who had not been traced. On seeing reviews of the exhibition, she contacted the Gallery and Meredith Frampton, and visited the exhibition, in which she was photographed with her portrait. One of the photographs was published twice (see reference above). Miss Kelsey had married and lived for many years in New Zealand, from where she returned to England not long before the Frampton exhibition opened.

Marguerite Kelsey wrote (letter, 23 June 1982) that Frampton:

> was very kind to me when [I] kept the pose for so long, and I got worked up like him when he was painting the magnolias before they faded. He suffered from headaches and had to have good light. One day I was booked and it was a very grey light. He had to stop work . . . In end if day did not improve he paid me and I went on to another artist.

In an interview with the compiler on 9 October 1985, Miss Kelsey added that as Frampton required a perfect light several sittings were abandoned. The painting required at least twelve and possibly as many as twenty-four sittings, which occurred about twice a week. They took place in the morning as Frampton tired easily and also wanted the model to be at her least tired. The pose was chosen in part because it was comfortable to maintain. The dress, for which she was measured, was made by the artist's mother, Lady Frampton, and the artist also provided the shoes.

At the same time Marguerite Kelsey recalled that she had been the model for as many as seven works, each by a different artist, in the Royal Academy Summer Exhibition in which the Tate's picture was first shown. The painter Jacomb-Hood had introduced her to Alan Beeton (for whom she was to work for ten years) who had in turn introduced her to Sir Gerald Kelly and it was he who introduced her to Frampton, to whom she had also been recommended independently by Sir William Reid Dick. She sat to all the artists mentioned in this paragraph except Kelly. Other artists to whom she sat included Dame Laura Knight, Augustus John, Sir William Russell Flint, A.R. Thompson, Arnold Mason, Harry Jonas, George Spencer Watson, Whitney Smith, Sir John Lavery, Henry Poole, F. Cadogan Cowper, Charles Shannon, Dame Ethel Walker, Sir Thomas Monnington and Mark Gertler. In Leonard Campbell-Taylor's well-known painting 'The Sampler' 1932 (Lady Lever Gallery, Port Sunlight) she was the model for the seated figure and also to some extent for the standing one. She was also the model for the Tate's 64 inch high bronze of a leaping nude, 'Spring' 1929-30 (N 04548) by Sir Charles Wheeler.

Dame Elisabeth Frink b.1930

T 03416 In Memoriam I 1981

Bronze $50\frac{1}{4} \times 43\frac{1}{4} \times 26\frac{3}{4}$
$(1275 \times 1100 \times 680)$
Inscribed 'Frink 3/6' on left shoulder
Purchased from Waddington Galleries
(Grant-in-Aid) 1982

Lit: Sarah Kent, *Elisabeth Frink, Sculpture in Winchester*, exhibition catalogue, Great Courtyard, Winchester, 1981, unspecified cast repr. (n.p.); Peter Burman, Father Kenneth Nugent (eds.), *Prophecy and Vision*, exhibition catalogue, Arnolfini Gallery, Bristol, 1982, unspecified cast repr. (n.p.); Bryan Robertson, Sarah Kent et al., *Elisabeth Frink, Sculpture, Catalogue Raisonné*, 1984, no.265, unspecified cast repr. pp.88 in col., 195, cover in col.
Also repr: unspecified cast in *Arts Review*, XXXV, no.14, 22 July 1983, cover in col., unspecified cast, in *Elisabeth Frink, Open Air Retrospective*, exhibition catalogue, Yorkshire Sculpture Park, West Bretton, 1983 (n.p.)

Elisabeth Frink made her first series of heads in 1959. In the mid 1960s she began work on series of heads which demonstrated her attitude towards violence. 'Soldier's Head' I-IV 1965 and 'Heads' 1967 led to 'Goggled Heads' 1969, in which the artist's feelings about the Algerian war and the aggression of the Moroccan strongmen are reflected.

Later, in 'Tribute Heads' I-IV 1975, Frink turned

her attention from aggressors to the victim. These heads are:

a tribute to all people who have died or suffered for their beliefs. These men are heroes in the sense that they are survivors, but they are also victims stripped of everything but their human courage. (Elisabeth Frink in conversation with Sarah Kent, quoted in the catalogue of the exhibition *Elisabeth Frink, Sculpture in Winchester*, July–September 1981 (n.p.).

'In Memoriam I' and 'In Memoriam II' relate very closely to the 'Tribute' series in that they are also a tribute to people who have suffered for their beliefs. Man's inhumanity to man is a subject that has concerned the artist since the early 1950s when she made her prize winning maquette for the 'Monument to the Unknown Political Prisoner' 1953. Both the 'Tribute' and the 'In Memoriam' heads are a tribute to Amnesty International, whose work Elisabeth Frink has supported over the years. In an interview with Norman Rosenthal in 1985 the artist commented:

My recent heads – the monumental ones – are to do with Amnesty and human rights because they are memorials to people who are suffering for their beliefs (catalogue of Frink retrospective exhibition, Royal Academy, February–March 1985, p.25)

The 'In Memoriam' heads represent all victims of state persecution, not individuals; according to the artist they represent the 'thousands of people who are being tortured today' (letter to the cataloguer, February 1986).

The profiles of T 03416 and T 03417 have been thinned down from the thick set jaws of the 'Goggled' and 'Soldier' heads; unlike the 'Tribute' heads their eyes are open, staring ahead. In *Elisabeth Frink, Sculpture, Catalogue Raisonné* Sarah Kent characterises them as personifying stoic resistance:

Lips are sealed into hard lines of endurance ... the blank stare that indicated dumb stupidity ['Goggled Heads'] now becomes an inward gaze produced by suffering and isolation (p.64).

The artist originally intended the heads to form a pair, but two individual casts of each head have been sold. Individual casts of 'In Memoriam I' are in private collections in Australia and Greece and individual casts of 'In Memoriam II' are at Margam Sculpture Park and Yorkshire Sculpture Park.

The complete edition of six has been cast at the Meridian Bronze company in Peckham, London.

A third head, 'In Memoriam III', made in 1983, is related to the earlier two heads and is 55 in. high. It is reproduced in *Elisabeth Frink, Sculpture, Catalogue Raisonné*, no.284, p.199.

This and the following entry have been approved by the artist.

T 03417   **In Memoriam II 1981**

Bronze 49 × 46 × 26¾ (1245 × 1170 × 680)
Inscribed 'Frink 3/6' on left shoulder
Purchased from Waddington Galleries (Grant-in-Aid) 1982

Lit: Sarah Kent, *Elisabeth Frink, Sculpture in Winchester*, exhibition catalogue, Great Courtyard, Winchester, 1981, unspecified cast repr. (n.p.); Pamela Wedgwood, '20th century sculpture', *Arts Review*, XXXIV, nos. 17 and 18, 13 and 27 August 1982, p.441, unspecified cast repr. p.421; Terry Dintenfass, 'Elisabeth Frink', *Art News*, New York, LXXXIII, no.2, February 1984, unspecified cast repr. p.162; Bryan Robertson, Sarah Kent et al., *Elisabeth Frink, Sculpture, Catalogue Raisonné*, 1984, no.266, unspecified cast repr. pp.89 in col., 195, cover in col. *Also repr:* unspecified cast in *Arts Review*, XXXV, no. 14, 22 July 1983, cover in col.; unspecified cast, in *Elizabeth Frink, Open Air Retrospective*, exhibition catalogue, Yorkshire Sculpture Park, West Bretton, 1983 (n.p.)

See entry on T 03416.

Henri Gaudier-Brzeska 1891-1915

T 03726 **The Dancer** 1913

Plaster, painted brown 31 × 9 × 8½
(787 × 230 × 216) including base
Inscribed 'H Gaudier-Brzeska 1913' on
the base
Transferred from the Victoria and Albert
Museum 1983

Prov: Sydney Schiff *c.* 1913; presented by
Sydney Schiff to Sophie Brzeska for the
purpose of presenting it to the Victoria and
Albert Museum 1918; presented by
Sophie Brzeska to the Victoria and Albert
Museum 1918 (A. 89–1918)

Exh: *Henri Gaudier-Brzeska 1891-1915*,
Towner Art Gallery, Eastbourne, July
1977 (74)

Lit: Stanley Casson, *Some Modern Sculptors*,
1928, pp.97–9 and 108 (repr. pl.34); H.S.
Ede, *A Life of Gaudier-Brzeska*, 1930,
pp.178 and 204 (repr. pl.11 as 'Statuette of
Sophie Brzeska: The Dancer' and pl.XL as
'The Dancer'); J. Wood Palmer, 'Henri
Gaudier-Brzeska (1891–1915)', *Studio*,
CLIII, June 1957, p.178; Mary Chamot,
Dennis Farr and Martin Butlin, *The
Modern British Paintings, Drawings and
Sculpture*, Tate Gallery, 1964, I, p.208
(repr. p.127); M. Ménier, 'Nouvelle
Présentation. Musée National d'Art
Moderne. La Salle Gaudier-Brzeska', *La
Revue du Louvre*, no.3, 1965, pp.144–5;
Tate Gallery Report 1965–66, 1966, p.29;

Mervyn Levy, *Gaudier-Brzeska Drawings
and Sculpture*, 1965, pp.16–17; *Henri
Gaudier-Brzeska (1891–1915) Sculptures*,
exhibition catalogue, Scottish National
Gallery of Modern Art, Edinburgh,
August–September 1972, pp.21–2 (repr.
pl.5); Richard Cork, *Vorticism and
Abstract Art in the First Machine Age*,
1975, I, p.176 (bronze cast repr.); Roger
Cole, *Burning to Speak. The Life and Art
of Henri Gaudier-Brzeska*, Oxford, 1978,
pp.32–3 and 81 (bronze cast repr.); Brice
Rhyne, 'Henri Gaudier-Brzeska: The
Process of Discovery', *Artforum*, XVI,
May 1978, p.35; Serge Fauchereau,
'Gaudier-Brzeska: Animalist Artist',
*Henri Gaudier-Brzeska, Sculptor 1891-
1915*, exhibition catalogue, Kettle's Yard
Gallery, Cambridge, October–November
1983, p.8 and catalogue entry 41 (repr.)

T 03726 is in plaster painted the colour of bronze and is
supported by a wooden armature at the figure's right
knee. There are also traces of green and red pigment.

According to Ede, 'The Dancer' is 'a statuette of
Sophie Brzeska' although it has also been suggested that
it is a portrait of Nina Hamnett (see J. Wood Palmer
and catalogue entry 41 in the catalogue to the exhibition
at Kettle's Yard Gallery). There is considerable facial
resemblance between Nina Hamnett and this sculpture
(for further reference to Nina Hamnett see entry for
T 03731 below).

T 03726 originally belonged to Sydney Schiff. He
described it in a letter to Cecil Smith as 'the original
plaster model' (undated letter, after 11 July 1918, Victoria and Albert Museum). The sculpture would have
been modelled in clay and cast in plaster. By 1918 there
were two bronze casts, one of which was exhibited at the
Memorial exhibition held at the Leicester Galleries
in May–June 1918, but it is still unclear whether they
were cast during Gaudier's lifetime. According to Ede
(letter of 1 October 1966) 'there was no bronze originally
made by the artist'. The bronzes belonged to Schiff and
to George Eumorfopoulos. By 1966 the cast belonging
to the former had entered the collection of Sir Edward
Beddington Behrens. The other cast is now in a private
collection in London. Since then at least six more casts
have been made which are in the following collections:
Christ Church Picture Gallery, Oxford, Mr and Mrs
David Wynne, London, Tate Gallery (T 00762), Musée
National d'Art Moderne, Paris, Musée des Beaux-Arts,
Orléans and Kettle's Yard, Cambridge. They were all
cast from the original plaster by the Fiorini and Carney
Foundry. The first five were cast in 1965 under the
supervision of David Wynne. Although uncertain, he
thinks that six may have been cast at that time (con-

versation with the compiler on 22 May 1986). The cast belonging to Kettle's Yard was made in 1967.

The sculpture is relatively naturalistic – although the distance between the knees and the feet has been considerably foreshortened – but was made shortly before or at the same time as Gaudier was experimenting with primitivism.

Cole intimates that Rodin's 'Invocation' (Musée Rodin, Paris) may have been the source for this work but Fauchereau suggests that the 'Dancer' of the Gallo-Roman period, on display in Gaudier's youth in the Municipal Museum, Orléans, may have been at the back of his mind. He writes:

> One may not fairly talk of reminiscences here since Gaudier never returned to Orléans after 1910, but it must be acknowledged that the little Gallo-Roman dancer has the same limb movement, especially the arm over the head, which we find in several of Gaudier's nude figures.

'The Dancer' is one of three works on the theme of dancing executed by Gaudier. The first such work was entitled 'The Firebird' 1912 and depicts a man and a woman dancing in Stravinsky's ballet of the same name which was being performed in London to great acclaim at that time by Diaghelev's 'Ballets Russes'. This sculpture is far more static than 'The Dancer'. Gaudier also executed a 'Wrestler' in the same year. The other sculpture on the theme of dancing is 'Red Stone Dancer' 1914 (N04515).

Schiff purchased 'The Dancer' for £10. Gaudier wrote to Schiff:

> I am naturally glad that Mme Schiff likes the statuette. It is a sincere expression of a certain disposition of my mind, but you must know that it is by no means the simplest nor the last. The consistency in me lies in the design, and the quality of surface – whereas the treatment of the planes tends to overshadow it (Ede, p.178)

This might suggest that Gaudier was beginning to concern himself more with the organisation of planes rather than with naturalistic representation, a concern which would be important in the creation of 'Red Stone Dancer' 1914 (N04515).

In the *Modern British Paintings, Drawings and Sculpture* catalogue of the Tate Gallery a text by Ezra Pound has been erroneously interpreted as describing T03726. It actually describes N04514. similarly, Cole writes that 'The Dancer' was recorded by Gaudier in his 'List of Works' which he compiled on 14 July 1914. This list is in the archives at Kettle's Yard, Cambridge and the entry for 'The Dancer' is written in pencil in the hand of H.S. Ede. All other entries are in ink in the hand of Gaudier. In the *Modern British Paintings, Drawings and Sculpture* catalogue of the Tate Gallery T03726 was

described as having been transferred to the gallery in 1952 and was given an accession number (6092). According to records at the Victoria and Albert Museum this work was transferred to the Tate Gallery in 1952 only on 'permanent long loan'.

T03727 Fallen Workman 1912

Bronze, on a green marble base
$11\frac{5}{8} \times 15\frac{1}{4} \times 14\frac{1}{8}$ (295 × 388 × 359),
dimensions do not include base
Not inscribed
Transferred from the Victoria and Albert Museum 1983

Prov: ...; Presented by A.E. Anderson to the Victoria and Albert Museum 1921 (A. 88–1921)

Exh: *Henri Gaudier-Brzeska (1891–1915) Sculptures*, Scottish National Gallery of Modern Art, Edinburgh, August–September 1972, City Art Gallery, Leeds, September–October 1972, National Museum of Wales, Cardiff, October–November 1972 (13, as 'Workman Fallen from a Scaffold'); *Pioneers of Modern Sculpture*, Hayward Gallery, July–September 1973 (106, as 'Man Fallen from a Scaffold'); *Henri Gaudier-Brzeska 1891–1915*, Towner Art Gallery, Eastbourne, July 1977 (79)

Lit: H.S. Ede, *A Life of Gaudier-Brzeska*, 1930, p.204 (plaster version repr. from rear, pl.IX as 'The Fallen Workman'); Horace Brodzky, *Henri Gaudier-Brzeska 1891–1915*, 1933, pp.123–4 (plaster repr. facing p.79 as 'Man Fallen from Scaffold'); William C. Wees, *Vorticism and the English Avant-Garde*, Toronto, 1972, p.134;

Henri Gaudier-Brzeska (1891–1915) Sculptures, exhibition catalogue, Scottish National Gallery of Modern Art, Edinburgh, August–September 1972, p.18 (repr.); Roger Cole, *Burning to Speak. The Life and Art of Henri Gaudier-Brzeska*, Oxford, 1978, p.64 (repr.)

Brodzky records that the subject of this work was based on 'an incident that Brzeska remembered having seen in Paris'. He suggests that the work is a fragment of the original since the figure once had arms 'and depicted the man in the act of raising himself from the ground in agony'. This would explain the angle at which the figure is fixed to the base. The figure was made in clay and given to Major Charles Wheeler. According to Brodzky it was exhibited as a clay sculpture in the Memorial exhibition of 1918 (16) but was already, by that time, in a damaged state.

Brodzky also remarks that the arms, 'which were eventually found and annexed by [Wheeler's] charlady', were used 'for whitening the doorstep of Wheeler's house'. According to Ede, however, a plaster version belonged to Wheeler, while by 1930, the original clay version belonged to Ede. Cole records that two bronze casts were made, of which T 03727 is one, and that two plaster casts were executed (one since destroyed). He does not indicate whether the plasters were cast posthumously but it seems likely they were cast during Gaudier's lifetime.

Cork observes that T 03727 is an attempt by Gaudier at 'a direct emulation of his great countryman, Rodin. Its forms are modelled with the intensely fluid, almost molten texture that was Rodin's sculptural signature.' In 1912 Gaudier wrote letters to Sophie Brzeska on several occasions acclaiming the work of Rodin and, in particular, his 'St John the Baptist' which he described as 'a beggar who walks along, who speaks and gesticulates – he belongs to my own time, is in my epoch, he has a twentieth century workman's body just as I see it and know it' (quoted in Jeremy Lewison, 'A Note on Chronology', Kettle's Yard Gallery exhibition catalogue, p.29). The musculature of the figure is also reminiscent of Michelangelo whose sculptures Gaudier had copied in drawings in 1910.

T 03728   **Sleeping Fawn** 1913

Plaster, painted brown $4\frac{1}{2} \times 10 \times 8\frac{1}{2}$ (114 × 254 × 216)
Not inscribed
Transferred from the Victoria and Albert Museum 1983

Prov: Raymond Drey after 1914; Leicester Galleries 1918; presented by Messrs E. Brown and Phillips (The Leicester Galleries) to the Victoria and Albert Museum 1939 (A. 25–1939)

Exh: *Henri Gaudier-Brzeska (1891–1915) Sculptures*, Scottish National Gallery of Modern Art, Edinburgh, August–September 1972, City Art Gallery, Leeds, September–October 1972, National Museum of Wales, Cardiff, October–November 1972 (30, repr. pl.18); *Henri Gaudier-Brzeska, Sculptor 1891–1915*, Kettle's Yard Gallery, Cambridge, October–November 1983, City Museum and Art Gallery, Bristol, November 1983 – January 1984, York City Art Gallery, January–February 1984 (50, repr.)

Lit: Stanley Casson, *Some Modern Sculptors*, 1928, pp.98 and 109 (bronze cast repr. pl.36 as 'Fawn'); H.S. Ede, *A Life of Gaudier-Brzeska*, 1930, pp.170 and 196–7 (marble version repr. pl. XXXVI); Horace Brodzky, *Henri Gaudier-Brzeska 1891–1915*, 1933, pp.88 and 96; E.H. Ramsden, *Sculpture: Theme and Variations*, 1953, p.32 (repr. pl.58a); *Henri Gaudier-Brzeska (1891–1915) Sculptures*, exhibition catalogue, Scottish National Gallery of Modern Art, Edinburgh, August–September 1972, p.23 (repr. pl.8); Roger Cole, *Burning to Speak. The Life and Art of Henri Gaudier-Brzeska*, Oxford, 1978, p.90 (repr.); Serge Fauchereau, 'Gaudier-Brzeska: Animalist Artist', *Henri Gaudier-Brzeska, Sculptor 1891–1915*, exhibition catalogue, Kettle's Yard Gallery, Cambridge, October–November 1983, p.13 and catalogue entry 50

According to Ede T 03728 and T 03729 (see entry below) were 'the result of [a] vision of deer' in Arundel Park which Gaudier visited for the day with Sophie Brzeska. Cole states that these animal sculptures were 'created in spare moments and often [given] as presents to friends' but does not provide evidence for this assertion.

In his list of works Gaudier notes the prices at which he sold his animal sculptures and where no prices are given he does not record having disposed of the works.

T 03728 is a unique plaster cast, probably of the original version listed in Gaudier's list of works, which was made from Seravezza marble and belonged to Raymond Drey. Drey purchased the original marble for £5. The marble was exhibited in *Twentieth Century Art* at the Whitechapel Art Gallery, May–June 1914 (208) and at the Memorial exhibition at the Leicester Galleries in 1918 (98). According to Ede, by 1930 the marble version belonged to Mrs W.W. Crocker of San Francisco and in 1959 Mr W.W. Crocker confirmed that the work was in his possession.

Between 1918 and 1939 twelve casts in bronze were made of T 03728 for the Leicester Galleries as they were required (letter from Oliver Brown, 30 August 1960). In 1952 T 03728 was catalogued as 6093 and was erroneously described as having been transferred to the Tate Gallery. According to records at the Victoria and Albert Museum this work was transferred only on 'permanent long loan'.

T 03729   **Crouching Fawn** 1914

Plaster, painted brown 10 × 12 × 5 (254 × 305 × 127)
Not inscribed
Transferred from the Victoria and Albert Museum 1983

Prov: ...; Leicester Galleries after 1918; presented by Messrs E. Brown and Phillips (The Leicester Galleries) to the Victoria and Albert Museum 1939 (A. 26–1939)

Exh: *Henri Gaudier-Brzeska (1891–1915) Sculptures*, Scottish National Gallery of Modern Art, Edinburgh, August–September 1972, City Art Gallery, Leeds, September–October 1972, National Museum of Wales, Cardiff, October–November 1972 (34); *Henri Gaudier-Brzeska, Sculptor 1891–1915*, Kettle's Yard Gallery, Cambridge, October–November 1983, City Museum and Art Gallery, Bristol, November 1983 – January 1984, York City Art Gallery, January–February 1984 (51)

Lit: Ezra Pound, *Gaudier-Brzeska, a Memoir*, 1916, p.161 (stone version repr. pl.IX); H.S. Ede, *A Life of Gaudier-Brzeska*, 1930, pp.170 and 198 (stone version repr. pl.XXVI as 'Seated Fawn'); Roger Cole, *Burning to Speak. The Life and Art of Henri Gaudier-Brzeska*, Oxford, 1978, p.91 (repr.); Judith Collins, *The Omega Workshops*, 1983, p.70

T 03729 is a unique plaster cast. Although the Leicester Galleries acquired it sometime after 1918 there are no records indicating exactly when the cast was made. T 03729 is a plaster cast of a work in Bath stone. According to a relative of the owner of the stone version the plaster cast was made in the twenties (letter to the compiler 16 November 1983). The stone version was listed by Gaudier as having been sold to Mrs Mayor of Campden Hill, probably through the Omega Workshops since the symbol of the Omega is placed next to it. Cole, however, suggests that Mrs Mayor's carving 'was worked to the design of the plaster'. This seems less likely than that the plaster was made at the time of making the bronze casts. In 1913 Gaudier concentrated primarily on carving stone and the sculpture has the crispness of a carving rather than the appearance of a work modelled in clay. The original carving sustained damage to one ear and, according to the correspondent cited above, although it has been mended, the break remains visible. The carving is now in a private collection.

The dating of the original marble and stone versions of T 03728 and T 03729 by Cole to 1913 is disputed by Jeremy Lewison in the catalogue of the exhibition held at Kettle's Yard Gallery. Lewison states that in his list of works Gaudier clearly records that the fawn sold to Drey (T 03728) was executed in 1913 whereas the stone fawn sold to Mayor (T 03729) was made in 1914. Cole dates Drey's work to 1913 and T 03729, which he considers preceded Mayor's stone version, also to 1913. Given the argument that the plaster succeeded the Bath stone carving it is arguable that one should not doubt Gaudier's dating. The issue is further complicated, however, by the fact that the sizes of the sculptures, as recorded by Gaudier, do not fully coincide with those of the works under discussion but this may be accounted for by the fact that Gaudier compiled his list from memory. Therefore the recorded sizes were probably approximations. Finally, according to Collins, the fawn belonging to Mrs Mayor was exhibited (47) at the Second Grafton Group exhibition at the Alpine Club Gallery which opened on 2 January 1914, the same exhibition in which he exhibited the 'Red Stone Dancer' (N 04515) for the first time, a work which is accepted as dating from 1914. If this is correct then 'Fawn Crouching' was probably completed at the very end of 1913 or beginning of 1914 and Gaudier chose to record it as being made in 1914. There is some doubt, however, as to whether the fawn exhibited was this particular one since Brodzky, whose account of Gaudier's life is admittedly highly inaccurate, records that the fawn exhibited was purchased by Princess Lichnowsky (p.176). Pound, however, states that 'A Faun, [sic] crouching, [was] sold at Alpine Club Show several years ago' thereby describing the kind of fawn exhibited. He also stated that the fawn in question was reproduced in his *Memoir* (pl.IX), which is indeed 'Fawn Crouching'. Pound's 'Partial Catalogue of the Sculptures', however, is unreliable in many respects and therefore the statement above cannot be accepted with complete confidence.

Gaudier's fawn carvings were characterised by Brodzky as 'Chinese' for he felt they had been inspired by Chinese carvings in the British Museum. He wrote that 'In no sense is the "Fawn" academic or realistic; it is a summary – like the Chinese – of a beautiful creature expressed by the simplest means.' Fauchereau, on the other hand, claims that the fawns 'are stylised with a tenderness which has more in common with the work of fashionable contemporary animalists', although he implies that the 'rather daring simplifications ... of the eyes and hooves' owe something to Gallo-Roman sculpture on display during Gaudier's youth at the Municipal Museum, Orléans (Kettle's Yard Gallery exhibition catalogue, p.13).

The stone version of T 03729 was exhibited in the Memorial exhibition (94), as 'A Little Fawn'. T 03729 was previously catalogued as 6094 and described, in error, as having been transferred to the Tate Gallery in 1952 (see above).

T 03730   The Idiot *c.* 1912

Plaster $7\frac{1}{8} \times 5\frac{1}{2} \times 6\frac{1}{2}$ (181 × 140 × 165)
Not inscribed
Transferred from the Victoria and Albert Museum 1983

Prov: Haldane McFall; Zwemmer Gallery before June 1943; presented by Anton Zwemmer to the Victoria and Albert Museum 1951 (Circ. 47–1951)

Exh: *A Memorial Exhibition of the Work of Henri Gaudier-Brzeska*, Leicester Galleries, May–June 1918 (21, as 'Head of an Idiot');

Henri Gaudier-Brzeska (1891–1915) Sculptures, Scottish National Gallery of Modern Art, Edinburgh, August–September 1972, City Art Gallery, Leeds, September–October 1972, National Museum of Wales, Cardiff, October–November 1972 (14, as 'Head of an Idiot'); *Henri Gaudier-Brzeska 1891–1915*, Towner Art Gallery, Eastbourne, July 1977 (77); *Henri Gaudier-Brzeska, Sculptor 1891–1915*, Kettle's Yard Gallery, Cambridge, October–November 1983, City Museum and Art Gallery, Bristol, November 1983 – January 1984, York City Art Gallery, January–February 1984 (13, as 'Head of an Idiot')

Lit: H.S. Ede, *A Life of Gaudier-Brzeska*, 1930, p.205; R.H. Wilenski, foreword to *Drawings and Sculptures by Some Contemporary Sculptors*, exhibition catalogue, Zwemmer Gallery, November–December 1930 (n.p.); Mervyn Levy, *Gaudier-Brzeska Drawings and Sculpture*, 1965, p.29; *Henri Gaudier-Brzeska (1891–1915) Sculptures*, exhibition catalogue, Scottish National Gallery of Modern Art, Edinburgh, August–September 1972, p.18; Roger Cole, *Burning to Speak. The Life and Art of Henri Gaudier-Brzeska*, Oxford, 1978, pp.28 and 65 (bronze cast repr.); *Henri Gaudier-Brzeska, Sculptor 1891–1915*, exhibition catalogue, Kettle's Yard Gallery, Cambridge, October–November 1983, p.36 and catalogue entry 13

According to the catalogue of the exhibition of work by Roy de Maistre and Henri Gaudier-Brzeska held at Temple Newsam, Leeds (June–August 1943), there are two plaster versions of this work; one belonged to Alan Fraser and, before that, to Claud Lovat Fraser as recorded by Cole, and the other one belonged to Haldane McFall. T03730 is the latter.

According to Cole this work is to be considered as a satirical self-portrait but it has also been referred to as 'Head of a Jew'. He states that Fraser's version was exhibited at Dan Rider's bookshop in St Martin's Court, off Charing Cross Road, under this title. Wilenski, in 1930, wrote that he thought he could 'discern the outline of the sculptor's own features' in the work, which appears to be one of the earliest references to the notion of the self-portrait. Cole suggests that 'it was the subject of much ridicule between [Gaudier] and Fraser'. In the catalogue to the exhibition at Kettle's Yard, Lewison notes the resemblance between T03730 and Rodin's portrait of Baudelaire of 1898.

Cole states that seven casts of this sculpture were made in bronze. They were executed posthumously. The Temple Newsam catalogue states that six casts were made for Zwemmer. Ede dates the work to 1914 but this is unlikely from a stylistic point of view. Furthermore Gaudier rarely modelled sculpture after the beginning of 1914.

This work does not appear in Gaudier's list of works.

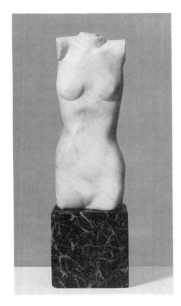

T03731　**Torso** 1914

Grey veined white marble on a base of Tinos marble $9\frac{7}{8} \times 3\frac{7}{8} \times 3$ ($252 \times 98 \times 77$), dimensions do not include base
Not inscribed

Transferred from the Victoria and Albert Museum 1983

Prov:　Presented by Sophie Brzeska to the Victoria and Albert Museum 1915 (A. 96–1915)

Exh:　*The First Exhibition of the London Group*, Goupil Gallery, March–April 1914 (115); *Henri Gaudier-Brzeska (1891–1915) Sculptures*, Scottish National Gallery of Modern Art, Edinburgh, August–September 1972, City Art Gallery, Leeds, September–October 1972, National Museum of Wales, Cardiff, October–November 1972 (23, repr. pl.4); *Pioneers of Modern Sculpture*, Hayward Gallery, July–September 1973 (109); *Henri Gaudier-Brzeska 1891–1915*, Towner Art Gallery, Eastbourne, July 1977 (78); *Rodin Rediscovered*, National Gallery of Art, Washington, D.C., June 1981–May 1982 (360, as 'Female Torso I'); *Henri Gaudier-Brzeska, Sculptor 1891–1915*, Kettle's Yard Gallery, Cambridge, October–November 1983, City Museum and Art Gallery Bristol, November 1983–January 1984, York City Art Gallery, January–February 1984 (54)

Lit:　Ezra Pound, *Gaudier-Brzeska a Memoir*, 1916, p.169 (repr. pl XII as 'Torse'); Roger Fry, 'Gaudier-Brzeska', *Burlington Magazine*, XXIX, August 1916, pp.209–10; Stanley Casson, *Some Modern Sculptors*, 1928, p.98; H.S. Ede, *A Life of Gaudier-Brzeska*, 1930, pp.177 and 200–1 (repr. pl.XXXIX); Nina Hamnett, *Laughing Torso*, 1932, pp.39–40 (repr. as frontispiece); E.H. Ramsden, *Sculpture: Theme and Variations*, 1953, p.32 (repr. pl.57); Mervyn Levy, *Gaudier-Brzeska Drawings and Sculpture*, 1965, p.13; *Henri Gaudier-Brzeska (1891–1915) Sculptures*, exhibition catalogue, Scottish National Gallery of Modern Art, Edinburgh, August–September 1972, pp.20–1 (repr. pl.4); Richard Cork, *Vorticism and Abstract Art in the First Machine Age*, 1975, I, p.167 (repr.); Roger Cole, *Burning to Speak. The Life and Art of Henri Gaudier-Brzeska*, Oxford, 1978, pp.32 and 78 (repr.); *Henri Gaudier-Brzeska, Sculptor 1891–1915*, exhibition catalogue, Kettle's Yard Gallery, Cambridge, October–November 1983, p.30 and catalogue entry 54; *Also repr: A Memorial Exhibition of the Work of Henri Gaudier-Brzeska*, exhibition catalogue, Leicester

Galleries, May–June 1918, facing p.7;
Herbert Read, The Art of Sculpture, 1956,
pl.193

In the autumn of 1915 Sophie Brzeska offered to present to the Victoria and Albert Museum a collection of twelve drawings and 'Torso' by the late Henri Gaudier-Brzeska to whom she referred as her 'brother'. She wrote in a letter to the museum that Gaudier had regularly visited it. On 16 November the gift was accepted. Twelve further drawings were turned down and returned to Ezra Pound who, to some extent, was acting as an agent for Sophie, particularly in regard to purchases by the American lawyer, John Quinn. Sophie Brzeska's contact with the museum continued until 1922 when she was certified 'lunatic'. The museum stored a number of sculptures for her both during and after the First World War when she was living principally at Wotton under Edge, Gloucestershire. At the time of giving the 'Torso' she was living at 185 Munster Road, London sw6.

The 'Torso' can be seen both as an answer to Gaudier's critics who disliked his primitive, modernistic approach to sculpture and as the culmination of an ambition to make a sculpture in the classical style. On 3 June 1911 he wrote to Sophie Brzeska: 'I long to make a statue of a single body, an absolute, truthful copy – something so true it will live when it is made even as the model himself lives' (Ede, p.64). He described the 'Torso' to Major Smythies, of whom he had made a portrait bust, as 'a marble statue of a girl in a natural way, in order to show my accomplishment as a sculptor' (Ede, p.177). Smythies had apparently criticised Gaudier's more abstract work and Gaudier continued: 'We are of different opinions about naturalism. I treat it as hollow accomplishment, the artificial is full of metaphysical meaning which is all important.'

Gaudier spent many hours making drawings after sculpture by Michelangelo at the beginning of the decade but never produced such a naturalistic work other than the portrait busts. In his list of works he dates the 'Torso' to the year 1914. Cole disagrees with this dating but does not give reasons. There seems to be no reason, however, to doubt Gaudier's dating.

Gaudier records that the sculpture was a 'Portrait of the painter Nina Hamnett' who describes, in *Laughing Torso*, the circumstances surrounding the making of this piece. She met Gaudier in 1913 during his exhibition of drawings at Dan Rider's bookshop and arranged to have lessons in sculpture from him. She relates that:

One day he came to my room and said, 'I am very poor and I want to do a torso, will you sit for me?' I said, 'I don't know, perhaps I look awful with nothing on,' and he said 'Don't worry'. I went one day to his studio in Fulham Road and took off all my clothes. I turned round slowly and he did drawings of me . . . From the drawings he did two torsos.

She also records that he stole the marble from a stonemason's yard in Putney.

Cork remarks that 'Torso' is 'a polished imitation of a Greek original – extended even to the broken arms and neck', although he probably does not intend to imply by this that Gaudier actually copied a particular sculpture. The torso is executed in grey veined white marble which Gaudier records as Sicilian. Two casts have been posthumously made of this marble; one is in the collection of Kettle's Yard, Cambridge, the other is in the collection of the Musée National d'Art Moderne, Paris.

Gaudier made at least two other torsos of which he listed one, namely a torso in Seravezza marble purchased by Olivia Shakespeare, the mother-in-law of Ezra Pound, now in a private collection in Italy. The other torso was made in clay and cast in plaster. According to Cole two plaster casts were made from the aforementioned plaster; one was given to Alfred Wolmark (now in the collection of the Musée des Beaux-Arts, Orléans) and the other was given to Horace Brodzky. An unrecorded number of bronze casts have been made posthumously from these plasters.

The catalogue to the Memorial exhibition held at the Leicester Galleries in May–June 1918 lists a plaster cast of 'Torso' as having been exhibited (8). This is unlikely. Either T03731 was exhibited as no. 8 or one of the plasters described above was mistaken for a cast of T03731. It seems likely that T03731 was exhibited, since it was illustrated in the catalogue, although records at the Victoria and Albert Museum do not indicate that it was lent.

T03732 **Figure** *c*. 1913–14

Bronze $4\frac{3}{4} \times 2 \times 1\frac{1}{2}$ (121 × 51 × 38)
Not inscribed
Transferred from the Victoria and Albert Museum 1983

Prov: . . .; Dr G.A. Jellicoe (date of purchase not known); The Leicester Galleries (date of purchase not known); Dr N. Goodman 1933 by whom presented to the Victoria and Albert Museum 1971 (A. 23–1971)

Exh: On loan to the Victoria and Albert Museum

Lit: Roger Cole, *Burning to Speak. The Life and Art of Henri Gaudier-Brzeska*, Oxford, 1978, p.128 (repr. as 'Figure Study')
Also repr: Henri Gaudier-Brzeska (1891–1915) Vu et Raconté par les Elèves du Lycée Professionel de Saint-Jean-de-Braye, Saint-Jean-de-Braye, 1986, p.117

This sculpture is in Gaudier's Vorticist style and is not listed by Gaudier in his list of works. It depicts a seated figure. Cole dates it to 1912–13 but the compiler considers this to be too early in view of its primitive idiom.

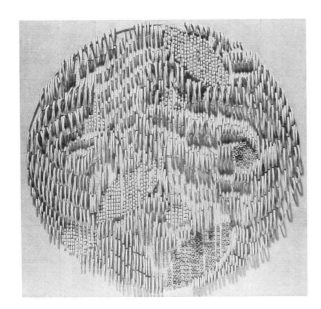

Arthur Giardelli b.1911

T03799 **The Sea is All About Us** 1982

Acrylic, watercolour and paper construction on plywood 32 × 32 (813 × 813)
Inscribed '30 April 17 July 1982' and 'The Sea is all about us, Arthur Giardelli' on reverse
Presented by Mr & Mrs Eric Estorick 1983
Prov: Purchased from the artist by Eric Estorick

Giardelli has for a long time worked in two different techniques, making watercolour landscapes and abstract constructions. Unusually, both these materials are included in this construction, since the coils of paper consist of his own discarded watercolours torn into strips. The constructions have often referred indirectly to landscape, and have incorporated coloured slates or natural materials that evoke particular places. They are characteristically designed with repeated shapes, particularly circles and half-circles, and their backboards are covered with pages from old printed books. These features apply to 'The Sea is All About Us', which is made of coils of watercolour paper glued onto a board covered with overpainted pages of a book.

The design is made up of circles – 'The circle is appropriate to a work about the sea. The whole round earth has more sea than anything else and all sea forms are curved' (letter from the artist, 2 January 1984). The overall pattern is taken from a roundel on the tomb slab of Cosimo dei Medici in the Old Sacristy of San Lorenzo in Florence. The complex interlocking shapes are followed in the different depths of cut in the board, in the coils of paper on three different axes and in their various sizes. The artist's letter enclosed his outline sketch of this design in Florence, drawn on 29 March 1982, which appealed to him primarily for its qualities of design rather than its association with Italian art.

The title is taken from T.S. Eliot's *The Dry Salvages* (1941, line 15), at the beginning of a section describing the action of the sea against the land. Giardelli's exhibition at the Aberystwyth Arts Centre in December 1983 was titled 'At the Sea's Edge', and several of the constructions had similar marine titles.

Giardelli lives in an isolated house on a headland in Dyfed, where he frequently sketches on the beach, and the subject of this construction is the waves: 'I cut into the wooden base to different depths so as to be able to show waves and also ripples and heads of water in shallow places.'

Stephen Gilbert b.1910

T03698 **Untitled** 1948

Oil on canvas 21 × 28¼ (535 × 715)
Inscribed 'Stephen Gilbert 1948' on reverse

[175]

T 03698

Sheet no.5

Purchased from the artist (Knapping
Fund) 1983

Exh: *Stephen Gilbert, Cobra Paintings 1940–
1950*, Court Gallery, Copenhagen,
October 1971 (23, repr. in col.); *Aftermath,
France 1945–54, New Images of Man*,
Barbican Art Gallery, March–June 1982
(87, repr. p.105, in reverse)

Lit: Sarah Wilson, 'Stephen Gilbert',
*Aftermath, France 1945–54, New Images
of Man*, exhibition catalogue, Barbican Art
Gallery, 1982, p.103

Stephen Gilbert was invited to join the Cobra group of
artists in Paris, where he lived, in the year of this painting. He had been painting similar subjects for some
years beforehand.

Gilbert and George b.1943, b.1942

T 03452 The Nature of Our Looking 1970

Permanganate splashes, graphite red and
black chalk on five separate sheets of
paper.

(1) 'THE NATURE OF OUR LOOKING',
103 × 46 (2630 × 1180)
Inscribed 'George and Gilbert/June
1970'/London' b.l.

(2) 'THE NATURE OF OUR LOOKING',
103 × 35 (2630 × 900)
Inscribed 'George and
Gilbert/June/1970' b.r.

(3) 'HERE IN THE COUNTRY'S HEART WHERE
THE GRASS IS GREEN, WE STAND VERY
STILL AND QUIET', 152 × 106
(3850 × 2700)
Inscribed 'George and Gilbert June
London/1970' b.r.

(4) 'FOREVER WE WILL SEARCH AND GIVE
OUR THOUGHTS TO THE PICTURE WE
HAVE IN OUR MIND. WE ARE WALKING
ROUND NOW AS SAD AS CAN BE',
137 × 93 (3480 × 2360)
Inscribed 'George and Gilbert/June
1970'/London' b.l.

(5) 'WE BELIEVE THAT LOVE is the PATH for
a BETTER WORLD of ART in which GOOD
and BAD GIVE WAY for GEORGE and
GILBERT TO BE', 110 × 143
(2785 × 5620).
Inscribed 'George and Gilbert/June
1970'/London b.l.

Each of the five sheets is inscribed 'Art for
All 1970 The Sculptors Gilbert and
George' along the bottom.

Purchased from Anthony d'Offay Ltd
(Grant-in-Aid) 1982

Prov: Barbara Neusse, Germany, 1970; Anthony
d'Offay Gallery through Konrad Fischer
Gallery, Düsseldorf, 1981

Exh: *Frozen into the Nature for Your Art*,
Françoise Lambert Gallery, Milan, June–
July 1970, Heiner Friedrich Gallery,
Cologne, Autumn 1970 (no catalogue);
Gilbert and George 1968–1980, Stedelijk
van Abbemuseum, Eindhoven, November–
December 1980, Kunsthalle, Düsseldorf,
January 1981, Kunsthalle, Bern, February
1981 (repr.); *Westkunst*, Cologne, May–
August 1981 (830, one panel ('Here in the
country's heart … ') repr. p.489); *Gilbert*

and George, Richard Long and Bruce McLean, Anthony d'Offay, May–June 1982 (no catalogue); *New Art at the Tate Gallery*, Tate Gallery, September–October 1983 (not in catalogue); *Gilbert and George The Charcoal on Paper Sculptures 1970–1974*, Musée d'Art Contemporain, Bordeaux, May–September 1986 (3, repr.)

During the summer of 1970, a friend of Gilbert and George took a series of photographs of the artists in the countryside near Colchester on the Suffolk–Essex border. These formed the basic imagery of 'The Nature of Our Looking' which was executed in London at their Studio, 'Art for All', 12 Fournier Street, Spitalfields. In an interview with Démosthène Darretas (*Gilbert and George, the Charcoal on Paper Sculptures 1970–1974*, cited above) the artists commented, 'We did not know at that time how to make large photo-pieces. Still, each 'Charcoal-on-Paper' piece is based upon a photograph broadly enlarged by drawing.'

Known as a 'charcoal-on-paper sculpture', 'The Nature of Our Looking' is the third work by Gilbert and George in this medium. It is composed of five parts, each section created by joining together small pieces of paper with masking tape, to produce mural-sized sheets of paper. The smaller units of paper measure from $17\frac{1}{4} \times 23$ to $17\frac{3}{4} \times 23\frac{1}{2}$ and are arranged in a grid pattern, which is clearly visible. This arrangement enables the sheets to be folded in upon themselves and to be packed neatly into an accompanying cardboard storage case. This box is labelled 'Art for All Gilbert and George' and facilitates easy handling and storage of T 03452 as well as protecting the fragile sheets. Gilbert and George had previously used a box to carry work in 1969. This was their 'Life-Box' which functioned as an artist's portfolio.

The paper of T 03452 has been artificially antiqued with permanganate splashes creating localised areas of brown discolouration. This ageing effect can be found in 'All my life I give you nothing and still you ask for more' (1970, Anthony d'Offay) and 'Walking, Viewing, Relaxing' (1970, private collection, Germany). In the booklet, 'The Pencil on Paper, Descriptive Works of Gilbert and George' 1970 by Gilbert and George, the sculptors talk of 'the potential life of that paper'.

The 'Nature of Our Looking' initiates the compositional formula of the image, bordered along the bottom with extracts of language, which is subsequently adopted in later charcoal-on-paper works such as 'The General Jungle' (1971, Sonnabend Gallery, New York).

The hand-printed text of T 03452 incorporates upper and lower case letters, while in later works only capital letters are used. The text in the section listed number 3, is adapted from Norman Gale's 'The Country Faith' (*The Collected Poems of Norman Gale* 1914):

Here in the country's heart
Where the grass is green,
Life is the same sweet life
As it e'er hath been.

Gilbert and George also used the above text in their 18 minute video sculpture 'The Nature of Our Looking' (1970, Anthony d'Offay) and for the video's accompanying announcement card.

Along the top edge of each piece, loops of red satinized ribbon are used to hang the piece. These are fixed on the reverse with red sealing wax, similar to that used by Gilbert and George in their postal-sculptures of 1969. In the 1986 interview with Démosthène Darretas, the artists said:

They were not drawings. They were more like a means of communicating with the world around us. As if we had been writing huge letters. We thought of them as big letters or documents.

Gilbert and George have used a hanging arrangement for T 03452 which is centred on the large horizontal piece, flanked by the two smaller vertical pieces, and adjacent to these, the larger vertical pieces, as can be seen below:

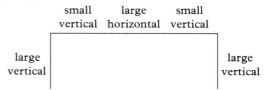

This arrangement, though favoured by Gilbert and George, is not obligatory.

A reworking of T 03452 can be found in the 'Painting Sculpture', 'The Painting (with Us in the Nature)' 1971 (collection Gilbert and George). This consists of six triptychs in oil on canvas; the triptych format echoes the preferred arrangement of the horizontal and two small vertical panels in T 03452. On the accompanying guide to the painting, Gilbert and George wrote 'It was the summer of 1970. Then came the winter and we re-created these senses.' The reworking consists of a transposition from black-and-white into colour of the same imagery – the self portraits, George's walking stick and the countryside.

Eric Gill 1882–1940

T 03449   Christ Child 1922

Painted wood (reverse bears outline
drawing in red ink) 5½ × 13½ × ½
(141 × 341 × 12) excluding base
Not inscribed
Purchased from Anthony d'Offay Ltd.
(Grant-in-Aid) 1982

Prov: Purchased by Anthony d'Offay from the
artist's family

Exh: *British Sculpture in the Twentieth Century*,
part 1, Whitechapel Art Gallery,
September–November 1981 (49, dated
1910); *Eric Gill*, Anthony d'Offay, May–
June 1982 (56, repr. dated 1910)

Lit: Walter Shewring, ed., *Letters of Eric Gill*,
1947, p.150

Written under the base of this carving is 'Original carving made by Eric Gill to decorate a baby's crib'. Gill made a figure of the Christ Child for a Christmas crib in the chapel at Ditchling in 1921, using a card cut out and painted, with a wooden support (the other figures were made by David Jones, and Joseph Cribb made the animals). The following year he made for the crib a Christ Child carved in wood and painted, which is mentioned in his diaries for 17–18 and 21 December, 1922. In the absence of other evidence it is likely that the Tate Gallery's carving is this one. (Information from Gill's diaries at the William Andrews Clark Memorial Library, University of California, Los Angeles.)

T 03477   Ecstasy 1910–11

Portland stone 54 × 18 × 9
(1372 × 457 × 228)
Inscribed with monogram of an eye on a
hand on r. edge
Purchased from Mrs D. Webber (Grant-
in-Aid) 1982

Prov: Probably purchased from the artist in 1912
by Edward Perry Warren, Lewes; H.A.

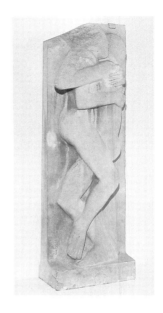

Thomas, sold Sotheby's, 9 March 1949
(158), bt Leger, from whom purchased by
Mrs Webber in 1954

Lit: Walter Shewring, ed., *Letters of Eric Gill*,
1947, p. 46; Robert Speaight, *The Life of
Eric Gill*, 1966, p.53; Richard Cork, *Art
Beyond the Gallery in Early 20th Century
England*, 1985, p.92, repr. p.95

The title 'Ecstasy' is not recorded before the Sotheby sale of 1949, and is unlikely to be the artist's own.

The sculpture can be identified with a carving listed by the artist in his diaries as 'They', on which he worked from August 1910 to January 1911 (and perhaps slightly later). The evidence for this is:

a) it is in style an early carving, comparable to the frontal female nude in the relief 'A Roland for an Oliver' 1910 (University of Hull Art Collection)

b) only the early carvings are signed with the monogram of an eye on the palm of a hand

c) there is a slight drawing by Gill for this group (at the British Museum, in a folder 'Love drawings, etc') dated 1910, although this date seems to have been added later. The heads are positioned differently, and it is squared for transfer to a larger sheet

d) in the record book for 1 January 1911, Gill refers a sculpture as ' "They" group "fucking".' No other such subject is known by him from that date, apart from the small relief inscribed 'Votes for Women', which would not have taken so much time to carve

e) the provenance from E.P. Warren's purchase in 1912 is probable. The artist's daughter, Mrs Petra Tegetmeier, does not recall ever seeing the relief in the studio, which confirms that it left his possession early.

Gill's record books also list a small version of 'They', which was probably a model in clay.

The sculpture is mentioned in letters written by Roger Fry to Gill in February 1911 (in the William Andrews Clark Memorial Library, University of California, Los Angeles). Fry acquired for himself two sculptures by Gill. The earlier of these is a 'Cupid', which he had received by September 1910. The second, referred to by Gill as a 'Statue of the Virgin', was a full size half nude, and was sketched in November 1910 and carved between February and June 1911, and is now in the Dutch Garden, Holland Park. Fry was further involved with Gill as he acted on behalf of the Contemporary Art Society to purchase his two reliefs exhibited at the Chenil Gallery in January 1911, 'A Crucifix' (N03563) and 'A Roland for an Oliver' (University of Hull Art Collection). Fry's letter to Gill of 18 February 1911, quoted in Robert Speaight (loc.cit.) is about the latter relief, and not one of the sculptures he owned: 'We have had to stand a pretty racket over your reliefs. I'll tell you about it when we meet. Also how I want you to do away with the gilding of the necklace on Her. It is a false note I think ... '

Gill wrote that these reliefs were a pair (see entry on N03563), and although they were not exhibited together it appears from Fry's letters that Gill thought of them as a series with the Tate Gallery's 'Ecstasy'. He sent Fry a photograph of this latter sculpture just finished, to which Fry responded in a letter of 15 February 1911:

The last thing is the best of all. I find it strangely beautiful and noble. I think it is wonderful that you have gone so straight – not influenced in the least by all the associated ideas mostly impertinent that have gathered round the act in the turbid course of human life. This is real religious art. I long to see the thing itself. I hope you'll have it better photographed and let me have some.

Fry wrote again on 18 February:

The more I look at Them the more I like it. You have to me at all counts said all that you wanted and it ought to be put up in a public place. It can't be till we're much more civilized in the real sense. Do send me some photos of it. I want to send one to Ed Carpenter who will welcome it immensely.

The capital letter suggests that Gill called this group 'Them', as in his diary for 1 January 1911 where he lists it as 'They'. Fry's reference to 'A Roland for an Oliver' as 'Her' implies that least in conversation Gill linked these three sculptures together.

A 'relief group (Man and Woman embracing)' was offered by Gill to E.P. Warren on 23 April 1912 for £60 (Walter Shewring, loc.cit.). Warren was an American who lived in Lewes, not far from Gill's studio at Ditchling, who collected classical works of art and modern sculptures by Rodin and Dalou. In 1904 he took delivery of Rodin's marble 'Kiss' (N06228) which he had commissioned as a replica from the artist four years before. Gill's carving is not listed in the sale catalogue of Warren's collection in 1929, and the evidence that he did acquire it is that its vendor at Sotheby's in 1949 was H.A. Thomas, who was presumably Warren's heir H. Asa Thomas (the Sotheby records of this sale are lost).

With Rodin's 'Kiss' and this Gill, Warren owned two of the most sexually explicit modern sculptures, although neither had been commissioned by him in the first place. Such subjects were important to Gill in his career both as a sculptor and graphic artist. Augustus John wrote to his patron John Quinn in New York on 10 February 1911 that Gill had 'recently started doing figures', and was 'impressed by the importance of copulation', probably referring to this sculpture. The group is startling for its date, and was influenced by Indian art, which Gill then admired. For Gill there was also a religious aspect to lovers, although this is not made apparent in this sculpture. He made several engravings of the same group in the 1920s, and in some the figures have haloes and are titled 'Divine Lovers'. The carved reliefs of 1910, 'A Crucifix' (N03563) and 'A Roland for an Oliver' he considered a pair, in which the body of Christ was paralleled by that of the woman.

The relief 'The Lovers' by Walter Ritchie made of carved bricks (1976, Delapré Park, Northampton) is very similar to 'Ecstasy', but was taken from one of Gill's later prints of this subject.

The relief was accidentally damaged in the top left corner before acquisition by the Tate Gallery, and the back of the woman's head and the man's left wrist are missing.

T 03733 **Alphabet and Numerals** 1909

Hoptonwood stone 13 × 24$\frac{3}{8}$ × 2$\frac{3}{8}$
(329 × 618 × 60)
Inscribed in raised characters
'ABCDEFGHIJ/KLMNOPQR/STUVWXY
&Z/123/456/789 TAX AD/A.E.R. GILL
Lettercutter Pub. by JOHN HOGG
Paternoster Row, London C. SMITH &
SONS Moulders, Kentish Town, London'

Transferred from the Victoria and Albert
Museum 1983

Prov: Presented by the artist to the Victoria and
Albert Museum 1931 (A. 25–1931)

Exh: British Institute of Industrial Art, Victoria
and Albert Museum, 1931 (no catalogue);
travelling exhibitions of the Department
of Circulation, Victoria and Albert
Museum; *Eric Gill*, Dartington Cider
Press Centre, Dartington, July–August
1979, Kettle's Yard, Cambridge, October–
November 1979

Lit: Edward Johnston, *Manuscript and
Inscription Letters*, 1909, plate 15
(photograph taken before 'John Hogg' text
added, and signed lower right 'A.E.R.G.
1909'); Evan R. Gill, *The Inscriptional
Work of Eric Gill an Inventory*, 1964, 168 C;
Robert Harling, *The Letter Forms and
Type Designs of Eric Gill*, 1976, p.22.
Also repr: Reproduction in plaster by John
Hogg, 1909; coloured reproduction
published by Victoria and Albert Museum

The three inscribed alphabets T 03733–5 were carved in
April 1909 for reproduction in the portfolio by Edward
Johnston, 'Manuscript and Inscription Letters for
Schools and Classes and for the use of Craftsmen'
(1909).

Gill first met Johnston at the Central School of Arts
and Crafts in 1899, as his teacher of letter design. Johnston was a calligrapher rather than a carver, and for his
book 'Writing and Illuminating and Lettering' (1906)
he included an appendix by Gill on 'Inscriptions on
Stone'. Gill there recommended Hoptonwood stone and
slate as the best materials for inscriptions to be placed
out of doors. The plates in 'Manuscript and Inscription
Letters . . . ' were intended to be further illustrations
to be used with the earlier book, and were not bound
together so that they could be more easily copied. Gill
made five plates for it. The three carved inscriptions
were to illustrate:

1. Roman capital letters (plate 13) T 03735
2. 'Lower case' italics and numerals, to match the
   capitals (plate 14) T 03734
3. 'Raised letters' – capitals and numerals (plate 15)
   T 03733

Gill's two other plates were of 'Roman Capitals . . .
and Arabic Numerals . . . ' written with a brush (plate
16) and, at the head of the Section, 'Alphabet from the
Inscription on the Trajan's Column, Rome . . . Drawn
by A.E.R. Gill from a photograph' (plate 17). The
inscription on Trajan's Column is described by Johnston as 'the root form of Western European lettering'
and he instances Gill's two inscriptions in capital letters

as modern alphabets 'founded on such root forms'. Gill
himself pointed out that he was not strictly dependent
on the Trajan lettering, in a letter to the Director of the
Victoria and Albert Museum in June 1931:

> I'm sorry the E and F of the incised capitals have
> such short middle bars – I suffered a reaction at the
> time against the Trajan snobbery of the Art Schools.

The extra text at the lowest line of T 03733, 'TAX AD'
was intended to demonstrate channelled and rounded
sections to the letters. The commentary explained 'The
forms and sections of the large letters at the foot . . . are
only appropriate for isolated letters or words or for
obviously ornamental uses.'

The three inscriptions were included in an exhibition
at the Victoria and Albert Museum in 1931 organised
by the British Institute of Industrial Art, and were
given to the Museum by the artist during the course of
the showing. Gill had corresponded with the Museum
frequently during the 1920s, and the Museum had
already acquired several inscriptions by him for educational purposes.

T 03734 Two Alphabets and Numerals 1909

Hoptonwood stone, the letters painted
$10\frac{1}{2} \times 15\frac{3}{4} \times 1\frac{1}{8}$ (265 × 400 × 28)
Inscribed
'Aabcdefghijklmno/pqqrstuvwxyz
&/*abcdefghijklmnopqrst*/*uvwxyz*
1234567890/A.E.R. Gill Letter-cutter.
Pub. by JOHN HOGG Paternoster Row,
London, C.SMITH & Sons, Moulders,
Kentish Town, London'
Transferred from the Victoria and Albert
Museum 1983

Prov: Presented by the artist to the Victoria and
Albert Museum 1931 (A. 26–1931)

Exh: British Institute of Industrial Art, Victoria
and Albert Museum, 1931 (no catalogue);
travelling exhibitions of the Department

of Circulation, Victoria and Albert Museum; *Eric Gill*, Dartington Cider Press Centre, Dartington, July–August 1979, Kettle's Yard, Cambridge, October–November 1979; *Strict Delight, the Life and Work of Eric Gill*, Whitworth Art Gallery, Manchester, March–April 1980 (L,17)

Lit: Edward Johnston, *Manuscript and Inscription Letters*, 1909, plate 14; Evan R. Gill, *The Inscriptional Work of Eric Gill an Inventory*, 1964, 168 B; Robert Harling, *The Letter Forms and Type Designs of Eric Gill*, 1976, p.22 and repr. opp. p.17

Also repr: Reproduction in plaster by John Hogg, 1909; coloured reproduction published by Victoria and Albert Museum; a rubbing reproduced as end papers in Robert Speaight, *The Life of Eric Gill*, 1966

See entry on T 03733. The commentary under the reproduction of T 03734 in Edward Johnston, op.cit., is:

LOWER-CASE ITALICS and NUMERALS incised with 'V' section ... These letters are appropriate for all ordinary inscriptions in stone. While they are as easily and quickly made as the more common 'sans-serif' or 'block' letters, they are at the same time more legible ...

This, with T 03745 for capital letters, was of considerable influence in Britain, by means of reproductions in Edward Johnston's 1909 portfolio and the plaster casts of the same year.

Amongst the artist's photographs of his own works, sold from the Hague family collection at Sotheby's, 9 November 1981, were photographs of two carved inscriptions by Gill of letters and numerals, both signed and dated 1909. These are similar to T 03734 and T 03735, but are arranged differently, and they were perhaps intended to be kept by the artist as fair copies.

In T 03734 the first two lines of figures are painted red, the third blue and the last blue (the letters) and red (the numbers).

T 03735   **Alphabet** 1909

Hoptonwood stone, the letters painted $12\frac{3}{4} \times 17 \times 1\frac{1}{8}$ ($325 \times 431 \times 28$)
Inscribed
'ABCDEFGH/IJKLMNOP/QRSTUVW/XYZ/A.E.R. GILL/Letter-cutter
Pub. by JOHN HOGG Paternoster Row, London/C.SMITH & Sons Moulders/Kentish Town, London'
Transferred from the Victoria and Albert Museum 1983

Prov: Presented by the artist to the Victoria and Albert Museum 1931 (A. 27–1931)

Exh: British Institute of Industrial Art, Victoria and Albert Museum, 1931 (no catalogue); travelling exhibitions of the Department of Circulation, Victoria and Albert Museum; *Eric Gill*, Dartington Cider Press Centre, Dartington, July–August 1979, Kettle's Yard, Cambridge, October–November 1979; *Strict Delight, the Life and Work of Eric Gill*, Whitworth Art Gallery, Manchester, March–April 1980 (not catalogued)

Lit: Edward Johnston, *Manuscript and Inscription Letters*, 1909, plate 13; Evan R. Gill, *The Inscriptional Work of Eric Gill an Inventory*, 1964, 168 A; Robert Harling, *The Letter Forms and Type Designs of Eric Gill*, 1976, p.22 and repr. opp. p.16

Also repr: Reproduction in plaster by John Hogg, 1909; coloured reproduction published by Victoria and Albert Museum

See entries on T 03733 and T 03734. The commentary under the reproduction of T 03735 in Edward Johnston, op. cit., is:

ROMAN CAPITAL LETTERS ... Inscriptions in stone or marble may be gilt or coloured with advantage. For 'lower-case' and italic letters to match these capitals see Plate 14 ...

The letters are painted red.

T 03736   **Crucifix** c.1913

Hoptonwood stone $17\frac{3}{4} \times 6\frac{3}{4} \times 1\frac{1}{2}$
($455 \times 175 \times 38$)
Inscribed 'O.¯E. FELICEM' at foot of cross
Transferred from the Victoria and Albert Museum 1983

T 03736

T 03737 The North Wind 1929

Portland stone 10 × 27½ × 4
(254 × 698 × 101)
Not inscribed
Transferred from the Victoria and Albert
Museum 1983

Prov: Frank Pick; presented by Mrs Frank Pick
to the Victoria and Albert Museum, 1942,
(A. 10–1942)

Exh: The Goupil Gallery Salon, 1929 (192, as
'South Wind (Original Design in stone for
the Underground Railway Building)');
Eric Gill, Dartington Cider Press Centre,
Dartington, July–August 1979, Kettle's
Yard, Cambridge, October–November
1979; Strict Delight, the Life and Work of
Eric Gill, Whitworth Art Gallery,
Manchester, March–April 1980 (S 13);
British Sculpture in the Twentieth Century,
part 1, Whitechapel Art Gallery,
September–November 1981 (132).

Lit: Oliver Bernard, 'Tunnelling and
Skyscraping', The Studio, XCVIII, 1929,
pp.556–8; 'Sculpture. The Temple of the
Winds', The Architectural Review, LXVI,
November 1929, pp.240–1; Kineton
Parkes, The Art of Carved Sculpture, I,
1931, pp.80–9; Kineton Parkes, 'The
Work of Eric Gill', Design and
Construction, V, April 1935, pp.185–7;
Walter Shewring, ed., Letters of Eric Gill,
1947, p.242; Robert Speaight, The Life of
Eric Gill, 1966, p.203; Denis Farr, English
Art 1870–1940, 1978, p.251; Malcolm
Yorke, Eric Gill, 1981, pp.228–9; Richard
Cork, 'Overhead Sculpture for the
Underground Railway', British Sculpture
in the Twentieth Century, ed. S. Nairne and
N. Serota, 1981, pp.91–101; Richard
Cork, Art Beyond the Gallery in Early 20th
Century England, 1985, pp.249–96

Prov: Frank Rinder; presented to the Victoria
and Albert Museum, Department of
Sculpture, by Mrs F. Rinder in memory
of her husband, 1938 (A.10-1938)

Exh: ?Eric Gill, Goupil Gallery, January 1914
(10) (possibly included); Eric Gill,
Dartington Cider Press Centre,
Dartington, July–August 1979, Kettle's
Yard, Cambridge, October–November
1979; Strict Delight, the Life and Work of
Eric Gill, Whitworth Art Gallery,
Manchester, March–April 1980 (S 1)

The first carving of this subject by Gill is the Tate
Gallery's 'Crucifixion' of 1910 (N 03563). Gill was not
converted to the Roman Catholic church until three
years later, and this first crucifixion is unconventional
both for the choice of the inscriptions and for its pairing
with a relief of a female nude.

After his conversion Gill carved several crucifixions
and small crucifixes. T 03736 resembles one of his earliest wood engravings, made in 1913 (Christopher Skelton, The Engravings of Eric Gill, 1983, p.16 and p.xviii)
and it is probably of the same date. His diaries record
that he carved a crucifix in Hoptonwood stone between
19 April and 2 May 1913 (William Andrews Clark
Memorial Library, University of California, Los
Angeles). The print does not have the inscription at the
foot, but the pose and proportions, and the emaciated
figure, are similar. Skelton records that the wooden
block of this print was made as a plaque, and offered
for sale at a bookshop in London belonging to Everard
Meynell. Gill had known Meynell from 1912 when he
sought his advice about Roman Catholicism. Meynell
lent a crucifix of Hoptonwood stone by Gill to his
exhibition at the Goupil Gallery in January 1914, which

may be this one. It is not known when Frank Rinder
acquired T 03736, but he was in contact with Gill at
least by 1918, when he commissioned from him an
inscription for a holy water stoup (Evan R. Gill, The
Inscriptional Work of Eric Gill an Inventory, 1964, 350).

The letters of the inscription are painted red.

'The North Wind' and 'The East Wind' (N 04487) were carved by Gill after his designs for large reliefs in Portland stone on the London Underground Headquarters building in Broadway, Westminster. The history is described by Richard Cork in *Art Beyond the Gallery in Early 20th Century England* (1985, op.cit.)

It has been thought that these two carvings were models for two of the three full size reliefs which were made by Gill. His diaries record however that both were begun and completed in October 1929 some time after the building had been finished, and immediately before he exhibited them at the Goupil Gallery (William Andrews Clark Memorial Library, University of California, Los Angeles). Gill did make models for the reliefs, but these are not known to survive. The sequence of events given by his diary is:

22, 30 March 1928. Drawings for the designs.
9 June. Designs for North, South and East winds.
10–13 July. Carves a model for the sculptures.
18 September. Stone delivered to his house, Pigotts.
13–30 October. Draws sculptures on stone and sends off the stone.
13, 15–17 and 19 November. Draws on stone and makes models, at Piggotts.
20 November–8 February 1929. Carves full size sculptures in London.
11–21 October. Carves 'South Wind'. (T 03737)
21–26 October. Carves 'East Wind'. (N 04487)
29 October. Delivers 'Winds' to Goupil Gallery.

The design of the building by Charles Holden was cross shaped in plan, with wings at North, South, East and West. The relief sculptures were sited above the eighth floor, and were intended to make reference to the ancient Greek 'Tower of the Winds' in Athens, with two carved reliefs for each wind, each flying outwards from the centre. Gill made three of these, and was in charge of the five assistant sculptors, including Henry Moore, each of whom made one each. The reliefs are all generally similar, and it is not clear whether it was Gill or someone else who specified the type of figures wanted, although they generally depend on the Greek reliefs of the first century BC. 'The Tower of the Winds' at the Radcliffe Observatory, Oxford which has similar relief sculpture is a probable more immediate source.

The sequence of events also leaves unclear the function of the preparatory models made by Gill in July and in November 1928, and the size and function of the stone that he drew on in October 1928. The two small reliefs at the Tate Gallery are exact copies of the large sculptures, except that 'The North Wind' is in reverse. Richard Cork (op.cit.) published photographs of the designs drawn by Gill on 9 June 1928 (collection of the William Andrews Clark Memorial Library, University of California, Los Angeles). One of these is for 'The North Wind' in the same direction as the final sculpture,

but is inscribed by Gill 'figure reversed' and 'Make model 1/4 fs'. The size of the Tate Gallery reliefs is approximately one quarter full size. Evidently when making them for the Goupil Gallery exhibition in October 1929 he used as a guide either the earlier drawings or models, before the placing of his design had been finally determined. It is possible that the 'models' made in November 1928 were of clay, and the two stone reliefs in the Tate Gallery were precise copies of them. If the North and South Winds by Gill on the building had been interchanged and reversed, then each representation of each of them by the various artists would have been consistent as to sex – the North and East female, and the West and South male.

In his letter to Graham Carey of 2 December 1928 (Walter Shewring, ed., loc.cit.) Gill refers to the commission slightingly, because of the sculptors' dependence on the architecture, the short time in which he had to work and the different attitude to art of the builders.

T 03738   **Inscription 'Ex Divina Pulchritudine' 1926**

Hoptonwood stone, the letters painted
$12 \times 18 \times 1\frac{1}{2}$ (306 × 457 × 38)
Inscribed 'EX DIVINA
/PVLCHRITVDINE/ESSE
OMNIVM/DERIVATVR' and 'EG' b.r.
edge
Transferred from the Victoria and Albert Museum 1983

Prov: Commissioned from the artist by the Department of Circulation, Victoria and Albert Museum 1926 (Circ. 959–1926)

Exh: Travelling exhibitions of the Department of Circulation, Victoria and Albert Museum; *Eric Gill*, Dartington Cider Press Centre, Dartington, July–August 1979, Kettle's Yard, Cambridge, October–November 1979; *Strict Delight, the Life and Work of Eric Gill*, Whitworth Art

Gallery, Manchester, March–April 1980
(L. 18)

Lit: Evan R. Gill, *The Inscriptional Work of Eric Gill an Inventory*, 1964, 479 A. *Also repr*: Coloured reproduction published by the Victoria and Albert Museum

This text was chosen by Gill in response to a commission from Eric MacLagan, the Director of the Victoria and Albert Museum, who wrote to him asking for an 'inscription for Department of Circulation ... on hoptonwood or other stone ... sufficiently light in weight to be transportable ... both Roman capitals and italics' (26 April 1926). Gill made two tablets on August 18-21 (recorded in his diaries, William Andrews Clark Memorial Library, University of California, Los Angeles), this one and one painted on wood which still belongs to the Victoria and Albert Museum (Evan R. Gill, op. cit., 479). He wrote to MacLagan 'As to the text, I reckon I have given the art students something to chew and, that there may be no doubt of the meaning, I have done it in Latin, French and English' (21 August 1926).

The Latin is from St Thomas Aquinas's commentary on Dionysius, *De Divinis Nominibus*, (ch. 4, lect. 5). It is translated into French and English in the painted version, and the latter text is 'The Beauty of God is the cause of the being of all that is'.

The top line is painted red, the second black, the third blue and the last black.

T 03739   Alphabet of Raised Letters 1927

Hoptonwood stone 21 × 21½ × 1¾
(533 × 546 × 44)
Inscribed in raised letters

'ABCDEF/GHIJKLM/NOPQRST/UV WXYZ' and 'EG 27' b.r.

Transferred from the Victoria and Albert Museum 1983

Prov: Commissioned from the artist by the Department of Circulation, Victoria and Albert Museum 1927 (Circ. 531–1927)

Exh: Travelling exhibitions of the Department of Circulation, Victoria and Albert Museum

Lit: Evan R. Gill, *The Inscriptional Work of Eric Gill an Inventory*, 1964, 498A; Robert Harling, *The Letter Forms and Type Designs of Eric Gill*, 1976, p.27
Also repr: David Kindersley, *Eric Gill*, 1982, opp. p.5

Eric MacLagan, the Director of the Victoria and Albert Museum, wrote to Eric Gill at Capel-y-ffin on 23 February 1927, asking for a stone panel with an alphabet, incised or in relief, which he felt he should commission 'considering the part you have played in the revival of good lettering'. In July, Gill wrote to say that he was making the two alphabets, which he finally sent to the Museum in September (correspondence at the Victoria and Albert Museum). His diaries record that they were carved on 8–9 August (William Andrews Clark Memorial Library, University of California, Los Angeles).

A rubbing of the inscription in the St Bride Printing Library is signed by the artist 'For SKM., E.G. del; L.C. and E.G. Sc. Aug. 1927', meaning that it was made for the South Kensington Museum, and carved by Gill with the assistance of Lawrence Cribb.

T 03740   Alphabet 1927

Hoptonwood stone 20⅛ × 21⅛ × 1¾
(512 × 543 × 44)

Inscribed 'ABC/DEFGHIJKL
/MNOPQRST/UVWXY&Z' and 'E.G. 27'
b.r.
Transferred from the Victoria and Albert
Museum 1983

Prov: Commissioned from the artist by the
Department of Circulation, Victoria and
Albert Museum 1927 (Circ. 530–1927)

Exh: Travelling exhibition of the Department
of Circulation, Victoria and Albert
Museum

Lit: Evan R. Gill, *The Inscriptional Work of
Eric Gill an Inventory*, 1964, 498; Robert
Harling, *The Letter Forms and Type
Designs of Eric Gill*, 1976, p.27

See entry on T 03739. The signature on the rubbing
of T 03740 at the St Bride Printing Library is the same
as on T 03739.

T 03741　Inscription 'Homines Divites' 1922

Portland stone $9\frac{1}{2} \times 35\frac{1}{4} \times 1$
($237 \times 897 \times 35$)
Inscribed 'HOMINES . DIVITES . IN .
VIRTUTE/PULCHRITUDINIS .
STUDIUM . HABENTES/
PACIFICANTES . IN DOMIBUS . SUIS'
Transferred from the Victoria and Albert
Museum 1983

Prov: Commissioned by Lord Carmichael, 1922;
bequeathed to the Victoria and Albert
Museum by Lady Carmichael, through the
N A-C F, 1947 (Misc. 1–1947)

Exh: Tancred Borenius, *Lord Carmichael of
Skirling, A Memoir*, 1929, pp.272–7; Evan
R. Gill, *The Inscriptional Work of Eric Gill
an Inventory*, 1964, 413

Lord Carmichael of Skirling, First Baron (1859–1926),
who collected, amongst other things, medieval and
renaissance sculpture, commissioned the three inscriptions and the sundial (T 03741-4) for the garden of his
house at 13 Portman Street. The garden also contained
other inscriptions and some of his sculpture collection.
The artist's diaries record that they were not all carved
together (William Andrews Clark Memorial Library,
University of California, Los Angeles):

28–29 August 1922. Carved 'Homines Divites . . . '
on stone
29–30 December 1922. Carved 'In Terra Pax . . . '
and 'Gloria in Altissimis Deo . . . ' on slate
29 December 1923–22 January 1924. Carved Sundial
'Pensa che questa di . . . ' on slate

The text 'Homines Divites' had earlier been used by
Gill in a watercolour inscription drawn by a pupil in
June 1920 (Evan R. Gill, op.cit., 379B). It is from
Ecclesiasticus in Apocrypha, chapter 44 verse 6: 'Rich
men furnished with ability, living peaceably in their
habitations.'

Rubbings from the inscriptions for Lord Carmichael
are in the collection of the St Bride Printing Library.

T 03742　Inscription 'In Terra Pax' 1922

Slate $6 \times 32\frac{3}{4} \times 1$ ($155 \times 830 \times 30$)
Inscribed 'IN TERRA PAX
HOMINIBUS/BONAE VOLUNTATIS'
Transferred from the Victoria and Albert
Museum 1983

Prov: As T 03741 (Misc. 2–1947)

Exh: *Strict Delight, the Life and Work of Eric
Gill 1882–1940*, Whitworth Art Gallery,
Manchester, March–April 1980 (L 21)

Lit: Evan R. Gill, *The Inscriptional Work of
Eric Gill an Inventory*, 1964, 412

See entries on T 03741 and T 03743.

T 03743 Inscription 'Gloria in Altissimis Deo' 1922

Slate 10 × 21 × 1 (255 × 530 × 25)
Inscribed 'GLORIA/IN
ALTISSIMIS/DEO'
Transferred from the Victoria and Albert
Museum 1983

Prov: As T 03741 (Misc. 3–1947)
Exh: *Strict Delight, the Life and Work of Eric
Gill 1882–1949*, Whitworth Art Gallery,
Manchester, March–April 1980 (L 19)
Lit: Evan R. Gill, *The Inscriptional Work of
Eric Gill an Inventory*, 1964, 412

See entry on T 03741. T 03742-3 together form part of
the same text, which had already been used by Gill
in 1903 in one of his earliest inscriptions, which he
continued to display on his studio wall (Evan R. Gill,
op.cit., 22). It is from the beginning of the Gloria in the
Mass, and is translated 'Glory to God in the highest,
and on earth peace to men of good will'.

A photograph of another carving of this inscription
('Gloria in ALTISSIMIS/DEO/ET IN TERRA PAX'),
not recorded by Evan R. Gill, was in the collection of
the artist's photographs sold at Sotheby's, 9 November
1981.

T 03744 Sundial 1923–4

Slate, with metal gnomon 18⅛ × 15 × 8¼
(460 × 381 × 222)

Inscribed 'PENSA . CHE . QUESTO .
DI/MAI . NON .
RAGGIORNA/VI/VII/VIII/IX/X XI XII
I/II/III/IV' and on reverse a monogram
Transferred from the Victoria and Albert
Museum 1983

Prov: Commissioned by Lord Carmichael, 1923;
bequeathed to the Victoria and Albert
Museum by Lady Carmichael, through the
N A-C F, 1947 (Misc. 4–1947)
Exh: *Strict Delight, the Life and Work of Eric
Gill 1882–1940*, Whitworth Art Gallery,
Manchester, March–April 1980 (L 20)
Lit: Evan R. Gill, *The Inscriptional Work of
Eric Gill an Inventory*, 1964, 442

See entry on T 03741. The text is from Dante (*Purga-
torio*, Canto XII, line 84), and was chosen, according to
the Victoria and Albert Museum's records, by Lord
Carmichael. It was translated for this entry by Tom
Phillips as:

Just think; this day will never dawn again.

At the St Bride Printing Library there is both a rubbing
of the inscription and a layout design. Evan R. Gill
records (op.cit.) that 'the border and dial lines were cut
by Phillip Hagreen'. The '*o*' of 'questo' is smaller than
the other letters and was recut from an '*a*'.

T 03745 St Sebastian 1920

Portland stone 41 × 8 × 10
(1040 × 202 × 254)
Not inscribed
Transferred from the Victoria and Albert
Museum 1983

Prov: Commissioned from the artist by André Raffalovich, 1919; bequeathed by him in 1934 to Rev. Canon John Gray, who presented it in the same year to the Victoria and Albert Museum, in memory of A. Raffalovich (A. 10–1934)

Exh: *British Sculpture in the Twentieth Century*, part 1, Whitechapel Art Gallery, September–November 1981 (95)

Lit: Walter Shewring, ed., *Letters of Eric Gill*, 1947, p.138; Peter F. Anson, 'Random Reminiscences of John Gray and André Raffalovich', in Brocard Sewell, ed., *Two Friends, John Gray and André Raffalovich*, 1963; Robert Speaight, *The Life of Eric Gill*, 1966, p. 73; Malcolm Yorke, *Eric Gill*, 1981, p.215
Also repr: J.K.M. Rothenstein, *Eric Gill*, 1927, plate 20 (two views)

André Raffalovich (1864–1934) commissioned several sculptures, a book plate and a portrait drawing of himself from Eric Gill. They first met in Edinburgh, where Raffalovich lived, in 1914, and maintained contact through Canon John Gray, who often visited Gill in Buckinghamshire. The artist's diaries record work on this sculpture in March and April 1920 (William Andrews Clark Memorial Library, University of California, Los Angeles).

Gill's letter to Raffalovich of 16 June 1920 thanks him for letting him know that the sculpture had arrived, and he explains that it was made after a study of his own body in a mirror. Peter Anson (op.cit.) records being shown it when it first arrived in Edinburgh. It is likely that the subject was given by Raffalovich, but it is not recorded as a design for a particular setting.

Charles Ginner 1878-1952

T03841 Victoria Embankment Gardens 1912

Oil on canvas 26⅛ × 18³⁄₁₆ (664 × 461)
Inscribed 'C. Ginner' b.r.
Purchased from Anthony d'Offay Ltd. (Grant-in-Aid) 1984

Prov: ... ; Anton Lock, London, by whom sold Christie's 9 June 1978 (59, repr.) £10,000 bt Anthony d'Offay Gallery

Exh: *The 5th London Salon*, A.A.A., Royal Albert Hall, July 1912 (75); *Camden Town Group Exhibition*, The Little Gallery, February 1914 (no catalogue); *Harold Gilman and Charles Ginner*, Goupil Gallery, April–May 1914 (57, as 'Victoria Gardens'); *Charles Ginner 1878–1952 paintings and drawings*, AC tour, Art Gallery, Darlington, November 1953, City Art Gallery, Bristol, November–December 1953, Art Gallery, Carlisle, January 1954, Tate Gallery, January–February 1954, Art Gallery, Southampton, February–March 1954, Assembly House, Norwich, March–April 1954 (4); *British Paintings 1890–1928*, Columbus Gallery of Fine Art, Ohio, February–March 1971 (32, repr.); *Post Impressionism: cross-currents in European painting*, R.A., November 1979 – March 1980 (297, repr.); *The Camden Town Group*, Yale Center for British Art, New Haven, April–June 1980 (42, repr.); *British Painting 1895–1965*, Anthony d'Offay Gallery, March–April 1982 (no catalogue no., repr.)

Lit: C. Ginner, '*Notebooks Volume I*', unpublished, p.57; 'Paintings by the Camden Town Group', *The Athenaeum*, No.4504, 1914, p.281; 'Charles Ginner: Memorial Exhibition at the Tate', *The Times*, 30 January 1954, p.8; Malcolm Easton, 'Charles Ginner: Viewing and Finding', *Apollo*, XCI, 1970, pp.205–6, repr. fig.4; Alexander Robertson, 'Charles Ginner, Camden Town and Neo-Realism', *Leeds Arts Calendar*, No.80, 1977, p.10; Bernard Denvir, 'Individual Temperaments', *Art and Artists*, XIV, 1980, p.16, repr. p.17

Ginner first exhibited T03841 in the 5th London Salon of the Allied Artists Association, which ran for the month of July 1912. Roger Fry, anxious to promote modern English art to a Parisian audience, had organised an exhibition of paintings by several English artist friends, including Ginner, at the Galerie Barbazanges, Paris, from 1–15 May 1912. Ginner showed three works in this Parisian show, 2 still-lifes and one London view entitled 'Les Affiches, Londres'. Since Fry was looking for recent paintings to send to Paris and since T03841 was not included, it might be possible to suggest that T03841 was painted between April 1912, when Fry collected the paintings for Paris, and July 1912 when the 5th London Salon of the Allied Artists Association opened. Certainly the lush foliage of the trees and plants in Victoria Embankment Gardens could suggest a seasonal date of around May–June.

After Ginner's decision to settle in London in late 1909, it is noticeable that he seemed keen to paint several pictures recording aspects of London life and its topography; Piccadilly Circus (Tate Gallery Collection) and Leicester Square (Brighton Art Gallery), both also of 1912, are two notable examples. The subject of T03841 is the view of the Palace of Westminster, the Houses of Parliament, from Victoria Embankment Gardens. From Westminster Bridge to Blackfriars Bridge, the road which runs along the north bank of the River Thames is known as Victoria Embankment. There are two garden plots along Victoria Embankment, and the plot between Hungerford Bridge and Waterloo Bridge is Victoria Embankment Gardens. Ginner has painted the view looking west, towards the horizontally-striped architecture, chimneys and crown-like ornamentation of Norman Shaw's New Scotland Yard (1890, partially obscured by foliage), and beyond it to the clock tower of Big Ben and, in the distance, the Victoria Tower area which flies the flag. In the middle ground is Edgar Boehm's eleven foot high bronze statue, unveiled in May 1884, of William Tyndale (the pre-Reformation reformer and translator of the New Testament into English from Greek). The view is unchanged today except for the absence of the park benches.

Dora Gordine b.1906

T03746 Guadaloupe Head c.1925–7

Bronze 14¼ × 9⅛ × 9⅛ (360 × 230 × 230)
Inscribed 'Dora Gordine 8/8' on back of head and 'VALSUANI CIRE PERDUE BRONZE' on back of neck
Transferred from the Victoria and Albert Museum 1983

Prov: Mrs A.Q. Patullo (probably purchased at the Leicester Galleries in 1938);

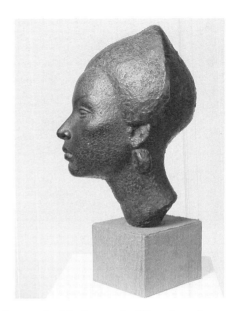

bequeathed by her to the Victoria and Albert Museum 1952 (Circ. 80–1952)

Exh: ? Salon des Tuileries, Paris (date unknown, unspecified cast); ? *An Exhibition of Sculpture by Dora Gordine*, Leicester Galleries, October 1928 (7, repr., as 'Guadaloupe Head (Negress)', unspecified cast); ? *Exhibition of Recent Sculpture and Drawings by Dora Gordine*, Leicester Galleries, November 1938 (24, under 'Earlier Sculpture', unspecified cast); ? *Junge Künstler, Dora Gordine, Fritz Kronenberg, Paul Strecker*, Galerie Alfred Flechtheim, Berlin, September–October 1929 (4, repr. as 'Negerin' unspecified cast); travelling exhibitions of Department of Circulation, Victoria and Albert Museum; *British Sculpture in the Twentieth Century*, Whitechapel Art Gallery, September–November 1981 (79)

Lit: Arthur Symons, 'Sculpture, Dora Gordine', *The Spectator*, 4 November 1938

The artist (the Hon Mrs Richard Hare) has stated that this is the earliest of her four bronze heads of African and Oriental women that belong to the Tate Gallery. She made the sculpture while still a student at Paris University, and modelled it from the life from a girl whom she met by chance, and 'struck by her dignity', asked to sit for her.

The edition of eight casts was completed, and the artist recalled that all were sold to private collectors by 1938.

This information was given by the artist on 7 February 1985.

Spencer Gore 1878–1914

T03561 The Artist's Wife 1913

Oil on canvas $30\frac{1}{8} \times 25\frac{1}{16}$ (765 × 636)
Not inscribed, but bears studio stamp

S.F. Gore , b.r.

Presented by the artist's son, Frederick
Gore, 1983

Prov: Mary Gore; Frederick Gore
Exh: *Spencer Gore*, The Minories, Colchester,
March–April 1970, Ashmolean Museum,
Oxford, April 1970, Graves Art Gallery,
Sheffield, May–June 1970 (60, repr.)
Lit: John Woodeson, 'Spencer Gore', *The
Connoisseur*, CLXXXV, March 1974,
pp.174–80, repr. 179; Simon Watney,
English Post-Impressionism, 1980, repr.
p.122

After Gore's death in 1914 Harold Gilman labelled all
the paintings left in his studio. The Gilman label on the
back of T03561 states that it was painted at 2 Houghton
Place [London]; Gore lived at this address from the
time of his marriage until the summer of 1913 when he
moved to Richmond, Surrey.

The artist married Mary Johanna Kerr (known as
'Mollie') in 1912. He met her in 1911 and painted her
portrait several times before and after their marriage.
'The Gas Cooker' 1913 (T00496), acquired by the Tate
in 1962, depicts Mrs Gore working in the kitchen at 2
Houghton Place. Other portraits of the artist's wife
include 'Mrs S F Gore in the Garden of Rowlandson
House', summer 1911 (repr. in Gore exhibition catalogue, Anthony d'Offay 1983, no.17), 'The Artist's

Wife, Mornington Crescent' 1911 (National Art
Gallery, Wellington) and 'The Artist's Wife' 1911 (repr.
in Gore exhibition catalogue, Anthony d'Offay 1983,
no.14).

Anthony Gormley b.1950

T03681 Natural Selection 1981

Twenty-four objects [ball, melon, ball of
string, coconut, bottle, marrow, pestle,
parsnip, glue brush, pear, light bulb,
lemon, grenade, goose egg, plumb bob,
cucumber, bradawl, courgette, vibrator,
banana, chisel, carrot, pencil, pea] encased
in lead, 499 × 6 × 6 (11960 × 150 × 150)
Not inscribed
Presented by the Contemporary Art
Society 1983

Exh: *Anthony Gormley: Sculpture*, Whitechapel
Art Gallery, March–April 1981 (not in
catalogue); *The Sculpture Show*, Hayward
and Serpentine Galleries, August–October
1983 (27)
Lit: Lynne Cooke, 'Anthony Gormley at the
Whitechapel', *Artscribe*, June 1981 no.29,
pp.56–7, repr. p.57; *Objects and Sculpture*,
exhibition catalogue, ICA and Arnolfini
Gallery, Bristol, 1981, p.18; Stuart
Morgan, 'Genesis of Secrecy',
*Transformations, New Sculpture from
Britain*, exhibition catalogue, XVII Bienal
de São Paulo, 1983, pp. 36–7, repr. p.37

The following entry, which has been approved by the
artist, is based on conversations between him and the
compiler on 25 and 31 July 1986.

'Natural Selection' was conceived towards the end of
1979 and executed during the following two years. It
belongs to a body of related works which includes:
'Land, Sea and Air 1' 1977–9, 'Fruits of the Earth'

1978–9, 'Full Bowl' 1979 and 'Three Bodies' 1981 (all repr. in Lynne Cooke, *Anthony Gormley*, New York 1984, ills.6, 7, 4, 10) which are also made in lead, as well as sculptures in other materials, notably 'Last Tree' 1979 (repr. *Objects and Sculpture*, 1981, p.13) and 'Bed' 1980–1 (repr. Cooke 1984, ill.8) which are made out of wood and slices of bread respectively. These were all produced during the period 1977–81 and Gormley regards them as 'analytical works which explore the objective world' [this and all subsequent quotations, unless stated otherwise, by the artist in conversation with the compiler].

'Natural Selection' consists of twenty-four objects. Half are man-made and half are natural in origin. They are arranged in a canon of ascending size in which manufactured objects alternate with natural ones. Each object is encased in one layer of lead. Casing objects in lead is a means of separating the object's image from its substance, thereby creating an analogue. The lead skin 'frees the object from time and function' and, by removing it from direct apprehension, 'allows it to be made anew in the viewer's mind'. A basic tenet of Gormley's art is that the creative act is collaborative, and involves the participation of both the artist and the viewer. His intention is to set up a dialogue in which the spectator can 'energise' the work with his own ideas and imagination, while at the same time the work may inhabit the viewer's 'mental landscape' and alter his view of the world.

'Natural Selection' arose out of Gormley's desire to make a progression piece indicating the principle, articulated in 'Fruits of the Earth', that he could take a manufactured object and connect it to an organic force. The title 'Natural Selection' is an obvious reference to Darwin's theory of evolution but at the same time is intended to be ironic. The objects included are 'a very unnatural selection' and are a mix of natural and 'distressingly unnatural inventions'. Gormley has explained that his primary consideration in the selection of these particular objects was for their formal values and the way in which they could be harnessed in order to give a sense of progression and direction which would pull the observer forward. His intention is to make the act of looking a physical process: an idea which he also explored in 'Breadline' 1978 (repr. Cooke 1984, ill.5) and 'One Apple' 1981–2 (not illustrated in any publication). He recalls that he started with the idea of something small and organic – the first object in the progression is a pea – and the choice of subsequent objects followed quickly. While many of these are found objects and were readily available, others were more difficult to obtain and necessitated a search lasting many months for objects of precisely the required type and shape. Some objects have obvious morphological associations, for instance, the pear with the light bulb and the banana with the vibrator. However, the overall selection

is evidence of an underlying dialectical method. Gormley holds that the practice of his work in general is based on the dialectic of destruction and creation. Referring to 'Natural Selection' in particular, Gormley has described how

the dialectic I have used in opposing cultural and natural objects and trying to reconcile their differences whilst at the same time underlining them, relates also to the similarity of the urges of creativity with urges of aggression, the urge of sexuality and the urge towards destruction. In 'Natural Selection' for example, those two dialectics are very implicit. By alternating a man-made object with a god-made object I also uncover a sexual division – objects of aggression are naturally phallic; objects which present a containing oval are naturally female. However, the central elements in 'Natural Selection' are an egg and a grenade. The opposition has been levelled out in a morphological sense, where an object associated with aggression is morphologically close to an object naturally associated with creativity (quoted in *Objects and Sculpture*, 1981, p.18).

The dialectic of man-made and god-made objects in 'Natural Selection' is made up of tools and fruits and vegetables. They are perceived as complementary opposites which pass from one 'orbit' to another and cross in so doing. Fruit comes from 'closed ground' and 'passes into our field'; tools extend the 'closed ground of our bodies' and, in being put to use, penetrate the environment. Their opposition here generates an additional resonance in referring to the relationship between work and food which, in modern times, have also become separated. The opposition and reconciliation of cultural and natural objects is further suggestive of the relationship between growth and destruction, and life and death.

'Natural Selection' does not make a statement in any literal or finite sense. Gormley's intention is that the work should invite speculation and provide an 'open ground for experience and reflection' in which the spectator is invited to make connections between the forms.

Sir William Goscombe John
1860–1952

T 03747 **Pan** 1901

Bronze $26\frac{3}{4} \times 8\frac{1}{4} \times 4\frac{3}{4}$ (680 × 210 × 120)
Inscribed 'Goscombe John to Frank Short' on r. of base
Transferred from the Victoria and Albert Museum 1983

Prov: Sir Frank Short; his daughter Dorothea Short, by whom bequeathed to the Victoria and Albert Museum 1973 (A.7–1973)

Lit: Fiona Pearson, *Goscombe John at the National Museum of Wales*, 1979, pp. 36 and 80; Susan Beattie, *The New Sculpture*, 1983, p.180

Goscombe John's sculptures can be dated from his regular exhibitions at the Royal Academy between 1886 and 1948. The model for this 'Pan' was the bronze statuette 'Joyance' shown there in 1901, and this was itself a reduction of a large plaster 'Joyance' shown in 1899. A bronze cast of the larger sculpture was commissioned to ornament a fountain in Thompson Park, Cardiff, and had always been displayed there until it was recently destroyed by vandals. A later cast, 69½ ins. high, is in the collection of the National Museum of Wales, Cardiff. Another cast of the statuette, titled 'Hermes' and with wings on his feet and a different base, was at the St Louis International Exhibition of 1904 (207, repr.).

The Tate Gallery cast has been made into a 'Pan' by the addition of pipes on the base, but whatever he may have held in his hands is missing.

Alan Green b.1932

T 03443   One to Four 1982

Oil on canvas, three panels, each $67\frac{1}{8} \times 67\frac{1}{8}$ (1706 × 1706), overall dimensions $67\frac{1}{8} \times 201\frac{3}{8}$ (1706 × 5118)
Inscribed 'ALAN GREEN/1982/ONE TO FOUR/I OF 3 (LEFT PANEL)/← CENTRE' on reverse of left canvas, 'TOP/ALAN GREEN 1982/ONE TO FOUR (2 OF 3)/←(CENTRE PANEL)→' on reverse of centre canvas and 'ALAN GREEN 1982/ONE TO FOUR/3 OF 3/(RIGHT PANEL)/CENTRE→' on reverse of right canvas
Purchased from Juda Rowan Gallery (Grant-in-Aid) 1982

Exh: *Alan Green, Recent Paintings and drawings*, Juda Rowan Gallery, April–May 1982 (no catalogue, repr. in col. on folded card); *Also repr: Alan Green Neue Bilder*, Gimpel-Hanover and André Emmerich, Zurich, repr. in col. on folded card but not shown in exhibition

beneath a diagram illustrating the main formal divisions in 'One to Four'

ONE	I	2	3
			4

the artist has written (letter to the compiler, 18 May 1986):

At its simplest level this painting is about three squares. One fully occupied, one cut vertically, one cut horizontally. These three activities have different properties which form the subject of the painting:

Panel 1:   The fullness of the left hand square; hence the underlying left-right and right-left diagonal structure.

Panel 2:   The speed of the vertical cut in the middle panel, although barely visible, echoes the physical vertical divisions of the junctions between the three panels.

Panel 3[4]: The natural slowness of the horizontal division in the right hand panel opposes the previous verticals and ceases to be linear, becoming instead the junction between two opposing colour areas; thus both questioning and reinforcing the existing order created in the two previous panels.

Since the mid-seventies Green has intermittently produced multi-panelled paintings. This triptych – the three panels are joined together – was completed during the first two months of 1982, when he was experimenting with broader and bolder textures, often using a palette knife to score, cross-hatch or flatten his built-up surfaces (the left-hand canvas of T 03443 has been diagonally scored in this manner). The major divisions within the composition are: Section *One* (see Green's diagram above) a deep blue-purple ground cross-hatched as described; section *1* a broad vertical stripe of black-purple and *2* a similar stripe of dark plum colour – both of these laid over a crimson ground so that the division between them shows as a narrow strip of crimson; *3* a broad horizontal band of Prussian blue above *4* a crimson area of similar dimensions. This provides a challenge to the compositional balance of the painting which is otherwise quite closely balanced in colour and tone.

In a letter to Alan Bowness (22 July 1982) the artist wrote:

I . . . feel it [T 03443] was an ambitious painting and reflects one side of my work – the use of disparate areas combined in one large canvas. I have produced about six or seven such paintings in recent years – almost as a foil to the more apparently simple works . . .

This entry has been approved by the artist.

T 03835   **Check** 1973

Acrylic on cotton canvas, 84 × 108 (2134 × 2743)
Inscribed 'ALAN GREEN 73/CHECK' on reverse

Purchased from Juda Rowan Gallery (Grant-in-Aid) 1984

Prov: Mr Gert and Mrs Rosi Diefenthal, Freimersdorf, 1973–83, Juda Rowan Gallery 1983–4

Exh: *Prospekt 73*, Kunsthalle, Düsseldorf, September–October 1973 (6, slide No.6); *Alan Green, Paintings 1969–1979*, Kunsthalle, Bielefeld, September–October 1979 (6, repr. p.46)

Lit: 'Alan Green on his paintings', *Studio International* CLXXXVI, No.959, 1973, pp.144–5 (repr. as 'Chek' p.144); Martine Lignon 'Alan Green', *Alan Green, Paintings 1969–1979*, exhibition catalogue, Kunsthalle, Bielefeld, 1979, pp.12–13; Catherine Lacey in *Alan Green, Recent Paintings and Drawings*, exhibition catalogue, Juda Rowan Gallery, August 1985, p.9, repr. in col. p.8

Green's earliest mature paintings (c.1967–9) operate within a rigid grid format but around 1972 he began to make what he refers to as 'block' paintings, much more loosely painted works which nevertheless retain (though more informally) the blocked-out division of the earlier grids. In the block paintings, Green first began to experiment with achieving unity of surface predominantly through paint rather than through underlying geometric structure. Around 1972–3 he began to emphasise what had been the upright divisions in the original grid lay-outs, in a series of vertical columnar compositions which contrasted hard-edged with more informal passages of paint but which, like the 'blocks' were made by contrasting near transparent washes with built up areas – usually opaque bands of paint in near monochrome blues or blacks. 'Check', which is an early example of these 'column' works, is closely related in size, treatment and composition to a number of Green's paintings of the same year, in particular to the following, all illustrated in the catalogue for Green's exhibition at the Kunsthalle, Bielefeld in 1979: 'Side by Side' (62); 'Towards Grey' (7); 'Status Quo' (10); 'Limbo' (9) and the slightly earlier 'Four in the Morning' 1972 (5).

In 1973 Green wrote (*Studio International*, loc.cit.) that the works of 1973 and the 'block' paintings before them came about through 'a need to use more of myself, having felt completely hemmed in by the grid paintings'. He started working in a freer way around the summer of 1971 when he first laid a piece of unstretched canvas over a small table and ran a paint roller over it, then moved the canvas and repeated the operation. In the same article, written in the year when most of the 'column' paintings were produced, Green wrote, 'I think what I like about columns is that they have a different kind of speed from blocks. I did try to go straight into columns. But it doesn't really work, because they end up like stripes. The best paintings with columns happen because they merge together, and I find this merging a very difficult situation to force.' He also noted that at this stage, he liked his paintings to 'declare their history' and how the progress of a painting might be conditioned by certain painterly occurrences (for example dripping paint), which were originally accidents.

He admitted to being wary of the intrusion of too many chance elements but 'I find you've got to have a few bonuses in a painting. For instance, how it dries. I put in more cobalt in a painting illustrated here (T 03835) and when it dried the violet took over more than I thought it would. I think this one came a bit early, it put me off my stride.'

By 1974, paintings like 'Four Greys Don't Make Black' (Bielefeld, 1979, 12) with its more regular vertical banding, signalled the advent of simpler monochrome compositions and hint at Green's later polyptych arrangements, which the strong vertical emphasis in paintings like 'Check' also appears to anticipate.

The artist has written (letter to the compiler, 18 May 1986):

'Check' was one of the first attempts to move from block paintings to a less divided field. I remember at the time I felt slightly 'expressionist' because of the large colour washes eventually covered by black. It must also be the first time I really used details like taped lines to slow some areas down against the free washes of acrylic.

This entry has been approved by the artist.

Philip Guston 1913–1980

T 03364   **Black Sea** 1977

Oil on canvas 68⅛ × 117 (1730 × 2970)
Inscribed 'Philip Guston' b.r.
Purchased from David McKee Gallery, New York (Grant-in-Aid) 1982

Exh: *New Paintings, New York*, Hayward Gallery, May–June 1979 (not numbered); *Philip Guston*, San Francisco Museum of Modern Art, May–June 1980, Corcoran Art Gallery, Washington, D.C., July–September 1980, Museum of Contemporary Art, Chicago, November 1980–January 1981, Denver Art Museum, Colorado, February–April 1981, Whitney Museum of American Art, New York, June–September 1981 (82, repr. in col.); *Philip Guston: Paintings 1969–80*, Whitechapel Art Gallery, October–December 1982, Stedelijk Museum, Amsterdam, January–February 1983, Kunsthalle, Basle, May–June 1983 (23, repr. in col.); *Forty years of Modern Art*, Tate Gallery, February–April 1986 (not numbered, repr. in col.)

Lit: Ross Feld, 'Philip Guston. An Essay by Ross Feld', *Philip Guston*, exhibition catalogue, San Francisco Museum of Modern Art, San Francisco, 1980, p.30, pl.72 in col.; John Clark, 'Philip Guston and Metaphysical Painting', *Artscribe*, 30, 1981, pp.24–5 (repr.); *The Tate Gallery Illustrated Biennial Report 1982–84*, p.57 (repr. in col.)

In 1970 Philip Guston exhibited a group of paintings at the Marlborough Gallery, New York which shocked the art world and which marked a radical departure from his previous Abstract Expressionist style. These and subsequent paintings, which seemed to owe much to the imagery of cartoons, have become known as the 'late paintings' and are often autobiographical. T 03364 is a 'late painting' and was made in 1977 when Guston had achieved a maturer, more classical figurative style.

Guston's 'conversion' to figurative painting dates from 1968 when he began to paint images of hands, shoes, books and lamps on panel. Always deeply pre-occupied with the difficulty of making paintings and particularly 'pure' paintings, he decided that he 'wanted to tell stories' (quoted in Norbert Lynton, 'An Obverse Decorum', *Philip Guston: Paintings 1969–80*, exhibition catalogue, Whitechapel Art Gallery, 1982, p.11). After an exhibition of recent paintings held at the Jewish Museum in 1966, Guston decided he:

> wanted to go on and deal with concrete objects. I got stuck on shoes, shoes on the floor. I must have done hundreds of paintings of shoes, books, hands, buildings and cars, just everyday objects. And the more I did the more mysterious these objects became ('Philip Guston Talking', in the Whitechapel Art Gallery exhibition catalogue, p.52).

These became some of the stock items in the vocabulary of Guston's 'late paintings'. The image of the shoe and the shoe heel were prolifically used by Guston in the 'late paintings' and the latter forms the central motif of 'Black Sea'.

Guston had already used the shoe motif as early as 1947 in 'Porch No.2' (repr. San Francisco exhibition catalogue, pl.6 in col.) and, according to Ross Feld, 'Guston was not alone among the Depression-developed painters in finding them usable and repeatable images' (p.17). Furthermore the shoe heel shape is remarkably similar to some of the shapes Guston employed in his abstract paintings of the fifties.

In 'Black Sea' the heel of a shoe is located on the horizon of a sea which paradoxically is predominantly green. The painting is composed of two colour-fields, blue-pink and green-black. The shoe heel, which is largely pink with heavy black contours, is set centrally against the blue field at a slight angle and is painted illusionistically to suggest depth. By contrast the two colour-fields are painted in such a way as to suggest flatness. The configuration of the heel resembles the outline of the head of the artist's wife Musa as depicted in 'Red Blanket' of 1977 (repr. San Francisco exhibition catalogue, pl.70) and 'Source' (repr. ibid., pl.59 in col.), a painting of the previous year. 'Source' is considered to make reference to Piero's 'Madonna de Parto' (Roberta Smith, 'The New Gustons', *Art in America*, LXVI, January/February 1978, p.105). It is possible therefore that one of the intended references of 'Black Sea' is to the artist's wife.

In 1976 and 1977 Guston made several paintings in which objects were set on an horizon and where the breadth of the painting was emphasised by the juxtaposition of a compact form within a broadly formatted painting. It has been suggested by John Clark that this practice reflects Guston's long-held interest in films which are 'strips of horizontally presented images' (p.24). By 1976 Guston had begun to make greatly simplified images often containing only one form and painted in two or three predominant colours. The arrangement of colours in broad bands in 'Black Sea' may lend substance to Norbert Lynton's belief that Guston's last paintings are 'monuments against Rothko, Still and Newman, or at any rate against the easy piety and ready greed they engender – sublime ripostes to their much vaunted sublimity' (Whitechapel Art Gallery exhibition catalogue, p.14). Unlike the mature paintings of Rothko, however, Guston's application of paint is more vigorous and the brush marks themselves remain strongly visible. The broad vertical and horizontal brushstrokes, which are highly evident, assert the flatness of the picture surface and the breadth of the painting.

The subject of the sea was employed by Guston in a number of previous paintings, notably 'Red Sea' 1975 (part of a triptych, repr. San Francisco exhibition catalogue, pl.50a in col.), 'Wharf' 1976 (repr. ibid., pl.56 in col.), which depicts a black sea with green highlights, and 'Source' 1976, which may depict a river rather than a sea. With the exception of 'Red Sea', these works are clearly divided into colour fields in the manner of 'Black Sea' and depict motifs located on an horizon suggesting either the sinking or the rising of the object portrayed. Shoe heels and shoes are depicted in 'Wharf' but as part of a greater configuration of objects. 'Black Sea' is the only painting by Guston where one heel has been isolated and is one of only a few where a single object is depicted. The central location of the object is consistent with Guston's practice as an abstract painter in the fifties of centring forms within his paintings.

Although 'Black Sea' was acquired after the artist's death, David McKee stated that it was the painting that Guston wanted the Tate to own.

This entry has been approved by the artist's daughter, Musa Mayer.

Maggi Hambling b.1945

T03542　Max Wall and his Image 1981

Oil on canvas 66 × 48 (1677 × 1219)
Inscribed 'Hambling/1981' on reverse
Presented by the Trustees of the Chantrey Bequest 1983
Exh:　*Max Wall. Pictures by Maggi Hambling*, National Portrait Gallery March–May 1983, John Hansard Gallery, Southampton, May–June 1983, Newlyn Art Gallery, Penzance, September–

October 1983 (1, repr. in National Portrait Gallery catalogue); *The Hard-Won Image*, Tate Gallery, July–September 1984 (66, repr.); *Artist and Model*, Whitworth Art Gallery, Manchester, May–July 1986 (19, repr.)

Lit: *Maggi and Max*, Channel 4, 27 March 1983, directed by Judy Marle

The actor Max Wall was born in London in 1908. He has been well-known for many years as a music-hall entertainer; his performances include Jarry's 'Ubu Roi' at the Royal Court, Beckett's 'Krapp's Last Tape' at Greenwich Theatre and Riverside Studios, and the BBC and Roundhouse productions of 'Waiting for Godot'. Extensive biographical notes on Max Wall are given in the catalogue of Maggi Hambling's Max Wall exhibition at the National Portrait Gallery (cited above) pp.32–3.

The following information is based on a conversation with the artist on 14 April 1986.

Maggi Hambling first saw Max Wall when he was performing as Ubu in Jarry's 'Ubu Roi' at the Royal Court Theatre in 1966. In spring 1981, towards the end of her appointment as first Artist in Residence at the National Gallery, she saw him in his one man show, 'Aspects of Max Wall' at the nearby Garrick Theatre. After seeing the show for a second time, again moved by his performance, Maggi Hambling wrote to Max Wall asking him if he would sit for a portrait. This was the first time that she had approached a sitter in this way. In the catalogue of her Max Wall exhibition at the National Portrait Gallery (cited above), p.10, Maggi Hambling wrote:

He has the true face of the sad clown, and possesses that power I can only call magical to make one laugh and cry at the same moment. My first painting in oils at the age of fourteen was of a clown, and at various times over the years I have attempted this subject. The contradictory aspects of the clown's nature fascinate me. I believe that the art of the clown in demonstrating to us the absurdities of life is a very necessary part of life.

'Max Wall and his Image' is Maggi Hambling's first painting of Max Wall. It was painted in five sittings in the spring of 1981. The setting is the artist's studio in Tennyson Street in South London. Maggi Hambling set the stage by hanging up a black curtain and placing stools on drawing boards, themselves raised on crates. When setting up this precarious arrangement Maggi Hambling did not realise that Max Wall had been an acrobat during his early career. To decide on the pose she made two quick working drawings. They are reproduced in the catalogue of the National Portrait Gallery exhibition (cited above), p.11.

The artist borrowed a large photograph of Max Wall's celebrated character Professor Wallofski and pinned it to the wall of her studio, beside the black curtain, before his first visit. In T03542 the shadow of Wallofski hovers behind his right shoulder. This is the image that is most generally associated with the actor. During sittings Max Wall referred to it as 'the monster'; he felt that he was followed everywhere by Wallofski. The artist feels that the portrait shows him 'as he is, my response to him, as I saw him'. The Wallofski section of the painting was repainted several times, including three different versions of the shadow walking from behind the curtain. The final version has been turned around and simplified almost to a silhouette.

The artist asked Max Wall to wear for the sittings the costume he had worn during the first half of his one man show, the part of the performance that had particularly moved her.

The first ovoid shape to appear in the painting was the door handle, which from a particular angle appeared to resemble an egg. During a rest between sittings Max Wall picked up a white alabaster egg and demonstrated one of his conjuring tricks to the artist. He later gave Maggi Hambling a black glass egg as a present. A white and black egg can be seen flying in the picture space in the Tate's painting.

The moon, in the top left hand corner, is a doubly significant reference to night time. Max Wall's working life as an actor takes place mostly in the evenings. Also Maggi Hambling fetched the actor for sittings at lunchtimes, and contrary to her normal practice, the sitting and conversations went on well into the night.

Max Wall smoked continuously between sittings and his butts and St Moritz cigarette packet appear in the foreground of the painting. Most of the Tate's picture is painted from life, directly representing Max Wall as he appeared on the stage Maggi Hambling had arranged, with the studio door beyond. Only the part of the painting to the left and immediately behind the sitter (the wall colour, the eggs, the moon and the final image of Wallofski) come from the imagination. Maggi Hambling points out that for her 'a portrait is first and foremost a painting and secondarily a portrait'.

Starting with the Tate's picture Max Wall became the subject of Maggi Hambling's work for nearly two years. The catalogue of her Max Wall exhibition lists thirty-eight works (fifteen of them canvases) representing him with subjects connected with him. Almost all are reproduced; they include 'Max's Egg' 1982, in which one of the items seen on the crowded mantelpiece of Maggi Hambling's studio is a photograph of the Tate's painting.

This entry has been approved by the artist.

upside down, is the shape of the stepped hemispherical seats and the row of columns behind them. The drawing of the other half of the painting is taken from the large hanging plants and the metal window of his studio. The geometry of these is distorted, and they are shown as they would appear in a concave mirror. In both halves the design was made from a recollection of the subjects, and not copied from them. The artist said in conversation (2 February 1983) that he thought of these two shapes on either side of the canvas as if each was a projection of the other in coordinate geometry.

The reds and the oranges in the painting are fluorescent paint, which Hayter has used in his work for more than twenty years. The purpose is to increase the depth and ambiguities of the space, as well as to reveal the colours beneath, since the paint is translucent. This configuration of space, with a central perspective with orthogonals converging from either side, Hayter had used in prints slightly earlier, such as the large colour etching 'Serre' (1979).

This entry has been approved by the artist.

Stanley William Hayter b.1901

T 03407 **Teatro Olimpico** 1980

Acrylic on canvas $44\frac{3}{4} \times 57\frac{1}{2}$ (1137 × 1458)
Inscribed 'Hayter 80' b.r. and 'June 17 80 Teatro Olimpico' on reverse
Presented by the artist 1982

The architectural shapes used in this painting are taken from two interiors: the auditorium of Palladio's Teatro Olimpico at Vicenza, and the artists' studio at the rue Cassini, Paris, where it was painted.

The artist visited Vicenza for the first time in February 1980, with the particular purpose of seeing Palladio's buildings, which Joseph Losey's film of *Don Giovanni* (1979) had recently brought to his mind. He made a sketch in the theatre, but it is represented only schematically in this painting, and the detail is not important. In the right hand half of the painting, shown

T 03408 **Ophelia** 1936

Oil, casein tempera and gesso on canvas
$39\frac{1}{2} \times 57$ (1000 × 1445)
Inscribed 'Hayter 36' t.l. and 'Ophelia 36' and 'No.11' on reverse, and 'No.1 S.W. Hayter' on stretcher
Purchased from the artist (Grant-in-Aid) 1982

Exh: *Exposition Internationale du Surréalisme*, Galerie Robert, Amsterdam, June 1938 (50); *Abstract and Surrealist Art in the United States*, Cincinnati Art Museum, February–March 1944, Denver Art Museum, March–April 1944, Seattle Art Museum, May–June 1944, Santa Barbara Museum of Art, June–July 1944, San Francisco Museum of Art, July 1944 (55, repr.); *S.W. Hayter, Paintings*, Corcoran

Gallery of Art, Washington, May–June
1973; *Dada and Surrealism Reviewed*, Arts
Council of Great Britain, Hayward
Gallery, January–March 1978 (12. 66,
repr.)

Lit: Jacob Kainen, 'An Interview with Stanley
William Hayter', *Arts Magazine*, LX,
no.5, January 1986, pp.64–7

'Ophelia' was painted in Paris, where Hayter had lived since 1926, in his studio at 17 rue Campagne-Première. It remained in his possession until purchased by the Tate Gallery. There is an abstract painting, over-painted, on the reverse.

The title refers to Millais's painting in the Tate Gallery of the drowned Ophelia, which Hayter had known from the time of childhood visits. He described the Millais in conversation (2 February 1983) as a 'good bad painting', and there is no direct connection between the two works. Hayter's 'Ophelia' is one of his few paintings of this period which has no figurative subject, but he imagined the elements in it to be floating on the surface of water, and hence the association with the Millais.

There exists a more general connection in that Hayter had made drawings 'after' paintings in the surrealist technique of 'automatic writing', looking at the object he was copying but not at his hand. Although he did not make such copies after the Millais this type of hidden subject lies behind the status of this title. 'Ophelia' was exhibited specifically as surrealist in Amsterdam in 1938, and Hayter's similar 'Pavane', 1935, was one of the first paintings by a British artist to be published as surrealist (in David Gascoyne, 'Premier Manifeste Anglais du Surréalisme', *Cahiers d'Art*, 1935, p.106).

Several of Hayter's works of 1936–9 have casein tempera as an underpainting, although most of these were on wooden board and not canvas. This medium was purchased in Paris already made up, and was not unusual. There is a marked variety of surface texture in the painting, with some colours applied as a relief of about ⅛ in. deep, made by mixing them with plaster of Paris. There are traces of pencil drawing visible at the margins, and the artist said that he made no preparatory drawings apart from those on the canvas itself.

This entry has been approved by the artist.

Dame Barbara Hepworth 1903–1975

T 03399   Ball, Plane and Hole 1936

Teak 8 × 24 × 12 (205 × 610 × 305)
Not inscribed

Purchased from Waddington Galleries
(Grant-in-Aid) 1982

Prov: Acquired from the artist by Sir Leslie and
Lady Martin; Sotheby's, 31 March 1982
(105, repr.) bt Waddington

Exh: *1937 Exhibition: Unity of Artists for Peace,
Democracy and Cultural Development*,
A.I.A., 41 Grosvenor Square, April–May
1937 (90, 91, 93 or 94); *Sculpture by
Barbara Hepworth*, Alex Reid and Lefevre
Ltd, October 1937 (4); *British Art and the
Modern Movement*, Welsh Committee of
the Arts Council of Great Britain,
National Museum of Wales, Cardiff,
October–November 1962 (58, as
'Sculpture c.1935'); *British Sculpture in the
Twentieth Century, Part I: Image and
Form 1901–1950*, Whitechapel Art
Gallery, September–November 1981
(168)

Lit: J.P. Hodin, *Barbara Hepworth*, 1961 (81);
A.M. Hammacher, *Barbara Hepworth*,
1968, repr. fig.48; Barbara Hepworth, *A
Pictorial Autobiography*, 1970, repr. 120 (as
at 'New Movements in Art' Exhibition at
the London Museum, but of 1937 A.I.A.
exhibition)

This is no.81 of the artist's catalogue of her sculpture (Tate Gallery Archive). J.D. Bernal, in the foreword to the Lefevre Gallery exhibition of 1937, describes it and two others as 'cup and bar ... [which] bring out the theme of complementary forms, each solid structure being contrasted sharply with a hollow smaller, or larger, than itself'. The photograph in the artist's catalogue emphasises the relation of solid and hollow in the work by taking a low viewpoint from centrally in front of the longer side, so that the ball is contrasted to the hole beside it.

The rectangular shapes are unusual for Hepworth in 1936–8, when her sculpture (although exclusively abstract) more often used spheres or rounded columns. However her largest work of this time, the six foot carving in blue Ancaster stone 'Monumental Stela', is designed as a series of near rectangles, and 'Ball, Plane and Hole', which is slightly earlier, is in effect a study of these more architectural shapes.

[197]

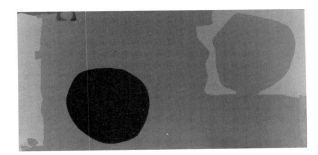

T 03749   **Involute II** 1956

Bronze $16\frac{1}{4} \times 16\frac{1}{2} \times 14\frac{1}{4}$ (410 × 420 × 360)
Not inscribed
Transferred from the Victoria and Albert
Museum 1983

Prov: Purchased by the Department of
Circulation, Victoria and Albert Museum,
from the artist through Gimpel Fils 1960
(Circ.249–1960)

Exh: Travelling exhibitions of the Department
of Circulation, Victoria and Albert
Museum

Lit: J.P. Hodin, *Barbara Hepworth*, 1961,
no.218 (repr.)

A cast of this sculpture was first exhibited at Gimpel
Fils in June 1956. It is numbered '11' as a small study
for it, titled 'Involute' (9½ in. high, Hodin, op.cit.,
no.214) was cast in 1956. These were amongst Hepworth's first sculptures made to be cast in bronze, a
technique she used only from that year. It resembles
the earlier sculptures of cut and bent sheet metal such
as 'Orpheus' 1956 (T 00955), and was made by adding
plaster to an armature of bent metal.

The sculpture is fixed at the base by a pin, which
allows it to be revolved. There is a total of six casts.

Patrick Heron b.1920

T 03660   **Cadmium with Violet, Scarlet, Emerald, Lemon and Venetian: 1969** 1969

Oil on canvas $78\frac{1}{4} \times 156\frac{1}{2}$ (1985 × 3790)
Inscribed 'Patrick Heron/1969' on reverse
and 'Cadmium with Violet, Scarlet,
Emerald, Lemon and Venetian: 1969' on
stretcher
Presented by Lord McAlpine 1983

Prov: Alistair McAlpine (now Lord McAlpine)
1972 (on loan to Leeds City Art Gallery
1974–7).

Exh: *Patrick Heron Recent Paintings*,
Waddington Gallery, January–February
1970 (not in catalogue); *Patrick Heron
Recent Paintings and selected earlier
canvases*, Whitechapel Art Gallery, June–
July 1972 (25, repr. in col.); *British
Painting 1952–77*, RA, September–
November 1977 (173); *Paintings by
Patrick Heron 1965–1977*, University of
Texas at Austin Art Museum, March–
May 1978 (6)

Lit: Patrick Heron, 'The Shape of Colour' (text
of the Power Lecture in June 1973,
Australia), *Studio International*,
CLXXXVII, 1974, pp.73–4, repr. in col.
p.75); Patrick Heron, *The Colour of Colour*
(E. William Doty Lectures in Fine Arts
1978), Austin Art Museum, 1979, p.17,
pl.no.1 (col.); Bernard Smith (ed.),
'Concerning Contemporary Art: The
Power Lectures 1968–73', Oxford, 1975,
pp.176–7, 179, pl.84

In a letter to the compiler (dated 14 July 1986), the
artist wrote:

> In the summer of 1967 I broke my right leg very
> badly in an accident in the sea at Lamorna Cove
> involving a canoe. My entire leg was encased in
> plaster for nine months – for four of which I
> afterwards discovered the surgeon had contemplated
> amputation at the knee. As a result I was unable to
> paint a single canvas for nearly a year – as distinct
> from works on paper, which could be done in a
> sitting position. When I finally started painting
> canvases again I for some reason decided very greatly
> to enlarge their scale, setting to work on a series of
> paintings measuring nine, eleven, thirteen and even
> fifteen feet in length. This painting was one of that
> series, all of which were exhibited in January 1970
> at Waddington's original gallery at number 2, Cork

Street, where they were slightly cramped for space, of course.

Unlike Rothko, who, in 1960, showed me the flat in Manhattan where he'd been living *and* painting until well after he'd enlarged the scale of his canvases to the familiar size of his mature style, with the result that his paintings were *touching* each other all around the walls of his living-room-cum-studio, as he explained to me – I, myself, have always needed very considerable space for showing my paintings. I've always felt that my canvases simply cannot be *seen* if they are not more or less *isolated* by expanses of white wall all around them. Rothko, in total contrast, actually *prescribed* very close hanging – about 18 ins. between each work. I therefore most enjoyed seeing this painting of mine at the Royal Academy's 1977 exhibition *British Painting 1952–1977*, where it was isolated on a specially built screen in the centre of one of the galleries, from where it was visible from down a vista of several rooms. The result was that it *floated*.

About the painting itself, it so happens that I mentioned it in the Power Lecture, entitled 'The Shape of Colour', which I gave in Australia in 1973. The following is part of what I said there:

For instance, in 1969, I arrived at a series of very large paintings ... 'Cadmium with Violet, Scarlet, Emerald, Lemon and Venetian: 1969' is an example. Looking back, the object here seems to have been to see how far a few of the familiar elements could be stretched out sideways, with this long horizontal composition (and there's a word, 'composition', we needn't run away from), without that *largest* area of cadmium-red disintegrating back into that vacuous background of neutral nothingness I so much despise! I used to say, as far back as 1959, that what one was looking for, in stretching out a single colour-plane across four-fifths of a canvas, was a full emptiness or an empty fullness. In these very long, very large paintings of 1969 and after, I think one has added to that earlier requirement of 'full emptiness' this new one: to see how *big* a colour-area can become physically while still retaining a visible compactness in its image, a tightness in its design and organisation that remains totally readable, despite the expanded scale of that design, of those images. How far could one *expand* one's colour-areas without appearing to be *distending* any or all of them? I have painted a version of this 'Cadmium with Violet', with the same colours but on a format only nine inches long. One of the mysteries of scale which seeing the two versions together would demonstrate is to do with what I call the physicality of mere size: the plain physical impact of a large painting, the sheerly quantitative

bombardment by the vibrations of really big areas of colour – these constitute a totally new factor. It was simply a fact that, in painting large, one was entering a field of physical sensation which just was not given off by smaller paintings.

It used to be felt that two adjacent areas of flat but differing colours – say a red or a blue – would always take up a fixed spatial position in relation to one another along the line dividing them. It used to be said that the red would always appear to come in front of the blue. My own experience suggests that this is quite untrue. When your eye alights on the sharp linear frontier separating two colour-areas, your sensation that one of those colours is 'nearer' to you than the other – this sensation, this conviction that space-in-depth *separates* the two colour-areas, is overwhelmingly definite as a sensation. Its cause, however, is enormously difficult to pinpoint. In these large recent paintings such as 'Cadmium with Violet' one is extremely conscious, as one's eye moves along the frontiers of the various areas, that these areas actually alternate with one another (as one's eye moves) in seeming to be *behind* or *in front of* one another – according to whatever loop or angle in the frontier one happens to be focusing upon. For instance, the cadmium-red ground (if you'll excuse the term) does not appear to be uniformly either behind or in front of the more orange 'harbour-shape' which extends downwards from the top right-hand corner of the painting. On the contrary, as your eye slides round those outlines the cadmium and the orange [scarlet] appear to keep exchanging their spatial positions. In 'Colour in My Painting: 1969' I said 'Complexity of the spatial illusion generated along the frontier where the two colours meet is ... enormously increased if the linear character of those frontiers is irregular, freely drawn, intuitively arrived at.' It is the totally regular, the perfectly geometric lines between colours in the movement known as Op Art which distinguishes it entirely from my own – despite our shared interest in optical after-images, and so on. The after-image is for me merely a welcome by-product, not a calculated end-product.

The period of my work to which this painting belongs came to an end with the paintings I made for my retrospective at the University of Texas at Austin Art Museum during 1977, the year before that exhibition was held (1978). I called them 'wobbly hard-edge' when I showed in Australia. Since 1980 the interests pursued in my painting have moved away from the rather exclusive preoccupations described in the long passage from 'The Shape of Colour' which I've quoted above.

Anthony Hill b.1930

T 03750 **Relief Construction** 1963

Construction of perspex and aluminium
24 × 30 × 4 (610 × 762 × 100)
Inscribed on reverse '↑24
CHARLOTTE/STREET W./ANTHONY
HILL/1963/B 17/AH/63'
Transferred from the Victoria and Albert
Museum 1983

Prov: Purchased from the artist by the
Department of Circulation, Victoria and
Albert Museum, 1968 (Circ.581–1968)

Exh: *Four Artists: Reliefs, Constructions and
Drawings*, Victoria and Albert Museum
exhibition, 1969 (12 repr.); *Anthony Hill.
A Retrospective Exhibition*, AC, Hayward
Gallery, May–July 1983 (50, repr.)

John Hoskin b.1921

T 03752 **Black Beetle** 1957

Welded iron wire 6¾ × 6¾ × 13½
(172 × 172 × 314)

Not inscribed
Transferred from the Victoria and Albert
Museum 1983

Prov: Purchased by the Department of
Circulation, Victoria and Albert Museum,
at Lords Gallery 1957 (Circ.188–1957)

Exh: *Sculpture by John Hoskin*, Lords Gallery,
October–November 1957 (8); travelling
exhibitions of the Department of
Circulation, Victoria and Albert Museum

John Hoyland b.1934

T 03701 **April 1961** 1961

Oil on canvas 60 × 60⅛ (1525 × 1527)
Inscribed on canvas overlap 'HOYLAND
April 61'
Presented by E.J. Power 1983

Prov: E.J. Power 1962; Tate Gallery 1983

Lit: *Neue Malerei in England*, exhibition
catalogue, Stadtisches Museum,
Leverkusen, September 1961; Bryan
Robertson, 'Introduction', *John Hoyland,
paintings 1960–67*, exhibition catalogue,
Whitechapel Gallery, April 1967

Describing Hoyland's paintings of the period 1960–1 in
the catalogue for the 1967 retrospective exhibition at the
Whitechapel Gallery (cited above), Bryan Robertson
wrote:

In 1960–62, the theme was thin or thick lines, straight
or curved, in close or more widely separated

alignment, invariably travelling horizontally across a square or just vertical canvas. When the lines are thicker they can more properly be read as bars. The lines are one colour against a contrasting coloured ground; or in two or more colours, light and dark, opposition to the ground. The purpose of these lines is to animate the ground, obviously enough, as well as to divide it into calculated areas – straining towards shapes.

Until the mid-seventies, Hoyland generally restricted the titles of his works to the date on which each was completed. The Whitechapel catalogue listed seven paintings from 1961, five having been completed in the spring of that year: 2. '20.3.61', purple and blue, oil on canvas, 76 × 66″; 3. 'EASTER 1961', blue, with violet, oil on canvas 68 × 68″; 4. 'April 1961', Lilac, with green, oil on canvas 68 × 68″; 5. '25th MAY 1961', dark plum and black, oil on canvas 60 × 60″; 6. '25.5.61', plum, black and amber, oil on canvas 68 × 60″. Three of these, including No.4, a work very similar in composition to T 03701 but larger and identically titled are illustrated in the catalogue and the artist has confirmed that he made a number of closely related works at about this time, which makes identification by catalogue more difficult.

In 1960 Hoyland was included in the influential *Situation* exhibition held at the RBA Galleries in London. In his catalogue introduction, Roger Coleman identified a group of artists making works which were 'cartographically simple but perceptually complex – a kind of stable/unstable surface'. He grouped Hoyland with Robin Denny, Bernard Cohen, Peter Stroud, Gordon House and John Plumb as using forms that could be identified with reference to geometric figures but also as emphasising the equality of the relationship between the parts of a painting and a unity between figure and ground, so that it would be difficult for the spectator to 'satisfy himself that he has located all forms in a final spatial order. Yet in spite of their perceptual instability, the pressure of the painting as a surface is never lost.'

By 1961, Hoyland was teaching at Hornsey College of Art and he exhibited paintings similar to T 03701 in the exhibition *New London Situation* (Marlborough New London Gallery, August–September, No.12 (3 in the Whitechapel catalogue) and No.13 (5 in the Whitechapel catalogue). The same year he also exhibited at the Stadtisches Museum, Leverkusen (*Neue Malerei in England*, September–November 1961). According to the catalogue this exhibition also included six paintings of the same type as T 03701, nos. 20, 21, 22, 23, 24 and 25, although neither of those titled 'April 1961' (Nos. 20 and 22) corresponds in dimensions to T 03701.

John Hoyland told the compiler (telephone conversation, 26th June 1986) that 'April 1961' was painted at a time when he, like many artists of his generation,

was trying to come to terms with the impact of American painting – he mentioned that he was particularly impressed by the paintings of Mark Rothko and Barnett Newman. At the time he was teaching a basic design course at Hornsey and was involved with problems of visual perception but was also trying to follow the lead of such painters as Rothko and solve the problem of eliminating traditionally rendered form in his paintings. At this stage he already knew artists pursuing similar lines of investigation (Stroud, Turnbull and Denny had also been involved in the 'Situation' exhibition), but he had not, for example, seen a painting by Vasarely.

He remembers that he was concerned to try to make paintings which worked all over the surface but which still retained the possibility of space and illusion. Working with lines he could suggest depth and volume with very simple means or elements. He stressed that the climate within which T 03701 and related works were made was one where problems of perception, within the framework of the current art school teaching, were constantly being debated (Newman was also particularly influential in this respect).

By 1961, Hoyland was beginning to feel that he was not temperamentally suited to the rigid framework that his work was operating within but still felt the need to react (like many of his contemporaries) against the more painterly excesses of the followers of, for example, de Kooning. However, after this point his work became more direct and full-bodied in its execution and imagery.

This entry has been approved by the artist.

John Hubbard b.1931

T 03371   **Light Structure** 1966

Oil on canvas 68 × 80 (1727 × 2030)
Inscribed 'JOHN HUBBARD – 1966'
incised b.l. and 'OC
66.2/OWNER:/KATE HUBBARD/"Light Structure"/68″ × 80″ 1966/John Hubbard' on reverse
Purchased from Fischer Fine Art (Grant-in-Aid) 1982

Prov: Kate Hubbard; Fischer Fine Art
Exh: *John Hubbard*, Newlyn Art Gallery, May 1978 (4); *John Hubbard, Paintings and Drawings 1962–80*, Warwick Arts Trust, January–March 1981
Lit: John Hubbard, *John Hubbard Paintings and Drawings 1962–80*, exhibition catalogue, Warwick Arts Trust, 1981, n.p.

This painting was not displayed in the artist's exhibition at the New Art Centre in November 1967, although it is listed in the catalogue.

It was painted in his studio at Swyre, on the Dorset coast, and was based on this landscape, although it does not show any particular features and was 'essentially dealing with atmosphere rather than features like woodland or hills' (letter of 25 May 1986). It is one of about ten paintings of this kind made during the years 1964–6, which he studied in charcoal drawings and small oil sketches, all also made in his studio. The artist wrote of the painting (letter of 2 March 1982):

> I consider this one of my most successful Dorset landscapes of the 1960s, belonging to the lyrical more extrovert group based on the movement of light across the hills near the sea. The composition is less overtly dramatic than in other paintings of this period, also the brushwork, and I was trying (in Turner's words) to consider 'every part as receiving and emitting rays to every surrounding surface'.

In his introduction to the catalogue of his retrospective exhibition at the Warwick Arts Trust in 1981, the artist referred to the painting as an example of his interest in artists of the past (as opposed to being exclusively a 'modernist'):

> . . . many artists of the past [are] just as vital as my contemporaries, and many of my paintings contain certain deliberate references to them. 'Light Structure' (1966), for example, is one of several homages to Turner . . .

T 03372 **Haytor Quarry** 1980–1

Oil on canvas 80 × 76 (2032 × 1930)
Inscribed on back of canvas 'Haytor Quarry/1981 80" × 76'" and 'John Hubbard'
Purchased from Fischer Fine Art (Grant-in-Aid) 1982

Haytor is on Dartmoor, and Hubbard visited the granite quarry near there frequently from the late 1960s. In the late 1970s he made a series of charcoal drawings in the quarry of the rock faces, and some studies in oil on paper derived from these were exhibited at Fischer Fine Art in 1979. The Tate Gallery's is the latest of his oil paintings of the same subject. It was begun in London, but worked on again when it had been moved to his studio in Chilcombe, Dorset, where the light was better. The artist wrote of it (letter of 2 March 1982):

> I consider this to be a sort of culmination of the numerous drawings and oils on both paper and canvas based on the disused Haytor quarry. The shapes are more directly based on those of the quarry than in other works, but the colour is subjective, intended to suggest the quarry's sombre presence.

Malcolm Hughes b.1920

T 03753 **Maquette for 'Square Relief'** 1968

Construction, card on plywood, painted
13 × 12¼ (330 × 310)
Not inscribed

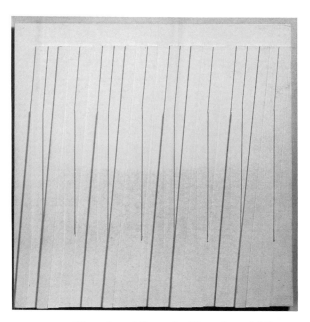

Transferred from the Victoria and Albert
Museum 1983
Prov: Purchased from the artist by the
Department of Circulation, Victoria and
Albert Museum, 1969 (Circ.76–1969)
Exh: *Four Artists. Reliefs, Constructions and
Drawings. John Ernest. Anthony Hill.
Malcolm Hughes. Gillian Wise*, Victoria
and Albert Museum, 1969 (21); travelling
exhibitions of the Department of
Circulation, Victoria and Albert Museum

See entry for T 03754.

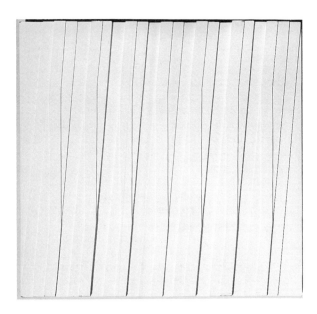

T 03754   **Square Relief. White** 1968

Construction, painted wood $24 \times 24 \times 2\frac{3}{8}$
($610 \times 610 \times 60$)
Inscribed on reverse 'MALCOLM
HUGHES 19 OXFORD RD: ↑TOP
LONDON SW15 * USE PERSPEX ANTI-
STATIC/POLISH'
Transferred from the Victoria and Albert
Museum 1983
Prov: Purchased from the artist by the
Department of Circulation, Victoria and
Albert Museum, 1969 (Circ.77–1969)
Exh: *Four Artists. Reliefs, Constructions and
Drawings. John Ernest. Anthony Hill.
Malcolm Hughes. Gillian Wise*, Victoria
and Albert Museum Exhibition, 1969
(17); travelling exhibitions of the
Department of Circulation, Victoria and
Albert Museum

The catalogue of the 'Four Artists' exhibition prints a
statement, dated December 1968, by the artist about
this group of constructions, and reproduces a drawing
on graph paper that is a study for this relief. A similar
drawing, lettered and numbered to show the basis of
the pattern, is reproduced in the exhibition catalogue
Malcolm Hughes, Ferens Art Gallery, Hull, September
1973.

Louise Hutchinson 1882–1968

T 03751   **Three-fold Head** c.1953

Terracotta and wax $13 \times 12\frac{3}{4} \times 7\frac{1}{4}$
($330 \times 320 \times 180$)

Not inscribed
Transferred from the Victoria and Albert Museum 1983

Prov: Purchased by E.C. Gregory for the Contemporary Art Society, c.1953; donated by the Society to the Department of Circulation, Victoria and Albert Museum 1964 (Circ.74–1964)

The artist, who was also known as a portrait photographer under her second married name Li Osborn, began to make sculpture in about 1942 while living in Ascona. She was self taught. She made a number of portrait heads in bronze and terracotta, and 'Three-fold Head' is unusual in her work as in a style between these and the abstract, root-like shapes that she also made.

Paul Huxley b.1938

T 03589   **Fable** 1982

Acrylic on canvas 77 × 77 (1956 × 1956)
Inscribed 'Paul Huxley ↑77 × 77' on reverse
Purchased from Juda Rowan Gallery (Grant-in-Aid) 1983

Exh: *Paul Huxley, Recent Paintings*, Juda Rowan Gallery, November–December 1982 (no catalogue)

The monochrome colours, shades of grey and black, are the same on both sides of the vertical division of the design, but are contrasted in the manner of painting.

The left side is evenly painted throughout, but on the right hand side the edges of some of the rectangles are faintly repeated as blurred shapes in the background. This follows earlier paintings by Huxley in which one half of the design was painted in greys and the other coloured.

Albert Irvin b.1922

T 03590   **Empress** 1982

Acrylic on canvas 84⅜ × 120 (2135 × 3047)
Inscribed 'Irvin '82' on reverse on canvas turnover t.r.
Purchased from Gimpel Fils (Knapping Fund) 1983

Exh: *Albert Irvin A Double Exhibition of New Works: Paintings, Watercolours, Prints*, Gimpel Fils, September–October 1982, Goldsmith's College Gallery, October–November 1982 (18, at Gimpel Fils only)

The following entry is based on a conversation with the artist on 8 April 1986. It has been approved by him.

'Empress' is a work which is invested, in Irvin's own words, 'with much personal significance'. By way of explanation, Irvin has recalled that it was the last work to be completed in a series of paintings which includes: 'Samson', 'Beatrice', 'Prospero', 'Pegasus' and 'Portal'. These were also executed in 1982. 'Empress' and 'Prospero' were shown at Gimpel Fils, 9 September–2 October 1982 and 'Samson', 'Beatrice', 'Pegasus' and 'Portal' were shown at Goldsmith's College Gallery 13 October–3 November 1982. Irvin feels that, because these shows were imminent, 'Empress' was executed in a spirit of great optimism and confidence and with a sense of freedom to take risks. This may partly explain why in a number of respects 'Empress' is a reaction to and a development from the paintings which he had produced since the late 1970s.

During this earlier period Irvin had become increasingly dissatisfied with his practice of painting directly onto the white canvas ground. He felt that this inhibited the feeling of space which he wished to create within the picture. His solution was to begin subsequent paintings by staining the canvas with a single overall colour thereby creating a space which he felt he could 'inhabit'. Between 1979 and 1982, all of Irvin's paintings, save 'Empress', were of this type. 'Empress' was mainly painted between June and September 1982. It is different in character from its immediate predecessors in that in this work Irvin reverted to the procedure which he had not used since 'Trafalgar' 1979. In 'Empress' Irvin began by making initial 'sullying' gestural marks on the periphery of the canvas (the green, oval and crossed forms in the final composition) and in its finished state areas of white ground are permitted to figure as part of the overall design. Irvin is unable to account for this isolated turnabout except by reference to the conditions under which the painting was created.

In 'Empress' the visual vocabulary employed in the works of the preceding five years achieves a greater state of refinement and is developed further through simplification of the constituent elements. With 'Albion' 1977, Irvin had broken with the landscape format which characterises the works exhibited at the New 57 Gallery, Edinburgh, and the Aberdeen Art Gallery in 1976. The common feature of these works is a thinly painted form at the top of the canvas suggesting sky above a more densely painted and textural area occupying the bottom half of the picture space. Irvin felt that this feeling of landscape was becoming too readily readable as such and was looking for a means of lending the dynamic elements within the picture greater possibilities of development. From 'Albion' onwards he evolved a structure which solved this problem. This consisted of a near diagonal set against a near horizontal suspended above the bottom edge. He found that this composition animated the rectangle better than before while the near diagonals directed from right to left were, in keeping with his right-handedness, a more effective 'container for feeling'. In 'Empress' Irvin takes this further. He has described how, after painting a number of large blue diagonals across the face of the canvas, the possibility of a single large diagonal form suggested itself as a means of activating the space more emphatically. Consequently he overpainted these with the massive red diagonal which is the dominant and distinctive feature of the painting. This passage is particularly painterly and, in addition to the usual range of brushes, Irvin also used four-ringed dusting brushes (tradesman's brushes consisting of four ferrules containing long bristles and normally used for dusting surfaces prior to painting) in order to animate the surface. Irvin feels that the sensuous handling of paint in this area is closely related to his experience of visiting the Soutine

exhibition at the Hayward Gallery, 17 July–22 August 1982, where the lively paint surfaces, particularly the red backdrops of such paintings as 'Pastrycook' 1918–19 and 'Young Man' 1920, made a profound impression. Irvin has stated that he feels a marked affinity with Soutine whom he regards as the paradigm of an artist who finds the image in the movement of paint.

A characteristic shared by 'Empress' with all Irvin's paintings since 1975 is that it is named after a street. In this case Empress Street is in Kennington, London SE17. Initially only London locations were used. However when the sheer number of paintings produced exhausted the availability of suitable names, Irvin began using titles from other places also. Prior to 1975 Irvin thought of his paintings as journeys. The titles of his paintings at this time – 'Travelling Alone', 'Excursion', 'Wanderer' – reflect this. Irvin maintains that he adopted this use of street names because he wanted a non-descriptive way of identifying his works without resorting to numbers or 'Untitled' labels. Nevertheless, although not used in any literal sense, the street names which Irvin selects have a significance above and beyond their function of identifying specific works. In some cases titles recall an acquaintance with or an experience of a place which has in some way contributed to or is connected with the making of the work in question. For instance, 'Sul Ross' 1981 is the address of the Rothko Chapel in Houston, USA. Irvin feels that the experience of his visit here subsequently fed into the making of this work. Alternatively, street titles are used because they have a 'ring of relevance'. In this way 'Boadicea' 1979 (repr. in col., on the front of *Albert Irvin*, exhibition catalogue, Bede Gallery, Jarrow, November–December 1980) was used because Irvin felt that it conveyed ideas of femininity, the Heroic, and majesty which Irvin feels are inherent in the work. Irvin has suggested that these are qualities which are shared by 'Empress' and because the two paintings are related in character he used a name which carried similar associations. Irvin's earlier insistence on having been actually acquainted with the street in question is now less important than the idea of streets symbolising the passage of the artist through the world.

On a formal level there is in 'Empress' a tension between its flat painted surface and the suggestion of complex spatial relations. This is created, not by perspectival means but through a progressive overlapping of elements beginning at the bottom edge of the canvas with the circular and inverted 'V' shape in the foreground working through to the half-covered green forms at the top left of the painting. Irvin feels that this instinct derives in part from Kenneth Martin who was teaching at Goldsmith's College when Irvin was a student there. Its aim is to create what Irvin calls 'a basket of space', in which the spectator is free to exercise his own imagination. In subsequent works this is a tendency which has become more complex and sophisticated as forms are increasingly plaited and overlapping.

As with all his work, Irvin maintains that 'Empress' is not *of* anything. The subject is the painting and what has been 'found' in its making. The statement it makes is the record of how it was made. However he allows that its source is human activity and the experience of 'being in the world'. As it was created at a time of singular optimism there is also a sense that 'Empress' is a celebration of this experience.

William Johnstone 1897–1981

T 03659   **Large Brush Drawing** c.1975–6

Black ink on paper 36 × 51⅞ (916 × 1318)
Inscribed 'W. Johnstone' b.l.
Presented anonymously in memory of
Terence Rattigan 1983

Prov: Purchased from the artist by the donor
1976

Exh: *William Johnstone*, Hayward Gallery,
February–March 1981, AC tour, Towner
Art Gallery, Eastbourne, April–May 1981,
Talbot Rice Art Centre, Edinburgh, July–
August 1981 (148)

The artist first made a series of small abstract ink drawings in the 1930s and continued to do so at intervals throughout the 1950s and 1960s. Towards the end of 1974 the scale of the drawings increased and T 03659 is an example of this new found expansion. Johnstone's autobiography *Points in Time*, published in 1980, offers an explanation:

I was delighted to receive as a birthday present in
1974 a most beautiful architect's drawing table, and
in excitement, we drove to Edinburgh to buy reams
of the finest drawing paper. It seemed sacrilegious

to destroy the pristine clarity of these lovely sheets of paper, such marvellous quality, such inviolate whiteness. This barrier had to be broken and for two years I enjoyed myself enormously making large drawings in Indian ink and watercolour.

Johnstone's ink drawings were done spontaneously, not copied from any external motif. With its horizontal format, T 03659 has resonances of landscape subject matter and the donor told the compiler that the artist recalled how 'Large Brush Drawing' was done from memory in response to the Roxburghshire landscape which meant so much to him. Johnstone was born on a border farm, and when he retired from art teaching in London in 1961, he returned to his roots and bought a farm on the borders. In his autobiography, he wrote of the importance of that landscape:

Always I have made drawings of the Border
landscape which, by now, has become so ingrained
in my system that whatever I do my own countryside
comes through. My art is, therefore, not really
'abstract' art, although it is certainly abstracted from
my own landscape – elemental, but located
geographically in the Scottish Borders.

Allen Jones b.1937

T 03379   **Wet Seal** 1966

Oil on canvas and wood with attached
melamine 36⅞ × 36 × 4 (934 × 915 × 100)
Inscribed 'Allen Jones Wet Seal
1966/36″ × 36″' on stretcher and 'Allen

Jones 1966' on back of canvas
Purchased from Waddington Galleries
(Grant-in-Aid) 1982

Prov: The artist; Waddington Galleries 1982
Exh: *Allen Jones*, Arthur Tooth and Sons, June–
July 1967 (3, repr.); *Pop Art in England*,
BC tour, Kunstverein, Hamburg,
February–March 1976, Stadt Galerie im
Lenbachhaus, Munich, April–May 1976,
City Art Gallery, York, May–July 1976
(42, repr.); *Allen Jones Retrospective of
Paintings 1957–1978*, organised by Walker
Art Gallery, Liverpool, ACGB, BC and
Staatliche Kunsthalle Baden-Baden;
Walker Art Gallery Liverpool, March–
April 1979, Serpentine Gallery, May–
June 1979, Sunderland Museum and Art
Gallery, June–July 1979, Staatliche
Kunsthalle, Baden-Baden, September–
October 1979, Kunsthalle, Bielefeld,
November–December 1979 (26, repr.)
Lit: Paul Overy, 'On the Streets', *Listener*,
LXXVIII, July 1967, p.45, repr.; Marco
Livingstone, '*Allen Jones, Sheer Magic*'
1979, pp.76, 108, 130, repr. in col.
pp.62–3; *Also repr*: Advertising space in
Studio International, CLXXIII, June 1967,
p.276, announcing the artist's exhibition
at Arthur Tooth and Sons

'Wet Seal' was painted in London immediately after
Jones's return from a stay in America. He lived in New
York from 1964–5 and then travelled throughout the
Unites States by car. Jones created the image of the
lower half of the female figure from an advertising
source. The artist wrote (letter to the compiler, April
1986):

> The stance of 'Wet Seal' comes from an image seen
> in a mail order brochure . . . at that time [1966] I
> used a stylization of the figure from popular sources
> as a way of re-inventing the figure – this of course
> was something done by American Pop artists too.

'Wet Seal' was the first in a series of five three-foot
square canvases with attached shelf which the artist
exhibited as a group at Arthur Tooth's gallery in June
1967; the others were 'Drama' 1966–7 (collection Hans
Neuendorf, Hamburg), 'Sheer Magic' 1967 (private
collection, London), 'Gallery Gasper' 1966–7 (private
collection, Belgium) and 'Evening Incandescence' 1967
(private collection, London) and all but the last work
were illustrated in the catalogue. The artist wrote that
'all the titles [of these three-foot square canvases] are
names of shoes that appeared in the Fredericks of Hollywood mail order catalogues of the time'. A page of shoes
from a Fredericks mail order catalogue was reproduced
on the fourth page of an unpaginated catalogue, *Allen*

Jones New Paintings and Sculpture, which accompanied
the artist's show at Marlborough Fine Art in September
1972. Also, Jones produced a work 'Shoe Box' in 1968
which contained, besides an embossed screenprint of
a ballet shoe, seven lithographs based on mail order
catalogue reproductions of shoes, and the overall shape
of the shoe in 'Wet Seal' is like that of lithograph No.5
from 'Shoe Box'. Prior to his series of three-foot square
canvases of 1966–7 concentrating on the legs and feet
of female figures, Jones had worked on a larger scale,
favouring a canvas height of six feet, approximately the
size of an average adult, for paintings containing full-
size male and female figures. Even though 'Wet Seal'
contains a fragment, the lower half of a female figure,
'anatomically the image seems life-size on a 3′ × 3′ size
canvas'.

Although Jones had begun in 1966 to introduce the
painted image of a highly modelled, life-size leg and
foot in a high-heeled shoe, with the shoe resting along
the lower edge of the canvas, 'Wet Seal' was the first
work to include a small melamine covered wooden shelf,
made by the artist himself, which protruded forward
four inches from the canvas surface. The artist wrote:

> The shelf was to encourage the notion that the image
> might enter *our* space (something posited by all
> illusionistic painting). In actuality the 'fact' of the
> shelf served to underline the flatness of the canvas –
> paradoxically allowing the possibility of extreme
> modelling to take place – without the picture space
> collapsing! Enough modelling to provoke the sense
> of touch, but not enough to suggest that *someone* was
> being depicted.

The left leg in 'Wet Seal' is highly modelled and offers
a convincing three-dimensionality whereas the right leg
is painted flatly and left unfinished at the foot, with
the unmodulated pigment necessary for its realisation
daubed along the edge between canvas surface and shelf
surface.

The motif of legs and shoes in 'Wet Seal' is seen again
in two works by Jones of 1968, 'Desire Me' (Victoria and
Albert Museum) and 'Man Pleaser' (private collection,
Italy). The artist wrote that those

> pictures had the lower half of 'Wet Seal'
> photographically enlarged, requiring me to
> complete the rest of the figure using another
> technique . . . I liked the idea of re-using a unique
> image (hand-painted), for multiple purposes. The
> repetition of an image demotes its literal significance
> and can underscore thereby the formal
> preoccupation present.

David Jones 1895–1974

T 03677 **Sanctus Christus de Capel-y-ffin** 1925

Gouache and pencil on paper $7\frac{5}{8} \times 5\frac{1}{4}$
(193 × 133)
Inscribed 'DMJ 25' b.l. and
'S/AN/CT/VS/CH/R/IST/VS/DE/CAPEL
-Y-FFIN' in sky
Presented by the Friends of the Tate Gallery 1983

Prov: Given (?) by the artist to Elizabeth Gill (daughter of Eric Gill); her estate; Edgar Holloway, c.1957, from whom purchased by the Friends of the Tate Gallery 1983
Exh: *David Jones*, Tate Gallery, July–September 1981 (30, repr.)
Repr: Eric Rowan, *Art in Wales 1850–1980*, 1985, p.97; *2 Plus 2*, Spring/Summer 1986, p.101

Capel-y-ffin was the former monastery in the Monmouthshire Black Mountains where Eric Gill and his family moved in August 1924. David Jones first visited them there the following December, and the building at the left of this drawing loosely resembles the monastery, in its winter landscape. Eric Rowan (loc.cit.) compares this drawing to a wall painting of the Crucifixion made by David Jones at Capel-y-ffin in the same winter.

Karin Jonzen b.1914

T 03755 **Head of a Youth** c.1947–8

Terracotta $6\frac{1}{4} \times 4 \times 5\frac{1}{2}$ (160 × 100 × 140)
Inscribed 'KJ' on back of neck
Transferred from the Victoria and Albert Museum 1983

Prov: Purchased from the artist by Sir Edward Marsh and given by him to the Contemporary Art Society, and by them given to the Victoria and Albert Museum in 1964 (Circ.95–1964)
Exh: Travelling exhibitions of Department of Circulation, Victoria and Albert Museum

The artist wrote (2 August 1984) that no casts were made from this terracotta, and that it was an imaginary head.

Peter Joseph b.1929

T 03467 **No.55 Green with Dark Blue Surround** 1981

Acrylic on canvas $64\frac{5}{16} \times 73\frac{15}{16}$
(1648 × 1876)
Inscribed 'Peter Joseph Oct '81' on top overlap and 'Green with Dark Blue Surround 55 65″ × 74‴' on stretcher
Purchased from Gillespie-Laage-Salomon, Paris (Grant-in-Aid) 1982

Exh: *Peter Joseph*, Gillespie-Laage-Salomon, Paris, December 1981–January 1982 (no catalogue)

The artist was asked about the making of T03467 and he replied (in a letter to the compiler, 7 May 1986):

You ask me whether there was significance for me in selecting the blue and the green. Yes, there was the utmost significance and all the more significance because I cannot state what significance is, other than through colour.

Yes there was a specific necessity (not reason) for the ratio of green to blue, just as there were certain proportions to the canvas shape and size, and to the tone and hue of the colours.

What was I being influenced by at the time ... by that which suggests more than I know – a passage of sounds and tones in a sonata by Schubert and perhaps the fall of shadow under a tree.

There is a certain sensibility that one needs to evoke in painting a canvas, and a certain meaning to be evoked which cannot be understood but is immanently experienced.

There is little space left in the industry of art exhibiting for a dream or reverie. What you see in my work is perhaps a momentary attempt to establish this space.

Anish Kapoor b.1954

T03675 **As if to celebrate, I discovered a mountain blooming with red flowers** 1981

Wood, cement, polystyrene and pigment, 3 elements, $38\frac{1}{4}$ (at highest point) × 30 (at widest point, × 63 (970 × 762 × 1600); 13 × 28 × 32 (330 × 711 × 813); $8\frac{1}{4}$ × 6 × $18\frac{1}{2}$ (210 × 153 × 470), overall

dimensions variable
Not inscribed
Purchased from the artist through Lisson Gallery (Grant-in-Aid) 1983

Exh: *British Sculpture in the 20th Century. Part 2: Symbol and Imagination 1951–1980*, Whitechapel Art Gallery, November 1981–January 1982 (158 in brochure); *Anish Kapoor: As If to Celebrate, I Discovered a Mountain Blooming with Red Flowers*, Walker Art Gallery, Liverpool, March–April 1982; *Aperto, XL Biennale Venice*, June–September 1982 (listed in general catalogue with incorrect illustration p.227); *Anish Kapoor*, Rotterdamse Kunststrichting, Galerie 't Venster, Rotterdam, January–February 1983 (6, repr. p.6); *New Art at the Tate Gallery 1983*, September–October 1983 (not listed, repr. in col. p.47); *An International Survey of Recent Painting and Sculpture*, Museum of Modern Art, New York, May–August 1984 (repr. p.180); *Forty Years of Modern Art 1945–1985*, Tate Gallery, February–April 1986 (not listed, repr. in col. p.118)

Lit: Steve Baker, 'Anish Kapoor at the Walker Art Gallery, Liverpool', *Artscribe*, no.35, June 1982, p.67, repr.; Michael Newman, 'Anish Kapoor', *Englische Plastik Heute/British Sculpture Now*, exhibition catalogue, Kunstmuseum, Lucerne, July 1982 (n.p.); Marco Livingstone, catalogue introduction, *Anish Kapoor, Feeling into Form, Le Sentiment de la forme, La Forme du Sentiment*, exhibition catalogue, Walker Art Gallery, Liverpool, March 1983 (not listed, repr. in col. p.6); Mark Francis, 'Anish Kapoor', *Transformations: New Sculpture from Britain*, exhibition catalogue, XVII Bienal, São Paulo 1983,

p.49, repr.; Lynne Cooke, 'Mnemic Migrations', *Anish Kapoor*, exhibition catalogue, Kunstnernes Hus, Oslo, 1986, repr. fig. VIII
Also repr: *Paris Biennale*, exhibition catalogue, Paris, October 1982, p.136; *Artforum*, XXI, November 1982, p.85 in col.; *Tema Celeste*, exhibition catalogue, Museo Civico d'Arte Contemporanea di Gibellina, Sicily, January 1983, p.54; Jean-Louis Pradel, *World Art Trends 1982*, New York 1983, p.117 in col.; introduction, *The 'Poetic' Object*, exhibition catalogue, The Douglas Hyde Gallery, Dublin 1985, p.7

Unless otherwise stated this entry is based on an interview with the artist (2 July 1986).

Kapoor made this work for the exhibition *British Sculpture in the 20th Century*, held at the Whitechapel Art Gallery in 1981–2. The invitation to exhibit at the Whitechapel came at a point when he was feeling the need to synthesise and to condense his previous larger installations into no less powerful but smaller and more specific groupings.

'As if to celebrate ...' and the works which directly preceded and followed it, 'To reflect an intimate part of the red' 1981, 'Part of the red' 1981, and 'White Sand, Red Millet Many Flowers' 1982, coll. Arts Council (documented by Michael Newman in the catalogue for *Englische Plastik Heute*, and reproduced in colour in *Anish Kapoor, Feeling into Form*, both catalogues cited above), all consist of small groups of between three and five objects. While based on the same repertoire of largely geometric and architectural forms Kapoor had been using in his earlier work, these and other works of around the same time herald the introduction of more obviously organic shapes into his sculpture (although they also appear to develop naturally from the hemispheres, stepped ziggurat shapes and mounds, of, for example the *1000 Names* series (1979–80), his first works made with pure pigment.

In the catalogue cited, Michael Newman pointed out that, whereas previous works had been more site specific, these new groups, while still creating a 'sense of place', put more emphasis on the internal relationships between forms:

> The objects were formed to be placed in the relationship with each other such that the charge of the whole would be greater than the sum of its parts ...

With the third group [T 03673], the geometrical architectural element has become a spectacular three-peaked mountain (the Hindu temple takes the form of a mountain and uses the metaphor of the body); the characteristic rounded form with an indentation like a cup has doubled and become like a pear or petal, making the connotation of breast more overt; and the third object, which is the smallest, is lifted off the ground on a curved surface and with its triangular, boat-like appearance suggests a directional movement. The three objects thus make a 3-2-1 sequence, and there is the suggestion that the 'triple mountain' is somehow related to the unity of 'breasts' and 'boat'. In colour the latter is yellow while the other two objects are red. A wide range of movement is implied, ground-hugging, travelling, rising. As is often the case, the title provides a complement to the work, expressing its joy and exuberance.

The exact significance of T 03673 remains private but according to Kapoor, the title comes from two main sources. The first part, 'As if to celebrate ...' is taken from a Haiku poem which he remembers reading on a train and deciding to use (he felt that the precision and economy of classical Haiku was appropriate to the spirit of the new work).

The second part of the title he invented but it relates to his having read the Hindu myth of the Goddess, who was born out of a fiery mountain which was composed of the bodies of male gods. Kapoor was interested in this image of the transmission and transmutation of power, the idea of the energy of one force giving way to or being translated into the energy and substance of another.

Although all his work of this period was beginning to hint at more organic presences, Kapoor feels that 'As if to celebrate ...' and its companions are more specifically about physicality and in the case of T 03673, birth, as denoted by the mythological reference in the title. However, despite his symbolic use of imagery (for example the two linked shapes suggesting breasts which are at the same time containers or pots, the proliferation of objects, from one single item to the tripartite red 'mountain') he is not interested in a narrow sexual interpretation.

Lynne Cooke (op.cit.) points to the importance of metonym in Kapoor's art and Kapoor stresses that work concerned only with formal arrangement or pleasing internal relationships, but without any suggestion of evolution and transformation, is not of interest to him. The objects or images must be worked to a point where they appear as symbols. However, formal considerations, for example the relationship between the elements, do contribute to what Kapoor likens to grammatical sense in a sentence – unless the works are grouped in the correct order, the sense is lost.

He also has a strong feeling for ritual, the bringing together of objects imbued with significance, as on an altar or shrine, where it is the combination of items in very precise relationships coupled with the particular site which is important for the believer.

In 1979, Kapoor returned to India for a visit after some years' absence. He feels that, in the past, too much has been made of this trip in relation to subsequent developments in his technique and imagery (which have been seen as having a specifically Indian quality or character). He sees the trip as having acted as a catalyst (as Lynne Cooke suggests, article cited above) and endorsing existing channels of investigation. On his return he made his first works out of coloured pigment. The use of powder, for which there is a precedent in Indian daily life and ritual, he also equates with the deliberate choice of 'poor' materials in the tradition of Arte Povera.

Kapoor describes 'As if to celebrate . . .' as being about the colour red, not only in relation to the colour's more traditional symbolic attributes but also having a specific space/shape relationship. The small yellow wedge acts as a point of punctuation in relation to the whole. Kapoor makes drawings for his sculpture but in the case of T 03673 these were all made direct on his studio wall while he was working on the shapes. The basic structure of this work is wood cement and polystyrene and when all the shapes (the three 'cones' of the mountain shape have now been mounted on one base) are in position, they are first painted with a weak pigment solution and afterwards covered with loose dry pigment which is flicked on to them with a brush so that no hand marks are made. (This perfection or absence of 'hands' also relates to religious rituals in various other cultures.) Ideally the audience should be able to circulate freely round the sculpture when it is in position.

This entry has been approved by the artist.

Alex Katz b.1927

T 03805 **Hiroshi and Marsha** 1981

        Oil on canvas 72 × 96 (1828 × 2437)
        Not inscribed
        Presented by Paul Schupf 1983
Prov: Paul Schupf 1981 (purchased from
        Marlborough Gallery Inc., New York)
Exh: *Alex Katz*, Marlborough Fine Art,
        January–February 1982 (4, repr.)

The subject of this painting is friends of the artist, Hiroshi Kawanishi, a silkscreen printer who lives in New York near the artist, and Marsha, his wife. They have subsequently divorced. They are depicted against the background of lower Manhattan, looking from SoHo towards the financial district of Wall Street. The view is that from the art critic Irving Sandler's home in

Bleecker Street, which Katz had decided was suitable for the subjects.

Katz does not use photographs when he begins the work but draws from life on location. Initially he works in pen and pencil on small pieces of paper and produces many variants showing different poses and combinations of the participants. On this occasion he made nine, each 9 inches by 11 inches, and a drawing of the same size which combined aspects of several of these. He then made a small painting in oil on a pressed wood board (gesso ground prepared by the artist) to establish the subject and colour values; this was 18 × 24in. Having decided on the subject he returned to the location with the sitters and made a drawing of approximately 15 × 22in., which was followed by two more delicate and detailed ('finished') drawings of a similar size. The time devoted to these 'finished' drawings amounted to four sessions with one additional session to adjust (or 'wreck' as he puts it) these drawings. One of these drawings was enlarged conventionally to make full-size cartoons for the painting on kraft paper. Katz used a pinned wheel to prick the cartoons and ochre pounce to transfer the image to the canvas. Katz found this image particularly rich and he made three finished paintings from it – the Tate's painting; a portrait, 60 × 100in., of Hiroshi, now in the artist Joel Shapiro's collection; and a canvas 120 × 100in., of Marsha, now in a private collection in New York. The cartoons for each version were developed independently from the finished drawings.

Katz is a meticulous, conservative craftsman who prepares his own canvases using traditional sizes and grounds; he mixes all the colours required for painting, a process which may take as long as painting the work itself. The painting is executed relatively quickly with large brushes, usually working wet pigment into a wet base colour. Katz seeks to create the most particular rendition of person, to achieve a likeness with the greatest economy of means. He has been told that his works reveal careful observation of psychological inter-relations, although he does not set out to do this.

Sir Gerald Kelly 1879–1972

T 03650   **Boulevard Montparnasse** 1904

Oil on panel $7 \times 4\frac{3}{8}$ (180 × 120)
Inscribed 'Kelly' b.centre and on reverse
'Boulevard Montparnasse '04'
Presented anonymously in memory of
Terence Rattigan 1983

Prov: Purchased from the artist by the donor in
1969

Exh: *Sir Gerald Kelly K.C.V.O., P.P.R.A.,*
Royal Academy of Arts, Diploma Gallery,
October–December 1957 (54)

Sir Gerald Kelly had in his studio at 117 Gloucester
Place, Portman Square, W1, 'an enormous number of
little pictures' left from the early part of his career (letter
to the donor, 10 March 1969). These appear not to have
been exhibited at the time of their execution, and were
only revealed to the public at the artist's retrospective
exhibition at the Royal Academy in October–December
1957. These little oil on panel pictures, or 'sketches' as
Sir Gerald also called them, were always done en plein
air in front of the motif and were not intended as studies
for bigger pictures. Sir Gerald kept them stored in date
sequence in boxes in his studio.

Kelly's studio in 1904 was in the rue Victor-Con-
siderant, close to the Boulevard Montparnasse. Several
other small sketches exist of the same boulevard.

T 03651   **Alex and Demary Dancing in a Music Hall at Algiers** 1906

Oil on panel $5\frac{5}{8} \times 7$ (148 × 180)
Inscribed 'Kelly' b.l. and on reverse 'Alex

& Demary dancing in a Music hall/At
Alger at Alg/1 March 1906'
Presented anonymously in memory of
Terence Rattigan 1983

Prov: ...; Galerie Wenning; Roland, Browse and
Delbanco March 1967; the donor
November 1967

Exh: *Sir Gerald Kelly K.C.V.O., P.P.R.A.,*
Royal Academy of Arts, Diploma Gallery,
October–December 1957 (107); *Christmas
Present Exhibition*, Roland, Browse and
Delbanco, November–December 1967
(80)

The donor, after purchasing this panel, took it to Sir
Gerald Kelly who recalled, on seeing it again, that he
had visited the music hall in Algiers in the company of
his great friend Somerset Maugham. Kelly also remembered that the panel was painted in the music hall during
the performance and that Maugham was seated in the
audience, although he is not actually distinguishable.
Nothing further is known about the name of the music
hall nor about the performers on stage.

Kelly first met Somerset Maugham in autumn 1903
and they remained firm friends for the next sixty years.
Kelly had moved to Paris in 1901 and early in 1905 he
found Maugham an apartment close to his own studio
in Montparnasse. Kelly's movements for early 1906 are
not well documented whereas Maugham's are. He is
recorded as travelling for the first three months of 1906
in Greece and Egypt. In January he was in Alexandria
having taken a boat from Venice to Port Said. Later he
spent a month in Cairo and was back in London in
April. Kelly equally was back in Paris in April 1906
because he painted a scene of the Luxembourg Gardens
and dated it April 1906. Three other paintings of Algerian scenes by Kelly exist, one entitled 'Algiers: Evening' is dated 4 March 1906, and these were shown in a
Sir Gerald Kelly exhibition organised by the Fine Art

Society, December 1975–January 1976 (7, 10, 11). Possibly Maugham persuaded Kelly to join him on the North African Coast.

Kelly painted the first of his eighteen portraits of Maugham in 1907, and the Tate Gallery owns one painted in London in July 1911 – N 04703 'The Jester (W. Somerset Maugham)'.

T 03652   Terrace at Monte Carlo 1908

> Oil on panel $5\frac{7}{8} \times 7\frac{1}{8}$ (149 × 180)
> Inscribed on reverse "Terrace at Monte Carlo/Febry.1908/Gerald Kelly"
> Presented anonymously in memory of Terence Rattigan 1983
>
> *Prov:*   Purchased from the artist by the donor in 1969
> *Exh:*   *Sir Gerald Kelly K.C.V.O., P.P.R.A.*, Royal Academy of Arts, Diploma Gallery, October–December 1957 (121); *Sir Gerald Kelly*, City Art Gallery, Plymouth, June–July 1958 (44); *Sea Pictures: British Impressionist Pictures of the Sea*, Brighton Polytechnic, May 1974 (12)

From the evidence of several small oil on panel sketches dated by the artist, Kelly spent part of the months of January and February 1908 painting views in Marseilles and Monte Carlo.

T 03653   Beach at Etretât 1908

> Oil on panel $8\frac{1}{2} \times 10\frac{5}{8}$ (215 × 270)
> Inscribed on reverse 'Etretat 29 July 08/Gr. Kelly'
> Presented anonymously in memory of Terence Rattigan 1983
>
> *Prov:*   Purchased from the artist by the donor in 1969

> *Exh:*   *Sir Gerald Kelly*, City Art Gallery, Plymouth, June–July 1958 (67); *Sea Pictures: British Impressionist Pictures of the Sea*, Brighton Polytechnic, May 1974 (11)

The artist told the donor that he painted this panel while seated on a raft moored a short distance from the water's edge and that the people on the beach are facing away from the artist since they were appalled by his clothes. Two other panels exist painted under the same circumstances: they are *Etretât: From the Sea!* oil on panel $5\frac{7}{8} \times 7\frac{1}{8}$ (149 × 180) shown at Kelly's retrospective exhibition at the Royal Academy in October–December 1957 (101) and *Etretât – The Beach From a Raft*, oil on panel $8\frac{1}{2} \times 10\frac{1}{2}$ (215 × 266), dated on the reverse '30th July 1908', shown at the Sir Gerald Kelly exhibition at the Fine Art Society, December 1975–January 1976 (25). T 03653 appears to have been painted on a wooden box lid, since there is a screw hole for a knob on the reverse of the panel.

Zoltan Kemeny 1907–1965

T 03595   Moonlight 1948

> Oil on incised strawboard $47\frac{3}{4} \times 29\frac{3}{8}$ (1212 × 747)
> Not inscribed
> Presented by Mrs Madeleine Kemeny 1983
>
> *Exh:*   *Zoltan Kemeny*, Kunstmuseum, Berne, March–May 1982 (not numbered, as 'Mondschein' and 'Clair de Lune', repr. p.51)

T 03596   Cat Mask 1947

> Plaster, woven canvas, scrim, rope and braiding glued on to a fibre board and

T 03595

Prov: The artist
Exh: *Anselm Kiefer*, Galerie im Goethe –
Institut/Provisorium, Amsterdam,
September–October 1973

T 03596

painted $16\frac{3}{4} \times 23\frac{1}{2} \times 3\frac{1}{8}$ (410 × 585 × 79)
Inscribed with studio stamp 'zk' b.r.
Presented by Mrs Madeleine Kemeny
1983
Exh: *Zoltan Kemeny*, Galerie Maeght, Paris,
1968

Anselm Kiefer b.1945

T 03403   Parsifal I 1973

Oil on paper laid down on canvas
$127\frac{7}{8} \times 86\frac{1}{2}$ (3247 × 2198)
Inscribed 'Herzeleide' above centre r.
Purchased from Galerie Paul Maenz
(Grant-in-Aid) 1982

T 03404   Parsifal II 1973

Oil and blood on paper laid down on canvas
$126\frac{5}{8} \times 86\frac{1}{8}$ (3217 × 2188)
Inscribed 'Parsifal' above centre r. and
'ither' above centre l.
Purchased from Galerie Paul Maenz
(Grant-in-Aid) 1982

Prov: The artist
Exh: *Anselm Kiefer*, Galerie im Goethe –
Institut/Provisorium, Amsterdam,
September–October 1973

T 03405 **Parsifal III** 1973

Oil and blood on paper laid down on canvas
$118\frac{3}{8} \times 171\frac{1}{16}$ (3007 × 4345)
Inscribed 'Gamuret' and 'Fal parsi' centre
top, 'Amfortas' and 'Titurel' centre right,
'Kundry' bottom right, 'Klingsor' bottom
left, and 'Oh, wunden-wundervoller
heiliger Speer!' along bottom edge
Purchased from Galerie Paul Maenz
(Grant-in-Aid) 1982

Prov: The artist
Exh: *Anselm Kiefer*, Galerie im Goethe –
Institut/Provisorium, Amsterdam,
September–October 1973

Ken Kiff b.1935

T 03612 **Person Cutting an
Image** 1965–71

Tempera on hardboard 24 × 24
(610 × 610)
Inscribed 'Ken Kiff' on reverse
Purchased from Nicola Jacobs Gallery
(Grant-in-Aid) 1983

Exh: *13 Britische Kunstler: eine Austellung über
Malerei*, BC tour, Neue Galerie –
Sammlung Ludwig, Aachen, December
1981–February 1982, Kunstverein,
Mannheim, February–April 1982,
Kunstverein, Brunswick, June–
September 1982 (repr. p.46); *New Art at
the Tate Gallery 1983*, Tate Gallery,
September–October 1983 (repr. p.18);
Ken Kiff, Paintings 1965–85, AC tour,
Serpentine Gallery, January–February
1986, Ferens Art Gallery, Hull, March–
April 1986, Arnolfini, Bristol, May–June
1986 (3, repr. in col.)
Lit: Timothy Hyman, 'Coming to terms with
the Time-Spirit', *London Magazine*,
XXIII, nos. 9 and 10, December 1983–
January 1984, p.88. *Also repr*: Martha
Kapos, 'Chagall and Figurative Painting',
Artscribe, 52, May–June 1985, p.32

The lengthy period of execution of this painting, from
1965 to 1971, is associated with the artist's choice of the
medium of tempera and pastel. It is one of his earliest
paintings in the style he now recognises as a part of all
his subsequent work, and it was, for instance, the third
in date order in his retrospective exhibition at the Serpentine Gallery in 1986. The artist wrote (letter of 6
August 1984):

At the time when I began that painting, being very
unsure where I was going with painting, I started
working on gesso on hardboard so that the images
could be scraped off or radically changed many many
times, and yet a paintfilm which was clear, probably
translucent, and above white, could be kept. I didn't
see, nor do I see now, how this could be done with
any other medium. Though I'd used tempera before,
mixing it myself, with *these* paintings (of which there
were six in all) I used Rowney's 'egg' (ie. egg-oil
emulsion) tempera. It behaves much like tempera
and was convenient for paintings which really have
nothing of the laboriousness and attention to detail
which the purist tempera painters usually have.

The group of early paintings (in fact more than six) in this medium were shown at the Serpentine Gallery in 1986 as numbers 2 to 8, where they were dated from 1965 to 1979, and there is also, in addition, another painting 'Woman Taking her Clothes' (24 × 24 ins.) which was not exhibited since it was still unfinished. All of these were altered considerably during the painting, although 'Person Cutting an Image' less so:

The 'Man Cutting an Image' (like the pastel, which was begun earlier) was always a figure against a dark background. But other presences in the darkness, a window, the table and whatever was happening on it, all these things came and went, and changed the picture fundamentally. Doing two versions – I suppose always a way of thinking about what one is doing – may have had a technical point with this painting: a soft matt translucent black is easier in pastel or tempera than in oil (letter of 24 August 1984).

The pastel version (22 × 30 ins., private collection) has the same composition, but the table is a darker colour and the features of the head are drawn in a different way, as if also seen in profile inside the full round of the head.

In these two letters the artist gave no direct account of the subject, but described some of its associations:

I hope that [these] paintings, having become whole as one works on them, become more serene for the viewer as he continues to look at them. That the black background dovetails into the figure, reaches into it as the head reaches into the darkness, or that other sharper black shape, the scissors, reaches into the image on the table . . .

And the general implications of the subject:

Things being split apart, divided or even destroyed – I think I do a lot of subjects like that, but always I hope the real subject is wholeness, or the movement towards wholeness.

The image is related to that of another painting of similar date. 'Man Reading with a Paraffin Stove' (oil on canvas, 60 × 48 ins., 1964–5, collection of artist) shows a seated figure, full length and in a comparable pose, staring at a painting of a head that is probably his own, or even a mirror. A pair of scissors is open on the floor near his feet. That the 'image' he looks at is a self-portrait is far more explicit than in the Tate Gallery's painting, but there is a possibility that this identification is continued there as well.

Peter Kinley b.1926

T 03476 **Fire** 1982

Oil on canvas, 66 × 84 (1676 × 2134)
Inscribed 'Fire 66 × 84 1982 P. Kinley' on stretcher
Purchased from Knoedler Gallery (Grant-in-Aid) 1982

Exh: *Peter Kinley: Paintings 1956–1982*, Museum of Modern Art, Oxford, May–June 1982 (65)

Kinley worked on 'Fire' during the winter of 1981–2 while he was living in Wiltshire. The subject is essentially autobiographical, the artist watching his daughter kneeling to make up the fire. It marks a return to the theme of figure and interior which had interested him throughout the 1950s and 60s, during a period mainly preoccupied with the landscape and the depiction of animals.

Kinley stresses that the description of the particular and narrative content was not what interested him. Rather he was concerned with the transformation of personal observation and experience into an immediate yet lasting image. He was interested in the complex assymetry and rhythm of the kneeling figure and its formal, functional relationships. It is in the definition of these precise relationships that he seeks to convey the essential significance of the image. 'I do not want my paintings to be read (from left to right as it were) but intend them to be seen.'

His working process is revealed by three studies (oil on paper, the artist) in which he makes changes to colour and line and introduces the rectangle of the ceiling at top right.

The above entry is based upon a discussion with Peter Kinley (3 March 1986) and has been approved by him.

Oskar Kokoschka 1886–1980

T 03829 Study for 'Ambassador Ivan Maisky' 1942

Coloured pencil on paper 14 × 10
(355 × 253)
Not inscribed
Presented by Mrs Olda Kokoschka 1984

Exh: *Oskar Kokoschka 1886–1980*, Tate
Gallery, June–August 1986, Kunsthaus,
Zürich, September–November 1986,
Guggenheim Museum, New York,
December–February 1987 (208, repr. in
col.)

Lit: Oskar Kokoschka, *My Life*, translated by
David Britt, 1974, p.34

T 03830 Study for 'Ambassador Ivan Maisky' 1942

Coloured pencil on paper 14 × 10
(355 × 253)
Not inscribed
Presented by Mrs Olda Kokoschka 1984

Exh: *Oskar Kokoschka 1886–1980*, Tate
Gallery, June–August 1986, Kunsthaus,
Zürich, September–November 1986,
Guggenheim Museum, New York,
December–February 1987 (209, repr. in
col.)

Lit: As for T 03829

These two studies are for the Tate Gallery's portrait
of Ivan Maisky 1942–3 (N 05432). Ivan Mikhailovich
Maisky (1884–1975) was Soviet Ambassador to London
for eleven years from 1932 until 1943.

There were about thirty sittings for the portrait; these
took place in Maisky's study at the Soviet Embassy, 13
Kensington Palace Gardens. The first sitting was on 19
March 1942, during which Maisky read *The Times*.
Kokoschka recalled it in his autobiography:

> I could not get him to talk; perhaps he regarded a
> portrait as some new form of brainwashing. Finally,
> after hours of sitting, I suggested he reverse the
> paper behind which he was hiding, for I had finished
> reading the part turned towards me. At length he
> became more talkative, and told me about his
> student days in Vienna and Munich.

The two sketches concentrate on Maisky's head. In the
finished portrait Maisky is depicted writing at his desk;
behind him, echoing the round shape of his head, is a
globe which is turned to display the USSR. On the left
there is a statue of Lenin who, with upraised arm,
gestures towards the globe.

T 03834 The Crab 1939–40

Oil on canvas 25 × 30 (634 × 762)
Inscribed 'OK' b.l.
Purchased from the estate of the late Sir
Edward Beddington-Behrens through
Marlborough Fine Art (Grant-in-Aid)
with the aid of the NACF 1984

Prov: Lady Knott; Major (later Sir) Edward
Beddington-Behrens, by 1946

Exh: *Unesco: Exposition Internationale D'Art
Moderne*, Musée Nationale d'Art
Moderne, Paris, November–December
1946 ('Artistes Réfugiés de l'Europe

T03834

This picture was painted while Kokoschka was living in Polperro, Cornwall at the outbreak of the Second World War. The crab which dominates the composition has been described by Richard Calvocoressi in the catalogue for the 1986 Kokoschka exhibition at the Tate Gallery as having:

> a malevolent human appearance, towering over the harbour and threatening the tiny, vulnerable figure of the swimmer struggling to reach the safety of the pier.

In his autobiography, *Look Back, Look Forward*, 1963, Edward Beddington-Behrens recalled that Kokoschka told him that the swimming figure (a self-portrait) represented Czechoslovakia and the crab, Neville Chamberlain, who 'would only have to put out one claw to save him from drowning, but remains aloof'. (At the time, Kokoschka held Czech citizenship, and had arrived in England as a refugee in 1938.)

Kokoschka also told Edith Hoffmann that what started off as a straightforward realistic landscape had the habit of turning into a political allegory, especially if he brought the painting back to London unfinished.

A crab first appears in Kokoschka's 'Polperro I' 1939 (Courtauld Institute Galleries). The view of the jagged rocks in the background, known as The Peak, is close to that in the watercolour 'Polperro IV' 1939 (Lord Croft), which also includes a female figure sitting underneath the cliff at the extreme right and a shell or lobster pot in the foreground to the left. 'The Crab' is also related to the oil 'Polperro II' 1939 in the Tate's collection (N05251), a non-allegorical representation of almost the same land- and seascape. A watercolour study for 'The Crab' (16 × 20⅛ ins., private collection) is reproduced in colour in the catalogue of the Tate's Kokoschka retrospective of 1986 (204).

Centrale' 10); *Oskar Kokoschka*, Kunsthalle, Basle, March–April 1947 (83); *Oskar Kokoschka*, Kunsthaus, Zürich, July–August 1947 (54); *Oskar Kokoschka*, Haus der Kunst, Munich, March–May 1958 (112, repr. p.76); *Oskar Kokoschka in England and Scotland*, Marlborough Fine Art, November–December 1960 (14); *Kokoschka*, Tate Gallery, September–November 1962 (124); *Oskar Kokoschka*, Kunstverein, Hamburg, December 1962–January 1963 (62, repr.); *Oskar Kokoschka*, Kunsthaus, Zürich, June–July 1966 (80); *Oskar Kokoschka, Cityscapes and Landscapes. A 90th Birthday Tribute*, Marlborough Fine Art, March–April 1976 (12, repr.); *Oskar Kokoschka (1886–1980)*, *Memorial Exhibition*, Marlborough Gallery, New York, May–June 1981, Marlborough Fine Art, June–July 1981 (39, repr. p.62); *Oskar Kokoschka*, Galerie des Beaux Arts, Bordeaux, May–September 1983 (39, repr.); *Oskar Kokoschka 1886–1980*, Tate Gallery, June–August 1986, Kunsthaus, Zürich, September–November 1986, Guggenheim Museum, New York, December 1986–February 1987 (87, repr. in col.)

Lit: Edith Hoffman, *Kokoschka, Life and Work*, 1947, pp.224, 232–3, 336, no.294, repr. in col. pl.2; Hans M. Wingler, *Oskar Kokoschka. The Work of the Painter*, 1958, p.328, no.319, repr. pl.102; Richard Calvocoressi and Richard Morphet, 'Three Mid-twentieth Century Acquisitions', *National Art-Collections Fund Annual Review*, 1985, p.97, repr. in col.

Stanislav Kolíbal b.1925

T03806 Identity 1982

Plaster, string, iron rod, nails, oil and crayon on wood 57½ × 62¾ × 10 (1460 × 1595 × 250)
Inscribed 'Kolíbal' on back of panel
Presented by Illa Kodicek 1983

Prov: Purchased by the donor from the artist through Riverside Studios 1983

Exh: *Stanislav Kolíbal*, Studio Carlo Grosetti, Milan, March–April 1983 (not numbered, repr. as 'Differenza e Breve Accordo' 1982); *Adriena Šimotavá and Stanislav Kolíbal*, Riverside Studios, October–November 1983 (works not numbered)

Prov: Acquired by the donor from the Beaux Arts Gallery

Exh: *Heinz Koppel*, Beaux Arts Gallery, May–June 1958 (26)

The artist said on 12 October 1984 that he would prefer his work to be called 'Identity' rather than 'Difference and Brief Accord', which is the title under which it was first exhibited in Milan. He finds it very difficult to choose the right title and only rarely finds words which express exactly what he has in mind. The title is not just for identification.

The recurrent theme of all his work, he said, is fascination with the paradox of something that is related and not related. For example in this particular work, if you stand in a certain position but in that position only, the line formed by the string at the top right corresponds with the line in the painted image. This momentary relationship is firm yet fragile, unstable, and he sees it as an existential symbol for life situations. When making this work he also had an image of two cubes partly in mind and one could even call it 'Two Cubes' except that this would be an over-simplification and miss the point.

As is his usual practice, he made several very small sketchy preparatory drawings for this work, but in the end the finished work was different from the sketches.

Although this work was listed in the catalogue of his exhibition at the Padiglione d'Arte Contemporanea in Milan in 1983, it was not actually shown there but in a parallel exhibition at Studio Carlo Grossetti, Milan.

Heinz Koppel 1919–1980

T 03798 **Snow, Sunshine, Rain** 1957

Oil on canvas 48 × 86 (1220 × 2190)
Inscribed 'Snow. Sunshine. Rain.' at lower edge
Presented anonymously 1983

'Snow, Sunshine, Rain' has a complex subject which was not discussed by the artist. This entry is based on conversations with his widow and with his pupil and friend Charles Burton. The date of the painting is given in the catalogue of the Beaux Arts Gallery exhibition.

Each detail of the painting had for the artist a specific meaning, although this is as likely to have been found after it was finished as before. There are several large paintings by Koppel like this in which the subject is seen in separate compartments, which were intended to be seen both as a sequence in time and all together. The precedent for this work is 'Merthyr Blues' (1955–6, oil on canvas, private collection, America. Repr. *Heinz Koppel*, Beaux Arts Gallery 1958 (25)). Both paintings show parts of Merthyr Tydfil and its suburb Dowlais, where the artist lived from 1944 to 1956, and both have a foreground that is part of, yet separate from, each of the three main compartments. In a large drawing for 'Merthyr Blues' the compartments are labelled 'Ego, Superego, Id', yet in the painting these names are omitted and replaced with lines from pop songs ('I could go for you baby' and 'I wanna be good, moima'), so the subject was evidently considered by the artist both in terms of psychoanalysis and of local popular culture. In the foreground the artist's corgi is shown four times, walking from left to right or being thrown to the ground, possibly with reference to Koppel's own movements, and comparable to the car in the foreground of 'Snow, Sunshine, Rain'.

Koppel often painted landscapes which refer to his life in places which he had left, and he had moved to London in 1956, the year before he painted Dowlais in 'Snow, Sunshine, Rain'. In the foreground, separated by design and colour from the larger part of the canvas is a bridal couple, seated with a chauffeur and another man in a wedding car decorated with ribbons. At the centre of the painting a bird opens its beak to catch a butterfly, which possibly refers to its name in German 'vogeln', meaning in slang to make love. Behind the bird a girl talks to a man on a bicycle, the outlines of both figures merged into one. It is likely that the different types of weather of each section refer also to the mood of the onlooker, or of the artist, as in 'Merthyr Blues'. It has been suggested that there are figures deliberately hidden within the painting, intended to be understood subliminally, particularly in the snow scene a face on the roof looking at a female nude drawn in the snow on the road.

The subject of this painting is the artist's parents. The Oxford catalogue of 1981, cited above, reproduces a closely related drawing (p.30) and 'Two Seated Figures No.1' 1980 (oil on board, 48 × 60 ins., p.39).

Jannis Kounellis b.1936

T 03796   **Untitled** 1979

Wall drawing, two impaled stuffed birds and five charcoal drawings on paper; height of birds 25 (63) and 17 (43), dimensions of drawings each $27\frac{3}{4} \times 39\frac{1}{4}$ (70.3 × 100); overall dimensions variable
Not inscribed
Purchased from Galleria Christian Stein, Turin (Grant-in-Aid) 1983

Exh: *Jannis Kounellis*, Galleria Christian Stein, Turin, October–November 1979 (no catalogue); *Kounellis*, Musée d'Art Moderne de la Ville de Paris, Paris, April–June 1980 (not listed in catalogue, repr. in col. (30)); *Jannis Kounellis*, Musei Comunali Sale d'Arte Contemporanea, Rimini, June–September 1983 (117, repr.); *New Art at the Tate Gallery 1983*, September–October 1983 (not numbered in catalogue, repr. p.12 as 'View of Streets drawn in charcoal on wall with 2 crows and 5 drawings on adjacent wall')

Lit: Giuseppe Risso 'Jannis Kounellis a Torino' *Domus*, DCII, January 1980, p.53, repr. in col.; Dadamaino, 'Jannis Kounellis, Christian Stein Turin', *Flash Art* No.94–5, January/February 1980, p.59, repr.; Marlis Grüterich, 'Jannis Kounellis, les pouvoirs de l'art', *Art Press*

Leon Kossoff b.1926

T 03680   **Two Seated Figures No.2** 1980

Oil on hardboard 96 × 72 (2438 × 1829)
Not inscribed
Purchased from Fischer Fine Art (Grant-in-Aid) 1983

Exh: *Leon Kossoff: Paintings from a Decade 1970–1980*, Museum of Modern Art, Oxford, May–July 1981, Graves Art Gallery, Sheffield, July–August 1981 (43, repr. in col.); *The Hard-Won Image*, Tate Gallery, July–September 1984 (85, repr. in col.)

Lit: Peter Fuller, 'Visions from an E8 Landscape', *New Society*, LVII, issue 978, 1981, pp.272–3
Also repr: *Leon Kossoff, Recent Work*, Fischer Fine Art, exhibition catalogue, 1984, repr. in col. front cover but not exhibited

XXXVII, May 1980, pp.14–15, repr. p.15;
*Identité Italienne, L'art en Italie depuis
1959*, exhibition catalogue, Musée
National d'Art Moderne, Paris, June–
September 1981, p.608, repr.
Also repr: *Kunstforum* No.39, March 1980,
p.35; 'Jannis Kounellis', exhibition
catalogue, Stedelijk Van Abbemuseum,
Eindhoven, 1982, pp.74–5, dated 1980;
Tema Celeste, exhibition catalogue, Museo
Civico d'Arte Contemporanea di Gibellina,
Sicily, January 1983, p.68, as 'Hotel
Louisiane (III stanza) 1979'; Germano
Celant, *Arte Povera*, Milan, 1985, p.201

This work was first exhibited as one part of a three
part installation, referred to in contemporary reviews
(erroneously, according to the artist) as 'Hotel Louisiane' or 'Louisiana'. The individual sections of the
work have been untitled in subsequent literature and
Kounellis confirms that this is correct. ('Hotel Louisiane' was also the title of an earlier work by Kounellis,
installed in a Rome hotel, the Albergo della Lunetta,
the reference being to a hotel in Paris associated with
the heyday of Existentialism, see pp.108 and 169 in the
Rimini catalogue and p.56 in the Eindhoven catalogue,
both cited above).

In its original site, T03796 was installed in the third
of three intercommunicating rooms. The first room was
empty and in the second, thirteen works on paper were
placed around the room at the height of the cornice.
These were described by the reviewer in *Domus* (op.cit.)
as having been 'sensitised' with coal dust dissolved in
glue, and their position as resembling metopes in a
Doric frieze. The last room (containing T03796) was
described by the reviewer as:

almost square, a small town is drawn on the far wall –
profiles of houses – over which two stuffed ravens
loom, transfixed with arrows. The scene, which
overthrows traditional perspective planes, takes on
a tri-dimensionality in its cross-reference to the
invisible archer from whose bow the arrows flew
(*Domus*, op.cit.).

When installed (on two adjacent walls) the work comprises an urban and industrial landscape with houses
and smoking factory chimney, simply drawn in sharp
perspective, in charcoal outline with the aid of a
template. The drawing extends across the right angle
separating the two walls. Above the drawn roof tops but
below the cloud of smoke, two large stuffed birds (a
jackdaw and a hooded crow) are impaled on arrows,
which pin them to the wall; the attitudes of the birds
suggest that they have just been shot and are about to
fall to earth. At a right angle to the townscape, five
drawings on paper are pinned to the wall in a vertical
column. These carry simple images in outline of

women's heads and landscapes which have been drawn
by engraving lines with a sharp-ended instrument into
the thick layers of black carbonised material. The drawings appear to confront the chimney from which the
smoke billows.

Questioned about the significance of the imagery in
this work (conversation with the compiler, 14 March
1986) the artist said that although the urban landscape
is reminiscent of those in Northern Italy and the work
was first shown in Turin, he had not intended any
specific reference to that city but sought to portray
an archetypal and imaginary nineteenth century
townscape, hence the smoking chimney. The drawings
on paper were also imaginary – he compared them to
drawings made on the surface of the water or on a pond
which last only for a second. The artist declined to
comment on the specific significance of the birds but
drew a comparison between the work and an earlier
untitled work of 1975 (repr. in the Rimini catalogue,
fig.119), where a fragmented classical plaster cast of
Apollo is spread out on a table above which a 'cloud' of
black hair billows out. Kounellis had also used the image
of a chimney before, for example in 'Untitled' 1976–81
(Rimini fig.118) and frequently uses carbon or charcoal
in his installations. He included a stuffed bird (again a
crow) in an earlier installation of 1973 (Rimini fig.69).
Elsewhere he has commented on his use of fire imagery
as having to do with medieval legends, the suggestion
of punishment and purification (in *View* I, no.10, California 1979).

In his catalogue essay for the Eindhoven exhibition
('Fourth Story', p.42), Rudi Fuchs suggests that for
Kounellis the chimney in the post-industrial age can be
seen as a museum or monument to the drama of the
Industrial Revolution and that Kounellis uses it as an
allegory of progress, and a 'memento mori'. However
the chimney 'can burn ... can blow smoke and produce
wonderful figures whirling in the black clouds. The
chimney can be the furnace of creative invention, like
the mind.'

In his catalogue essay for Rimini (op.cit., 'L'urto e
l'urlo', p.21), Germano Celant suggests that the dead
birds surmounting the work represent the end of freedom of the imagination.

When this work was first exhibited, a reviewer (in
Flash Art, cited above) suggested that the smoke had
multiple associations and many meanings in the context
of the installation, ranging from the smoke of the crema-
torium to smoke as a metaphor for the unconscious. The
reviewer stated that, according to the artist, the two
birds represent:

the romantic aspect of this work, the unsuppressible,
emotional 'quid' that goes hand in hand with
creation.

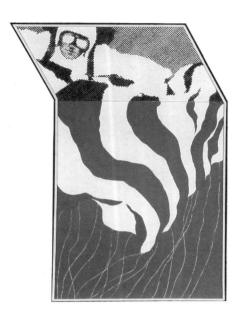

Gerald Laing b.1936

T 03842 **Skydiver VI** 1964

Oil and pencil on canvas mounted on two
stretchers attached to one another, top one
$22 \times 57\frac{3}{4}$ (559×1467), lower one $58 \times 47\frac{5}{8}$
(1473×1210), overall dimensions
$80 \times 57\frac{3}{4}$ (2032×1467)
Inscribed 'SKYDIVER 6 1964/GERALD
LAING' on back of top canvas
Purchased from the artist (Grant-in-Aid)
1984

Exh: *4 Young Artists*, ICA, October–November
1964 (4); *Gerald Laing*, Scottish National
Gallery of Modern Art, Edinburgh, June–
August 1971 (2); *Gerald Laing Paintings
and Sculpture 1963–1983*, Herbert Art
Gallery, Coventry, September–October
1983, (2, repr.)

Gerald Laing studied at St Martin's School of Art,
London, from 1960–4, and 'Skydiver VI' was painted
during his last year at St Martin's, at home in his studio
at 12 Fournier Street, Whitechapel. On graduation from
St Martin's, the artist lived in New York from 1964 to
1969, having already spent the summer of 1963 there.

The previous summer [1963] I spent in New York,
working for Robert Indiana at his studio at Coenties
Slip. During the summer I met Lichtenstein, Warhol
and Rosenquist, who were at that time having their
first group show at the New York Museum [*Six
Painters and the Object*, The Solomon R.
Guggenheim Museum, New York, March–June
1963] and who were still more or less unknown.

Before this visit to New York I had already begun to
paint paintings of photographs (to which the
'Skydiver VI' has an obvious debt); this was a sort
of notion of the time, I suppose – the notion that
reproduced media images had a stronger sense of
reality than reality itself; not an idea which I'd
subscribe to now. (letter to the compiler, 4 April
1986).

Laing, in his student years, began to restrict himself
to magazine and newspaper photographs as the sources
for his subject matter.

During this period of painting, which lasted from
1963 to 1965, I was interested only in what I
considered to be contemporary 'heroic' themes, and
I worked on them all concurrently, scouring
magazines and billboards, etc, for source material.
The themes were Skydivers, Astronauts, Drag
Racers and, I'm afraid, Starlets. (I claim absolution
on the grounds of youth!)

In a catalogue note written by Laing to accompany
'Skydiver VI' when it was shown at the Herbert Art
Gallery, Coventry in 1983, the artist reiterated his early
interest in deriving his subject matter from

contemporary mass-produced images of women,
drag-racing cars, astronauts and skydivers – typical
concerns of a young man, I suppose, but also
endorsing the technological optimism of the early
1960s at a time when all things seemed possible, and
that man would be able to dominate his environment
and solve all his problems through science. This
hubris was soon to end in disillusion.

When asked by the compiler if this was his first
shaped canvas, the artist replied:

It was not ... I had made four previous to this one.
The reason for the shaped canvas was two fold: a) to
assert what used to be called the 'objecthood' of the
painting – ie. the existence of the painting as an
object rather than as a window or hole with
atmospheric perspective, leaning towards the Italian
primitives such as Cimabue or to Uccello, rather
than to later paintings of the C17th say; b) to make
the painting imply a physical 3-D volume; in
'Skydiver VI' the shape refers to a cube, for example.
Later on I developed the skydiver paintings, much
abstracted, into a sort of environmental sculpture
with an illusory volume, later still these became
properly volumetric sculptures ... I had one or two
favourite photographic sources but composed the
image myself. For instance in 'Skydiver VI' two
separate incidents which occur at different moments
are seen in the same painting: a) the skydiver has
just jumped out of the aeroplane and his parachute
is still in its pack and b) he is on the ground (below

the bottom edge of the painting) and his parachute is collapsing since it is no longer bearing his weight (safe arrival). This again refers to, say, Italian primitive painting where the saint may be depicted involved in several different incidents in his life.

Since T 03842 is 'Skydiver VI', the artist was asked how big the series was and where the related paintings are or were. He replied:

There were Skydivers I–VIII, and also 9 other paintings with skydivers as the subject but with other titles; also a portfolio of 6 silkscreen prints which was in an edition, I think, of 75. And the skydiver content was the one which I used in the move towards abstraction in 1965–7, so there are also a few transitional ones. Skydiver VIII was painted in New York in the autumn of 1964 – I went there straight from Art School. As far as I can ascertain, the rest of the series are in the following locations (they may have been resold, of course):

Skydiver I   – destroyed
Skydiver II   – Harry Abrams, Publishers, NY
Skydiver III – ditto [repr. *Art in America*, Vol.52, no.130, Oct. 1964]
Skydiver IV – Academy for Educational Development, NY
Skydiver V   – [Private Collection] Boston
Skydiver VI – [The Tate Gallery]
Skydiver VII – Armand Bartos, NY
Skydiver VIII – University of New Mexico Art Museum, Albuquerque

All of them have been exhibited in various places, particularly in Feigen Gallery, New York, Chicago, and Los Angeles soon after they were painted. However for some logistic reason, 'Skydiver VI' was not shown at this time ...

When, in 1963, Laing began to devise his subject matter from newspaper and magazine photographs, he also began to organise his own technical system for representing this subject material, utilising a parody of cheap printing methods, ie. rows of black dots set out in a grid format on a white background. In New York in the summer of 1963, Laing learnt that 'Lichtenstein had also begun to use dots in his paintings; he came to my first show at the Feigen Gallery [New York] and we agreed that there was no conflict because the approaches were so radically different.' Laing worked on the two canvases of T 03842 at the same time, fixed together, and only the top canvas bears black dots. Over the whole area of this top canvas is visible a preparatory criss-cross grid of pencil lines and these diagonal lines:

are to position the dots. The establishment of the appropriate areas between dot centres was something I considered very carefully; the idea of

the whole technique used was to avoid any possibility of accident or of 'now you see it, now you don't' effect. It was an attempt to be absolutely particular and exact. The pencil lines are a definite part of the pictures, makes it very difficult to clean, though, and now I wish I'd varnished them.

Both canvases also have loose curving pencil contour lines drawn on the white primer coat and these were 'a guide to the painting of the forms ... and I sometimes altered these forms while painting, hence [the] discrepancy between, say, coloured areas and pencil lines'.

Although Laing was interested in the way black dots in the top canvas create a sense of volume, he attempted to deny volume in the lower canvas, which is painted with flat, strong colour; unmodulated red and white for the parachute stripes and blue for the sky. The paint 'was applied in a manner which referred deliberately to printing techniques especially to silkscreen printing' and 'the idea was to get the strongest and clearest colours possible. [I] Found yellow very difficult to handle. I developed a private theory that the primary colours were red, white and blue, science and politics notwithstanding.'

In 1963–4 both Allen Jones and R.B. Kitaj painted works with parachutists as subject material; those of Jones include 'Wundebare Landing' 1963, 'Parachutist I' 1963, 'Figure Falling' 1964 and 'Aureolin' 1964, and a Kitaj example is 'A Disciple of Bernstein and Kantsky' 1964. The artist was asked whether he was aware of this shared subject matter at the time. His reply was that he was 'not particularly aware of Kitaj/Jones use of parachutes, would not have approved of the way they did it anyway! But it is worth noting that a parachute is a good way to get large fields of colour onto the canvas while still retaining a figurative connotation.'

Maurice Lambert 1901–1964

T 03756   **Man with a Bird** 1929

Serravezza marble 35 × 8 × 7½
(890 × 203 × 190)
Inscribed 'ML' r. of base
Transferred from the Victoria and Albert Museum 1983

Prov: ...; presented by D.H. Conner to the Department of Architecture and Sculpture, Victoria and Albert Museum 1930 (A.35–1930)

Exh: *New Sculpture by Maurice Lambert*, Arthur Tooth and Sons, June–July 1929 (8)

T 03756

Lit: Edmund Dulac, 'The Work of Maurice
Lambert', *Studio*, XCVIII, 1929,
pp.504–8, repr. p.506

This sculpture was previously catalogued as 6096 and
described in error as having been transferred to the
Tate Gallery in 1952. The artist wrote to the Gallery
on 8 September 1957:

> 'Man with a Bird', a very early work in marble ... I
> suppose it made its way to the Tate, and I rather wish
> it hadn't.

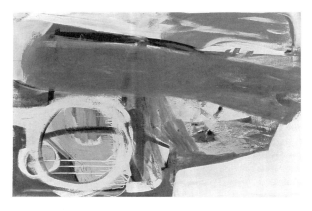

Peter Lanyon 1918–1964

T 03693 Wreck 1963

Oil on canvas 48 × 78 (1220 × 1830)
Inscribed 'Lanyon 63' lower centre and
'Lanyon 63' near right edge towards
middle and 'Lanyon 63' slightly to lower
left of this and 'Wreck Lanyon Dec 63' on
reverse
Presented by the Friends of the Tate
Gallery 1982

Prov: Mrs Sheila Lanyon (until 1967); Peter
Stuyvesant Foundation (until 1976);
private collection, sold to Redfern Gallery
1982, from whom purchased for the Tate
Gallery

Exh: *54/64 Painting and Sculpture of a Decade*,
Tate Gallery, April–June 1964 (212,
repr.); *Peter Lanyon, Bilder 1960–64*,
Gimpel und Hanover Galerie, Zurich,
September–October 1964 (12); *Recent
British Painting*, Tate Gallery,
November–December 1967 (25, repr.) and
extensive subsequent tours of Peter
Stuyvesant Collection including *Recent
British Painting*, Sixth Adelaide Festival
Of Arts, Art Gallery of South Australia,
1970 (24); *Forty Years of Modern Art*,
Tate Gallery, February–April 1986 (works
not numbered, repr. in col. p.57)

Lit: Andrew Causey, *Peter Lanyon: His
Painting*, 1971, no.201, p.68

Alan Bowness wrote (letter to the compiler of 29 April
1986):

> 'Wreck' was one of the last important paintings that
> Peter made, completed in December 1963.
> Immediately after it was finished he began to
> experiment with a brighter palette – which is already
> hinted at in some earlier 1963 pictures, like Margaret
> Gardiner's 'Heather Coast'. But 'Wreck' was a
> winter picture, and Peter didn't move far away from
> the blue sea-and-sky colours that he always
> preferred.

The first title of this work was 'Untitled, Jeanne
Gougy', but Peter Lanyon seems to have decided to call
the painting 'Wreck' when he sent it to London for the
'54/64' exhibition at the Tate Gallery (letter to Alan
Bowness from Peter Lanyon, 8 March 1964). Alan Bowness wrote 29 April 1986), that:

> new paintings were usually left in the studio and in
> the house for several months, so that Peter could
> live with them and make sure they were all right. At
> this period the titles often changed.

The inspiration for this painting came from the wreck
of a French trawler, Jeanne Gougy, bound for Dieppe
from Irish fishing grounds, in November 1962 (the
correct name of the ship was confirmed by the Ministry
of Defence, Hydrographic Office in Taunton; it has
sometimes been incorrectly called 'Jean Gougy'). The
ship ran aground at Land's End during sudden squalls

of rain and heavy seas. 'It was one of the most dramatic wreck and rescue stories off the Cornish Coast' (David Mudd, *The Cruel Cornish Sea*, 1981). Mrs Sheila Lanyon wrote (letter of 19 April 1986) that 'the wreck was one of the more horrifyingly memorable ones' and the whole Lanyon family went down to Land's End to see the wreck a few days after the event.

Lanyon painted this subject in the garage studio at his home 'Little Park Owles', Carbis Bay, Cornwall, a year later. According to Alan Bowness it was certainly painted between October and December 1963, as 'it didn't exist when I left St Ives in September 1963; and I saw it in late December/early January 1964'. There were no preliminary drawings or sketches, apart from two photographs by the artist of the grounded ship (two slides, copies of the original photographs, are in the Tate Gallery Archive). Alan Bowness recalls that 'Peter was very happy with "Wreck"'. In the catalogue of the exhibition *Recent British Paintings*, Tate Gallery, 1967, he characterised this work as 'one of the most dramatic before his untimely accidental death'.

Purchased from the artist (Grant-in-Aid) 1983

Exh: *John Latham*, Stadtische Kunsthalle, Dusseldorf, September–October 1975 (no catalogue no., repr.); *Arte inglese oggi 1960–76*. Palazzo Reale, Milan, February–March 1976 (no catalogue no., repr.); *John Latham*, Tate Gallery, June–July 1976 (8); *John Latham*, Fruit Market Gallery, Edinburgh, September–October 1976 (5); *Forty Years of Modern Art 1945–1985*, Tate Gallery, February–April 1986

Christopher Le Brun b.1951

T 03454   **Dream, Think, Speak** 1981–2

Oil on canvas 96 × 90 (2440 × 2285)
Inscribed on reverse '19.12.81 → 13.1.82/Christopher Le Brun/Dream, Think, Speak', and the following inscriptions cancelled but legible 'Aram Nemus Vult'/Building, Dwelling, Thinking/"PASSAGE" 'CLEARING'.
Inscribed on right tacking edge and adjacent rear canvas turnover '19.12.81' and an illegible date and (cancelled) '18.12.81'
Purchased from Nigel Greenwood Inc. Ltd (Grant-in-Aid) 1982

Exh: *Christopher Le Brun*, Nigel Greenwood Inc., May-June 1982 (no catalogue); *Zeitgeist*, Martin-Gropius-Bau, West

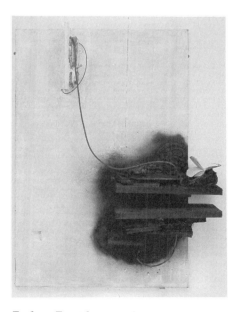

John Latham b.1921

T 03706   **Observer IV** 1960

Mixed media, plaster, books, metal, spray-paint on linen canvas glued on to hardboard 96 × 72 × 15 (2440 × 1830 × 380)
Not inscribed

Berlin, October–December 1982 (142, repr., dated 13.1.82); *New Art at the Tate Gallery*, Tate Gallery, September–October 1983 (catalogue not numbered, repr., dated 1981); *Forty Years of Modern Art 1945–1985*, Tate Gallery, February–April 1986 (works not listed)

Lit: 'Twentieth-Century Acquisitions at the Tate Gallery' *The Burlington Magazine*, cxxvi, December 1984, pp.810–13 (repr.), as 'Dream, think, speak' *Also repr.*: *La Forma e L'Informe*, exhibition catalogue, Galleria d'Arte Moderna, Bologna, April–May 1983, p.63 (dated 1982); Sarah Kent, 'Between two territories: a way forward in British painting', *Flash Art*, Summer 1983, pp.40–6, repr. p.42 (dated 1982)

Except where noted otherwise the following entry is based on the artist's replies to specific questions about 'Dream, Think, Speak' in conversation on 14 March 1986, and has been approved by him.

'Dream, Think, Speak' was painted in Le Brun's studio in 234 Burdett Road, London E14, which has since been demolished. It was painted on a wall only slightly larger than itself, in a narrow room which prevented Le Brun from viewing it from more than a short distance. It was painted over a period of weeks, during part of which time Le Brun was also working on a painting with very similar imagery, 'Trophy (Anger, Reverie)' 1982 (oil on canvas, 93 × 84 inches, collection Granada Television, Manchester), which is reproduced in colour in *Artforum*, xxi, December 1982, p.48. Le Brun customarily works on more than one painting at a time, but thinks that the dates 19 December–13 January, inscribed on 'Dream, Think, Speak', denote the starting and finishing points of the culminating period of work on this picture, during which he worked on it exclusively.

Le Brun believes 'Dream, Think, Speak' and 'Trophy (Anger, Reverie)' to be his only paintings in which a central image of a horse is accompanied by the head of a second horse to one side. He sees the central head as being more pronounced in 'Trophy (Anger, Reverie)' partly because, unlike the head in 'Dream, Think, Speak', it is almost severed. In this connection the dominant word of the title would be 'Trophy', a reading also associated with another title Le Brun considered for 'Trophy . . .', namely 'Falada', which in one of Grimms' Fairy Tales, *The Goose Girl*, is the severed horse's head, above the gate, that speaks the truth. Le Brun thinks of each of these paintings as representing two horses, though some viewers see suggestions, in fainter form, of a third, or even more. A distinct kind of auxiliary horse image is the 'shadow' image of the central horse

in 'Dream, Think, Speak', which (as it transpires) anticipates the emergence of further such shadow images in Le Brun's recent work. Le Brun does not conceive of the horses in 'Dream, Think, Speak' or 'Trophy (Anger, Reverie)' as winged. As will be explained below, the horse image in his work does not 'stand for' anything in a literary sense. Commentators have often noticed a broad similarity (which exists in respect of 'Dream, Think, Speak') between the clusters of tall dark trees in Le Brun's paintings and Böcklin's 'The Island of the Dead'. While Le Brun admires Böcklin, 'The Island of the Dead' did not directly influence his work but rather confirmed for him intuitions he had already felt.

As is customary in Le Brun's work, there were no preparatory notes, studies or sketches for 'Dream, Think, Speak'. Like his other paintings it was developed on a single canvas by means of a succession of separate images the nature of which Le Brun could not predict before they appeared. He cannot recall the motifs of the images which preceded the final appearance of 'Dream, Think, Speak' on his canvas, but many of them were probably, as usual, unrelated to each other. In this, as in other works, as many as thirty or forty images may have preceded the final one. Such paintings proceed by means of a sequence of cancellations of images. The succession of cancelled images builds up the surface, though not in the sense of refining the painted texture towards one particular image. Rather it is a case of the often contradictory images forming an accretion, through which what is to become the final image begins eventually to emerge. This stage is reached when in the course of the painting Le Brun comes across an image which he 'recognises' as answering his need, in a search the goal of which he had not consciously identified when it began. From this point the painting process becomes directed by the nature of the particular image. The title 'Trophy (Anger, Reverie)' was conceived as a description of Le Brun's painting process, in which each successive 'skin' of imagery constitutes a discovery or 'trophy', an achievement which can then turn to frustration before he realises, as in a 'reverie', what form the succeeding image must take.

For many years at the outset of his career, images in Le Brun's work had only a secret life. In his abstract paintings he used representational images covertly. An aspect of which Le Brun is conscious in the discrete horizontal bands of paint in 'Dream, Think, Speak' and similar works is the way their discontinuity breaks up the surface, so that the viewer's imagination is working all the time on the paint and on the possible implications of any mark in terms of imagery. These bands of paint descend from the oblong slabs in paintings he made when a student at Chelsea – slabs which (as with their successors) he tried to make expressive in themselves, and which overlaid figurative images previously painted beneath. Commenting on this passage in draft, Le Brun wrote to the compiler on 7 April 1986 that:

> The suppression of the image was less to do with the 'climate' than with the question of what was then the nature of risk, because I saw that the recognised image was now the carrier of openness and doubt in contradiction to the accepted wisdom for which it represented an understood and conventional meaning.
>
> The roles suddenly reversed, a new and open place, a 'region' of images, broke out ahead.
>
> Of course this is in retrospect, and at the time was immensely confusing, for to go on towards paradox seemed not only potentially disastrous but also required the invention of an almost Byzantine technique to hold the layering of opposites within an overall form that held the Gestalt and spoke with a timeless lack of an eccentricity – a form that seemed entirely natural ... The only method that seemed possible was to embody experience or sense in the structuring, not in the image, and yet *necessarily employing the image.*

The strong and longstanding element of ambiguity or elusiveness in Le Brun's imagery is at the heart of its nature. As it does not start from a particular image, each of his paintings lacks the particular kind of focus possessed even by pictures which abstract *from* a given motif. Rather, in each picture Le Brun is working towards something which, while in one sense it has always been there, like a buried archetype, and demands to be given representational form, is at the same time not only an image but also an idea. Thus it does not have a given iconographic source. To restate known motifs in art (whether figurative or abstract) is not the point of Le Brun's work. Strong imagery and strong forms are essential to him, but they have to arise not from a detached or calculated process of construction but through their being discovered at the centre of the lived experience at once of the artist, of the culture and of the art of painting.

Thus while, for example, he admires greatly some of the major colour field and Minimal artists, he finds that in this respect the artists are somehow 'outside' the idea of the work they make, by contrast with artists he admires even more, such as Turner and Delacroix, who were, in this sense, in the middle of theirs. Like Turner and Delacroix, a Rothko or a Judd produce kinds of archetypal structure, but in the case of Turner or Delacroix such structure cannot be identified without reference to the whole aim and process of depicting, with which they were centrally concerned. This is why Le Brun's inspiration in painting is drawn predominantly from the Western European heritage. The account that has been given of his search for the subject, in each work afresh, and of its inseparability both from his own inner being and from the act of painting, offers interesting parallels with Abstract Expressionism, but for Le Brun the Abstract Expressionists too often stopped short of a necessary association of a painting with the recognisable image. While in Abstract Expressionist painting, as in Le Brun's, the nature of the final statement made by the painting depends on the finality of the last marks made, for Le Brun the intensity of the final configuration consists crucially in its also being the completion of an image. For him, the risk involved in the process lies not in the authenticity or otherwise of the statement made by painterly gesture alone but in the successful identification, through such gesture, of the image – a kind of engagement which for him is at once broader and more acute. Each picture is the record of a behavioural pattern associated, vitally, with the experience of painting 'in the midst of images'.

To Le Brun it is essential that the painter should take on everything and delegate nothing. This includes the heritage of great painting, with which the painter must engage because it has an insistent momentum of its own in which the painter participates almost by definition, and which is only understood by a recognition of the pivot, the hidden image at the heart of the tradition. The early 1970s were a key period in Le Brun's development. In the humiliating position (as he saw it) of painting at that time he found a spur to his conviction of the necessary fullness of painting's ambition. He resented both the excessive reductiveness of much painting of the time and the attacks that were being made on painting's metaphysical claims. His view, by contrast, was and remains that far from restricting himself to the material characteristics of painting (important though these are) the artist's task is to respond to the need of the culture for those open to images who, through the ancient art of painting, will represent deep-seated needs and desires.

Both the final title of the Tate's work and all the titles which Le Brun considered for it earlier (inscribed on the reverse, but in the end crossed out) relate to this conviction. The phrase 'Building, Dwelling, Thinking' is the title of an essay by Heidegger first published in 1954 in German and translated into English by Albert Hofstader in M. Heidegger, *Poetry, Language, Thought* (New York 1971, pp.145–61). For Le Brun this phrase suggested not so much a specific image as the sense of the clear centre of a place where thought is possible. (Another of the titles considered for this work, 'Clearing', bears a similar meaning. Le Brun used it for a painting exhibited at the Sperone Westwater Gallery, New York, in June 1986. He gave the title 'Passage' to a painting of 1984–5). It brought to mind for him the notions of classicism, the centre, permanence and the ideal. As this example shows, discussion of the specific motifs in the Tate's painting is an inadequate means of explaining their subject. In Le Brun's words, he aims in a work 'to bring in *every* association in order to pinpoint *one* association'. Integral to the subject of each work are the concepts of memory, centrality and permanence and the aim of reconnecting with the key sources of Western painting. Le Brun's search for a central archetype is recalled in another title he considered for the Tate's painting, 'Aram Nemus Vult'. This Latin phrase, which Le Brun found in Ezra Pound's *Pisan Cantos*, where it occurs three times in slightly different forms (*The Cantos of Ezra Pound*, 1960, pp.473, 512, 525), may be translated as 'The Grove Requires an Altar'. It is associated in Pound's work with his use of the pictogram 𓏲 . For Le Brun the key word in Pound's phrase is 'vult' (requires), for this carries the sense of the final image's absolute *necessity*. Le Brun observes that this sense distinguishes his work fundamentally from that of the Italian 'Trans-Avant-Garde' painters, with which his has on occasion been linked on account of a shared concern with associational imagery. On this passage, Le Brun comments in the letter already quoted that in the phrase:

> ARAM NEMUS VULT each is a key word: and 'requires' for VULT seems a polite translation. Also GROVE (NEMUS – Latin) must lead us back to HYLE – Greek – 'The Uncut Forest', thus material nature. The connection for me is therefore clear – out of the material nature, the uncut forest, the natural history of the canvas, the image (ARAM, The Altar) MUST rear itself.

Le Brun combined the 𓏲 pictogram with the image of a central horse's head in the drawing 'Untitled' 1983, graphite and watercolour, 75.8 × 61 cms. (repr. in col. in CDR Fine Art, catalogue 1, *Twentieth Century Works on Paper*, Spring/Summer 1986, p.47).

The title finally chose for the Tate's work, 'Dream, Think, Speak', was adapted by Le Brun from a sentence in the *Journal* of Delacroix, which he recollects as 'Colour dreams, thinks, speaks'. Like 'Trophy (Anger, Reverie)', this sequence of words suggests that of making something, and thus an assertion about the nature of the process of painting the picture which bears it as title. But Le Brun deliberately gave the words of the title the form of an exhortation *to the painting*. He felt that in observing that colour dreams, thinks and speaks, Delacroix implied that the life of the material itself was not metaphorical but real. In selecting as this picture's title his own version of Delacroix's words, he wished to affirm his belief that both the materials of this painting and painting itself were alive; and further, that by the act of addressing them he was demonstrating his conviction that, far from being separate phenomena, the painter, the painting and the life of images become, through the act of painting, a single thing. 'The image completely penetrates the painter, the painting and the surroundings.' Le Brun observes that while we are accustomed

to speak of painting's 'development', its 'growth', etc., in a metaphorical way, he works as if painting is literally a live thing. As much as the horses it depicts, the exhortation to painting to 'Dream, Think, Speak' is itself the subject of this painting.

Julio Le Parc b.1928

T 03774 **Virtual Forms in Various Situations, multiple** 1965

Construction of wood and aluminium $14\frac{3}{4} \times 23\frac{3}{4} \times 14\frac{1}{2}$ (375 × 600 × 370) with four double-sided printed cards, each 14 × 14 (355 × 355)
Not inscribed
Transferred from the Victoria and Albert Museum 1983

Prov: ...; purchased from Hanover Gallery by the Department of Circulation, Victoria and Albert Museum, 1966 (Circ.130–1966)

Repr: *Le Parc, 33 Biennale de Venise 1966*, Galerie Denise René (13, as 'Formes virtuelles à situations variées, 1965, reliefs à déplacement du spectateur')

This sculpture is a 'Multiple', published by the Galerie Denise René, Paris: different printed cards are slid into the central slot, to make reflections in the curved metal.

Jacques Lipchitz 1891–1973

For T 03397 and T 03479 to T 03534 the foundry inscriptions, and reproductions of casts in other materials in the books listed below, are recorded. Abbreviations used:

Arnason 1969   H.H. Arnason, *Jacques Lipchitz: Sketches in Bronze*, 1969

Lipchitz 1972   Jacques Lipchitz, *My Life in Sculpture*, 1972

Stott 1975   Deborah A. Stott, *Jacques Lipchitz and Cubism*, 1975 (reprinted 1978)

Otterlo 1977   A.M. Hammacher, *Lipchitz in Otterlo*, Rijksmuseum Kröller-Müller, Otterlo, 1977

Centre Pompidou 1978   Nicole Barbier, *Lipchitz: oeuvres de Jacques Lipchitz (1891–1973) dans les collections du Musée National d'Art Moderne*, Paris, 1978

Arizona 1982   *Jacques Lipchitz. Sketches and Models in the collection of Arizona Museum of Art*, Tucson, Arizona. Introduction and catalogue by Peter Bermingham, 1982

T 03397   **Sculpture** 1915–16

Limestone $38\frac{1}{2} \times 11 \times 7\frac{1}{8}$ (980 × 280 × 180)
Inscribed 'J *Lipchitz*/16' on base and '#137' in red paint under base
Purchased from Marlborough Fine Art (London) Ltd. (Grant-in-Aid) with the assistance of the Friends of the Tate Gallery, Mrs T. Steinberg and the Rayne Foundation 1982

Prov: Estate of the artist
Exh: ? Galerie Léonce Rosenberg, Galerie de l'Effort Moderne, Paris, 1920 (probably); ? *Jacques Lipchitz à la Renaissance*, La Renaissance, Paris, June 1930 (16. Sculpture (pierre) 1916) (perhaps); ? *Les Maîtres de l'Art Indépendant 1895–1937*, Petit Palais, Paris, June–October 1937 (3. Figure (1916) Pierre) (perhaps); ? *Jacques Lipchitz*, Galerie Maeght, Paris, 1946 (9. Sculpture (mi-corps) Pierre 1916) (perhaps); *The Essential Cubism 1907–1920*, Tate Gallery, April–July 1983 (211, as 1915)
Lit: Robert Goldwater, *Lipchitz*, 1958, n.p. (as 'Standing Half Figure (1915)'); Douglas Cooper, *The Cubist Epoch*, 1971, p.250; Lipchitz 1972, p.32; Otterlo 1977, n.p. (under 1915, as 'Standing Figure'); Stott 1975, pp.19, 234, 272 fig.2 (bronze), 257 (22 as 'Half-Standing Figure, 1915, bronze, 28″h)
Repr: Maurice Raynal, *Lipchitz*, 1920, n.p.; Roger Vitrac, *Jacques Lipchitz*, 1929 (27, as 'Sculpture (pierre) 1916')

The first cubist stone carvings by Jacques Lipchitz were made in 1916. No more than a few were carved by Lipchitz himself, although he always supervised them, and all were made from original models in clay. In the winter of 1916 he made a contract, his first, with the dealer Léonce Rosenberg, and this enabled him to employ a stone carver as an assistant. Some of the carvings were made after models of the previous year, and the style of all these sculptures is a development of that of the wooden constructions of 1915. The date cut into this carving has been read as '15', but although it is not absolutely clear it is more likely to be '16'. It is not known when Lipchitz made this inscription, which is not on the stone in an early photograph from the Fonds Léonce Rosenberg (Caisse Nationale des Monuments Historiques et des sites, Paris), and it may refer only to the making of the stone, and not the model from which it was copied.

In his autobiography Lipchitz makes clear that these 'abstract architectural sculptures' needed 'the architectural mass of stone' (Lipchitz, op.cit., p.33), and that he had always intended them to be carved. The Tate Gallery's 'sculpture' is not reproduced in this book, but as it is the only such piece with a circular part as the base it is probably that described on p.34:

> The next several pieces, from 1915 and 1916, illustrate what I mean. The first of these is a half-standing figure which rises from a circular base that is like the top of a table at which he is sitting. This and the others that followed it were made in clay, then in stone, and later in bronze. All of these, in the construction of interlocking planes, are developments from the earlier demountable figures. In them I was definitely building up and composing the idea of a human figure from abstract sculptural elements of line, plane, and volume; of mass

contrasted with void completely realized in three dimensions.

This group of carvings are the most abstract of Lipchitz's sculptures, and in early reproductions are titled merely 'sculpture', yet all are of the figure. In the conversations of 1968–70 recorded by Deborah Stott he described the parts of the body in two of these sculptures, and in the passage quoted above he describes the Tate Gallery's sculpture as a figure seated behind a table. The alternative title for this of 'Half Standing Figure' was first published in an exhibition catalogue of 1957 (*Jacques Lipchitz*, Otto Gerson Gallery, New York, March 1957, '45. Half-Standing Figure. Bronze, 1916. 39"H'. It is not reproduced, but no other sculpture of this date is this size) and is probably a translation of the French 'sculpture (mi-corps)', used, for instance, by the Galerie Maeght in 1946. This sculpture is one of his most abstract within this group, and the only one to incorporate a cone, a shape associated with wooden or paper constructions.

It is not certain that this carving was included in the exhibitions in Paris listed above, as the titles are not explicit. The first record of it is in the book by Maurice Raynal of 1920, and since this was published at the time of Léonce Rosenberg's exhibition it is likely that it was included in it. The photographs in this book, although not titled, are stated to be in chronological order from 1915 to 1919 inclusive, and the reproduction of this carving is the second of twenty (the first is made of wood).

The plaster of this sculpture belongs to the Kröller-Müller Museum (Otterlo 1977, n.p., repr. as 'Standing Figure (1915)'). There are several drawings by Lipchitz related to this and the similar carvings of 1916. The tallest part of the sculpture was at one time broken off, and was repaired under the direction of Lipchitz by George Koras in New York.

T 03479 **Portrait of Gertrude Stein** 1938

Terracotta and pigment 12 × 10 × 8 (305 × 259 × 203)
Inscribed 'J Lipchitz' on back of neck
Presented by the Lipchitz Foundation 1982

Lit: Bert van Bork, *Jacques Lipchitz, The Artist at Work*, 1966, p.129 (bronze); Arnason 1969, repr. 124 (bronze); Lipchitz 1972, pp.63 and 140, repr. 127 (bronze)

Lipchitz made portrait heads of Gertrude Stein on two occasions, first in 1920–1 and again in 1938. The plaster of the earlier head is in the collection of the Kröller-Müller Museum (Otterlo, 1977, repr., n.p.). In 1938 he made two similar terracottas of the same size, again of

the head alone, the Tate Gallery's and another now in the collection of the University of Arizona Museum of Art (Arizona, 1982, no.44).

A number of years later, in 1938, I met Gertrude after a long interval and found that she had lost a great deal of weight. She looked now like a shrivelled old rabbi, with a little rabbi's cap on her head. I was so struck by the contrast that I asked if I could make another portrait of her. I made two different sketches, one with the cap and one without. She preferred the one without the cap, perhaps because it looked more feminine, but I liked the other one better. I did not carry the second portrait beyond the sketch stage because of the interruption of the Second World War, although I made a variant of it for a university in Houston, Texas, I think after that war. I liked these later sketches very much, particularly that with the cap. They have a strongly lifelike appeal. The massive, self-confident Buddha has become a tired and rather tragic old woman (Lipchitz, loc.cit.).

This portrait was not a commission, and Lipchitz had made few portraits since the early 1920s, apart from the imaginary head of Géricault. It anticipates the style of the realistic heads of artists and patrons which Lipchitz began in New York in 1942.

The terracotta has been prepared for display, with white colour brushed into the crevices of the surface. There is a repair in plaster over the figure's right ear.

was to enable him to carry out the tasks set by Zeus before he would be allowed to marry his daughter. According to Lipchitz Pegasus represents 'the wild forces of nature', which are captured and used by the intelligence of man. This is related to the origin of law, and so appropriate for Columbia School of Law, since correct behaviour follows also from the observation of nature (Lipchitz does not, in his autobiography, make the more obvious parallel between Bellerophon's taming of Pegasus and the restraints of law on the naturally wild nature of man, and his reference to the observation of nature puts the subject into the context of the morality of the artist's life and the rules of art, derived from nature).

The completed monument at Columbia University was unveiled after Lipchitz's death, in November 1977.

T 03480　Sketch for Bellerophon Taming Pegasus 1964

Plaster 20¾ × 16 × 5 (522 × 407 × 127)
Not inscribed
Presented by the Lipchitz Foundation 1982
Lit:　Lipchitz 1972, pp.xxxii–xxxiii, 168 and 213–14; Albert Elsen, *Duets of Line and Shadow*, Art News, LXXVII, March 1978, pp.64, 66

Lipchitz was commissioned in 1964 to make a sculpture to be placed over the entrance of the Columbia University School of Law, New York. This new building had then been designed but not constructed, and Lipchitz made his first maquettes, of which this plaster is one, after studying a model and talking to the architect, Max Abramovitz. Lipchitz chose the subject, on the basis first of all of the shape needed to contrast with the building, and then for a subject which included a horse (Lipchitz, loc.cit.). He had previously made different sculptures of Bellerophon in 1929 (a 'transparent') and in 1944–50 ('Pegasus Giving Birth to the Muses').

Four other maquettes of the same date, cast in bronze, are illustrated in the autobiography (reprs. 195a–d). The Modern Art Foundry, New York, were at this time casting Lipchitz's collection of his own maquettes, and were therefore ready to preserve an unusually large number of his studies for this commission. Another cast of the Tate Gallery's plaster, slightly damaged, is in the collection of the Kröller-Müller Museum (Otterlo 1979, n.p., repr.).

Bellerophon is shown capturing the flying horse Pegasus by tying a rope around his neck. In Lipchitz's account (which varies from the usual Greek myth) this

T 03481　Sketch for Government of the People 1967–8

Plaster, coated with glue 34 × 10¼ × 10¼ (864 × 260 × 260)
Not inscribed
Presented by the Lipchitz Foundation 1982
Lit:　Lipchitz 1972, p.222 and repr. 200 (as '51"h'); A.M. Hammacher, *Jacques Lipchitz*, 1975, repr. 161

This group was designed by Lipchitz in response to a commission for the Muncipal Plaza in Philadelphia. He was asked to choose his own subject, and the title was only given by the committee after seeing a sketch (probably the plaster in the collection of the Kröller-Müller Museum (Otterlo 1977, n.p., repr.), which is smaller than the Tate Gallery's and better fits Lipchitz's description of the upper tier as a flag):

There was a new commission for a monumental sculpture in 1967 to be placed in the Municipal Plaza in Philadelphia. The Plaza involves in addition to the City Hall, a modern building and a number of heterogeneous nineteenth-century buildings; the original City Hall, nineteenth-century Victorian, is very interesting with the sculptural decorations done by Alexander Milne Calder, the grandfather of the sculptor Alexander Calder. So it has been quite a job to create a work that would unite these different buildings. I was not given a specific commission or theme but simply asked to make a monumental work. I did a sketch which was sort of a totem pole. At the base there is a couple, and then another couple, and this develops in groups to a climax of the Philadelphia city flag. So those concerned entitled it Government of the People. There have been many changes since the original design. In my studio I have several photographic montages which show the site with the sketch superimposed, a technique I had never used before, but which has helped me a great deal. It is on this that I am working with my assistants, the two young sculptors (Lipchitz, loc.cit.).

its reproduction in Bert van Bork's book of 1966, but otherwise this is presumably an original plaster of 1912.

The structure of this composition resembles 'Our Tree of Life' (T 03491) in the way the upper group is supported. Three pairs of nudes are represented, in three tiers: at the base a couple are touching heads and hands; at the centre two nudes turn in a spiral, reaching upwards; at the top, designed to be seen only from below, the figures are indistinct but lie horizontally.

The completed bronze was installed in Philadelphia in 1976. A photograph of the full size plaster in the foundry in Italy is reproduced in *Lipchitz, Sculpture and Drawings*, Marlborough Fine Art, May 1983, opp. p.22 (it is clearer in this that the group at the top are reclining figures).

T 03482   **Pregnant Woman** 1912

> Plaster, coated with shellac $25\frac{1}{4} \times 5\frac{3}{4} \times 5$ ($642 \times 146 \times 122$)
> Inscribed '13' under base in red paint
> Presented by the Lipchitz Foundation 1982
>
> *Lit:*   Bert van Bork, *Jacques Lipchitz. The Artist at Work*, 1966, p.88; Lipchitz 1972, p.11 and repr. fig.6 (bronze); Stott 1975, pp.186 and 256 (2, bronze)

The artist associated this sculpture with the 'Woman with Gazelles' group of the same year, although it was an independent sculpture.

There is no record of a bronze cast before the reproduction in Lipchitz's autobiography. The figure's hair appears to have been remodelled at some time before

T 03483   **The Rape of Europa** 1938

> Painted plaster $16 \times 23\frac{1}{2} \times 13\frac{1}{4}$ ($407 \times 597 \times 337$)
> Not inscribed
> Presented by the Lipchitz Foundation 1982
>
> *Lit:*   Lipchitz 1972, p.140

A bronze cast of this sculpture was included in Lipchitz's retrospective exhibition at the Galerie Maeght, Paris, in 1946 (66 or 67, repr.). There is another version the same size as this and almost identical, the plaster of which is in the collection of the Kröller-Müller Museum (Otterlo 1972, repr., n.p.) and Lipchitz mentions a third version of this date in his autobiography.

He took up the subject again in America in 1941, but with the underlying theme of Europa killing the bull Hitler, which is not implied in the 1938 versions.

... I also made three small sculptures of the 'Rape of Europa'. The latter derived from my continually increasing interest in classic myth, and also it had a personal association. All of my sculpture derives from something in my life, a desire or a dream. In the bull who carries off Europa and swims with her to Crete, the appendages at the back suggest a fishlike form. In my collection there is an extremely rare bronze Coptic piece in which the bull takes on different aquatic shapes. I think that I may have been influenced by this. The general forms of the bull and Europa probably derive from the earlier bull and condor, although, as is so frequently the case with my sculpture, the conflict and terror of the earlier version is here transformed into erotic love. I used the theme of the 'Rape of Europa' later in a quite different context, the Europa as a symbol for Europe and the bull as Hitler, with Europe killing Hitler with a dagger. This reverses the concept to one of terror, whereas in the original sculptures of Europa the entire theme is tender and erotic love; the bull is caressing Europa with his tongue (Lipchitz, loc.cit.).

The plaster was painted at the Modern Art Foundry at New York, in a dark colour to match the black patina of the bronze. The plaster base was probably cast at a later date to the original plaster of 1938, and added to it.

T 03484 The Joy of Orpheus II 1945–6

Plaster, partly coated with shellac
$20\frac{1}{2} \times 13\frac{1}{2} \times 10$ ($521 \times 342 \times 254$)
Not inscribed
Presented by the Lipchitz Foundation 1982

Lit: Bert van Bork, *Jacques Lipchitz, The Artist at Work*, 1966, repr. p.182 (bronze); Lipchitz 1972, p.168

A bronze cast of this sculpture was exhibited at the Buchholz Gallery, New York, in 1946 (*Jacques Lipchitz*, March–April 1946, 20). Also included was 'The Joy of Orpheus I' 1949 (19, repr.), which is the same composition and size, but has thinner shapes, cut to an edge.

Lipchitz described the subject as a woman seated in a man's lap, the whole composition also resembling the shape of a harp:

Another piece I made before going to Europe was the 'Joy of Orpheus', 1945. It has to do with the love of my wife. The woman is sitting on the man's lap. They are happy and her arm is raised in the air; and

all of it takes on the form of a harp. I think of it as a very interesting sculpture, poetic and beautiful. It comes so directly from my emotions, although everything I do comes from emotions (Lipchitz, loc.cit.).

A large drawing of the subject was reproduced in 1944 and dated to the preceding year ('Le bonheur d'Orphée', tempera, 25×19 ins. Curt Valentin, *The Drawings of Jacques Lipchitz*, 1944).

The plaster is probably a cast of 1945–6. It has been repaired with new plaster at two of the feet, probably after damage caused by taking a mould. The outlines of the repair differ slightly from those of the bronze reproduced by van Bork.

T 03485 Spanish Servant Girl 1915

Plaster $35 \times 9 \times 5\frac{1}{2}$ ($889 \times 228 \times 139$)
Inscribed 'Lipchitz', moulded at back of base, with a thumbprint
Presented by the Lipchitz Foundation 1982

Lit: Stott 1975, p.256 (17, bronze)

The 'Spanish Servant Girl' is not recorded before Lipchitz's exhibition at the Marlborough-Gerson Gallery, New York, in 1968, which included a bronze cast, dated in the catalogue 1915 (*Lipchitz. The Cubist Period 1913–1920*, March–April 1968, 14, repr.).

Lipchitz made four sculptures of standing Spanish figures, all about 30 ins. high, in 1914–15, of which this is the latest and the most advanced stylistically. The rigid pose, with hand on hip and face in profile, is similar to that of the 'Toreador' (1914–15, T 03487) and

T 03485

the 'Woman with Braids' (1914). The figure is not nude and the flat pieces attached to the arms and legs represent the flounces of the costume. It was made in Paris after his return from Spain, and is a reworking of his Spanish figures in a different style.

The figure is similar to the 'Detachable Dancer' of 1915 (private collection, New York) which is made of flat wooden pieces screwed and glued together. The original is the 'Demountable Figure: Dancer' (1915, painted wood) in the collection of Mrs Lipchitz (exhibited in *Qu'est-ce que la sculpture moderne*, Musée National d'Art Moderne, Centre Pompidou, Paris July–October 1986 (37, repr.)). The plaster was not, however, cast directly from this construction, since: a) it shows no sign of the wood grain b) the signature and thumbprint at the base are moulded, and have been transferred from another original c) no casts have been taken from it, as would be the case were it an old cast and the source of the bronze. The flat pieces on the wooden construction are removable, and differ from those in the Tate Gallery's plaster. It is likely that the bronze exhibited in 1968 was cast indirectly from the construction, perhaps via another plaster cast. The flat pieces were modelled anew in order to make the bronze, and were added to the wax. The Tate Gallery's plaster was then cast from the bronze as a record of the completed work. The Marlborough-Gerson catalogue of 1968 states that the bronze was made in an editon of only two, although Lipchitz's practice was otherwise to cast an edition of seven.

Two drawings of this subject by Lipchitz, undated but labelled in the exhibition '1914', were shown at Marlborough Fine Art in 1978 (*Jacques Lipchitz, Sculpture and Drawings from the Cubist Epoch*), October–November 1978, not catalogued).

The plaster is missing two small pieces broken from the left arm.

T 03486 **Bather III** 1917–18

Plaster 29 × 10 × 10½ (737 × 254 × 267)
Not inscribed
Presented by the Lipchitz Foundation 1982

Lit: Lipchitz 1972, pp.46–7; Stott 1975, pp.134–6, 257 (35, stone) and 285–9, reprs. 27–9 (stone and bronze)

The stone carving of this sculpture, dated 1918, is in the collection of the Barnes Foundation, Merion, USA, and was purchased from the artist by Dr Barnes in Paris in 1922 (Maurice Raynal, *Lipchitz*, 1920, n.p., repr.). The original plaster belongs to the Musée National d'Art Moderne, Paris (Centre Pompidou 1978, 11).

There are no sculptures specifically titled 'Bather I' and 'Bather II', and the present title for this sculpture was first used at the Marlborough-Gerson Gallery in 1968 in an exhibition which included two other 'Bathers' of 1917 (*Lipchitz. The Cubist Period 1913–1930*, 26, 28 and 29). This plaster is of poor quality, and has not been finished, and was cast during the 1960s from a mould used to cast a wax.

T 03487 **Toreador** 1914–15

Plaster, painted 33¼ × 10½ × 10
(845 × 267 × 254)
Not inscribed
Presented by the Lipchitz Foundation 1982

Lit: Irene Patai, *Encounters, The Life of Jacques Lipchitz*, 1961, pp.143–4, 152–3 and 156; Bert van Bork, *Jacques Lipchitz, The Artist at Work*, 1966, repr. p.90 (as 'bronze'); Lipchitz 1972, pp.18–19, 23 and repr.13 (bronze); Stott 1975, p.256 (14, bronze)

Lipchitz left Paris for a long visit to Spain and Majorca in 1914, with Diego Rivera and both their families. In Madrid he became enthusiastic about bullfighting, and became a friend, according to Patai, of the toreador Joselito, who posed for this sculpture. Lipchitz and Rivera, although neither of them French citizens and so not liable for military service, were unable to return to France at the outbreak of war in August and remained in Spain until the New Year. Lipchitz finished the sculpture in Paris in early 1915.

An undated drawing by Lipchitz of this figure shows the head facing the front, and was probably made during the modelling of the sculpture (*Jacques Lipchitz, Small Sculptures, Maquettes and Drawings 1915–1972*, Marlborough Gallery Inc., New York, March 1979, repr. p.5).

A bronze cast of the 'Toreador' was shown in Lipchitz's retrospective exhibition at the Galerie de la Renaissance in Paris in 1930. Patai records that three of the Spanish sculptures were cast in bronze by Valsuani in Paris in about 1915, and so T 03487 was probably the model for one of these casts. This plaster is presumably an original of 1915. Its surface was cleaned and painted with shellac and pigment in the 1970s.

T 03488   Seated Man with Clarinet I
1920

Plaster coated with shellac $30\frac{1}{2} \times 11\frac{1}{2} \times 11$ (775 × 293 × 280)
Inscribed on reverse at base 'JL – V – 20' moulded into the plaster, and '96' on top of base at front, in pencil
Presented by the Lipchitz Foundation 1982

Lit: Stott 1975, 58 (bronze, as '1919')
Repr: *L'Esprit Nouveau*, 1920, p.182

The plaster of a different version of this, 'Seated Man with Clarinet II' is in the collection of the University of Arizona Museum of Art (Arizona 1982, 1, repr, $30\frac{1}{2}$ ins. high). It differs from the Tate Gallery plaster throughout, particularly in the shape of the feet, which are pointed. Bronze casts of both sculptures were exhibited in *Jacques Lipchitz*, Stedelijk Museum, Amsterdam, March–May 1958 (31 and 32).

The plaster is presumably an original of 1920. The signature was transferred in the mould from the clay. A stone carving is not recorded, although a carving of the plaster at Arizona is illustrated in the catalogue *Les Maîtres de l'Art Indépendant*, Petit Palais, Paris, June–October 1937 (6, as 'L'Homme Assis').

T 03489   Song of Songs   1945

Plaster, coated with shellac and painted $5\frac{1}{2} \times 8\frac{1}{2} \times 3\frac{1}{2}$ (139 × 216 × 89)
Not inscribed
Presented by the Lipchitz Foundation 1982

Lit: Lipchitz 1972, pp.107–8 and 167

T 03489

A bronze cast, gilt, of this sculpture was exhibited at the Buchholz Gallery, New York in 1946 (*Jacques Lipchitz*, March–April 1946, 16, repr.). The exhibition also included a larger bronze, 20½ ins. high, of the same composition but with much smoother shapes. T 03532 is a development of this subject.

The subject is King Solomon playing a harp. The general appearance of the sculpture is reminiscent of the later version of 'Prometheus Strangling the Vulture' (1943) in which the hero grasps the vulture with both hands, his cloak fluttering behind him so as to make the piece horizontal. Lipchitz evidently saw this further possibility of changing the mood of the subject within the same configuration. It also in part represents the sculptor working his material, and it was among a list of subjects described by the artist as of an 'encounter ... an encounter between the artist, the material, and the forms he is using' (Lipchitz, op. cit., p.108).

The plaster is an original cast of 1945.

T 03490 **Picador, Bas Relief** *c.* 1932

> Terracotta with plaster back 20 × 25½ × 4
> (508 × 647 × 102)
> Not inscribed
> Presented by the Lipchitz Foundation
> 1982

A similar terracotta bas relief of 'Bull and Condor' is in the collection of the University of Arizona Museum of Art (Arizona 1982, 12, repr., 14¾ × 19⅛ × 1⅜ ins.). Neither was included in the collection of small bronzes published by Arnason in 1969, but the Arizona relief is mentioned by Lipchitz in his autobiography, where it is dated 1933 (Lipchitz 1972, p.128). It is possible that they were included in Lipchitz's exhibition at the Galerie Maeght, Paris, in 1946 (catalogue nos. 53–5 were each titled 'Bas–Relief. Terre cuite. 1932'). A bronze cast of the Tate Gallery relief is in the collection of the Israel Museum, Jerusalem (Martin Weyl, *Jacques*

Lipchitz, Bronze Sketches, 1971, 100, repr., as 'man on horseback fighting bull, 1932').

Lipchitz had not used bullfighting subjects before this since 1915, but there is an association with the 'Bull and Condor' subjects of 1932 (see T 03513).

T 03491 **Sketch for Our Tree of Life** 1962

> Plaster, coated with shellac and pigment
> 32½ × 10 × 10½ (825 × 254 × 267)
> Not inscribed
> Presented by the Lipchitz Foundation
> 1982
> *Lit:* Lipchitz 1972, pp.198–9; *the Jacques Lipchitz 'tree of life'*, Hadassah University Hospital, Jerusalem, n.d.

See entry on T 03525. A mould has been taken from

T 03491, but no bronze cast has been illustrated. The plaster itself was cast in two pieces, and repaired with fresh plaster at the joins. It differs only in detail from the complete sculpture of T 03525.

Müller Museum, Otterlo, from the Lipchitz Foundation.

The shape that makes the right-hand shoulder and knee of this figure is repeated from the earlier 'Sculpture 1916' (T 03397).

T 03492 Sculpture 1916

Plaster, coated with shellac 46 × 14½ × 13½ (1169 × 368 × 342)
Not inscribed
Presented by the Lipchitz Foundation, 1982
Lit: Stott 1975, pp.129–31, 237–8 (transcript of tape), 243–4, 257 (27) and repr. 23 (stone)

The stone carving of this sculpture, formerly in the collection of the Norton Simon Museum of Art, Pasadena, is in a private collection, Dallas.

The sculpture was discussed at length by the artist on 14 August 1969 with Deborah Stott. He confirmed that he had started the carving himself, rather than asking his assistant to copy the model. The subject is a woman, seated with her legs crossed, and the tall block is a part of the head – 'to give value to the head, the back of the head, you know' (op.cit. p.238) – and not a raised arm.

This plaster was cast from the stone carving and has the same detailed surface pattern. There is a network of pencil crosses over the shellac surface, which mark 'points' for another carved copy to be made. This copy is not known, but may be connected with the three marble enlargements made in the 1960s from sculptures of 1919–21 and which are now on loan to the Kröller-

T 03493 Sketch for Enterprise 1953

Plaster coated with shellac and pigment 11¾ × 13 × 6 (218 × 330 × 152)
Inscribed '#1' incised into top of base, and '218' incised and '396 4 off' in black paint under base
Presented by the Lipchitz Foundation 1982
Lit: Arnason 1969, repr.150 (bronze); Lipchitz 1972, p.187

See entry on T 00320 (Ronald Alley, *The Tate Gallery's Collection of Modern Art*, 1981). Arnason reproduces two other small maquettes of this subject. The commission for 'The Spirit of Enterprise' overlapped both with the fire in Lipchitz's New York studio on 5 January 1952 and with the period after the death of Curt Valentin in 1955 when he had no dealer, and these maquettes were not exhibited at the time they were made.

The plaster was presumably cast in 1953, and has been painted light red. It was dismembered for casting, probably at the Modern Art Foundry, New York, in the early 1960s. It was repaired with fresh plaster, and not repainted.

[237]

and he made no other such references to artists. His other portraits of 1932–3 have not been published, but the Géricault head is much less idealised than the 1920s portraits, and in the sculpture he exaggerated the lack of symmetry between left and right, and the sloping jaw of the painter.

T 03494   Géricault 1933

Terracotta $9\frac{1}{2}$ × 7 × 8 (241 × 177 × 202)
Inscribed '13' inside neck, in black paint
Presented by the Lipchitz Foundation
1982

Lit: Irene Patai, *Encounters: The Life of Jacques Lipchitz*, 1961, p.262; Arnason 1969, repr.104 (bronze); Lipchitz 1972, p.128 and repr.115 (bronze)

Arnason reproduces four different bronze heads of Géricault by Lipchitz, including this one, all studies for a large bronze 24 ins. high of the same year (A.M. Hammacher, *Jacques Lipchitz*, 1975, repr. p.108). A plaster from the Tate Gallery's terracotta is in the collection of the University of Arizona Museum of Art (Arizona 1982, 43, repr.).

Lipchitz wrote that he intended this portrait to be as accurate a likeness as possible:

> During 1932 and 1933 I returned to portraiture, of which the most interesting to me was the portrait of Géricault. I have always been a great admirer of this painter, a genius who died young, and I have some paintings of his. There exists a death mask of Géricault of which I acquired a cast. I wanted to make the portrait as realistic as possible, so I checked documents and existing portraits of him. This was my homage to a great artist whom I loved very much. I think it is a good portrait. Even the Museum at Rouen, which has a lot of his works because Géricault was born there, bought a copy. My American dealer, Curt Valentin, bequeathed me a small sculpture by Géricault of a fawn and a nymph (Lipchitz, loc.cit.).

This imaginary portrait is unusual in Lipchitz's work,

T 03495   David and Goliath, on a Column 1933

Terracotta 13 × $5\frac{1}{4}$ × $5\frac{1}{4}$ (330 × 133 × 133)
Inscribed 'J Lipchitz 1933' incised under base, and '806 5 off' in black paint, both under base
Presented by the Lipchitz Foundation
1982

Lit: Arnason 1969, repr.100 (bronze); Lipchitz 1972, pp.127 and 131–2

See entry on T 03515. Lipchitz (loc.cit.) referred to this as the 'final sketch'. The composition differs slightly from the preceding plaster, as here David places both feet against Goliath's back and pulls himself off the ground.

T 03496   Head and Hand 1932

Terracotta $7\frac{3}{4}$ × $6\frac{1}{4}$ × $3\frac{3}{4}$ (197 × 158 × 95)
Inscribed 'Lipchitz' incised under base, and '427' in black under base
Presented by the Lipchitz Foundation
1982

Lit: Arnason 1969, repr.74 (bronze); Lipchitz 1972, pp.115 and 124–5

This terracotta is similar to the 'Head, Bust and Arms' T 03498 and 'Bust of Woman' T 03504 of the same year, and both are part of a numerous group of such small studies.

Lit: Arnason 1969, repr.121 (bronze); Lipchitz 1972, pp.136–40

See entry on T 03500. These two 'Prometheus' maquettes are both of the first idea for a commission from the 'Palais de la Découverte' at the Grand Palais, Paris, and show the reclining figure of Prometheus safeguarding the flame with one hand, while with the other holding back a vulture.

T 03498 Head, Bust and Arms 1932

Terracotta $7\frac{3}{8} \times 6\frac{1}{2} \times 3\frac{3}{4}$ (187 × 165 × 95)
Inscribed under base '979 6 off' in black ink
Presented by the Lipchitz Foundation 1982

Lit: Arnason 1969, repr.78 (bronze); Lipchitz 1972, pp.115 and 124–5

See entry on T 03496.

T 03497 Study for Prometheus 1936

Terracotta, partly coated with shellac
$10\frac{1}{8} \times 9 \times 4\frac{1}{2}$ (260 × 227 × 114)
Inscribed 'J Lipchitz' incised under base and '4' and '421' in black paint under base.
Presented by the Lipchitz Foundation 1982

T 03499 Seated Bather 1916–17

Plaster, coated with shellac and pigment
29 × $9\frac{3}{4}$ × 10 (736 × 247 × 254)
Inscribed '742' incised into top of base and 'SEATED BATHER/17' (partly illegible) in black paint under base
Presented by the Lipchitz Foundation 1982

Lit: Lipchitz, 1972, pp.42–5 and repr.30 (bronze); Stott 1975, pp.131–3 and 257 (30, stone)

T 03499

The stone carving of this sculpture is recorded in 1975 in a private collection in New York (A.M. Hammacher, *Jacques Lipchitz*, 1975, repr.72). It was first reproduced in the monograph of 1920 by Maurice Raynal.

Lipchitz describes this work in his autobiography, pointing out that it was more effectively three-dimensional than were his preceding cubist sculptures, which had been strictly vertical and horizontal. As a result there was a more emotional feeling to the figure, 'a brooding quality emphasized by the shadowed face framed in the heavy, hanging locks of hair' (op.cit., p.45). In conversation with Stott he dated it late 1916 or early 1917 (op.cit., p.131).

The coating of shellac is terracotta colour, and has been prepared for exhibition, although it is now chipped through to the plaster in many places. The plaster is presumably an original of 1916–17.

T 03500 **Study for Prometheus** 1936

Painted plaster $7\frac{1}{2} \times 9 \times 3\frac{1}{2}$
(190 × 228 × 890)
Not inscribed
Presented by the Lipchitz Foundation 1982
Lit: Arnason 1969, repr.122 (bronze); Lipchitz 1972, pp.136–40 and repr.122 (bronze)

See entry on T 03497. The terracotta of this sculpture is in the collection of the Musée National d'Art Moderne, Paris (Centre Pompidou 1978, 35, repr.). The Tate Gallery's plaster does not show marks of a cast having been taken from it, and is likely to date from the early 1960s.

T 03501 **Figure** 1915

Plaster $19\frac{3}{4} \times 5\frac{3}{8} \times 4$ (502 × 136 × 101)
Not inscribed
Presented by the Lipchitz Foundation 1982
Lit: Arnason 1969, repr.2 (bronze); Lipchitz 1972, p.37 and repr.26 (bronze); Stott 1975, p.257 (26, bronze)

A bronze cast of this sculpture was shown at the exhibition of *Jacques Lipchitz: 157 Small Bronze Sketches* at the Otto Gerson Gallery in New York in 1963 (2). It was the only cubist sculpture included, perhaps because of its small size and status as a study for a larger work. Lipchitz referred to it as 'a small sketch that still has much of the machine world of my demountables' (Lipchitz, loc.cit).

The Modern Art Foundry in New York, which cast the bronzes for this exhibition, have a polaroid photograph of the original of this sculpture (probably also a plaster), marked on the reverse:

Figure 1915 19" high 7 / 6 off 1 plaster / 722/
Billed 5/4/64/ 19" H – if he adds base add 5

The Tate Gallery plaster was therefore cast in 1964 from one of the moulds of the bronzes cast for the Otto Gerson Gallery exhibition. The surface has not been cleaned, and the sculpture was not intended for exhibition.

Bronze casts have been exhibited with the title 'Half Standing Figure', first at the Marlborough-Gerson Gallery in 1968 (*Lipchitz. The Cubist Period*, March–April 1968 (20)).

T 03502　**First Study for Pastoral**　1934

> Terracotta on a plaster base, varnished
> 4¾ × 5 × 3¼ (120 × 127 × 82)
> Inscribed '104' in black paint under base
> Presented by the Lipchitz Foundation 1982
>
> *Lit:*　Arnason 1969, repr.105 (bronze)

The sculpture represents the nose and eyebrows of a head, looking rather like a pig, with a horizontal shape below the nose, which in other sculptures is more clearly seen as a clenched hand. There is a connection with the fragmentary heads of 1932, such as 'Head and Hands', T 03496, but the title is unexplained.

A large, undated drawing of the subject is reproduced in Lipchitz 1972 (repr.110) as 'Pastorale, 1933', and a similar drawing was reproduced much earlier as '1942' (in Curt Valentin, *The Drawings of Jacques Lipchitz*, 1944, as 'Pastorale 1942'). There is no connection with the sculpture 'Pastorale, 1947', which has two figures (A.M. Hammacher, *Jacques Lipchitz*, 1975, repr.132).

The foundry notes were written on a label tied onto the sculpture ('"Study for Pastoral"/6 off. make thick plate', with an indication that three of the casts had been made).

T 03503　**Reclining Figure**　1929

> Terracotta 6 × 10 × 4¾ (152 × 254 × 120)
> Not inscribed
> Presented by the Lipchitz Foundation 1982
>
> *Lit:*　Arnason 1969, repr.36 (bronze); Lipchitz 1972, p.103

The pose of this figure resembles the 'Reclining Nude with Guitar' (see T 00311), Lipchitz's major sculpture of 1928, but according to the sequence of his autobiography it follows this work. Another terracotta maquette, with a more naturalistic figure not punctured with holes, preceded it (Arnason 1969, repr.28 (bronze)).

The base is made of plaster. The foundry notes were written on a label tied onto the sculpture ('"Bigger Reclining Woman"/ 7 off. make plate', with an indication that three of the casts had been made.

T 03504　**Bust of a Woman**　1932

> Terracotta 7½ × 4¼ × 4¼ (190 × 108 × 108)
> Not inscribed
> Presented by the Lipchitz Foundation 1982
>
> *Lit:*　Arnason 1969, repr. 76 (bronze)

See entry on T 03496.

T 03504

that time, the 1930 'Figure' (85 ins. high). Lipchitz wrote in his autobiography that he enlarged this idea at the request of a patron, and he had not thought of such a change of scale when he made the terracottas.

This sketch represents a figure, although it also borrows from the idea of the abstract zigzag pedestal of the 1921 'Study for a Garden Statue' (T 03523). In one of the other terracottas this connection is clearer, and Lipchitz modelled a relief of figures within the 'head' part, implying that the remainder was a pedestal. The large sculpture 'Ploumanach', 1926, is also ambiguous in this way, and can either be seen as a single head and shoulders, or as a rock with a small figure on it.

T 03505 Sketch for a Figure 1926

Terracotta $8\frac{1}{2} \times 4\frac{1}{4} \times 1\frac{1}{2}$ (216 × 108 × 48)
Inscribed 'L' incised under base
Presented by the Lipchitz Foundation
1982

Lit: Bert van Bork, *Jacques Lipchitz, The Artist at Work*, 1966, repr.157 (as 'Maquettes for Figure, 1926', with two other terracottas); Arnason 1969, repr.24 (bronze); Lipchitz 1972, pp.89 ff.; Stott 1975, p.174

This is the earliest of three small terracottas, later used as studies for one of Lipchitz's largest sculptures up to

T 03506 The Snuffer 1930

Painted plaster 7 × 6 × 6 (177 × 152 × 152)
Inscribed '40' in blue paint inside the hollow cast, twice
Presented by the Lipchitz Foundation
1982

Lit: Arnason 1969, repr.57 (bronze); Lipchitz 1972, p.119

Lipchitz implies that this was an unimportant piece:

There were other curious and sometimes funny maquettes from this period suggesting caricature heads that I entitled 'Cinderella', the 'Snuffer', and 'Head of a Woman' (Lipchitz, loc. cit.).

The title presumably refers to the large nose of the head. The plaster, cast in the early 1960s, is painted a dark terracotta colour.

T 03507 **Head** 1932

Painted plaster $9 \times 5\frac{3}{4} \times 5\frac{1}{2}$
($228 \times 146 \times 139$)
Not inscribed
Presented by the Lipchitz Foundation
1982

Lit: Arnason 1969, repr.80 (bronze); Lipchitz
1972, p.127 and repr.112 (bronze)

There is another plaster of this sculpture in the collection of the Kröller-Müller Museum (Otterlo 1977,
n.p., repr.), and the terracotta original is reproduced in
Maurice Raynal, *Jacques Lipchitz*, 1947. It is likely that
the plaster in the Kröller-Müller Museum, which is a
better cast, was made at the same time as an early cast
of a bronze, and that the Tate Gallery's plaster was
made in the early 1960s. The monograph by Raynal
also reproduces a similar terracotta of the same date
with much larger cavities around the left eye and the
left side of the skull. This 'Head' is a unique subject in
Lipchitz's work, and he compared it to his sculptures
of fragments of heads such as 'Head and Hand' (T 03496)
and 'Head, Bust and Arms' (T 03498):

> Some of these studies of head and hands were formal
> explorations of interior or negative sculptural space,
> and the interest in this problem led me in 1932 to a
> series of sketches of helmet or skull heads in which
> the interior space is open and enveloped by a skin or
> bone structure pierced with great eye holes
> (Lipchitz, loc.cit.).

T 03508 **Head of a Woman** 1911–12

Plaster, the head coated with shellac
$6\frac{1}{4} \times 2\frac{1}{2} \times 2\frac{1}{8}$ ($158 \times 63 \times 54$)

Inscribed '491' on back of head in black
paint
Presented by the Lipchitz Foundation
1982

Lit: Arnason 1969, repr. A (bronze); Lipchitz
1972, p.4 and repr.1 (bronze)

This very small head of a girl (without the support it is
about 3 ins. high) is related to Lipchitz's 'Woman with
Gazelles' which he exhibited in the Salon d'Automne
in November 1913, where it became his first public
success. It is the same scale as the head of the woman
in this group, but although it is broken around the neck
it is not a fragment of the original plaster for this figure
as it differs in detail, particularly the position of the
headband and the slope of the neck at the left.

Lipchitz records (op.cit., p.7) that he originally made
this group in 1911, with only one gazelle, and that
the small head was associated with work he did at the
Académie Julian, which he attended from about early
1910.

There is no specific record of an early bronze cast of
this head. The plaster returned into Lipchitz's possession during the preparation of Arnason's catalogue
of his *Sketches in Bronze* in 1968–9. A bronze cast,
considerably reworked in the wax, was reproduced in
this book as an extra illustration. Another cast, more
faithful to this plaster, was reproduced in Lipchitz's
autobiography. Neither of these bronzes has the same
plaster support as T 03508, which was evidently made
in the 1970s.

The plaster is presumably an original cast of 1911–
12. Part of the headband at the crown was cut away at
an early date. The original metal armature has been cut
below the neck, and slightly protrudes.

T 03509 Musical Instruments, Bas Relief 1923

Plaster coated with shellac, the reverse
painted 6¼ × 8 × 1 (158 × 203 × 25)
Not inscribed
Presented by the Lipchitz Foundation
1982

Lit: Lipchitz 1972, p.73

During 1923 and 1924 Lipchitz made a number of small
relief sculptures as studies for a commission from Dr
Albert Barnes, who had asked him to make several relief
carvings to go over lintels on the outside of his house
and art gallery at Merion, Philadelphia, then being
built. This, T 03618 and T 03526 are all versions of the
same composition, not used at Merion but similar in
subject to some of the reliefs:

> T 03509 is a plaster cast in about 1923 from a small
> scale preliminary study,
>
> T 03518 is a plaster cast in the 1960s when this small
> study was cast as a bronze, and has the addition of
> a display stand,
>
> T 03526 is a plaster cast in about 1923 from a larger
> development of this composition, and was itself used
> as a model for a bronze edition.

For this commission Lipchitz returned to the still
lifes of musical instruments that he had already used
for his first cubist reliefs in 1917–18. The guitar and
open book were typical subjects of Lipchitz's friend
Juan Gris, as for example in the Tate Gallery's 'Violin
and Fruit Dish', 1924 (N 05935), but also in many earlier
paintings. These carvings were completed before the
commission given by Dr Barnes to Matisse in 1930.

The plaster has been coloured to resemble terracotta.
Plaster, painted light red, has been brushed onto the
reverse, possibly hiding a foundry inscription.

T 03510 Meditation 1931

Plaster 7¾ × 7 × 5¾ (197 × 178 × 146)
Inscribed '14.' in blue paint, twice, under
the base of the arms
Presented by the Lipchitz Foundation
1982

Lit: Arnason 1969, repr.63 (bronze)

The terracotta of this sculpture, which has in addition
a thin base, is in the collection of the University of
Arizona Museum of Art (Arizona 1982, 54, repr.).

Lipchitz made a number of similarly abbreviated
sculptures of heads and hands in the early 1930s, which
develop his interest in the idea of a hollow space within
the body. This particular pose goes back to the 'Man
Leaning on his Elbows', 1925 (Arnason 1969, repr.21),
which is itself related to the 'transparent' sculptures of
that year.

This plaster was cast in the early 1960s.

T 03511 Woman with Hair 1932

Plaster, partly stained from the mould
5 × 3½ × 2½ (127 × 89 × 63)
Not inscribed
Presented by the Lipchitz Foundation
1982

Lit: Arnason 1969, repr.77 (bronze); Lipchitz
1972, pp.115 and 124–5

See entry on T03496. The terracotta original of this sculpture is in the collection of the University of Arizona Museum of Art (Arizona 1982, 36, repr.) and this plaster was cast in the early 1960s.

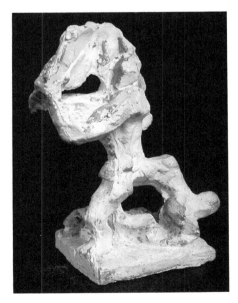

T03512 First Study for 'Toward a New World' 1934

Plaster, partly stained from the mould
$4\frac{1}{4} \times 3\frac{1}{2} \times 2$ (108 × 89 × 51)
Not inscribed
Presented by the Lipchitz Foundation
1982

Lit: Arnason 1969, repr.107 (bronze); Lipchitz 1972, p.132

Arnason reproduces three further studies for this subject, each with two standing figures. A plaster was included in Lipchitz's exhibition at the Galerie Maeght, Paris, in 1946 (58), probably the one which is illustrated in Maurice Raynal, *Jacques Lipchitz*, 1947 (50 ins. high).

Lipchitz's account points out that the subject was connected with a commission from Russia for a monument to the Russian revolution. He visited his family in Russia in 1935, after his first designs for the monument. His project was not accepted, and after the war he used the composition as a starting point for the commission in America for a monument to 'Enterprise' (see T03493 and T00320 of 1953).

> Most of the surviving maquettes of 1934 and 1935 are projects for monuments. Aside from the 'David and Goliath' and the Soviet Monument, I made the initial designs entitled 'Toward a New World', which I was finally able to complete as 'Enterprise' for Fairmount Park in Philadelphia, in the 1950s. The four surviving maquettes show with increasing complications figures carrying a flag. They are organized in a violently agitated pyramid, interpenetrated spatially, with the great flag in undulating motion, sweeping over and encompassing the group. 'Toward a New World' was also one of the very few political sculptures I have made, suggestive of my momentary enthusiasm for the revolutionary cause of Russia, an enthusiasm which did not survive very long, because I have always been and continued to be on the side of freedom and against any form of oppression or dictatorship (Lipchitz, loc.cit.).

An invoice of 1 June 1965 from the Modern Art Foundry, New York, refers to this plaster or to another version. The plaster was cast at about that time, and is not of high quality. The five-pointed Jewish star on the banner was cut into the plaster.

T03513 Bull and Condor 1932

Plaster $8\frac{1}{4} \times 12\frac{1}{2} \times 6\frac{1}{4}$ (209 × 317 × 158)
Inscribed 'J Lipchitz' incised under base, and '152' in blue paint under base
Presented by the Lipchitz Foundation 1982

Lit: Irene Patai, *Encounters: The Life of Jacques Lipchitz*, 1961, pp.260–1; Arnason 1969, repr.82 (bronze); Lipchitz 1972, pp.127–8

Two maquettes were made of this subject in 1932, but Lipchitz did not make a larger version. Bronze casts of

T 03513

both were exhibited in 1958 (*Jacques Lipchitz*, Stedelijk Museum, Amsterdam, March–May 1958, nos. 65 and 69). In his autobiography Lipchitz stresses that he used a rough technique for these, appropriate to the violent subject:

> In 1932, when my friend the poet Larrea returned from Peru, he told me a story about fiestas where the feet of a condor are sewn into the back of the bull and they are then let loose in an arena. There results a fantastic and horrible battle until one or both are killed. This story moved me deeply. At the moment when Hitler and the Nazis were in power in Germany, I was entering upon a period of profound depression and I felt that the bull and the condor, and particularly the human beings who delighted in their struggle, signified the insane brutality of the world.
>
> I made two maquettes of the theme in 1932 as well as a relief in 1933, in all of which I tried to express the horror and the furious struggle of the event. These are modelled with a passion that reflects my emotions in the face of this frightening conflict. The clay is scarred, undercut and torn like the bodies of . the fighters. The jagged textures and contours emphasize further the violence of the scene. This is a work that I should have made into a large sculpture: why I did not do so, I do not know. In its violence and textural freedom it looks forward to the most expressive sculptures of the 1940s and 1950s, in many of which the bull, which appears here for the first time, again becomes a symbol of suffering in many different contexts (Lipchitz, loc.cit.).

The Spanish poet Juan Larrea, who lived near Lipchitz in Boulogne-sur-Seine in the 1930s, later published a book on Picasso's 'Guernica' (Curt Valentin, New York, 1957) and both he and Lipchitz spoke at a symposium on 'Guernica' at the Museum of Modern Art, New York on 25 November 1947.

The plaster was signed under the base when wet, and was cast in the early 1960s. An undated wash drawing (Lipchitz 1972, repr.114b) is close in appearance to this model, and was probably drawn after it.

T 03514 **Study for a Monument** 1934

Plaster, partly stained from the mould
$12\frac{1}{2} \times 3\frac{1}{2} \times 3\frac{1}{2}$ (317 × 89 × 89)
Not inscribed
Presented by the Lipchitz Foundation
1982

Lit: Arnason 1969, repr.112 (bronze); Lipchitz 1972, p.131

The terracotta of this sculpture is in the collection of the University of Arizona Museum of Art (Arizona 1982, 13, repr.) and includes at the top the raised arm of the figure, which has broken off this plaster. Arnason reproduces two other studies for this momument, and in all of them the reliefs, as well as the figure, are only sketched, and evidently had not been considered in detail in subject.

The monument was a commission from Russia, as T 03512:

> During 1935 I spent some time in Russia, which I had always wanted to visit again. As a result of my early experiences, I had been sympathetic to the Russian revolution, but I must say that my three months' sojourn there disillusioned me. I designed a project for a monument to the Russian revolution, a maquette of dancing figures on a column decorated with reliefs. The dancing figures derived from my sculpture 'Joy of Life', and the entire monument was intended to extol the liberation of the Russian people through industry and agriculture. The Soviet Arts

Commission was interested in the project and asked me to submit a large sketch. I sent a plaster version, which was not accepted (Lipchitz, loc.cit.).

It is not clear if Lipchitz made the studies on his own account as a suggestion for a commission, or if the commission came first, but he dated them the year before his Russian visit.

T 03515 **David and Goliath** 1933

> Plaster 11 × 11 × 6 (279 × 279 × 152)
> Not inscribed
> Presented by the Lipchitz Foundation 1982
> *Lit:* Arnason 1969, repr.99 (bronze); Lipchitz 1972, pp.127 and 131–2

Arnason reproduces four sketches for this subject, including this one and T 03415. A large plaster, 30 ins. high, was exhibited in the Paris Salon of 1934 (Maurice Raynal, *Lipchitz*, 1947, n.p., repr.). This plaster was one of the most explicit of Lipchitz's references to the Nazis, as the figure of Goliath had a swastika inscribed on his chest (not visible in Raynal's illustration) and the Old Testament subject makes clear that it was the Jews who were retaliating.

> During 1933 I had designed a series of maquettes on the theme of David and Goliath that were specifically related to my hatred of fascism and my conviction that the David of freedom would triumph over the Goliath of oppression. In the first of the four remaining maquettes (1933) David stands over the recumbent Goliath, twisting a cord around his neck. In the subsequent sketches, the figures are reversed, with the huge Goliath rising up vertically and David pulling back with all his strength on the great cable cord which he has twisted around the throat of the giant. The final sketch, placing the

figures on a column, reduces the size of the giant to a more human scale. The two figures straining mightily against one another establish a terrific state of tension. The project was executed on a somewhat larger scale and the plaster was exhibited in 1934 at the Salon des Surindépendants. I wished there to be no doubt about my intent so I placed a swastika on the chest of Goliath. The statue cost me considerable difficulty with German agents who in the guise of art critics began to show intense interest in visiting and examining my studio. However, it remained unharmed in the basement of the Musée National d'Art Moderne during the entire German occupation (Lipchitz, loc.cit.).

The group shows David pulling a noose around the neck of Goliath from behind, which the giant tries with both hands to tear off. This is a variation of the story in the Bible, in which David cuts off his head.

This plaster is listed in the accounts of the Modern Art Foundry, New York, for 1 February 1963.

T 03516 **Jacob and the Angel** 1931

> Plaster 9¾ × 13¾ × 7¼ (247 × 349 × 184)
> Inscribed 'J. Lipchitz' incised into wet plaster under base, and '53.' in blue paint under base
> Presented by the Lipchitz Foundation 1982
> *Lit:* Arnason 1969, repr.67 (bronze); Lipchitz 1972, pp.100, 120 and repr.104 (bronze)

This and another study of a similar size (Arnason 1969, repr. 66) preceded a large bronze which was exhibited at the Petit Palais, Paris, in 1937 (*Les Maîtres de l'Art Indépendant 1895–1937*, June–October 1937 (24). Lipchitz 1972, repr.105, 47¾ins. long). Lipchitz gives his own account of the subject:

The theme of the struggle of Jacob and the angel began to obsess me in 1941. This is a curious story. Jacob was sleeping and the angel came to him and woke him and challenged him to do battle, so that Jacob began to fight. Although the angel was a messenger of the Lord, and Jacob could not overcome him, he did fight nevertheless, and after that, the Lord rewarded him for having fought and named him Israel. To me, this meant that God wants us to fight with him. From these tentative ideas emerged many sketches and, finally, a complete sculpture made in 1932. Again, I realize that there is always the theme of the embrace, which is also a struggle, a tension of opposites that seems to occur continually in my sculpture (Lipchitz, op.cit., p.120).

This is the earliest narrative subject by Lipchitz in the collection, although it was preceded in his work by 'First Idea for Sacrifice', 1925 and 'Leda and the Swan', 1929.

The plaster has not been completed after the casting, and casts of the dividing material have not been removed. It was cast in the early 1960s, and was signed under the base before it had set.

Lipchitz made sculptures of two incidents from the myth of Prometheus (see also T01755, T03500 and T03497). This plaster illustrates the end of his story, when he was punished for stealing fire from the gods by being chained to a rock, with a vulture gnawing at his liver. According to Lipchitz there was originally a vulture with this figure:

> During 1931 I made a small sketch of a 'Prometheus', a reclining figure with arched back and screaming mouth. There was originally a vulture who was tearing at his liver, but this part of the sculpture disappeared or was destroyed and I preserved only the figure. This, again, is important to me as one of my earlier uses of a theme from classical mythology to illustrate some of my thoughts about the world, in this case specifically about the intellectuals who were moving into a period of darkness and persecution. I was haunted by the specter of fascism in Germany, and this little piece reflected some of my feeling (Lipchitz, loc.cit.).

The pose of the man with head leaning back and mouth open had already been used as an expression of extreme emotion in the small study 'Mother and Child', 1929 (Lipchitz 1972, repr. 92).

The plaster was cast in the early 1960s.

T03517 **First Study for Prometheus** 1931

Plaster $4\frac{3}{4} \times 11 \times 5\frac{1}{2}$ (120 × 279 × 140)
Inscribed '67.' in blue paint under base
Presented by the Lipchitz Foundation 1982

Lit: Irene Patai, *Encounters: The Life of Jacques Lipchitz*, 1961, p.281; Arnason 1969, repr.68 (bronze); Lipchitz 1972, repr.113 (bronze) and p.127

The terracotta original of this sculpture belongs to the University of Arizona Museum of Art (Arizona 1982, 9, repr.)

T03518 **Musical Instruments, Relief on a Stand** 1923

Plaster $9\frac{3}{4} \times 8 \times 2\frac{1}{4}$ (248 × 203 × 57)
Not inscribed
Presented by the Lipchitz Foundation 1982

Lit: Arnason 1969, repr.13 (bronze); Lipchitz 1972, p.73

See entry on T 03509. This plaster was cast in the 1960s at the time that the bronze reproduced by Arnason was cast, although the stand differs. The surface markings are identical to those of T 03509, and were evidently moulded from it. There are a number of faults in the casting from air bubbles, notably in the centre of the guitar's sound hole.

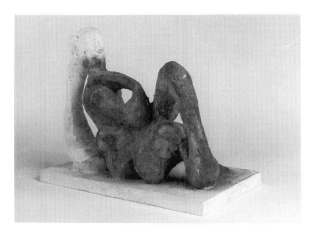

T 03519   **Hagar** 1948

Plaster, partly painted $6 \times 7\frac{1}{4} \times 4\frac{1}{4}$
($152 \times 184 \times 108$)
Not inscribed
Presented by the Lipchitz Foundation
1982

Lit: Ziva Amishai, 'Lipchitz – Themes within a Jewish Context', exhibition catalogue, *Jacques Lipchitz at Eighty*, Israel Museum, Jerusalem, 1971, n.p.; Lipchitz 1972, pp.183–4

The final bronze of 'Hagar', which also has the figure of her son Ishmael, was exhibited at the Buchholz Gallery, New York, in 1951 (*Jacques Lipchitz*, May 1951, as '22, Agar, 23″ high', repr.). Also included, as a single catalogue number covering more than one work, were 'Studies for Agar, 1948, bronze, $6\frac{1}{4} - 9\frac{3}{4}$ ins. high', which probably refer to bronze casts of this sculpture and T 03527 and T 03534.

This is probably an original plaster of 1948, from which the right arm and head were completely removed and replaced at a later date with new plaster, when the base was also made. The terracotta from which the figure was first cast is in the collection of the University of Arizona Museum of Art (Arizona 1982, 29, repr.).

The limbs of this early study for Hagar can be read ambiguously, with the right hand at either end of the arm, and the raised leg indeterminate.

Lipchitz makes clear in his autobiography that the subject referred to the foundation of Israel in 1948. Hagar, in Genesis 16, was the mother of Abraham's illegitimate son Ishmael, who was the ancestor of the Arabs. They were exiled by Abraham's wife Sarah, who was the mother of Isaac, the ancestor of the Jews. The subject therefore appeals for sympathy for the Arabs, but Lipchitz also goes on to refer to his own situation as an exile in America, with his second wife and their child:

> The two concepts, my feeling for Israel and my feeling for the mother and child, came together in the Hagar I of 1948, which has to do with Israel and the conflict between Israel and the Arabs. Despite my admiration for and love of Israel, I feel strongly that the Jews and the Arabs should make peace, that they should live together as brothers, which they were able to do for many centuries. Hagar was a concubine of Abraham and when he married Sarah, Sarah did not wish to have her or her child, Ishmael, so Abraham finally sent them away. They suffered in the desert until they were rescued by an angel. I wished to show my sympathy for Ishmael, who is thought of as the father of the Arabs in the same manner as the Hebrews are the sons of Abraham; so this is a prayer for brotherhood between the Jews and the Arabs. It is a concept which combines tragedy and suffering with tenderness and hope for the future (Lipchitz, loc.cit.).

T 03520   **Reclining Woman** 1921

Plaster, coated with shellac $3 \times 4\frac{1}{4} \times 1\frac{1}{2}$
($76 \times 108 \times 38$)
Inscribed with illegible number in brown paint under base
Presented by the Lipchitz Foundation
1982

Lit: Lipchitz 1972, p.67 and repr. fig.51
(bronze); Stott 1975, p.259 no.68 and repr.
fig.45 (bronze); Arnason 1969, repr. pl.6
(bronze)

There are two very similar versions of this 'Reclining
Woman' of 1921, of which this is the slightly larger. It
is the earliest in the Tate Gallery's collection of the
small maquettes which Lipchitz had cast in bronze at
the Modern Art Foundry in New York in the early
1960s (apart from the cubist 'Figure 1915' (T03501)),
and exhibited together at the Otto Gerson Gallery (*157
Small Bronze Sketches*, April–May 1963). Nearly all of
these were cast then for the first time, and the shellac
surfaces of the plasters were cleaned and prepared both
before and after this casting. T03520 is presumably an
original cast of 1921.

The origin of this almost abstract figure is explained
by Lipchitz in his autobiography. Coco Chanel commissioned from him, in addition to a portrait head, a
pair of firedogs for a rococo style fireplace.

> I realized that I must change my entire approach for
> this commission, and the experiment in curvilinear
> forms was to have a most profound effect on my
> sculpture of the next decades (Lipchitz, loc.cit.).

Each firedog took the form of a reclining woman, formed
from figure of eight curves. This piece of decorative
art immediately influenced a further commission from
Coco Chanel for a sculpture for her garden. The plaster
'Reclining Figure' is a study for this, in which the shape
of the figure on the firedog has become a spiral. The
garden sculpture was never made, but this study was
an important departure for Lipchitz both in its subject
of a reclining woman and its treatment, and as one of
the first of his hand size modelled maquettes.

T03521   Woman Leaning on a Column 1929

Painted plaster 10 × 5¼ × 3½
(254 × 133 × 89)
Inscribed '32.' in blue paint under base
Presented by the Lipchitz Foundation
1982
Lit: Arnason 1969, repr.40 (bronze); Lipchitz
1972, p.107

There are three versions of this maquette (Arnason
1969, reprs.38–40) and a similar 'Reclining Woman on
a Puff' (Arnason 1969, repr.41). No larger version was
made, but Lipchitz links these studies with the much
later striding figure in 'The Spirit of Enterprise', 1953
(T03493 and T00320).

The terracotta original of this sculpture is in the
collection of the University of Arizona Museum of Art

(Arizona 1982, 32, repr.). This plaster is painted in
three shades of brown, and was cast in the early 1960s.

The title was probably given by the artist before the
exhibition of the bronze at the Otto Gerson Gallery,
New York, in 1963. The 'Column' is not represented,
although the massive right leg and torso of the woman
are rather columnar. She rests both hands under her
chin, and her eyes and nose are incised into the concave
surface of her face.

T03522   Dancer with Veil 1928

Terracotta 6⅞ × 3¼ × 2¾ (174 × 79 × 70)
Inscribed 'J Lipchitz' incised under base,

and '143 3 off' in black ink under base
Presented by the Lipchitz Foundation
1982

Lit: Arnason 1969, repr.31 (bronze)

There are two sculptures by Lipchitz with this title made in 1928, and bronze casts of both were exhibited in the Otto Gerson Gallery in 1963 (*Jacques Lipchitz: 157 Small Bronze Sketches*, 29 and 31). The other sculpture is a relief on a stand, and was associated by Lipchitz with the idea of a memorial for his sister Jenny, who died in 1928 (Lipchitz 1972, p.104). He wrote also that he 'wished to explore subjects of greater freedom and movement'. T 03522 was his most unbalanced and twisted figure up to that time, although preceded by a group of 'transparents' of circus figures cast from strips of wax bent like wire.

The subject is a single figure of a woman standing on her right leg, the other bent at the knees, with the foot placed against the standing leg. Three long scarves hang from her waist, one of them reaching the ground behind her. The upper half of her body, with both hands extended and head leaning back, is twisted around to her left so as to almost face behind her.

T 03523 Study for a Garden Statue 1921

Plaster, coated with shellac $5\frac{1}{2} \times 1\frac{3}{8} \times 1\frac{1}{2}$ (140 × 35 × 38)
Inscribed '144' in brown paint under base
Presented by the Lipchitz Foundation
1982

Lit: Lipchitz 1972, pp.67–8, 110 and repr. fig.52 (bronze); Arnason 1969 repr. fig.7 (bronze)

This sculpture was identified by Lipchitz as a preliminary model for a garden sculpture for Coco Chanel 'intended to be seen in a vista of forest at the end of an alley of grass' (loc.cit). It was never carried out, like the 'Reclining Woman' of the same date (T 03520), which was also a study for a sculpture for the same place.

The subject is a couple embracing, and this group is placed on a tall geometrical column. This dominant pedestal looks back to the near abstract 'Sculpture, 1916' in which the figure of a pregnant woman is almost invisible inside a cleft column, and forward to the large bronze 'Figure', 1926–30, for which there is a small terracotta study in the Tate Gallery ('Sketch for a Figure', 1926, T 03505. Both are reproduced in *Lipchitz. The Cubist Period 1913–1930*, Marlborough–Gerson Gallery, New York, March–April 1968, nos.24 and 62).

The plaster is presumably an original cast of 1921. The instructions to the foundry were on an attached label '"Sketch for a garden statue" /3 7/ off make plate' with an indication that three bronzes had been cast.

T 03524 Portrait of Coco Chanel *c.*1921

Terracotta 12 × 8 × $8\frac{1}{4}$ (335 × 203 × 209)
Inscribed 'J Lipchitz' incised at rear of neck, and '77' (twice) in black paint under neck.
Presented by the Lipchitz Foundation
1982

Lit: Lipchitz 1972, p.63

Another version of this head was apparently preferred by the sitter, who had commissioned it, since it was that version that was cast in bronze, and one of the casts belonged to her. This bronze differs from the Tate Gallery's terracotta chiefly in the more realistic treatment of the hair, which is brushed forward across the forehead.

Lipchitz remarks in his autobiography that he was not happy with the result of this commission, which was 'too much of an official or commissioned portrait' (loc.cit. The bronze version is reproduced). After leaving his dealer Léonce Rosenberg in 1920 Lipchitz looked for portrait commissions as a source of income. Although he also modelled Gertrude Stein (T 03479 of 1938 is a later portrait of her by Lipchitz) these heads are for the most part of his friends and were not commissioned. Neither of the heads of Coco Chanel is of the quality of the best of these, such as the 'Portrait of Raymond Radiguet' (1920) which demonstrate more clearly that a precisely classical style interested Lipchitz least as much as the possibility of commissions.

T 03525   Sketch for Lower Part of Our Tree of Life 1962

Plaster 22 × 7 × 9 (558 × 177 × 228)
Not inscribed
Presented by the Lipchitz Foundation
1982
Lit: Arnason 1969, repr.157 (complete plaster, another cast); Lipchitz 1972, pp.198–9 (complete bronze repr.181); *The Jacques Lipchitz 'tree of life'*, Hadassah University Hospital, Jerusalem, n.d.

This plaster is the lower half of a 34 ins. high study, which is reproduced complete in Arnason. For some reason Arnason illustrates a plaster, and not a bronze, but a bronze cast was made, and is reproduced in A.M. Hammacher, *Jacques Lipchitz*, 1975, repr.165.

Six studies for this composition, all on the same scale, have been published:

1   'The Sacrifice of Abraham', plaster in the collection of the Kröller–Müller Museum (Otterlo 1977, n.p., repr., dated in the catalogue 1960–1). Lowest part only
2   T 03525. Study for complete composition
3   T 03491. Study for complete composition
4   'Study for the lower part of *Our Tree of Life*', 1970, bronze, 11½ ins., in A.M. Hammacher, op.cit., repr.166.
5   'Sketch for Our Tree of Life', 1971–2, bronze, in *Jacques Lipchitz: Sculptor and Collector*, exhibition catalogue, Albert and Vera List Visual Arts Centre, Massachusetts Institute of Technology, March–June 1985 (15, repr.).
6   'Our Tree of Life (last working model)', plaster, in A.M. Hammacher, op.cit., repr.167.

Lipchitz records that there were many other studies, the earliest of which were destroyed in the studio fire in 1952.

The final version of 'Our Tree of Life' was installed on Mount Scopas, Jerusalem, in 1978 (after Lipchitz's death). He had received this commission in 1967, from the Hadassah University Hospital, and enlarged and developed the studies for a Jewish monument which he had already been making for years beforehand. The origin of this scheme was his wish to make a monumental sculpture for the Hebrew religion that was a parallel to the sculpture of the Virgin Mary which he had been commissioned to make for the church of Notre Dame de Liesse at Assy, near Chamonix, in 1947. There is a similarity between the structures of 'Our Tree of Life' and the last models for 'Between Heaven and Earth' (the title of the Assy monument) made in 1958, particularly in the way the separate subjects are piled on top of each other. In both sculptures the uppermost group rests on a similar support of curving shapes, so that in a general view the design of the earlier group is continued in the later, although the subjects differ.

The subject of 'Our Tree of Life' has several overlapping interpretations, as described by Lipchitz in his autobiography (which was based on taped conversations of 1968–70, while he was still working on the later models of the sculpture). As a whole, the composition was seen as a tree, and as a sequence of subjects illustrating the development of Judaism. A later description published by the Hadassah University Hospital, Jerusalem (op.cit) refers to the whole monument as a seven branched candelabrum. The particular groups from which it is made, are, numbering upwards from the base:

1   The sacrifice of Isaac by Abraham, interrupted by an angel (this is the only group in T 03525)

2 The three Patriarchs
3 The flames of the burning bush, which enclose
  Moses, kneeling in front of the tablets of the law.
4 The phoenix.

This plaster has not been broken, but is one of the
two halves in which the clay model was cast.

T 03527 Variation on the Theme of Hagar 1948

Plaster, coated with shellac 6 × 9 × 4
(152 × 228 × 102)
Inscribed '2 off' in black paint under base,
and with illegible letters
Presented by the Lipchitz Foundation
1982
Lit: Lipchitz 1972, pp.183–4

See entry on T 03519. This study is closer than is T 03519
to the 23 ins. bronze of this subject which was exhibited
in 1951 (*Jacques Lipchitz*, Buccholz Gallery, New York,
May 1951, 22, repr.). This bronze also included the
figure of the baby Ishmael, being suckled at his mother's
left breast.

The plaster was cast in 1948, and a bronze cast from
it was probably also included in the 1951 exhibition (21,
'Studies for Agar. 1948. Bronze, H. 6¼–9¾). The base is
a separate piece, but was probably made at the same
time as the figure. The present title was not used at the
time it was made.

T 03526 Musical Instruments, Standing Relief 1924

Plaster coated with shellac 15¼ × 19 × 3¾
(388 × 482 × 95)
Inscribed 'I. I.' and 'L.' in red paint on the
reverse, and '554 B 3 OFF' in brown ink
along lower edge
Presented by the Lipchitz Foundation
1982
Lit: Lipchitz 1972, p.73

See entry on T 03509. There is a small terracotta study
for this relief (Centre Pompidou 1978, 25). Another
plaster is of the same dimensions but stands on two
short, bent legs (Otterlo 1977, n.p., as 'Standing Bas
Relief (1923–26').

Unlike the smaller design T 03509, no part of the
surface of the relief is in the same plane as the surround,
and the surface of the guitar is inclined slightly. The two
eye shapes at top and bottom are most easily imagined to
be some still life objects, but Lipchitz had not before
used them in such an ambiguous way, and there is also
a suggestion of his wish to integrate the human figure
with the instruments.

It is possible that this plaster is one of two sculptures
exhibited at the gallery La Renaissance in Paris in June
1930 as 'Nature morte, bas-relief (plâtre). La pierre se
trouve à la Barnes Foundation'. The plaster is an original of 1924.

T 03528 Sketch for Duluth Monument 1963

Plaster, coated with shellac and pigment
21 × 5 × 5 (533 × 127 × 127)
Not inscribed
Presented by the Lipchitz Foundation
1982
Lit: Lipchitz 1972, pp.210, 213

Lipchitz made the first studies in 1963 for a commission
from the Tweed Museum of Art, University of Min-
nesota, Duluth for a monumental portrait of the founder
of the city, Daniel Greysolon, Sieur du Luth. He had
been asked about this commission a few years earlier,

T 03528

in the collection of the University of Arizona Museum of Art (Arizona 1982, 22, repr., 24 ins. high) and was cast in bronze (Arnason 1969, repr.159).

but had refused because it was too large a bronze for the Modern Art Foundry in New York. The Tommasi Foundry in Pietrasanta, Italy, were able to cast on this scale, and the plaster studies were made in Lipchitz's Italian studio.

The proportions of the figure were adjusted to suit the viewpoint on the restricted site of the museum's extension:

> The Duluth monument was interesting because it was a portrait of a man of whom no portraits existed. Therefore, I had to create an idea of the explorer rather than a specific portrait. The result was that I made a great number of sketches, including a nude model for which a man at the foundry posed one morning. The sculpture was designed to be placed on a high pedestal in a rather narrow courtyard between buildings. So I actually distorted the figure in order to correct the perspective from which it would normally be seen, with the upper part of the body larger than would be natural. The sculpture is about nine feet high and the base about ten feet or more, eighteen feet in all. I worked on it in Italy during 1963 and it was installed in 1964 (Lipchitz, loc.cit.).

Apart from the posthumous memorials to Senator Taft and John F. Kennedy (1964) this was the most conventional of Lipchitz's public monuments, as an imaginary over life size portrait of the figure commemorated.

A different plaster study of the whole monument is

T 03529 Guitar Player in Armchair 1922

Plaster, coated with shellac $15\frac{1}{2} \times 11\frac{1}{2} \times 12$ (394 × 292 × 304)
Inscribed '1922 J Lipchitz' moulded into plaster at back of chair, and painted under base 'W.' in red, and over that '3 off/ GUITAR PLAYER/IN ARMCHAIR/1922/251' IN BLACK
Presented by the Lipchitz Foundation 1982
Lit: Lipchitz 1972, p.70

The stone carving of this sculpture, in granite, belongs to a private collector in New York (A.M. Hammacher, *Jacques Lipchitz,* 1975, repr.86). The years 1921–2 were difficult for Lipchitz financially – apart from the commissions from Coco Chanel – and it is unlikely that he could then have afforded then to have this carving made, and it is probably of a later date. At his retrospective exhibition of 1930 Lipchitz included a cast of this sculpture in artificial stone (*Jacques Lipchitz à la Renaissance,* June 1930 (49). It is reproduced in *Documents,* 1, 1930, p.20).

A small plaster at the Kröller–Müller Museum, Otterlo, 'Seated Man with Guitar' (1921) is a study for this sculpture. This study was not cast in bronze with other sketches reproduced by Arnason. The origin of this composition in such a small clay model accounts for the flowing lines, in contrast to the preceding cubist work. The study also resembles the firedogs made for

Coco Chanel in its curved legs, the internal corner and the way in which the figure merges with the guitar. This double use of shapes, as also with the figure's legs and those of the chair, is pointed out by Lipchitz in his autobiography with reference to this sculpture (op.cit., p.70).

The plaster is presumably an original cast of 1922.

T 03530 **Mother and Child I** 1949

Plaster coated with shellac and pigment
19 × 11¼ × 10 (483 × 285 × 254)
Not inscribed
Presented by the Lipchitz Foundation
1982

Lit: Lipchitz 1972, p.183; Michael Parke-Taylor, *Jacques Lipchitz: Mother and Child,* exhibition catalogue, Norman MacKenzie Art Gallery, Regina, Saskatchawan, 1983, p.25

A bronze cast of this sculpture was exhibited at the Buchholz Gallery, New York, in 1951 (*Jacques Lipchitz,* May 1951 (28, repr.)) with 'Mother and Child, II' of the same date, which is a different composition standing on four legs. The large bronze 'Mother and Child' (A.M. Hammacher, *Jacques Lipchitz,* 1975, repr.137, 52 ins. high) is close in appearance to T 03530. In both the mother suckles the baby at her right breast, and is enclosed by flowing drapery with pronounced folds.

Lipchitz described the subject as the birth of his first child in October 1948:

After the 'Miracle' and 'Sacrifice' series, which were very different from almost anything I had ever done before, reflecting a spirit of anger and even

pessimism, my mood changed dramatically as a result of the birth of my daughter, Lolya. It was a fantastic experience at the age of fifty-nine finally to have my own child, particularly a daughter, which is what I wanted, partially because I wanted her to have my mother's name. The result in my sculpture was a series of extremely lyrical works on the theme of the mother and child. These have the curvilinear movement in-the-round of the dancers of the earlier 1940s, but the mood is now much more tender and obviously maternal (Lipchitz, loc.cit.).

Another large 'Mother and Child' bronze was included in the 1951 Buchholz Gallery exhibition, and 'The Cradle', 1949, takes up the same theme.

The base of this plaster was added later, and still has underneath a scrap of newspaper of the 1960s which stuck to it when it was cast. The figure is probably a cast of 1949, and both it and the base have been painted at the same time in two shades of brown.

T 03531 **Dancer** 1929

Plaster, partly stained from the mould
3¼ × 2½ × 2 (82 × 63 × 51)
Not inscribed
Presented by the Lipchitz Foundation
1982

Lit: Arnason 1969, repr.42 (bronze)

This 'Dancer' was cast from the terracotta T 03535 in the early 1960s.

T 03532 Song of Songs 1946

Plaster coated with shellac $18\frac{1}{2} \times 38 \times 10\frac{3}{4}$
($470 \times 965 \times 273$)
Inscribed 'Lipchitz.' incised under base
Presented by the Lipchitz Foundation
1982
Lit: Lipchitz 1972, p.167

See entry on T 03489, which is an earlier version of the same subject.

Lipchitz chose this subject in response to a commission for a sculpture to hang on a wall, and there is a slot in the base to receive a wall hook. The plaster is cast as a thin shell, and is probably the version 'first done in stucco' that Lipchitz describes:

The next maquette I made in 1944 was a rough design for the 'Embracing Couple', which was to develop into the 'Song of Songs'. At the time I was working on this sketch, a friend of mine, an architect, told me that he wanted to give his wife a present, a sculpture for her music room. I looked at the apartment and felt that the idea involved in this piece might be appropriate; so I made a somewhat larger sketch in 1946, still rough and free, and finally the finished sculpture, which was first done in stucco to have it light for hanging on the wall. The forms as finally realized have a curvilinear flow appropriate to the musical theme. I finally made a bronze version, changing the shapes and proportions somewhat. It was thought of first as a relief, but then I placed it on a support, transforming it into a free-standing sculpture that suggests a relief form. This I had done many years earlier when I transformed some of my cubist reliefs into free-standing sculptures by placing them on a base, and the idea actually led to that interest in severe frontality that dominated in such works of the twenties as the 'Ploumanach'. The title, 'Song of Songs', of course comes from the Old Testament, and the theme is a love song, extremely lyrical and tender, since it was made for a very loving couple (Lipchitz, loc.cit.).

T 03533 Study for a Monument *c.*1936

Plaster, partly coated with shellac
$20\frac{1}{4} \times 10 \times 8\frac{3}{4}$ ($514 \times 254 \times 222$)
Not inscribed
Presented by the Lipchitz Foundation
1982
Lit: Lipchitz 1972, pp.135–6

This is a unique sculpture, which Lipchitz altered after it had been coated with shellac as if finished, adding plaster and working it with a file. No bronze cast is known of a previous version, and it is too large to have been made as a terracotta, and so the original part is a contemporary plaster. It is possible that the plaster alterations were made at a later date, but this is unlikely, and more probable that Lipchitz worked on the plaster soon after it had been cast, but then did not take it further. It is larger than the maquettes of the 1930s and is an advanced study for a sculpture to be exhibited, whether as a bronze or a plaster for a bronze.

The sculpture resembles the 'Song of the Vowels', a monumental bronze commissioned in 1931, and derived in subject from studies of musicians playing the harp. However, although the subject of T 03533 is difficult to read it is not of harpists, and is closer in appearance to the group of people waving flags at the top of the 'Study for a Bridge Monument' of 1936 (Arnason 1969, repr.119). Lipchitz (loc.cit.) writes of this study as a further case of his wish to make 'a great architectural sculpture', a 'statue on a bridge with flags and people', which was never realised. It is possible that T 03533 continued the general outline of the 'Song of the Vowels' without any particular subject in mind, before the group waving flags was seen as a theme.

The plaster has been damaged at the top, where a fragment is missing.

T 03535 Dancer 1929

Terracotta $3\frac{1}{2} \times 2\frac{1}{2} \times 2$ (82 × 63 × 57)
Inscribed 'JL' incised under base and '159'
in black ink under base
Presented by the Lipchitz Foundation
1982

Lit: Arnason 1969, repr.42 (bronze)

This, and the plaster cast from it (T 03531), are the smallest sculptures by Lipchitz in the collection. The twisting movement of this piece is similar to 'Dancer with Veil' of 1928 (T 03522).

T 03534 Study for Hagar 1948

Plaster and iron filings $9\frac{1}{2} \times 8\frac{3}{4} \times 8$
(241 × 222 × 203)
Inscribed 'JL 3/10' moulded at back
Presented by the Lipchitz Foundation
1982

Lit: Lipchitz 1972, pp.183–4

See entry on T 03519. This sculpture, despite its origin in the studies for the Hagar and Ishmael group, is an independent work and was cast in reinforced plaster in an edition of ten. Iron filings mixed with the plaster have rusted at the surface, as intended, to give a reddish colour. Another cast in the collection of the Kröller–Müller Museum (Otterlo 1977, n.p., repr.).

No other sculptures by Lipchitz were cast in an edition in plaster in this way, but the sculpture is not listed in his exhibition catalogues of the time.

Richard Long *b.*1945

T 03808 A Sculpture in Bristol 1965/83

Seven black and white photographs mounted on board and one title panel hand-lettered in pencil on board, each panel $10\frac{7}{8} \times 10\frac{7}{8}$ (276 × 276)
Inscribed 'A SCULPTURE IN BRISTOL/1965' on title panel and 'R.Long' on reverse of each board
Purchased from Anthony d'Offay Ltd. (Grant-in-Aid) 1983

Exh: *Richard Long, Touch Stones: Words after the fact,* Arnolfini Gallery, Bristol, March–May 1983 (not numbered); *1965–1972 When Attitudes Became Form,* Kettle's Yard, Cambridge, July–September 1984, Fruit Market, Edinburgh, October–November 1984 (not numbered)

In a letter to the compiler (22 April 1986), the artist commented:

Though not my first outdoor work ('A Snowball Track' 1964), 'A Sculpture in Bristol' was my first work actually digging into the ground. I wanted to make work both below ground level and in the ground. It was made in the garden of a derelict house at the time of doing various labouring jobs before I came to London.

The work consisted of a roughly circular hollow, a meandering channel or small trench, and two holes. The hollow and a part of the channel were lined with white plaster, the two holes were filled with plaster (one full, the other half full) and a section of the channel was just earth. The work was loosely based on rivers; sources, and inlets flowing into a lower riverbed (which can be seen in the River Avon. I

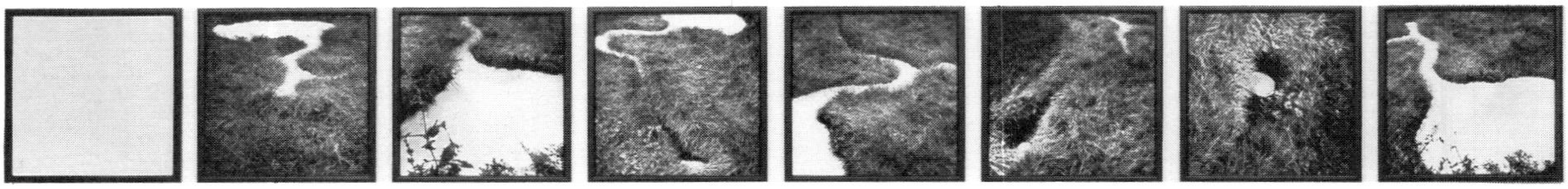

T03808

had always been interested in the negative space and shape of the Avon at low tide). So the sculpture was made by digging, lining and pouring, and was a sort of fictional abstracted river system without water, or with the tide out.

The photos were taken casually, and only made into a photo-work, to my specifications, eighteen years later, for the occasion of my show at the Arnolfini in Bristol in 1983.

Robert Longo *b.*1953

T03782 **Sword of the Pig** 1983

Left section: paint on melamine laminate on wood relief $82\frac{3}{8} \times 87\frac{1}{8} \times 20\frac{1}{8}$ (2090 × 2210 × 510); Centre section: charcoal and acrylic on paper $97\frac{3}{4} \times 49\frac{5}{8}$ (2480 × 1260); Right section: silkscreen on aluminium $48\frac{5}{8} \times 96\frac{1}{2}$ (1235 × 2435); Overall dimensions $97\frac{3}{4} \times 231\frac{5}{8} \times 20\frac{1}{8}$ (2480 × 5880 × 510)
Not inscribed
Presented by the Patrons of New Art through the Friends of the Tate Gallery 1983

Exh: [*Group Exhibition*], Metro Pictures, New York, May–June 1983 (no catalogue); *New Art at the Tate Gallery,* Tate Gallery, September–October 1983 (not numbered, repr. in col.)

Lit: Robert Longo, *Talking about Sword of the Pig,* Patrons of New Art, 1983; *The Tate Gallery Illustrated Biennial Report 1982–84,* Tate Gallery, 1984, repr. p.65; Maurice Berger, 'The Dynamics of Power: An Interview with Robert Longo', *Arts Magazine,* LIX, January 1985, pp.88–9, repr. p.89; Carter Ratcliff, *Robert Longo,* Munich, 1985, pp.23–5, repr. in col. pl.20; *Robert Longo: Studies and Prints,* exhibition catalogue, Norman MacKenzie Art Gallery, Regina, 1986 (n.p.)

Leonard McComb b.1930

T03601 **Portrait of Zarrin Kashi Overlooking Whitechapel High Street** 1981

Watercolour on paper (watermark 'Hayle Mill Handmade') laid on cotton duck $72\frac{3}{8} \times 74\frac{1}{4}$ (1840 × 1885)
Inscribed 'Leonard/McComb/1981' b.l. and 'My name is Zarrin I am my fathers daughter and my father loves me' along lower edge
Presented by the Trustees of the Chantrey Bequest 1983

Prov: Purchased from the artist by the Trustees of the Chantrey Bequest 1983

Exh: RA 1983 (808, as 'Portrait of Zarine Kashi, Whitechapel'); *Leonard McComb Drawings Paintings Sculpture,* AC tour, Serpentine Gallery, October–November 1983, Museum of Modern Art, Oxford, November 1983–January 1984, City Art Gallery, Manchester, January–March 1984, Gardner Art Centre, University of Sussex, Brighton, March–April 1984, Fruit Market Gallery, Edinburgh, May–June 1984 (68, repr. in col.); *Representation Abroad,* Hirschhorn Museum, Washington, June–July 1985 (92, repr. as 'Zarrin Kashi Overlooking Whitechapel High Street')

Lit: Timothy Hyman, 'Leonard McComb: Body and Spirit', *London Magazine,* XXII, August–September 1982, pp.64–73 (detail repr. p.69); Timothy Hyman, 'Leonard McComb: Body and Spirit', *Artscribe,* No.37, October 1982, pp.38–43 (repr. p.42). *Also repr.*: Elma Mitchell, *Furnished Rooms,* Liskeard 1983 (detail repr. on front cover)

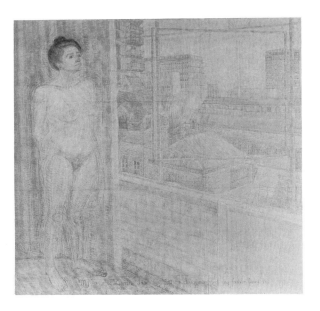

because our studio was needed for an annual exhibition of students' work David Graham, teacher and painter, very kindly organised another studio for us to continue working – so we had about 12 days in all on the work ...

In addition to the time I spent at the Cass I must have worked here at least another 18 days on the painting and 3 days designing and making up the frame, with Barbara's [his wife] help in this.

In a letter of 30 May 1986, McComb added:

The studio where the painting was made is on the 5th floor of the Sir John Cass School; the studio is directly opposite the roof of the Whitechapel Art Gallery, Whitechapel High Street.

The cityscape is very much a composed aspect of the painting; the buildings have been freely selected from a 180 degree eye sweep of the view; as seen through the window. In essence, the cityscape space has been sandwiched closer. Moving backwards from left to right, in the picture's cityscape, is Canon Barnet Primary School, Commercial Street, with the corner of Denning Point G L C Flats behind; these have been brought forward displacing the buildings in front of them on Whitechapel High Street.

The centre foreground-end of the School, with grid windows, has been enlarged and lowered.

The iron railed wall, and windowed slate roof corner, which completes the right foreground of the painting is of Whitechapel Art Gallery, and although without decorative columns, is pretty well unchanged in scale and position. The middle distance back to the chimney, is a selection of the linen merchants and clothing manufacturers' buildings, which border Wentworth Street, Thrawl Street, Loleworth Close, and Fashion Street; these run parallel to Whitechapel High Street and in between Commercial Street, and Brick Lane. Behind Fashion Street provided my major omission, where I left out Hawksmoor's Christ Church, Spitalfields with its surround of splendid plane trees. These I replaced with a taller and slimmer version of Trumans (I left out the name) brewery factory chimney which has been brought forwards from far distant end of Brick Lane. In the painting the chimney acts as a smoking centre for the space of the cityscape, echoing the vertical column of Zarrin herself; the top of the chimney being parallel to her head. The flats left and right behind the chimney are enlarged and have been brought forwards from their Hoxton horizon. The view of Hampstead seen behind the church on a fine day has been omitted. One of the visual aspects of the painting which became increasingly interesting as the work developed, was the variety and almost Byzantine beauty of the brickwork in this part of the East End

Zarrin Kashi is an Iranian who at the time of this picture was working as a professional model. The setting is a room in the Sir John Cass Faculty of Art (City of London Polytechnic), London E1. All quotations in this entry are from a letter from the artist dated 1 April 1986, except where otherwise indicated.

The artist has presented for the Gallery's files 'the first scribblings for the picture taken from my sketchbook at the time'. These are three pencil drawings, all 6½ × 6½ (165 × 165), numbered to show their sequence. McComb writes that 'glancing at these sketches I realise I ... redesigned the studio – made the window lower – and redesigned the relationship between the wall and the window-frame'. In addition there was a preparatory drawing in coloured crayons (private collection) and a working drawing (the artist) in which 'the whole composition is quite carefully worked out – squared off – and was used to transcribe onto the finished painting'.

The artist writes that:

The painting was made at the Sir John Cass School and here in my studio [in Brixton]. It was transported each Saturday on the roof rack of my Morris car for 10 consecutive Saturdays to the John Cass School, where I was a student with about 8 other students, who worked from the same model (Zarrin Kashi), same pose each Saturday from 10 a.m. to 5 p.m. The teacher was Frederick Dean, portrait painter, who allowed us to set up the pose as we wished. My fellow students were part-time artists, retired workers, amateurs, 'A' level students, etc. The painting was made in the summer term and

of London. I used opera glasses extensively in studying the cityscape.

In the painting 'the window was opened as a device to connect Zarrin and the internal room with the unsympathetic city landscape outside. Zarrin standing with natural dignity, a creature of the sun, against the mishmash of Victorian and contemporary tower blocks. Timothy Hyman's article expresses very well the thoughts and feelings which I tried to convey in the painting, including the relevance of the quote.' The relevant passage in Hyman's article (cited above; it was published twice in slightly different forms) reads as follows:

In the strangest work of all, the same model stands like a sentinel, over and against a roofscape of the tower blocks and small factories of the industrial East End: shoulders thrust back and head uplifted in a motion that seems to speak of endurance. The wavy lines and arcs around her body contrast with the cityscape's steady pulse of horizontal and vertical (though the smoke billowing from the distant chimney acts as a sudden all-important eruption of curves). This city-figure is like an emblem; one's bound to see her somehow embodying a value, a meaning.

On the general level, there seems to be the polarisation of mankind against the hostile environment we have created – the organic against the inorganic. But there is also the meaning specific to the individual sitter. She was from the Middle East, and the mental suffering born of her displacement fed into the work; several times as she stood there, McComb heard her repeat 'My name is Zarrin: I am my father's daughter, and my father loves me', and he ended by inscribing this poignant chant along the bottom of the picture. She is, then, in part an emblem of solitariness; and I think we can recognise in all McComb's single colossal figures an air both of the tragic, and of aspiration.

McComb has provided a sketch showing his and Zarrin Kashi's positions in relation to the room as a whole and its windows, during work on the Tate's picture. This room 'is top floor and flanked by windows on two sides. ... By changing one's position in the studio a variety of cityscapes are possible.' McComb confirms that the following works represent scenes in the same room: 'Portrait of John' 1976 (repr. 1983 Serpentine Gallery catalogue cited above, p.14), 'Nude by City Window' 1978 (repr. ibid., p.7) and 'Nude by Window, Whitechapel' 1980 (not repr.). In the following further works the model was Zarrin Kashi: 'Zarrin Sleeping' 1980 (repr. ibid., p.48) and 'Zarrin Seated' 1981 (detail repr. in colour, ibid.; a larger detail repr. Hyman article in *Artscribe* cited above). McComb recalls that these

other portraits of Zarrin Kashi were also 'made as a Saturday student at the Cass and carried each Saturday, to and from here on top of my car'.

Stephen McKenna b.1939

T 03540 **An English Oak Tree** 1981

Oil on canvas $78\frac{3}{4} \times 59$ (2000 × 1500)
Inscribed '^{S}M^{c}K' b.r. and 'Stephen McKenna/1981/OIL ON OIL' on reverse
Purchased from the artist (Grant-in-Aid) 1982

Exh: *Stephen McKenna*, Patrick Verelst, Antwerp, February–March 1982 (no catalogue); *documenta 7*, Kassel, June–September 1982 (works not numbered, repr. in col. as 'Oak Tree in Dulwich Park' in Vol 11 of catalogue, p.223); *Stephen McKenna*, Museum of Modern Art, Oxford, September–November 1983 (50); *The Hard-Won Image*, Tate Gallery, July–September 1984 (97); *Stephen McKenna*, Stedelijk van Abbemuseum, Eindhoven, October–November 1984 (50)

This image was developed from drawings made from nature, in 1981, of a particular oak tree in Dulwich Park, south London. In addition to many rough sketches, McKenna made two large drawings on the spot, from which he worked directly when painting 'An English Oak Tree' in the studio. He owns one of these; the other (private collection) is repr. Stephen McKenna, *On Landscape*, Berlin, 1984, p.33. In Dulwich Park

McKenna first worked from a large oak tree but then decided to work instead from one – the basic source for the Tate's picture – which, though smaller, seemed to him to have more of the essential characteristics of an oak. However he did not alter the intention he had already conceived that his eventual painting should represent a large oak. Thus in view of the relatively small size of the second and final tree from which he worked the painted image departs in some degree from its observed source. McKenna's aim was to produce a generalised image both of the whole tree and its setting and of the detailed descriptions of foliage and branches. To this end he also made many detailed drawings of oak leaves and individual branches, working from nature in this respect both outdoors and in the studio. Two resulting paintings of oak leaves and branches are 'Oak Leaves' 1982 (oil on canvas 800 × 1000mm, private collection, Berlin; repr. in col. in catalogue of exhibition *Stephen McKenna,* Galerie Isy Brachot, Brussels, April–May 1983 (7)) and 'Oak Leaves and Apples' 1982 (oil on canvas 402 × 501mm, private collection). Also related is the central panel of 'The City of Derry' 1982 (oil on three canvases, repr. in col. in catalogue of exhibition *Stephen McKenna,* Institute of Contemporary Arts, October–November 1985, pp.16–18). Around three sides of this central canvas is painted a garland of oak leaves, in reference to the fact that the place-name Derry means 'Hill of Oaks'.

In painting 'An English Oak Tree' McKenna was very much aware of the importance of the oak tree both as an English national symbol and as having a long history of deep-seated religious significance in certain cultures. It was, for example, sacred both for the Druids and for the ancient Greeks. While many primitive societies imposed penalties for cutting down trees in general, those for felling oaks were particularly severe.

The moment at which McKenna determined to paint 'An English Oak' was when he saw in the Castle Museum, Norwich a painting by Crome of a large oak tree. Seeing the Crome recalled for McKenna his response to Courbet's 'The Oak at Flagey, known as "The Oak of Vercingétorix"' 1864 (oil on canvas 890 × 1100mm, Pennsylvania Academy of Arts, Philadelphia) when he saw it in the Courbet retrospective at the Grand Palais, Paris, October 1977–January 1978. This work is reproduced in the catalogue of the same exhibition, *Gustave Courbet,* Royal Academy of Arts, January–March 1978 (73). The Courbet excited McKenna on account of its content. Although it was relatively small it had a monumental quality; its grandeur of scale inspired him in principle to paint a single oak very large. The importance for him of subsequently seeing the Crome was that it showed him that the kind of painting he had in mind was a technical and visual possibility. The Tate Gallery owns a large Crome of a single tree, 'The Poringland Oak' *c.*1818–20 (oil on

canvas 1251 × 1003mm), which McKenna did not know at the time.

'An English Oak Tree' is the pendant to 'L'Hêtre au Bois de la Cambre' 1981, which is the same size and is reproduced in colour in *Artforum,* XXIV, October 1985, p.114 (where reversed in reproduction and mistakenly stated to belong to the Tate Gallery) and also (the right way round) in the catalogues of McKenna's exhibitions at Brussels, Oxford and Eindhoven cited above. This represents a single oak tree which McKenna observed in a large park in Brussels. Two large drawings for it, made from nature, are reproduced in Stephen McKenna, *On Landscape,* (op.cit.), p.32, opposite one (already cited) for the Tate's painting. In recent years McKenna has been dividing his time principally between two homes, in London and Brussels. The beech tree painting was painted entirely in Brussels and the Tate's painting almost entirely in London (though finished in Brussels). McKenna cannot recall which work he began first, but he worked on them alternately as he moved between the two cities. The conspicuously exposed roots of the beech tree were as observed. Along with a number of other beeches in the Bois de la Cambre with similarly exposed roots it has since been felled, as it had become dangerous. The contrast between the topographically specific title of the beech tree painting and the generalised one of the Tate's is owing to the fact that in Belgium the beech plays no role in national consciousness comparable to that of the oak in England.

In painting the Tate's picture McKenna was very conscious also of Caspar David Friedrich's painting 'Oak Tree in the Snow' *c.*1828–30 (oil on canvas 440 × 345mm, Wallraf-Richartz Museum, Cologne; repr. catalogue of exhibition *Caspar David Friedrich,* Tate Gallery, September–October 1972 (93)). However, he wanted to avoid painting the oak tree as a romantic symbol (as Friedrich had done) and also to avoid the slight sense he found in the Friedrich of immateriality, in part derived from Friedrich's metaphysical purpose. Both in the Tate's painting and in its pendant, McKenna painted the tree before painting its background. In each case the landscape background (which is imaginary) was essential in order to counter the tendency towards the metaphysical and immaterial, which McKenna considers the beech tree painting does not quite avoid. McKenna's article 'Caspar David Friedrich' in *Studio International,* CLXXXIV, September 1972, pp.69–72, reproduces in colour and discusses another painting of a single oak, 'The Solitary Tree' 1823 (oil on canvas 550 × 710mm, Nationalgalerie, Berlin).

McKenna's 'Rhododendrons' 1982 (oil on canvas 1200 × 1600mm, repr. in colour in catalogues of Brussels, Oxford and Eindhoven exhibitions cited above) is related to 'An English Oak Tree' in being another work derived from nature in Dulwich Park and representing a whole single plant. In recent years McKenna has painted many pictures of city parks, his interest in which includes their carefully-controlled cultivation and the coming together in them of the natural and the man-made. Though derived from motifs observed in such parks, 'An English Oak Tree' and its pendant are not particularly related to this theme, but they led directly to McKenna's interest in the work of Constable and are thus direct antecedents of works such as 'Richmond Park' 1983 (oil on canvas 2000 × 2750mm, repr. in colour in catalogue of exhibition *The Hard-Won Image*, 1984, cited above, p.47).

This entry is based principally on an interview with the artist on 19 April 1986, and has been approved by him.

T 03541   **Venus and Adonis** 1981

Oil on canvas 59 × 78¾ (1500 × 2000)
Inscribed "ᵋMᶜK' b.r., and 'Stephen McKenna/1981/OIL ON CANVAS/OIL GROUND' on reverse
Purchased from the artist (Grant-in-Aid) 1982

Exh: *Stephen McKenna,* Patrick Verelst, Antwerp, February–March 1982 (no catalogue); *documenta 7,* Kassel, June–September 1982 (works not numbered; repr. in Vol. 11 of catalogue, p.222, as 'The Blind Orion with Eos and Artemis'); *New Art at the Tate Gallery,* Tate Gallery, September–October 1983 (works not numbered, repr. in colour p.27); *The Hard-Won Image,* Tate Gallery, July–September 1984 (98, repr.)

In a statement for the Tate Gallery, dated 10 November 1982, Stephen McKenna wrote about this work:

The use of mythology in Painting gives the possibility of referring to particular human situations as part of the general natural condition. The Venus and Adonis myth grows out of the winter/summer cycle, and represents the yearly death and re-birth of vegetation. This is paralleled in the two halves of the background, which also refers to the differences between the natural, or divine, and the cultivated, or human.

In a more directly human sense, the story contains elements of love, mourning, jealousy and rashness, with the expressive possibilities which go with these. There is also the relationship between men and the gods, or man and animals.

The . . . descriptive techniques vary from the naturalistic to the theatrically artificial.

McKenna owns a number of informal sketches for this painting and a finished sketch in pen and watercolour. Related to the subject of the scene at top right in the Tate's painting is 'The Destruction of Actaeon' 1983 (oil on canvas, 2000 × 1500mm; repr. catalogue of exhibition *Stephen McKenna,* Museum of Modern Art, Oxford, September–November 1983, p.9) and a charcoal study for it (repr. ibid., p.51).

The two separate episodes represented in the Tate's painting are derived from passages in Ovid, *Metamorphoses,* where the story of Venus and Adonis is recounted in Book x. Myrrha, daughter of Cinyras, King of Cyprus, conceived a child by unwitting incest with her father. Ashamed, she begged the gods to change her into another form. They granted her prayer by turning her into a tree, after which she gave birth to a son, Adonis. When Adonis (who was mortal) grew up, the goddess Venus fell in love with him. She warned him to beware of – and not to provoke – various species of wild animals, including boar. But in Ovid's words (*The Metamorphoses of Ovid,* translated Mary M. Innes, Harmondsworth 1955, p.244), Adonis's:

natural courage ran counter to her advice. By chance, his hounds came upon a well-marked trail and, following the scent, roused a wild boar from its lair. As it was about to emerge from the woods, the young grandson of Cinyras pierced its side with a slanting blow. Immediately the fierce boar dislodged the bloodstained spear, with the help of its crooked snout, and then pursued the panic-stricken huntsman, as he was making for safety. It sank its teeth deep into his groin, bringing him down, mortally wounded, on the yellow sand.

Venus, as she drove through the air in her light chariot drawn by winged swans, recognised the groans of the dying Adonis from afar. As she looked down from on high she saw him, lying lifeless, his limbs still writhing in his own blood. Leaping down from her car she . . . cried . . . There will be an everlasting token of my grief, Adonis, your blood will be changed into a flower . . .

With these words, she sprinkled Adonis's blood with sweet-smelling nectar and, at the touch of the liquid, the blood swelled up, just as clear bubbles rise in yellow mud. Within an hour, a flower sprang up, the colour of blood ... its name, anemone.

In the Tate's painting the central tree represents the transformed Myrrha and the fissure in its trunk the point through which she gave birth to Adonis. In the centre of the painting lies the dead and wounded Adonis, tended by the grieving Venus, with Cupid beyond (his bow broken) and the boar to the right. The red flowers closest to the wounds in Adonis's groin are the anemones into which his blood has been turned.

The scene at top right represents the death of Actaeon (Ovid, *Metamorphoses*, III), of whom the *Oxford Classical Dictionary* relates that 'a keen hunter, he one day came upon Artemis [Diana] bathing; offended at being seen thus naked by a man, she turned him into a stag and he was chased and killed by his own hounds ... [Actaeon was] torn by hounds under Artemis's eyes.'

McKenna had long been a close reader of Ovid. He was further inspired to paint 'Venus and Adonis' by the large number of memorable treatments of this subject (and of that of Diana and Actaeon) in past art. However, while many of his paintings are inspired by particular works from the past there was no particular source for the composition or style of 'Venus and Adonis' as a whole.

As the foregoing account of the subject of 'Venus and Adonis' shows, McKenna's picture brings together three separate instances of the transformation of human substance into some other form, and a corresponding number of demonstrations of the relationship between mortals and the gods. McKenna emphasises that (as here in the case of Actaeon) such transformations, which more often than not were disadvantageous for the lesser being that was transformed, were usually the result of presumption on the part of the mortals in coming too close to the gods. This last point is exemplified also in the fate of Adonis, for not only was he loved by a goddess, but their continued association contravened an agreement that after half a year he would return to Venus's rival, Persephone.

McKenna divided the composition of 'Venus and Adonis' into contrasted zones – the right side dominated by movement and mayhem, in a principally wintry setting, the left characterised by peace and by the abundance of Spring. The image of the death of Actaeon was derived from Titian's 'Diana and Actaeon' (National Gallery); the dog at b.r. from Stubbs's 'Park Phaeton with a Pair of Cream Ponies in Charge of a Stable-lad with a Dog' 1780–5 (Mr and Mrs Paul Mellon); Adonis and the sleeping dog from an engraving after Martin De Vos (*c*.1531–1603) of which McKenna saw a reproduction in a catalogue not confined to the work of De

Vos; the boar from an engraving in *Johnsonus*, a seventeenth century book of engravings on subjects in natural history; the plants from McKenna's garden in Brussels; Venus partly from invention and partly from a model; and Cupid, the herm, the trees and the landscape from invention alone. For the oak branches in the foreground, see the entry on T 03540 'An English Oak Tree'. The stone in the foreground, with marks incised in its surface, was conceived as suggesting both a natural, weathered form, a weapon and a sculpture, thus occupying a position open to associations, midway between the natural and the man-made.

Closely related to 'Venus and Adonis', though not a pendant, is an oil of the same dimensions, also on the theme of transformation and the gods, 'Apollo and Daphne' 1981 (repr. in catalogue of exhibition *Stephen McKenna*, Galerie Isy Brachot, Brussels, April–May 1983 (4)).

This entry draws substantially on an interview with the artist on 19 April 1986, and has been approved by him.

Bruce McLean b.1945

T 03411 **Study for 'Possibly a Nude by a Coal Bunker'** 1980

Black oil pastel and acrylic on photographic paper, five panels, each $157\frac{1}{2} \times 54\frac{5}{8}$ (4000 × 1387)
Not inscribed
Purchased from Anthony d'Offay Ltd. (Grant-in-Aid) 1982

Prov: Anthony d'Offay 1981

Exh: *Bruce McLean*, Kunsthalle, Basel, May–June 1981 (not in catalogue); *New Art at the Tate Gallery*, Tate Gallery, September–October 1983 (no catalogue number)

Lit: Annelie Pohlen, 'Bruce McLean (Kunsthalle Basel, Switzerland, exhibition review)', *Artforum*, XX, 1981, p.92

During 1980, the artist had been working in one of the studios at the Riverside Studios, Hammersmith. T03411 was painted there immediately prior to the performance of 'Possibly a Nude by a Coal Bunker' on 20 September 1980. A photograph of this performance is printed on p.53 of *Bruce McLean,* exhibition catalogue, Whitechapel Art Gallery, 1981. In a telephone conversation with the compiler (2 July, 1986), Bruce McLean commented:

> They were like working notations done in the foyer of the Riverside Studio, on the wall, in front of which the performance took place called 'Possibly a Nude by a Coal Bunker', done the day or night before the performance, which was just me and the naked lady who was standing by a coal shuttle. The piece [the performance] was to do with how nothing works so slides were projected but failed to come through.

Asked about the title of T03411, the artist said:

> – autobiographical, well, Scotland has an obsession with coal bunkers, I don't know why. I was thinking of those beautiful classical nude figures which are always attached to a tree stump, never attached to anything like a wheel-barrow, so I thought why not attach it to a coal scuttle, well this became a coal bunker [in T03411].

While McLean was working on the piece, the panels were fixed to the wall by large tacks reinforced with masking tape. The entire work was trimmed and individually framed under the artist's instructions in 1982 at the Tate Gallery. When arranged in the correct sequence (the pieces were numbered temporarily from 1–5 in black felt pen on masking tape on the reverse; the tape has since been removed) the total width of the work is approximately 26 feet. McLean continued some imagery directly across panels 3 and 4; two similar shapes, one large and one small face-motif, are divided by the frame/border line. The work reveals his pre-occupation with 'lines of movement' which are complemented by the contrasting black ground and the unmixed vibrant colours, mint green, dark lilac and blue.

A related work to T03411, also titled 'Study for "Possibly a Nude by a Coal Bunker"' 1980, Anthony d'Offay), explores similar ideas on a smaller scale, which Hetty Einzig refers to as 'mini-performances – memories of past works' ('Bruce McLean (Anthony d'Offay Gallery)', *Arts Review,* Vol.33, November 1981, p.502).

Similar figuration to T03411 can be seen in 'Pillar to Pillar, Post to Post' (1980, acrylic and wax crayon on photographic paper, Anthony d'Offay) and 'Yucca Gloriosa (with trellis)' (1980, acrylic and wax crayon on photographic paper, Anthony d'Offay) although neither has such a dramatic colour scheme as T03411.

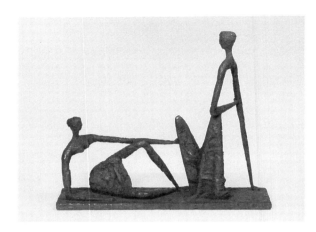

F.E. McWilliam b.1909

T03758 **Mother and Daughter** 1951

Plastic wood and 'Loy' plastic metal
$12\frac{1}{2} \times 15 \times 5\frac{1}{4}$ (320 × 380 × 120)
Not inscribed
Transferred from the Victoria and Albert Museum 1983

Prov: Purchased from the artist by Department of Circulation, Victoria and Albert Museum, 1953 (Circ. 2–1953)

Exh: *McWilliam, Sculpture and Drawings, Robin Campbell, Paintings,* Hanover Gallery, October–November 1952 (no catalogue)

McWilliam made in the early 1950s a number of such small sculptures out of plastic wood applied to a metal armature, and many of these have family subjects. It was an alternative technique at a time when he could not afford bronze, and he worked directly, and not from drawings (letter from the artist, 5 December 1984). His major work in this style on a large scale is the metal 'Matriarch', which was shown in 1953 at the exhibition *20th Century Form* at the Whitechapel Art Gallery, and which is similar in design to the Tate Gallery sculpture.

Heinz Mack b.1931

T03748 **Relief** 1964

Aluminium relief over hardboard
$14\frac{1}{4} \times 16\frac{3}{8} \times 1\frac{5}{8}$ (365 × 415 × 40)
Not inscribed
Transferred from the Victoria and Albert Museum 1983

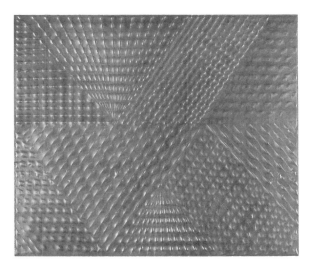

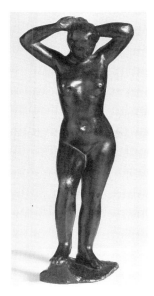

Aristide Maillol 1861–1964

T 03757 **Girl Arranging her Hair** *c.*1898

Bronze $10\frac{3}{8} \times 4\frac{3}{8} \times 4\frac{3}{8}$ ($264 \times 112 \times 112$)
Inscribed 'A M' in monogram on base
Transferred from the Victoria and Albert Museum 1983

Prov: ...; bought at Goupil Gallery by A.E. Anderson, who presented it to the Department of Architecture and Sculpture, Victoria and Albert Museum 1928 (A. 38–1928)

Exh: *Aristide Maillol. Sculpture, Drawings, Wood Engravings,* Goupil Gallery, October 1928 (not identified in catalogue); *Sculpture in France,* Auckland City Art Gallery, September–December 1963 (24, as 'Bather Arranging her Hair', repr.)

Lit: John Rewald, *Maillol,* 1939 (repr. 70 and 71)

Rewald reproduces a bronze and a plaster of this subject, and dates the original statuette to about 1898, with an enlargement made in 1932. There are two enlargements, $31\frac{1}{2}$ins. and 63ins. high.

Paul Maitland 1863–1909

T 03622 **Hyacinth** *c.*1883

Oil on canvas $12 \times 9\frac{7}{8}$ (305×250)
Inscribed 'P F Maitland' b.l.
Presented anonymously in memory of Terence Rattigan 1983

Prov: The artist's family; ...; Leicester Galleries; Peyton Skipwith; the donor 1968

Exh: *The First Annual Exhibition of Flowers by Modern Flower Painters, and Water Colours by Vignoles Fisher,* Baillie Gallery,

March–April 1906 (22); *Water Colours by Owen Merton. Paintings of London by Paul Maitland. Paintings by J.D. Innes,* Leicester Galleries, May 1928 (43, as 'Hyacinth in a ginger bowl'); *First Exhibition of Paintings by Barbara Gilligan. Exhibition of Paintings by Paul Maitland,* Leicester Galleries, November 1948 (67, as 'Flowerpiece'); *Clifford Hall, Recent Drawings. Felix Kelly, Paintings of America, Spain, Italy and New Zealand. Bateson Mason, Recent Paintings. Paul Maitland, An Exhibition of Little Paintings,* Leicester Galleries, December 1952 (40, as 'A Hyacinth in a ginger-jar'); *Paul Maitland,* Leicester Galleries, November 1962 (55, as 'A Hyacinth in a ginger-jar'); *The Early Years of the New English Art Club,* Fine Art Society, February–March 1968 (65, as 'Still Life – Hyacinth and Ginger-Jar')

Maitland enrolled as a student at the Royal College of Art in 1879. He took a year's leave of absence in 1880 due to illness, but he continued his studies from 1881–3. T 03622 is thought to be a mature student work. Its subject matter, that of a still life closely observed, is rare in Maitland's oeuvre and could well be still indebted to subjects chosen for students to paint at the Royal College. Also, in contrast with the swift handling of Maitland's later pictures, this painting is quite heavily worked.

Maitland signed this painting with a prominent signature and included his middle initial of F, for Fordyce, his grandmother's maiden name, a practice which only occurs with his early paintings.

T 03623 Factories Bordering the River *c.*1886

Oil on canvas $10\frac{1}{8} \times 14\frac{1}{2}$ (257 × 370)
Inscribed 'P Maitland' b.l.
Presented anonymously in memory of Terence Rattigan 1983

Prov: The artist's family; . . . ; John Baillie, New Zealand; Bartholomew Bailey; the donor 1965

This, along with most of the other Maitland entries, has no exhibition history listing, or at best an incomplete one. The difficulties of researching an accurate exhibition history and a provenance for these works are two-fold. The first difficulty concerns the titles of the works: many works share the same title and equally many works have had their titles altered over the years so it is usually not possible to be sure whether the title is the original one or a later variant. Since early twentieth century catalogues rarely gave dimensions along with titles, it has not been possible to turn to such material to assist in identifying works with titles, and therefore to identify which work with which title appeared in a particular exhibition. Secondly, on Maitland's death in May 1909, he left everything to one of his two sisters, Maggie Maitland. In July 1909, a private memorial exhibition of Maitland's work was mounted, for one week, at 7 More's Gardens, Chelsea, and because of this, his two sisters put their own paper labels on the back of all the works in their care, with their own titles and dates, caring little for art-historical cataloguing accuracy. These labels therefore have only added to the confusion surrounding the possible identification of exhibited works. As a result, the paintings have been dated on stylistic grounds and through changes in the artist's signature.

From 1878 to 1889 the Maitland family – Paul, his mother and his two sisters Maggie and Ada – lived at 7 Edith Terrace, London, SW10. Edith Terrace is a short stretch of road parallel to the King's Road and to the Thames, and Maitland in the late 1880s painted numerous small works en plein air recording the topography of the Chelsea and Battersea banks of the river.

T 03624 The Sun Pier, Chatham *c.*1897

Oil on panel $9\frac{5}{8} \times 10\frac{3}{4}$ (246 × 272)
Inscribed 'P Maitland' b.l.
Presented anonymously in memory of Terence Rattigan 1983

Prov: The artist's family; . . . ; Leicester Galleries; Mrs Harold Bompas 1928; sold *Modern British Drawings, Paintings and Sculpture,* Christie's, 18 July 1969 (59, as 'Off Sheerness') bt the donor 1969

Exh: *Exhibition of Paintings by the Late Paul Fordyce Maitland,* The Chelsea Association, July 1909 (84, as 'Near Southend'); *Exhibition of Paintings by the Late Paul Fordyce Maitland,* Baillie Gallery, January 1910 (6, as 'Near Southend'); *Watercolours by Owen Merton, Paintings of London by Paul Maitland, Paintings by J.D. Innes,* Leicester Galleries, May 1928 (83, as 'Off Sheerness')

T 03624 shows the Sun Pier at Chatham, Kent to the right of the painting, with a flour mill and its high chimney, and a timber wharf, to the left. The chimney of the flour mill has now been reduced in height. The Sun Pier, designed for sunbathing, was built in 1884, blown down in 1885 and rebuilt in 1886. It was extended in 1902, and since Maitland's painting does not include these extensions, it must have been painted between 1886 and 1902. The picture is likely to have been painted from a barge moored in the middle of the river Medway, for the use of bathers.

After his student days at the Royal College of Art, Maitland turned to Theodore Roussel for tuition. Roussel had a studio home in Chelsea but also a country house near Rochester, and it could well be a painting trip in Kent with Roussel that brought Maitland to Chatham.

T 03625 The Gardens, Chelsea Embankment *c.*1889

Oil on panel 11 × 10$\frac{7}{16}$ (280 × 265)
Not inscribed
Presented anonymously in memory of Terence Rattigan 1983

Prov: The artist's family; ... ; Leicester Galleries; ... Colnaghi and Co. Ltd; sold *Modern British Prints, Drawings, Paintings and Sculpture,* Christie's 24 April 1964 (178, as 'A Spring morning with the statue of Carlyle in Kensington Gardens') 50 gns, bt G. Shankland; the donor

Exh: *London Impressionists,* Goupil Gallery, December 1889 (47); *Twenty-Ninth Exhibition of Works of Modern Artists,* Glasgow Institute of the Fine Arts, Glasgow, February–April 1890 (673); *Coronation Exhibition,* Goupil Gallery, June 1902 (5, as 'Chelsea Embankment Gardens'); *Water Colours by Owen Merton. Paintings of London by Paul Maitland. Paintings by J.D. Innes,* Leicester Galleries, May 1928 (59, as 'Chelsea Embankment Gardens in Spring'); *First Exhibition of Paintings by Barbara Gilligan. Exhibition of Paintings by Paul Maitland,* Leicester Galleries, November 1948 (14, as 'The Carlyle Statue, Chelsea Embankment'); *Clifford Hall, Recent Drawings. Felix Kelly, Paintings of America, Spain, Italy and New Zealand. Bateson Mason, Recent Paintings. Paul Maitland, An Exhibition of Little Paintings,* Leicester Galleries, December 1952 (33, as 'Carlyle Statue, Chelsea Embankment, morning'); *The Leicester Galleries New Year Exhibition,* Leicester Galleries, January 1962 (57, as 'The Carlyle Statue, Chelsea')

T 03625 depicts a small strip of public gardens situated between Chelsea Embankment and Cheyne Walk, level with the intersection of Cheyne Row and Cheyne Walk. Thomas Carlyle, the writer, lived in Cheyne Row from 1834 to his death in 1881 and this statue of Carlyle, by Edgar Boehm, was unveiled in 1882. Chelsea Embankment roadway has since been widened and the garden area to the right of the wide path has been reduced to a small area of grass without trees. The railings around the gardens and around the base of the statue are no longer there. The statue of Carlyle faces the Thames with Albert Bridge to its left and Battersea Bridge to its right. It appears that the very spot at which Maitland set up his easel to paint the view shown in T 03625 also served as the place from which he painted T 03635, 'The Embankment after a Shower'. All that was necessary for this view, including Albert Bridge, was for the artist to turn to the right.

T 03626   Surrey Side of the River – Grey Day c.1886

Oil on panel (cigar box lid) $4\frac{1}{4} \times 8\frac{3}{16}$ (107 × 208)
Inscribed 'P Maitland' b.l.
Presented anonymously in memory of Terence Rattigan 1983
Prov: The artist's family; . . . ; Leicester Galleries; the donor 1967

T 03626 is an accurate view of an industrial section of the bank of the river Thames. For similar views see T 03627, T 03628 and T 03629. T 03626 has an unusually large signature.

T 03627   Riverside Industries c.1889

Oil on panel $5\frac{3}{8} \times 9\frac{1}{4}$ (137 × 235)
Inscribed 'P Maitland' b.l.
Presented anonymously in memory of Terence Rattigan 1983
Prov: The artist's family; . . . ; Leicester Galleries; the donor 1967
Exh: *Exhibition of Paintings by the Late Paul Fordyce Maitland*, The Chelsea Association, July 1909 (78); *Exhibition of Paintings by the Late Paul Fordyce Maitland*, Baillie Gallery, January 1910 (17)

T 03628   Warehouse Across the River c.1886

Oil on panel $4\frac{1}{2} \times 6$ (110 × 152)
Inscribed 'P Maitland' b.r.
Presented anonymously in memory of Terence Rattigan 1983
Prov: The artist's family; . . . ; Fine Art Society; the donor 1979

T 03629   Battersea Boat Houses c.1888

Oil on panel $6\frac{1}{2} \times 5\frac{1}{4}$ (165 × 130)
Inscribed 'P Maitland' b.l.
Presented anonymously in memory of Terence Rattigan 1983
Prov: The artist's family; Baillie Gallery 1910; John Baillie, New Zealand; Bartholomew Bailey; the donor 1965
Exh: N.E.A.C., April–June 1889 (76); *Exhibition of Paintings by the Late Paul Fordyce Maitland*, The Chelsea Association, July 1909 (19); *Exhibition of Paintings by the Late Paul Fordyce Maitland*, Baillie Gallery, January 1910 (30)

T 03629

dens and the streets bordering Kensington Road. Maitland's health was always poor, after an injury to his back as a baby. This resulted in curvature of his spine which worsened with the years, effectively curtailing his painting activity. He could not walk far, particularly if carrying easel, panel and paints, and Chelsea and the Thames were obviously too far for pedestrian trips from a base in Kensington. In the last decade of his life he recorded the seasonal and atmospheric changes of a section of Kensington Gardens. For other views of this subject, see T 03631, T 03632, T 03633 and T 03634.

T 03631 Fall of the Leaves, Kensington Gardens *c.*1900

Oil on panel $5\frac{3}{8} \times 8\frac{1}{8}$ (136 × 206)
Inscribed 'P M' b.l.
Presented anonymously in memory of
Terence Rattigan 1983
Prov: The artist's family; ... ; Leicester
Galleries; the donor

T 03630 By Hyde Park Gate, Kensington Gardens *c.*1906

Oil on panel (cigar box lid) $3\frac{7}{8} \times 7\frac{1}{8}$
(99 × 180)
Inscribed 'P M' b.l.
Presented anonymously in memory of
Terence Rattigan 1983
Prov: The artist's family; ... ; John Baillie, New
Zealand; Bartholomew Bailey; the donor
1965

From 1895 to 1897 Maitland lived in a studio at 45 Roland Gardens, s w, and then from 1897 until his death in 1909 he lived at 3 Cheniston Gardens Studios, Cheniston Gardens, W. He actually died at a friend's house at Shottermill in Surrey. The decision to move from the Chelsea area to Kensington brought about an attendant change in his subject material. From the late 1890s his views of Chelsea and the banks of the Thames diminished and instead he began to concentrate on scenes found in the southern half of Kensington Gar-

T 03632 Autumn, Kensington Gardens *c.*1906

Oil on panel $4\frac{1}{4} \times 6\frac{3}{4}$ (102 × 173)
Inscribed 'P M' b.l.
Presented anonymously in memory of
Terence Rattigan 1983

Prov: The artist's family; ...; Leicester Galleries; the donor

Exh: *First Exhibition of Paintings by Barbara Gilligan. Exhibition of Paintings by Paul Maitland*, Leicester Galleries, November 1948 (37)

T03633 The Flower Walk, Kensington Gardens *c.*1897

Oil on panel $5\frac{1}{16} \times 7$ (128 × 178)
Inscribed 'PM' b.r.
Presented anonymously in memory of Terence Rattigan 1983

Prov: The artist's family; ...; Leicester Galleries; ...; Hugh Beaumont; the donor 1973

Exh: *Water Colours by Owen Merton. Paintings of London by Paul Maitland. Paintings by J.D. Innes,* Leicester Galleries, May 1928 (52); Bury Street Gallery, June 1980 (no catalogue)

T03634 Kensington Gardens with Chairs and Figures *c.*1907

Oil on panel $4\frac{1}{4} \times 6\frac{7}{8}$ (108 × 175)
Inscribed 'P Maitland' b.l.

Presented anonymously in memory of Terence Rattigan 1983

Prov: The artist's family; ...; John Baillie, New Zealand; Bartholomew Bailey; the donor 1965

T03634 shows a section of Kensington Gardens with the chairs for hire tipped diagonally against one another or against a tree. Park attendants used to tip them in this manner in the evening to prevent rain or dew collecting on the seats. The Ashmolean Museum, Oxford owns a Maitland, 'Park Scene', oil on canvas ($10\frac{1}{4} \times 18\frac{1}{8}$ins.) which shows these chairs in their upright position.

T03635 The Embankment after a Shower *c.*1888

Oil on panel $5\frac{3}{8} \times 8\frac{5}{8}$ (136 × 220)
Inscribed 'P Maitland' b.l.
Presented anonymously in memory of Terence Rattigan 1983

Prov: The artist's family; ...; Leicester Galleries; ...; Colnaghi & Co Ltd; Lord Ilford (Geoffrey Hutchinson); sold *Impressionist and Modern Pictures and Sculptures* Phillips 30 October 1978 (129) bt Fine Art Society; the donor 1979

See entry on T03625 for another work painted from the same spot. T03635 depicts Cheyne Walk and the embankment wall with a lamp-post in the middle ground and the Albert Bridge crossing the river Thames beyond. The Albert suspension bridge dates to 1873. When Maitland painted T03635 the bridge was painted a uniform grey whereas in recent times it has been treated to a colourful display of blue, green, white and pink paint. The embankment lamp-post is still present today as are the warehouses on the opposite bank.

T03636 In Buckinghamshire *c.*1890

Oil on panel $5\frac{3}{4} \times 9\frac{1}{2}$ (146 × 240)
Inscribed 'P Maitland' b.l.

Presented anonymously in memory of
Terence Rattigan 1983
Prov: The artist's family; . . . ; Leicester
Galleries; the donor

Country landscapes are very rare in Maitland's oeuvre.
It is known that he went to Ludlow to stay with his
friend, the painter William Osborn, whose wife worked
in a school there, and to Buckinghamshire to stay with
his relations, the Snows. There are no significant features in this view which could assist in an identification,
thus it could be either Shropshire or Buckinghamshire.
An old handwritten label cites it as Buckinghamshire.

T 03637 **A Yacht off Sheerness** *c.*1896

Oil on panel 9¼ × 5⅜ (236 × 136)
Inscribed 'P M' b.l.
Presented anonymously in memory of
Terence Rattigan 1983
Prov: The artist's family; . . . ; Leicester
Galleries; the donor 1966

Exh: *Clifford Hall, Recent Drawings. Felix
Kelly, Paintings of America, Spain, Italy
and New Zealand. Bateson Mason, Recent
Paintings. Paul Maitland, An Exhibition of
Little Paintings*, Leicester Galleries,
December 1952 (14); *Paul Maitland*,
Leicester Galleries, November 1962 (51)

Sheerness is situated at the furthest north-western tip
of the Isle of Sheppey, Kent, where the river Medway
runs into the Thames estuary. See the entry on T 03624
for information on Maitland in Kent.

T 03647 **The Three Public-Houses,
Morning Sun Light** *c.*1889

Oil on canvas 30 × 27¾ (760 × 705)
Not inscribed
Presented anonymously in memory of
Terence Rattigan 1983
Prov: The artist's family; . . . ; Leicester
Galleries; Hugh Beaumont; the donor
Exh: *London Impressionists*, Goupil Gallery,
December 1889 (49); *Twenty-Ninth
Exhibition of Works of Modern Artists*,
Glasgow Institute of the Fine Arts,
Glasgow, February–April 1890 (734, £40);
*Munchner Jahres-Ausstellung im
Glaspalast*, Munich, 1891 (922d, as 'Die
Drei Wirtshäuser'); *Artists at the Leicester
Galleries from 1902–1969*, Morley Gallery,
October–November 1969 (39, as 'Cheyne
Walk'); *British Art 1890–1928*, The
Columbus Gallery of Fine Arts,
Columbus, Ohio, February–March 1971
(58, as 'Cheyne Walk', repr.)

Lit: 'The London Impressionists', *The Sunday Chronicle*, 15 December 1889, repr. p.5

This view is Cheyne Walk, Chelsea, between Blantyre Street and Riley Street, looking east towards Battersea Bridge. J.M.W. Turner once lived in the house to the left of the ivy covered building.

Maitland lived in the family home at 7 Edith Terrace, Chelsea from 1878 to 1889. In 1887 and 1888 he also used 12 Bolton Studios, the home of Theodore Roussel, as an address from which works were sent to exhibitions. Roussel (1847–1926) came to England from France in 1874.

'The Three Public-Houses, Morning Sun Light' was painted after Maitland met Roussel and became his part-time student. It is one of Maitland's largest paintings. According to the donor Roussel encouraged Maitland to exhibit his paintings and to paint larger works which could more suitably be exhibited.

Raymond Mason b.1922

T03678　Barcelona Tram 1953

Bronze relief $30\frac{3}{4} \times 49\frac{1}{4} \times 9\frac{3}{4}$
($780 \times 1250 \times 250$)
Inscribed on lower front edge at extreme l. with foundry mark 'A.BRUNI FUSE.ROMA'; towards l. [in artist's hand] 'Barcelona'; towards r. [in artist's hand] 'Raymond Mason 1953 3/8'.
Purchased from Pierre Matisse Gallery, New York (Grant-in-Aid) 1983

Prov: The artist; Pierre Matisse Gallery, New York, 1968
Exh: *Raymond Mason*, Pierre Matisse Gallery, New York, October–November 1968 (2, as 'Barcelona Street Car', the plaster repr.); *Forty Years of Modern Art 1945–1985*,

Tate Gallery, February–April 1986 (works not numbered)
Lit: [David Sylvester], 'A new sculptor', in 'Mr. Moore's New Bronzes', *The Times*, 15 February 1954; David Sylvester, 'Two Exhibitions of Sculpture', *The Listener*, 15 November 1956, p.795; Michael Peppiatt, introduction to *Raymond Mason*, exhibition catalogue, Serpentine Gallery, 1982, pp.5–11; Raymond Mason, 'responses by Raymond Mason to questions by Michael Peppiatt', ibid., pp.12–16 (the plaster repr. p.24); Helen Lessore, 'Raymond Mason', in *A Partial Testament*, 1986, pp.168–83 (the plaster repr. p.170)
Repr: The plaster, in *Raymond Mason*, exhibition catalogue, Musée National d'Art Moderne, Paris, 1985, p.87 and photograph by Douglas Glass *c*.1955 (mistakenly captioned as 1953) of the artist with the plaster, p.146

In a letter of 6 April 1986 (from which all quotations in this entry are taken except where stated otherwise) the artist wrote:

If I have to talk about the 'Barcelona Tram' I must begin by saying that it is a subject seen in Spain by an Englishman, sculpted in France and cast into bronze in Italy.

By my second trip to Barcelona in 1952 I had already returned to figuration and had begun my first low-reliefs. However when I began to draw the Catalan scene, the strong sun and the opulent, sculptural forms of the people, particularly the women, literally impelled the idiom of high-relief upon me. The almost ritualistic arrival of the trams before the solemn, sunlit grandeur of the Estacion di Francia railway station was irresistible. My personnages stood as little statues until the tramcar came – and then away. In the tram itself a handsome group of people sat at the glass-less windows like spectators in theatre boxes.

It has been said that one can detect an influence of Piero della Francesca in this work but this is erroneous. Piero became of interest for me when I encountered Balthus and his paintings and this was only in 1955. The echo comes more likely from de Chirico, as David Sylvester had detected in relation to an earlier sculpture in his *Times* article of 1954. Statues and the somnambulism of great Mediterranean cities.

But *I* thought I was dealing with reality at its strongest. This sculpture was my first high-relief and I just made a box and put into it all that had caught my eye. The spread-out and a certain frontality of the figures are the beginning of my detachment from the art of Giacometti.

At the same time there was an attempt to suggest that the people depicted were being carried away to their destiny and I even placed the window-bars before the driver in the form of a cross.

When Mason began work on the plaster he had still never had a studio of his own. He 'began it in the studio of Joseph Erhardy, rue de Verneuil, Paris and completed it in the top-room flat of the Paris-Match photographer [Tony Saulnier], rue Jacob, Paris ... I only entered into possession of the 60 rue Monsieur le Prince studio in middle 1953 when the sculpture had just been completed.' The Tate has a photograph of Mason working on the plaster in rue Jacob in early 1953. The first display of any example of 'Barcelona Tram' was of the plaster, in Mason's first one-man exhibition, at the Beaux-Arts Gallery, London, February–March 1954. The first showing of a bronze cast was in Mason's exhibition at the Galerie Claude Bernard, Paris, May 1965. At the time of writing, six of the intended eight bronze casts of 'Barcelona Tram' have been made. The Tate's cast was made in 1968.

All the reproductions of the plaster cited above are of the artist's preferred photograph of it, by Tony Saulnier. Mason prefers that photographs of the work (bronzes included) should be taken, like Saulnier's, by daylight without flash and that (as in the Tate's photograph) the principal view should be from the angle and height adopted by Saulnier.

Mason first visited Barcelona in 1950 to work on a portrait bust in terracotta. He felt immediate enthusiasm for the city but did not become interested in the subject of the Tate's work until his second long stay there in 1952. Mason's exhibition at the Musée National d'Art Moderne, Paris in 1985 included two related ink drawings both titled 'Le Tramway de Barcelone'. One of these (3, repr., coll. John Lessore) is one of two 'Barcelona Tram' drawings in London private collections drawn in 1953, not from observation. It shows tram and tram-stop from approximately the same angle as in the Tate's relief but with different figures and background. It represents the tram-stop at the port, as does the other drawing in the 1985 exhibition (2, not repr., coll. the artist), which was made in 1952 from observation and shows two trams in the middle distance with trees (two of them palms) and shipping in the background. The Tate has a photograph of this work, as well as photocopies of two further 'Barcelona Tram' drawings of 1952 (private collection, New York) which are among several which Mason made from observation in front of the Estacion di Francia (which forms the background to the scene in 'Barcelona Tram') with the intention of making the sculpture.

'Barcelona Tram' was the first work in which Mason dealt with a group of figures. He cites a remark of André Malraux's which he recalls as 'Low relief and high relief permit the representation of people who are not in contact with one another and do not know each other, as compared with sculpture in the round which supposes that the protagonists are in direct contact or know each other.' But Mason explains:

I must underline that at no time was I trying to develop the mode of relief or the high-relief or any other form of sculpture and I have to this day never gone out of my way to examine the reliefs of Italy which abound nor, for instance, the calvaries of Brittany which seem to have reference to my later crowds. It was simply because I wanted to encompass a *whole scene* which obliged me initially to adopt the relief form and when my figures developed in form I had to mount the walls of the frame to semi-enclose the scene. This tendency culminated in the 'Departure of Fruit and Vegetables ...' [1969–71] after which the frame became extraneous to the sculpture and was abandoned.

In an interview with Richard Cork broadcast on Radio 3 on 25 April 1985, Mason observed that it was not until rather later than 'Barcelona Tram' that figures in his sculpture came to be more united to each other. In his letter of 6 April 1986 he added:

When my subject ceased to be uniquely the street-scene, when my passers-by started to assume their new role as members of humanity, then naturally the decor of the buildings, which linked them together, disappeared and only the uniting of the figures one to another could make up the sculptural mass. But by then the union of people was itself a theme.

In answer to a question about the prevalence of trams and cars in his work of the 1950s, Mason replied:

I cannot see how an artist who concerns himself with *the* great subject – the world which moves around him – can avoid treating what you call modern forms of transport. Thus cars, which appear in the 1953 'Place St. Germain-des-Prés', 'Place de l'Opéra' 1956, 'La Rue' 1964, and buses, 'Boulevard St. Germain '58', 'Carrefour de l'Odéon '58–59' and the 'Place de l'Opéra'. [All these works are reproduced in the catalogues of Mason's retrospectives at the Serpentine Gallery in 1982 and at the Musée National d'Art Moderne, Paris in 1985]. There were no longer any trams in Paris on my arrival after the war. All these conveyances placed people on different levels from that of the street and added interest to the specifically human element. Of course trams and buses were a major part of my childhood in Birmingham as was the motor-car since my father was a pioneer motorist.

Probably the tram has a link with the later polychrome compositions where the figures, although numerous, are isolated one from another. The link with the 'Carrefour' is not, of course, the tram since, as I have said, the 'Carrefour' and the 'Place de l'Opéra' vehicles are the platformed buses of that period. 'Le plate-forme de l'omnibus parisien – haut lieu de la civilisation' Jean-Paul Sartre. Rather it is what you detected so exactly as being the opposition of spread-out and frontality and a sharp counter-axis which disappears into the distance, described in the 'Barcelona Tram' by a mere diminution of size and in the 'Carrefour' with greater emphasis by the grouping of all the windows and doors of the Boulevard St. Germain into a multiplication of fine stigmats. With the intention, as you correctly say, of pulling the spectator's eye straight in.

The compiler asked about the interest in 'Barcelona Tram' shown by Picasso, Bacon and Balthus. Mason replied:

Since you ask me pointedly to speak on the matter, it is true that this single work, the 'Barcelona Tram', was responsible for my three contacts with three famous artists. At the age of 31 in 1953 I was personally unknown.

Picasso, I went to see on the beach of Golfe Juan, in the summer of 1954. I had already met him, and, recovering from a peritonitis operation in the south of France, I hoped he could introduce me to a ceramist in Vallauris where I would be able to do terracottas which were all my strength could allow. Showing him photographs of my work as it stood to date, the only work of any consequence was the 'Tram' done the year before. Naturally the subject of Barcelona was enough to interest him in the work and he praised it highly, saying that it wasn't compilation art but something personal. Following which, as I have related elsewhere, he added that I was an English artist and, seeing my admittedly crestfallen face, he continued by saying that he admired English art deeply and proceeded to name all our important artists from Hogarth onwards ... After which he called over – all this had taken place at the lunch to which he had kindly invited me – a famous French sculptor to look at this photograph of the Tram. 'Not bad,' said the friend, 'but it's not sculpture.' 'And that's exactly why I like it,' retorted Picasso, 'because sculpture-sculpture gives me the shits.' To cap it all he proposed me an introduction to his dealer Kahnweiler, which I never used.

Francis Bacon asked to meet me on seeing the 'B.T.' at my first exhibition at Helen Lessore's. So I got Helen to arrange a dinner-party for us both and

David Sylvester and in effect, my friendship with Francis dates from then.

I met Balthus one evening at Carmen Baron's [flat in Paris] sometime in spring 1955. Late at night he walked me home and as the conversation continued, I walked him back to his place. No less English in his habits than me, Balthus then accompanied me a second time to my studio and it was then, in the early hours of the morning, that he saw my 'Barcelona Tram' and 'the Idyll', now destroyed [repr. Mason retrospective catalogue, Paris, 1985, fig.25]. He approved of them enough to return the following day to examine them afresh. We were friends from then on.

About the same time the great poster artist and stage designer A.M. Cassandre fell in love with the 'Tram' to the point where a well-wisher bought the original plaster from me and gave it as a gift to Cassandre. He kept it a nominal year and then returned it to my studio so that I could put it into bronze.

And finally I will mention that at the time of my 1954 show at the Beaux Arts Gallery, my father-in-law of the time wanted to have it put into bronze in order to present it to the Tate. I refused this proposition deeming that it wasn't in that way that I wanted to enter the Tate. I felt also, and doubtless correctly, that the Tate would have, in 1954, refused the offer.

Close-up of view through window

T 03797 St Mark's Place, East Village, New York City 1972

Acrylic on epoxy resin in glazed and painted wood box with integral base, $27 \times 49\frac{3}{16} \times 19\frac{1}{2}$ (686 × 1249 × 495) Inscribed 'Raymond Mason/1973 5/6' on upper face of horizontal board at bottom front of interior of box (nearest figures to inscription are those with turban and with shoulder bag), and 'ST. MARK'S PLACE EAST VILLAGE N.Y.C. as seen through the window of the Village East Coffee Shop. 1972' along front edge of integral base

Presented by Mme Andrée Stassart 1983
Prov: Galerie Claude Bernard, Paris; Mme
Andrée Stassart

Exh: *The Hard-Won Image,* Tate Gallery, July–
September 1984 (100, repr.); *Raymond
Mason,* Musée National d'Art Moderne,
Centre Georges Pompidou, Paris,
September–November 1985, Musée
Cantini, Marseilles, December 1985 –
February 1986 (65, unspecified cast repr.
in col., pp.114–15)

Lit: Raymond Mason, *St Mark's Place East
Village, N.Y. Sculpture by Raymond
Mason,* exhibition catalogue, Pierre
Matisse Gallery, New York, November
1974 (eight different views of unspecified
cast repr. in col.); Phyllis Derfner,
'Raymond Mason at Pierre Matisse', *Art
in America,* LXIII, May–June 1975,
pp.90–1 (detail of unspecified cast repr.);
anon., entry on this work in *Raymond
Mason,* exhibition catalogue, Serpentine
Gallery, 1982, p.40 (unspecified cast repr.;
also repr. in col. p.16)

This sculpture was made in Paris in 1972 in recollection of a scene observed by Mason in New York in 1971. He still owns the original plaster, from which the full edition of six casts in epoxy resin has been made in the studios of Robert Haligon at Perigny-sur-Yerres and at Brie-Comte-Robert in the suburbs of Paris. There will also be two casts hors-edition. Each cast is painted individually by Mason.

The dates inscribed by the artist along the lower front edge of the work and inside its glazed box are each in error by one year. Mason stencilled the inscription on the lower edge in June 1984, to make this example consistent with the others in the edition, but in the final digit he inadvertently gave the date at which the work was sculpted, rather than the date of the original scene which it depicts. In the inscription made several years earlier in the interior of the work he inadvertently gave the date at which this cast was painted, rather than the date at which it was sculpted.

The following account by Raymond Mason of the origins and meaning of this work was published by Pierre Matisse Gallery, New York in November 1974 on the first occasion of the exhibition of any example of the edition:

The sobering thought is that almost every person who sees my sculpture of St Mark's Place, East Village, in the Pierre Matisse Gallery, must know that district a hundred times better than I do.

At the least. I saw this particular scene once, for two hours, in November 1971.

It was quite by accident. I went to visit my old friend Jason Harvey who lives on Cooper Square and coaxed him into making me a drawing-board to fit the piece of paper I'd brought down-town for that purpose. I was waiting for the showing of my Paris market sculpture in this same Gallery [this refers to 'Le Départ des Fruits et Légumes du Coeur de Paris, 1969' which is reproduced in colour in the catalogues of Mason's retrospective exhibitions at the Serpentine Gallery, 1982 and at the Musée National d'Art Moderne, Paris, 1985] and in the meantime I hoped to draw some of the skyscrapers in central New York, particularly the curved one then just nearing completion on 57th Street. With this intention in mind I was re-entering the subway in the same Cooper Square when I realized that it was lunch-time and that I'd more easily find food where I was, than up-town on a Saturday mid-day. I went to the first eating-house I saw on a corner of Third Avenue. It was Tony Provenzano's 'Village East Coffee Shop'.

I sat down by the window which on that side looks out onto the first four buildings of St Mark's Place. During the meal I greedily ate up the spectacle outside where an extravagant populace trouped the sidewalks in sharp noon sunlight. All travellers enjoy sitting watching a foreign world pass by. I felt particularly fortunate because I soon noticed that some of the more curious faces in that street outside passed by my window again and again as though incapable of breaking through an invisible barrier at the end of the block. Maybe, too, my heart was being warmed by the sight of the brick fronts opposite. I was born in Birmingham, England and had spent a sickly childhood looking through curtains at a brick-lined street – except that my bricks had been red, to be sure, while these were painted black or white. In any case I forgot that I had intended to draw buildings which scrape the sky. Here were people very much down to earth, some perhaps barely risen from it, judging by their strange outfits that suggested a bivouac way of life. And here, too, at my side was my brand new drawing-board with its fresh sheet of paper. Not having drawn in days – and feeling hungry in that way too – I took out my pen and ink. The coffee-shop proprietor had no objections. On the contrary, he stood behind me and told me all he knew about each face or feature as it appeared on the paper. It takes an Italian to recognise things that fast. (If St Mark's Place is East Village mythology, Tony Provenzano was my Homer. If it is Hell, as some say, then he was my Dante.)

From then on I can't honestly say whether this or that detail of the scene struck me at the time or only seemed to grow significant when looking at the drawing a month or two afterwards in Paris or at an even later date when I had begun the sculpture and things were becoming more defined. When did I first give importance to the word 'Pazza' which is situated in the exact center of the composition and which in Italian means 'mad'? Was it before or after my coming to the very conclusion that a certain streak of folly ran through my little group of characters – the drunkard mad from drink, and his neighbour from smoking God knows what, the girl mad for her man who, with a cycling helmet on his head and some sort of palm-branch in his hand hardly appears an embodiment of reason. As for the man wandering around dressed as a soldier of the War of Independence ... Of course, I'd better mention that I saw these individual people exactly as I attempt to show them here and they all appear in the original sketch. Two moments do come to my mind which made a mark at the time and, as it were, a move in my direction. I had begun by drawing the police-car stationed just outside the window because it had a sculptural silhouette with its siren and the alarm-signal on the roof. The policemen seemed to have the same battlemented fixity so I was surprised when I realised that they had left the car and were sitting drinking on my side of the glass in the coffee-house. Less large than life they looked, like actors got down from a stage. The second occasion was the arrival of the drunk. He came feeling his way across the window, moving clumsily like a lobster in the aquarium of a sea-food restaurant. That hand on the glass gave a relief to the drawing and another significance to the window as I realised later on once back in Paris. I had left New York shortly afterwards without returning to East Village and the drawing lay amongst others in the studio.

It returned to my mind because in the midst of my winter's work of finishing and painting the remaining copies of the Market sculpture (32 apples, 80 oranges, 108 leeks, 160 faces, etc.) I felt I needed some 'light relief' and the mid-day scene in St Mark's Place seemed just the thing. However I was aware that a deal of concentration would be involved and for a time I was content to imagine the sculpture as it would be when finished. At the same time I described it to one or two people giving them the impression that it was already half-done. One night sitting on the glass-enclosed terrace of a café I was speaking of it again to friends just arrived in Paris. 'And the best of it,' I concluded, 'is the hand pressing against the window, just like here, before our very noses.' My friend's wife is a sculptor and her approval of the idea put me to shame and the next day to work. I've related this random succession of events to show with what 'irresponsibility' I finally sat down – to do what? Solely, I must admit, to reproduce as guilelessly as possibly and within drastic limits of scope and scale my brief vision of that vivid thoroughfare. The general concept of the sculpture was accordingly simple. It would consist of a windowed-box in which I could stage the scene and place the various dramatic personae just as they had played before my eyes. The notable difference would necessarily be that whereas I had sat within and watched them without, now they would be inside and myself the outside spectator.

Given these conditions, what kind of sculptural interest could I hope for?

Essentially it would have to stem from the very heteroclitic nature of that crowd of figures. In the foreground, an uninspired Hindu, a mystical intellectual, the drunk, the smoker, the lovers, the hippy, a bum. Behind them, the two policemen, a cosy Negress, a Latin-type running, the man with the feathered helmet, a bruiser and his Portuguese pal. On the sidewalk opposite, though hardly to be seen, are nevertheless the man who sits on the steps (all day and every day according to Tony), a girl in hot-pants, a dog, an Arab, a Negro stooping for a cigarette-butt, a girl off to visit the shops, the cook serving a pizza to a truck-driver, a loafer, a Negro mammie with her little girl, a bearded guy, an old man, a young Negro and, at her window on the second floor, a dejected blond. If I can group these people together I also have to consider that they must reorganise themselves in a dozen other ways so as to present a coherent picture to the viewer who will change his angle before the window. The moving eye will give momentum to the separate elements so that they can come and go in a continual metamorphosis, sharply emphasised by the colour employed. This bristling between the figures should be measured and intensified by the rigid window-bars and the geometry and lettering of the facades across the street. If the little space can come alive its inmates might seem to breathe. Accordingly I must accept all incidents, all accessory facts, as vivifying since they enrich the outlines; their crenellation claws and stirs the air around. (As I have said I was at the onset fascinated by the turreted-roof of the police-car.) Similar attempts to tap the vitality of out-door life have been evident in most of my street scenes and more particularly in the Market sculpture where I first used colour to detach and personalise a quantity of separate elements. This isolation of various groups in the latter sculpture had its counterpart in my direct modelling in plaster to make component forms, hollow from the back – thus easier to cast into the resin – the edges of which being defined by the very limit of the spectator's vision.

I sat down to sculpt the East Village scene along precisely similar lines.

While engrossed in the making of my little peep-show, various thoughts came my way which I'll mention for what they're worth.

There was an Arab looking rather lost on the sidewalk opposite. In the sculpture he stands close to the Irish cop beside the police-car; a couple of inches away – maybe three. Now there's a greater gap than three inches between an Arab and a Irishman. So there comes a push of space between them, or so it seems to me. And accordingly between the other racial and social types which mingle in that exotic street. A difference in sentiment or in expression also creates a gap. Travelling from the convulsed face of the drunk to the pacified grimace of the smoker represents a break in space and time, yes, a journey. I once noticed this on an alabaster Roman column featuring on alternate sides the masks of tragedy and comedy. There was no knowing the slenderness of that column. I had forgotten this.

In the same line of thought, it occurred to me, while I was painting the sheet-iron chimney beside the drab lace curtains, that the more I made it look like a chimney and the closer I could get to making a curtain – the more, in short, that they showed likeness to themselves – then the more they would differ from each other. They would thus tend to move apart to a minute degree. Minute but immeasurable so therefore why not infinite?

I've already said on another occasion that I expect a work of art to speak of everything. What I saw through Tony Provenzano's window gave me an inkling that there may be a sculptural way of expressing it.

Mason's only drawing of St Mark's Place, described above, is in a New York private collection and has not been reproduced.

In a letter of 6 April 1986, from which all the following quotations are taken, Mason wrote that this was the first of his sculptures 'to attempt the reading of emotions, giving an added complexity to the sculptured web'.

Mason has made several other works in which notional or represented glazing is interposed between the viewer and the depicted human image. One was:

a plaster sculpture in my 1956 show at the Beaux Arts Gallery which represented a nude girl behind a glazed window where the shadow of the window-bars emphasized the curves of the body. All this in a box approximately 110 × 70 × 40cms. The sculpture was destroyed afterwards in the friend's house where I had left it. As far as I know, no photograph exists although I have some drawings.

The Tate has photocopies of these two drawings. The catalogue of Mason's retrospective at the Musée d'Art Moderne, Paris, 1985 reproduces as fig.11 part of the plaster of Mason's sculpture 'Le Voyage' 1966 which was to have represented a family in a car, seen through the windscreen. The couple in the front seats are looking towards the viewer. The very small original model for this work (private collection, Paris) was in colour, and included the car's windows. In 1976 Mason made a drawing (of which the Tate has a photocopy) titled 'Vous êtes la Gioconde'. This represents a dense crowd of people in the Louvre, seen from the viewpoint of the 'Mona Lisa' of Leonardo da Vinci, at which almost all those in the crowd are staring intensely and with varying emotions. Mason writes that 'most of my groups look at something or other but particularly, of course, the Illuminated Crowds which did begin ... with "Vous êtes la Gioconde" '.

Henri Matisse 1869–1954

T 03568 Cap d'Antibes 1922

Oil on canvas $19\frac{7}{8} \times 24\frac{1}{16}$ (506 × 612)
Inscribed 'Henri-Matisse' b.r.
Bequeathed by Mrs A.F. Kessler 1983
Prov: Bernheim-Jeune, Paris (purchased from the artist); Percy Moore Turner (Independent Gallery), February 1923; William Boyd, Dundee; Reid and Lefevre; Mrs A.F. Kessler 1943
Exh: *Henri Matisse*, Bernheim-Jeune, Paris, February 1922; *Loan Exhibition of Pictures*, Norwich Castle Museum, October–November 1927 (73, as 'Antibes', lent by William Boyd); *The Kessler Collection*, Wildenstein Gallery, October–November 1948 (19); *Les Fauves und die Zeitgenossen*, Kunsthalle, Bern,

April–May 1950 (102); XXV Biennale, Venice, June–October 1950 (Fauves 49); *The Kessler Bequest*, Tate Gallery, February–April 1984 (not numbered, repr. in col.)

A view at Cap d'Antibes on the French Riviera, painted in January 1922. The figure seated on the right is probably the artist's daughter Marguerite, as the black-and-white check coat appears to be the one she is wearing in 'The Scottish Coat' 1918 (coll. Dubi Müller, Geneva) and its related version 'Mlle Matisse in a Scottish Coat' of the same year, in which the pattern is less clear, more abstracted. However, Matisse sometimes used the same clothes on different models, so one cannot be certain of this (information from Wande de Guébriant and Dominique Fourcade).

Bernard Meadows b.1915

T 03409   **Black Crab** 1952

Bronze $16\frac{3}{4} \times 13\frac{3}{8} \times 9\frac{1}{2}$ (425 × 340 × 242)
Inscribed 'M /º/8' on underside of larger oval form
Purchased from the artist through Whitechapel Art Gallery (Grant-in-Aid) 1982

Prov: Mrs Marjorie Meadows
Exh: ? *British Pavilion XXVI Biennale*, Venice, 1952 (135, unspecified cast); ? *Sculpture in the Home*, Arts Council, 1953 (27, repr., unspecified cast); ? *British*

Pavilion XXXII Biennale, Venice, 1964 (53, repr., unspecified cast); *Forty Years of Modern Art*, Tate Gallery, February–April 1986 (not numbered, repr. in col.)

Lit: W.J. Strachan, 'The Sculptor and his drawings. 2. Bernard Meadows', *The Connoisseur*, April 1974, CLXXXV, no.746, pp.288–93, repr. p.289 (Clare College, Cambridge cast); *British Sculpture in the 20th Century. Part 2: Symbol and Imagination 1951–1980*, Whitechapel Art Gallery leaflet 1981 ('V. Animals and Beasts') and list of works (52, another cast).

T 03759   **Crab** 1953

Bronze, partly painted $5\frac{1}{8} \times 3\frac{1}{2} \times 4\frac{3}{8}$ (155 × 90 × 110)
Not inscribed
Transferred from the Victoria and Albert Museum 1983

Prov: Purchased from the artist 1953, by the Victoria and Albert Museum (Circ. 4–1953)
Exh: Travelling exhibitions, Department of Circulation, Victoria and Albert Museum
Lit: *British Sculpture in the 20th Century. Part 2: Symbol and Imagination 1951–1980*, Whitechapel Art Gallery leaflet 1981 ('V. Animals and Beasts') another cast repr., as '1955'.

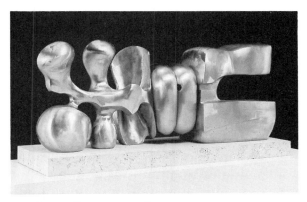

T 03811   **Lovers** 1980

Bronze on marble base $25\frac{1}{2} \times 55\frac{1}{2} \times 17\frac{3}{4}$
($670 \times 1410 \times 450$) including base
Not inscribed
Presented by the Friends of the Tate
Gallery 1983

Lit: *The Friends of the Tate Gallery Annual
Report 1st May 1983–30th April 1984*,
1984, p.14, repr.

Else Meidner b.1901

T 03694   **Death and the Maiden**
*c.*1918–25

Charcoal on paper $21\frac{3}{4} \times 19\frac{3}{4}$ (550×497)
Not inscribed
Presented by Dr J.P. Hodin 1983

Prov: Dr J.P. Hodin (from the artist)
Exh: *Else Meidner*, Ben Uri Gallery, June–July
1972 (30)

Mrs Meidner said that this was probably one of the
drawings which she executed when she was a teenager
in Berlin. As her father was a doctor and she was sensitive in her early youth and afraid of death, her drawings and writings of that period were predominantly on
the subject of death (information from H.R. Holme on
behalf of the artist, 12 December 1984).

She already had a great admiration at that time for
the work of Käthe Kollwitz, whom she went to visit in
1918, taking some of her own drawings with her, and
with whom she remained in touch for some years afterwards.

Mario Merz b.1925

T 03673   **Fibonacci Tables** *c.*1974–76

Charcoal, acrylic and metallic paint with
neon on cotton canvas $105 \times 150\frac{1}{2}$
(2667×3822)
Not inscribed
Purchased from Anthony d'Offay Ltd
(Grant-in-Aid) 1983

Exh: *Mario Merz, Important Works 1966–83*,
Anthony d'Offay Ltd, February–March
1983 (no catalogue);

Lit: 'Mario Merz, An interview with Caroline
Tisdall', *Studio International*, CLXXXXI,
January/February 1976, pp.11–17; *Mario
Merz*, exhibition catalogue, Palazzo
Congressi ed Esposizioni, San Marino,
November 1983

This work was originally dated *c.*1970 but appears
to relate closely to a group of drawings made by
Merz between 1974–6 (repr. *Mario Merz Arbeiten auf*

Papier, exhibition catalogue, Kestner-Gesellschaft, Hannover, July–September 1983, figs.18, 25–39, 45–6).

The painting combines three images or elements which have recurred in Merz's work since the late 1960s/early 1970s, neon, numbers and tables.

From 1965 he has used neon tubing (first on three dimensional objects and later on paintings) to denote a state of flux or transformation and, after 1970, to record in numerals a process of proliferation of objects.

Since 1970, Merz's work has been based on the number series known as the Fibonacci System (Fibonacci was the nickname of the medieval Italian mathematician, Leonardo da Pisa, who wrote the *Liber Abaci* in 1202). The number series (originally applied to the understanding of reproduction in rabbits) can extend infinitely and was seen by da Pisa to correspond to proliferation in nature. The numbers increase by the addition of each preceding pair, for example, $1 + 1 = 2 + 1 = 3 + 2 = 5$; thus 1 1 2 3 5 8 13 21 etc.

Here, as in many of Merz's works, images of tables are linked to the number system by neon numbers which spiral out from the centre in the following sequence. 1, 1, 2, 3, 5, 8, 13, 21. Glasses drawn on each table correspond to these numbers, suggesting an increasing number of diners, and the sizes of the tables increase as the spiral widens, implying an open-ended development.

Merz has investigated different forms (all either linked closely to man's use or to nature, which illustrates the principle of dynamic growth (see also the entry for T 03674). The image of a table, suggesting social grouping and interaction and the breakdown of hierarchies, is one which Merz has used from the early seventies. Germano Celant writes (*Mario Merz*, exhibition catalogue, Museum Folkwang, Essen, January 1979, pp.56–7, translated for the later Whitechapel showing):

As the igloo represents Merz's idea of territory and materials, the table comes to stand for the social interaction of the local community. Thus the table, through the rites of reunion and eating, transcends the boundaries between people and objects. Merz is no longer in the centre, but seated next to the others. Everyone in the ceremony has a sense of rapport with the others, a defined place in the entire space. A group or an individual can draw back into a private zone or can reunite with the others under the roof of branches or panes of broken glass. In this moment, the nomad, in the centre of a system of relations, becomes sedentary. He begins to occupy precise confines, placing himself near the other nomads and living with them, organising the space according to the presence of others. In this way tables are formed for one person, for two, for three, for five, for eight, for 13, for 21, for 34, for 55, for 89. As they

proliferate they arrange themselves in spirals, in relation to the increase in people.

The artist discussed his table works, both paintings and drawings, with Caroline Tisdall in an interview in 1976 (cited above).

In 1973, Merz wrote:

I reject linear, one by one, or assembly-line fabrication of spaces. I reject the idea that there can be a fixed number of people in a space.
Tables which belong to the reality of daily life have to be made either for a full space or for an empty space ...
For one person.
For another person.
For two people then.
For three people.
For five people.
For eight people.
For thirteen people.
For twenty-one people.
For thirty-four people.

[From exhibition catalogue, *it is possible to have a space with tables for 88 people ...*, John Weber Gallery, New York, November–December 1973, n.p.].

This painting may have been one of those exhibited in Merz's one-man exhibition at the Institute of Contemporary Arts (September–October 1975). According to the catalogue for his exhibition in San Marino in 1984 (see entry for T 03674) two 'Table paintings' from 1975, and one from 1974, were included.

T 03674 **Cone** *c.*1967

Willow basket work 87 × 51 × 51 (2210 × 1295 × 1295)
Not inscribed
Purchased from Anthony d'Offay Ltd (Grant-in-Aid) 1983

Exh: *Mario Merz, Important works 1966–83*, Anthony d'Offay, February–March 1983 (no catalogue, dated 1966 on hand list)

Lit: M. Sonnabend, 'Mario Merz', *Mario Merz*, exhibition catalogue, Galerie Sonnabend, Paris, April 1969, another version repr. as 'Cestone di Vimini 1966'; Germano Celant, in *Mario Merz*, exhibition catalogue, Museum Folkwang, Essen, January–March 1979, and travelling, p.15; *Identité Italienne, L'art en Italie depuis 1959*, exhibition catalogue, Musée National d'Art Moderne, Paris, June 1981, pp.267, 269, another version repr. as 'Cestone' 1968; *Mario Merz*, exhibition catalogue, Palazzo Congressi ed

Esposizioni, San Marino, November 1983, pp.43–4, 50, 209–16; Germano Celant, *Arte Povera*, Milan, 1985, p.95, another version repr. as 'Untitled, 1968 (wicker cone containing a pot of boiling beans)'; *Mario Merz*, exhibition catalogue, Kunsthaus, Zürich, April 1985, p.31

In a telephone conversation with Helen van der Meij (July 1986), Mario Merz dated this work *c.*1967. According to him, there are now two wicker cones in existence (an earlier cone was destroyed). The other surviving cone is in the collection of the Stadtisches Museum Abteiberg, Mönchengladbach (see *Stadtisches Museum Abteiberg, Mönchengladbach, Bestandskatalog II*, Mönchengladbach, 1980, p.140, 'Cono' 1965, 200 × 100 × 20cm, repr.). Merz himself cannot remember which of the two (and originally three) cones has been the one most exhibited but the catalogue for his exhibition in San Marino in 1984 (cited above) lists the following exhibitions as having included wicker cones: *Prospect 68*, Stadtische Kunsthalle, Düsseldorf, September 1968, 'Cono' 1966 (not listed in exhibition publication); *Arte Povera + azioni povera*, Arsenali dell'Antica Repubblica, Amalfi, October 1968, 'Cono' 1966. The San Marino catalogue describes this as a structure in wicker in the shape of a cone, inside which boils a pot of beans. The same work is reproduced by Germano Celant in *Arte Povera* (see above) as 'Untitled 1968 (Wicker cone containing pot of boiling beans)'; The catalogue for the Paris exhibition, *Identité Italienne*, also cited above, reproduces the same work as 'Cestone' or hamper and again dates it 1968 (see p.269). What could be the same cone (the same height but appearing thinner than T 03674) is illustrated in the exhibition catalogue *Mario Merz*, Galerie Ileana Sonnabend, Paris, April

1969 as ' "Cestone di Vimini" 1966 h.220cm (Con acqua all'interno in ebollizione)' although it does not appear to have been included in the exhibition itself.

Merz himself has suggested that a cone might have been included in his exhibition held at the Sperone Gallery in Turin in January–February 1968 and the San Merino catalogue lists a 'Cestone' (or hamper) 1966. However, an installation photograph of the exhibition, in the same catalogue (29), shows another wicker work, shaped like a hamper or basket, fastened to the wall. (To further confuse matters, the work in the photograph is listed as 'Cestone' 1967.) What appears to be the same wall work is reproduced in the catalogue for Merz's Essen exhibition (cited above) as 'Cestone/Korb' 1964 (pp.32–3). However in an essay in this catalogue, Germano Celant describes a cone like that exhibited in Amalfi and described in the Sonnabend catalogue, in the context of what he refers to as the 'illogical and functionless assemblies' exhibited at Sperone in 1968:

> Freedom to perceive 'things' prompts one to 'reconstruct' or 'construct' ideas, like the idea of that light-spear, which turns into one spear or two spears in wood and perspex struck into a vacuum, which is represented by a transparent rectangle, or remaking the 'projecting structure' as an object in the 'hamper' which perfectly reproduces the structure's volume, or the *cone* made of a vast wicker which refers back to the cone in bits pierced by a neon strip, the wicker chest being further transformed by placing inside it a saucepan of boiling water.
>
> This boiling of the material due to the coming together of two energies leads on to *sit-in* and *solitaio solidale* where wax and light acting as heat work together, and to the igloos where writing/structure/material are uplifted osmotically. [Germano Celant 1971 (translated by Anthony Melville)].

In an excerpt from an interview with Germano Celant, reproduced in the catalogue for his Zürich exhibition in 1985 (cited above) Merz referred to a 'Cone' and 'Basket' made in 1966/67, describing how he decided to have 'a giant basket hanging on the wall' (presumably 'Cestone', already referred to) and a 'giant cone' made by craftsmen in basket-work. Merz refers to making one cone himself but this could be the cone in pieces, pierced by neon, referred to by Celant (above) and exhibited by Sperone in 1968. (Installation photographs of the Sperone exhibition do show an earlier two-part plaster cone, pierced by neon.)

The San Marino catalogue also lists the following exhibitions as having included cones: *Palermo, Mario Merz, Gerhard Richter*, Galerie Konrad Fischer, Düsseldorf, 1979, 'Cone 1966'; *Mario Merz*, Museum Folkwang Essen, January–March 1979, Whitechapel Art Gallery, January–March 1980, Van Abbemuseum, Eindhoven, April–May 1980 'Cono' 1966 ('Stuttura in

Vimini a forma di Cono'). (This cone, installed at the Van Abbemuseum and surrounded by other objects, is reproduced in *Kunstforum International*, 39, March 1980, p.41.). A cone dated 1969 is reproduced in colour in *Mario Merz*, the catalogue for his exhibition at the Musée d'Art Moderne de la Ville de Paris (May–September 1981 (n.p.).

The cone, because of its everyday materials, is an archetypal 'arte povera' object. Merz's work concerns archetypes: igloos (as shelters but also metaphors for a democratic architecture), spirals, echoing nature and suggesting infinity, tables (see T 03673), social groupings and so on. 'Cone' is man sized and suggests a shelter or hiding place.

Despite the fact that Merz began consciously to apply a mathematically based system after he made the cone-related works, Celant suggests (in the article already cited) that the idea of proliferation developed in later Fibonacci works (see entry for T 03673) was already present in the earlier work. A drawing in the Essen catalogue of 1979 (cited above) and titled 'Igloo Fibonacci' 1970 (pl.3), resembles a tall cone constructed of numbers built up on the Fibonacci system from 1 (suggesting the apex) to 139583861555, suggesting the broad base of the cone.

Joan Miró 1893–1983

T 03401 **Woman** 1949

Bronze $7\frac{3}{8} \times 10\frac{3}{8} \times 8\frac{3}{8}$ (186 × 264 × 224)
Inscribed 'Miró $^7/_8$' and stamped with foundry mark inside cast
Purchased from Waddington Galleries (Grant-in-Aid) 1982
Prov: ... ; Perls Gallery, New York

Exh: *Sculptures de Miró, Céramiques de Miro et Llorens Artigas,* Fondation Maeght, St Paul, April–June 1973 (17, unspecified cast); *Exposition Miró Sculptures,* Seibu Museum of Art, Tokyo, February 1979 (2, repr. in col., unspecified cast); *Joan Miró/Sculptura 1931–72,* Palazzo Pretoria, Prato, May–September 1979 (2, repr., unspecified cast); *Joan Miró,* Waddington Galleries, December 1981 (1, repr.); *The Touch of Dreams, Joan Miró, Ceramics and Bronzes 1949–80,* Sainsbury Centre for Visual Arts, Norwich, October–December 1985 (3, repr.)

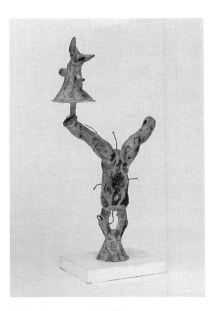

T 03402 **The Tightrope Walker** 1970

Bronze and steel on wooden base
$22 \times 11 \times 5\frac{7}{8}$ (560 × 280 × 150)
Inscribed 'Miró 2/2' and stamped with foundry mark on back
Purchased from Waddington Galleries (Grant-in-Aid) 1982
Prov: ... ; Galerie Maeght, Zürich; Waddington 1981
Exh: *Joan Miro, Das Plastische Werk,* Kunsthaus, Zürich, June–July 1972 (23, repr., unspecified cast); *Exposition Miró Sculptures,* Seibu Museum of Art, Tokyo, February 1979 (44, repr. in col., unspecified cast); *Miró Milano,* Comune di Milano Mazzatta, October–December 1981 (repr.); *Joan Miró,* Waddington Galleries, December 1981 (16, repr.); *The Touch of Dreams, Joan Miró, Ceramics and*

Bronzes 1949–80, Sainsbury Centre for
Visual Arts, Norwich, October–
December 1985 (3, repr.)

T 03690   A Star Caresses the Breast of a Negress (Painting Poem) 1938

Oil on canvas 51 × 76½ (1295 × 1943)
Inscribed 'miró' b.l. and 'une
étoile/caresse le sein d'une/négresse' t.l.;
also 'JOAN MIRÓ./peinture-poème./IV-
938' on reverse
Purchased from Pierre Matisse Gallery,
New York (Grant-in-Aid) 1983

Exh: *Joan Miró*, Tate Gallery, August–October
1964, Kunsthaus Musée des Beaux-Arts,
Zürich, October–December 1964 (158);
Joan Miró, Haus der Kunst, Munich,
March–May 1969 (53, repr.); *Joan Miró*,
Réunion Des Musées Nationaux, Grand
Palais, Paris, May–October 1974 (55,
repr.); *Dada and Surrealism Reviewed*,
Hayward Gallery, January–March 1978
(12.100, repr.); *Miró Selected Paintings*,
Hirshhorn Museum and Sculpture
Garden, Smithsonian Institution, March–
June 1980 (29, repr. in col.); *Joan Miró*,
Museum of Modern Art, New York,
November 1981–January 1982 (not
numbered, repr. p.74); *Miró in America*,
Museum of Fine Arts, Houston, April–
June 1982 (20, repr. in col.); *Miró's People*,
Scottish National Gallery of Modern Art,
Edinburgh, August–October 1982 (24,
repr. in col.)

Lit: Cirici-Pellicer Alexandre, *Miró y la
Imaginacion*, Barcelona, 1949, pp.37, 51;
James Thrall Soby, *Joan Miró*, New York,
1959, pp.96–8, pl.97; Roland Penrose,

Miró, 1970, 65, pl.65; Rosa Maria Malet,
Joan Miró, Stuttgart, 1984, pp.17, 31, pl.50
(col.); *Also repr.;* Jacques Dupin, *Joan
Miró; Life and Work*, 1962, pl. 496;
Alexandre Cirici, *Miró et son Temps*,
Barcelona, 1985, pl.231 (col.)

T 03691   Message from a Friend 1964

Oil on canvas 103¼ × 108½ (2620 × 2755)
Inscribed 'MIRÓ. "MESSAGE/D'AMI"'
and '12/4/64' on reverse
Purchased from Galerie Maeght, Paris
(Grant-in-Aid) with a substantial
contribution from funds bequeathed by
Miss H.M. Arbuthnot through the
Friends of the Tate Gallery 1983

Exh: *Joan Miró*, Grand Palais, Paris, May–
October 1974 (81, repr.); *Un Cami
Compartit (Miró-Maeght)*, Galeria
Maeght, Barcelona, December 1975–
January 1976 (24, repr. in col.); *Joan Miró,
Peintures, Sculptures, Dessins, Céramiques
1956–76*, Fondation Maeght, Sâint Paul,
July–September 1979 (6, repr. in col.)

Lit: Yvon Taillander, '"Message to a Friend".
Miro's Journey to Van Gogh Via Calder
in Homage to Joan Miró, Special issue of
XXe Siècle, 1972, p.87, repr. in col.; Rosa
Maria Malet, *Joan Miró*, Stuttgart, 1984,
pp.17, 31, pl.50 (col.)

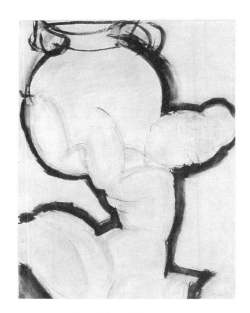

Amedeo Modigliani 1884–1920

T 03569 Madame Zborowska 1918

Oil on canvas 25⅜ × 18⅛ (645 × 460)
Inscribed 'modigliani' b.r.
Bequeathed by Mrs A.F. Kessler 1983

Prov: L. Zborowski, Paris; J. Netter, Paris; Lepoutre, Paris; Reid and Lefevre, London; Mrs Kessler

Exh: *Paintings by Modigliani*, Lefevre Gallery, March 1929 (15); *French Paintings from the Kessler Collection*, York Art Gallery, May 1948 (8); *The Kessler Collection*, Wildenstein Gallery, October–November 1948 (20); *The Kessler Bequest*, Tate Gallery, February–April 1984 (works not numbered, repr.)

Lit: Arthur Pfannstiel, *Modigliani*, Paris, 1929, p.42; Arthur Pfannstiel, *Modigliani et son Oeuvre*, Paris, 1956, no. 260, p.140; J. Lanthemann, *Modigliani 1884–1920: Catalogue Raisonné*, Barcelona, 1970, no.334, p.130, repr. p.248 as 'La Zborowska en Buste' 1918

Mme Zborowska was the common-law wife of the Polish poet and dealer Leopold Zborowski, who became Modigliani's agent from the summer of 1916 onwards. Although usually known as Zborowska, her original name was Hanka Sierspowska, and she came of an aristocratic Polish family. Both she and her husband posed for Modigliani many times. According to Pfannstiel, this portrait was painted in 1918 at Nice, where Modigliani spent much of his time from about July 1918 until May 1919.

T 03570 Caryatid with a Vase c.1914

Watercolour and crayon on paper 25 × 19 (633 × 481)
Inscribed 'modigliani' b.r.
Bequeathed by Mrs A.F. Kessler 1983

Prov: Paul Guillaume, Paris; Mme Paul Guillaume, Paris; Arthur Tooth & Sons, 1936; Mrs Kessler 1936

Exh: *The Kessler Collection*, Wildenstein Gallery, October–November 1948 (21); *The Kessler Bequest*, Tate Gallery, February–April 1984 (not numbered, repr.)

Lit: Adolphe Basler, *Modigliani*, Paris, 1931, p.7; Gotthard Jedlicka, *Modigliani 1884–1920*, Erlenbach – Zürich, 1953, pp.33–4; J. Lanthemann, *Modigliani 1884–1920: Catalogue Raisonné*, Barcelona, 1970, no.586, p.141, repr. p.305 as 'Cariatide à la Potiche' 1914

Modigliani made a large number of drawings of caryatids, some partly or wholly coloured in watercolour, pastel or coloured pencil. Lanthemann reproduces 74 of various kinds, and there may well have been more. According to Basler, who knew Modigliani at the time, many of them were done before the artist embarked on carving. 'For several years, Modigliani did nothing but draw ... those numerous caryatids, which he kept promising himself to execute in stone ... Then one day he began to carve figures and heads directly in stone.' Jedlicka relates that Paul Guillaume told him Modigliani even had a fantastic project to make a temple not in honour of God, but of humanity, which was to be surrounded by hundreds of caryatids, 'columns of tenderness'. Nevertheless, out of the twenty-five or so sculptures by Modigliani that are known, only one (now in the Museum of Modern Art, New York) is of a caryatid.

As none of the caryatid drawings are dated, it is difficult to date them with certainty, but it is generally assumed that those which are highly stylised in a manner reminiscent of negro art were the earliest, and that those like this which are very rhythmical, with oval heads and almond eyes, were among the last.

There are nine other related drawings and watercolours which show a figure in a very similar attitude (Lanthemann 575 and 578–85), but in most cases with little or no indication of the object she is supporting. The version closest to the present work, and probably made at the same time, is Lanthemann 585, in which the figure is holding exactly the same type of large rounded vase.

T 03760 **Head** *c.*1911–12

> Euville stone 25 × 5 × 13⅞
> (635 × 125 × 350)
> Inscribed 'MODI/GLIANI' on back of base
> Transferred from the Victoria and Albert Museum 1983

This sculpture has already been catalogued when on loan from the Victoria and Albert Museum, see entry in Ronald Alley, *Collection of the Tate Gallery's Collection of Modern Art other than works by British Artists*, 1981, pp.526–7

Sir Thomas Monnington 1902–1976

T 03832 **Trees and Rocks** 1952

> Pencil on paper 19¾ × 25 (503 × 635)
> Not inscribed
> Purchased from Lady Monnington (Grant-in-Aid) 1984
>
> *Exh:* RA 1952 (1126, as 'Study: Trees and Rocks'); *Drawings and Paintings by Sir Thomas Monnington PRA 1902–1976*, RA, October–November 1977 (38)

Lady Monnington writes (letter, 22 May 1986): 'I clearly remember him doing a lot of drawings, and one or two small oils, in the quarry behind our house [near Groombridge, Kent] in the years 1949–1954.' Lady Monnington owns one of the oils, which is on canvas and measures 24 × 20 ins.

The most finished of the known drawings of this motif is 'Trees and Rocks' 1954 (chalk heightened with white, on waxed tracing paper, 24 × 24 ins., coll. Royal Academy of Arts, to which bequeathed by Marshall Sisson RA in 1978). This drawing is reproduced in *RA Illustrated* 1954 (pl.74), and in the catalogue of Monnington's memorial retrospective at the Royal Academy in 1977 (pl.6). In the latter catalogue Judy Egerton writes that the Academy's drawing:

> treats the same trees and rocks [as represented in the Tate's drawing] as if they were part of a structure with geometric proportions, taking the subject several degrees nearer to abstraction and compressing the design into a veritable square. Monnington later referred to [the Academy's drawing] as the best drawing he ever did.

The present location of a drawing representing an

intermediate stage in the process of abstraction (exh. RA 1952, 1117, repr. *RA Illustrated* 1952, pl.80) is unknown.

The dimensions of this latter drawing are 24 × 26 ins.

T 03833 **Trees** *c*.1938

Oil on canvas 14 × 17⅞ (350 × 452)
Not inscribed
Purchased from Lady Monnington
(Grant-in-Aid) 1984

The reverse bears a Roberson's stamp which suggests that the canvas was bought at some point in the years 1937–9 inclusive. The character of the paint is consistent with the picture's having been painted in the same period. Lady Monnington writes of this work (letter, 22 May 1986):

> I do not remember Tom painting it, so I think it must have been painted in the late 1930s before I met him, and it looks like a view down the valley below Leyswood [his home, near Groombridge] – a valley he often painted in.

Henry Moore, O.M. 1898–1986

T 03761 **Reclining Figure** 1939

Lead 5⅞ × 11 × 4 (150 × 280 × 100)
Inscribed 'CIRC 17–1940' underneath
Transferred from the Victoria and Albert
Museum 1983

T 03762 **Head** 1928

Cast concrete 7⅞ × 7⅞ × 5⅛
(200 × 180 × 130)
Inscribed 'CIRC 11–1950' at r. side
Transferred from the Victoria and Albert
Museum 1983

T 03763 Three Motifs against a Wall No. 1 1958

Bronze $19\frac{7}{8} \times 42\frac{1}{2} \times 17\frac{7}{8}$ (505 × 1080 × 440)
Inscribed 'CIRC 234–1961' on reverse
Transferred from the Victoria and Albert Museum 1983

Sir Cedric Morris, Bt 1889–1982

T 03831 Frances Hodgkins c.1917

Gouache on paper $9\frac{1}{2} \times 6\frac{3}{8}$ (242 × 162)
Not inscribed
Presented by the surviving executor of Frances Hodgkins 1984
Prov: Frances Hodgkins (d.1947); her estate
Exh: *Cedric Morris*, Tate Gallery, March–May 1984, Bowes Museum, Barnard Castle,

May–July 1984, National Museum of Wales, Cardiff, August–September 1984, The Minories, Colchester, September–October 1984 (104, repr.)

A portrait of the well-known New Zealand-born painter (1869–1947). On the reverse is a pencil drawing of Cedric Morris's head in profile, pipe in mouth. John Piper confirms its attribution to Frances Hodgkins, in whose hand the pencil inscription below the portrait of Morris appears to be. This reads 'painted by/Cedric Morris/ Newlyn 1917?'.

During parts of 1917 and 1918 Cedric Morris lived at Zennor, Cornwall, near St Ives where Frances Hodgkins was based then and until 1920. In 1919 when Morris and Arthur Lett-Haines moved to Newlyn, Cornwall, they retained a London base by sub-leasing Frances Hodgkins's studio in Kensington. In that year Morris painted a watercolour portrait of Frances Hodgkins, head and shoulders in profile (repr. catalogue of Tate Gallery Morris exhibition, 1984 (105) in which the course of Morris's and Lett-Haines's friendship with Frances Hodgkins, which lasted until her death, is traced on pp.36–7). Morris successfully proposed Hodgkins for membership of the Seven and Five Society in 1929. Morris's oil portrait of Frances Hodgkins, 1928, is in Auckland City Art Gallery, New Zealand, and hers of him, 'Man with a Macaw' 1930, is in the Towner Art Gallery, Eastbourne.

T 03592 Patisseries and a Croissant c.1922

Oil on canvas, $14\frac{1}{8} \times 12\frac{7}{8}$ (359 × 327)
Inscribed 'C. MORRIS' and indecipherable date b.r.

Presented by the artist's sister, Miss Nancy Morris 1983

Prov: Given to Miss Nancy Morris by the artist

Exh: *Cedric Morris,* Tate Gallery, March–May 1984, Bowes Museum, Barnard Castle, May–July 1984, National Museum of Wales, Cardiff, August–September 1984, The Minories, Colchester, September–October 1984 (12, repr.)

Croissants, steeply-raking surfaces and intense side-lighting are all features of the somewhat earlier paintings of Giorgio de Chirico, whom Morris admired and whose first one-man exhibition was held, in 1919, at the same gallery as Morris's in 1922, the Casa d'Arte Bragaglia, Rome.

David Nash b.1945

T 03471 **Rostrum with Bonks** 1971

Pine, ash, horse chestnut and birch wood
$68\frac{1}{2} \times 24\frac{3}{4} \times 24\frac{3}{4}$ (1740 × 630 × 630)
Not inscribed
Purchased from the artist (Grant-in-Aid) 1982

Exh: *Briefly Cooked Apples,* Queen's Hall, York, summer 1973, Oriel, Bangor 1973 (no catalogue); *David Nash, Loosely Held Grain,* Arnolfini Gallery, Bristol, October–November 1976 (not listed in catalogue)

Repr: *David Nash,* International Contemporary Sculpture Symposium, Shiga, Japan, 1984,

p.83; *Sixty Seasons, David Nash,* exhibition catalogue, Third Eye Centre, Glasgow, 1983, pp.12, 41

The pedestal and top of the sculpture are made of pine, and the balls are of ash, horse chestnut and birch, looking from the front (the lowest) to the back.

'Rostrum' was made at the artist's studio, a converted chapel at Blaenau Ffestiniog, Gwynedd. It is one of the first of a group of sculptures which he made in the early 1970s in the shape of tables, and in the Tate Gallery's 'Family Tree' drawing (T 03473) it is illustrated with several others. This drawing demonstrates that these followed from the very tall, Brancusi-like columns of cone shapes that he made in 1970 after leaving Chelsea School of Art. Two relevant interests persisted from these columns, the shaping of the individual parts and the way in which they were displayed. The balls, or 'bonks', on the rostrum were shaped with an axe into approximations of spheres, and show their different resistances to this by their rough shapes. One, of ash, has split when drying, like Nash's earlier 'Nine Cracked Balls' (1970). The three are displayed on different levels like the sections of the columns, on a pedestal of different wood, sawn and pegged by hand. The tapered shape of the base and its top are also like two sections of the columns, and this part was made out of pieces from one of the columns, and retains its shape. A quotation from the artist in the catalogue *Sixty Seasons* (op.cit., p.40) explains the origin of the word 'Bonk' in a nickname given by a neighbour to a rock outcrop in a field, and Nash further glossed this (letter of 15 June 1986) as 'outcrop – isolated place island-like, contained observed as places, points across the land'.

The arrangement of the bonks on the steps was spoken of by the artist as 'foreground, middle ground and background' (conversation of 29 March 1982). In his next large sculpture 'Table with Cubes' (1972, National Museum of Wales, Cardiff) he originally intended that the cubes could be moved around by the spectator, although this was impractical.

A very small version of the top of the 'Rostrum' was carved at the same time as a study for it (collection of the artist).

T 03472 **Wood Quarry – Beech, Otterlo** 1982

Charcoal and earth on paper $48 \times 95\frac{1}{4}$ (1219 × 2426)
Inscribed top centre 'Wood Quarry – Beech/Otterlo, May 1982/David Nash' and with the titles of sculptures
Purchased from the artist (Grant-in-Aid) 1982

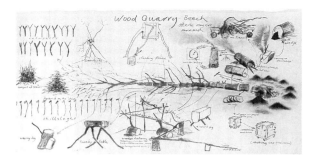

Two drawings, this and 'Family Tree 1970–1982' were made for the Tate Gallery in late 1982 in association with the purchase of 'Rostrum with Bonks' and 'Standing Frame'. 'Standing Frame' was exchanged with the artist for 'Flying Frame' (T 03932) in 1984.

The 'Wood Quarry' drawings are made by Nash to show the origin of particular sculptures in one tree, all of which is used, and to show how the sculptures can be imagined in the reverse process to fit together again to make the growing shape. They are begun on site where the tree is felled, and use earth from around the roots to colour some areas. The Tate Gallery's drawing is a version of another of the same tree which was exhibited at the Kröller-Müller Museum, Otterlo, in May–July 1982, and is reproduced in the catalogue (the exhibition was itself subtitled 'Wood Quarry'). The catalogue also reproduces a photograph of the tree in the Kröller-Müller park before it was felled, and the exhibition included all the sculptures illustrated. Another 'Wood Quarry – Otterlo' drawing is reproduced in the catalogue *Fellowship '81–'82, David Nash*, Yorkshire Sculpture Park (1982). The two trees which supplied the exhibition were not cut down especially for it, since one had to be removed for a new avenue and the other was dying.

The Tate Gallery's drawing was begun on site at Otterlo, and finished in the studio. At the artist's request it was framed by the gallery in beech wood.

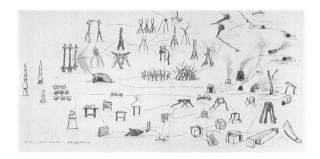

T 03473   Family Tree, 1970–1982 1982

Charcoal on paper 38 × 74¼ (965 × 1884)
Inscribed '"FAMILY TREE", 1970–1982.

David Nash '82' and with the titles and dates of sculptures
Purchased from the artist (Grant-in-Aid) 1982

See entry on T 03472. Nash's 'Family Tree' drawings illustrate the development of one of his sculptures from another, and this one includes the Tate Gallery's 'Rostrum with Bonks' (1971, T 03471). It is drawn on Japanese wood bark fibre paper bought by the artist in Japan, and was framed by the Gallery in oak at his request.

Paul Nash 1889–1946

T 03820   The Colne 1925

Watercolour and pencil on paper 15½ × 22¾ (390 × 570)
Inscribed 'Paul Nash/1925' b.r.
Bequeathed by Mrs Ernestine Carter 1984
Prov: ...; Desmond Coke, sold by his estate, Sotheby's, 25 July 1931 (107) bt John Carter; his widow Mrs Ernestine Carter
Exh: *Paul Nash*, Mayor Gallery, November 1925 (8); *Paul Nash, Paintings and Watercolours*, Tate Gallery, November–December 1975 (89, repr.)
Lit: Margot Eates, *Paul Nash*, 1973, p.119 (as 'The Colne, watercolour, 1924'), repr. pl.30 (as 'Bridge over the Dyke', 1924); Andrew Causey, *Paul Nash*, 1980, p.391 cat. 489, repr. pls. 124 and 125; *Also repr*: E. Bernard Lintott, *The Art of Watercolour Painting*, 1926, opp. p.267

The River Colne at Hillingdon was near the house of Paul Nash's parents-in-law. Andrew Causey points out that the figures of two men bathing, drawn in pencil to the left of the bridge and visible in the photograph published in Lintott (loc.cit.) have been erased, probably by the artist shortly after the watercolour was acquired by John Carter.

C.R.W. Nevinson 1889–1946

T 03676 **Bursting Shell** 1915

Oil on canvas 30 × 22 (760 × 560)
Inscribed 'C R W Nevinson' bottom centre
Purchased from Maclean Gallery (Grant-in-Aid) 1983

Prov: . . . ; Mrs Manuel Cansino; her children, from whom purchased by Maclean Gallery

Exh: *The London Group*, Goupil Gallery, November–December 1915 (66); ? *C.R.W. Nevinson*, Leicester Galleries, September–October 1916 (24); ? *C.R.W. Nevinson*, City Art Gallery, Manchester, July–August 1920 (14, as 'Shell Bursting. Lent by the Lady Tredegar'); *Artists at War, 1914–1918*, Kettle's Yard Gallery, Cambridge, October–November 1974 (47); *C.R.W. Nevinson, The Great War and After*, Maclean Gallery, February–March 1980 (1); *Futurismo e Futurismi*, Palazzo Grassi, Venice, April–September 1986 (repr. in col. p.310)

Lit: *The Daily Graphic*, 26 November 1915, repr.; Richard Cork, *Vorticism and Abstract*

Art in the First Machine Age, 1976, I, repr. in col. p.296

The reproduction in the *Daily Graphic* (Tate Gallery Archive) proves that this was the painting exhibited at the Goupil Gallery in November 1915, but there was another painting by Nevinson with the same title (*C.R.W. Nevinson*, introduction Campbell Dodgson, 1918, repr. 10 in col.; another version sold Sotheby's, 21 May 1986, 114, repr.) so it is not certain that it was again shown at the Leicester Galleries in 1916 and 1918. From the beginning this painting has been seen as a conjunction of Nevinson's futurist style of painting with the demands of a war subject. The reviewer of *The Observer*, 28 November 1915, commented in this way:

'Bursting Shells' is Futurism pure and simple, without a remnant of realistic tendencies. An extraordinary sense of irresistible, destructive force is conveyed by that revolving rainbow-coloured spiral from which radiate black, orange bordered shafts.

It appears from this reproduction that the colour of the radiating black wedges has darkened, and the buildings in the background were originally clearer.

The painting was purchased by Mrs Cansino in the mid 1950s in response to an advertisement in the *New Statesman*, which offered for sale two paintings by Nevinson.

Sir William Nicholson 1872–1949

T 03792 **Harbour in Snow, La Rochelle** 1938

Oil on canvas laid on board $13\frac{3}{4} × 17\frac{3}{4}$ (350 × 450)
Inscribed '.N.' b.l.

Presented by the Friends of the Tate Gallery 1983

Prov: . . . ; Roland, Browse and Delbanco; sold to A.D. Peters; bequeathed to a private collector; sold Christie's, 12 March 1982 (144, repr.), bt Browse and Darby, from whom purchased by the Friends of the Tate Gallery 1983

Exh: *Exhibition of Paintings by Sir William Nicholson and Jack B. Yeats,* National Gallery, January 1942 (73a); *British Painting 1925–1950, 2nd Anthology,* AC, New Burlington Gallery, June–July 1951, Manchester City Art Gallery, August–September 1951 (92); *William Nicholson, Centenary Exhibition,* Roland, Browse and Delbanco, April–May 1972, Aldeburgh Festival, June 1972 (37)

Lit: Marguerite Steen, *William Nicholson,* 1943, pp.197 ff.; Robert Nichols, *William Nicholson,* 1948 (15, repr. in col.); Lillian Browse, *William Nicholson,* 1956, cat. no. 481, p.108

Nicholson stayed in La Rochelle during the winter of 1938–9. Marguerite Steen, who was with him, describes his affection for the town, and the preoccupation of the people there with news of the expected war. Lillian Browse lists nine paintings of La Rochelle of 1938–9, all of about this size, and refers to them (loc.cit):

the lovely group of La Rochelle pictures, most of them looking down upon the harbour from his window, represent Nicholson's swan-song of landscape.

Hermann Nitsch b.1938

T 03412   Blood Picture 1962

Blood on three linen or cotton squares laid down on coarse canvas $41\frac{7}{8} \times 31\frac{5}{8}$ (1062 × 804)
Inscribed 'hermann nitsch 1962' on stretcher
Purchased from Galerie Heike Curtze, Düsseldorf (Grant-in-Aid) 1982

Sir Sidney Nolan, O.M. b.1917

T 03553   Desert Storm *c.*1955

Oil on hardboard 36 × 48 (914 × 1219)
Not inscribed
Presented by Lord McAlpine 1983

Prov: Lord McAlpine (purchased from the artist)

The artist says that this was inspired by the sight of the desert landscape of central Australia after drought, but was actually painted in London about 1955.

T 03554   Woman in a Hat *c.*1964

Oil on hardboard 48 × 48 (1219 × 1219)
Not inscribed
Presented by Lord McAlpine 1983

Prov: Lord McAlpine (purchased from the artist)

Exh: *Nolan,* David Jones; Art Gallery, Sydney, May 1965 (one of 18–22, all this size and all entitled 'Head')

This was one of six paintings of heads of women wearing monstrous hats decorated with artificial flowers which

were shown together at David Jones' Art Gallery, Sydney, in May 1965. It was suggested then by one of the critics (*Morning Herald*, Sydney, 5 May 1965) that they had been inspired by the sight of women wearing hats like these at the garden party at the 1964 Adelaide Festival of Arts, which Nolan had attended; however Nolan says that he was thinking more of Australian country women with their 'dried, sad look', who get dressed up to come into town for country agricultural shows and the like. He had himself worked for four years as a young man in the art department of a hat factory, designing men's and women's hats.

T 03555   **Carcase in Swamp** 1955

Oil on hardboard 36 × 48 (914 × 1219)
Inscribed 'N.' b.r. and 'CARCASE IN SWAMP./1955', 'Nolan', 'ABANDONED MINE' and 'DUR' on reverse
Presented by Lord McAlpine 1983

Prov: Lord McAlpine (purchased from the artist)

Nolan was commissioned in 1952 by *The Courier-Mail* of Brisbane to make a series of drawings of the effects of a catastrophic drought in central Australia. He and his wife flew to Darwin in August 1952 and then travelled by road over two of Australia's pioneer cattle routes: the Murranji track along which all cattle from the Victoria River country travel across to Newcastle Waters, and then the Barkly stock route eastwards into Queensland. Everywhere they went they saw the bodies of animals that had died of thirst and starvation, with twisted bones and decaying ligaments. (Already by August 1952 some 1,250,000 head of cattle had been lost in Queensland and the Northern Territory combined). Then, early in 1953, he followed the Birdsville route from Maree, in South Australia, to Birdsville, in Queensland. Besides making drawings from memory of what he saw on these journeys, he took numerous photographs of the carcasses of animals (though not of the landscape itself).

His paintings on this theme were made between 1952 and 1955, this work being one of the last of the series.

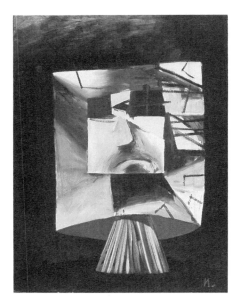

T 03556   **Armoured Head** 1956

Oil on hardboard 48 × 36 (1219 × 914)
Inscribed 'N.' b.r. and 'HELMET./1956/Nolan', 'NOV. 16th 1956' and 'NOLAN/NOVEMBER 16th/1956' on reverse
Presented by Lord McAlpine 1983
Prov: Lord McAlpine (purchased from the artist)

Exh: *Sidney Nolan,* Whitechapel Art Gallery,
         June–July 1957 (68, as 'Mask'); *II.*
         Documenta, Kassel, July–October 1959
         (Nolan 2, as 'Helmet')
Repr: *Encounter,* VIII, January 1957, facing p.16

The artist says that this picture, dated 16 November 1956, is one of three or four paintings inspired by the Hungarian uprising which took place that month. Soviet tanks entered Budapest early in the morning of 4 November and savage fighting broke out; but large-scale hostilities were over within a fortnight.

This work was reproduced in *Encounter* a couple of months later with a quotation from a news item: 'All the people in the street could see of the driver of the tank was his face reflected in the driving mirror' (apparently the Hungarians tried to immobilize the tanks by smashing the mirrors). This description also inevitably reminded Nolan of Ned Kelly in his helmet, and the image turned into a kind of fusion between the two. Although it is inscribed with the title 'Helmet', Nolan would now prefer it to be called 'Armoured Head'.

T 03557   **In the Cave** 1957

Polyvinyl acetate on hardboard 48 × 60 (1219 × 1524)
Inscribed 'N.' b.c. and 'MRS FRASER/1957', '1957/CAVE/(MRS FRASER/Series)', 'No 53', 'FOR/BRITISH/COUNCIL' and '2' on reverse
Presented by Lord McAlpine 1983

Prov: Lord McAlpine (purchased from the
         artist)
Exh: *Sidney Nolan,* Whitechapel Art Gallery,
         June–July 1957 (81, as 'In the Cave');
         Nolan, Hatton Gallery, Newcastle, March
         1961 (53, repr.)
Repr: Kenneth Clark, Colin MacInnes and
         Bryan Robertson, *Sidney Nolan,* 1961,
         p.150, repr. pl.92

This is one of a series of pictures based on the true story of Mrs Fraser and the convict, Bracefell. Mrs Fraser was a Scotswoman emigrating to Australia in the 1860s who was shipwrecked on an island (now known as Fraser Island) off the coast of Queensland. She lived for several months with the aborigines, who gave her food but stripped off all her clothes, until she was found by an escaped convict who offered to take her across country to a settlement if she would intercede on his behalf.

Nolan first heard of Mrs Fraser when he spent several months on Fraser Island in 1947 and painted his first pictures of her soon afterwards. He then took up the theme again in London in 1957 when preparing work for his retrospective exhibition at the Whitechapel Art Gallery. What particularly fascinated him was the bizarre conjunction of a naked white woman and a convict in his black-and-white striped convict clothes in a lush tropical rain forest; also that, when the pair finally reached the neighbourhood of the settlement, Mrs Fraser reneged on her promise and told the convict to be off or she would hand him over to the police.

In this picture Mrs Fraser is splayed across the face of a rock like an aboriginal drawing, and Bracefell emerges from a cave in the rock.

T 03558   **Antarctica** 1964

Oil on hardboard 48 × 48 (1219 × 1219)
Inscribed '30.Aug 1964/nolan' b.r.
Presented by Lord McAlpine 1983

Prov: Lord McAlpine (purchased from the
artist)

Sidney Nolan visited Antarctica for about eight days in January 1964. He and the author Alan Moorehead (who was preparing a book on the exploration and settlement of the South Pacific) went as guests of Rear Admiral J.R. Reedy, Commander of the United States Navy Antarctic Support Force, and were flown by the U.S. Navy from Christchurch, New Zealand, to the American base at McMurdo Sound. Nolan was greatly impressed not only by the vast, desolate emptiness, but by the colours, far from just white, and the light:

> It [the Antarctic] is black, ochre, dark green, and blue, with an oyster-coloured sky and an indigo sea. The colours appear as if under intense moonlight (quoted in *The Australian Women's Weekly*, 15 September 1965).

He painted some fifty pictures of Antarctica in the following eighteen months, including some which are not simply landscapes but with figures of explorers. This particular work shows McMurdo Sound on the right, with Mount Erebus looming in the background.

T 03559 Camel and Figure 1966

Oil on hardboard 47⅝ × 48 (1210 × 1219)
Inscribed 'nolan/1966' b.r. and '20
Sept/1966/nolan' on reverse
Presented by Lord McAlpine 1983
Prov: Lord McAlpine (purchased from the
artist)
Exh: *Sidney Nolan: Retrospective Exhibition*,
Art Gallery of New South Wales, Sydney,
September–October 1967 (143); National
Gallery of Victoria, Melbourne,
November–December 1967 (143);
Western Australian Art Gallery, Perth,
January–February 1968 (143); *Sidney
Nolan: Retrospective Exhibition*, Arts
Centre, New Metropole, Folkestone,
February–April 1970 (50); *Sidney Nolan:
Gemälde und Druckgraphik*, Kunsthalle,
Darmstadt, May–June 1971 (38, repr. in
col.); *Sidney Nolan*, Marlborough Galerie,
Zürich, October–November 1973 (9, repr.
in col.); *Sidney Nolan*, Moderna Museet,
Stockholm, January–March 1976 (56, repr.
in col.)
Repr: *Art and Australia*, v, no.2, 1967, p.464;
Elwyn Lynn, *Sidney Nolan: Myths and
Imagery*, London–Melbourne, 1967, pl.68
in col.

This is one of a considerable number of paintings which Nolan made from 1948 onwards inspired by the exploits of the ill-fated explorers Burke and Wills. Robert O'Hara Burke, a police inspector with neither scientific training nor experience of the bush, was appointed leader of an expedition (also including William John Wills, an English surgeon) which set out from Melbourne in August 1860 to make the crossing of Australia from south to north. After setting up a base camp at Cooper's Creek, roughly the half-way point, Burke pushed on with three companions and managed to reach a swamp close to the Gulf of Carpentaria. However on the way back one of the party died, and by the time the others staggered into Cooper's Creek in April 1861 the base party had just left. When a rescue party arrived five months later, they found that Burke and Wills were dead and there was only one survivor.

Nolan says that he thought of the figure in this picture as Burke, who was the more manic of the two. The whitish, iridescent area in the distance, to the right, is a salt lake: actually Lake Frome, north of Adelaide. The explorers would not have seen this, as it was off their route, so its inclusion is an example of artistic licence.

The expedition included a number of camels, most of which had been specially imported from India. Burke is shown naked, an omen of disaster. In mid-Australia, stripping off clothes is legendarily the last crazed, automatic act of a man dying for lack of water in a wasteland.

T 03560 Peter Grimes's Apprentice 1977

Oil and PVA on hardboard 36 × 48
(914 × 1219)
Inscribed 'Aldeburgh/Britten Grimes'

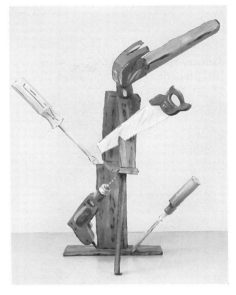

Apprentice/Nolan 27 March 1977' on
reverse
Presented by Lord McAlpine 1983

Prov: Lord McAlpine (purchased from the
artist)

Exh: *Sidney Nolan*, 30th Aldeburgh Festival,
Aldeburgh, June 1977 (26)

Sidney Nolan has been a regular visitor to the Aldeburgh Festival for many years and was a friend of Benjamin Britten. He contributed exhibitions to several of the Festivals, including a series of studies of Shakespeare's Sonnets in 1964 and a series of flower paintings in 1968.

This particular picture was painted specially for the 30th Festival, where his exhibition was subtitled 'An artist's response to the music of Benjamin Britten'. The theme of this work is taken from the opera *Peter Grimes* and shows the death of Grimes's second apprentice. Grimes, a fisherman, had seen a large shoal of fish and dragged his apprentice back to work although it was a Sunday and his day off. Making his way over-hastily down a cliff, the boy slipped and fell to his death. His dead body is seen floating among the fishes; he is still wearing the jersey with an embroidered anchor which was later found washed up on the shore.

Julian Opie b.1958

T 03783 Making It 1983

Painted steel construction $102\frac{3}{4} \times 46\frac{1}{2} \times 75\frac{3}{4}$
$(2610 \times 1180 \times 1925)$
Inscribed 'Julian Opie 83' and 'Julian
Opie' on back
Presented by the Patrons of New Art
through the Friends of the Tate Gallery
1983

Prov: Lisson Gallery, from whom bought by
Patrons of New Art

Exh: *Making Sculpture,* Tate Gallery, July 1983
(not numbered, repr. Julian Opie leaflet);
Julian Opie, Lisson Gallery, September–
October 1983 (no catalogue, repr. in col.
private view card); *Forty Years of Modern
Art 1945–1985,* Tate Gallery, February–
April 1986 (not numbered, repr. in col.)

Lit: Paul de Monchaux, Fenella Crichton, Kate
Blacker, *The Sculpture Show,* exhibition
catalogue, Hayward and Serpentine
Galleries, August–October 1983, repr.
p.78; William Feaver, 'The New British
Sculpture', *Art News,* LXXXIII, January
1984, pp.71–5, repr. in col. p.75; Kenneth
Baker, *Julian Opie,* exhibition catalogue,
Kölnischer Kunstverein, Cologne,
September–October 1984, repr. in col.
p.33

This work was exhibited at the *Making Sculpture* exhibition at the Tate Gallery from 4–24 July 1983.

Opie made larger than life models of tools and planks using sheet steel on which he drew their outlines with chalk. The steel was then cut using an oxyacetylene welding torch, and bent into shape. The components were assembled from pen sketches and welded together, this method enabling him to arrange the tools in precarious positions, which few other techniques would allow. As a result, the tools appear to be in the process of carrying out their normal function – the work is the description of an event. In addition, all the components were primed and painted using oils, this technique being a product of Opie's view that sheet metal could be regarded as a canvas and that his work falls somewhere in a category between painting and sculpture. To emphasize this point further, 'Making It' and most of his work is not painted on the reverse.

Although he admits that most observers are intrigued by the method of construction and materials used, he maintains that this is not important and that his work is about illusion.

His palette is bright, influenced by comic strips and advertising. Each tool itself is in this tradition in that it is 'typical, standard, even if you hardly ever see one exactly like it, it must be the classic idea of that object, the kind you would draw for a person who couldn't read.'

By making all the elements in his sculpture rather than using found objects, he rids the objects of as many worldly connotations as is possible while maintaining the items' essential identity. Thus, transforming the item to a sign for itself. 'Making It' is narrative and he thinks that using found objects would not enable him to transform them into signs in the same language. By constructing the objects himself he can reduce the detail and increase or decrease the scale at will. Of 'Making It' he says:

It is a self-conscious sculpture. It's aware of itself being made and that makes it into a very different thing. The tools swamp the conventional wooden sculpture, in the same way that being aware that you are making art changes the art.

He also suggests that the human presence is subordinated, and the objects are allowed an intentionality and interdependency:

It is about the sculpture of the seventies, a lot of which tried to iron out any sign of human interference, whereas with 'Making It' you get to see behind the scenes, but really its reason for being is gained by one thing doing something to another like a match lighting a cigar. This gives a reason to the match and cigar, or the tools and the sculpture. They support each other – visually and physically.

All quotations are from an interview with the compiler 1984.

Dennis Oppenheim b.1938

T03468 **Life Support System for a Premature By-Product** 1981

Dry powdered pigment in metallic silver with bronzing liquid and pencil on paper, 2 panels framed as one $38\frac{1}{4} \times 100\frac{1}{4}$ (971 × 2546)

Inscribed 'LIFE SUPPORT SYSTEM FOR A PREMATURE BY-PRODUCT/(FROM A LONG DISTANCE) 1981/SONNABEND GALLERY NEW YORK/THE CONTEMPORARY ARTS CENTER CINCINNATI, OHIO. THE LOWE ART MUSEUM/MIAMI FLORIDA. DIMENSIONS 15' × 40' × 80'/Dennis Oppenheim 1981' on rt. panel
Purchased from the artist through Lewis Johnstone Gallery (Grant-in-Aid) 1982

Exh: *Dennis Oppenheim 'Vibrating Forest'*, Ikon Gallery, Birmingham, April–May 1982

Lit: Steve Wood, 'An Interview with Dennis Oppenheim', *Arts Magazine*, LV, June 1981, pp.133–7; Emily Braun, 'Dennis Oppenheim: The Factories', *Arts Magazine* LV, June 1981, pp.138–41; Robert Ayers, unpublished untitled interview with the artist edited and circulated in typescript by the Ikon Gallery, Birmingham, April 1982

William Evelyn Osborn 1868–1906

T03648 **Royal Avenue, Chelsea** c.1900

Oil on canvas $19\frac{7}{8} \times 24$ (505 × 610)
Not inscribed
Presented anonymously in memory of Terence Rattigan 1983

Prov: Augustus John; Admiral Sir Caspar John, by whom given to the donor 1979

Exh: *Autumn Exhibition of Pictures and Sculpture*, Walker Art Gallery, Liverpool, September–December 1901 (133, as 'The Avenue'); *A Memorial Exhibition of Pictures by the late W. Evelyn Osborn*, Wm.B Paterson, October–November 1906 (4)

In this painting Royal Avenue, Chelsea is seen from King's Road looking towards Sir Christopher Wren's

Royal Hospital (1682–c.1691). Sir Caspar John remembered the painting hanging in his father's home; for many years Sir Caspar and others believed it to be by Paul Maitland. Owing to a certain similarity in style, Osborn's and Maitland's paintings are sometimes confused and this is exacerbated by the fact that after Osborn's death his paintings were left with Maitland, one of his few close friends.

In *Chiaroscuro* (1952), Augustus John wrote about meeting Osborn in the Blue Kailin Restaurant, Chelsea:

In the corner by the fireplace, a rather silent and dejected figure used to sit: this was William Osborne [sic]. Henry Lamb, then a young artist lately arrived from Manchester, and I soon got to know him, and the three of us became intimate and spent a good deal of time together. We found a common interest in the subject of painting, for Osborne [sic] too was an artist. Our senior in years, 'Billy' seemed vastly our superior in knowledge ... A once elegant but now dilapidated row of houses in the King's Road, with their peeling stucco, reminded Billy of a bevy of elderly ladies vainly trying to camouflage the ravages of time under a reckless application of rouge. This sort of thing was very 'ninetyish' of course, but it was new to us. Our friend claimed that this method permitted him to paint in any light: by a learned transposition of colour he could deal with Nature in any mood. This was theory: practically, he preferred the weather to accommodate itself to his palette, as in London it often did. He used few colours and those sparingly. Black was his basic pigment. 'As for the rose of bricks', he said, 'a little burnt umber and white suffices' (pp.228–9).

At different times Osborn was known variously as William Evelyn, Will E., W. Evelyn and Billy.

T 03649   **Beach at Dusk, St. Ives Harbour** *c.*1895

Oil on canvas 24 × 20⅛ (610 × 510)
Inscribed 'Will. Osborn' b.l.
Presented anonymously in memory of Terence Rattigan 1983

Prov: ... ; Charles Murrish, sold W.H. Lane & Son, Penzance, 28 November 1978 (88, as 'Landing the Catch, Evening St Ives') bt Nicholas Skeaping; bt the donor 1981

A view of the harbour at St Ives, Cornwall, with Smeaton's Pier to the right. William Osborn lived in Draycott Terrace, St Ives in 1893 and at The Terrace, St Ives from 1894–6. Research by the donor among elderly residents of St Ives suggests that Osborn frequently needed to exchange paintings for food and lodgings, bartering works to earn a living.

A label on the back of the work suggests that the painting might have been exhibited at or purchased from Lanhams, St Ives.

Eduardo Paolozzi b.1924

T 03764   **Mr Cruickshank** 1950

Polished bronze 11⅜ × 11⅜ × 7⅞ (290 × 290 × 200)
Inscribed 'E Paolozzi 1950' and 'MORRIS SINGER FOUNDER LONDON' behind left shoulder
Transferred from the Victoria and Albert Museum 1983

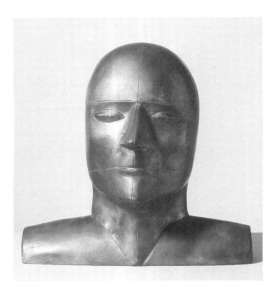

Prov: Given by the artist to the Department of
Circulation, Victoria and Albert Museum,
1971 (Circ. 682–1971)
Exh: ? *Eduardo Paolozzi*, Tate Gallery,
September–October 1971 (30, unspecified
cast)
Lit: Winifried Konnertz, *Eduardo Paolozzi*,
1984, pp.60–7

This bronze, and the plaster from which it was cast,
were given by the artist to the Department of Circulation, Victoria and Albert Museum, after his exhibition
at the Tate Gallery in 1971. Since the plaster is not
listed as included in this exhibition, it is not certain that
this particular cast of the bronze was shown there.

Winifried Konnertz (op.cit.) reproduces on p.60 a
double page from one of Paolozzi's scrapbooks of 1950
which includes two pages cut out from a magazine. This
describes an experiment at the Massachusetts Institute
of Technology in which a dummy head of a man was
bombarded with X–rays, in order to study the treatment
of brain tumours, under the title

Wooden Head is Target for X-ray Research.

Paolozzi's head is copied closely from the head illustrated, including the lines marked geometrically around
the surface. The head in the experiment came to pieces
in sections so that film could be inserted to measure the
penetration of the rays, and was called by the scientists
'Mr Cruickshank', but apparently

His name, picked at random, has no special
significance

One of the three photographs, titled

Block-headed 'Mr Cruickshank' Plays a Brainy Role
in Crucial X-rays

shows the bust on a table with the X-ray apparatus
pointing straight at it.

This head was one of the first sculptures made after
Paolozzi's move in the autumn of 1949 from Paris to
London, and is unlike his preceding works, such as
'Forms on a Bow', 1949 (T 00227).

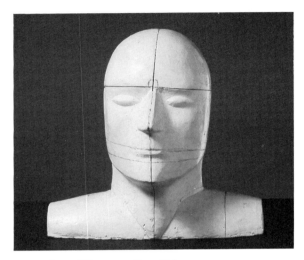

**T 03765 Plaster for 'Mr
Cruickshank' 1950**

Plaster and pencil, in two pieces, when
assembled 11⅜ × 11⅜ × 7⅞
(290 × 290 × 200)
Not inscribed
Transferred from the Victoria and Albert
Museum 1983
Prov: Given by the artist to the Department of
Circulation, Victoria and Albert Museum,
1971 (Circ. 683 and 683a–1971)

See entry for T 03764.

Giuseppe Penone b.1947

T 03420 Breath 5 1978

Terracotta 61 × 32¾ × 33
(1540 × 830 × 840)
Not inscribed
Purchased from Galerie Durand-Dessert,
Paris (Grant-in-Aid) 1982
Exh: Galerie Durand-Dessert, Paris, June–
August 1979 (no catalogue); *Giuseppe
Penone*, Stedelijk Museum, Amsterdam,
February–March 1980 (15, as 'Soffio 5',
repr. in col.); *Giuseppe Penone*, Gewad,

Ghent, 1980 (no catalogue); *Identité
Italienne, l'Art en Italie depuis 1959*,
Museé National d'Art Moderne, Centre
Georges Pompidou, Paris, June–
September 1981 (repr. p.618); *Biennale de
la Critique*, Palais des Beaux Arts,
Charleroi, December 1981–January 1982
and Internationaal Cultureel Centrum,
Antwerp, January–February 1982
(catalogue not numbered); *New Art at the
Tate Gallery*, Tate Gallery, September–
October 1983 (repr. p.18); *Falls the
Shadow: Recent British and European Art*,
Hayward Gallery, April–June 1986 (not
listed)

Lit: Germano Celant, 'Die archetypischen
Verbindungen bei Giuseppe Penone',
Giuseppe Penone, exhibition catalogue,
Museum Folkwang, Essen, 1978, pp.29–
62; *Identité Italienne, l'Art en Italie depuis
1959*, exhibition catalogue, Museé
National d'Art Moderne, Centre Georges
Pompidou, Paris, 1981, pp.582, 585 and
591; Marlies Gruterich, 'Italienische
Identität oder reiche arme Kunst', *Kunst-
Bulletin des Schweizerischen Kunstvereins*,
February 1982, pp.2–9, repr. p.8;
Giuseppe Penone, exhibition catalogue,
Kunstmuseum, Lucerne, 1977, p.47;
Jessica Bradley, 'The Poetics of
Representation', *Giuseppe Penone*,
exhibition catalogue, National Gallery of
Canada, Ottawa, 1983, pp.10–15, repr. in
col. on cover; Jessica Bradley, 'La Vision
poétique de Giuseppe Penone', *Giuseppe*

Penone, exhibition catalogue, ARC, Musée
d'Art Moderne de la Ville de Paris, Paris,
1984, pp.9–14, repr. p.43
   *Also repr: Art 11, '80, Die internationale
Kunstmesse Basel,* June 1980, p.66; *An
International Survey of Recent Painting
and Sculpture,* Museum of Modern Art,
New York, 1984, p.247

'Breath 5' is one of six similar terracottas of 1978, the
first three made in the artist's studio in Turin, and the
others at the pottery at Castellamonte, where they were
all fired.
   These sculptures, titled in Italian 'Soffio', are now in
these collections:

1. Stedelijk Museum, Amsterdam
2. FER Collection, West Germany
3. Private collection, Italy
4. Galerie Rudolf Zwirner, Cologne
5. Tate Gallery
6. Musée National d'Art Moderne, Centre Georges
Pompidou, Paris

Their first publication was the reproduction of two
of them in the catalogue of the artist's exhibition at
the Museum Folkwang, Essen, of September–October
1978. This catalogue is also illustrated with Penone's
studies of breath in two types of drawing, one in the
style of Leonardo da Vinci showing currents of air
blown from the mouth like waves, and another showing
studies of human lips, pursed as if to blow. These give
a key to the subject of this sculpture.
   The clay is modelled as if it were the imagined shape
of a breath of air, shortly after being exhaled from the
artist's mouth, when the first part of it has just reached
the ground. The frontispiece of the Essen catalogue is
a drawing by Penone of a man blowing into a funnel,
with the pattern of air breaking over the surface in
front of him like waves. The top of the Tate Gallery's
sculpture represents the cavity of the funnel into which
he is blowing, and in the centre of this uppermost
section is the shape of the interior of his mouth,
squeezed into the clay, and so making positive the shape
of the air coming from his throat. Photographs in the
catalogue show Penone taking a bronze cast of such a
shape out of his mouth, to demonstrate what it
represents. The impression along the side of the clay is
of the artist's clothed body, as he leans forward to blow
down to the ground. The Tate Gallery's version has the
impression only of one leg, wearing jeans, as if he leaned
forward on that one with the other stretched behind.
The lumps at the edge of this impression represent
billows of air rebounding from his body.
   An explanation by the artist in the Essen catalogue
enlarged the association of his clay breath with that of
a god in the act of creation:

according to a myth the creator of man was the god Khnum, who is represented as a potter shaping man on his wheel. In another myth, Athena breathes life into men whom Prometheus had made from clay and water (translated from the French in *Identité Italienne, l'Art en Italie depuis 1959*, 1981, p.585).

Penone has often made works concerned with the direct impression of the human onto nature. Before making the 'Breaths' he was interested in an ancient terracotta vase, comparable to them both in the material used and in that he was fascinated by the fingerprints of the potter, apparently noticeable on the surface, which he enlarged as a relief. The clay of the 'Breaths' similarly receives the touch of the artist. The marks of the potter Penone compared also to the creation of man by God, since the creator's touch must leave his imprints on the surface of what he creates:

> The hand that modelled man has left upon him the prints filled by water and air as our movements vary. Indeed, air in filling the prints re-creates the maker's skin; the skin of whoever touches the man tends to acquire at that point the shape of the maker's skin. With the negative of his skin impression one can make an infinite number of positives, just as many positives as there will be contacts with the surface of the future. (*Giuseppe Penone*, Kunstmuseum, Lucerne, 1977, p.78).

The breath of the artist was exhibited more directly in 1979, in the form of leaves on the gallery floor which he had blown into various shapes (*Giuseppe Penone*, ARC, Musée d'Art Moderne de la Ville de Paris, Paris, July–September 1983, repr. 17, 'Souffle de feuilles').

Sir Roland Penrose 1900–1984

T 03377   The Last Voyage of Captain Cook 1936/67

Oil on wood, plaster and steel
$27\frac{1}{4} \times 26 \times 33\frac{1}{2}$ (692 × 660 × 825)
Inscribed 'Roland Penrose 1936–1967/assisted by Anthony' on base b.r. and 'The Last Voyage/of Captain Cook' on base centre
Presented by Mrs Gabrielle Keiller through the Friends of the Tate Gallery 1982

Prov: Purchased from the artist by Mrs Keiller, 1979

Exh: *First International Surrealist Exhibition*, New Burlington Gallery, June–July 1936 (286); *Roland Penrose and Ithell*

Colquhoun, Mayor Gallery, June 1939 (6); *Dada and Surrealism Reviewed*, Hayward Gallery, January–March 1978 (14.44, repr. pp.367, 370); *Roland Penrose*, AC tour, Fermoy Arts Centre, King's Lynn, July–August 1980, I C A, August–September 1980, Arnolfini, Bristol, October–November 1980, Harris Museum and Art Gallery, Preston, November–December 1980, Ferens Art Gallery, Hull, December 1980–January 1981 (12, repr.); *Roland Penrose*, B C, Fundacio Joan Miró Centre d'Estudis d'Art Contemporani, Barcelona, February–March 1981 (14, repr.); *Paul Eluard et ses amis peintres 1895–1952*, Musée National d'Art Moderne, Paris, November 1982–January 1983 (no catalogue no., repr. 159)

Lit: Benjamin Péret, *Surrealist Exhibition*, Gordon Fraser Gallery, Cambridge, November 1937 (n.p.); Marcel Jean, *The History of Surrealist Painting*, Paris, 1959, p.271, repr.; Simon Wilson, *Surrealist Painting*, 1976, no.42, fig.32; Richard Shone, 'Roland Penrose at the I C A', *Burlington Magazine*, C X X I I, no.931, 1980, p.705; John Golding, 'Obituary: Roland Penrose 1900–84', *Burlington Magazine*, C X X V I, no.980, p.699; *Also repr: International Surrealist Bulletin*, no.4, September 1936 (on back cover); Herbert Read, *Surrealism*, 1936, repr. no.75; *London Bulletin*, no.17, June–July 1939, p.16; André Pieyre de Mandiargues, 'Objets Surréalistes', *XXe siècle*, no.42, June 1974, p.25; Roland Penrose, *Scrap Book 1900–81*, 1981 (repr. 9, 143 and repr. in col. 142); *British Surrealism Fifty Years On*, Mayor Gallery 1986 (on back cover)

'Captain Cook's Last Voyage' was made during 1936 and was first shown at the International Surrealist Exhibition at the New Burlington Galleries, London in 1936; André Breton was photographed next to it when he delivered his opening speech at that exhibition. Penrose had returned from Paris, where he had become close friends with several of the surrealists, in 1935 and began work immediately both on the organisation of the exhibition and this work.

Penrose incorporated a plaster model that he had purchased in Paris; the white plaster bust was sold as a decorative object in many shops around Montmartre. He commissioned the metal globe from a bicycle repairer in London. The first version was destroyed in storage during the war and the artist made a second version, with his son Anthony Penrose, in 1967. The artist made the base, giving it both a rounded and sharp profile to suggest movement and to reduce the sense of it being hard and fixed. The saw came from a tool he had in the workshop.

Penrose found it difficult to define the meaning of the work, which he regards as poetic, and which developed as the work was being made rather than established or brought out in advance. He suggests that the woman is equivalent to the earth (*la terre* is feminine) and the painted stripes on the body and the base are the strata of the earth revealed by cutting (also suggested by the saw handle). The body and base are also sliced, cut, in order to represent movement: he was anxious to avoid stasis. They are imprisoned in a scientific cage, the metallic globe. The title was an invention of the artist, a 'surrealistic title' made to name the work for the International Surrealist Exhibition.

This work is the most important of a number of objects made by Penrose in the mid-1930s.

T03400   Portrait 1939

Oil on canvas 30 × 25 (760 × 640)
Inscribed 'R Penrose '39' t.l.; there are also numerous inscriptions integrated into the composition
Purchased from the Mayor Gallery (Grant-in-Aid) 1982

Prov: Diane Deriaz; Mayor Gallery 1982

Exh: *Roland Penrose*, AC tour, Fermoy Arts Centre, King's Lynn, July–August 1980, ICA, August–September 1980, Arnolfini, Bristol, October–November 1980, Harris Museum and Art Gallery, Preston, November–December 1980, Ferens Art Gallery, Hull, December 1980–January 1981 (31, repr.); *Roland Penrose*, BC, Fundacio Joan Miró Centre d'Estudis d'Art Contemporani, Barcelona, February–March 1981 (35, repr.)

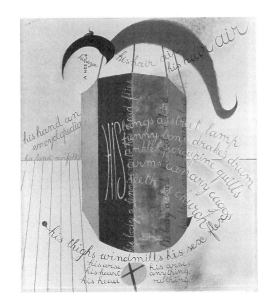

Lit: Claude Michaelides, 'Vous montre la maison d'un collectionneur fermier', *L'Oeil*, no.67–8, July–August 1960, p.66, repr.; Roland Penrose, *Scrapbook 1900–1981*, 1981, p.126, repr. 305

T03819   House the Light-House 1983

Pencil, gouache, ink and collage on paper 23½ × 33⅛ (590 × 840)
Inscribed 'Roland Penrose 1983' b.r. and 'House the Light-House 1983' on reverse
Presented anonymously 1984

Exh: *Roland Penrose, Recent Collages*, The Mayor Gallery, November–December 1983 (no catalogue)

Pablo Picasso 1881–1973

T 03670 **Nude Woman with Necklace** 1968

Oil and oil/alkyd on canvas $44\frac{11}{16} \times 63\frac{5}{8}$ (1135 × 1617)
Inscribed 'Picasso' t.l. and '8.10./68./I' on reverse
Purchased from Galerie Louise Leiris, Paris (Grant-in-Aid) 1983

Prov: Acquired from the artist by Galerie Louise Leiris

Exh: *Picasso: exposition organisée par le comité central du parti communiste français et l'Humanité, 1973*, La Courneuve, Paris, 5–9 September 1973 (111); *Picasso*, Musée Ingres, Montauban, June–September 1975 (17); *Exposition Picasso*, Metropolitan Museum of Art, Tokyo, October–December 1977, Prefectural Museum, Aichi, December 1977, Cultural Centre, Fukuoka, January 1978, National Museum of Modern Art, Kyoto, January–March 1978 (80, repr. in col.); *Pablo Picasso: Das Spätwerk – Themen 1964–1972*, Kunstmuseum, Basel, September–November 1981 (28, repr. in col., as 'Nu couché'); *Picasso*, National Gallery of Victoria, Melbourne, July–September 1984, Art Gallery of New South Wales, Sydney, October–December 1984 (164, repr. in col., as 'Reclining Nude with Necklace/Nu Couché')

Lit: Christian Zervos, *Pablo Picasso*, Paris, 1973, XXVII, no. 331, repr. p.126 as 'Nu couché'; Richard Morphet, 'A Late "Reclining Nude" by Picasso: a new acquisition for the Tate', *The Burlington Magazine*, CXXVI, February 1984, pp.84–8, repr. p.84 and in col. on cover as 'Reclining Nude with Necklace'; *The Tate Gallery Illustrated Biennial Report 1982–84*, 1984, repr. in col. p.55 as 'Reclining Nude with Necklace'

Though titled 'Nu couché' in Zervos, this work was acquired from Galerie Louise Leiris as 'Femme nue au collier' and its first exhibition was under the same title. Picasso's inscription on the reverse suggests that he completed at least one other work on the same day as this (8 October), but no such work is cited in Zervos or known to Galerie Louise Leiris.

The Tate's picture was completed only three days after Picasso had executed the final work in his suite of 347 engravings often known as 'Suite 347', on which, alongside works in other media, he worked at Mougins from 16 March to 5 October 1968. If the supplement is included, all 347 works are reproduced in the catalogue of the exhibition *Picasso 347 Engravings*, Institute of Contemporary Art, March–April 1970. As Roland Penrose wrote (*Picasso, His Life and Work*, third edition, 1981, p.451), although Picasso:

> had the expert help of the brothers Piero and Aldo Crommelynck ... they were hard put to keep pace with the speed of Picasso's output ... It would be difficult to find in the history of art a more extraordinary example of perfection and mastery of drawing in old age expressed with such variety and in such abundance.

Four of the nudes in 'Suite 347' wear necklaces (nos.289, 314, 325 and 338). Of these, only one is reclining and none is alone like the nude in the Tate's painting. The reclining nude in no.59 (30 April) has certain points in common with that in the Tate's painting, one of which is that the bracelet on her right wrist almost reads as a necklace. Gert Schiff (letter to the compiler, 26 March 1986) draws a parallel between the image in the Tate's painting and no.6 in 'Suite 347', 'where the large woman plays in the same autoerotic manner with her nipple'.

Zervos (op.cit., where all are repr., as nos.330, 331, 333, 334, 337) shows that Picasso completed at least one large oil painting of an unaccompanied reclining female nude per day from 7 to 10 October 1968 inclusive, two being completed on the 9th. Each of these five works is horizontal and of the same width, and the first canvas of 9 October is of exactly the same dimensions as the Tate's work. In all five works the body stretches across the whole canvas, with the head being located near the right edge, and each nude reclines on her left lower arm in a similar manner. Zervos reproduces (ibid. nos.321, 322) two closely-related drawings made on 9 October. 'Nu couché' 13 (11) October 1968 (repr. ibid., no.342) is a further oil of a reclining nude, with the same dimensions as the Tate's painting.

In a letter cited above, Gert Schiff draws attention to the similarity between the Tate's image and those of the upright reclining nudes in the oils Zervos XXVII, 35 (14 June 1967) and XXXI, 315 (10 July 1969). Morphet (loc.cit.) points out the parallels with the following horizontal oils in each of which, despite stylistic dissimilarities, an unaccompanied reclining nude, again with head to the right, rears towards the viewer while resting on her left arm: Z.XXXI, 454 (8 October 1969); Z.XXXI, 448 (2 November 1969); Z.XXXIII, 170 (7 September 1971).

Agreeing with Morphet that there remains an ambiguity in the Tate's image between an interior and a waterside location, Gert Schiff adds that drawings of February 1968 such as Z.241, 243 and 245 (each of which has the word 'Courtisane' in the title) makes inevitable the identification of the red shape at the right in the Tate's painting as a cushion.

Cirque et Enfant' Paris 1905; Christian Zervos, *Pablo Picasso*, Paris, 1970, XXII, no.224, repr. p.81 as 'Saltimbanque au Diadème, allaitant son Bébé' 1905

The girl, wearing a tiara and dancing shoes, and feeding her baby, appears to be a circus artist. Picasso made many drawings and paintings of the private life of circus folk at this period. This drawing was probably done from life on the page of a sketchbook, and is not related to any other known work.

T 03572 **Dish of Pears** 1936

Oil on canvas $14\frac{15}{16} \times 24$ (380 × 610)
Inscribed '15D.XXXVI.' b.l. and 'Picasso' b.r.
Bequeathed by Mrs A.F. Kessler 1983

Prov: Rosenberg & Helft; Mrs Kessler c.1939
Exh: *Picasso: Recent Works*, Rosenberg & Helft, March–April 1939 (3, as 'Compotier de Poires'); *French Paintings from the Kessler Collection*, York Art Gallery, May 1948 (9, as 'Les Fruitiers'); *The Kessler Collection*, Wildenstein Gallery, October–November 1948 (24, as 'Le Compotier'); *Picasso*, Tate Gallery, July–September 1960 (141, repr. as 'Still Life'); *The Kessler Bequest*, Tate Gallery, February–April 1984 (not numbered, repr. in col.)
Lit: Christian Zervos, *Pablo Picasso*, Paris, 1957, VIII, no.311, repr. p.147 (as 'Nature Morte')

This still life is dated 15 December 1936.

T 03571 **Circus Artist and Child** 1905

Indian ink and watercolour on paper
$6\frac{5}{8} \times 4\frac{1}{8}$ (168 × 105)
Not inscribed
Bequeathed by Mrs A.F. Kessler 1983

Prov: C. Frank Stoop; Mrs Kessler 1933
Exh: *The Kessler Collection*, Wildenstein Gallery, October–November 1948 (23, as 'The Circus Artist'); *The Kessler Bequest*, Tate Gallery, February–April 1984 (not numbered, repr.)
Lit: Pierre Daix and Georges Boudaille, *Picasso 1900–1906: Catalogue Raisonné de l'Oeuvre Peint*, Neuchâtel, 1966, no.D.XII.8, p.269, repr. as 'Artiste de

John Piper b.1903

T03818 Covehithe Church 1983

Oil on canvas 34 × 44 (863 × 1118)
Inscribed 'John Piper' b.r. and 'Covehithe
Church (Suffolk) 1983' on reverse
Presented by the artist 1984

Exh: *John Piper*, Tate Gallery, November 1983–
January 1984 (170)

Covehithe is in Suffolk. A film made for London Weekend Television in the summer of 1983 to coincide with
the Tate Gallery exhibition shows the artist sketching
the church.

Vivian Pitchforth 1895–1982

T03661 Seated Model c.1950–60

Brown ink and brown pastel on cream
wove paper 12¾ × 10 (325 × 254)
Not inscribed
Bequeathed by the artist 1983

Lit: Mervyn Levy, 'Draughtsman without
portfolio', *Studio*, CLXIII, January 1962,
pp.11–18; Lord Thorneycroft, *The
Amateur, A Companion to Watercolour*,
1985, pp.33, 35, repr. pl.12

T03662 Model Seen from the Back c.1950–60

Brown ink and brown pastel on cream
wove paper 10 × 13⅛ (254 × 334)
Not inscribed
Bequeathed by the artist 1983

Lit: See catalogue entry T03661

T03661

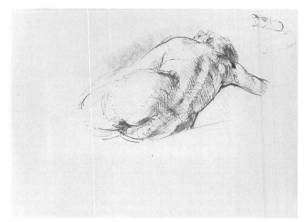

T03662

Vivian Pitchforth taught life drawing at London art
schools throughout his career: Camberwell 1926–65,
Clapham 1926–39, St Martin's 1930–65, RCA 1937–9,
Chelsea 1948–65 and John Cass 1965–73/4. These two
drawings in pastel and brown ink applied with pen
and brush were made as practical demonstrations for
his students. Peter Coker, RA, has described Vivian
Pitchforth's classes at St Martin's School of Art:

> The strength in his teaching was due in large measure
> to the clarity of his illustration. In spite of his
> deafness or perhaps because of it, his life classes
> became more concentrated and animated. One could
> also hear much of what was being said to the other
> students with the word 'form' echoing round the
> room ... At the end of the day he would produce his
> book and draw for himself which was particularly
> stimulating and many of his demonstration drawings

were kept by the students (*Times* Obituary, 8 September 1982).

'Seated Model' has been identified by Walter Woodington, curator of the Royal Academy Schools (retired) as Pat Horne, who sat for all the major London art schools in the late forties, fifties and sixties.

Pitchforth's emphasis on volume and form in these drawings was probably the result of his early admiration for Cézanne and also due to the teaching of Leon Underwood at the Royal College of Art and later at Girdlers Road. To explain the importance of form, Pitchforth sliced sections through the figure and marked out the bulk and weight of the body with dotted lines. The artist told Mervyn Levy:

> One begins by thinking the three masses of the skeleton, the head, the thorax, the pelvis ... I must observe the alignment of the three masses and in relation to these the rhythm that runs through the figure, and the angles of the limbs. These are the basic anchors that will hold my drawing securely in place ... Feel the sections of the limbs, the sections through them ... I am drawing with a lump of brown chalk; later I'll work into this with pen and ink ... I begin to draw over and into the broad masses and shapes of my preliminary drawing. Cutting and refining, polishing, shaping, describing with the incisive descriptive point of the pen (or pencil).

T 03663   View of Harbour – Folkestone *c*.1920

Watercolour and pencil on wove cartridge paper 19¼ × 29⅛ (489 × 740)
Watermark J & J.H. Kent
Not inscribed
Bequeathed by the artist 1983

This large watercolour has recently been identified as a view of Folkestone harbour. On the left is the harbour wall known as East Head and the headland beyond it is Copt Point. On the right is the end of South Quay.

Vivian Pitchforth painted from a point just off the Fishmarket, behind the slipway.

The painting can be dated to between 1908 and 1921 from the fishing boat *The Bonny Margaret* FE67 which was in service between those years, but it seems probable that it was done in the early twenties, after Pitchforth served in the First World War and when he returned to Leeds School of Art to continue his interrupted studies (1913–15, 1918–22). FE64 has been identified as the *Britannia* built in 1895 and the large vessel in the distance is a frozen meat and passenger ship bound for Fray Bentos in Argentina or for Australia.

'View of a Harbour' is an early example of Vivian Pitchforth's use of watercolour which was generally a prelude to oil painting until the late thirties when he abandoned oils, took up watercolour as his medium and the British coastline, estuaries and rivers in different weather conditions as his subject matter. This was an interest which evolved from unlikely beginnings as Pitchforth explained in a handwritten, unpublished manuscript in the Tate Gallery archive, written towards the end of his life, for unknown placement. He described how he moved from Cézannesque studies of mountains and being a follower of the Impressionists towards his new medium and subject matter.

> My friend (Eric C) Gregory (Founder of the Gregory Arts Fellowships at Leeds University) bought a boat and invited me to join him round the Medway estuaries and creeks. I was bored to tears the first week ... nothing but water and sky. However you can't stop a chap working so I got going and really enjoyed this sort of pansey (sic) art, but was secretly ashamed after being 'with it' with the then revolutionary Impressionists.

The compiler is indebted to Mr R. Mansfield of E.T.W. Dennis, publishers of Olsen's Fisherman's Nautical Almanack for identifying the harbour and dating and identifying the boats.

T 03664   Wet Windscreen, Ramsgate Harbour after 1971

Watercolour on mouldmade drawing paper
18¾ × 24⅝ (477 × 625)
Watermark 'Montgolfier St Marcel-les-Annonacy' and a lion rampant holding a sword. 'INGRES' countermark
Inscribed on verso 'Wet Windscreen/Ramsgate Harbour'
Bequeathed by the artist 1983

'Wet Windscreen, Ramsgate Harbour' shows the left arm of the harbour wall with the lighthouse and some boats. The other side of the harbour is obscured by

The habit grew so as to be able to extract from nature the effects which last only minutes and also to be able to control subtleties which are difficult on the spot ... I know exactly what I want before I start. The notes I make are rather poor as drawings and marked all over with references to colour value, but allied to memory they are adequate.

All the above quotations are taken from the handwritten, unpublished manuscript in the Tate Gallery archive, written towards the end of Pitchforth's life for unknown placement, already referred to in T 03663.

mist. A sketch for this work in a sketchbook owned by the Royal Academy dates the painting after 1971. Since the sketchbook bears a decimal currency price, it can be assumed that it was bought after February 1971.

There are precedents for Pitchforth sketching subjects from vehicles. Two other works of his in the Tate Gallery, N 05173 'Night Transport' (1939–40) and T 00037 'Floods, Port Madoc Valley, North Wales' 1954, were both subjects seen in the first instance from motor vehicles. The inclusion of the distinct foreground plane of the car windscreen in this painting is a new device which enables the artist to depict the moment when the rain begins to clear. The 'lovely English climate of all over greys with its mists, rain and subtle nuances' is the true concern of his later work, and led Pitchforth to devote at least half the space in watercolours such as this to the sky, and the rest often to wide expanses of reflective water.

The artist's brother, Gerald, owns a similar, less finished, version of 'Wet Windscreen, Ramsgate Harbour' with additional boats in the foreground. It was Vivian Pitchforth's habit, in later years, to make two versions of his more successful works. There are a number of other watercolours by Pitchforth of Ramsgate Harbour. The Royal Academy owns two undated views, no.119, which depicts a trawler and a fishing boat within the harbour wall and no.277 showing the view from one end of Ramsgate harbour with the lighthouse as the central feature. Pitchforth's Royal Academy Diploma work of 1954, 'Ramsgate Harbour', looks back from the harbour to the town, as do two other views of Ramsgate which were exhibited at the Royal Academy Summer Exhibition of 1950. 'Wet Windscreen, Ramsgate Harbour' may be considered as a late study of a subject matter long favoured by Pitchforth.

For his watercolours, Vivian Pitchforth worked in his London studio, or sometimes in hotel bedrooms near to the scene, from 'notes' made in front of the motif with indications of colour. The Royal Academy sketch $4\frac{3}{8} \times 6$ (110 × 154) for this work is such a note:

Nicholas Pope b.1949

T 03536   **Big Hoos** 1982

Silver birch $91\frac{3}{4} \times 68 \times 35$
(2330 × 1740 × 890)
Not inscribed
Purchased from Waddington Galleries
(Grant-in-Aid) 1982

Exh: *Sculpture*, Waddington Galleries, September–October 1982 (37, repr.)

Lit: Rasaad Jamie, 'Mixed Shows at Waddington's, Nicola Jacobs and Blond', *Artscribe*, 37, October 1982, pp.57–9; recorded interview with artist 2 July 1983, Tate Gallery Archives

'Big Hoos' was the last sculpture completed by Nicholas Pope in his studio in Hampshire before he moved in April 1982 to Herefordshire. It was first displayed with pieces standing directly on the floor. The base was made for it by the artist in June the following year so that it could be displayed more safely, in part in response to discussion with the Tate Gallery at the time it was acquired.

During the period 1982–3, Nicholas Pope changed decisively the kind of sculpture that he made, and 'Big Hoos' is transitional between styles. It resembles his earlier works in the precarious balance of the wooden tree trunks standing on end, particularly so before the base was added, and also in the character of the work as an accumulation of similar objects. Unlike earlier work, however, are the human associations of the shapes and the skill of its carving in the traditional sense of shape and surface texture.

The title, onomatopoeic and humorous, is similarly unlike both the titles of earlier works which referred to the process by which they were made, and to more recent titles with references to landscape. 'Big Hoos' has no specific meaning, except that it is a larger version of 'Hoos', a five piece sculpture of Wellingtonia wood, which itself took its name from 'Yoo Hoo', a punning title for a sculpture made of yew.

'Hoos' was made in the autumn of 1981. The pieces are about four feet tall, and Pope made use of the shape of the wood so that each piece divides, including one horizontal protuberance. 'Big Hoos' was similarly dependant on the original shape of the silver birch, and there were no preparatory studies apart from some outline drawings in a sketchbook. It is not itself a study for anything else, unlike some of his wooden sculptures made shortly afterwards, which were intended as maquettes for very large sculptures in stone.

Mabel Pryde 1871–1918

T 03464   The Harlequin c.1910

Oil on canvas 40 1/16 × 25 5/16 (1018 × 643)
Inscribed 'The Harlequin by Mabel
Nicholson' on stretcher
Presented by Timothy Nicholson 1982

Prov: Possibly Ben Nicholson (inscribed 'B
Nicholson, 97 King's Road, Chelsea' on
stretcher); Nancy Nicholson; Timothy
Nicholson

Exh: *Paintings by the late Mabel Nicholson,*
Goupil Gallery, April 1920 (9, as
'Harlequin No.2')?

A portrait of Nancy Nicholson, the third child of Mabel Pryde and William Nicholson. Nancy was born Annie Mary Pryde Nicholson in 1899. She married Robert Graves in 1918 after meeting him in Harlech in 1916. She died in 1977.

William Nicholson and Mabel Pryde painted several portraits of their children. Mabel Pryde's exhibition at the Goupil Gallery in 1920 lists 'Nancy with the Rabbit' and 'Nancy' among the 28 works in the exhibition.

William Nicholson's 'Nancy in Profile' 1912 (private collection) was painted at about the same time as the Tate picture and it also shows Nancy against a dark background. It is illustrated in colour in the Arts Council catalogue, *William Nicholson, Paintings, Drawings and Prints,* July 1980–January 1981, p.7.

The theatre held a particular attraction for Mabel Pryde. Her brother, James Pryde, had a brief career as an actor. She and William Nicholson admired Henry Irving and Ellen Terry; Terry's son Edward Gordon Craig was a close friend.

According to the donor (the artist's grandson) Nicholson and Pryde kept a large chest of dressing-up clothes. He believes that the Harlequin outfit was probably one of the costumes kept in this chest and that the Harlequin was probably chosen for this portrait as it fitted Nancy best at the time. Mabel Pryde's 'Portrait of Kit as a Child' (private collection), a portrait of her fourth child, shows a Harlequin's outfit draped over a box with a red-handled sword leaning against it.

The Harlequin appears to have been one of Mabel Pryde's favourite subjects. The Goupil Gallery exhibition included four Harlequin paintings – 'The Silver Harlequin', 'Harlequin No. 1', 'Harlequin No. 2' and 'Harlequin Asleep'. 'The Columbine' also appears among the exhibits, Columbine being Harlequin's sweetheart in the Commedia dell'Arte. 'Harlequin No. 1' (repr. *Country Life,* 17 April 1920, p.509) depicts a Harlequin against a dark background, facing right with its arms folded. It almost certainly represents Nancy. 'Harlequin Asleep' (private collection) may also represent Nancy.

The artist wrote in a letter to Max Beerbohm (? 1911) 'Nancy is getting lovely. So tall and so fascinating.'

In 1909 Mabel Pryde and her family moved to the Old Vicarage, Rottingdean. It is possible that this work was painted there. 'The Grange, Rottingdean' (private collection) shows Nancy sitting in front of a tall window with long red curtains. It is possible that this is the window depicted in the Tate picture.

Mabel Pryde lived as a child in 10 Fettes Row, a north-facing Edinburgh house. Derek Hudson writes in *James Pryde*, 1949, 'The impression is one of narrowness and semi-darkness, a weird half-light illuminating the entire perpendicular lines of the interior' (p.13). This might partly account for the sombreness which prevails in Mabel Pryde's work and the work of her brother, and which is evident in 'The Harlequin'.

Inscribed 'R.' b.r.
Purchased from Galerie Heike Curtze, Düsseldorf (Grant-in-Aid) 1982

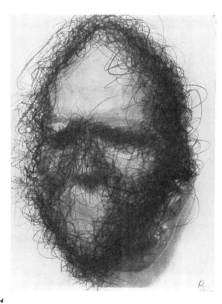

Arnulf Rainer b.1929

T 03385 **Untitled (Death Mask)** 1978

Oil pastel on black and white photograph
$23\frac{3}{8} \times 16\frac{3}{4}$ (594 × 425)
Inscribed 'R.' b.r.
Purchased from Galerie Heike Curtze, Düsseldorf (Grant-in-Aid) 1982

T 03386 **Untitled (Death Mask)** 1978

Ink drawing on black and white photograph
$23\frac{1}{4} \times 16\frac{1}{2}$ (592 × 415)

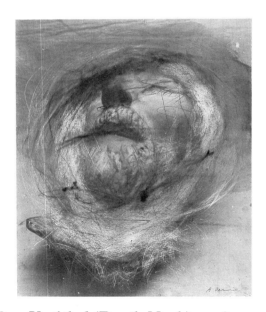

T 03387 **Untitled (Death Mask)** 1978

Oil pastel on black and white photograph
$24 \times 19\frac{7}{8}$ (609 × 505)
Inscribed 'A Rainer' b.r.
Purchased from Galerie Heike Curtze, Düsseldorf (Grant-in-Aid) 1982

T 03388 **Untitled (Body Language)** *c*.1973

Oil pastel on black and white photograph
$23\frac{7}{8} \times 19\frac{3}{4}$ (595 × 501)
Inscribed 'A. Rainer' b.r.
Purchased from Galerie Heike Curtze,
Düsseldorf (Grant-in-Aid) 1982

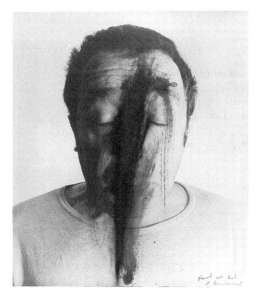

T 03390 **Untitled (Face Farce)** *c*.1971

Oil pastel and oil paint on black and white
photograph
24 × 20 (608 × 507)
Inscribed 'A Rainer' b.r.
Purchased from Galerie Heike Curtze,
Düsseldorf (Grant-in-Aid) 1982

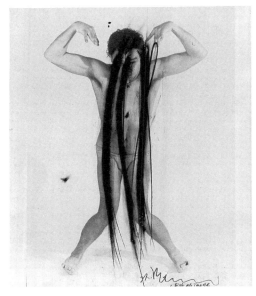

T 03389 **Two Flames (Body Language)** 1973

Oil on black and white photograph
$19\frac{7}{8} \times 23\frac{7}{8}$ (505 × 607)
Inscribed '2 Flammen/ 'A Rainer' t.l.
Purchased from Galerie Heike Curtze,
Düsseldorf (Grant-in-Aid) 1982

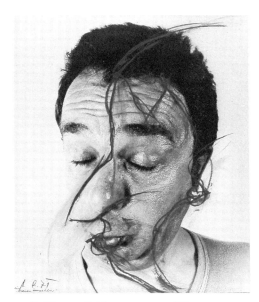

T 03391 **A Nose Adjustment (Face Farce)** 1971

Oil pastel on black and white photograph
24 × 20 (608 × 507)

Inscribed 'A.R.71/eine nasen korrektur'
b.l.
Purchased from Galerie Heike Curtze,
Düsseldorf (Grant-in-Aid) 1982

T 03671   Wine Crucifix 1957/78

Oil on canvas 66¼ × 40¾ (1680 × 1030)
Inscribed 'AR57/78' b.r. and 'Dunkel-
/Rotes ᴋʀᴇᴜᴢ A Rainer 57/1972...
[illegible] und/neu aufgezogen/dabei
restaur... [illegible]/A. Rainer' on back of
lining canvas
Purchased from Galerie ak, Frankfurt
(Grant-in-Aid) 1983

William Ratcliffe 1870–1955

T 03359   Clarence Gardens 1912

Oil on canvas 20 × 30 (570 × 760)
Inscribed 'W. Ratcliffe 1912' b.l.
Purchased from Anthony d'Offay Ltd.
(Grant-in-Aid) 1982

Prov: ...; Contemporary Art Society; given by
the Society to Russell-Cotes Art Gallery
and Museum, Bournemouth, 1945, by
whom sold at auction; ...; Anthony
d'Offay

Exh: *The London Salon of the Allied Artists'
Association Ltd*, Royal Albert Hall, July

1912 (187 or 188); ? *The Camden Town
Group,* Carfax & Co. Ltd., December 1912
(42); ? *Twentieth Century Art,* Whitechapel
Art Gallery, May 1914 (20); *Paintings of
London by Members of the Camden Town
Group,* Anthony d'Offay Gallery,
October–November 1979 (29)

Lit: Wendy Baron, *The Camden Town Group,*
1979, p.322 and repr. p.323; William
Ratcliffe, exhibition catalogue,
Letchworth Museum and Art Gallery,
1982, p.6

At the Allied Artists' Exhibition of July 1912, Ratcliffe
showed two paintings titled 'Clarence Gardens', priced
at £12 and £10. Wendy Baron (loc.cit.) suggests that
T 03359 was the more expensive painting, and a smaller
oil of a different view of the same square (10½ × 19¾
ins., private collection, London, repr. *Camden Town
Recalled,* exhibition catalogue, Fine Art Society, 1976,
p.112) is the other one.

Clarence Gardens was a square in London ɴᴡ1, and
has been completely rebuilt.

Robert Rauschenberg b.1925

T 03376   Revenue (Spread) 1980

Mixed media on wooden support with
collaged elements
96 × 104 × 26⅜ (2435 × 2640 × 670)
Inscribed on reverse: left panel
'80.50ʀᴇᴠᴇɴᴜᴇ (sᴘʀᴇᴀᴅ)/ᴘᴀɴᴇʟ ᴀ/ 1
ᴏꜰ 2/ʀᴀᴜsᴄʜᴇɴʙᴇʀɢ, '80' c., drawing,
assembly instructions t.l.; centre panel
'ɪʀᴏɴɪɴɢ ʙᴏᴀʀᴅ ɪs ɴᴇᴠᴇʀ ᴛᴏ ʙᴇ
ʀᴇᴍᴏᴠᴇᴅ' t., drawing, assembly
instruction b.; right panel '80.50
ʀᴇᴠᴇɴᴜᴇ (sᴘʀᴇᴀᴅ)/ᴘᴀɴᴇʟ ʙ/ 2 ᴏꜰ
2/ʀᴀᴜsᴄʜᴇɴʙᴇʀɢ '80' c.

Purchased from Sonnabend Gallery,
New York (Grant-in-Aid) 1982

Prov: Lent to Tate Gallery by Sonnabend
Gallery, New York, from April 1981 until
date of purchase

Exh: *Robert Rauschenberg*, Tate Gallery,
April–June 1981 (75)

Martial Raysse b.1936

T 03383 Necropolis I 1960

Plastic assemblage $23\frac{1}{2} \times 5 \times 5$
(597 × 125 × 125)
Inscribed 'MARTIAL RAYSSE 60' on top
Purchased from Galerie Bonnier, Geneva
(Grant-in-Aid) 1982

Paula Rego b.1935

T 03839 Nanny, Small Bears and Bogeyman 1982

Acrylic on paper $47\frac{1}{4} \times 59\frac{7}{8}$ (120 × 152)
Inscribed 'Nanny/Paula Rego 1982' on
back of paper
Presented by the Patrons of New Art
through the friends of the Tate Gallery
1984

Prov: Edward Totah Gallery 1982, from whom
purchased by the Patrons of New Art,
1984

Exh: *Paula Rego, Paintings and Prints*, Edward
Totah Gallery, September–October 1982
(7); *Paula Rego Paintings 1982–83*,
Arnolfini Gallery, Bristol, September–
October 1983 (3)

In an interview with the compiler on 24 April 1984
Paula Rego described the subject of the picture as follows:

The story of the picture comes from an episode in
the autobiography of Elias Canetti which a friend of
mine told me about (I have not read the book myself).
Canetti had a nanny whose boyfriend always wanted
to cut out the little boy's tongue. I started to do this
picture because I knew the story; to do a picture I
always need a story to start with, although as I go
along the story may change or the picture may
change. I did this bogeyman, on the left, who is the
boyfriend of the nanny and who is going to cut off
the tongue of the little boy who, in the picture, is a
little bear. The bear is tied to the nanny; the one
who is most wicked is not the bogeyman but the
nanny who has strapped him up. She is so possessive
and horribly evil that while I was painting the front
bear another little bear appeared behind it. This
little bear is like the twin of the other one – it's really

the shadow if you like, the shadow also in a sort of psychological sense of the good little bear and the bad little bear. The bad little bear is sad and they are both bewildered and frightened because they are going to have their willies cut off.

The picture refers very loosely to Rego's experience of human personalities during her childhood in Portugal. She uses animals to stand for people because their features may be exaggerated without reaching the point of caricature. The animals are not chosen in advance to represent specific people 'but the animals appear and then I recognise certain people after that'.

T03839 is one of a series of works on paper. Rego stated that she always works in series. The figures were drawn in first and then the paint was applied with sponges and then brushes. She employs paper because it is absorbent and smooth and she 'can make an absolutely clean mark. You don't need priming, you don't need stretchers and when you have finished you just draw out the next sheet and it doesn't stop the flow.'

This entry has been approved by the artist.

Sir Norman Reid b.1915

T03478 Mr Pencil at Annestown 1960–81

Oil on canvas laid on hardboard $17\frac{15}{16} \times 20\frac{3}{8}$ (452 × 518)
Inscribed 'Sir Norman Reid [the artist's address]' and ' "Mr Pencil at Annestown" ' on the back of the board
Presented by Lady d'Avigdor Goldsmid through the Friends of the Tate Gallery 1982
Exh: RA 1982 (1501)

Sir Norman Reid joined the staff of the Tate Gallery in 1946, rising to Deputy Director in 1954 and Keeper in 1959, becoming Director from 1964 until 1979. He was trained as a painter at Edinburgh College of Art and won a postgraduate scholarship there, but his duties at the Tate left him little time for painting. A portrait of Sir Norman Reid, painted by Sir Lawrence Gowing in 1980, is in the Tate Gallery's collection (T03208).

Sir Norman spent a summer holiday in Annestown, Eire in 1952 and executed a number of gouaches on that occasion. Annestown is a small village on the coast, about ten miles south-west of Waterford. The artist wrote to the compiler (letter of 15 April 1986) that:

> The Tate painting is fairly close to one of these gouaches although the design is much modified. I had always had it in mind to develop some of these sketches and decided to try out this one when I came across it in a portfolio.

The twenty-one year span for the execution of the painting is explained by the artist:

> After the painting was begun in 1960 it stood around for a number of years when I was making collages – this being a more convenient medium than oil paint for the short periods of time then available. I had a fresh look at it some few years before it reached its final state and it was during this time that it was modified to read upside down.

The title of the painting includes not only the venue, Annestown, but a reference to 'Mr Pencil'. Monsieur Pencil is the cartoon strip figure of an artist created by Randolphe Toepffer in 1830 and reproduced in A. Ozenfant's *Foundations of Modern Art,* 1931, p.74. Monsieur Pencil makes 'a drawing from nature' and the caption then reads:

> looks at what he has done with pleasure, and remarks he is pleased with it. M. Pencil . . . remarks that upside down it pleases him too. And even if he looks at it over his shoulder. And having tried to see it from behind, M. Pencil, who is an artist, remarks with pleasure that he is still pleased with it.

T03478 went through various stages including being turned upside down. Its agreed orientation now is the way it originally was painted. The artist recalls:

> I think it is more satisfactory as it hangs now although for a long while I was pleased to have it standing the other way up. My wife called this 'doing a Mr Pencil' after the sly cartoon by Randolphe Toepffer . . . Hence the title 'Mr Pencil at Annestown' which was intended as a family joke but has gone by chance into the record.

T03478 depicts the village of Annestown seen from the beach below. The main street in the centre of the picture runs uphill and divides a large manor house with grounds and outbuildings on the left from smaller massed buildings, including a former police station, on the right. A lighthouse painted with stripes stands out against the coastline.

The artist intended the picture to be readable either way up even though only one of the orientations is now the proper way.

Auguste Renoir 1841–1919

T03573 **Nude on a Couch** 1915

Oil on canvas 21⅜ × 25⅜ (518 × 652)
Inscribed 'Renoir.' b.l.
Bequeathed by Mrs A.F. Kessler 1983

Prov: Ambroise Vollard, Paris (purchased from the artist); Reid and Lefevre; Mrs Kessler 1938

Exh: *Corot to Cézanne,* Lefevre Gallery, June 1936 (43, as 'Nu à la Méridienne' *c.*1914); *The 19th Century French Masters,* Lefevre Gallery, July–August 1937 (38); *Twentieth Century French Masters,* Whyte Gallery, Washington, D.C., November–December 1938 (11); *Milestones in French Painting,* Lefevre Gallery, June 1939 (38); *French Paintings from the Kessler Collection,* York Art Gallery, May 1948 (10, as 'Gabrielle'); *Renoir,* Lefevre Gallery, June 1948 (33, repr.); *The Kessler Collection,* Wildenstein Gallery, October–November 1948 (27); *The Kessler Bequest,* Tate Gallery, February–April 1984 (not numbered, repr. in col.)

Lit: Ambroise Vollard, *Tableaux, Pastels et Dessins de Pierre-Auguste Renoir,* Paris, 1918, I, no.498, repr. p.125 with the date 1915 and listed p.180 as 'Femme nue sur un Canapé'; *Burlington Magazine,* LXXIII, 1938, advertisement supplement to December issue, pl.15

Although this picture has usually been known since at least 1936 as Nu à la Méridienne' (Nude having a Siesta), it was reproduced by Vollard in 1918 with the title of which an English translation is used here.

The model was Gabrielle Renard (1878–1959), a cousin of Mme Renoir's from Essoyes, who joined the Renoir household in the summer of 1894 to help Mme Renoir, who was then expecting her second child. She later combined the duties of being in charge of the housework with those of serving as Renoir's favourite model, including often posing for him in the nude from the age of twenty onwards.

T03574 **Peaches and Almonds** 1901

Oil on canvas 12¼ × 16¼ (312 × 413)
Inscribed 'Renoir.' b.l.
Bequeathed by Mrs A.F. Kessler 1983

Prov: Ambroise Vollard, Paris; Reid and Lefevre; Mrs Kessler

Exh: *Milestones in French Painting,* Lefevre Gallery, June 1939 (33, as 'Pèches et Amandes' *c.*1898); *The Kessler Collection,* Wildenstein Gallery, October–November 1948 (25, repr. as 'Nature Morte: Pèches et Amandes'); *Renoir,* Royal Scottish Academy, Edinburgh, August–September 1953 (15); *The French Impressionists and Some of their Contemporaries,* Wildenstein Gallery, April–May 1963 (56); *The Kessler Bequest,* Tate Gallery, February–April 1984 (not numbered, repr.)

Lit: Ambroise Vollard, *Tableaux, Pastels et Dessins de Pierre-Auguste Renoir*, Paris, 1918, II, p.100

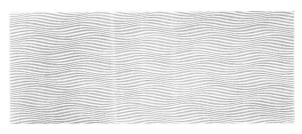

Bridget Riley b.1931

T 03375   **To a Summer's Day 2** 1980

Acrylic on canvas $45\frac{1}{2} \times 110\frac{3}{4}$ (1155 × 2810)
Inscribed 'RILEY '80' on edge of canvas
t.l., 'RILEY/TO A SUMMER'S/DAY 2',
'1980/ACRYLIC/ON LINEN', 'TOP↑'
and $45\frac{5}{8} \times 110\frac{5}{8}$ INS' on reverse, 'RILEY
TO A SUMMER'S DAY 2 1980 ACRYLIC
ON LINEN' along centre bar of stretcher
and 'TOP' on vertical bar of stretcher.
Purchased from the artist through Juda
Rowan Gallery (Grant-in-Aid) 1982
Exh: *Bridget Riley,* The Warwick Arts Trust,
June–July 1981 (5, as '1979')

The painting titled 'To a Summer's Day' was made in 1980. It is in acrylic on canvas, $45\frac{3}{4} \times 99$ ins., and is of the same design as T 03375. It was sold at Christie's 25 March 1986 (41, repr.).

'To a Summer's Day 2' was painted at the artist's studio in West London. There were no small scale preparatory studies particularly for it, although the colours and their combinations in groups were studied in numerous gouaches. As for all her paintings the artist first made a full size cartoon, in pencil and gouache on cartridge paper, drawn flat on the floor. The function of this was to test if the design and colours would work as a painting, in the sense of producing an active optical mixture, and the cartoon was displayed on her studio wall for study. The cartoon was subsequently destroyed by the artist.

The drawing of the cartoon and later of the painting was made using three templates cut from hardboard. One of these was as wide as the painting, with one edge cut in regular waves, and was used to draw the top and bottom of the waves, which are set at a diagonal. The lines that mark the borders between colours within the waves were made from two double sided templates of a single wavelength, the top and bottom marked 'shorter' and 'longer'. These borders run from every trough and crest. Since the outlines of the waves are at a diagonal these curves are either of shorter or longer wavelength, corresponding to the two sides of the template. It was found in practice that in order to balance the colours correctly these curves could not be regular, and two templates were used as alternatives for each.

There are two variables in the drawing of 'To a Summer's Day 2' within this scheme, the direction of advance of the waves (caused by their diagonal alignment) and the direction of the twist of the colours within each wave. The direction of advance changes seven times, and is arranged in such a way that the most rapid change occurs just above the wave at the central horizontal. This more active centre and calmer top and bottom is referred to by the artist in terms of landscape, as if there were a horizon just above the centre, with the implication that the spectator has a certain point of view. The direction of the twist changes alternately from wave to wave throughout the design.

The margins of the design were adjusted by eye, both in design and colour, so as not to draw attention to any obtrusive fragments.

The positions of the four colours – blue, violet, pink and ochre – were determined by the artist when looking at the completed cartoon. They are not repeated in order, either along each wave or from one wave to another, although the same colour is not repeated across a border within a wave. The colours were considered as pairs, in combinations that were warmer or colder, and placed in clusters at certain places. These clusters of similar colours do not follow the changes in the design. Each wave has three colours at any one point and one starts and another ends at every crest or trough, each colour persisting for one and a half wavelengths. The choice of colours was intended to provoke an optical mix in the eye, with as much interaction as possible between colours, and hence mixed rather than pure colours were used.

When the cartoon was approved, the design was redrawn onto the canvas in pencil and ink pen, using a padded template, and painted with acrylic. The colours were made up as equivalent to the overall effect of the gouache colours, and not matched mechanically.

The title refers in a general way to the feeling of the painting, using a phrase from Shakespeare's sonnet 'Shall I compare thee to a summer's day'.

In both colour and drawing this painting is one of the most complex arrangements of wave patterns used by Bridget Riley, although others have used up to six colours. In paintings of the later 1960s such as 'Cataract 3' (1967) the waves are all of the same size (so that the colours do not twist) and progress evenly so that all the crests fall on parallel diagonal lines. Twisting colours were first used in paintings of parallel stripes, and then in wave paintings from 1976. The further variation, changes of direction in the waves, was introduced in the paintings of 1980 exhibited the following summer at the Warwick Arts Trust.

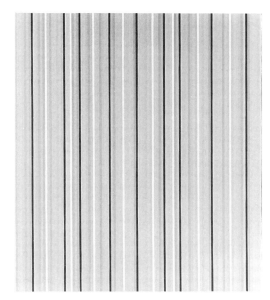

T03816 Achaian 1981

Oil on canvas 94 × 79¾ (2390 × 2023)
Inscribed 'Riley/'81' on edge of canvas b.l.,
'ACHAIAN, Riley 1981 Oil on linen' along centre bar of stretcher, and 'ACHAIAN, /Riley 1981/Oil on linen, 94 × 79⅝', 'This painting looks/best in natural/daylight' and 'TOP↑" (twice) on reverse
Purchased from the artist through Juda Rowan Gallery (Grant-in-Aid) 1983

Lit: Robert Cumming, 'Colour and Light: the Visit to Egypt', *Working with Colour, Recent Paintings and Studies by Bridget Riley*, Arts Council, 1984 (n.p.)

'Achaian' is one of the 'Egyptian' series of paintings by Bridget Riley, which use a palette of colours derived from her experience of the landscape and tomb paintings of Egypt, seen on a visit in autumn 1981. Particular shades of these colours – yellow, blue, red and turquoise – she regarded as a breakthrough in that they gave the optical effect which she sought and are brighter and purer than the colours she had previously been using.

The cartoons for the paintings in this series were made from coloured strips of gouache, which were laid flat as if in a painting and yet could be rearranged. There is no regular system in the placing of the colours, which is not symmetrical, although in some places the sequence has the appearance of a reflection about a central colour.

The artist reads the painting horizontally across the bands, pointing to variations of hot and cold colour, with 'accents' in the design in certain places. The title was given after the painting was finished, and refers to the Greeks who made 'the finest early sculpture – vigorous but simple' (conversation of 11 April 1986) and which corresponded to the character of the painting as 'dark and Mediterranean'.

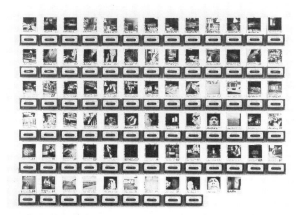

Dieter Roth b.1930

T03610 Harmonica Curse 1981

74 audio cassettes inscribed 'Dieter Roth' and numbered 1 to 74 t.r.
76 Polaroid photographs each 4¼ × 3½ (109 × 90); each inscribed 'Harmonica Curse Dieter Roth' and numbered b.r., also dated variously from 14 February 1981 to 8 August 1981 and number of edition noted
Edition of 5
Purchased from Audio Arts (Grant-in-Aid) 1983

This work was published by Audio Arts, London.

Sir William Rothenstein

1872–1945

T03682 **Study for the Attendant in 'The Princess Badroulbadour'**
*c.*1908

> Red chalk on paper $15\frac{1}{4} \times 11$ (387 × 281)
> Not inscribed
> Presented by Sir John Rothenstein through the Friends of the Tate Gallery 1983

This drawing is a study for Rothenstein's painting 'The Princess Badroulbadour' (1908, N03953), a portrait of his three children, John, Betty and Rachel, in fancy dress. It is of his son, but in the painting the pose with folded arms was used for one of his daughters. Sir John Rothenstein gave to the Tate Gallery in 1970 another drawing of himself by his father, also a study for this painting (T01248).

Pierre Roy 1880–1950

T03537 **Boris Anrep in his Studio, 65 Boulevard Arago** 1949

> Oil on canvas $25\frac{3}{4} \times 19\frac{5}{8}$ (653 × 501)
> Inscribed ' P. Roy/1949' b.r. and 'BORIS ANREP IN HIS STUDIO/65 BOULEVARD ARAGO/1949' on back of canvas
> Bequeathed by Mrs M.J.A. Russell 1982
> *Prov:* Mrs M.J.A. Russell (bequest from the artist)

An imaginary portrait of the painter and mosaicist Boris Anrep (1883–1969), who was born in St Petersburg and studied art in Paris and Edinburgh. He lived for some years in England, where he made his first mosaics, and then from 1926 mainly in Paris. His works include the mosaic floor for the entrance hall and upper landing of the National Gallery, London (1927 and 1952) and the floor for the former Blake Gallery at the Tate (1923).

He met Pierre Roy when both were studying at the Académie Julian in Paris in 1908, and they remained life-long friends.

Igor Anrep, Boris Anrep's son, says that this studio at 65 Boulevard Arago in Paris (Studio 4) originally belonged to Roy, on a long lease, and Boris Anrep lived next door. But when Anrep parted from his wife Helen in 1926 he got this studio from Roy and it remained his until about three or four years before his death.

The sculpture head is imaginary. The general appearance of the studio is fairly accurate, except that most of the floor was occupied by a very large table and there were not so many pictures. Most of the works on the walls are probably cartoons for mosaics, though hanging high up to the top left of the doorway (above the head) one can see the picture by Pierre Roy 'A Naturalist's Study' of 1928 which was bequeathed to the Tate by Anrep in 1969 (T01182). Anrep worked on mosaics in this studio and bought brioche tins to keep his tesserae in. Justin Vulliamy describes Anrep's studio in his introduction to the catalogue of the Anrep retrospective at Gallery Edward Harvane, January–February 1973.

In a private collection there is another portrait of Anrep by Roy painted in 1912 which is realistic and romantic, showing him with a laurel wreath on his head and poems in his hand.

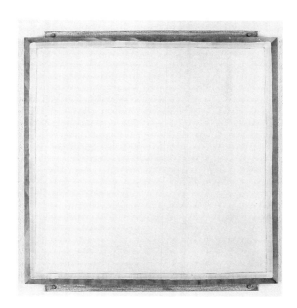

Robert Ryman b.1930

T 03550 **Ledger** 1982

Enamelac on fibreglass with aluminium
support $30\frac{1}{16} \times 28 \times 1\frac{5}{8}$ ($763 \times 711 \times 36$)
Inscribed on reverse, top 'RYMAN '82↑
"LEDGER"'
Purchased from Mayor Gallery (Grant-in-
Aid) 1983

Exh: Robert Ryman, Recent Paintings, Mayor
Gallery, November–December 1982
(repr. in col.)

T 03824

Niki de Saint Phalle b.1930

T 03824 **Shooting Picture** 1961

Paint on plaster relief $56\frac{3}{8} \times 30\frac{3}{4} \times 3\frac{1}{8}$
($1430 \times 780 \times 81$)
Not inscribed
Purchased from Jean Tinguely (Grant-in-
Aid) 1984

David Salle b.1952

T 03444 **Walking the Dog** 1982

Two panels – figures: acrylic, oil and
charcoal on cotton $86\frac{1}{8} \times 56\frac{1}{8}$
(2188×1425), dog: acrylic and oil on linen
$86\frac{1}{8} \times 56\frac{1}{8}$ (2188×1425), overall
dimensions $86\frac{1}{8} \times 112\frac{1}{4}$ (2188×2850)
Not inscribed
Purchased from Anthony d'Offay (Grant-
in-Aid) 1982

*Exh: Chia, Clemente, Kiefer, Salle, Schnabel,
New Paintings,* Anthony d'Offay, June–
July 1982 (works not numbered)

'Walking the Dog' was painted on two supports; on the
left, on cotton duck, the artist used acrylic paints to
colour the ground and for the images of the body parts.
On the right, on fine Belgian linen, he used cadmium
oil paint to draw the woman and dog. The anatomical
images are taken from magazines; the woman walking
the dog is an image recalled from a nineteenth century

French print that he had seen in a flea market in Paris about a month before making the painting. Salle began with the left hand panel without the impastoed areas and then painted the right hand panel. When he put them side by side he realised that the dog-walking figure 'made the other part very poignant; in a way it made the other half alienated and sad'. He decided that he should take the image further and laid the left-hand panel on the ground and started to squeeze tubes of acrylic paint in empty spaces. These colours 'more or less arbitarily squished together' resemble his recollection of a 1956 painting by Jean Paul Riopelle (Canadian, b.1923) which had been reproduced in an auction catalogue that Salle had seen at a friend's house.

Two circular areas of paint occur above and to either side of the walking figure; this device has been used by Salle since 1976 in paintings that he has subsequently destroyed. Salle relates them 'in a very simplistic (Freudian) way (to) the body orifices, they're really like two holes...'

Salle is concerned that the source of the images is not regarded as more significant than the resonances and connections that occur between the images. He describes the process of his thinking about a painting as follows (interview with the compiler 19 May 1983):

> I think that a lot of work is involved with the ways in which we find ourselves calling attention to something ... it goes in stages – paying attention to something, noticing that we're paying attention to something and, then, noticing both the desire and the means by which we call attention to it ... It seems to me that from having to confront what's called attention to, to the way in which attention is called is ... the subject of the painting.

A second version of the figure with dog appears in a painting made soon after the Tate's painting had left the studio; it is now in the collection of Raymond Learsy, New York.

Julian Schnabel b.1951

T 03441   Humanity Asleep 1982

Mixed media on wooden support
$108\frac{1}{4} \times 144 \times 11$ ($2743 \times 3656 \times 280$)
Inscribed 'HUMANITY ASLEEP' c.r.
Purchased from Mary Boone Gallery, New York (Grant-in-Aid) 1982

Exh: *Julian Schnabel*, Tate Gallery, June–September 1982 (not in catalogue); *New Art at the Tate Gallery*, Tate Gallery, September–October 1983 (works not

numbered, repr.); *Forty Years of Modern Art 1945–1985*, Tate Gallery, February–April 1986 (works not numbered)

'Humanity Asleep' was made in the month preceding the Tate Gallery's small exhibition of Schnabel's work in 1982. It is painted in oil on a panel prepared by assistants under the artist's supervision. This consists of four plywood and softwood boxes, with the outer edges chamfered to make the work appear to float and to concentrate attention on the centre of the image. Before painting began, shards of domestic pottery were attached to the front surfaces of the boxes, using a filled polyester resin adhesive (normally used to repair car bodies), and the four boxes were bolted together and hung on the wall. In this painting the shimmering effect is produced by painting over dark imagery with white paint mixed with a varnish medium; in previous works the pottery fragments had been left unpainted to produce a similar effect.

The artist knew that the work would be included in the Tate exhibition and named it 'for William Blake' although he acknowledges that the title is not a direct quotation from Blake's poems or from the titles of his works. The title also describes the central image which depicts two heads floating on a raft at night, hopelessly lost. The image of the raft comes from a photograph of soldiers clinging to driftwood taken during the Second World War and was also used in a larger painting entitled 'The Raft' (1982). The angel with a sword and wings was painted from life from a Puerto Rican santos figure that the artist had purchased from an antique dealer.

Schnabel commented:

> Anyway I was interested in the shape of them because when you paint something from life, it has a kind of believability or contour that's different from something that's flat...

Around the saint the artist has outlined a circle, indicating a mirror, on which he has inscribed the title of the work. He talks of this image being painted on top of the whole painting as if by another hand:

> Not my hand, necessarily, but maybe God's hand. So it's the scale of it, and the parenthetical quality of it [that] alludes to something outside of the painting.

The portraits which form the centre of the image are of the Italian artist Francesco Clemente in front of a self-portrait of Schnabel. The Clemente portrait was painted from life and represents Schnabel's wish to envisage him as both a significant moral component in the art world and an heroic figure, a good artist. The self-portrait is less heroic, as if, as the artist describes it, 'more like my skin's been peeled off', which emphasises the humanness. The two figures are joined in a worthwhile enterprise, that of making art, but restricted by the difficulty of communicating this project. Schnabel describes it as 'just some kind of existential analogue of just being in the world – in my case making a work or thinking that there might be any significance in making art...' He describes the painting and the process of its reception in an interview with the compiler (18 May 1983):

> The sea is the 'Humanity Asleep'; the sea is the sort of black, it's the sea at night, it's a place where your voice won't be heard, and it's a place that we're surrounded by ... But I don't think it's cynical as it is just realistic in the sense of the difficulties of communication or the kind of, the high sea that is the sea of mis-understanding. Or the sea could be like ignorance.... I mean I'm working on these things but who understands my work? I'm curious about what I'm trying to find out about, but in fact what happens is, with each step further on I get, it makes people more confused somehow. On the other hand some people feel that it clarifies things. I believe that it clarifies things ... It seems to me that it's like a real metaphor for painting.

Emile Schuffenecker 1851–1934

T 03639   **Spring-like Morning** *c.*1896

> Pastel on paper 13 × 17¾ (330 × 452)
> Inscribed with studio stamp (design with a flower) b.r.
> Presented anonymously in memory of Terence Rattigan 1983
> Prov: Galerie Les Deux-Iles, Paris (purchased from the artist's daughter); Anthony d'Offay Fine Art; the donor

> Exh: *Claude-Emile Schuffenecker (1851–1934),* Anthony d'Offay, December 1965– January 1966 (no catalogue)

This drawing has a label of Anthony d'Offay Fine Art on the back, with the date *c.*1896. It was presented as 'Matin Printanier'.

T 03640   **Seascape (Cliffs)** *c.*1895

> Pastel on paper 5¼ × 8¼ (135 × 209)
> inscribed with studio stamp b.l.
> Presented anonymously in memory of Terence Rattigan 1983
> Prov: Galerie Les Deux-Iles, Paris (purchased from the artist's daughter); the donor *c.*1966

The view is probably a Breton one, and the site may be quite close to those of the two following works T 03641–2; indeed they may even all have been done on the same visit.

Although Schuffenecker was a member of Gauguin's circle for a number of years, his own work remained Impressionist in character.

T 03641   Cliffs and the Sea *c.*1895

Pastel on paper $5\frac{1}{2} \times 8\frac{1}{4}$ (140 × 210)
Inscribed with studio stamp b.r.
Presented anonymously in memory of
Terence Rattigan 1983

Prov: Galerie Les Deux-Iles, Paris (purchased
from the artist's daughter); Anthony
d'Offay Fine Art; the donor

Exh: *Claude-Emile Schuffenecker (1851–1934)*,
Anthony d'Offay, December 1965–
January 1966 (no catalogue)

T 03642   Cliff, Grey Weather *c.*1895

Pastel on paper $8\frac{3}{4} \times 10\frac{7}{8}$ (222 × 275)
Inscribed with studio stamp b.l.
Presented anonymously in memory of
Terence Rattigan 1983

Prov: Galerie Les Deux-Iles, Paris (purchased
from the artist's daughter); the donor
*c.*1966

This work was presented as 'Falaise, Temps gris'.

Kurt Schwitters 1887–1948

T 03766   The Autumn Crocus 1926–8

Plaster, $32 \times 11\frac{1}{2} \times 11\frac{1}{2}$ (810 × 293 × 293)
Inscribed 'DIE HERBSTZEITLOSE' on
side of base
Transferred from the Victoria and Albert
Museum 1983

Prov: The artist, from whom inherited by Ernst
Schwitters, 1948; Philip Granville, Lords
Gallery, 1958; lent to Arts Council
November 1959–May 1960; purchased by
Victoria and Albert Museum 1964
(Circ.242–1964)

Exh: *Kurt Schwitters*, Lords Gallery, October–
November 1958 (92, repr.); *Kurt
Schwitters*, AC tour, Arts Council Gallery,
Cambridge, November–December 1959,
Glynn Vivian Art Gallery, Swansea,
January 1960, Graves Art Gallery,
Sheffield, January–February 1960,
Museum and Art Gallery, Leicester,
February–March 1960, Herbert Art
Gallery, Coventry, March–April 1960,
University Print Room, Glasgow, April–
May 1960 (17); travelling exhibitions of
the Department of Circulation, Victoria
and Albert Museum

Lit: John Elderfield, *Kurt Schwitters*, 1985,
p.191, repr. in col. no.247. *Also repr*: Kurt
Schwitters Supplement, *Ark*, 23, Autumn
1958, pl.J; Herbert Read, *A Concise
History of Modern Sculpture*, 1964, ill.126

Terry Setch b.1936

T 03591 **Once upon a Time There was Oil III, panel 1** 1981–2

Oil, wax, scrim and paper on canvas
$102\frac{7}{8} \times 171\frac{5}{8}$ (2600 × 4360)
Not inscribed
Purchased from Nigel Greenwood Inc. Ltd., (Grant-in-Aid) 1983

Exh: *Terry Setch*, Nigel Greenwood Inc. Ltd., September–October 1982 (8); *Paintings by Terry Setch*, Arnolfini Gallery, Bristol, October–December 1982 (not numbered); *New Art at the Tate Gallery*, Tate Gallery, September–October 1983 (not numbered)

Lit: John McEwen, 'Fruits of battle', *Spectator*, 25 September 1982, pp.25–6; Sanda Miller, 'Les paysages de cire de Terry Setch', *Art Press*, no.64, November 1982, pp.12–13, repr. p.12; Derek Southall, 'Terry Setch at the Arnolfini', *Artscribe*, no.38, December 1982, pp.47–8, repr. p.47; Adrian Searle, 'On the beach', *Artscribe*, no.41, June 1983, pp.26–30, repr. p.28; Sarah Kent, 'Between two territories: a way forward in British painting', *Flash Art*, no.113, Summer 1983, pp.40–6; Martin Holman, 'Terry Setch', *London Magazine*, December 1984/January 1985, pp.109–13, repr. p.111

Terry Setch went to South Wales in 1964 to lecture at Cardiff College of Art. In 1969 he went to Penarth, in South Wales and began to take the beach there as a subject for his work. In the early 1970s Setch made painted installations taking canvases down to the beach and using industrial and domestic waste from the sea-shore; later he painted large pictures in his studio, beginning with the 'Car Wreck' series in 1978–9.

'Once upon a Time There was Oil III, panel 1' depicts a person carrying a sheep on a beach littered with debris. Terry Setch painted this work in his studio in Bute Street, Cardiff, though he frequently visited the beach to make studies. Studies for T 03591 are included in a sketchbook owned by the artist. The work is painted on unstretched cotton canvas and during painting it was bolted through the eyelets on to a large metal frame.

In an interview with Adrian Searle (loc.cit.) the artist said:

> The work comes from direct experience: seeing extraordinary things on the beach – clothing, cars, which start out often looking fairly new and in a few weeks they're transformed.
>
> It's a quest of discovery, seeing the separateness of these objects, then moving them, piling them up, shifting and changing them. Lighting fires … the painting is a metaphor for all this.

Setch's work is about losing and discovery; images disappear and reappear on the canvas just as the objects on the beach are in the process of being lost to the human world and returning to nature.

Setch told the cataloguer that the paintings are not in themselves political statements but that social and political issues may be raised by them. Although the 'Once' in the title of T 03591 appears to refer to the past, the painting itself is about present and future predicaments.

The Tate's painting is one of Setch's earliest large paintings to include a human figure. The first to do so was 'Once upon a Time There was Oil' 1981 (Nigel Greenwood). The inclusion of figures enabled him to view the landscape through them. In his more recent work, groups of figures appear frequently.

A smaller related picture, 'Once upon a Time There was Oil III, panel 11' (Nigel Greenwood), measuring 100 × 101 ins., was painted at the same time. This work is illustrated in colour in *Flash Art* (loc.cit.), p.44.

This entry has been approved by the artist.

Joel Shapiro b.1941

T 03697 **Untitled** 1978

Bronze $13\frac{1}{4} \times 21\frac{3}{4} \times 6\frac{1}{4}$ (337 × 553 × 157)
Inscribed 'SHAPIRO' on underside and stamped '78$\frac{3}{8}$'
Purchased from Paula Cooper Gallery, New York (Grant-in-Aid) 1983

Exh: *Made by Sculptors*, Stedelijk Museum, Amsterdam, September–November 1978 (6, repr.)

Lit: *Joel Shapiro*, exhibition catalogue, Whitechapel Art Gallery, 1980, unspecified cast repr. p.33; *Joel Shapiro*, exhibition catalogue, Whitney Museum of

American Art, New York, 1982 (La Jolla Museum of Contemporary Art, California's cast repr. p.57); *Joel Shapiro*, exhibition catalogue, Stedelijk Museum, Amsterdam, 1985, unspecified cast repr. p.50

Walter Richard Sickert 1860–1942

T 03360 **Miss Earhart's Arrival** 1932

Oil on canvas $28\frac{1}{8} \times 72\frac{1}{8}$ (717 × 1832)
Not inscribed
Purchased from C.G.C. Hyslop (Grant-in-Aid) 1982

Prov: Frederick Lessore 1932, by whom sold (1947) to Raymond Mortimer, by whom bequeathed to C.G.C. Hyslop, 1979

Exh: Beaux Arts Gallery, May–June 1932 (no catalogue); *Thirty-First Annual International Exhibition of Paintings*, Carnegie Institute, Pittsburgh, October–December 1933 (150, repr.); *61st Autumn Exhibition*, Walker Art Gallery, Liverpool, October 1935–January 1936 (97); *Late Sickert*, AC tour, Hayward Gallery, November 1981–January 1982, Sainsbury Centre for the Visual Arts, University of East Anglia, Norwich, March–April 1982, Wolverhampton Art Gallery, April–May 1982 (97, repr. in col. p.48)

Lit: 'Artist Inspired by a Photograph', *Daily Sketch*, 31 May 1932 (repr. in an earlier state); 'Mr Sickert's New Picture', *Morning Post*, 31 May 1932; P.G.K[onody]. 'Painting of Miss Earhart', *Daily Mail*, 31 May 1932; 'High Speed Art', *Edinburgh Evening News*, 31 May 1932; ' "Miss Earhart's Arrival" ', *The Times*, 3 June 1932; 'Mr. R. Sickert's Latest', *The Observer*, 5 June 1932; 'The Painting and the Photograph', *British Journal of Photography*, 10 June 1932; Wendy Baron, in *Late Sickert*, exhibition catalogue, Hayward Gallery, 1981–2, p.108; Tate Gallery monthly Calendar, March 1983 (repr.); *The Burlington Magazine*, CXXVI, February 1984, supplement p.3 (repr.); *The Tate Gallery Illustrated Biennial Report 1982–84*, 1984, p.47 (repr. in col.)

The *Encyclopaedia Britannica* describes the American Amelia Earhart (1898–1937) as 'probably the world's most celebrated aviatrix'. In 1928, as a passenger, she became the first woman (and only the third person) ever to fly the Atlantic. The subject of this painting is Miss Earhart's arrival at an airport near London the day after she landed at the conclusion of her solo flight across the Atlantic, the first to be undertaken by a woman. This transatlantic flight, which was from West to East, took place on 20–21 May 1932 and Miss Earhart's landing was in Ireland. After other remarkable flying exploits, Amelia Earhart disappeared in the South Pacific in 1937, towards the end of her attempted flight round the world. There is no conclusive explanation of her fate. The chapter 'Women Pilots and the Selling of Aviation' in Joseph J. Corn, *The Winged Gospel, America's Romance with Aviation, 1900–1950*, New York, 1983, gives an account of the wider ramifications of the pioneering role played by Miss Earhart and other women aviators.

Miss Earhart's solo transatlantic flight, which took 14 hours, 56 minutes, began at Harbour Grace, Newfoundland, on the evening of 20 May 1932. *The Times*, 23 May 1932, p.14 gives a vivid account of the problems of the flight, which included bad weather, having to fly blind for several hours, the failure of the altimeter and a fire which caused part of the plane to fall off into the sea. A fuller account is given in the biography of Miss Earhart by her widower, George Palmer Putnam, *Soaring Wings*, London, 1940. Miss Earhart's landing on 21 May 1932 was at Culmore, near Londonderry, in a field belonging to a farm in which she spent the night. On 22 May she was flown in a Paramount News aeroplane from Londonderry to Stanley Park Aerodrome, Blackpool, where she changed to another plane and was flown to Hanworth Air Park, Middlesex (in the outskirts of London). On alighting from the aeroplane Miss Earhart was greeted by a party which included the Master of Sempill, who read her a message of congratulations from the Prime Minister, and the United States Ambassador, with whom she stayed in London. At her landing point in Ireland, Miss Earhart had supervised the dismantling of the plane in which she had just flown the Atlantic. It was later displayed in Selfridges department store in London.

Sickert based the Tate's painting on the largest of the five photographs published on the front page of the *Daily Sketch* of 23 May 1932. Miss Earhart is wearing a flying helmet. Her face, in profile, can be seen between the umbrella at top right and the large hat nearest to the right edge of the picture. It is not known whether Sickert worked from the actual newspaper or from a photographic print of the original photograph. However his painting makes use of only approximately half of the source photograph as printed in the *Daily Sketch*, which there continues both above, below and to the right. Within the area selected, Sickert transcribed the forms broadly accurately, but with certain adjustments. These included small changes of scale (two heads, including Miss Earhart's, being slightly reduced in size and the width of the streaks of rain being widened slightly) and the suppression of the upper part of the head of a woman in the foreground (replaced, in the picture, by the horizontal part of the left arm of the third foreground figure from the left). In the transition from his black and white source, Sickert inevitably invented the colours used; he also clarified certain forms which were vague in the original, made others that were clearer more imprecise, and altered certain tonal relationships, notably that between the shadowed under-wing and the space beyond.

The first part of the caption to the source photograph as printed in the *Daily Sketch* read 'A storm of thunder and lightning and a cheering crowd of several hundred people greeted Miss Amelia Earhart, heroine of the record lone flight across the Atlantic, when she landed at Hanworth Aerodrome last evening from Londonderry. She is seen stepping out into the rain'. The headline at the top of the page read 'SERIOUS FLOOD DAMAGE OVER HALF ENGLAND'. The monthly weather report of the Meteorological Office for May 1932 shows that the month was considered the wettest over England and Wales as a whole for 160 years. Three of the five photographs on the page were of a *Daily Sketch* photographer and air pilot who had been killed when their plane crashed in thick fog near Stranraer as they were returning to London after having flown to Londonderry in connection with Miss Earhart's landing.

The Tate's picture was placed on view at the Beaux Arts Gallery only seven days after the source photograph had been published. (Sickert had had a one-man exhibition, largely of 'Echoes', at the Gallery from 11 April to 14 May). The gallery's card announcing 'Miss Earhart's Arrival' does not name the painting but is headed 'GREAT NEW PAINTING BY RICHARD SICKERT, A.R.A.' and states that it will be shown from 30 May to 26 June. As reported in the *Daily Mail* of 31 May, it was hung high up. Mrs Helen Lessore recalls that this was in an arch above the hanging line. The painting was reported in so many newspapers in May–June 1932 that the references listed above have been restricted to the more interesting. In a single-line review in *New Statesman and Nation*, 18 June 1932, T.W. Earp observed that 'Miss Earhart's Arrival' was 'like a fragment of a magnificent modern fresco'. A recurrent report (presumably from a single original source, the authority of which is not known) was that 'Mr Sickert ... is painting her as a head of a comet with the crowd rushing toward her through the rain forming the tail' (*New York Times*, 29 May 1932, datelined 28th).

The *Daily Sketch*, 31 May 1932, juxtaposed a photograph of Sickert's painting, in its present frame, with the corresponding section of the newspaper's own photograph from which it was derived. This reproduction of the painting shows it in an earlier state in several respects, which include a much lighter ground at t.l. and beneath the wing of the plane, and above all the marked prominence of squaring-up over a large part of the picture surface. The report in the *Daily Mail*, 31 May 1932, shows that the picture was exhibited at the Beaux Arts Gallery with the squaring-up still in place. However by the time it was photographed for the reproduction in the catalogue of the 1933 Carnegie International Exhibition (see above), the squaring-up had been removed. It is not known in what material Sickert executed the squaring up. In late May 1932, several newspapers reported that Sickert was working twelve to fourteen hours a day on 'Miss Earhart's Arrival', but Mrs Helen Lessore, later his sister-in-law, who was working at the Beaux Arts Gallery at the time, doubts that this is likely. On the other hand she feels certain that none of this painting was executed by Sickert's wife, Thérèse Lessore (who in later years did assist him in this way), or by anyone else.

In view of the fact that the most immediately noticeable feature of 'Miss Earhart's Arrival' is the bold diagonal strokes representing falling rain, the following observation by Sickert over twenty years earlier is of interest. In his essay 'The Post-Impressionists' in *The Fornightly Review*, January 1911 (reprinted Osbert Sitwell, ed., *A Free House, The Writings of Walter Richard Sickert*, 1947, pp.97–108), Sickert denigrated van Gogh's execution but continued 'But ... *Les Alyscamps* is undeniably a great picture, and the landscape of rain really does rain with furia. Blond dashes of water at an angle of 45° from right to left, and suddenly, across these, a black squirt. The discomfort, the mystery, the hopelessness of rain are there. Such intensity is perhaps madness, but the result is interesting and stimulating.' Although this passage is part of a review of *Manet and the Post-Impressionists*, Grafton Galleries, November 1910–January 1911, in which twenty-four paintings by van Gogh were exhibited, it is not known to which of van Gogh's works Sickert was referring here. None of van Gogh's paintings of Les Alyscamps, Arles, include diagonal strokes of rain and none of his paintings in which strokes representing rain are prominent (for example, 'Landscape at Auvers in the Rain' 1890, National Museum of Wales, Cardiff) is known to have been included in the exhibition Sickert was reviewing.

T 03548　**La Hollandaise** *c.*1906

Oil on canvas 20⅛ × 16 (511 × 408)
Inscribed 'Sickert' b.r.
Purchased from Mrs Janet Shand-Kydd through Browse & Darby (Grant-in-Aid) 1983

Prov:　...; Bernheim Jeune, Paris, by whom offered for sale in *Vente de 84 Oeuvres de Walter Sickert*, Hotel Drouot, Paris, 21 June 1909 (54); ...; William Marchant & Co., sold Christie's, 28 January 1927 (148), bt Cremette £46.4.0; ...; Mark Oliver, sold Sotheby's 29 November 1944 (129), bt Arthur Tooth & Sons £120; Roland, Browse & Delbanco, 1959; Peter Shand-Kydd 1960; Mrs Janet Shand-Kydd

Exh:　*Sickert*, Berheim Jeune, Paris, January 1907 (33); *84 Oeuvres de Walter Sickert*,

Bernheim Jeune, Paris, June 1909 (54); *Summer Exhibition*, Goupil Gallery, 1925 (months not specified) (79); *The Redfern Gallery Coronation Exhibition*, Redfern Gallery, Summer 1953 (49, repr.); *Sickert: Paul Delance*, Roland, Browse & Delbanco, May–June 1957 (24, as 'La Belle Hollandaise'); *Sickert 1860–1942*, Roland, Browse & Delbanco, March–April 1960 (30, repr.); *Sickert: Paintings and Drawings*, Tate Gallery, May–June 1960, Southampton Art Gallery, July, Bradford City Art Gallery, July–August (100, repr.); *Sickert*, Fine Art Society, May–June 1973 (49); *Sickert*, Browse & Darby, November–December 1981 (14, repr.)

Lit:　Lillian Browse, *Sickert*, 1960 (no.46, repr. pl.46); Wendy Dimson, 'Four Sickert Exhibitions', *The Burlington Magazine*, CII, October 1960, pp.438–43 (repr. fig.29); Sir John Rothenstein, *Sickert*, 1961, text to pl.7 (repr. in col.); Ronald Pickvance, *Sickert*, 1967, pp.5 and 8 (repr. in col. pl.VIII); Wendy Baron, *Sickert*, 1973, p.86 and no.211 (repr. fig.144); Wendy Baron, catalogue entry in *Sickert*, exhibition catalogue, Fine Art Society, 1973; Tate Gallery monthly calendar, November 1983 (repr.); *The Burlington Magazine*, CXXVI, February 1984, supplement p.3 (repr.)

The style and palette and the design of the bed combine to indicate that this picture was painted soon after Sickert's return to London in 1905. At this time he had studios in Mornington Crescent, Fitzroy Street and Charlotte Street.

Baron, 1973, reproduces as fig.145 a charcoal drawing (National Gallery of Canada, Ottawa) in which the angle of view, the lower part of the body and the disposition (reversed) of bed and mirrored wardrobe are almost the same as in the Tate's picture. In the oil 'Nuit d'Été' *c.*1906 (ibid., no.212, repr. fig.147), which also represents a reclining nude seen from beyond the end of the bed, bed and wardrobe are positioned as in the Tate's picture. Baron considers that all three works show the same model.

The meaning of the title is unknown, though the discussion in *The Burlington Magazine*, 1984 (loc.cit.) associates it with Sickert's admiration for Balzac, and with the nickname 'la belle Hollandaise' given to the prostitute Sara Gobseck in Balzac's *Gobseck* (1830).

John Skeaping 1901–1980

T 03767 **Buffalo** 1930

Lapis lazuli $3\frac{1}{8} \times 7\frac{1}{8} \times 4\frac{3}{8}$ (80 × 180 × 110),
on marble base $\frac{7}{8} \times 7 \times 3\frac{1}{8}$ (20 × 175 × 80)
Inscribed 'JRS' incised under marble base
Transferred from the Victoria and Albert
Museum 1983

Prov: ...; purchased 1931 by Mrs A.A.
Cresswell, and bequeathed by her to the
Department of Architecture and
Sculpture, Victoria and Albert Museum,
1941 (A.20–1941)

Exh: *An exhibition of sculpture by John Skeaping
and Barbara Hepworth*, Arthur Tooth and
Sons, October–November 1930 (26)

T 03768 **Burmese Dancer** 1928

Alabaster $18\frac{1}{2} \times 6\frac{3}{4} \times 5\frac{1}{2}$ (470 × 170 × 140)
Inscribed 'J. SKEAPING 28' r. side

Transferred from the Victoria and Albert
Museum 1983

Prov: ...; Edward Marsh; ...; given by the
Contemporary Art Society to the
Department of Circulation, Victoria and
Albert Museum 1964 (Circ.79–1964)

Exh: *XVIII Esposizione Biennale
Internazionale*, Venice, May–September
1932 (Great Britain, 139); travelling
exhibitions of the Department of
Circulation, Victoria and Albert Museum

Lit: John Skeaping, *Drawn From Life. An
Autobiography*, 1977, pp.75, 82–3

Skeaping's exhibition at the Lefevre Gallery in September 1928 included a 'Burmese Girl. Head (Pentelicon marble)', which is perhaps of the same model. Sir Edward Marsh was one of Skeaping's early patrons.

Jack Smith b.1928

T 03812 **Written Activity No.7** 1969

Oil on canvas 60 × 60 (1530 × 1530)
Inscribed on reverse 'Written Activity
No:7' and 'JACK SMITH 1969'
Purchased from Ken Powell (Knapping
Fund) 1983

Prov: Monika Kinley (until 1978); Ken Powell
Exh: *Jack Smith*, University of Hull Gallery,
April–May 1969 (39); *Jack Smith.
Paintings and Drawings 1949–1975*,
Sunderland Arts Centre, January–

February 1977 (35, repr. back cover); *Jack Smith. The Written and the Diagrammatic, Paintings and Drawings 1965–1977*, Serpentine Gallery, January–February 1978 (14, repr. p.9)

Lit: Alan Bowness, Helder Macedo, Jack Smith, 'Jack Smith, Paintings and Drawings 1949–1976', p.14 (repr. front cover and pl.39)

This painting forms part of a series of eight works, each entitled 'Written Activity', which was completed in 1969. It has previously been dated 1967 and 1968, but the artist has confirmed that he painted it in 1969. He states in a letter (22 February 1986) that the ideas behind this series do not move towards a conclusion, but instead represent the desire 'to perfect an image' which he finally achieved in 'Written Activity: No.8' 1969 (collection National Museum Wales, Cardiff; repr. Bowness et al., op.cit., p.36)

This series of paintings was begun in 1963, the date which Smith has stated marked his dramatic break away from the traditional style of his earlier work towards paintings that were like a list or an inventory. Initially this change necessitated finding equivalent 'forms' for objects in his studio (ibid., p.10). In the earlier works of the series the marks bear a closer resemblance to handwriting, with letters that appear to be decipherable, although the paintings can in no sense be interpreted (as in 'Written Activity No.2' 1966 and 'Written Activity No.3' 1967, repr. *Jack Smith*, Marlborough Fine Art, January 1968 (11 and 17)). However in 'Written Activity No.7' the notations have become more ordered and are arranged in neat rows across the canvas. The marks resemble hieroglyphs or ancient manuscripts, with spaces that imply pauses in sentence making, although the vocabulary cannot be deciphered. Using a sentence from a book or newspaper as his starting point he would break the sentence down into its different sounds 'and invent a form for each sound' (Bowness et al., op.cit., p.14). Having interpreted one sentence with forms, he would then invent the next sentence of forms in relation to the previous ones. 'When my sense of invention ran out, I would return to the written word again, and take the next sequence of sounds, and so that painting developed. Each line took me one day to make' (Bowness et al., op.cit., p.14). This 'language' is therefore personal; as it describes his own experiences its message remains detached from the viewer, who cannot translate any precise meaning. On completion of this series the artist wrote 'I seem now to be able to build up a visual written language that can deal with any experience or sensation. A written page can be remade in the same way that an artist remakes an object. WORDS BECOME OBJECTS, (*Journal of Typographical Research*, III, no.3, July 1969, reprinted Bowness et al.,

The artist stresses that these works cannot be read,

but are to be looked at solely from a visual point of view. 'There are no preparatory studies, only small individual visual notes and the paintings are allowed to evolve in their own way' (letter of 22 February 1986). As there is no paraphrasable sound and no meaning, the marks have more to do with the sensations and sounds which words make. In this sense the marks are phonetic and inform the viewer about sound. 'I wanted to use a script and make people read each form.'

This entry has been approved by the artist.

T 03813 Activities, Major and Minor 1972

Oil on plywood $48\frac{1}{8} \times 48$ (1222 × 1219)
Inscribed on reverse 'JACK SMITH 1972' and 'ACTIVITIES MAJOR + MINOR'
Purchased from the artist through Fischer Fine Art (Grant-in-Aid) 1983

The title of the painting 'refers to the forms used and has musical connotations' (letter from the artist, 22 February 1986). The artist is concerned with music not only in representing the notational sounds, but also the silences and pauses that occur; hence the cool lime green background which creates an atmosphere of calm against which these 'sound boxes' are superimposed. The 'Activity' is provided by the strong lively colours and also by the marks, which 'fall' diagonally across the work. Some of the forms appear to move rapidly, others move more slowly and leave a trail, and one (top left) stops altogether, creating a shadow.

The artist comments that the images for this painting have many sources 'very often evolving from other paintings ... all forms need to be continually remade' (ibid.). The painting is similar to 'Activities: 16 Major 7 Minor' 1972 (repr. *Jack Smith, Paintings and Drawings 1949–1976*, Sunderland Arts Centre, 1977, p.86, private collection) but does not belong to a particular series. The artist did not make any preliminary drawings or studies, and the work was painted 'intuitively'.

This entry has been approved by the artist.

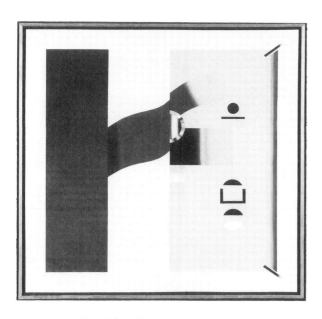

T 03814   **Inside, Outside 3**   1980

Oil on hardboard $36\frac{1}{8} \times 36\frac{1}{8}$ (920 × 920)
Inscribed on reverse 'INSIDE OUTSIDE 3' and 'Jack Smith/1980'
Purchased from the artist through Fischer Fine Art (Grant-in-Aid) 1983

Prov: Monika Kinley (until 1978); Ken Powell
Exh: *Jack Smith Recent Paintings*, Fischer Fine Art, March–April 1981 (32)
Lit: Alan Bowness, Helder Macedo, Jack Smith, 'Jack Smith, Paintings and Drawings 1949–1976'

The artist first used this title in the 1960s, for example a painting exhibited in *Jack Smith recent paintings and sculptures*, Grosvenor Gallery 1965 (13), where he also showed sculptures with similar titles.

'Inside, Outside 3' was painted in the artist's studio in in Hove where he had recently moved, and was affected by his interest in the quality of light reflected from the sea. As often in Jack Smith's works the support is square. Initially he chose this format in the early 1960s as he did not want to be dominated by the shape of his canvas, but subsequently became fascinated by the regularity of the square, and has continued to use it for the majority of his work (see Alan Bowness et al., op.cit., p.15).

This entry has been approved by the artist.

Jesus-Raphael Soto   b.1923

T 03769   **Twelve Blacks and Four Silvereds**   1965

Construction of wood and metal, painted $41\frac{3}{4} \times 41\frac{3}{4} \times 6\frac{3}{8}$ (1060 × 1060 × 162)
Inscribed on reverse 'HAUT Soto 1985'
Transferred from the Victoria and Albert Museum 1983

Prov: Purchased by the Department of Circulation, Victoria and Albert Museum, from Signals London, 1966 (Circ.38–1966)
Exh: *The Achievements of Jésus-Raphael Soto: 1950–65, Fifteen Years of Vibrations*, Signals London, October–December 1965 (as 'Grand Relation – Vibration with 4 silver plaques and 12 black plaques'); travelling exhibitions of the Department of Circulation, Victoria and Albert Museum
Repr: *Signals*, 1, November–December 1965, p.17

The original title of this relief is '12 noirs et 4 argentés'. It is similar to the Tate Gallery's 'Relationships of

Contrasting Elements', 1965 (T 00806) which is on the same scale, but larger overall since it has two more rows of plaques. Soto began to make these reliefs in 1964–5, and a number of other versions are listed in Ronald Alley, *The Tate Gallery's Collection of Modern Art*, 1981, p.698.

Joseph Edward Southall 1861–1944

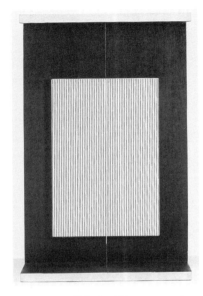

T 03770 **Light Trap** 1965

Construction of wood and nylon with printed paper 18½ × 11¾ × 5⅜ (470 × 298 × 131)
Not inscribed
Transferred from the Victoria and Albert Museum 1983

Prov: Purchased by the Department of Circulation, Victoria and Albert Museum, from Signals London, 1966 (Circ.140–1966)

Exh: Travelling exhibitions of the Department of Circulation, Victoria and Albert Museum

Previously listed in error at the Victoria and Albert Museum as 'Spiral Relief', this is a reproduction of a 1964 construction by Soto titled 'Piège de Lumière' which he published with Editions MAT as a multiple. In the original the background lines are white on black, and in the multiple they are black on white.

T 03699 **Belgium Supported by Hope** 1918

Tempera on canvas 12½ × 16¼ (318 × 410)
Inscribed 'EJS 1918' b.r. and 'COLOUR BEGUN VIII 1918' on canvas turnover and 'Marian E. Longford/Christmas 1918/HGL [in monogram] With Love' on reverse
Purchased from Fine Art Society (Grant-in-Aid) 1983

Prov: Marian E. Longford 1918; . . .; Fine Art Society

Lit: George Breeze, *Joseph Southall 1861–1944, Artist-Craftsman*, exhibition catalogue, City Museum and Art Gallery, Birmingham, 1980

A cartoon for 'Belgium Supported by Hope' (whereabouts unknown) was exhibited at the Royal Birmingham Society of Artists, 1919 (342); Alpine Club Gallery, 1922 (55), Manchester City Art Gallery, 1922 (4), RBSA, 1933 (103) and Dudley Art Gallery, 1934 (75). T 03699 appears never to have been exhibited.

Southall did very little painting during the First World War, devoting most of his time to the cause of Pacificism. He was a member of the Independent Labour Party and at the outbreak of the First World War was Chairman of the Birmingham Auxiliary of the Peace Society; in the same year he was one of the two Vice-Presidents of the Birmingham and District Passive Resistance League. He produced a series of illustrated fables (1915–18) in which the political message is very clear; in T 03699 it is much more subtle.

After German troops entered Belgium in August 1914 King Albert of Belgium appealed for help from the other signatories of the 1839 Treaty of London. He received support from France and Britain. Allegorical posters and prints in support of Belgium were made at this time, although generally they were more impassioned than T 03699. E.R. Frampton's 'A Maid of Bruges' exh. 1919 (repr. in col. in Sotheby's sale of 19th century European paintings and drawings, 21 June 1983, 101) is more comparable to T 03699; it shows a large scale female figure in profile against a Belgian scene.

In 'Belgium Supported by Hope' Southall seems to be encouraging Belgium to renew and rebuild her country despite the ravages sustained during the war. The figure on the right personifies Hope, one of the three theological virtues, and the left hand figure personifies Belgium. Hope is pointing towards an idyllic scene, unspoilt by war, while Belgium holds in her hand ears of wheat, a symbol of rebirth.

Southall's sketch books contain careful studies of costumes and Lot 155 in the sale of Mrs Southall's estate (6 April 1948) was 'a box containing a quantity of fancy clothing for studio posing purposes' (George Breeze, op.cit., p.15).

Southall first used tempera after his visit to Italy in 1883. He became a firm admirer of early Italian art and resolved to study tempera techniques. He wrote:

> I saw Carpaccio's pictures in St Giorgio degli Schiavoni in Venice and read in Ruskin's St Mark's Rest that they were painted in tempera. I resolved then to paint in tempera, but I knew no one who could instruct me and had only Sir Charles Eastlake's 'Materials for a History of Oil Painting' as a guide.
>
> ('Notes on the Revival of Tempera Painting by Joseph E. Southall' found in the front of Maxwell Armfield's own copy of his *A Manual of Tempera Painting* (coll: Alexander Ballard) George Breeze, op.cit., p.18).

The frame is original. With the assistance of his wife, Anna Elizabeth, Southall made many of his own frames. He usually carved the frame and she was responsible for gilding and decoration.

T 03382

Daniel Spoerri b.1930

T 03382 Prose Poems 1960

Assemblage of objects on wooden board
27⅛ × 21⅜ × 14¼ (690 × 542 × 361)
Inscribed 'Tableau Piège:/"Poèmes en Prose/sur Fond Vasarely"/Daniel Spoerri/Nov. 60' on back of board
Purchased from Galerie Bonnier, Geneva (Grant-in-Aid) 1982

Theophile-Alexandre Steinlen 1859–1923

T 03771 A Cat

Bronze 5 × 2 × 2½ (130 × 50 × 65)
Inscribed 'Steinlen' l. of base
Transferred from the Victoria and Albert Museum 1983

Prov: ...; bequeathed by Mr Henry L. Florence to the Department of Architecture and Sculpture, Victoria and Albert Museum, 1917 (A.34–1917)

The collection of Henry L. Florence of 9 Princes Gate, which was offered to the Victoria and Albert Museum in 1911, consisted of paintings and furniture, with decorative sculpture.

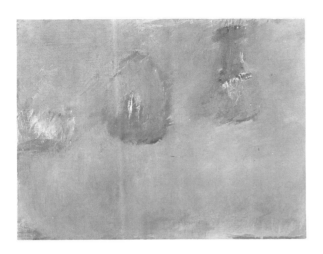

Adrian Stokes 1902–1972

T 03579 **Still Life: Last Eleven (No.4)** 1972

Oil on canvas marouflaged onto board,
$12\frac{7}{8} \times 16\frac{1}{8}$ (328 × 410)
Not inscribed
Purchased from Mrs Ann Stokes Angus
(Grant-in-Aid) 1983

Exh: *The Last Paintings of Adrian Stokes*, Tate
Gallery, February–March 1973 (no
catalogue); *Adrian Stokes*, Serpentine
Gallery, June–July 1982 (119); *The Hard-
Won Image*, Tate Gallery, July–September
1984 (126)

Lit: Richard Wollheim, 'Adrian Stokes', *The
Listener*, 28 December 1972, p.900;
Lawrence Gowing, 'True to Form', *New
Statesman*, 2 March 1973, p.316; Marina
Vaizey, 'Adrian Stokes, John Hubbard',
Financial Times, 5 March 1973;
Christopher Fox, untitled review of Tate
Gallery exhibition of the Last Eleven
paintings, *Studio International*, CLXXXV,
April 1973, p.153; Keith Roberts,
'Current and Forthcoming Exhibitions',
The Burlington Magazine, CXV, April
1973, p.263; Richard Wollheim, 'Adrian
Stokes, critic, painter, poet', *Times
Literary Supplement*, 17 February 1978,
pp.207–9; Richard Wollheim, 'Adrian
Stokes, critic, painter, poet', *PNReview*,
15, VII, 1980, pp.31–7; Richard
Wollheim, Lawrence Gowing, in *Adrian
Stokes*, exhibition catalogue, Serpentine
Gallery, 1982, p.18; Richard Wollheim,
'An artist who practised what he
preached', *The Times Higher Education

Supplement, 18 June 1982, pp.12–13;
Robert Melville, 'The Last Eleven',
London Review of Books, 15 July–4 August
1982, p.18

T 03579 to T 03587 inclusive are the last nine paintings
Adrian Stokes made. Along with Stokes's two immediately preceding paintings they were all made after the
onset of his final illness, the nature of and treatment for
which help account for their particular character. As
recalled below, Stokes stated that during this last period
he achieved the kind of results in painting which he was
seeking. The catalogue of the exhibition *Adrian Stokes*,
Serpentine Gallery, 1982, cited above, reproduces in
colour (on p.23) one of Stokes's paintings of 1972 made
before the onset of his final illness. It and all his last
eleven paintings were made at his home in Hampstead,
London NW3. A number of the vessels represented in
the last eleven paintings are pots made by Stokes's wife
Ann (now Mrs Ann Stokes Angus), whose pottery was
in the same house.

Within days of Adrian Stokes's death Richard
Wollheim wrote of the last eleven paintings (published
in *The Listener*, 28 December 1972 as cited above):

There is much to be said about these last paintings.
When they are shown – and there is reason to hope
that they will be in the near future – I think that they
are likely to be found one of the most arresting
groups of work in 20th-century British painting.
They are the products of development – of a slow,
uneven, ruminative development – so that they have
the unmistakable character of 'late' work imprinted
on them. They are the kind of work that an Old
Master would achieve in his final years, and of which
this century can provide us with no more than a
handful of examples. But at this distance in time,
the paint and the painter's death so fresh, I find it
almost impossible to think continuously of them
except in one way: as evidence of the survival of the
person through the decay of senses and faculties. In
the last few weeks Stokes had increasing difficulty in
bringing the canvas into focus; his grip on the brush
was uncertain; he did not always pick up from the
palette the colour he sought. None of this matters.
The hand and the eye, so long the agents of the mind,
turned incapacity into freedom, and the last
paintings look like the earlier paintings burst into a
final flame.

It was the same with the man. It didn't matter that
the words would sometimes come out wrong, or that
trains of thought might cross over, or that the mind
inevitably tired after a quarter of an hour of talking.
The character was as strong as ever. When Stokes
began to speak of his last great enthusiasm, the
magnificent exhibition of Islamic carpets arranged
by his friend David Sylvester, or described with

startling frankness the progress of his illness and the kindness of the nurses in hospital, or expressed pleasure at some green travertine beads that I had brought him back from Afghanistan, knowing his love for the material, it was the sense of continuity with the old self that hit me: the same powerful impact made by a very gentle character.

Mrs Ann Stokes Angus states (letter, 2 April 1986) that the last eleven paintings were made in the following order. First the one in the collection of David Plante (oil on canvas, 20 × 23¾ (508 × 603), repr. in col. in catalogue of Serpentine Gallery exhibition 1982, cited above). Second, the one in the collection of Andrew Forge (oil on canvas, 20 × 24 (508 × 610), not repr.), and then the Tate's nine paintings, in the following order – 3rd T 03587, 4th T 03579, 5th T 03582, 6th T 03680, 7th T 03584, 8th T 03583, 9th T 03586, 10th T 03585, 11th T 03581.

Mrs Ann Stokes Angus continues:

Adrian began getting ill in late July – he suddenly found himself on the top floor having missed the door to the sitting room and study off it. He was trying to do his income tax and called me to say he simply could not add up. I thought he was joking at first. He asked me to put his page proofs for his last book, 'The Game that must be Lost' in order as he simply could not do it himself. He was writing or arranging this book and not painting so much and his poems were very much in his mind. He very soon became unable to write but could paint. August was almost the worst moment for us both since he was given a brain scan which showed he had cancer on the right side and he realised he would die.

He painted these pictures between September and December 1972 until two days before he died [on 15th December].

When Adrian Stokes went into University College Hospital on 18 or 19 September he had begun only the first of the last eleven paintings (coll. David Plante). On his return home on 21 September he began to take Cortisone, taking that day:

the highest dose of Cortisone and various other pills which did have a great effect. He said his head felt like boxes banging together but by 22nd September he was more cheerful and we walked on the Heath almost every day after his morning's painting which was in the top room studio where Bill Coldstream has painted since 1973 or 74 (since he began using the sitting room and later moved up to the studio). [...] Without [the Cortisone] there would have been very few pictures [...] About David P[lante]'s picture; he had painted the right hand half before going to U.C.H. and was unable to paint the left hand half, which he was able to do as soon as he got back. It seemed to me strange, or significant rather than strange, that his right brain which, I am told, orders or commands actions to the left and vice versa, should demonstrate so clearly that it was clouded.

The dark picture T 03587 and the next smaller one, T 03579, also dark [...] to me both were unhappy, rather desperate pictures [which] he went back to, to improve but mainly repainted No. T 03579 which he felt a lot for and was pleased when friends singled it out.

He did not paint more than one at a time but he did review them and change them a little but mainly T 03579. [...]

It was after Adrian gave Andrew Forge No.2 that I suggested Adrian should keep these pictures both for his own sake and mine. He was very glad to do so and in fact had a fit of persecution mania thinking his friends only came to get his pictures. This did not last long. While Adrian was painting in the top studio [Colin St John Wilson] gave Adrian the two valuable books on Matisse by Aragon and Adrian said 'too late' – he could no longer read nor write and had to strain to make his sig. on pictures but worse on cheques. He liked having them none the less.

We got to Gabo's filmshow of his sculptures in London. John G[olding] and James Joll drove him over to David Sylvester's terrific oriental carpet exhibition at the Hayward [19 October–10 December 1972] where Adrian was provided with a pushchair and hated having to succumb to sitting in it to be pushed round (in every sense). He enjoyed the carpets very much though. I think that was his last outing – unless the Gabo came after.

When he took to falling over (twice I found him flat on the studio floor quite unable to get up on his own) I felt I must be able to keep a closer eye and to be able to hear if he needed help. This only took place for the last three pictures nos. T 03586, T 03585 and T 03581. The date must have been late in November. I cannot swear that he did not paint no. T 03583 in the pottery too but I think it was upstairs. Sometime in November, in the pottery, Adrian said 'This is how I should have painted'. He said he felt without any restraint and able to paint exactly as he wanted.

There was no big gap from 3rd November to 9th December but Adrian took longer over the last 3 and was unable to start the no. 10 for several days.

No. 11 was very, very difficult to start – by the time he was painting in the pottery Adrian could scarcely stand by himself so I arranged the vases and cups etc. as he indicated. All those he painted upstairs were arranged by himself. It was either 9 or 10 which David P. failed to arrange satisfactorily.

An account of the painting of No.11 (T03581) is given in the entry for that work. Mrs Ann Stokes Angus cites as one key to Stokes's attitude to his paintings the text of 1968 published posthumously as 'A drama of modesty: Adrian Stokes on his paintings', *Studio International*, CLXXXV, April 1973, p.153.

The following account of Adrian Stokes during the period of his last eleven paintings was written by the novelist David Plante on 16 March 1986 in answer to enquiries from the compiler.

In the early seventies I used to make pottery with Ann. At tea-time, she'd ask me up to Adrian's study, where he'd be working at his desk, and we'd all have tea from Ann's cups. I would bring him little gifts, mostly post-cards. One was of an Indian miniature, which he liked. Another was of a Surrealist painting (can't recall which) and this he did not like, though his way of indicating he didn't like something wasn't to say, but to laugh a little. Later, he told me he didn't like the Surrealists, but as if as an aside.

I had no idea what Adrian's likes and dislikes were, and I realise now that this both intimidated me and excited me. Not yet having read his work, all I knew for sure was that he *had* a vision. I was intimidated by this vision because I suspected it was entirely beyond me to understand it, and it excited me because of the possibilities I sensed in it. My little gifts – besides postcards, a volume of three modern Greek poets, fancy cakes from a pastry shop in Hampstead, etc. – were offered partly with the wonder of how he would react to them.

Once, having been first to Stephen Buckley's studio, I went to Church Row with a little work of Stephen's under my arm which I showed to Adrian at the time; he looked at it for a long while on his desk, and I, standing by, wondered what he was thinking. When he said 'Yes, I like it', I was very pleased.

You might ask me what, after a time, I began to imagine his vision to be from his reactions. I certainly didn't intuit his theories on why one appreciates an art object, but I was always aware that his appreciation was, in a way, reflective, that it had to do with *deciding* something about the object. You waited in silence while Adrian looked at something, and you thought, he is making up his mind about it. If it was a gift, you of course hoped he liked it. He wouldn't say he liked it just to be friendly. If he didn't, he laughed a little. His appreciation was, I felt, based on the object's standing up or not to Adrian's awareness of it. You didn't feel: Adrian is coming to terms with the object. But: The object is trying to come to terms with Adrian.

After tea, he'd come down to Ann's pottery studio to look at what we'd done. I had been coiling a big pot, my first. He studied it. He said, 'I like the hole at the top.' I hadn't thought about the hole, which, I realised, justified the entire pot, gave it the quality it needed for Adrian to see in it something more than clay. Without knowing what the principles of his vision were, I had a strong sense from Adrian of its all encompassing ability to explain why, say, the hole made the pot worth looking at.

On September 14th (1972) Ann told me that Adrian was dying of cancer of the brain. I didn't do any pottery, but went directly up to his study to see him. He was very weak, but refused to sit; he had to hold on to the back of a big armchair to keep himself from falling. His skin looked grey and matt. Ann had warned me that he had very little concentration, but he seemed pleased to have a visitor, however embarrassed he also seemed to be about his undignified state. Finally, he sat at his desk, and for some reason laughed, in a totally expressionless way. Ann put a cup on his desk, but he simply looked at it and said he wouldn't have any. I realised he said he wouldn't because he couldn't lift the cup, and didn't want to ask for help. Ann held the cup up for him to drink. Again, he laughed, but always without any expression. After he finished his tea, we talked a little. He said, 'I feel very calm.' Then he said he would like to be alone. When I went back about ten days later (September 23rd), Adrian was different. [. . .] He was painting when I went in. A large, loose, but finished painting was propped against the fireplace, and when I saw it, I said, 'It's so beautiful!' He laughed, now expressing warmth and, at the same time, a curious detachment (Adrian had the ability to be both warm and detached at once, in the same way, I suppose, as one can be both pleased by praise and indifferent to it). He immediately said, 'You must have it.' I said I couldn't. He said I must. I looked towards Ann, who said yes, I must. This was the first of the series he started after he was given pills to relieve him of pain – pills that also, he said, made him 'very happy'. [Ann Stokes Angus comments that this painting was in fact started before Stokes began to take Cortisone and that when, on his return from hospital, he was boosted by this drug, he was also able to complete the left side of the picture, which the clouding over of his right brain had hitherto prevented.]

He was, however, more confused than ever, and at moments he knew this. He said, 'I'm not really very normal, you know.'

Ann told me [this quotation corrected by Ann Stokes Angus, April 1986], 'You see, the intellectual part of his brain is deteriorating. The emotional side is as it's always been.'

While Ann and I potted, always to Greek bouzouki music, Adrian [upstairs] painted.

By late November, Adrian was hardly able to support the brush. [...] As he wasn't able to move without Ann's help, I [tried] to arrange the bottles he was painting as he wanted them arranged [...] He wasn't able to articulate his wishes, and I could never understand what he wanted me to do with the bottles. He'd point with his brush and say something incomprehensible, and I, feeling that I should understand, would place a bottle upright, or on its side, but the arrangement was never what he wanted. I said, 'Just say yes if I do the right thing, no if I do the wrong thing', but this didn't work any better. - He became impatient, and said, 'It doesn't matter.' Then he seemed to become resigned. He'd gone far from seeing objects in terms of his ideas about them; in the last eleven paintings, he had to take objects as they were, beyond his control in every other way but by painting them.

T 03580   **Still Life: Last Eleven (No.6)** 1972

Oil on canvas 14 × 18 (356 × 457)
Inscribed on top canvas turnover 'A D S '72' by artist and '3/11/72' by Ann Stokes
Purchased from Mrs Ann Stokes Angus (Grant-in-Aid) 1983

Exh: *The Last Paintings of Adrian Stokes*, Tate Gallery, February–March 1973 (no catalogue); *Adrian Stokes*, Serpentine Gallery, June–July 1982 (125, repr.); *The Hard-Won Image*, Tate Gallery, July–September 1984 (127)

Lit: As for T 03579

T 03581   **Still Life: Last Eleven (No.11)** 1972

Oil on canvas 14 × 18 (356 × 457)
Inscribed on top canvas turnover by Ann

Stokes '15/11 1972 Last "Last 11"'
Purchased from Mrs Ann Stokes Angus (Grant-in-Aid) 1983

Exh: *The Last Paintings of Adrian Stokes*, Tate Gallery, February–March 1973 (no catalogue); *Adrian Stokes*, AC tour, Serpentine Gallery, June–July 1982, Huddersfield Art Gallery, July–August 1982, City Museum and Art Gallery, Gloucester, September–October 1982 (127, repr. in col.); *The Hard-Won Image*, Tate Gallery, July–September 1984 (128)

Lit: As for T 03579

This is Adrian Stokes's last painting. The 1982 Serpentine Gallery exhibition catalogue states that it was painted between 10 and 13 December 1972. In a letter of 2 April 1986, Ann Stokes Angus explained that her inscribing of this work as having been painted in November was a mistake for December. The day of the month was also incorrectly inscribed; when making the inscription she had mistakenly thought that Adrian Stokes had died on 16 December. In fact, he died on Friday, 15 December 1972 and Mrs Angus (who has approved this entry and those on the other eight paintings by Adrian Stokes acquired at the same time) confirmed in the same letter that he finished T 03581 two days before he died. She later added (letter, 8 April 1986):

We shared a spoon or fork and the plate for our meals in the last month or so when he could not lift it to his mouth easily and finally on the last of the 'Last 11' ... he sat in front of the canvas and said, 'You paint it.' I said, 'How can I paint your picture.' He said, 'You paint it.' I said, 'I can do a lot for you but not that.' As he wouldn't start I sat close beside him and asked where he wanted it started and what colour, and though he could scarcely communicate with ordinary words he showed me what he wanted and, for an hour, we were in the most marvellous mental contact I can ever have known. Then to my relief he got interested in the brush, took it from me and scrubbed out what I had done but for a bit of background and did the whole picture himself. I think he finished it the next day [...]

At the end of the last painting session [...] he dropped his brushes deliberately, with a clatter, and murmured words to the effect that it was finished. I was quite aware that he meant everything was finished.

In his 'Adrian Stokes', *The Listener*, 28 December 1972, p.900, Richard Wollheim described the circumstances of the painting of T03581 as follows:

Working late into the evening of Wednesday, 13 December, Adrian Stokes completed a painting on which he had been engaged for the past few days. The painting is small, 14 inches by 18. It shows two bottles or jugs grouped together, one overlapping the other, placed slightly left of centre, with no line drawn between the level on which the bottles stand and the ground behind them. So described, the painting will seem of a very familiar kind to anyone who knows Stokes's work. Bottles, jugs, earthenware or china bowls, the utensils of domestic life, transformed into something like architectural members, the shapes discriminated but not opposed to one another – this is a theme or content to which he returned many, many times in forty or fifty years of painting.

But this painting was different. It belonged to a small group of paintings that Stokes began this autumn: in September, when he returned home after a few days in hospital, where he learnt that his body, including his brain, was incurably ravaged by cancer. All these 11 paintings express the victory of will, of life, over physical deterioration, but the one of which I speak represents the high point of that achievement. Never again, Stokes realised, would he be able to repeat the bodily effort. He called this small painting his Waterloo. His wife Ann – who had already done more than could be expected of a human being to ensure the serenity of these shortening winter weeks – has described to me how happily the next day and the following morning passed. He contemplated. On Friday he lay down for his rest after lunch, fell asleep more easily than he had managed recently, and he never woke.

T03582 Still Life: Last Eleven (No.5) 1972

Oil on canvas 14 × 18 (356 × 457)
Inscribed on top canvas turnover 'ADS '72'
Purchased from Mrs Ann Stokes Angus
(Grant-in-Aid) 1983

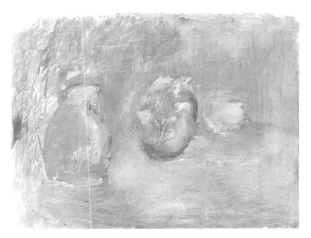

Exh: *The Last Paintings of Adrian Stokes*, Tate Gallery, February–March 1973 (no catalogue); *Adrian Stokes*, Serpentine Gallery, June–July 1982 (118); *The Hard-Won Image*, Tate Gallery, July–September 1984 (129)

Lit: As for T03579

T03583 Still Life: Last Eleven (No.8) 1972

Oil on canvas 20 × 16 (508 × 407)
Inscribed on top canvas turnover 'ADS '72'
Purchased from Mrs Ann Stokes Angus
(Grant-in-Aid) 1983

Exh: *The Last Paintings of Adrian Stokes*, Tate Gallery, February–March 1973 (no catalogue); *Adrian Stokes*, Serpentine Gallery, June–July 1982 (117); *The Hard-*

Won Image, Tate Gallery, July–September
1984 (130)
Lit: As for T 03579

Gloucester, September–October 1982
(126, repr.); *The Hard-Won Image*, Tate
Gallery, July–September 1984 (132)
Lit: As for T 03579

T 03584 **Still Life: Last Eleven
(No.7)** 1972

Oil on canvas 14 × 18 (356 × 457)
Inscribed on top canvas turnover 'ADS '72'
Purchased from Mrs Ann Stokes Angus
(Grant-in-Aid) 1983
Exh: *The Last Paintings of Adrian Stokes*, Tate
Gallery, February–March 1973 (no
catalogue); *Adrian Stokes*, AC tour,
Serpentine Gallery, June–July 1982,
Huddersfield Art Gallery, July–August
1982, City Museum and Art Gallery,
Gloucester, September–October 1982
(123, repr. in col.); *The Hard-Won Image*,
Tate Gallery, July–September 1984 (131)
Lit: As for T 03579

T 03585 **Still Life: Last Eleven
(No.10)** 1972

Oil on canvas 22 × 29⅞ (559 × 759)
Inscribed on top canvas turnover '9/12
ADS '72'
Purchased from Mrs Ann Stokes Angus
(Grant-in-Aid) 1983
Exh: *The Last Paintings of Adrian Stokes*, Tate
Gallery, February–March 1973 (no
catalogue); *Adrian Stokes*, AC tour,
Serpentine Gallery, June–July 1982,
Huddersfield Art Gallery, July–August
1982, City Museum and Art Gallery,

T 03586 **Still Life: Last Eleven
(No.9)** 1972

Oil on canvas 20 × 21 (508 × 534)
Inscribed on top canvas turnover 'ADS '72'
Purchased from Mrs Ann Stokes Angus
(Grant-in-Aid) 1983
Exh: *The Last Paintings of Adrian Stokes*, Tate
Gallery, February–March 1973 (no
catalogue); *Adrian Stokes*, Serpentine
Gallery, June–July 1982 (122); *The Hard-
Won Image*, Tate Gallery, July–September
1984 (133)
Lit: As for T 03579

T03587 **Still Life: Last Eleven (No.3)** 1972

Oil on canvas 20 × 24 (508 × 610)
Not inscribed
Purchased from Mrs Ann Stokes Angus
(Grant-in-Aid) 1983

Exh: *The Last Paintings of Adrian Stokes*, Tate
Gallery, February–March 1973 (no
catalogue); *Adrian Stokes*, AC tour,
Serpentine Gallery, June–July 1982,
Huddersfield Art Gallery, July–August
1982, City Museum and Art Gallery,
Gloucester, September–October 1982
(120, repr., as 'Still Life: Last Eleven
(No.4)'); *The Hard-Won Image*, Tate
Gallery, July–September 1984 (134, repr.)

Lit: As for T03579

Delbanco did not provide a title when they sold it.
Information held on the Tate Gallery's file on Arthur
Studd, provided by a cousin of the artist, reveals that
Studd remained a bachelor all his life. It is therefore
possible that Sir Eric Studd and his wife, when identifying the sitter as Mrs Studd, meant the mother of the
artist.

Arthur Studd 1863–1919

T03644 **The Mauve Hat (?)** c.1900–10

Oil on panel 8⅝ × 6¼ (220 × 157)
Not inscribed
Presented anonymously in memory of
Terence Rattigan 1983

Prov: ...; Roland, Browse and Delbanco; the
donor c.1965

In the spring of 1966, the donor visited the artist's
nephew, Sir Eric Studd, with a photograph of T03644.
Sir Eric and his wife identified the sitter as 'Mrs Studd'
and the donor assumed it was the artist's wife. When
T03644 was acquired by the Tate Gallery, it took the
title 'The Artist's Wife', since Roland, Browse and

T03645 **Venetian Lyric (San Giorgio) (?)** c.1900–10

Oil on panel 5 × 8½ (127 × 217)
Inscribed 'Studd' b.l.
Presented anonymously in memory of
Terence Rattigan 1983

Prov: ...; Mrs Elga Johnson, niece of a friend of
the artist; the donor 1966

See entry for T03646.

T 03646 Venetian Lyric (Santa Maria della Salute) (?) *c.*1900–10

Oil on panel 5 × 8½ (127 × 217)
Inscribed 'Studd' b.r.
Presented anonymously in memory of
Terence Rattigan 1983

Prov: . . .; Mrs Elga Johnson, niece of a friend of
the artist; the donor 1966

Arthur Studd's single one-man exhibition during his lifetime was held at the Alpine Club Gallery, London, in June 1911. Of the sixty paintings in the exhibition, at least twenty were views of Venice; even the catalogue cover was decorated with the reproduction of a swift pen sketch of the church of Santa Maria della Salute. No biographical details were offered in the catalogue so it is not possible to be precise about the date of Studd's working visit to Venice. Some of the works exhibited were entitled with the view they represented eg. 'Riva della Salute' whereas eight were shown under the generic term 'Venetian Lyric' followed by the first eight letters of the alphabet, A–H. Neither T 03645 nor T 03646 has an Alpine Club Gallery label which could securely link them to this exhibition, but T 03646 has a paper label with the number 51, and 51 in the Alpine Club Gallery exhibition was entitled 'Venetian Lyrics B (The Low Line of Light)'

The Tate Gallery acquired 'A Venetian Lyric', N 03275 in 1918, a similar small oil on panel, and this was believed to have been shown in the June 1911 Alpine Club Gallery exhibition under the title 'A Temple of Vulcan'. It was given the tentative date of (?) 1900–10.

Patrick Symons b.1925

T 03552 Oak Arch Grey (Wimbledon Common) 1977–81

Oil on canvas 35⅛ × 31¼ (892 × 795)
Inscribed 'Symons '77–81' b.r., and

various mathematical calculations on right hand canvas turnover
Purchased from Browse & Darby (Grant-in-Aid) 1983

Exh: *Patrick Symons recent paintings & drawings*, Browse & Darby, November–December 1982 (6, repr. in black and white; a detail, showing the self-portrait, repr. in col. on the cover); *The Hard-Won Image*, Tate Gallery, July–September 1984 (136, repr. in col. p.47)

Wimbledon Common is in south-west London. The image of a figure towards lower left, sitting on the ground near a tree trunk while drawing, is a self-portrait. Apart from the final sentence, which Symons added later, all the quotations in this entry are from a letter from the artist dated 19 March 1986, sent in reply to questions from the compiler.

Before beginning a painting Symons usually makes a drawing of the motif (to discover a proportional idea for the picture), which he describes as a 'scribble'. He writes of the drawing for this painting (private collection) that:

the 'scribble' best describes the area of the picture which consists of two horizontal rectangles one above the other, of which the centres were both deliberately used as focal points. The lower part, to do with the ground, is a double square (its diagonal measurement is the height of the whole picture). The upper part, more extended to do with looking up into the branches, is a golden rectangle. This idea would have been discovered in the 'scribble' but used deliberately from the start of the painting and frequently re-stated – for example to accommodate the self portrait and other incidents.

The artist has explained that he has been painting at Wimbledon Common, mostly in June and July, since 1967:

> moving progressively into the Oak wood just to the west of the Windmill car park. Some students, originally from Chelsea foundation course, still return from various schools or later and my former colleague Trevor Felcey brings others from the Byam Shaw and Wimbledon schools.

His first Wimbledon drawing, outside the wood, was 'Wimbledon Oaks' 1967, and this was followed by 'Wimbledon Oaks' 1968 (charcoal; Museum and Art Gallery, Doncaster), in which the view is down the path from the entrance. Around 1971:

> I painted the small Sycamore tree in the hollow over to the right. In 1972 I moved further down the path and made a drawing for 'Holly under Oak' which I painted from 1973–5 and which was bought by someone I think from Germany after being shown by William Darby and at the Royal Academy.

In 1976, the year of the drought, I moved further into the previous picture where I have been working ever since, and started 'Oak Arch Sunny' [repr. in catalogue of *Tolly Cobbold Eastern Arts, Fourth National Exhibition*, Fitzwilliam Museum, Cambridge, April–May 1983 and tour, p.34]. It took quite a long time to settle on the oak arch and to find a place to look at it from. I very much liked the arch formed by these two trees and the movement of the ground towards them, but was worried at first that it looked a bit too much like one of my pictures already. However, struggling to make sense of all those particular trees and the ever changing patches of sunlight soon took care of all that.

In 1977, which was much less sunny, I started your picture 'Oak Arch Grey'. Standing about five yards nearer and to the right, I found a quite different view to do with looking up into the branches above the arch as well as across the ground. It is a more complex space but I hoped to make the leaves more clearly about the growth of each branch uncomplicated by sunlight. Also, because of the even light, I was more aware of the movement of passers by and many different incidents have come and gone in the picture, including two horses, but I could not get them sufficiently settled without more than one sight of them. A student did pose for me briefly once or twice carrying his picture out of the wood on the left of the picture as I had originally seen him by chance.

The self-portrait began to appear in the third year I think. One particularly glorious sunny morning, that was hopeless for both the paintings, I had made an entirely separate empathy drawing about myself situated under that tree, and the delight of just being there. The drawing was a very slight one but I enjoyed the experience and began to like the idea of my own presence in the picture. But I could not combine the imagined space of the drawing with the observed and measured space of the painting; so the whole thing had to become a great deal more literal. I made measured marks off myself on the ground and on the tree and I set up my clothes and the drawing on sticks. I got one student to pose for me wearing my clothes on one occasion, but the figure was always unsatisfactory and I was accused of being sentimental.

In the last year of the painting I almost gave up in despair. I pruned the small holly tree (it grows a lot each year) beyond the figure very carefully in the hope of making its presence intense enough to replace the figure and after much deliberation came back from the country in August to paint the figure out, which I did, but later that entirely sleepless night found it unbearable and cleaned off all the new paint. By now several other people posed for me in my clothes and I made drawings at home of the back of my head in mirrors, but *I never painted on the picture at all in the studio* and I continued to work off the figure into the top of the picture, particularly in the right top corner, all the time.

(I also used the drawing of myself, with cast shadows from mistletoe, in a Christmas card that year, and a sculptor called Karel Zuvac made an amusing empathy drawing of himself posing as me and being painted by me.)

The main trees are all English oaks and holly. I avoid Turkey oaks and birches which seem to me more feathery and less powerful. There is a small shrub of Alder Buckthorn on the right of the small path leading to the Arch which I painted specially with different pigments not used elsewhere. The branches in the foreground are pruned each year. Both the Oak Arch pictures were finished in 1981 and since 1982 I have been working on a third picture of the oak arch from even closer and further to the right on sunny mornings. The painting is about the same width as 'Oak Arch Grey' and about four inches higher. I have also been working on a very long horizontal drawing (about 16″ × 42″) of the whole place including the Oak Arch and all the paintings (or models of them) I have painted there (including 'Holly under Oak') set up on easels in their places. I am not prepared to make photographs of these before they are finished. The painting is bound to take at least two more years but there is a chance the drawing might be done in 1986.

The figures on the back of your picture probably refer to scales of measurement between sight size (measurements made on a ruler held at arm's length), the scribble, and the painting.

I think the most conscious precedents in earlier art are probably to do with Theodore Rousseau (like the one in the Wallace collection or another in the Louvre) in which a forest picture is an unpopulated stage set, into which I have tried to introduce incidents of sunlight and of figures. I haven't seen the Wilson Steer but the photograph reminds me a bit of Monet – I find the Rousseau more particular. [The works referred to in this paragraph are Theodore Rousseau, 'Sortie de Forêt à Fontainebleau, Soleil Couchant', exh. 1850 (Louvre, Paris) and 'The Forest of Fontainebleau: Morning' c.1848–50 (Wallace Collection); and P.W. Steer, 'An Oak Avenue' 1897, repr. Bruce Laughton, *Philip Wilson Steer*, Oxford, 1971, pl.157.]

The frame is really just a coloured mount, the proportions of which are deliberate extensions of the geometry of the picture. (I've forgotten how but know I had several goes to find an idea that also looked right.) So that I do think of it as an extension of the painting. I have not been able to think of a properly separate frame that would contain the picture without imposing a style nor can I find any satisfactory way of framing the mount. It is painted with a complicatedly adjusted mixture of acrylic white (yellow ochre, ultramarine and Indian red) pigments and matt Liquitex.

Marlborough Fine Art (Grant-in-Aid) 1982
Exh: *Rufino Tamayo: Recent Paintings*, Marlborough Gallery, New York, November–December 1981 (14, repr. in col.); Marlborough Fine Art, February 1982 (14, repr. in col.)
Lit: Octavio Paz and Jacques Lassaigne, *Rufino Tamayo*, New York, 1982, pl.265 in col.

The artist has explained that the letter 'O' before the date in the inscription is a homage to his wife Olga, using the initial of her first name. He agreed that this picture could be said to convey 'the feeling of desolation we all have about this hostile world in which we unfortunately live today' (letter of 15 January 1985).

Geoffrey Tibble 1909–1952

T 03655   **Three Women** 1930

Oil on canvas 12 × 16 (305 × 406)
Inscribed 'G. TIBBLE/''THREE WOMEN''/ 1930' on reverse
Presented anonymously in memory of Terence Rattigan 1983
Prov: Sir Augustus Daniel; Leicester Galleries 1950–1970; ...; Abbot and Holder; the donor 1970
Exh: *London Group 28th Exhibition*, New Burlington Galleries, October 1930 (222); *Paintings in Oil by Anthony Devas and Geoffrey Tibble*, Claridge Gallery, January 1931 (38, as 'Women and Landscape'); *Summer Exhibition*, Leicester Galleries, August–September 1970 (42, as 'Group of Figures')

Rufino Tamayo b.1899

T 03370   **Man and Woman** 1981

Oil on canvas $49\frac{1}{8}$ × $70\frac{7}{8}$ (1247 × 1800)
Inscribed 'Tamayo/O.81' b.r. and HOMBRE Y MUSER/180 × 125/OLEO' on back of canvas
Purchased from the artist through

Tibble's 1931 joint exhibition with Anthony Devas at the Claridge Gallery was held two years after Tibble graduated from the Slade School and was the first time he had exhibited in depth. It is not known whether Sir Augustus Daniel purchased T 03655 from the Claridge Gallery exhibition or shortly afterwards. Daniel must have been an admirer of Tibble's early work since he purchased the artist's 'Interior' for the Contemporary Art Society in 1932 (now in the collection of Bradford City Art Gallery). The artist's widow told the donor that she went along with her husband to Sir Augustus Daniel's home in Hampstead to see this work in his collection; this most probably would have been after their marriage in July 1934. It is interesting that although the artist inscribed the work with the title, 'Three Women', and the date, presumably in 1930 when he finished it, he was prepared to exhibit it the following year under a different title, 'Women and Landscape', one which stressed the setting as well as the figures. Reviews of Tibble's early work tended to concentrate on the sculptural quality of his figures, and the name Cézanne was cited. Equally, the female figures in the foreground do share an affinity with contemporary British sculpture, especially the reclining nude on the right, which has much in common with Henry Moore's exactly contemporary work of 1928–30.

After Sir Augustus Daniel's death in 1950, the Leicester Galleries handled his collection, mounting in June 1951 a selective exhibition from it. T 03655 was not one of the works selected on that occasion, but was retrieved from storage for their 1970 Summer Exhibition.

T 03656   The Mug   1948

Oil on canvas $14\frac{5}{8} \times 17\frac{1}{2}$ (370 × 445)
Inscribed 'Tibble' b.l. and 'Tibble/Oct 48' on reverse

Presented anonymously in memory of Vivien Leigh 1983
Prov: Mrs Serena Hobbs, widow of the artist; the donor 1967
Exh: *Geoffrey Tibble*, Arthur Tooth and Sons Ltd., May–June 1949 (? 9, with dimensions given as 12 × 20)

The window and the balcony railings belong to the same studio flat as that depicted in T 03658, the home of Barbara Phillips. Although Tibble's settings have recognisable features copied from the motif, his female figures are never true portraits. The sitter in T 03656, his favourite female type, with dark hair piled high in a bun, was based on his wife, Serena, whose looks were most distinctive, owing to her Anglo-Indian ancestry.

T 03657   Interior with Self-Portrait and Two Women   *c.*1944

Conté crayon on paper $16\frac{3}{4} \times 12\frac{1}{2}$
(425 × 320)
Not inscribed
Presented anonymously in memory of Terence Rattigan 1983
Prov: Mrs Serena Hobbs, widow of the artist; the donor 1967

When the donor acquired this drawing from the artist's wife, she referred to it under the provisional title 'Artist and Model'. She told the donor that the male figure was a self-portrait of the artist, even though he did have a habit of portraying himself as much fatter than he was in actuality. Mrs Hobbs was asked if this squared-up drawing was ever worked up into an oil painting and she thought not.

T 03658 **Dressing** 1944

Oil on canvas 30 × 39 (762 × 990)
Inscribed 'Tibble' b.l. and 'Tibble' on
reverse
Presented anonymously in memory of
Terence Rattigan 1983

Prov: Mrs Serena Hobbs, widow of the artist;
Mrs Paula Barnett, daughter of the artist
1968; the donor 1969
Exh· *Paintings and Drawings by Geoffrey Tibble
1909–1952,* City Art Gallery, Manchester,
July–August 1958 (22)

It appears that Tibble first began a painting with the
canvas stretched the other way round. This painting
was then abandoned, the image painted out with a uniform coat of grey paint and the canvas reversed on the
stretcher for the painting of the present image. It is
highly likely that the first painting on the canvas of
T 03658 which Tibble subsequently painted out was
one of his earlier totally abstract paintings. The artist
participated with seven artist colleagues, Edgar Hubert,
Graham Bell, Thomas Carr, Rodrigo Moynihan, Ivon
Hitchens, Victor Pasmore and Ceri Richards in an exhibition entitled 'Objective Abstractions', held at the
Zwemmer Gallery, London, in March–April 1934, and
from 1934 to 1937 Tibble painted and exhibited abstract
paintings. However from 1938 until his death he abandoned abstraction and returned to painting representational images. William Townsend, the painter, and
Mrs Serena Hobbs, the artist's widow, both independently reported to the donor that after Tibble's
rejection of Objective Abstraction, he methodically
reviewed recent art history until he found an artist he
could believe in, and that artist was Degas. As Charles
Sewter, a friend of the artist, wrote in the catalogue
introduction which accompanied Tibble's 1958
posthumous retrospective exhibition at Manchester:

. . . it has proved impossible to trace a single surviving
example of this [abstract] phase of Tibble's work.
Nearly all of them were overpainted or the canvases
turned and reused during the years 1942 to 1946,
when good canvas was practically impossible to
obtain.

T 03658 most probably falls into this category.

The room depicted in 'Dressing' (and seen again in
T 03656 'The Mug'), with its large window and
wrought-iron balcony railings beyond, is based on one
in a large studio flat in Notting Hill, London, which
belonged to Barbara Phillips, a Polish-born sculptor
friend of the artist. She eventually re-married and
moved to New York. Tibble himself lived at 13 Fitzroy
Street, in a small studio flat, until 1939 when, with his
wife and baby daughter, he moved back to his home area
of Reading. He lived from 1942 to 1948 in Beaconsfield,
where T 03658 was painted.

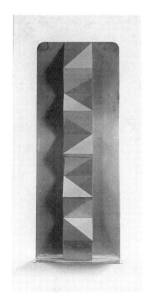

Joe Tilson b.1928

T 03772 **Ziglical Column** 1966

Screenprint on enamelled and stainless
steel $32\frac{1}{4}$ × 12 × $6\frac{1}{8}$ (820 × 305 × 155)
Not inscribed
Transferred from the Victoria and Albert
Museum 1983

Prov: Purchased by the Department of
Circulation, Victoria and Albert Museum,
from Marlborough Fine Art 1967 (Circ.
984–1967)

This was purchased by the Department of Circulation with a number of other screenprints, and is recorded on the invoice as number five of an edition of ten.

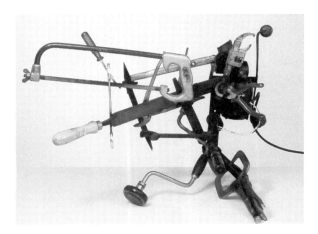

Jean Tinguely b.1925

T 03822 Débricollage 1970

Assemblage of household tools and welded metal 20 × 30 × 25½ (508 × 762 × 648)
Inscribed in relief 'TINGUELY' on metal bar on top
Purchased from the artist (Grant-in-Aid) with the help of the Friends of the Tate Gallery 1984

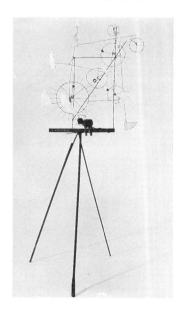

T 03823 Metamechanical Sculpture with Tripod 1954

Wire, painted cardboard and welded metal
93 × 32 × 36 (2360 × 815 × 915)
Not inscribed
Purchased from the artist (Grant-in-Aid)
1984

Henri de Toulouse-Lautrec 1864–1901

T 03575 Horsewoman 1899

Oil on gouache on board $21\frac{7}{8} \times 16\frac{3}{4}$ (555 × 425)
Inscribed 'HT Lautrec' (monogram) b.r.
Bequeathed by Mrs A.F. Kessler 1983

Prov: Pierrefort; Le Garrec; Alfred Lindon; Mrs Kessler

Exh: *H. de Toulouse-Lautrec*, Galerie Durand-Ruel, Paris, May 1902 (105, as 'Amazone', owned by M. Pierrefort); *Nineteenth Century French Paintings*, National Gallery, December 1942–January 1943 (40, as 'L'Amazone au Bois'); *French Paintings from the Kessler Collection*, York Art Gallery, May 1948 (12); *The Kessler Collection*, Wildenstein Gallery, October–November 1948 (29, repr.); *Henri de Toulouse-Lautrec 1864–1901*, Matthiesen

Gallery, May–June 1951 (33); *The French Impressionists and Some of their Contemporaries*, Wildenstein Gallery, April–May 1963 (83); *The Kessler Bequest*, Tate Gallery, February–April 1984 (not numbered, repr.)

Lit: Maurice Joyant, *Henri de Toulouse-Lautrec 1864–1901: Peintre*, Paris, 1926, p.298 as 'Amazone' 1899, owned by M. Le Garrec; M.G. Dortu, *Toulouse-Lautrec et son Oeuvre*, Paris, 1971, III, no.P.682, p.416, repr. p.417 as 'Amazone' 1899; Denys Sutton and G.M. Sugana, *The Complete Paintings of Toulouse-Lautrec*, 1973, no.500, repr. p.118 as 'Horsewoman'; M.G. Dortu and J.A. Meric, *Toulouse-Lautrec: The Complete Paintings*, London Toronto Sydney New York, 1981, II, no.590, p.80 repr. *Also repr:* *L'Amour de l'Art*, XII, 1931, p.139

It has been suggested that this horsewoman may be Mme Victorine Hansman, an Englishwoman who was a dealer in horses and ran a fashionable riding-school (Lautrec apparently met her at the racecourse at Auteuil and made a drawing of her in 1899), but the identification seems uncertain. There is a slightly smaller drawing (Dortu D.4.544) of 1899 in black and coloured crayons in which the horse and rider are almost exactly the same, but which shows more of the setting in the Bois de Boulogne, with a dog on the left and a man on horseback in the middle distance on the right. Lautrec also made a related lithograph in the same year ('Horse-woman and Dog', Delteil 285) of a rather similar horse and rider but in reverse, facing to the right, and with a small dog in the right-hand corner sitting in front of the horse.

Mrs Kessler was herself a keen horsewoman, and continued to ride to hounds, side-saddle, until she was in her eighties.

David Tremlett b.1945

T03689   The Cards 1972

Green felt-tip pen on commercial postcards, 81 cards framed in sets of 3, each card $3\frac{1}{2} \times 5\frac{1}{2}$ (88 × 140)
Each card inscribed by the artist with the name of a county in England, Scotland or Wales, b.r. or b.l.
Purchased from John Dunbar and J.E. Matthews (Grant-in-Aid) 1983

Prov: John Dunbar 1972–83, acquired from the artist

Card no.1

Exh: *British Thing*, Henie-Onstad Kunstsenter, Høvikodden, Norway, September–October 1972 (no catalogue); *Projects: 'The Spring Recordings' 'Green' a side show and other works made over the last three years by David Tremlett*, Museum of Modern Art, New York, March–April 1973 (no catalogue); *11 Englische Zeichner*, Gesellschaft der Freunde Junger Kunst in der Kunsthalle Baden-Baden, Kunsthalle, Baden-Baden, May–June 1973, Kunst-halle Bremen, July–August 1973 (1–81, as '81 Postcard Drawings – Spring 72', repr.)

Lit: *The Tate Gallery 1972–4 Biennial Report and Illustrated Catalogue of Acquisitions* (pp.243–5); Roberta Pancoast Smith, 'David Tremlett, the Museum of Modern Art', exhibition review, *Artforum* XI, May 1973, pp.83–4; Lizzie Borden, 'A note on David Tremlett's work', *Studio International* CLXXXV, June 1973, p.289

This work consists of eighty-one white, plain backed commercial postcards, on which the artist has executed a set of eighty-one simple landscape drawings in green felt-tipped pen. The drawings were made out-of-doors during May and June 1972, each in one of the (then) eighty-one counties of England, Scotland and Wales. Each drawing has been clearly inscribed on the front by the artist with the name of the county in which it was made. On completing each drawing, Tremlett posted it to John Dunbar in London. Where possible, the cards were posted soon after they had been drawn on. Later they were gathered together and framed in sets of three although a rather blurred polaroid taken during Trem-lett's project exhibition held at the Museum of Modern Art, New York in 1973 and sent by the artist to a curator at the Tate Gallery, shows that the cards (which were, according to the contemporary reviews cited above, hung in a long row 5ft 8in from the ground) were originally individually framed under perspex or glass. Tremlett has recently confirmed that he *prefers* the work to be displayed in a single line but has allowed the Tate to display it in three rows one above the other (each row containing 9 framed panels) when display space is limited.

'The Cards' is closely related to another work by Tremlett also in the Gallery's collection, 'The Spring Recordings' 1972 (T01742), acquired in 1973 (see the Tate Gallery's *Biennial Report and Illustrated Catalogue of Acquisitions 1972–74* (loc. cit.)). 'The Spring Recordings', 'The Cards' and an untitled companion set of 81 postcard drawings were all made in the same 81 secluded country locations during a journey round Britain which Tremlett made between 16 May and 11 June 1972. The Gallery's files contain a transcript of a diary Tremlett kept during the trip, which shows that he visited the counties in which he made the recordings and drawings in the following order: Tuesday 16 May, Essex, Hertfordshire, Buckinghamshire; Wednesday 17 May, Oxfordshire, Warwickshire, Northamptonshire, Bedfordshire, Huntingdonshire; Thursday 18 May, Cambridgeshire, Suffolk, Norfolk, Lincolnshire, Rutland; Friday 19 May, Leicestershire, Nottinghamshire, Derbyshire; Saturday 20 May, Staffordshire; Monday 22 May, Yorkshire, Durham, Northumberland, Roxburghshire, Selkirkshire, Peeblesshire, Berwickshire; Tuesday 23 May, E. Lothian, Midlothian; Wednesday 24 May, W. Lothian, Stirlingshire, Clackmannanshire, Fife; Thursday 25 May, Kinross-shire, Perthshire, Angus, Kincardineshire, Aberdeenshire, Banffshire, Moray, Nairnshire; Friday 26 May, Ross & Cromarty, Sutherland, Caithness; Saturday 27 May, Invernesshire, Argyll, Dunbartonshire; Sunday 28 May, Lanarkshire; Monday 29 May, Renfrewshire, Ayrshire, Wigtownshire, Kirkcudbrightshire, Dumfriesshire; Tuesday 30 May, Cumberland, Westmorland, Lancashire; Wednesday 31 May, Cheshire; Thursday 1 June, Flint, Denbighshire; Friday 2 June, Caernarvonshire, Merionethshire, Montgomeryshire; Saturday 3 June, Shropshire, Worcestershire, Herefordshire, Radnorshire, Breconshire; Sunday 4 June, Cardiganshire, Pembrokeshire, Carmarthenshire; Monday 5 June, Glamorgan, Monmouthshire, Gloucestershire, Berkshire, Wiltshire; Tuesday 6 June, Somerset, Devonshire, Cornwall; Friday 9 June, Dorset, Hampshire; Saturday 10 June, Sussex, Surrey, Kent; Sunday 11 June, Greater London. (In addition to county names and dates, Tremlett's diary contains very brief notes on approximate locations where the individual drawings and recordings were made and on the prevailing weather conditions, eg. 'Kent, Nr. Riverhead (N. Tonbridge) Day Fair'). It should be noted that the journey took place before the county boundaries and names were changed in the local government reorganisations of 1974; a number of the counties recorded no longer exist as such and some of the places Tremlett visited may have been absorbed into other counties.

Tremlett made only one recording in London but as the journey was circular, starting and ending in the capital, he used the London card to head the sequence. When the work was framed in panels of three, three cards, Staffordshire, Invernessshire and Midlothian were framed out of sequence by mistake.

As already noted (catalogue entry for T01742 op. cit.), Tremlett sought out quiet locations for all except the London recording and during the short period his tape-recorder was running, matched his action of recording the local sounds with quickly executed near identical sketches of the local landscape on two standard sized postcards. Having posted one set (T03689) to John Dunbar he decided to keep one set for himself. These were subsequently acquired by the artists Gilbert and George late in 1972. Tremlett has pointed out that while each drawing was posted in its county of origin the patterns of Post Office collection and sorting meant that some cards bear the postmark of a neighbouring county. In conversation with the compiler (4 March 1986) he mentioned that in addition to the cards, John Dunbar had a further work relating to the same journey which included a map of the route taken; Tremlett also retains such an annotated map. According to him, John Dunbar agreed to finance 'The Spring Recordings' project, on condition that he received a work and T03689 was originally conceived as a work to repay him.

Although 'The Cards' does not indicate it, the journey was divided into two parts. The first section was made by Tremlett on a bicycle; he slept in a tent which he carried with him. He thinks that around 6 June he returned to London and hired a green Volkswagen mini-bus from a fellow artist, before heading south. He slept in the van during the second part of the journey. He has confirmed that he had no particular system for seeking out the places in which to make his recordings (although he made the trip entirely on minor roads, never using motorways) but looked in each case for a quiet out-of-the-way place. Although 'The Cards' are not part of 'The Spring Recordings' they were made under identical conditions and are thus very closely linked. Tremlett deliberately kept the drawings very simple and this spare quality is further emphasised if they are hung in a single line. He has pointed out that his work has frequently involved what may be termed 'mail art', ranging from his private view cards which he always designs carefully and regards as limited edition works in their own right, to the 'informal works' he made in the early seventies when on long trips abroad (for instance to the Far East and Australia in 1973). He has regularly sent autographed postcards to certain friends and colleagues. He further draws a comparison between T03689 and 'Some Places to Visit', a limited edition book he published with the Nigel Greenwood gallery in 1974.

This entry has been approved by the artist.

William Turnbull b.1922

T 03773 **Mask I** 1953

> Bronze $9\frac{1}{8} \times 8\frac{1}{8} \times 2\frac{3}{4}$ (230 × 205 × 70)
> Not inscribed
> Transferred from the Victoria and Albert Museum 1983

Prov: Purchased by the Department of Circulation, Victoria and Albert Museum, Sotheby's, 15 April 1964, 149, as 'Mask II, 1955' (Circ. 194–1964)

Exh: *William Turnbull*, Tate Gallery, August–October 1973 (8, repr.)

The artist has confirmed the correct title and date of this sculpture (letter of 4 December 1984). There is one other cast, which belongs to the artist.

Euan Uglow b.1932

T 03418 **Zagi** 1981–2

> Oil on canvas $59\frac{1}{8} \times 42\frac{1}{8}$ (1500 × 1070)
> Inscribed on top canvas turnover
> '41.5″ × 58.7″. Varnish Rowneys No 800 /"Wax Matt Euan Uglow 1981–82 ⟨/oil on canvas'
> Purchased from Browse & Darby (Grant-in-Aid) 1982

Exh: *Euan Uglow: Paintings and drawings*, Browse & Darby, May–June 1983 (21, repr. in col. and black and white); *The*

Hard-Won Image, Tate Gallery, July–September 1984 (141, repr. in col. p.14)

Lit: Max Wykes-Joyce, 'Euan Uglow', *Art & Artists*, May 1983, p.33 (repr.); James Burr, *Apollo*, CXVII, June 1983, p.507 (repr.); Rasaad Jamie, 'Euan Uglow at Browse and Darby', *Artscribe*, 42, August 1983, p.60 (repr.);
Also repr: in advertisement for The Bath Festival Contemporary Art Fair, May–June 1983, in *Country Life*, 28 April 1983, p.1146; *Burlington Magazine*, CXXVI, October 1984, p.650

The following is largely based on the artist's replies to questions in conversation on 27 March 1986, and has been approved by him.

The model who posed for 'Zagi' was a New Zealander, Julia Burton, whom the artist had seen modelling at Chelsea School of Art; she posed for this painting for a period of a year, from Easter 1981, working five or six days a week, for up to five hours a day. The painting was executed in the artist's studio in Turnchapel Mews, Cedars Road, London SW4, using a wooden platform with a wedge-shaped addition to compensate for the angle of the studio floor, and a vertical wooden plank at its fore-edge, to which a horizontal bar, held by the model, had been attached.

Another source was a small toy made by the artist for this particular work, a figure with a carved wooden body and brass limbs attached to two steel rods, the counter-movement of which results in a sequence of acrobatic movements. The idea of the painting derived from the juxtaposition of the particular model and the poses generated by the acrobat-toy. 'Zagi' is a transliteration of the Chinese for 'acrobat' (the toy being based on a Chinese original).

The structure running down the right-hand edge of the painting curves at eye-level height, i.e. the height from which the painting should be seen; the purpose of the pattern of circles, made with a wooden cheese-top, is to define the surface of the structure – the circles themselves have no specifically analytical function. The curve in the left-hand edge of the structure allows the artist to retain the required distance between its base and the model's left foot, without having to make the arms unnaturally long. The same structure appears in 'Striding nude, blue dress II' (1978–81; illustration 15 in the 1983 Browse & Darby exhibition catalogue cited above), but with a less pronounced curve, since the figure is completely separated from the structure. The two paintings are related in terms of design, but are in no sense sequential.

The lower right leg and foot are painted using a change of scale, in order to accommodate the figure within the $\sqrt{2}$ rectangle with the foot fitting into the corner; this change of scale marked a late stage in the development of the painting. In common with other paintings by the artist, the numerous marks throughout the painting indicate transition-points in tone or structure, rather than serving any cartographic function.

Transferred from the Victoria and Albert Museum 1983
Prov: Presented by the artist to the Victoria and Albert Museum 1934 (A. 45–1934)

The artist said to the Tate Gallery's cataloguer in March 1961 that this work dated from 1932–3 and was the original matrix for the chased bronze cast, exhibited at *Leon Underwood*, Leicester Galleries, April 1934 (9). There were altogether three bronze casts. The same idea was used at a much later date, in 1957, for the maquette for a nine-foot figure intended for a building, but the project did not materialize. The maquette was exhibited at the Kaplan Gallery, March 1961 (14), with five other variations on the 'Herald' theme (15–19).

The sculpture is broken into several pieces. It was previously catalogued as 6127, and described in error as having been transferred to the Tate Gallery in 1952.

Keith Vaughan 1912–1977

T 03700 **Ninth Assembly of Figures (Eldorado Banal)** 1976

Oil on canvas $45\frac{1}{4} \times 60\frac{1}{4}$ (1150 × 1530)
Inscribed on reverse 'ELDORADO BANAL/(9th ASSEMBLY OF FIGURES 1976)/45 × 60/Keith Vaughan/"Quelle est cette île triste et noire – c'est Cythère/Nous dit-on un pays fameux dans les chansons/Eldorado banal de tous les vieux garçons/Regarde, après tout, c'est une pauvre terre"'
Purchased from Professor John N. Ball and Dr Gordon Hargreaves (Grant-in-Aid) 1983

Leon Underwood 1890–1975

T 03775 **Herald of New Day** 1932–3

Plaster $25\frac{1}{2} \times 11\frac{1}{2} \times 12\frac{1}{2}$ (647 × 292 × 317)
Not inscribed

Prov: Purchased by Professor John N. Ball and
Dr Gordon Hargreaves from Waddington
Galleries, 1976

Exh: *Keith Vaughan, New Paintings and
Gouaches*, Waddington Galleries, March–
April 1976 (no catalogue); *British Painting
1952–1977*, RA, September–October
1977 (371, repr.)

Lit: Linda Talbot, 'Lost Legend', *Express and
News*, 26 March 1976; 'Mr Keith
Vaughan. An individualistic British
painter' (obituary), *The Times*, 8
November 1977; G. Hastings, *Keith
Vaughan*, 1981 (unpublished B.A. thesis,
University College of Wales, Aberystwyth,
1981, pp.67–71)

The 'Ninth' was the last of the paintings titled by
Vaughan 'Assembly of Figures', and which had marked
his production from 1952, the date of the 'First', as key
works. It was painted in his studio in Belsize Park the
year before his death, when he already knew he was
suffering from cancer.

The composition was taken precisely from a small,
undated, pencil drawing, $6\frac{1}{2} \times 8$ ins. The artist gave this
to Professor Ball and Dr. Hargreaves when they jointly
purchased the painting, and told them it was made
much earlier. They date it on grounds of style to about
1960–2, and it was inscribed for them on the mount by
the artist 'To John and Gordon – March 1976 – Keith
Vaughan – 9th Assembly of Figures'. The drawing
is heavily worked, with many altered placings for the
figures before it was finally shaded over. The main
differences in the painting are that the central figure,
painted dark blue, is barely visible in the drawing, and
there is no suggestion of a landscape at the left, visible
in the drawing as two ellipse shapes.

It is likely that this drawing was itself also connected
to the verse from Baudelaire which is included in the
title of the painting, since the artist confirmed to Professor Ball that the right hand hanging figure is that of
the verse:

Perched on their provender, ferocious birds
were ravaging the ripe corpse hanging there.

He also identified the figure at the lower left, cut off
by the frame, as himself pictured as an observer. The
second verse, written in full on the reverse of the painting, also expresses disillusion with the ideal:

What is that dreary island – the black one there?
Cythéra, someone says, the one in the song
insipid Eldorado of good old boys:
it isn't much of a place, as you can see
(from Charles Baudelaire, *Les Fleurs du Mal*,
translated by Richard Howard, 1982)

Despite the reference to old age Vaughan had already
used this verse for a drawing of 1942, not connected
with the 'Ninth Assembly', titled 'Voyage à Cythère'
and inscribed 'Quelle est cette Triste Isle' (exhibited
The British Neo-Romantics, Fischer Fine Art, July–
August 1983 (67)). He was also in 1942–3 making drawings from Rimbaud's *Une Saison en Enfer*. A later painting titled 'Group of Figures, Eldorado Banal' (1965,
Huddersfield Art Gallery) equally has no connection in
composition with the 'Ninth Assembly'.

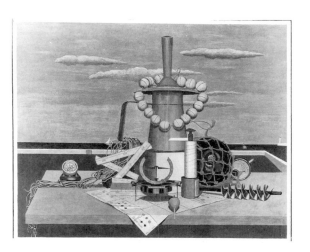

Edward Wadsworth 1889–1949

T 03398 **Regalia** 1928

Tempera with oil on canvas laid on
plywood $30 \times 36\frac{1}{8}$ (763 × 917)
Inscribed 'Edward Wadsworth 1928' on
painting of a label towards b.r.
Purchased from Mrs Barbara von
Bethmann-Hollweg through the Mayor
Gallery (Grant-in-Aid) with the help of
the Friends of the Tate Gallery 1982

Prov: The artist; Dudley Tooth after 1929 (?);
the artist after 1937; Fanny Wadsworth
1949; Barbara von Bethmann-Hollweg
1949

Exh: *An Exhibition of Tempera Paintings by
Edward Wadsworth*, Arthur Tooth and
Sons, May–June 1929 (11); *British
Contemporary Art*, Rosenberg and Helft,
January–February 1937 (30); *Exhibition of
Contemporary British Paintings*, Arthur
Tooth and Sons, December 1937 (50);
Contemporary British Art, Whitechapel
Art Gallery, May–July 1938 (76); *Edward*

Wadsworth Memorial Exhibition, Tate Gallery, February–March 1951 (17); *Painters of the Sea: an Exhibition of Contemporary Seascape*, AC Western Region touring exhibition (venues not known), May–October 1951 (23, repr., without painted border); *Edward Wadsworth 1889–1949. Paintings, Drawings and Prints*, P & D Colnaghi and Company, July–August 1974 (52, repr. in col.); *Tendenzen der Zwanziger Jahre*, Akademie der Künste, Berlin, August–October 1977 (4/191, repr. without painted border); *Edward Wadsworth 1889–1949. Paintings from the 1920s*, Mayor Gallery, April–May 1982 (9, repr. p.19 and in col. on the cover)

Lit: Mark Glazebrook, introduction to *Edward Wadsworth 1889–1949. Paintings, Drawings and Prints*, exhibition catalogue, P & D Colnaghi and Company, July–August 1974 (n.p., repr. in col. no.52); Christine Boyanoski, 'The Art of Edward Wadsworth', unpublished M.Phil. thesis, University of London, Courtauld Institute of Art, 1981, p.65; Mark Glazebrook, introduction to *Edward Wadsworth 1889–1949. Paintings from the 1920s*, exhibition catalogue, Mayor Gallery, April–May 1982 (n.p., repr. pl.9 and in col. on the cover); *The Friends of the Tate Gallery. Annual Report 1st May 1982–30th April 1983*, 1983, p.11 (repr. on front cover without painted border); *The Tate Gallery 1982–84. Illustrated Biennial Report*, 1984, p.45 (repr. in col. without painted border); *Also repr: Arts Review*, XXVI, 26 July 1974 (in col. on cover); Charles Harrison, *English Art and Modernism*, London, 1981, no.106 (without painted border)

Among other sources of information the following entry is based on letters from the artist's daughter, Mrs Barbara von Bethmann-Hollweg, dated 20 September and 21 September 1982, and 9 April, 14 May and 4 June 1986.

'Regalia' depicts marine instruments, grouped on a table, beyond which is a terrace overlooking the sea. From left to right the instruments may be identified as follows: compass, surveyor's chain, surveyor's rule, harbour signals chart, inclining sundial, fishing float, vertical sundial, glass net float, portable tachometer and auger. With the exception of the two sundials, which probably date from no later than the eighteenth century, the objects would have been in common use in the 1920s (information supplied by the National Maritime Museum in a letter of 26 March 1986). According to Mrs von Bethmann-Hollweg, the large red object, around which is draped a string of cork floats, is a ship's lantern (port) 'related to the type called Dark Lantern since its light could be shut off by a small door in its side'. She considers that the object identified above as an auger is 'an instrument for the cleaning of tubes, being a spiral of brass bristles on a metal stem, the tip of which is blunt'. The auger depicted in 'Shells with Auger' 1928 (repr. R.H. Wilenski, 'Modern "Still-Life". The Paintings of Edward Wadsworth', *Studio*, XCVII, June 1929, p.417) has a pointed, spiralled tip. Mrs von Bethmann-Hollweg states that the artist acquired these and similar objects in a number of ways: some were purchased at ships' chandlers, some he found discarded and others were given to him. Mrs von Bethmann-Hollweg no longer possesses any of the instruments depicted.

'Regalia' was painted in the artist's studio at Dairy House, Maresfield Park, Sussex in 1928 where he set up the instruments to contrive a still-life composition. Wadsworth was consistent in his practice of painting still-life from the motif but the view of the sea is imaginary. A number of the objects depicted are found in other paintings by Wadsworth of this period but one picture in particular closely resembles 'Regalia', namely 'Parergon' 1928 (private collection, London). Apart from the fact that 'Parergon' is smaller in size than T 03398, its composition is similar enough to suggest that the two works were painted successively. The principal differences between the two compositions are as follows: in 'Parergon' the chart on the table, one edge of which is curled upwards, is blue and does not depict harbour signals; the inclining sundial appears to be metallic; the surveyor's chain is missing but the composition contains a telescope; to the back of the composition stands a book, possibly a log book, which obscures the background on the left hand side; the table itself is yellow and is situated indoors before a window overlooking the sea (there is no terrace). In all other respects the composition is markedly similar. Other works which are less closely related but of relevance are 'Song of the Sea' 1928 (Swindon Museum and Art Gallery, Borough of Thamesdown, repr. R.H. Wilenski, p.413), 'Floats and Afloat' 1928 (repr. ibid., p.414), 'Wings of the Morning' 1928 (repr. ibid., p.416), 'Regatta' 1928, 'Bright Intervals' 1928 and 'Lamentations' 1928. All these works are still-lifes set before the sea; however, they all contain organic as well as man-made objects. 'Regalia', on the other hand, eschews the organic and in this respect is similar to 'Parergon', 'Log and Sextant' 1928 and 'Marine' 1928 (formally called 'Faithful Servants', Leeds City Art Galleries).

Wadsworth began to paint marine still-lifes in 1926 after a visit to Marseilles. Although it has sometimes been assumed that Wadsworth painted these first works during this visit, according to Mrs von Bethmann-Hollweg Wadsworth did not actually paint in France 'after the First World War', although he stayed 'in and around Marseilles between the two World Wars'. The subject of the marine still-life was to preoccupy him above all else until 1929 when his work began to move towards biomorphic abstraction. The vocabulary of the marine still-lifes generally includes both the organic and man-made, natural forms, such as shells, and instruments of measurement such as sundials. It was only in 1928 that he abandoned, temporarily, natural forms. The earlier still-lifes were juxtaposed with harbour scenes, thereby forming a link with the paintings of ships in harbour which directly precede these works, but the still-lifes of 1928 are mostly set against an empty or near-empty seascape. In 'Regalia' the sea is empty but for a small yacht and a buoy, the only indication of movement in an otherwise motionless scene. In 1926 the notion of setting a still-life before a landscape was becoming popular in England and by 1928 it had become typical of Seven and Five Society painting, notably in the work of David Jones, Ben and Winifred Nicholson and Christopher Wood, as well as in that of Paul Nash who was not a member. It was particularly popular on the Continent where de Chirico, Herbin, Metzinger, Léger, Matisse and Picasso were prominent practitioners, some of whose work Wadsworth knew in reproduction as early as 1921 as a result of his subscription to *L'Esprit nouveau*, of which he owned six volumes, and to Léonce Rosenberg's *Bulletin de L'Effort Moderne*, which he subscribed to from January 1924 until December 1927. According to Stephen Hayward, *L'Esprit nouveau* 'provided an important visual source for [Wadsworth's] contemporary port scenes and a theoretical justification for the compositional techniques he was to adopt in ... the later still-lifes of the mid-twenties' ('Metaphysical Painting in England during the 1920s and Thirties: the Work of Edward Wadsworth, Paul Nash, John Armstrong and Tristram Hillier', unpublished M.A. report, University of London, Courtauld Institute of Art, 1982, p.3, author untraceable, quoted without his permission). He cites, as an example, that triangular compositions were regularly endorsed in this magazine, a comment relevant to 'Regalia'. In 1927 Wadsworth spent three months in Paris where he became acquainted with a number of artists whose work was reproduced in these magazines, thereby gaining immediate access to their work.

L'Esprit nouveau and the *Bulletin de L'Effort Moderne* were both organs of those artists, critics and dealers who were advocating the 'rappel à l'ordre' after the First World War, a movement with which Wadsworth, after his Vorticist phase, appears to have had some sympathy. Indeed one of his paintings, 'Coast Guards' 1927, was reproduced in the *Bulletin* in December 1927 (issue 40 as 'Gardes-Côtes'). The return to the depiction of solid objects in an orderly, precise and clear manner was an important aspect of Wadsworth's work at this time, as indeed it was to his continental colleagues, notably Léger – by whom Wadsworth owned two works of 1928, 'Les Clefs (Composition)' (T 05990) and 'Carte et Pipe' (T 05991), the latter having an affinity with Wadsworth's work of the thirties – Metzinger and Pierre Roy whose surrealistic interiors would have been known to Wadsworth by 1928 and possibly as early as 1926, for Wadsworth painted 'Still-Life' c.1926 (N 05147) in order to demonstrate to Roy the use of tempera (letter from the artist dated 6 September 1942. According to Mrs von Bethmann-Hollweg, 'Still-Life' was painted in 1928, although on stylistic grounds alone the compiler considers that date less likely than 1926). The grouping of Wadsworth with Picasso, Roy and de Chirico was made by Wilenski in 1929 (Wilenski, p.414) and Frank Rutter compared Wadsworth with de Chirico and Metzinger in the same year ('Tempera Paintings Exhibited', *Sunday Times*, 26 May 1929). The work of Metzinger appears to be of particular relevance to 'Regalia', especially 'La Roulette' 1927 (repr. *Bulletin de L'Effort Moderne*, 31 January 1927) which depicts a still-life on a table top before a window overlooking a landscape. Among other objects the still-life comprises a roulette wheel, in the centre, which is placed on top of a green baize cloth, which protrudes beyond the front edge of the table. These aspects may be directly compared with the inclining sundial and the harbour signals chart in 'Regalia'. The roulette wheel is also suggestive of the compass in 'Regalia'. Furthermore, 'La Roulette' is painted predominantly in red and yellow, both keynote colours in T 03398. While Metzinger's picture may not have been a model for 'Regalia', Wadsworth would have known it in reproduction if not in actuality. Other works by Metzinger of some relevance are 'Astrologie' 1927 and 'Allégorie Maritime' 1927 (both repr. *Bulletin de L'Effort Moderne*, 36, June 1927). The latter is particularly of interest since it depicts a still-life comprising an instrument of measurement, among other items, set before the sea.

Although neither Rutter nor Wilenski mentioned the name of Jean Lurçat in their articles, his 'Fruits on a Table' 1927 (repr. *The Paintings of Jean Lurçat*, exhibition catalogue, Alex. Reid and Lefevre, May 1930, n.p.) bears a considerable compositional resemblance to 'Regalia', with its still-life of fruits set out in a basic pyramidal shape upon a table which stands before the sea, the horizon of which is depicted at approximately the same level as in 'Regalia'. Lurçat's application of paint, however, is expressive compared to Wadsworth's precise handling. It is possible that Wadsworth met Lurçat in Paris in 1927 and saw this work in the latter's studio. By 1930 Lurçat was painting still-lifes of tools and objects set in the landscape, as though viewed at close range, an idea markedly similar to Wadsworth's works of the late twenties and the late thirties and forties.

The depiction of still-life at close range, as in 'Regalia', was also favoured by Metzinger, Roy, Herbin and de Chirico for it endowed the objects with a Surrealistic quality, making them seem larger than they actually were. Although Wadsworth employed this strategy, according to Mrs von Bethmann-Hollweg he was not a Surrealist, 'although bewildered critics of his day, unable to "place" him, liked to hang this tag on his work'. De Chirico was also obsessed with notions of measurement and depicted instruments of measurement such as maps, rulers, set squares and clock (see, for example, 'The Melancholy of Departure' 1916, T02309). In the mid-thirties, when Wadsworth began once again to paint marine still-lifes, he regarded the objects as invested with symbolic qualities, but there is no evidence to suggest that he held the same attitude in the late twenties, although this may well have been the case. Such was the state of artistic debate in England at the time that reviewers insisted on the formal qualities of his paintings and Wadsworth's precision and accuracy in setting up and depicting the motif, rather than on any metaphysical or surrealistic intentions. The choice of the marine still-life was personal to Wadsworth. Ships and ports had always been in his repertoire of subjects even during the Vorticist period and he has always enjoyed visiting ports. Indeed during the First World War he had worked on the camouflaging of ships, an occupation recorded in his painting and prints of 'Dazzle Ships'. Wadsworth himself stated in 1933:

At no period has the aspect of things been a main consideration in my painting, although admittedly I have from time to time been stimulated by certain landscapes or objects, the realistic appearance of which I have promptly subdued in order to emphasise qualities which I considered more important. ('The Abstract Painter's Own Explanation', *Studio*, CVI, November 1933, p.275)

While this might imply that Wadsworth was interested in the formal and suggestive qualities of the object portrayed, he also implies that he was interested in qualities beyond naturalistic appearance, as would be the case in Metaphysical or Surrealist painting. In 1943, S.D. Cleveland stated that Wadsworth's fascination with nautical objects resulted from 'their aloof, symbolic and often nostalgic qualities' ('Recent Tempera Paintings', *Studio*, CXXV, June 1943, p.175). In the passage from 'The Abstract Painter's Own Explanation' quoted above, Wadsworth also indicates that he did not hesitate to alter the appearance of things to suit his intentions, a view confirmed by Michael Sévier who wrote, in 1933, in regard to the still-lifes and landscapes of the twenties:

He also realised ... that to confer upon a picture an autonomous and independent existence, he had to consider it as a total and coherent entity, governed only by the laws of harmony, detached from normal laws of nature and surpassing them by a long distance. He understood that in its superior manifestations painting is never imitative (even though it may suggest nature), that it resembles the art of pure music where the arrangement of sounds depends upon their own beauty and never on a more or less successful interpretation of sounds that one perceives in the universe such as, for example, the explosion of a shell, the blast of a hooter, the surf of the waves or the cracking of wood (*Séléction Chronique de la Vie Artistique*, XIII, 'Edward Wadsworth', Antwerp, 1933, p.24)

According to Mrs von Bethmann-Hollweg, however, the objects in 'Regalia' are faithfully reproduced. In regard to any meaning beyond the actuality of the objects little more may be said with certainty other than that the objects depicted are those connected with measurement, navigation and fishing. In 1929 most critics talked in formal terms about Wadsworth's paintings on view at Tooth's. Léonce Rosenberg, writing in the catalogue to this exhibition, exemplified this viewpoint:

To build a painting, the artist starts by choosing and grouping certain elements of the exterior reality; in other words, by synthesis, he draws out of a motive [sic], after having analysed it, the *elements* – colour and forms – necessary to the assemblage of his subject. The passage of the motive to the subject constitutes his aesthetic, the directing principles of which are reason and science. Afterwards, to pass from the subject to the work, he uses an ensemble of means suitable to the expression of his subject.

The composition of 'Regalia' is a basic triangle comprising circular, rectangular and triangular objects. It was carefully drawn in advance of applying the paint using compass and probably a ruler to ensure exactness. Pencil lines remain evident in a number of places and holes remain where the point of a compass has been inserted when mapping out the circular shapes. The equation of Wadsworth's paintings with science and mathematics was frequently remarked upon by the critics in 1929. The fact that 'Regalia' is painted in tempera, like all Wadsworth's paintings after 1921, necessitated careful preplanning and drawing prior to blocking in the colour, for the medium is fast drying and does not permit the mixing of colours or erasure by superimposition of colours. Wadsworth had been introduced to tempera painting as early as 1913 when, under the direction of Roger Fry, he helped to restore the Mantegna paintings at Hampton Court. In 1923, two years after he began to use tempera, he visited Italy, travelling through Tuscany among other places where, according to Hayward (op. cit.), he was particularly impressed by the paintings of Piero with their characteristic ultramarines, emerald greens and reds. Although Wadsworth's paintings prior to 1928 were generally subdued in tone, the paintings of 1928, notably 'Regalia' and 'Parergon', are more brightly coloured, particularly the former which seems directly to reflect the artist's interest in Piero's use of colour, an interest shared with other British artists in this period, such as Ben Nicholson. According to Boyanoski, de Chirico, who was himself a practitioner of tempera painting and was on friendly terms with Wadsworth by 1928, suggested that Wadsworth adopt a rich egg emulsion. This permitted the latter to use more saturated colour (letter from de Chirico to Wadsworth of 8 June 1928, Boyanoski, p.64 and p.71, note 28). Wadsworth's own latter day explanation for adopting stronger colours 'was to avoid dullness and a sort of fake mystery ... Also it seems to me that, as we can't compete with Nature's greatest weapon, the magic of light – our only foil is the magic of colour' (letter to Maxwell Armfield, 5 August 1942, Tate Gallery Archive). According to Mrs von Bethmann-Hollweg, 'Regalia' was considered unsaleable in 1929 because it was 'too loud in colour, therefore offensive ... That E.W. had faith in it is obvious by the fact that it still exists since ... he destroyed whenever he could all the work which he considered for one reason or another unsatisfactory.' Wadsworth's change in palette, as exemplified in 'Regalia', was remarked upon by Wilenski when he wrote in 1929: 'And now we have a further stage (due to a year's residence in Paris) [sic.] in which with an Italian palette enriched by strong scarlet he has rung the changes on a form of architectural still-life based on the experiments of Picasso, Chirico and Roy' (Wilenski, p.414).

Although T 03398 is executed predominantly in tempera, oil paint was also employed for the yellow border which surrounds it. It is not entirely clear whether the artist considered this to be a part of the work. According to Mrs von Bethmann-Hollweg he did regard it as part of the work but she also states that he may have painted it in lieu of a slip, because it was his practice, at this time, to frame all his works with a slip. The oil paint, she suggests, may have been a last minute expedient. However, Wadsworth was careful to ensure that this border reproduced the colour of the parapet of the terrace, perhaps indicating that the border was more significant than simply a framing prop. Indeed, it may describe the edge of a window frame such as that depicted in 'Parergon', the painting which most closely resembles 'Regalia', where the window frame is painted in two parallel, vertical stripes of green and yellow, the yellow being adjacent to the window opening. Never-theless the fact that it is painted in oil, not tempera, is a curious anomaly although oil being more durable than tempera, and the area in question surrounding the edge of the painting, Wadsworth may have decided to paint the edge in oil paint where it was vulnerable to damage from the frame itself. Since 'Regalia' was not illustrated in any publications during the artist's lifetime it is impossible to establish whether the border was an integral part of the work, although 'Wings of the Morning' appears to have a border, since it is reproduced in the Colnaghi exhibition catalogue with a substantial border, and is reproduced in Wilenski's article cited above with only a slight border. (Mrs von Bethmann-Hollweg doubts that it has a border but, since any possible border is covered by a fillet, it is not possible to tell without unframing the work.) It is not known, however, whether Wadsworth supervised the reproduction of his work in this article. Therefore, although it is impossible to be certain of Wadsworth's attitude towards the question of the border, on balance the compiler considers it likely that the border has both descriptive and practical functions.

Tempera was not widely used in England when Wadsworth began to employ it but during the course of the twenties The Society of Mural Decorators and Painters in Tempera, of which Wadsworth was a member, expanded. In 1930 Maxwell Armfield published a *Manual of Tempera Painting* summarising the techniques of Cennini's *Il Libro dell'Arte*. In the foreward to the *Manual*, Sir Charles Holmes equates the tempera revival with anti-Modernism but Wadsworth did not regard himself in this light. It is more likely that his choice of medium resulted from a desire to produce precisely painted images, for in his book of press cuttings (Tate Gallery Archive) he marked a number of passages which describe the possibilities of hard graver-like precision offered by tempera. On 1 November 1945 he wrote to Maxwell Armfield stating that the revival of tempera painting was the result of 'a nostalgia on the part of certain temperaments for some kind of basis of painting, a physical and esoteric aim of producing well-made pictures' (Tate Gallery Archive), thereby indicating that a further reason had to do with the actual craft of painting, a view with which de Chirico would have sympathised.

Wadsworth was aware of the fragility of tempera and the need to protect it and to this end he frequently applied a layer of wax to the surface. 'Regalia' is no exception but most of the wax has been removed since acquisition. In 1935 he wrote to Maxwell Armfield for advice on the protection of the paintings he was executing for the *Queen Mary* and stated that 'Wax is unsuitable as it collects dust and varnish is unsuitable as it cannot be applied until a year or so after and the protective covering – whatever it is – has to be applied within a week of the picture being finished' (letter of 20

November 1935, Tate Gallery Archive). Clearly Wadsworth did not regard the wax surface as important to the luminosity of the work but simply as an (inadequate) means of protection.

The question of the provenance of T 03398 is problematic. In his photographic record (Tate Gallery Archive) the artist wrote that the painting was 'in possession of Dudley Tooth Esq' but it is unclear from this inscription whether Tooth owned the work or had it on consignment. The photographic record of Arthur Tooth and Sons does not include a photograph of 'Regalia', which it would have done had the gallery sold the work. Nor does the gallery have any record of consignment in 1937 when it was re-exhibited. It is possible, therefore, that Dudley Tooth himself owned the painting since, in that case, it would not have appeared in the gallery's records. Mrs von Bethmann-Hollweg writes that

E.W. stated that it was in the possession of Dudley Tooth but he gave no date to this note. The work was certainly at some time during its earlier days with Tooth's and it is likely that the note was meant to mean the Tooth Gallery, which housed it when it was not on show elsewhere. I owned it for roughly 34 years, though I cannot be absolutely accurate about the date when I took it over from my mother, who had the care of all E.W.'s pictures after his death.

She also asserts that Boyanoski is wrong in stating that in c.1933 the painting belonged to Mrs F.C. van Duzer, a notable collector of Wadsworth's paintings in this period.

The title of T 03398 is a word normally used to describe the emblems and insignia of a king or queen which are used at coronations, such as crown, orb, sceptre, spurs, bracelet and chain. In Britain and elsewhere such royal ornaments are often displayed in a pyramidal arrangement, as they are in 'Regalia', and a number of items depicted in T 03398 seem broadly to correspond to the forms of the British regalia. For example, the glass fishing float relates to the orb, the auger to the sceptre, the surveyor's chain to the royal chain, the inclining sundial to the spurs. However Mrs von Bethmann-Hollweg denies that the artist had such associations in mind. In commenting on the significance of the title, she writes:

Wadsworth was a very international person and the regalia herein depicted is one belonging to the life of men upon or by the sea no matter where they happen to live. The regalia belongs to them and has nothing to do with the British Crown. Each of these objects has its practical value to those who have to do with the great waters of the world.

Edward Arthur Walton 1860–1922

T 03447 **Berwickshire Field-workers** 1884

Oil on canvas $35\frac{7}{8} \times 24\frac{1}{16}$ (914 × 609)
Inscribed 'E·A·Walton·84·' b.r.
Purchased from the Fine Art Society (Grant-in-Aid) 1982

Prov: Christie Brothers (latterly owners of Messrs Guthrie and Wells, Glasgow furnishers and stained glass manufacturers)

The field-workers are wearing head-dresses of cane and cotton known as 'uglies'. These bonnets were worn on both sides of the Border for protection against the sun. A piece of material was attached to the bonnet to protect the wearer's back.

Helen Weller in the E.A. Walton exhibition catalogue, Bourne Fine Art, Edinburgh, 1981, wrote

The subject matter [in Walton's work] is incidental, he was essentially a painter of atmosphere and the figures are used as punctuation in the composition or points of light in the chromatic scheme.

Stephen Willats b.1943

T03795 **Are you good enough for the Cha Cha Cha?** 1982

Collage and assemblage on paper, three
panels, each $58 \times 32 \times 2\frac{3}{4}$
($1473 \times 813 \times 70$); overall dimensions
when displayed $100 \times 185 \times 2\frac{3}{4}$
($2540 \times 4700 \times 70$)
Inscribed 'DO YOU THINK' t.l.,
'YOU ARE GOOD ENOUGH' b.
towards r. and 'FOR THE CHA CHA
CHA' t. towards r.; also with numerous
further inscriptions as part of the work
Purchased from Lisson Gallery (Grant-in-
Aid) 1983

Exh: *Inside the Night, Stephen Willats*, Lisson
Gallery, January 1983 (not numbered);
Under Cover, Stephen Willats, Arnolfini
Gallery, Bristol, May–June 1983; *New Art
at the Tate Gallery*, Tate Gallery,
September–October 1983 (not numbered,
repr.); *Striking Back, Stephen Willats*,
Mappin Art Gallery, Sheffield, March–
April 1986 (not numbered)

Lit: Christiane Bergob, 'Sprechen Sie Cha
Cha?', *Kunstforum*, CXI, May 1983,
pp.159–62, detail of panel repr. p.162;
Stephen Willats, 'Another City', *Studio
International*, CLXXXXVI, November
1983, p.30; Stephen Willats, *Means of
Escape*, exhibition catalogue, Rochdale Art
Gallery, 1984, p.6 (repr., detail of element
of collage, photograph of figures); Richard
Francis, 'Stephen Willats', *Stephen
Willats, Three Essays*, ICA/Mappin Art
Gallery, Sheffield, 1986, pp.8, 10–13
(repr. p.10, detail of each panel pp.11–13)
Also repr: Stephen Willats, *Cha Cha Cha*,
1982, details, elements of collage,
inscriptions and photographs of figures

This work is one of a group of four, shown together at
the Lisson Gallery in an exhibition entitled *Inside the
Night* in 1983, which were conceived and created with
the founders of groups of 'alternative' people who met
regularly in rented London venues. The other subjects
included androgynous women, a group who met at
Model Dwellings, an electronic futurist club, and a
group of mohicans who met at the Anarchy Centre, a
derelict ballroom in Hammersmith.

Willats had recently completed a work with a group
of young people in West London (Pat Purdy and the
glue sniffers' camp) where he had developed a conceptual model of the relationships between a normative
and therefore dominant social group with specific
behaviour patterns and an anarchic sub-group which
maintained a partly ritualised segregation through habits or actions which were regarded as taboo. Willats
recognised the creative potential in this second group
and their need to establish a 'capsule within a deter-
ministic society'. He had begun to look for new symbols
of this relationship and met, by chance, the two women
who participated in 'From the day into Night and the
Night into the day'. Their club allowed them freedom to
express their sensibilities, in this case their androgyny, a
concept of life in the future which they called futurism.
The work established an area of interest concerning
their relationship between night and day and a working
method.

Willats later met the main protagonists of the Cha
Cha Club, Scarlet and Michael, by chance in the studio
of a friend he was also working with. They introduced
him to the matt-black painted railway arches in Hungerford Lane below Charing Cross station where on one
night per week they operated a club with a strict admis-
sion policy typified by Scarlet's question 'Are you good
enough for the Cha Cha?'. Willats recalls this as a particularly exciting moment in the punk movement's
establishment of its own cultural boundaries. Several
such clubs existed; the Cha Cha was among the most
well known and its visitors included George O'Dowd
(Boy George, the leader of the popular music group,
Culture Club). The club was observed in operation over
several months, virtually its whole life. Willats began
fearfully, sitting in the corner and observing, continued
by explaining and then photographing the participants
and completed the work by collecting the debris from
the floor and taking it back to his studio.

He had decided to work with the founders of the club
and to treat them as creators of a particular situation
rather than portray the club itself. He therefore adopted
his usual procedure of tape-recordings and discussions
followed by a collaborative arrangement of material on
the panels. The purpose of this arrangement is to create
a work of art and this determines the topology of the
relationship; it allows the person working with the artist
to volunteer aspects of their life that they consider

relevant to the making of the work. The organisation of materials on the panel tends towards what Willats calls the 'democratic surface' where no particular view of reality is suggested by the predominance of one element. In addition the layering of types of material such as handwriting, objects and photographs tends to direct the work towards a more 'natural reality', that is towards a varied and confused position. The collaborators guided the creation of the work and had the right of veto but Willats remains the artist in the relationship. The subjects, for example, at Willats's prompting, collected household rubbish and incorporated this where they thought it useful in their panels. The panels reflect both the home and club life of the subjects and the triptych arrangement suggests three different aspects of the club's organisation.

The work's presentation in the gallery reflects the moment of its creation, the 'spontaneous tackiness' of the remnants of punk culture. Thus the wall around the work is roughly painted yellow and matt black in two overlapping coats and the panels were made quickly and originally shown unframed. Willats has agreed to the design of the frames for museum display and storage.

This work was important in that it offered Willats the opportunity to embody the phenomenon of self-organisation in recent youth culture that had interested him for almost ten years in a purposeful way and it introduced him to the participants in his next series of work.

In a telephone conversation with the compiler (15 July 1986), the artist commented:

> More than any other context that I had examined at the time it was a catalysis that embodied the sensibility of the moment which was influential in the whole post-punk movement. I used it to challenge the audience with the rawness of the moment which was spontaneous, tacky and black.

Gillian Wise-Ciobotaru b.1936

T 03776 **Relief Constructed from Unicursal Curve No.2** 1967

Construction of aluminium and perspex on wood $32 \times 32 \times 1\frac{5}{8}$ ($813 \times 813 \times 40$)
Not inscribed
Transferred from the Victoria and Albert Museum 1983

Prov: Purchased from the artist by the Department of Circulation, Victoria and Albert Museum, 1968 (Circ. 892–1968)

Exh: *Gillian Wise*, Axiom Gallery, September 1967 (12); *Four Artists: Reliefs, Construction and Drawings*, Victoria and Albert Museum, 1967 (29, repr.)

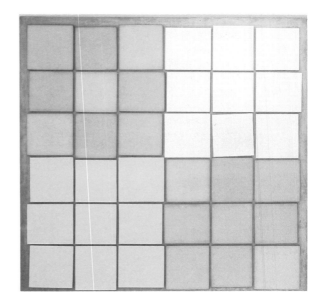

The Victoria and Albert Museum also purchased five drawings, all of 1967–8, from the artist at the same time (now in their print room). The materials of this relief are described in their records as 'Aluminium, Cobex and perspex on Dural'.

Francis Derwent Wood 1871–1926

T 03777 **Torso of a Girl** 1903

Plaster $42\frac{1}{2} \times 8\frac{1}{2} \times 12\frac{1}{4}$ ($1080 \times 216 \times 312$)
Inscribed 'F. Derwent Wood 1903' on r. of base

Transferred from the Victoria and Albert Museum 1983

Prov: Presented to the Victoria and Albert Museum by Mrs Derwent Wood 1927 (A. 52–1927)

Exh: *International Society of Sculptors, Painters and Carvers*, New Gallery, January–March 1904 (351); *Franco-British Exhibition*, 1908 (1411); *Works by the late Sir Hamo Thornycroft, R.A., and F. Derwent Wood, R.A.*, RA winter 1927 (168)

Repr: *Art Journal*, 1904, p.51; Eric G. Underwood, *A Short History of English Sculpture*, 1933, pl.34

The sculpture was previously catalogued as 6128, and described in error as having been transferred to the Tate Gallery in 1952.

Bryan Wynter 1915–1975

T 03362 **Saja** 1969

Oil and acrylic on canvas 83⅞ × 66⅜ (2130 × 1685)
Inscribed on back of canvas 'Bryan Wynter/"Saja" 1969/84 × 66'
Purchased from the New Art Centre (Grant-in-Aid) 1982

Prov: Monica Wynter (the artist's widow) 1975; New Art Centre 1982

Exh: *Painting and Sculpture 1970 (Alexander MacKenzie, John Skelton and Bryan Wynter)*, City Art Gallery, Plymouth, May–June 1970 (92); *Bryan Wynter*, Exhibition Hall, Devonshire House, Exeter University, April–May 1971 (5); *Bryan Wynter 1915–1975*, Falmouth School of Art, November–December 1975 (5); *Bryan Wynter 1915–1975, Paintings, Kinetics and Works on Paper*, Hayward Gallery, August 1976 (70); *Bryan Wynter 1964–1974*, New Art Centre, March–April 1982 (no catalogue no.); *St. Ives 1939–64, Twenty-Five Years of Painting, Sculpture and Pottery*, Tate Gallery, February–April 1985 (230, repr.)
Also repr: As a postcard for Bryan Wynter Exhibition at the New Art Centre 1982

Mrs Monica Wynter provided the following note on her husband's painting (letter of 2 October 1982):

'Saja' was one of three paintings completed in 1969 – his productivity during the late sixties and early seventies was very low for a variety of reasons, one being a kind of loss of confidence or an uncertainty over how he should develop images based on themes to do with the movement of water, which so preoccupied him.

It was painted in Trewarvereth Studio, Newlyn – originally [the studio of] Stanhope Forbes, which is where he worked on his paintings. As always, he brought paintings from there back to the house. We were now living at Treverven House . . . [The Wynters moved there in 1964.] He liked to see paintings in a different situation from where he painted them, sometimes hanging one in the bedroom, so that he could see it in that first moment of awakening, when the eye is not prejudiced by its previous acquaintance with the work. But this looking at the painting in the house was part of the "finishing off" process and essential to him, to be sure that the painting was indeed "finished" or ended. In April of 1969 we had a joint family holiday (his brother Eric and his family) in Northern Spain on the Atlantic coast and in the mountains inland – Los Picos de Europas. There was a lot of canoeing, exploration and photographing – colour slides – of the rivers in this area.

Patrick Heron, a close friend of Wynter's, wrote the introduction to his 1976 retrospective exhibition catalogue and he paid attention to Wynter's great interest in water:

. . . Wynter was fascinated by coasts and rivers and was an intrepid canoeist. There was not an inch of the savagely rocky coast extending from St Ives to Land's End and round into Mount's Bay which he had not investigated intimately by canoe; and hardly a river or stream in Cornwall he had not explored from its source down. Wherever he went – Wales, Scotland, the North of Spain – the canoes were carried on top of the car.

Mrs Wynter's letter continued:

I can't say now whether 'Saja' was begun before this holiday, but its title is the name of one of the rivers [along which] he and Eric canoed, as is 'Deva', one of the other paintings from 1969 of similar theme, but very different in colour and 'feel' ['Deva' is actually given the completion date of 1970] . . . the title ['Saja'] was given on completion. [Bryan Wynter's usual practice was to give his work a title only after the painting was finished.] 'Saja' has 'no direct reference to a particular landscape, *but* the paintings ['Saja' and 'Deva' for example] do express his enjoyment of water, rivers and all his activities connected with water, his preoccupation with the movement of water as well as the experience of these particular rivers. This interest in moving water, and his enjoyment of canoeing, were not pursued as a search for a 'theme' for paintings – I get the impression that some people get hold of this mistaken idea – but these activities were a part of his total personality, just as his paintings, and indeed anyone's paintings, were an expression of his total personality.

Mrs Wynter felt that the note which Bryan Wynter wrote in January 1960 for Alan Bowness and which was printed in the catalogue for Wynter's posthumous retrospective exhibition at the Hayward Gallery in 1976 was helpful in explaining the connection between a painting and its source material:

My paintings are non-representational but linked to the products of nature in as much as they are developed according to laws within themselves and are a static record of the processes that have brought them about.

A stream finds its way over rocks. The force of the stream and the quality of the rocks determine the stream's bed . . . There are no streams or rocks in my paintings but a comparable process of dynamic versus static elements has attended their development and brought about their final form.

T 03363 **Green Confluence** 1974

Oil on canvas $71\frac{3}{4} \times 47\frac{3}{4}$ (1825 × 1215)
Inscribed on back of canvas 'Green Confluence/(June)/72″ × 48″'
Purchased from the New Art Centre (Grant-in-Aid) 1982

Prov: Monica Wynter (the artist's widow) 1975; New Art Centre 1982

Exh: *Bryan Wynter 1915–1975*, Falmouth School of Art, November–December 1975 (8); *Exhibition of work by Roger Hilton and Bryan Wynter*, Penwith Society of Arts, St Ives, February–March 1976 (6); *Bryan Wynter 1915–1975, Paintings, Kinetics and Works on Paper*, Hayward Gallery, August 1976 (75, repr. in col.); *Bryan Wynter 1964–1974*, New Art Centre, March–April 1982 (no catalogue number)

Lit: Patrick Heron, introduction to 'Bryan Wynter', New Art Centre exhibition catalogue, 1982

Mrs Monica Wynter has provided the following note on her husband's painting (letter of 2 October 1982):

I can't say when the painting was started, but it was brought home, hung and declared finished in August or September 1974. In the last few years he produced very few paintings, partly as a result of working for three years to produce a commissioned show of mobiles (IMOOS) for Leslie [Waddington], (exhibition held October 1974 – Waddington Gallery) and partly because he felt a conflict having to produce a series of mobiles which for him had come to the end of their creative possibilities and a desire to get on with his painting – painting was always more important to him than the mobiles – but at the same time feeling he wanted to make some change in his paintings too. During mobile/painting years, say 1969 to 1974, he had made some paintings of a more 'hard edge' nature, still using the meander or confluence motif, but somehow more closely related to the kind of forms that he used in the mobiles. 'Green Confluence' is a move back towards a softer, more fluid (perhaps *not* a good choice of word in this context!) kind of painting, where the colour is more diffuse and not contained in definite boundaries. This softer, more 'landscapey' approach to colour is also apparent in the few very late gouaches he did towards the end of 1974 and the first weeks of 1975.

Bryan Wynter died suddenly on 11 February 1975, and 'Green Confluence' was his last painting.

Patrick Heron wrote an introduction to a Wynter exhibition catalogue for the New Art Centre, March–April 1982 and devoted most of his text to a consideration of the sort of shapes and marks most identified with the artist. The last phrase of this introduction draws the reader's attention to 'the wonderful blue-green light which emanates so steadily from the softer, almost furry touches of his last canvas, "Green Confluence" 1974'.

The Print Collection

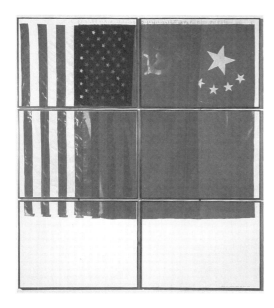

Vito Acconci born 1940

P 07639 **3 Flags for 1 Space and**
(i)–(vi) **6 Regions** 1979–81

Six sheet aquatint 95⅝ × 73¼ (2430 × 1860)
overall, printed by Nancy Anello at Crown
Point Press, Oakland, California, and
published by them in an edition of 25
Inscribed 'V A 79–81' and '2/25' and
'3 FLAGS FOR ONE SPACE AND 6
REGIONS' b.r. on P 07639(iv); impressed
with·the printer's and publisher's stamp
Purchased from Crown Point Press
(Grant-in-Aid) 1982

Acconci had made his first etchings at Crown Point
Press in 1977 and returned there in 1979 to make three
large pieces, '20ft Ladder for Any Size Wall', '2 Wings
for Wall and Person' and the present work. The use of
multiplied sheets, eight, twelve and six respectively,
was the result of Acconci's thinking in terms of making
etchings more like his installations and consequently
extending their scale far beyond conventional etching
sizes. Acconci has written:

> My tendency has been to use prints either as a
> summariser (the image 'puts something in print,'
> finishes it off) or as a precursor (the image announces,
> for me, to me, a future interest – the image, literally,

is 'etched' into my mind, to be dealt with later – the
image stands there, waving like a flag, beckoning like
an advertisement, urging me on) (letter to the
compiler, 18 July 1986).

P 07639 is a colour aquatint of the American, Russian
and Chinese flags hanging vertically and overlapping
each other; the image refers to the dominating presence
of the 'super-powers' and their potentially deadly
rivalry for terrestrial space. It is related to an installation
entitled 'Let's Pretend This Is An Apparatus For A
Political Kidnapping' (shown in the Kunstverein, Hamburg 1979) in which three flags hang side by side along
a fishing rod fixed to the back of a winged bicycle, to
whose handlebars a pram is attached, the whole construction being strung across the gallery space from
high on one wall. The flags are the Russian and American flags, both painted white, with a white flag of
truce. In an installation made in 1980 and titled 'Instant
House' four walls covered with American flags lie on
the floor and when the viewer sits on a swing in the
centre they rise to surround him with a house-shape,
the outer walls of which are covered with the Russian
flag. This extends the ideas in the present work by
literally containing the viewer, while hiding from him
the 'colour' of his house's outer walls and thus pointing
out the interchangeability of the powers represented by
the flags. Acconci is concerned with the space of the
gallery and with the work of art (the image) as a vehicle
of communication – he uses the words 'space' and
'vehicle' as well as using various literal forms of both as
active parts of his installations:

> ... the vehicle takes on the function of 'image'; the
> space, rather than *being* an image, is in the position
> of *having* an image, the space is 'embarrassed' by the
> imposition of ornament as symbol or, more
> precisely, by the ornament's announcement – almost
> with a fanfare – that symbolising can happen here:
> form, then, is separated from content, content is
> freed from form, allowing, e.g. an institutionalised
> form to be intruded on by (and to be the bearer of)
> radical content (the artist in *Cover*, II, no.1, 1980,
> pp.22–5).

This entry has been approved by the artist.

P08210 depicts the dark forms of monumental trees rising high above the ground. In an interview in the *Fine Art Letter*, 6, May 1982, p.17 Ackroyd stated that the impression he receives in this avenue is 'almost like a cathedral'. He also indicated that

> The trees at Avington were hand planted. They do excite me. I like the idea that the people who planted that avenue knew they would never live to see it in this kind of glory. It's the ultimate in unselfishness ... The people who planted these things for us, because we are seeing them, they have a feeling of timelessness about them.

This entry has been approved by the artist.

Norman Ackroyd born 1938

P08210 **The Avenue at Avington** 1982

> From 'Itchen Water: poems by Jeremy Hooker and etchings by Norman Ackroyd'
> Aquatint $3\frac{3}{4} \times 4\frac{5}{8}$ (950×117) on paper $12\frac{1}{2} \times 9\frac{3}{8}$ (317×239), printed and published by Winchester School of Art Press
> Inscribed 'Norman Ackroyd 82' b.r. and 'The Avenue at Avington' and '59/90'
> Transferred from the Library 1983

P08210 was printed to accompany the book *Itchen Water* which was published in a limited edition as follows: the first fifty copies numbered I to L contained ten initialled original etchings plus six artist's proofs and four presentation copies; one hundred copies numbered 1 to 100 with tipped in reproductions and one initialled original etching. P08210 was inserted into copy number 77 and is signed rather than initialled.

Itchen Water contains poems by Jeremy Hooker evoking locations in the Winchester area and impressions of natural phenomena. Each poem is accompanied by a reproduction of an etching by Norman Ackroyd. These images are not illustrations of the poems but parallel them. 'The Avenue at Avington' appears both as an inserted original etching and as a reproduction facing page 14. It accompanies a poem entitled 'Avington: the Avenue at Dawn'.

Avington is approximately five miles north east of Winchester and has been the subject of several prints by Ackroyd. The artist has stated, in answer to questions posed by the compiler in February 1986, that P08210 is a 'fairly true representation of this site' and that he drew on the plate 'almost entirely' on location.

P07811

John Baldessari born 1931

P07808 **Black Dice** 1982
–07816,
P07853   Nine etchings with squatint, each $6\frac{3}{8} \times 8$ (162×203) on Velin Arches paper $16\frac{1}{2} \times 19\frac{3}{4}$ (420×502), printed by Peter Kneubühler, Zurich, and one black and white photograph $8 \times 9\frac{1}{4}$ (203×235). The portfolio published by Peter Blum Editions, Zurich and New York
Each inscribed 'BALDESSARI' b.r. and '31/35'; P07853 not inscribed
Purchased from Peter Blum Editions (Grant-in-Aid) 1983

'Black Dice' is a set of nine etchings intended to be framed separately but shown together arranged in three rows of three. These prints are accompanied by a black and white photograph, a reproduction of a National

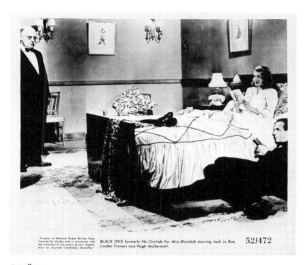

P 07853

Screen Service Corporation publicity still from the film of the same title made in 1948. The film was made in Britain and originally called *No Orchids for Miss Blandish*, from the story of that name by James Hadley Chase. The photograph, a piece of artificial action artificially stilled for the camera, is typical of the kind of source material Baldessari uses. He frequently uses 'found' photographs, or shots taken at random or by others to his instructions and puts them together according to a system of his own unrelated to their meaning or to any narrative. The format of 'Black Dice' is related to the kind of storyboards made for the preliminary planning of a film but it is made up of nine equal divisions of the original photograph. Baldessari had the sections blown up to the size of etching plate he planned to use, then drew over the photo-etched images using a mixture of soft-ground etching, sugar-lift and aquatint, introducing colour in an arbitrary way. He left wide borders on the prints so that, though their arrangement implies 'piecing together', it also implies unseen areas linking them. The image can still be deciphered though the work on the plates has disguised the image of the source photograph, which now takes on the role of a key to the work itself. It shows, in banal visual terms, a moment of ominous significance. It is an awkward composition in which the figures are placed at the edges of the frame, a satin bed cover with a gown hung over it and a patterned cushion beyond dominating the centre of the image. A girl sits in bed evidently feigning 'normality' in a most unnatural way; a man stands at the left, motionless but evidently posing a threat of some kind, and another man holding a gun hides – though evidently is not hidden – at the right. Baldessari's isolation and transformation of the compositional elements, separated out by his division of the photograph, refer to the use of one visual language as a

code for another, rather as the still refers to the film itself, in which all is obviously made clear in the usual language of mystery narratives.

Georg Baselitz born 1938

P 07737 **Rebel** 1965

Etching with drypoint and aquatint
$12\frac{5}{8} \times 9\frac{1}{4}$ (320 × 235) on paper $17\frac{7}{8} \times 12\frac{5}{8}$
(440 × 320), printed and published by the artist
Inscribed 'Baselitz 65' b.r. and '31/60'
Purchased from Maximilian Verlag, Sabine Knust, Munich (Grant-in-Aid) 1982

Repr: Fred Jahn, *Baselitz Peintre-Graveur*, I, Bern–Berlin, 1983, p.44; Siegfried Gohr, *Georg Baselitz–Druckgraphik 1963–83*, Munich, 1984, p.77

P 07738 **Untitled** 1965

Etching with open bite $12\frac{1}{4} \times 9\frac{5}{8}$ (310 × 245) on Richard de Bas paper $26\frac{3}{8} \times 19\frac{7}{8}$ (670 × 499), printed and published by the artist
Inscribed 'Baselitz 65' b.r. and '13/20'
Purchased from Maximilian Verlag, Sabine Knust, Munich (Grant-in-Aid) 1982

P 07738

Repr: Fred Jahn, *Baselitz Peintre-Graveur*, I, Bern–Berlin, 1983, p.39; Siegfried Gohr, *Georg Baselitz–Druckgraphik 1963–83*, Munich, 1984, p.71

P 07739 **Untitled (with Dog and Axe)** 1967

Etching and drypoint $13\frac{1}{8} \times 9\frac{5}{8}$ (334 × 245) on Richard de Bas paper $26\frac{1}{2} \times 20$ (672 × 509), printed and published by the artist
Inscribed 'Baselitz 67' b.r. and '7/20'
Purchased from Maximilian Verlag,

Sabine Knust, Munich (Grant-in-Aid) 1982
Repr: Fred Jahn, *Baselitz Peintre-Graveur*, I, Bern–Berlin, 1983, p.91

Unless otherwise stated all statements attributed to the artist in this and the following entries have been made in letters from Herr Detlev Gretenkort of 27 June and 10 August 1984 reporting answers by the artist to questions posed by the compiler. Herr Gretenkort is the artist's secretary.

P 07737 and P 07738 are etchings on the theme of the 'neuer Typ', a subject Baselitz explored in a variety of media between 1965 and 1966. P 07737 is closely related to a drawing entitled 'Hero' (repr. *Georg Baselitz Zeichnungen 1958–83*, exhibition catalogue, Kunstmuseum, Basel, March–May 1984, pl.64) and to a painting of the same name as P 07737 also in the collection (T 03442, see entry in this catalogue). The 'neuer Typ' (new man) represents a regenerated, restructured youth generally clad in battledress, looking with an air of ecstasy towards the future. The suggestion of the crucifixion and of a scarred landscape is typical of these works and indicate a legacy of Baselitz's earlier 'Pandemonium' pictures, which have been linked, in terms of source imagery, to the art of the insane and, in other respects, to the work of European artists of the fifties such as Fautrier and Wols. The two 'Pandemonium' manifestos which Baselitz issued in 1961 and 1962 express the frustration of working in Germany at a time of cultural impoverishment. The tone of the manifestos is often violent, sexual, and shocking and represents rebelliousness and anger. The 'Rebel' works emerged some three years later and represent a less aggressive approach to revolution. Richard Calvocoressi points out that

> The emergence of a mythic figuration in Baselitz's paintings was not a political act, although it is possible to recognise in the striding, monumental figure of the *neuer Typ* elements of both Fascist and Socialist Realist heroic iconography. However, the young pioneer in baggy battledress surrounded by attributes . . . is, as Gunter Gercken has pointed out, 'a peaceful fighter, a green hero, a partisan against war, armed not with a machine gun but with a paintbrush and palette' (*Georg Baselitz Paintings 1960–83*, exhibition catalogue, Whitechapel Art Gallery, September–October 1983, p.13).

Baselitz regards the rebel as an antihero who holds in his left hand a bag with a paintbrush and in his right hand 'an instrument of torture, made of a stone to squeeze the fingers'. The objects such as the fallen flag indicate 'a negative pathetic' and are signs of social disintegration. In P 07738, according to Baselitz, the figure is portrayed supporting a house in his right hand in order to 'protect the house against destruction'. The wing-like configuration behind the figure represents a tree stump. Although the artist states that there is no specific source for the rebel works they may be closely related to prints by northern Mannerist artists which he admires, in particular the work of Goltzius and Flotner. One work by Flotner (repr. *Georg Baselitz: Ein neuer Typ. Bilder 1965/66*, exhibition catalogue, Galerie Neuendorf, Hamburg, December 1973–January 1974, n.p.) seems especially close.

P 07739 is one of a series of prints depicting woodmen, huntsmen and animals in the landscape. Here the dog and the woodmen are camouflaged within the landscape so that the landscape becomes almost anthropomorphic. In the first 'Pandemonium' manifesto, Baselitz refers to 'Anthropomorphic pot-bellied putty rocks (without Archimboldi) ... Redon in the fleece of a one-eyed sheep, in the garden where the soft-leaved plants have faces' (Whitechapel Art Gallery exhibition catalogue, pp.23–4). The camouflage effect anticipates the so-called fracture paintings of 1967–9. According to the artist the woodmen refer 'to the so-called "Grünen", that are woodpartisans in the Russian Civil War'. He also states that they are neither asleep nor dead. Calvocoressi (ibid., p.14) writes that, 'The verdant, rustic world of the fracture paintings reflects Baselitz's total isolation from society' for in 1966 he moved from Berlin to the village of Osthofen, near Worms. Many of these works represent idyllic scenes but Baselitz's reference to the Russian Civil War may denote an underlying violence and rebellion. The axe is an instrument of death as well as a tool of trade.

This entry has been approved by the artist.

P 07779 **Eagle** 1981

from the series 'Sixteen Red and Black Woodcuts' 1981–2

Woodcut 25½ × 19½ (647 × 497) on offset paper 33⅞ × 24 (858 × 609), printed and published by the artist in an edition of 12
Inscribed 'Baselitz 82' b.r.
Purchased from Waddington Galleries (Grant-in-Aid) 1982

P 07780 **Head** 1982

from the series 'Sixteen Red and Black Woodcuts' 1981–2
Woodcut 25⅝ × 19¾ (651 × 502) on offset paper 33⅞ × 24⅛ (859 × 611), printed and published by the artist in an edition of 15
Inscribed 'Baselitz 82' b.r.
Purchased from Waddington Galleries (Grant-in-Aid) 1982

Repr: Siegfried Gohr, *Georg Baselitz – Druckgraphik 1963–83*, Munich, 1984, p.152

P 07779 and P 07780, from the series 'Sixteen Red and Black Woodcuts', are inverted images of an eagle and a head respectively. The eagle is an image found in a number of Baselitz's paintings from 1971 onwards. P 07780 is the first in the series and is printed in both red and black together; all the other prints in the series were printed in single tones, in the case of P 07779 five in brown and red-brown and twelve in black. P 07779 is a black version. Both P 07780 and P 07779 have been printed from two blocks. Baselitz has stated that he used red and black because they are traditional to the medium. In place of ink he has employed oil paint which when passed through the press causes the oil to bleed and to discolour the raised areas on the block. The use of red and black together in P 07780 was intended to create 'a doughy surface' in this area 'up to the white splintered contour'. As with all Baselitz's work since 1969 the images have been inverted so as to render insignificant a literal interpretation of the image in the quest for pure art. Accordingly the images have no symbolic meaning for the artist. Thus while a line may describe an image it is primarily emancipated from its descriptive role and becomes detached from the printed background.

Lately Baselitz has been making woodcuts and linocuts more than etchings. In an interview with Rainer Michael Mason (*Georg Baselitz, Gravures 1963–83*, exhibition catalogue, Cabinet des Estampes, Musée d'Art et d'Histoire, Geneva, June–September 1984, p.xxvi) Baselitz stated . . .

> when you are making etchings, working on copper or zinc plates, a certain concentration is demanded, a certain.isolation, almost singularity. One is a strange man when one scratches into these metal plates, and sometimes I am scared. I sought then to turn towards a more open object, to take a more open material. And, quite simply, to treat it generously, which etching or drypoint do not permit.

Baselitz relates his recent preference for woodcut and linocut to his practice as a sculptor. 'Sculpture is a very aggressive act. The same is true for woodcut and linocut' (ibid.).

This entry has been approved by the artist.

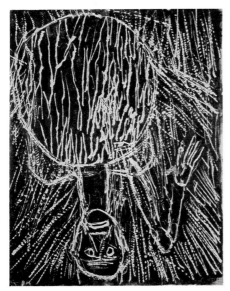

P 07998　**Drummer** 1982

Linocut 79⅛ × 59⅜ (2010 × 1508), printed and published by the artist in an edition of 10

Inscribed 'Baselitz' b.r. and '12.XII 82' and 'Nr.9'
Purchased from Maximilian Verlag, Sabine Knust, Munich (Grant-in-Aid) 1984

P 07998 is a large linocut. By employing the large format since 1977 Baselitz has broken with the convention of the cabinet print. In the interview cited in the entry above Baselitz stated that . . .

> the execution of the large format print requires the gestural, the corporal-gestural, in order to become master of such surfaces. It is not a matter of concepts or constructions which remain in the field of vision close to the face, as is the case with prints and drawings. The pictures have another origin, another basis. One works on surfaces not on projections. It is not indispensable that prints have a smaller space, that they are meanly arranged. Indeed I have tried to overcome that in my linocuts because their surfaces are very expansive.

Baselitz considers that the large scale allows the line to be liberated from its descriptive role and that the woodcut and the linocut eliminate the figure–ground relationship. These issues have been concerns in his paintings. Furthermore, relief printing is more flexible, especially on a large scale, than intaglio. He also saw in the large format an opportunity 'to schematize the pattern I use to make a picture. I wanted to show, in a very simple way, mostly in black and white, the model I use to make a painting. It is a demonstration of my method' (Henry Geldzahler, 'Georg Baselitz', *Interview*, XIV, April 1984, pp.83–4).

P 07798 is printed in brown. The drummer, according to Baselitz, is not a traditional but a symbolic figure 'signifying aggressiveness'.

This entry has been approved by the artist.

John Bellany born 1942

P 07901　**Death Knell for John Knox** 1972

Etching 18⅝ × 19¾ (473 × 500) on paper watermarked 'Arches France' 37⅞ × 29½ (955 × 750) printed by Jack Shirreff, Westbury and published by the artist
Inscribed 'John Bellany 72' b.r. and 'Death Knell for John Knox' bottom centre and '3/23'
Purchased from Monika Kinley (Grant-in-Aid) 1983

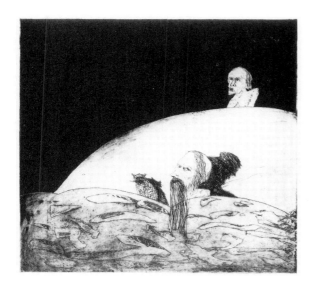

The following entry is based on information supplied by the artist in a letter dated 20 April 1986. It has been approved by the artist.

The subject of 'Death Knell for John Knox', according to the artist, is 'John Knox ... expiring'. In this work, two themes which recur in Bellany's iconography are fused into a single image. Both derive from the nature of Bellany's upbringing in Port Seton, Scotland. Bellany has identified the major influence in his childhood:

> John Knox dominated the thoughts of my formative years as a child brought up in a Calvinist dominated home and a Knox dominated fishing village in Scotland. Knox's 'bible thumping' and that of his followers runs through every strain of one's life in this situation. From education to physical and emotional outlets – SIN IS ALWAYS IN THE AIR with Knox looking over your shoulder.

During his early life in Port Seton, Bellany also gained a heightened awareness of human vulnerability and mortality. This was the result of first hand acquaintance with fishermen who earned their daily living by embarking on dangerous voyages and, consequently, from the recurrent tragedy of losses in the village community.

'Death Knell for John Knox' was directly inspired by Bellany's revelatory discovery in a biography of Knox that 'he was not as white as the driven snow'. He has explained that

> Knox's death was melodramatic to the point that Strindberg or Ibsen looked like Walt Disney in comparison. Knox's passion for his sixteen year old step daughter was at its highest peak, his wife, her mother turned a blind eye to the iniquities. Then Knox had a nightmare that he was in Hell and woke from his vision a distraught and terrorised man and

his death scene was hardly filled with singing of angelic choirs, but remorse and soul searching and extreme anguish of spirit and soul until the life left him.

In this work, Bellany depicts not simply the moment of Knox's death but also its nature and, in particular, 'the terror in Knox's tortured mind'. His stated aim is to communicate Knox's 'frenetic fear of fire and brimstone in everlasting damnation'. He achieves this through the cumulative effect of the image's constituent elements. Knox is seen in the foreground being literally overwhelmed by his 'various obsessions' which tax him with the knowledge that 'retribution will soon be at hand'. The black cat is 'Mephistophelian' and 'symbolises evil and the inner conflict Knox was fighting against. Good and Evil dominated the man's existence.' The female figure in the background is emaciated and resembles a Nazi concentration camp victim. Bellany visited Buchenwald in 1967 and its effect was traumatic. The presence of this image here links the scene with evil in modern times.

The work evolved from 'many many drawings – pencil – ink and wash and watercolour and several smaller etchings' most of which are in the artist's private collection. These were begun in 1971 and the etching was completed in 1972. Bellany felt that etching was the appropriate medium for this image because

> The clarity of the line was perfect for the 'carrion-pocked images' smothered in the death ridden rich heavy black of the atmosphere of the death scene with heavy heavy aquatint. One feels one can almost touch the air which is soot-sodden and stagnant awaiting the last gasp. This against the pristine clarity and light besmirched figures in the drama leaves one with the feeling – 'THERE IS ALWAYS HOPE' however minimal.

Bellany also executed two related oil paintings: 'Homage to John Knox' 1972 (repr. *John Bellany Paintings 1972–1982*, exhibition catalogue, AC tour, February 1983–September 1984, no.1) and 'John Knox on his Death Bed' 1972, which was accidentally destroyed while being moved.

P 07902 **Janus** 1982

> Screenprint 36 × 27 (915 × 685) on cream Velin Arches, printed by Chris Betambeau and Bob Saitch at Advanced Graphics, not editioned
> Inscribed 'Bellany '82' b.r. and 'A/P'
> Purchased from Monika Kinley (Grant-in-Aid) 1983

The following entry is based on information supplied

by the artist in a letter dated 20 April 1986. It has been approved by the artist.

'Janus' is 'a plea from the heart'. It was created at a time when Bellany's 'life and health were in a desperate state of peak emotional strain' during which his wife Juliet was suffering from a chronic illness which eventually proved fatal. Janus was the Roman god of doors, gates and entrances and is normally represented with two faces looking to past and future. It was an image which had haunted Bellany 'over a period of years'. In this work, and relating to the circumstances under which it was created, the double face is transformed into a self-portrait. As with the Roman original, the faces are turned to past and future but Bellany also uses the image as an icon of 'self-appraisal' and 'self-challenge'. It invokes the questions 'What are you? Where have you been? Whither do you go?' and represents 'an artist looking inwards on himself and on looking outwards is devastated by what he is seeing'.

This feeling of devastation and personal conflict with adverse external forces is amplified by and embodied in the words 'Spes Bona' which form part of the image at the bottom. Although these words may be translated, ironically, as 'good hope', they refer more directly to an incident in Bellany's childhood at Port Seton, Scotland which made an unforgettable impression. 'Spes Bona' was the name of a fishing boat which ran onto rocks during a heavy storm with the loss of all the crew. Bellany recalls that 'the skeleton of the boat lay on the rocks of the harbour bar ... until the timbers were eventually completely smashed to pieces by thunderous seas over the years'. Relating this to the meaning of the work as a whole, Bellany has stated that 'the paradox of the Latin name of the boat and her dreadful demise commemorates man's feebleness to contest in an elemental drama'. Bellany also produced a watercolour

with the title 'Spes Bona' 1985 (repr. *John Bellany*, exhibition catalogue, Fischer Fine Art, February–March 1986, no.26). On a wider level, the ideas of human vulnerability and personal conflict, which find metaphorical articulation in the image of sailors pitched against an overwhelming and irresistible sea, are further connected with the Roman Janus who was also a god of war and peace. That Bellany sees the work as a 'plea' stems from the heart-shaped motif containing the initials 'JB' drawn on the neck of the Janus head. 'JB' stands both for John and Juliet Bellany. This symbol was designed by the artist's wife and made into a love necklace which she wore as a 'ray of hope' during her illness. Bellany has stated that 'The prayer endemic in this is portrayed in the disturbing "Janus" silkscreen which is a plea from the heart.'

Although inscribed 1982, the work was executed between 1982–3. It evolved out of many preliminary watercolours and drawings including portraits made from life. All preparatory works were executed in the artist's London studio and are now in the artist's collection. The silkscreen was realised at Advanced Graphics in collaboration with Chris Betambeau and Bob Saitch at the same time as another silkscreen, 'The Gambler'. Bellany has indicated that silkscreen was the chosen printmaking technique for this work because he valued the directness of drawing on the screen and the richness of colour which he felt was required. He explored the image further in 'several [related] paintings and watercolours coming to a zenith in "Janus"' 1983, oil on canvas (repr. in col., *The British Art Show*, exhibition catalogue, AC tour, November 1984–December 1985, no.17).

Jonathan Borofsky born 1942

P 07817– **2740475** 1982
07829

Seven screenprints printed by H.M. Buchi, Basel, and six etchings printed by Robert Aull and Leslie Sutcliffe, Los Angeles, the portfolio published by Peter Blum, Zurich and New York, in an edition of 50
Purchased from Peter Blum Editions (Grant-in-Aid) 1983

P 07817
Screenprint $30\frac{1}{8} \times 22\frac{1}{8}$ (765 × 562) on grey paper
Inscribed 'Jonathan Borofsky' along left side and '39/50' b.l.; printed inscription '2739987'

P 07817

P 07822

P 07818
Etching (from a triangular plate) $3\frac{3}{4} \times 5$
(95×127) on paper $29\frac{7}{8} \times 22\frac{1}{4}$ (758×565)
watermarked 'ARCHES'
Inscribed 'Jonathan Borofsky' b.r. and
'39/50' b.l.; printed inscription (reversed)
'2739992'; impressed with the printer's
stamp

P 07819
Screenprint on grey paper $30\frac{1}{8} \times 22\frac{1}{8}$
(765×562)
Inscribed 'Jonathan Borofsky' bottom
centre and '39/50' b.l.; printed inscription
'2740152'

P 07820
Etching $2\frac{1}{4} \times 1\frac{3}{4}$ (58×45) on paper
$29\frac{7}{8} \times 22\frac{1}{4}$ (758×565) watermarked
'ARCHES'
Inscribed 'Jonathan Borofsky' b.r. and
'39/50' b.l.; printed inscription '2738104';
impressed with the printer's stamp

P 07821
Screenprint on grey paper $30\frac{1}{8} \times 22\frac{1}{8}$
(765×562)
Inscribed 'Jonathan Borofsky' b.r. and
'39/50' b.l.; printed inscription '2740225'

P 07822
Etching $2\frac{1}{2} \times 2\frac{1}{8}$ (64×54) on paper
$29\frac{7}{8} \times 22\frac{1}{4}$ (758×565) watermarked
'ARCHES'
Inscribed 'Jonathan Borofsky' b.r. and
'39/50' b.l.; printed inscription '2738105';
impressed with the printer's stamp

P 07823
Screenprint $30\frac{1}{8} \times 22\frac{1}{8}$ (765×562)
Inscribed 'Jonathan Borofsky' b.r. and
'39/50' b.l.; printed inscription '2740287'

P 07824
Etching (from two plates one above the
other) $6\frac{1}{2} \times 2\frac{3}{4}$ (165×70) overall on paper
$29\frac{7}{8} \times 22\frac{1}{4}$ (758×565) watermarked
'ARCHES'
Inscribed 'Jonathan Borofsky' b.r. and
'39/50' b.l.; printed inscription in top
plate (in reverse) '2739976' and bottom
plate (in reverse) '2739977'; impressed
with the printer's stamp

P 07825
Screenprint $30\frac{1}{8} \times 22\frac{1}{8}$ (765×562)
Inscribed 'Jonathan Borofsky' along left
side and '39/50' b.l.; printed inscription
'2740184'

P 07826
Etching $2\frac{3}{4} \times 1\frac{1}{2}$ (70×38) on paper
$29\frac{7}{8} \times 22\frac{1}{4}$ (758×565) watermarked
'ARCHES'
Inscribed 'Jonathan Borofsky' b.r.;
impressed with the printer's stamp

P 07827
Screenprint on grey paper $30\frac{1}{8} \times 22\frac{1}{8}$
(765×562)
Inscribed 'Jonathan Borofsky' along right
side and '39/50' b.l.; printed inscription
'2740396'

P 07828
Etching $2\frac{3}{4} \times 2$ (70 × 52) on paper $29\frac{7}{8} \times 22\frac{1}{4}$ (758 × 565) watermarked 'ARCHES'
Inscribed 'Jonathan Borofsky' b.r. and '39/50' b.l.; impressed with the printer's stamp

P 07829
Screenprint $30\frac{1}{8} \times 22\frac{1}{8}$ (765 × 562)
Inscribed 'Jonathan Borofsky' and '39/50' b.l.; printed inscription '2740474'

In 1969 Borofsky started writing numbers in sequence, starting with 1 and covering both sides of his sheets; he has continued this sequence at intervals ever since. In the early 1970s he found little drawings and scribbles intruding into the count and he began to make paintings of these images. He decided to identify them and all his subsequent works with the number he was on in his counting – hence the title of this portfolio is '2740475'. It contains seven screenprints and six etchings placed alternately (starting and finishing with a screenprint), thus creating a counterpoint of imagery from the flat silhouette of a figure wearing a hat and carrying a brief-case to the tiny etching plates on which a variety of images are drawn. Borofsky uses imagery developed from his own dreams and unconscious thoughts or fantasies and by repeated use some of his images become symbolic, as in the case of the silhouette figure used in the screenprints. It is based on a man Borofsky glimpsed in the street outside his house in New York City, and who he thought might be the man who had been putting sheets of paper through his letterbox anonymously. The sheets were covered in written names and addresses (mostly of well-known Black men) and Borofsky found in this presumably subconsciously motivated or psychotic behaviour an echo of his own written count. He has used the figure as it appears in these prints in a number of other works; here it appears first alone, then in two pairs, then in a group, then in two scattered groups and finally, alone again and upside-down. Each of these screenprints is numbered in the print, indicating the order in which they were done. The numbers are: 2739987, 2740152, 2740184, 2740225, 2740287, 2740396 and 2740474; the portfolio's title number is therefore the very next in sequence.

The first of the etchings (the second print) is on a triangular plate and includes a head with long animal ears which the artist has described as being a self-portrait as an animal, with a reference to the heightened sensitivity of animal ears. It and the sixth and tenth prints are all of heads enmeshed by wiry lines, planetary rings or other marks denoting mental turmoil. The second etching is related to Borofsky's 'Thought Book' drawings of 1968–9 and the third is another head. Borofsky is interested in the art of the mentally ill and of prisoners and frequently uses graphic conventions characteristic of such work, including opening up or adding to the crown of the head to denote the mental anguish within. The fourth etching is a repeated image of a head in a soft conical hat and with shoulders draped, related to a drawing made on the back of an envelope in about 1978–80 (see *Jonathon Borofsky Drawings 1960–83*, exhibition catalogue, Kunstmuseum, Basel, June–July 1983, no.131). The first four etchings have numbers, drawn on the plate and therefore printed backwards, which show they were not made in the sequence in which they appear: the first etching is 2739992, the second 2738104, the third 2738105 and the fourth, having two plates, is 2739976 and 2739977. The fifth etching contains columns of numbers like those of Borofsky's count with another head; the sixth contains only columns of numbers.

P 77008

Günter Brus born 1938

P 77001– **Night Quartet** 1982
77008
Eight drypoints each $9\frac{3}{8} \times 6\frac{3}{8}$ (238 × 167) on paper $15\frac{1}{2} \times 11\frac{5}{8}$ (394 × 295), printed at Druckerei Maly, Vienna and published by Galerie Heike Curtze, Düsseldorf and Vienna, and Edition Sabine Knust, Munich
Each inscribed 'G. Brus' b.r. and '19/30'; each inscribed in the plate as follows:
P 77001 'NACHTQUARTETT', P 77002 'I', P 77003 'NACHT, FREITOD|DES AUGES', P 77004 'II', P 77005 'TOD, DAUERTIEFSCHLAF|DER TRÄUME',

P 77006 'III', P 77007
'STILLSTANDREISE|DES LICHTS', and
P 77008 'IV'
Purchased from Galerie Heike Curtze
(Grant-in-Aid) 1983

P 07991

P 07992

P 07993

P 07991– Great Fear of the Earth 1982
07993

Three etchings (a title page and two plates)
each approx. $23\frac{3}{4} \times 35\frac{3}{4}$ (604 × 908) on
paper $30\frac{3}{4} \times 43\frac{3}{4}$ (781 × 1101) printed by
Lilah Toland and June Lambla at Crown
Point Press, Oakland, California and
published by them
P 07991, the title page, inscribed 'Günter
Brus 1982' b.r. and '1/5', and 'published
by CROWN POINT PRESS OAKLAND
CALIFORNIA' and 'printed by LILAH
TOLAND|and|JUNE LAMBLA' and
'G.BRUS|ENGELSTAMMEN|
LEIDER VON|MENSCHEN AB' and
'GROSSE ERDANGST' in the plate;
impressed with the printer's stamp
P 07992, 07993 inscribed 'Günter Brus
1982' b.r. and '1/15', and 'II' and 'III'
respectively; each impressed with the
printer's stamp
Purchased from Crown Point Press
(Grant-in-Aid) 1984

Stephen Buckley born 1944

P 07754 Flons Flons 1981–2

Screenprint $30\frac{3}{8} \times 40\frac{1}{8}$ (772 × 1018) on
Arches paper, printed by Douglas Corker
at Kelpra Studio and published by
Waddington Graphics
Inscribed 'Stephen Buckley 1981' b.r. and
'18/70'
Purchased from Waddington Graphics
(Grant-in-Aid) 1982

The title of this print is not translatable into English as
it means the sound and atmosphere of a fair or carnival;

the artist told the compiler it was 'maybe a bit like the smell of the greasepaint, the roar of the crowd' (this and other quotations from correspondence, March 1985). The print was made concurrently with a painting of the same title which was completed in January 1982. These were followed by a further four 'Flons Flons' paintings, the last of which was made in August 1982. All the 'Flons Flons' works are also related to the monoprints Buckley made at Alan Cox's workshop Sky in the Spring of 1982.

This print is one of three made at the same time at Kelpra, the others being 'Album' and 'Akenside' (the latter has sometimes been known as 'Jesmond'). This was the first and to date the only time Buckley worked at Kelpra. 'Flons Flons' was the first to be made; it is built up with drawings 'made actual size on tracing cloth using a water soluble opaque ink. There were seven screens/colours'. The orange mesh to the left was done 'from masking tape on tracing cloth exposed directly onto (the) screen'. The background was made up from two photographic separations from Buckley's original full size drawing and the leaf shapes and striped discs were done from two and three photographic separations respectively. The colours were finalised through 'instinct and trial and error plus an idea in my head that I wanted *print* colours rather than *paint* colours'.

This entry has been approved by the artist.

John Cage born 1912

P 07903 **Déreau No 33** 1982

Etching, engraving, drypoint and aquatint
18
¼ × 24¾ (463 × 629) on Japanese paper, printed by Lilah Toland at Crown Point Press, Oakland, California and published by them

Inscribed 'John Cage 1982' bottom centre and 'Déreau 33 two of two impressions'; impressed with the printer's and publisher's stamp
Purchased from Crown Point Press (Grant-in-Aid) 1983
Lit: Lilah Toland, 'Déreau, 1982', *John Cage Etchings 1978–1982*, Oakland, California, 1982, pp.20–1

The 'Déreau' portfolio consists of thirty-eight related works printed in two impressions each. P 07903 is the second impression of no.33 in the portfolio. They were printed by Lilah Toland with Paul Singdahlsen and Marcia Bartholme.

Cage began working on the series in January 1982. It was his seventh etching project at Crown Point Press. The title derives from the first syllable of the word 'décor' and the second syllable of the surname of Henry David Thoreau (1817–62), a close associate of Ralph Waldo Emerson (1803–82). Thoreau was a minor Transcendentalist who is best known for the two full length works published in his lifetime, *A Week on the Concord and Merrimack Rivers* (1849) and *Walden* (1854), and for his essays which have subsequently become classics in the literature of political dissent, 'On the Duty of Civil Disobedience' (1849) and 'A Plea for Captain John Brown' (1860). Although his publications were barely known in his lifetime they have come to be regarded as cornerstones in the mid-nineteenth century American Renaissance in literature. Thoreau was also the author of nearly forty journal-notebooks and of a number of posthumous 'travel' books. A fundamental tenet of his philosophy, as expressed in *Walden*, was 'to drive life into a corner and reduce it to its lowest terms'. Thoreau saw in nature's fine detail abiding spiritual meanings and saw nature as the repository of Emersonian-Transcendental spiritual 'laws' (see the entry on Thoreau by A. Robert Lee in Justin Wintle (ed.), *Makers of Nineteenth Century Culture 1800–1914*, London 1982, pp.619–22).

Cage had been familiar with Thoreau's *Journal* for many years before he became particularly interested in the drawings which the latter included to accompany observations of nature. Lilah Toland explains that Cage first gave them serious consideration when receiving an invitation in Paris to give a performance of 'Song Books' in Rome, which called for the projection of slides relevant to Thoreau, and he found that he did not have with him the slides of Walden Pond that he normally used. He recalled the sketches in the Journal and, knowing that Thoreau had drawn them, felt they could be used instead. He decided to use them as a basis for the Déreau etchings.

Cage used five intaglio processes in each print: drypoint straight lines, engraved curved lines, aquatint, a circular plate and photo-etched Thoreau drawings. Cage has written of these elements as follows:

> 'Déreau' uses 24 Thoreau drawings, four of which are represented and 12 of which disappear. For the 12 that disappear, substitutions were made: the first of which is a circle, the second, a horizon, the third, multiple parallel lines between chance-determined quadrants, the fourth, aquatints and the fifth, curves resulting from dropping a yard length of string on a plate each having the size and shape of the Kodalith film of the Thoreau drawing which disappeared (quoted in Toland, p.20).

According to Toland 'Déreau' 'marks the first time Cage has used both static and changing elements in the composition of a print. Although the photo images retain their positions throughout the series of 38 prints, all other images move freely about the paper. Thus the Thoreau drawings are a kind of stage set or "decor" for the other elements' (p.21).

Cage used the *I Ching* to determine the combinations of colours. He writes, 'Five palettes have been distinguished: Black, Yellow, Red, Blue and Earth. These appear alone or in combination with one of forty-five colours in chance-determined percentages with or without white. The whole series of prints is divided into 10 groups each having its own palette' (quoted in Toland, p.21). Cage began to structure his work by using chance operations derived from the *I Ching* in 1950. The *I Ching* provided him with a disciplined method of working which dispenses with intentioned decision-making and allows him 'to think of his work as an exploration of how nature functions rather than as a method of communicating his own ideas' (Kathan Brown, 'Changing Art: A Chronicle Centred on John Cage', *John Cage Etchings 1978–82*, p.7).

This entry has been approved by the artist.

P07755

P 07636

Patrick Caulfield born 1936

P 07755 **Brown Jug** 1982

Screenprint $39\frac{3}{8} \times 30\frac{1}{2}$ (1000 × 776) on Arches paper, printed at Kelpra Studio, published by Waddington Graphics
Inscribed 'Patrick Caulfield' b.r. and '2/80'
Purchased from Waddington Graphics (Grant-in-Aid) 1982

Sandro Chia born 1946

P 07632– **April Manual** 1981
07636

Five etchings with drypoint each approx. $11\frac{5}{8} \times 12\frac{1}{4}$ (295 × 312) on buff Velin Arches paper $29\frac{3}{4} \times 22\frac{1}{8}$ (757 × 563), printed by Sarah Feigenbaum at Aeropress, New York and published by Peter Blum Editions, New York and Zurich

Each inscribed 'Sandro Chia 1981' b.r. and '30/50'; each impressed with the printer's stamp
Purchased from Anthony d'Offay Gallery (Grant-in-Aid) 1982

Lit: Bice Curiger, *Looks et Tenebrae*, New York and Zurich 1984, pp.123–9, repr. pp.197–202; Danny Berger, 'Sandro Chia in his Studio: an Interview by Danny Berger', *Print Collector's Newsletter*, XII, January–February, 1982, pp.168–9; *Also repr: An Exhibition and Sale. Sandra Chia Prints 1973–1984*, exhibition catalogue, Metropolitan Museum of Art, New York, September–October 1984 pp.36–8

The title of the portfolio implies the notion of a manual, or book of instructions, and the notion of hand craftsmanship. Chia has stated:

Craftsmanship is very important in etching. The metal is treated for the purpose of expressing forms imprisoned in the metal. I chose the title 'April Manual', because it was April when I made it, and also because April stands for Spring, when the plants shoot up from the ground, precisely as in my work the pictures emerge from the metal. The general topic of the portfolio, though, is etching as such (quoted in Bice Curiger, p.126).

The portfolio consists of five etchings as follows: I 'The Artifice' (etching, drypoint, open bite and mezzotint); II 'To the Tower' (etching and drypoint); III 'About the Unseizable' (etching, drypoint and open bite); IV 'A Good Soul' (etching, drypoint, soft ground and aquatint); V 'And the Heroes at the Window' (etching, drypoint and aquatint). Although each print is an independent image, the titles of which in some cases were the starting point for the images, according to the artist the sequence of titles make up the story (from the written answer to questions posed by the compiler in a letter of 11 March 1985). Chia had made a number of etchings prior to the 'April Manual' and had printed them in small editions (approximately 10 impressions each). In an interview with Danny Berger he stated that etching 'is the technique I know best. Etching, aquatint, drypoint. In the editions I did recently I used all of these techniques, using several plates. Often using several techniques on the same image.'

The first print in the series depicts a young man hunting a hare with a knife. In his right hand he holds a torch. 'L'artificio' or 'the artifice' may also be translated as 'strategem', 'device' or 'deceit'. All these concepts are implied by the title. The image is closely related to a painting entitled 'Rabbit for Dinner' 1981 (repr. *Sandro Chia*, exhibition catalogue, Stedelijk Museum, Amsterdam, April–May 1983, n.p.) which

was executed at the same time. In the interview with Danny Berger Chia stated:

I have a studio in Ronciglione (outside Rome) which is set up for etching and where I do my etchings. It relaxes me from my painting. It is a communicative channel with painting. Sometimes something from my painting transfers to my prints, and sometimes it is the opposite. When I am in my studio, I have at my disposal the press, canvas, and pigments. I like to pass between the two disciplines.

According to Bice Curiger the young man stands for the artist in pursuit of a possible prey, presumably a subject. The hare represents emotion and instinct, the torch represents reason and intellect. Around the edge of the image Chia has drawn a margin because he 'needed to have a certain boundary in order to make the light on the inside spill out onto the page' (written answers).

The second image, 'To the Tower', depicts a medieval man plunging a knife into his fallen victim. Above the victim's upturned head is drawn a red question mark which the artist intends both literally to express surprise and as a pictorial device. The red, which complements the general green hue of the print, may be associated with blood which is otherwise not depicted in this print. The pose is one which might be associated with melodrama, although Chia maintains that the sources for all the images 'are found in the repertoire of art' (written answers). The image has a sculptural quality.

'About the Unseizable', the third in the series, loosely mirrors the image of the man in 'The Artifice' and relates to a painting of 1981 entitled 'Everything is Going Well' (repr. *Sandro Chia*, exhibition catalogue, n.p.). In this print Chia uses a large repertoire of etching techniques such as cross hatching, parallel hatching, hooks, points and wavy lines. It is the least imagistic work in the series.

The fourth work, 'A Good Soul' 'shows a boy as the emblem of (rediscovered) innocence and purification' (Curiger, p.128) and may serve as the complement to the final image in the series, 'And the Heroes at the Window', which according to Chia represents 'a group of rebels with somewhat stupid faces' (quoted in Curiger, p.129). 'A Good Soul' relates to the painting 'Idiots' 1981 (repr. *Sandro Chia*, exhibition catalogue, n.p.) and depicts a seated youth in a slightly contorted pose.

'And the Heroes at the Window' portrays a rather medieval looking group of warriors floating in the heavens. (Chia greatly admires the work of Chagall.)

This entry has been approved by the artist.

P 07637   **Running Boy with Strange Fingers** 1981

Etching and aquatint $25\frac{1}{2} \times 19\frac{1}{4}$ (650 × 490) on paper $39\frac{1}{4} \times 27\frac{1}{2}$ (993 × 700), printed by the artist (proof before the edition)
Inscribed 'Sandro Chia 1981' b.r. and 'prova d'artista'
Purchased from Anthony d'Offay Gallery (Grant-in-Aid) 1982

Repr: *An Exhibition and Sale. Sandro Chia Prints 1973–1984*, exhibition catalogue, Metropolitan Museum of Art, New York, September–October 1984, p.40 (editioned example)

This is a trial proof printed in sepia by Chia in his studio outside Rome prior to the publication in 1982 of the edition of 40 by Galerie Bruno Bischofberger, Zurich. The edition was printed in black by Studio Santa Reparta, Florence. In addition there were five artist's proofs and one 'bon à tirer'. The print is almost a mirror image of the painting entitled 'Fingers Crossed' 1981 (private collection, Washington, D.C.). In its proof stages the print has also been known as 'Man Running' and 'Back and Ground'. According to Chia this work and P 07638 'are different responses towards the cruelty that sometimes occurs within the world of art' (written answers). It is to some extent auto-biographical.

This entry has been approved by the artist.

P 07638   **The Butcher** 1981

Etching $25\frac{3}{8} \times 19\frac{1}{4}$ (645 × 490) on paper $38\frac{7}{8} \times 27\frac{1}{2}$ (990 × 696), printed by the artist (proof before the edition)
Inscribed 'Sandro Chia 1981' b.r. and 'prova d'artista'
Purchased from Anthony d'Offay Gallery (Grant-in-Aid) 1982

Repr: *An Exhibition and Sale. Sandro Chia Prints 1973–1984*, exhibition catalogue, Metropolitan Museum of Art, New York, September–October 1984, p.41 (editioned example)

Like P 07637 this is a trial proof, printed in sepia by the artist in his studio outside Rome. An edition of 40 with 10 artist's proofs and one 'bon à tirer' was published in 1982 by Emilio Mazzoli, Modena. The edition was printed in black by Studio Santa Reparata, Florence combining etching, brushed solvent and scraped aquatint. According to Chia, P 07637 was made at the same time as two paintings 'Brother' 1981 (private collection, London) and 'Son of Son' (both repr. *Sandro Chia*, exhibition catalogue, Stedelijk Museum, Amsterdam, April–May 1983, n.p.). He stated that 'They are all in the same family' (written answers). The final state of 'The Butcher' differs from P 07638 in the detailing on the man's sleeves and by the inclusion of a shaded area along the jaw line. The background in the final state is also considerably more worked. P 07658 has also been known as 'Man with Apron'. Like many of Chia's works this print is loosely autobiographical and refers to his association of the artist with the artisan.

This entry has been approved by the artist.

you see the Mona Lisa?' and is captioned 'A Paragon of Beauty'. The Dali image relates to Marcel Duchamp's 'L.H.O.O.Q.', a reproduction of the Mona Lisa with a small moustache and beard added; Duchamp's first version was made in 1919. The article in *Der Spiegel* is about the Mona Lisa as universally known symbol and as a vehicle for parodies of various kinds. The cover picture, with all its connotations of notoriety, art as news, as personality cult and as high-priced commodity is not hidden or disguised but transformed by being wrapped.

This entry has been approved by the artist.

Christo born 1935

P 07640   **Der Spiegel** 1963

Folded magazine wrapped in transparent plastic and tied with string, 12 × 4½ (305 × 115), wrapped and tied by the artist, published by Hans Moller, Düsseldorf, in an edition of 130
Inscribed 'Christo 63' b.r. and '96'
Purchased at Sotheby's, Los Angeles (Grant-in-Aid) 1982

Lit: Per Hovdenakk, *Christo Complete Editions 1964–82*, Munich 1982, no.1

Christo's first wrapped works were made in 1958 (see T 03290, *Tate Gallery Illustrated Catalogue of Acquisitions 1980–82*, pp.63–4), using cloth, or polythene for those in which he wanted to show the contents of the work. He made his first wrapped magazine in 1961. Other unique works related to 'Der Spiegel' include a wrapped post-card vending stand and magazines on a wire rack, both made in 1963. For the series 'Edition Original 1' in which Hans Moller published the work of fifteen artists, Christo wrapped 130 different copies of the German news magazine *Der Spiegel*. The work was a gesture of thanks to Moller, who had allowed Christo and his wife to share his apartment in Dusseldorf while Christo was preparing an exhibition at the Alfred Schmela Gallery in 1963. The Tate's work is the issue for Wednesday 7 October 1959, with a cover picture of the famous photo-collage of Salvador Dali as the Mona Lisa, from *Dali's Mustache* by Dali and Philippe Halsman, New York 1954, an interview in the form of questions with pictorial answers. The image is in answer to the question 'Dali, what do you see when

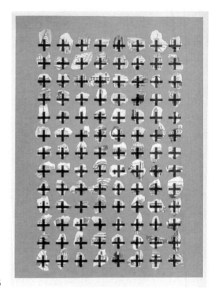

P 11066

Brian Clarke born 1953

P 11062–   **The Two Cultures** 1981
11069
Eight screenprints in range 29¾ × 19¾– 44⅛ × 27 (755 × 504–1120 × 685) on paper in range 42⅛ × 29¼–47¾ × 31¾ (1070 × 742– 1212 × 807) watermarked 'ARCHES FRANCE', printed at Kelpra Studio and published by Swellframe Ltd and Robert Fraser Gallery
Each inscribed 'Brian Clark' b.r. and '7.75'
Presented by Paul Beldock 1983

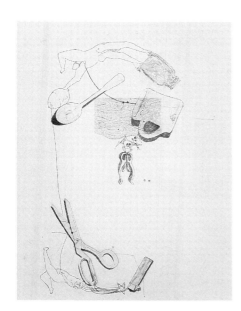

Francesco Clemente born 1952

P 07904   Seascape 1981

Softground etching from two plates
$24\frac{3}{8} \times 18\frac{1}{2}$ (619 × 470) on handmade paper
watermarked 'F', printed by Hidekatsu
Takada at Crown Point Press, Oakland,
California, published by them in an edition
of 10
Inscribed 'Francesco Clemente' bottom
centre and '6/10'; impressed with the
printer's and publisher's stamp
Purchased from Crown Point Press
(Grant-in-Aid) 1983

P 07905   Self Portrait No.6 (Stoplight) 1981

Softground etching $9\frac{1}{4} \times 13\frac{1}{4}$ (235 × 337) on
paper 16 × 20$\frac{1}{4}$ (405 × 515) watermarked

'ARCHES', printed by Hidekatsu Takada
at Crown Point Press, Oakland,
California, published by them in an edition
of 10
Inscribed 'Francesco Clemente' bottom
centre and '1/10'; impressed with the
printer's and publisher's stamp
Purchased from Crown Point Press
(Grant-in-Aid) 1983

These two etchings are from a group of 21 made at
Kathan Brown's Crown Point Press studio in California; they were Clemente's first etchings. The group
included six self portraits and three large prints in a
vertical, banner-like format. Clemente drew directly
on the plates, working from one point in the image
outwards, not standing back to consider or correcting
his drawing, but pursuing an intuitive form of
expression. In P 07904 he used a large plate (the plate
mark being beyond the edge of the sheet) with a small
rectangular plate at the centre. Clemente's imagery is
autobiographical, from the mundane details of daily life
to the central core of his physical and sexual persona;
his pantheistic, pan-cultural outlook is frequently concentrated into images of his own face and body with
imagery drawn from Hindu or Tantric art, as in P 07905
where his hands are placed palms outwards in a classic
Hindu gesture.

P 07830–   High Fever 1982
07838,
07848   Eight woodcuts with title page and
tailpiece on handmade paper, printed by
François Lafranca, Lugano, Switzerland,
published by Peter Blum, New York and
Zurich in an edition of 35
Each inscribed 'Francesco Clemente' b.r.
and '5/35', P 07848 and P 07838 not
inscribed
Purchased from Peter Blum Editions
(Grant-in-Aid) 1983

P 07848
Title page with woodcut on paper $26\frac{1}{2} \times 21\frac{5}{8}$–
(673 × 549)

P 07830
Woodcut $20\frac{1}{4} \times 16\frac{5}{8}$ (514 × 422) on paper
$27\frac{1}{2} \times 21\frac{1}{4}$ (698 × 540)

P 07831
Woodcut $18\frac{3}{4} \times 14$ (476 × 356) on paper
$26\frac{7}{8} \times 21\frac{1}{4}$ (683 × 540)

P 07832
Woodcut $21\frac{1}{8} \times 16\frac{1}{8}$ (536 × 410) on paper
$27 \times 21\frac{1}{4}$ (686 × 540)

P 07833

Though Clemente resists explaining his imagery, preferring to assert the intuitive nature of his work, 'High Fever' is said to be concerned with the birth of his daughter. The poem may therefore refer to his crying out against the anguish of childbirth. There is no narrative but from the simple heart, symbol of declared love with his and his wife's initials, on the title page to the circular tailpiece the prints are a single serial work, the order of which is established not by numbering but by the order of illustrations in the accompanying booklet. The heavy sheets of paper, made at the Lafranca studio, hold very strong impressions from the grainy woodblocks, Clemente's deep gouges and cut lines producing very clear white against a variety of blacks from sooty (P 07848, 07830, 07831, 07834) to prussian blue – (P 07832, 07835, 07837, 07838) or alizarin crimson – (P 07833, 07836) tinged black. The prints have a powerful material character, almost like paper sculpture, unlike his conventional prints but related to his handmade books. The blocks have a satiny grain, the natural pattern of which lies behind the cut image: 'The lines help avoid having the figures fall into emptiness. It is possible to follow the lines, and support is provided by the material of the structure of the wood. Whereas this question of support never occurs in works by American artists, who simply circumvent it, the German Expressionists were from an early period fully aware of this issue ...' (the artist, quoted in B. Curiger, *Looks et Tenebrae*, New York and Zurich 1984, p.158). Clemente has worked in Italy, America and India and the environment in which a particular work is made has always been an important factor in its evolution. Curiger refers to the disquieting effect of Switzerland's nordic landscape and Clemente's idea of woodcut as a nordic medium, ... 'Northern in the sense that light must be created from darkness' (p.157). In these prints, as in much of Clemente's work, he uses sexual imagery and symbols as they are used in Tantra, that is as a universal language referring to ultimate enlightenment, but also as direct autobiographical references both physical and spiritual. It is not Tantra as a religion that interests him, however, but its ability to express thought and ideas in its own visual language.

P 07833
Woodcut $21\frac{3}{8} \times 14$ (543 × 356) on paper
$27 \times 21\frac{1}{4}$ (686 × 540)

P 07834
Woodcut $21\frac{1}{4} \times 16\frac{1}{8}$ (540 × 410) on paper
$26\frac{3}{4} \times 21\frac{1}{4}$ (679 × 540)

P 07835
Woodcut $14 \times 14\frac{1}{4}$ (356 × 362) on paper
$26\frac{3}{4} \times 21\frac{1}{4}$ (679 × 540)

P 07836
Woodcut $21\frac{3}{4} \times 13\frac{7}{8}$ (553 × 353) on paper
$26\frac{3}{4} \times 21\frac{1}{4}$ (679 × 540)

P 07837
Woodcut $17\frac{1}{4} \times 20\frac{1}{2}$ (438 × 521) on paper
$21\frac{1}{2} \times 27\frac{1}{4}$ (546 × 692)

P 07838
Tailpiece with circular woodcut $13\frac{1}{2}$ (343)
diameter on paper $26\frac{3}{4} \times 21$ (679 × 533)

Clemente titled this portfolio in Italian, 'Febbre Alta'. It is accompanied by a booklet with a poem by Valerio Magrelli which the artist translates into English as follows:

I want one day
to turn into marble
without any nerves
or tendons or veins.
Dry stone only,
alive, profound and white,
keeping still and relying
only on itself

Prunella Clough born 1919

P 07906 Geological Landscape 1949

Lithograph $5\frac{7}{8} \times 7\frac{15}{16}$ (149 × 201) from two
stones (grey and a brownish yellow),
printed by the artist (not editioned)
Inscribed '1949' on the back
Purchased from the artist (Grant-in-Aid)
1984

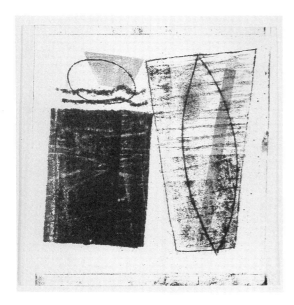

P 07907 Can and Basket 1950

Lithograph $6\frac{9}{16} \times 6\frac{3}{8}$ (167 × 162) from two
plates (black and a pale brownish green),
printed by the artist (not editioned)
Inscribed '1950' on the back
Purchased from the artist (Grant-in-Aid)
1984

P 07909 Float 1950

Lithograph $6\frac{3}{4} \times 4\frac{1}{2}$ (170 × 116) from one
stone, printed by the artist (not editioned)
Not inscribed
Purchased from the artist (Grant-in-Aid)
1984

These three lithographs were printed by Clough in her own studio where she had a lithography press set up. She did not make editions but printed five or ten copies of each image. She used stones, sometimes drawing on them directly and sometimes using transfer paper, treating the medium as experimental and exploring textures and tonal effects similar to those she was using in drawings, in which line and tone and rubbed textures like frottages were combined. 'Geological Landscape' is a relatively direct landscape image while in 'Float' an object like an improvised marker buoy with cork lashed to its post refers indirectly to the same kind of scene: Clough uses landscape as a source of visual ideas brought together from often fragmentary sensory memories, incorporating natural forms with the weathered detritus of industrial buildings, machinery, streets and derelict urban vistas. In 'Can and Basket' she explores the differing shapes and contours of the two objects.

This and the following entries have been approved by the artist.

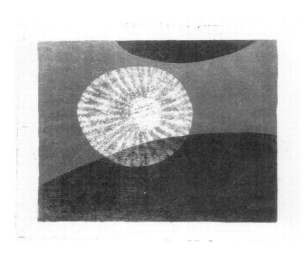

P 07908 **Jellyfish** 1950

Lithograph 10 × 12¾ (254 × 323) on thin
paper 14⅞ × 17¾ (377 × 452) from two
stones, printed by the artist (not editioned)
Inscribed '1950' and 'from 21 rue B' on
the back
Purchased from the artist (Grant-in-Aid)
1984

Also printed by the artist in her studio, and not more
than about ten impressions made.

P 07910 **Cranes** 1952

Lithograph 17 × 14½ (430 × 368) on paper
25¾ × 19¾ (655 × 502), printer unidentified

(see below), published by the Redfern
Gallery and Millers
Inscribed 'Clough' b.r. and '3/20'
Purchased from the artist (Grant-in-Aid)
1984

'Cranes' was one of a group of works commissioned by
Rex Nan-Kivell of the Redfern in collaboration with
Millers, a publishing house set up by Frances Byng-
Stamper and Caroline Lucas (who were sisters) to make
artists' lithographs. Other artists similarly commissioned at this time were Keith Vaughan, Robert
Colquhoun and Robert MacBryde. Like several of the
series 'Cranes' was drawn on transfer paper and sent
off to be printed: Clough saw and corrected proofs but
had no direct contact with the printers themselves. Two
printing studios were being used, Ravel in Paris and the
Chiswick Press in London. The image is related to the
relatively directly representational paintings of industrial scenes and lorries Clough was making at this date.
Imagery such as the silhouetted girders and strong dark
tonal blocks in this print later developed into a still
referential but much less specific pictorial language.

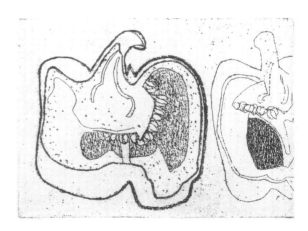

P 07913 **Pimentoes** 1954

Etching 3 × 4 (75 × 102) on paper 5⅜ × 7½
(135 × 190), printed by the artist (not
editioned)
Inscribed '1954' on the back
Purchased from the artist (Grant-in-Aid)
1984

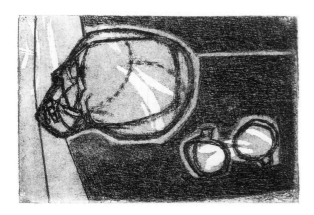

P 07914 **Skull and Pomegranate** 1954

Etching with aquatint $3\frac{3}{8} \times 5$ (85×125) on
paper $5\frac{1}{2} \times 7\frac{1}{2}$ (140×190), printed by the
artist (not editioned)
Inscribed '1954' on the back
Purchased from the artist (Grant-in-Aid)
1984

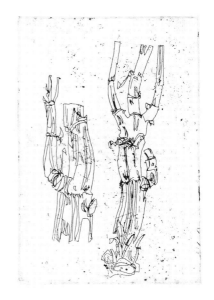

P 07912 **Marsh Plants** 1954

Etching $5\frac{7}{8} \times 4$ (150×100) on paper
$13 \times 11\frac{1}{2}$ (330×293), printed by the artist
(not editioned)
Not inscribed
Purchased from the artist (Grant-in-Aid)
1984

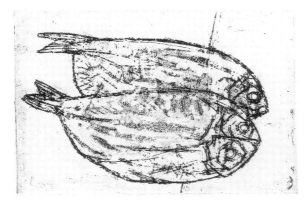

P 07911 **Kippers** 1954

Etching $4 \times 5\frac{7}{8}$ (100×149) on paper $6\frac{3}{8} \times 9\frac{5}{8}$
(162×244), printed by the artist (not
editioned)
Inscribed '1954' on the back
Purchased from the artist (Grant-in-Aid)
1984

P 07915 **Corrugated Fence** 1955

Etching $3\frac{3}{8} \times 4\frac{7}{8}$ (87×123) on irregularly
cut paper approx. $6\frac{1}{4} \times 7\frac{3}{4}$ (160×198),
printed by the artist (not editioned)
Inscribed '1955' on the back
Purchased from the artist (Grant-in-Aid)
1984

These four etchings were made at Chelsea School of
Art, where Clough was teaching. As it was a new

medium for her she turned to simple images which she drew on the plates through a hard ground. With the exception of 'Corrugated Fence', the images are still life subjects unrelated to the development of Clough's paintings at that time. She made a number of proofs but none of the etchings was editioned. As no satisfactory impression was available when this group of acquisitions was selected in 1983, the plate 'Marsh Plants' was printed specially for the Tate Gallery at Wimbledon School of Art.

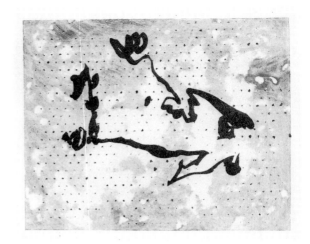

P 07917   **Fence/Climbing Plant** 1978

Screenprint $9\frac{1}{2} \times 11\frac{1}{2}$ (241 × 293) on paper $11\frac{1}{2} \times 13\frac{1}{2}$ (291 × 343) with hand colouring in watercolour, printed by the artist (not editioned)
Inscribed on the back 1978
Purchased from the artist (Grant-in-Aid) 1984

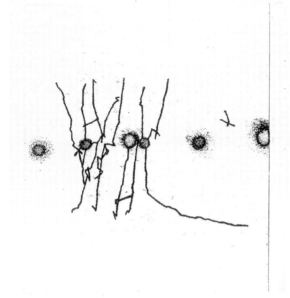

P 07916   **Off the Tracks** 1977

Etching 10 × $8\frac{5}{8}$ (254 × 220) on paper $15\frac{1}{8} \times 15\frac{1}{16}$ (384 × 383), printed by the artist (not editioned)
Inscribed 'Clough' b.r.
Purchased from the artist (Grant-in-Aid) 1984

This etching was made at Wimbledon School of Art while Clough was teaching there.

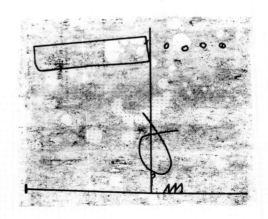

P 07918   **Gate Detail** 1980

Screenprint $19\frac{1}{16} \times 22\frac{9}{16}$ (484 × 573) with hand colouring in watercolour, printed by the artist (not editioned)
Not inscribed
Purchased from the artist (Grant-in-Aid) 1984

P 07919 **Gate** 1981

> Screenprint $7\frac{1}{2} \times 8\frac{7}{8}$ (190 × 225) on paper $15\frac{3}{8} \times 14$ (390 × 355) from three screens (white and two shades of greenish-blue) with hand colouring in watercolour, printed by the artist (not editioned)
> Not inscribed
> Purchased from the artist (Grant-in-Aid) 1984

These three prints were made at Wimbledon School of Art while Clough was teaching there. In P 07917 and P 07918 the image from a single screen was used as a basis on which to try a variety of different drawn and painted additions. Clough would prepare a sheet in her own studio and then take it to Wimbledon and print the screen image over it, sometimes adding more work by hand afterwards. In 'Fence/Climbing Plant' there is a washed rubbed ground of soft grey with some purple and orange; in 'Gate Detail' the ground is also washed and rubbed with powdery-looking pigment, predominantly grey but with some pale yellow. In 'Gate' a more substantial screenprinted image is over-worked in red watercolour and crayon.

P 07920 **Untitled** 1981

> Woodcut $10\frac{3}{4} \times 12\frac{1}{8}$ (274 × 308) on black paper, printed by the artist (not editioned)
> Not inscribed
> Purchased from the artist (Grant-in-Aid) 1984

One of a small group of unique prints using this woodblock in different configurations, made by the artist in her studio.

Bernard Cohen born 1933

P 07756 **Imitations** 1981

> Etching $27 \times 21\frac{1}{4}$ (686 × 541) on Velin Arches 36×27 (915 × 684), printed by Nigel Oxley at Kelpra Studio and published by Waddington Graphics
> Inscribed 'Bernard Cohen 1981' b.r. and 'IMITATIONS 6/60'; impressed with the printer's and publisher's stamp
> Purchased from Waddington Graphics (Grant-in-Aid) 1982

'Imitations' is from a group of four prints as follows: 'Concerning the Meal', 'Imitations', 'The Trace' and 'Things Seen'. All four prints refer to the ritual of dining in domestic surroundings. The central image of P 07756 is an aeroplane depicted as though reflected in a glass top table. The table itself appears to be cracked and shows signs of the meal having ended. The cracked

appearance is created by Cohen's use of deliberately fragmented plates, the edge of each plate revealing an unprinted, uneven line.

The imagery imployed in this work which includes aeroplanes, paddles, paw marks and hand prints is similar to that used in the other prints in the series and refer to Cohen's own living environment near the River Thames in Kew. For a discussion on the significance of these images see the entries on P 05547 'Concerning the Meal' 1980 and the painting T 03284 'Matter of Identity III – The Trace' 1977–9 in *The Tate Gallery Illustrated Catalogue of Acquisitions 1980–82*, pp.241 and 64–7.

This entry has been approved by the artist.

Robert Cottingham born 1935

P 07641 **Carl's** 1977

> Etching with aquatint $10\frac{1}{8} \times 10\frac{1}{4}$ (257 × 261) on paper $17\frac{1}{4} \times 17\frac{3}{8}$ (437 × 441), printed and published by Landfall Press, Inc., Chicago
> Inscribed 'Cottingham '77' b.r. and '30/50' and 'Carl's'; impressed with the publisher's stamp
> Purchased at Sotheby's, Los Angeles (Grant-in-Aid) 1982

P 07642 **Black Girl** 1980

> Lithograph $10\frac{1}{2} \times 10\frac{1}{2}$ (266 × 266) on paper $17\frac{1}{2} \times 17\frac{1}{2}$ (444 × 444), printed and published by Landfall Press, Inc., Chicago
> Inscribed 'Cottingham 1980' b.r. and '30/50'; impressed with the publisher's stamp
> Purchased at Sotheby's, Los Angeles (Grant-in-Aid) 1982

to the fast pace suggested by the urban context which Cottingham wishes to evoke. Although he is interested in typography and decorative lettering and prefers 'Downtown' street signs where there are numerous remnants from times when they were especially inventive and brash, this interest is not indulged simply for its own sake. Cottingham frequently modifies the appearance of a sign by cropping the image so that only a detail of the sign is included within the picture space. This enables him to invest the letters with a new, often incongruous, message or meaning, for example: 'Orph' 1972 (repr. *Photo-Realist Printmaking*, exhibition catalogue, n.p.) and 'Wool Ants' which figures in P 07641. In other works, this manipulation is evidence of an inventive verbal wit, as in 'Ode' (repr. Edward Lucie-Smith, *Super-Realism,* Oxford, 1979, ill.26).

P 07643   **Frankfurters** 1980

> Lithograph $10\frac{3}{8} \times 10\frac{1}{2}$ (265 × 267) on paper $17\frac{1}{2} \times 17\frac{1}{2}$ (444 × 444), printed and published by Landfall Press, Inc., Chicago
> Inscribed 'Cottingham 1980' and '34/50'; impressed with the publisher's stamp
> Purchased at Sotheby's, Los Angeles (Grant-in-Aid) 1982

These three prints belong to the Landfall Set, a group of 11 etchings and lithographs made at Landfall Press, Inc. between 1973 and 1978 (repr. *The Complete Guide to Photo-Realist Printmaking,* exhibition catalogue, Louis K. Meisel Gallery, New York, 1978). Cottingham's subjects are the advertising and neon signs on American shop fronts, an interest which arose out of his previous experience as an advertising executive. Although the images derive from photography, both in their genesis and in the printmaking technique (photolithography in the case of 'Black Girl' and 'Frankfurters'), the works demonstrate that Cottingham's aim is not merely to reproduce a ready-made photograph in order to achieve what would be known in commercial terms as a 'retouched image'. The artist has stated: 'I don't care about being realistic. In other words, I don't put in little rust spots or bolts that show. I'm not looking for that kind of realism. I'm just using the subjects as the stepping-off points to compose the painting' (quoted in *Pop Prints*, exhibition handlist, Walker Art Gallery, Liverpool, 1978). Cottingham's primary concerns are formal. In 'Frankfurters', for instance, Cottingham has cropped the image and in so doing emphasises the sharply converging verticals of the shop fascia. This ordering of forms is pursued with an inclination to their abstract values, but the resulting dynamics also relate

Simon Cutts   born 1944

P 08181   **Winter Fruit** 1980

> Letterpress $2\frac{1}{2} \times 3\frac{5}{8}$ (60 × 90) on paper $14\frac{1}{4} \times 10\frac{3}{4}$ (365 × 273), printed by the artist and published by Coracle Press
> Inscribed '26/50' on bottom of cover
> Transferred from the Library 1982

The artist has explained to the compiler that the image came from a label stuck on the end of a shoe box to identify the contents. He entitled it 'Winter Fruit' because 'it was exactly the same sort of label that one finds on boxes and trays of fruit in France. Clearly it's a Winter fruit.' He also stated that the image is in 'the grand tradition of found material. It helps that I knew I could print it reproductively, with the help of a superior engraved block maker, and thereby make an edition. Its significance grew on me as I admired it more and more, until I had a more formal object, with both title, content or "poem"'. The work is to a certain extent a homage to the Scottish artist Ian Hamilton Finlay. The artist remarked that 'I had seen Finlay wear those type of slippers, and to find that they were called Babouche Ecossais by the French had a suitable wildness to it'. A babouche is a Turkish slipper.

This entry has been approved by the artist.

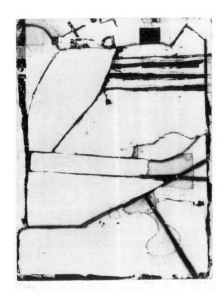

Richard Diebenkorn born 1922

P 07644 **No. 4 from Five Aquatints with Drypoint** 1978

Etching with open bite, aquatint and drypoint $10\frac{7}{8} \times 7\frac{7}{8}$ (277 × 200) on paper $18\frac{7}{8} \times 13$ (480 × 330) watermarked 'RIVES', printed by Lilah Toland at Crown Point Press, Oakland, California and published by them
Inscribed '4 RD 78' b.r. and '20/35'; impressed with the printer's and publisher's stamp
Purchased at Christie's, New York (Grant-in-Aid) 1982

Lit: *Richard Diebenkorn: Intaglio Prints*, exhibition catalogue, University of California, Santa Barbara, Art Museum, June–September 1979, no. 114 (trial proof repr. p.51)

Having previously had two stints making etchings at Crown Point Press, in 1963–5 and 1977, Diebenkorn returned there in December 1978 to make the set from which this print comes, a single etching and another set entitled 'Six Softground Etchings'. These prints explore the same subjects as Diebenkorn's paintings but though they are complete works in their own right they relate more closely to his working drawings and studies for compositions. This print, characteristically, relates to his extended series of 'Ocean Park' paintings, in which an up-tilted perspective of American West Coast suburban views criss-crossed with roadways is abstracted into a powerful formal vocabulary of shapes and lines: 'No. 4' 'is essentially abstract even with the whimsical landscape motif at the top' (letter from the artist, 1986).

This entry has been aproved by the artist.

Jim Dine born 1935

P 07757 **Two Hearts in a Forest** 1981

Woodcut over lithograph $36 \times 60\frac{1}{8}$ (915 × 1527) printed by the artist with his son at his studio in Putney, Vermont, published by Pace Editions, New York
Inscribed 'J Dine 1981' b.l. and '16/24'
Purchased from Waddington Graphics (Grant-in-Aid) 1982

Martin Disler born 1948

P 07839– **Endless Modern Licking of**
07846, **Crashing Globe by Black**
07990 **Doggie – Time Bomb** 1981

Eight etchings each approx. $20\frac{7}{8} \times 28\frac{3}{4}$ (530 × 730) on Van Gelder paper approx. $22\frac{7}{8} \times 29\frac{1}{2}$ (556 × 750), printed by Paul Marcus at Aeropress Inc., New York and

P 07846

published by Peter Blum Editions, New York and Zurich (the portfolio is accompanied by a cassette tape and a penknife mounted on board)
Each inscribed 'Martin Disler' b.r. and '49/49'; each impressed with the printer's stamp
Purchased from Peter Blum Editions (Grant-in-Aid) 1983
Lit: Dieter Hall, 'Eine Neue Grafik-Edition', *Du* no.9, 1981, p.124 (repr.); Bice Curiger, *Looks et Tenebrae*, New York and Zurich, 1984, pp.111–21 (repr. pp.187–95)

The following entry is based upon a conversation held between the artist and the compiler on 7 March 1985 and has been approved by the artist:

Although Martin Disler had had some experience of etching prior to making this portfolio, he had never before worked on a large scale. In this portfolio he embraces a wide variety of etching techniques, some of which he had never previously used, and explores the possibilities of the medium. He employs aquatint, soft and hard ground, sugar lift, drypoint and photoetching. Disler's paintings are gestural and improvisatory and his printmaking techniques reflect this approach; for example in one print he literally pressed his hand into the soft ground.

Disler has a preference for working at night but was unable to etch at night because the workshop facilities were not available. He therefore made a series of drawings and poems at night time which would put him in the mood for working on plates in the morning. Although the prints do not exactly resemble any particular drawings they are close to them in spirit. Disler has said of his method of working:

Manhattan seemed to me well suited for hanging out far above the rim of the world in order to see more sharply than ever what was going on in people's faces and in the streets. Every morning at 11.00 a.m., I went up to the fifth floor in Lafayette Street. Waiting

for me there was Paul Marcus, a printer who grew up in the Bronx and is incredibly experienced in the techniques of the trade. I had been drawing with charcoal and lithographic crayons all night, and I spoke with Paul about the drawings and how they might best be realized. In reality, I was fully determined to work in such a manner that it is impossible to recognize at a glance whether etching is the medium used. I noticed the staff's extremely orthodox attitude toward their craft, and knew I would not have an easy time. While I was smearing 'soft ground' (vernismou) with my finger onto the copper plate and looking deep into my picture through the mirror image, I actually got the impression that Pat, the supervisor at the printer's, would pass out. By the second copy, though, she found it 'magical', and Paul and I understood each other so well that I got the feeling that the etchings, although derived from my drawings, made at night, increasingly grew out of the conversation with him. The atmosphere was extremely tense because, on the one hand, Paul's preparations of the plate and tools proceeded slowly and ritualistically, and I, on the other hand, attacked the plates quickly and decisively. I had become aggressive from waiting, and as a consequence the tools often broke. We were determined to use every technique. Paul and I noticed how the etchings became several dimensions deeper than the drawings, and we smiled at each other (quoted by Curiger, pp.117–18).

The eight parts do not form a sequence or a narrative but are separate images and are accompanied by a cassette tape on which Disler recites a text entitled 'Nigger-Joint Cabaret'. The text was written at night and provides a link between the night time activities and the daytime etching, although it was not conceived specifically as an accompaniment. It incorporates the title of the portfolio and relates, 'the Story of Mr Feels Like a Million', who is a black dog, and makes reference to New York life. Like the drawings and the etchings it has an automatic quality and is not a straightforward narrative. Images of violence and sexuality pervade the text and relate perhaps to the inclusion of the knife. In addition certain images within it appear to relate directly to the etchings.

Disler considers etching to be an important aspect of his work. He has stated in conversation with the compiler that he regards it as 'alchemy to make a drawing on a plate and you do not know what is coming up'. He particularly likes the richness of black which can be achieved in printing.

With the exception of P 07841 which is made from two plates all the works are made from one plate each.

Jean Dubuffet 1901–1985

P 07781   **Man in a Cap** 1953

Lithograph 19¾ × 5⅞ (503 × 150) on Velin
Arches 23¾ × 12¾ (655 × 324), printed by
Henri Deschamps at Mourlot Frères, Paris
Inscribed 'J Dubuffet '53' b.r. and
'L'Homme à la Casquette' and '10/20'
Purchased at Sotheby's (Grant-in-Aid)
1983

Repr: *Catalogue des Travaux de Jean Dubuffet*,
IX, Paris, 1968, no.48

This is one of a series of lithographs which Dubuffet
made in the last months of 1953. At this time he was
also making collages of impressions in ink on lithographic paper which he called 'assemblages d'em-
preintes'. He executed 27 lithographs, 13 in colour and
14 in black and white, of which P 07781 is one, at the
Atelier Desjobert and at Mourlot Frères. In nearly all
cases the editions were limited to either 10 or 20
impressions. In his 'Memoir on the Development of my
Works' published in the catalogue of his retrospective
exhibition held in Paris (*Jean Dubuffet 1942–1960*, exhibition catalogue, Musée des Arts Décoratifs, Paris,
December 1960–February 1961, p.145) Dubuffet records that at this time he was making lithographs which

resulted from impressions [empreintes] made on
transfer paper with greasy ink. Then I cut some
pieces from these sheets, assembled them with glue,
and finally the whole was transferred onto the stone.
For those which were printed in colour I used many
impressions [empreintes] which were printed one
above the other in various tones, according to the

results of long sessions of tests that I held at the
printer's, where a spirit of improvisation reigned.

P 07781 is printed in black and, although it appears to
have been pulled from a heavily inked stone, it seems
not to have been made in the manner described above
but rather to have been drawn more conventionally.
Nevertheless the ink has a textured appearance.

During this period Dubuffet made a number of
images of people wearing caps or hats. P 07781 is
unusual among other lithographs of 1953 in that the
figure is depicted in a static pose and the torso is elongated. In this latter respect it resembles a sculpture in
sponge entitled 'The Duke' 1954 (repr. *Jean Dubuffet
1942–1960*, exhibition catalogue, pl.176). The depiction
of the figure is very flat which was consistent with
Dubuffet's approach to painting at the time. As he wrote
in his 'Notes pour les Fins-Lettrés' of 1945 (published
in 1946 in *Prospectus*);

The objective of a painting is to animate a surface
which is by definition two-dimensional and without
depth. One does not enrich it in seeking effects of
relief or trompe-l'oeil through shading; one
denatures and adulterates it ... Let us seek instead
ingenious ways to flatten objects on the surface; and
let the surface speak its own language and not an
artificial language of three dimensional space which
is not proper to it ... I feel the need to leave the
surface visibly flat. My eyes like to rest on a surface
which is very flat, particularly a rectangular surface.
The objects represented will be transformed into
pancakes, as though flattened by a pressing iron
(Hubert Damisch (ed.), *Jean Dubuffet, Prospectus et
Tous Ecrits Suivants*, Paris, 1967, I, p.74).

Mourlot Frères do not have records regarding the
publisher of P 07781 but think it likely that it was published by the artist.

Luciano Fabro born 1936

P 07994   **SS Redentore** 1972
(i)–(xii),
07995   Four-part screenprint, three parts
(i)–(xiv), composed of twelve sheets and one part
07996   composed of fifteen sheets; P 07994
(i)–(xii), 99⅝ × 85¾ (5300 × 1800) overall, P 07995
07997   94⅞ × 110⅝ (4100 × 8100) overall, P 07996
(i)–(xii)   99⅝ × 85⅝ (5300 × 1705) overall, P 07997
           97⅝ × 92⅛ (4800 × 3400) overall, printed by
           Alfredo and Enrico Rossi, Genova,
           published by them with the artist

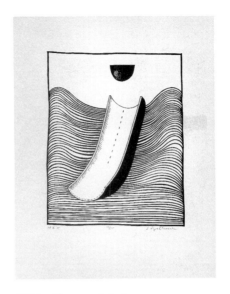

Stanislaw Fijalkowski born 1922

P 07921 **October 18, 1971** 1971

Linocut $15\frac{3}{4} \times 12\frac{1}{8}$ (400 × 308) on paper
$24\frac{1}{4} \times 17\frac{3}{4}$ (616 × 451), printed and
published by the artist
Inscribed 'S. Fijalkowski' b.r. and '14/35'
and '18 × 71'
Purchased from the artist (Grant-in-Aid)
1983

Inscribed 'Luciano Fabro' on the title
page and '51/120'
Purchased from Galeria Pieroni, Rome
(Grant-in-Aid) 1984

This work is a screenprinted line drawing of the façade
of SS Redentore with three variations on the proportions invented by Fabro: P 07994 is the façade and
P 07995–7 are the variations. Each part is accompanied
by a sheet printed with a small image of the façade
depicted in that part and there is a sheet headed 'Sinot-
tica degli insiemi e delle proporzione' with small images
of all four; there is also a title page bearing the artist's
signature and those of the printers.

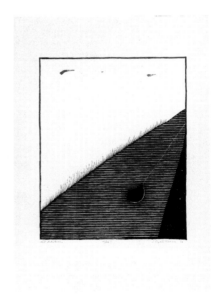

P 07922 **Motorway** XLV 1976

Linocut $20\frac{1}{2} \times 16\frac{1}{8}$ (521 × 410) on paper
$31\frac{1}{8} \times 21\frac{1}{2}$ (790 × 546), printed and

published by the artist
Inscribed 'S. Fijalkowski 76' b.r. and
'13/40' and 'XLV Autostrodov'
Purchased from the artist (Grant-in-Aid)
1983

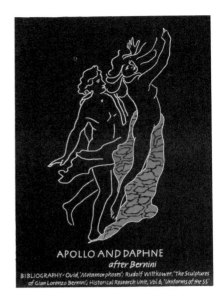

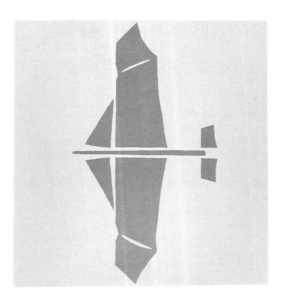

Ian Hamilton Finlay born 1925

P 07645 **Sailing Barge Red Wing** 1975

Screenprint $12\frac{7}{8} \times 12$ (328 × 305), printed
at Girdwood and published by the Wild
Hawthorn Press in an edition of 300
Inscribed 'Ian Hamilton Finlay' and '129'
on flyleaf of folder
Purchased from the artist (Grant-in-Aid)
1982

Made in collaboration with Ian Gardner, this work is
one of Finlay's characteristic images of visual coincidence. The image of a sailing barge and its reflection
printed in red make a bird shape on the green ground.
The Wild Hawthorn Press is Finlay's own publishing
press based at his home, Little Sparta, Stonypath, Lan-
ark (reference this and the other prints described here).
It is Finlay's habit to work with other artists and printers, using them to visualise his idea and his visual
concept by drawing or typography and then having the
result printed to his own specifications. In this case the
image was drawn by Gardner.

This and the following entries have all been approved
by the artist.

P 07931 **Apollo and Daphne** 1975

Screenprint $19\frac{1}{2} \times 14\frac{1}{8}$ (497 × 360), printed
at Girdwood, published by the Wild
Hawthorn Press in an edition of about 300
Not inscribed
Purchased from the artist (Grant-in-Aid)
1983

Text beneath the image indicates Finlay's idea of Apollo
with Daphne being engulfed by a green camouflage
smock: 'APOLLO AND DAPHNE/ after Berni-
ni/BIBLIOGRAPHY – Ovid, "Metamorphoses"; Rudolf
Wittkower, "The Sculptures of Gian Lorenzo Berni-
ni"; Historical Research Unit, Vol. 6, "Uniforms of
the SS"'. In conversation with the compiler the artist
mentioned that in the story of Apollo and Daphne the
gods and nature 'were behaving not unlike the Waffen
SS' (who were the first to use a smock with a leaf
camouflage pattern, hence its identification with them).
This image, in which Daphne is wearing a camouflage
smock which replaces 'nature', was used as the poster
for the exhibition 'Ian Hamilton Finlay: Collaborations'
at Kettle's Yard, Cambridge, 1977.

P 07934 **Venus of the Hours** 1975

Screenprint $29\frac{1}{2} \times 14\frac{1}{2}$ (749 × 368), printed
at Girdwood and published by the Wild
Hawthorn Press in an edition of about 300
Not inscribed
Purchased from the artist (Grant-in-Aid)
1983

Made in collaboration with Ron Costley, who did the
lettering – the words of the title together with a Venus

sign that is both an ancient and universal pictogram for female sexuality and a shorthand symbol for the dial of a vertical sundial constitute the image.

English at the right and an image of beehives with the names of ships at the left, represents the Japanese and American aircraft carriers whose planes, fuelled by petrol piped like honey through hives, flew far to engage the enemy, although the ships themselves did not come in sight of one another. The rosebushes represent the lush distances of ocean which concealed the rival fleets. Finlay frequently uses Latin, as in this and other works described here, to signify the epic or the arcane.

P 07932– **Midway I and II** 1977
07933

Two screenprints each approx. $22\frac{1}{4} \times 27$ (565 × 687), printed at Girdwood and published by the Wild Hawthorn Press in an edition of about 300
Not inscribed
Purchased from the artist (Grant-in-Aid) 1983

The Battle of Midway in June 1942 marked the turn of the war in the Pacific to America's favour. Finlay's image, composed of a sheet of lettering in Latin and

At the field's edge, on the vertiginous cliff-top, stood a solitary hut.

P 07646 **At the Field's Edge** 1978

Screenprint $11\frac{5}{8} \times 19\frac{7}{8}$ (296 × 504), printed at Girdwood, Edinburgh, published by the Wild Hawthorn Press in an edition of 300.
Inscribed 'Ian Hamilton Finlay' and '89' on a sheet of tracing paper
Purchased from the artist (Grant-in-Aid) 1982

This work consists of a folded sheet of paper (enclosing a separate sheet of tracing paper bearing the inscription and other information). On the right hand leaf of the open sheet is an image of the flat-topped prow of an aircraft carrier, from a drawing by John Borg Manduca;

text on the opposite leaf reads: 'At the field's edge, on the vertiginous cliff-top, stood a solitary hut'. The carrier is represented, as in other work by Finlay, as an aspect of the modern 'epic' and 'sublime'.

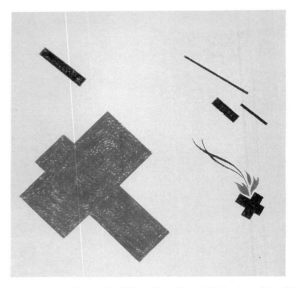

Inscribed 'Ian Hamilton Finlay' and '118' on folder
Purchased from the artist (Grant-in-Aid) 1983

This image refers to Malevich's own images of abstractions such as wireless waves or flying shapes. The artist, in conversation with the compiler, said that Malevich obviously pictured himself as 'the best aeroplane' and that the victim in the dog-fight might be the artist's rival Tatlin. Malevich's own writings make it clear that his abstractions are representations and not pure abstractions, though his commentators overlook this.

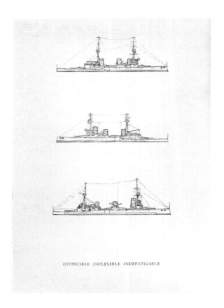

P 07647
(i) and
(ii)

Homage to Agam 1978

Two-sheet screenprint $15 \times 10\frac{3}{8}$ (380 × 264), printed at Girdwood and published by the Wild Hawthorn Press in an edition of 150
Inscribed 'Ian Hamilton Finlay' and '66' on flyleaf of cover
Purchased from the artist (Grant-in-Aid) 1982

This work, made in collaboration with David Button, consists of a sheet of cream paper printed with line drawings of three World War I warships and their names: 'INVINCIBLE. INFLEXIBLE. INDE-FATIGABLE' with a tracing paper overlay sheet which adds red diagonal strokes – the poles which held the ships' torpedo nets – along each hull. The words 'TRANSFORMABLE LINE SEGMENTS' are placed above the names and 'HOMAGE TO AGAM' below. The work is a visual pun on certain works by the Israeli artist Agam. It is enclosed in a grey cover.

P 07925 **Homage to Malevich** 1978

Screenprint $9\frac{7}{8} \times 9\frac{7}{8}$ (251 × 251) on paper $10\frac{7}{8} \times 10\frac{7}{8}$ (277 × 277), printed at Girdwood and published by the Wild Hawthorn Press in an edition of 300

P 07926 **Propaganda for the Wood Elves** 1981

Photograph $8\frac{1}{4} \times 5\frac{13}{16}$ (210 × 148)
Not inscribed
Purchased from the artist (Grant-in-Aid)
1983

Made in collaboration with Harvey Dwight from a photograph set up and taken in Finlay's garden at Little Sparta. In conversation with the compiler the artist described the image as 'an enigmatic emblem. Visual paradox is one mode of an emblem', adding that it referred to traditional German tree-worship and the violence of nature.

P 07927– **Posters from the Little Spartan**
07930   **War** 1982

Four linocuts each approx. 12 × 17 (305 × 432), printed by Nicholas Sloan at Parrett Press, Martock, and published by the Wild Hawthorn Press in an edition of about 100
Not inscribed
Purchased from the artist (Grant-in-Aid)
1983

P 07927
The Arts Council Must be Utterly Destroyed

P 07928
Death to the Arts Council

P 07929
Let Perish the Money Tyrants

P 07930
Peace to the Cottages – War to the Arts Council

Each poster is a Latin text, cut and printed by Nicholas Sloan. They are, respectively: 'CONCILIUM/ ARTUM/DELENDUM/EST', 'MORS/CONCILIO/ ARTUM/', 'PEREANT/TYRANNI/NUMMARI' and 'PAX.TUGURIIS/BELLUM.CONC/ARTIUM'; the translations are the artist's. In 1982, as part of Finlay's campaign against Strathclyde Region's attempts to extract rates for the Temple in his garden on the fallacious basis of it being a commercial gallery, these printed texts were fly-posted on the Scottish National Gallery, the Scottish Arts Council building and other places in Edinburgh. They were accompanied by a leaflet on revolutionary language alluding to Denis Roche, the poet who wrote a pamphlet on language and the French Revolution. The use of Latin here allegorises the neo-classical attitudes of Finlay and his supporters, the Sainte-Just Vigilantes. According to

Finlay, classicism supplied the entire 'iconography' of the French Revolution, which he has even described as 'a pastoral whose Virgil was Rousseau'. Two quotations from Finlay's 'Illustrated Dictionary of the Little Spartan War' (*MW Magazine*, Issue 3, February 1983) are relevant here: 'Neoclassicism, n. – a rearmament programme for architecture and the arts' (illustrated by a classical capital) and 'inscription, n. – an arcane communication often coded in Latin' (illustrated with one of the War Posters). 'Peace to the Cottages' is based on an actual slogan used by the Revolutionaries: 'Peace to the Cottages – War on the Castles'. 'The Arts Council Must be Utterly Destroyed' is derived from a phrase Cato would add to the end of every speech as a reference to his hatred of Carthage. The shortening of words as in 'CONC' follows normal usage in Roman inscriptions.

P 07923– **Two Trees** 1982
07924

Two woodcuts $3\frac{5}{8} \times 4\frac{5}{8}$ (92 × 116) and $4\frac{5}{8} \times 5\frac{7}{16}$ (116 × 138) respectively, printed by Richard Healy, published by the Wild Hawthorn Press in editions of 300
Not inscribed
Purchased from the artist (Grant-in-Aid) 1983

Each of this pair of woodcuts is marked out with a flap at the right side on which are printed instructions for folding and glueing the sheet into a rectangular column. They are printed in green and each has lettering down one face of what would be the column if so fixed. The idea is related to Finlay's installation at the Kroller-Muller Museum, near Arnhem, where he put stone column bases on actual trees. Finlay believes that this – or something like it – may have been done by the Romans.

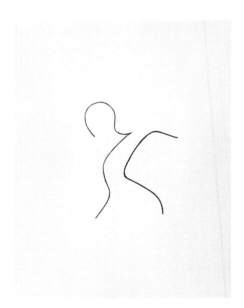

Joel Fisher born 1947

P 07758 **Untitled** 1981

Screenprint with collage $29\frac{7}{8} \times 22\frac{1}{2}$ on Somerset paper, printed by the artist, not editioned
Inscribed 'J Fisher 1981' on the back and 'unique screenprint and chine collé'
Purchased from Nigel Greenwood Gallery (Grant-in-Aid) 1982

Barry Flanagan born 1941

P 07935   Field Day 1983

Etching $7\frac{1}{4} \times 9\frac{1}{2}$ (184 × 216) on Velin
Arches paper $11\frac{1}{4} \times 15$ (285 × 381),
printed by the artist and Colin Dyer,
published by Waddington Graphics
Inscribed 'B F' b.r. and '47/75'; impressed
with the publisher's stamp
Purchased from Waddington Galleries
(Grant-in-Aid) 1983

Lit: David Brown, *Barry Flanagan Etchings
and Linocuts*, exhibition catalogue,
Waddington Galleries, May 1984 (n.p.
repr.)

The following entry is based on a conversation between
the artist and the compiler held on 21 August 1985 and
has been approved by the artist.

'Field Day' is one of a series of four etchings and
three linocuts all drawn before the model. They are
'Stepney Green', 'Mule', 'Cob Study', 'Field Day',
'Welsh Lights' and 'Ganymede' all dated 1983. Flanagan hired the horse for one day and had it brought to
the yard outside his studio. In conversation with the
compiler he stated: 'I called it "Field Day" because the
drawing has a beautiful form to it. It has fluency and
composure. That's reminiscent of racing and one can
have a field day in the sense of an enjoyable event.
Calling it "Field Day" was like naming the horse.'

The black rectangle at the bottom of the plate mark
results from the etching process. David Brown writes

> In the preparation of the etching plates, they are
> 'smoked' in a flame to produce a fine, even covering
> of wax, the plate being held by a pair of tongs.
> Normally the area covered by the tongs and
> therefore unaffected by the 'smoking' process would
> be waxed later, but with these prints, Flanagan chose
> to eliminate this final stage leaving a small area etched
> by acid and absorbing the ink.

The image was etched without any preliminary studies.
The fluency of the line results from Flanagan's general
approach to printmaking. He stated that 'the sculptor's
line is often gestural'.

P 07936   Welsh Cob

Linocut $14\frac{1}{4} \times 10$ (358 × 254) on Velin
Arches paper $22\frac{3}{8} \times 15\frac{1}{8}$ (568 × 384),
printed by the artist and Colin Dyer,
published by Waddington Graphics
Inscribed 'B F' b.r. and '2/50'; impressed
with the publisher's stamp b.l.
Purchased from Waddington Galleries
(Grant-in-Aid) 1983

Lit: David Brown, *Barry Flanagan Etchings
and Linocuts*, exhibition catalogue,
Waddington Galleries, May 1984 (n.p.
repr. in col.); also repr. *Barry Flanagan
Prints 1970–1983*, exhibition catalogue,
Tate Gallery, May–August 1986, p.27

The following entry is based upon a conversation
between the artist and the compiler held on 21 August
1985 and has been approved by the artist. Flanagan's
interest in depicting horses was sharpened by the
'Horses of San Marco' exhibition held at the Royal
Academy, London in 1979 and he has executed a number of sculptures and prints on this theme since then.
He stated that 'a Cob has a certain stocky nature, it's a
nice little work horse. The Morgan horse is the closest
survivor to the San Marco horse other than a cart horse.
A Welsh Cob is a similar sort of horse.'

'Welsh Cob' was cut direct before the model (see
entry for P 07935) but unlike the other prints in this
series contains a reference to the landscape. Referring

to the manner in which he executed the print Flanagan stated that 'making prints concentrates the mind. It is a commitment. It is intractable to a degree and requires a lot of attention. Pencil and paper I'm not really comfortable with ... I like to go into something and finish it.' He also remarked 'I like carving into lino, I like the challenge of achieving fluency of line and clarity of subject, the subtle variations of depth and wrist.' He regards printmaking as more suited to his 'sculptor's temperament' than drawing.

Inscribed 'Sam Francis' b.r. and '31/50'
Presented by J. G. Cluff 1984
Lit: Susan Einstein, 'The Prints of Sam Francis. Lithographs and Silkscreens', in Peter Selz, *Sam Francis*, New York, 1982, p.251
Repr: *Sam Francis*, exhibition catalogue, Kestner Gesellschaft, Hannover, April–May 1963, p.24 (col.)

In 1960 Sam Francis was living in Bern and suffering from tuberculosis. P 11070 and 11071 were made during this stay in Switzerland and were among the first lithographs that the artist produced. According to Susan Einstein he was urged to try lithography by E. W. Kornfeld and was introduced to the printer by Gottfried Honegger. Matthieu printed the first series of lithographs, to which these belong, in the summer of 1960. Einstein writes:

> Francis remembers this first session as being an intense learning experience. His fascination with lithography focusses on the stone itself – it is the basis for his imagery, the life-source of his prints. He perceives the stone as an animated substance with unique physical properties – 'you breathe on it and it shows.' Some of the first prints, bearing titles like *Blue Blood Stone*, *Coldest Stone*, and *Serpent on the Stone*, refer to his pursuit of a stone spirit. Thus, he acknowledges a mysterious element which remains partially beyond his control and which causes the image to rise out of the stone. When he comments, 'A dream is the way I work on stone – not something I think about or formulate in my mind, he does not diminish his own creative role, but, on the contrary,

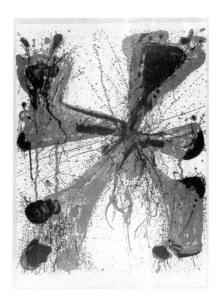

Sam Francis born 1923

P 11070 **Damn Braces** 1960

Lithograph 33½ × 24⅞ (851 × 632) on paper watermarked 'RIVES', printed by Emil Matthieu, Zurich and published by Klipstein and Kornfeld, Bern
Inscribed 'Sam Francis' b.r. and '27/75'
Presented by J. G. Cluff 1984
Repr: *Sam Francis*, exhibition catalogue, Kestner Gesellschaft, Hannover, April–May 1963, p.29 (col.)

P 11071 **Blue Blood Stone** 1960

Lithograph 33¼ × 24⅞ (844 × 632) on paper watermarked 'RIVES', printed by Emil Matthieu, Zurich and published by Klipstein and Kornfeld, Bern

professes that he is the unique medium through which these images can be revealed and preserved.

Although a number of the prints in this series relate to paintings made contemporaneously it was not Francis's intention to reproduce, on stone, ideas he had already used in paintings. Francis stated that 'Images sometimes spill over into a painting and vice versa, but each is worked out in its own way' (Einstein, p.252).

According to Wieland Schmied, writing in the Kestner Gesellschaft catalogue, the images in this series may refer to human organs and represent a 'stoical (and typically American) attitude towards death and pain' (p.14). During this period Francis made a number of paintings, commonly known as the 'Blue Balls' paintings, which seem to relate not only to human organs but also to Japanese art. Francis had visited Japan in 1957 and 1960. His treatment of space and the demonic nature of some of his images are likened by Selz to those found in Japanese art. P 11070 is an image of this kind.

Both works are printed in blue and red; P 11070 is predominantly blue and P 11071 is predominantly red. Both works were executed in tusche which suited the artist's desire to transpose the drips and splashes of his paintings directly into the lithographic medium and to make gestural marks. Although the size of the lithographs is smaller than anything Francis had previously painted, the scale of the markings is large. According to Selz 'the small size of the stone . . . affected his painting' (note 38, p.280) in that the paintings of the early 1960s were in a smaller format than preceding works.

In commenting on this catalogue entry the artist stated that the title of P 11070 'is part of one of W— Blake's aphorisms "Damn Braces Bless Relaxes".

'I speak to William Blake in my dreams & he sings to me.'

This entry has been approved by the artist.

Lucian Freud born 1922

P 07782 Head of a Woman 1982

Etching 5 × 5 (127 × 127) on paper $10\frac{3}{4} \times 8\frac{5}{8}$ (273 × 220), printed by Terry Willson at Palm Tree Editions, published by James Kirkman and Anthony d'Offay in an edition of 25 to accompany special copies of *Lucian Freud* by Lawrence Gowing, published by Thames & Hudson
Inscribed 'L.F.' b.r. and 'A/P IV/X';
impressed with the printer's stamp
Purchased from Anthony d'Offay Gallery (Grant-in-Aid) 1982

P 07783 The Painter's Mother 1982

Etching 7 × 6 (178 × 152) on paper $11\frac{3}{4} \times 9\frac{1}{2}$ (300 × 240), printed by Terry Willson at Palm Tree Editions, published by James Kirkman and Anthony d'Offay in an edition of 25 to accompany special copies of *Lucian Freud* by Lawrence Gowing, published by Thames & Hudson
Inscribed 'L.F.' b.r. and 'AP IX/X';
impressed with the printer's stamp
Purchased from Anthony d'Offay Gallery (Grant-in-Aid) 1982

Terry Frost born 1915

P07981 **Blue Moon** 1952

> Lithograph with linocut $14 \times 10\frac{7}{8}$
> (355×273) on paper 20×15 (508×380),
> printed by the artist and Henry Cliffe at
> Bath Academy of Art, Corsham, not
> editioned
> Not inscribed
> Purchased from the artist (Grant-in-Aid)
> 1983

This and the following entries are based upon information suppled by the artist, in answer to questions posed by the compiler, in August 1985 and on 16 April 1986.

Although 'Blue Moon' was the first print Frost made available for purchase it was not his first print. He had previously made woodcuts during the Second World War, while imprisoned in a camp, and lithographs at Camberwell School of Art. The print was originally envisaged as a lithograph but Frost decided to introduce linocut when 'it became difficult to obtain a welcome in the litho. dept. at Corsham'.

This entry has been approved by the artist.

P07982 **Boat Shapes** 1952

> Linocut $5\frac{1}{4} \times 5\frac{5}{8}$ (132×143) on paper
> $6\frac{1}{2} \times 6\frac{3}{8}$ (167×162), printed by the artist at
> No.4 Porthmeor Studios, St Ives, not
> editioned
> Inscribed 'Terry Frost' b.r. and 'linocut

printed in 52 but all different possibly 20 in all'
Purchased from the artist (Grant-in-Aid) 1983

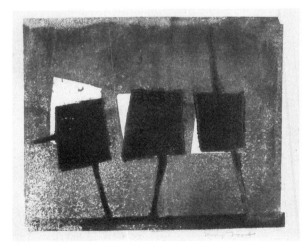

P07983 **Boat Shapes** *c.*1954

> Linocut $5\frac{1}{8} \times 6\frac{1}{4}$ (131×155) on paper
> $5\frac{5}{8} \times 6\frac{3}{4}$ (142×173), printed by the artist at
> No.4 Porthmeor Studios, St Ives, not
> editioned
> Inscribed 'Terry Frost' b.r.
> Purchased from the artist (Grant-in-Aid)
> 1983

P 07984 **Boat Shapes** 1954

Linocut $7\frac{3}{4} \times 10\frac{1}{2}$ (193 × 267) on paper
$8\frac{7}{8} \times 11$ (225 × 280), printed by the artist
at No.4 Porthmeor Studios, St Ives, not
editioned
Inscribed 'Terry Frost 54' b.r.
Purchased from the artist (Grant-in-Aid)
1983

P 07982 was printed by hand-pressure. Of the twenty
or so printed 'each one is pretty unique' in that most of
them were hand printed and Frost 'played about with
a bit of colour on the prints'. In some cases he used 'a
combination of press and hand', the press being an
etching press. The 'Boat Shapes' prints relate closely
to the motifs Frost was incorporating in his paintings
in the early 1950s inspired by the rocking movements
of boats moored in harbour (see Lawrence Alloway,
Nine Abstract Artists, 1954, pp.23–4 for an account of
the genesis of 'Blue Movement', repr. no.9, a painting
in this series, now in the collection of the Vancouver
Art Gallery). P 07982 is printed in blue, black and brown
from one block. Frost printed the block twice, once in
reverse, applying the colours with a brush in order to
be able to print more than one at a time. The lower half,
therefore, is a mirror reflection of the upper half. Frost
has written, 'It was most important to me, the accident
of that double print opened up the imagination to all
kinds of possibilities and I did do a super Blue ptg from
that double print which is in Vancouver.'

P 07983 is printed from two blocks in brown and
black, the black being printed last. The ink appears to
have been relatively dry, allowing the paper to show
through as a texture. P 07984, printed on off-white paper
in black, is also unevenly printed but is a more complex
image than the other two. According to Frost, 'This is
much more based on a painting idea and is a much
more complicated linocut.' The emphasis on the vertical
stripes in this work and the deep black tone anticipate

the paintings he would begin to make on taking up an
appointment as Gregory Fellow at Leeds University in
that year. This entry has been approved by the artist.

P 07985 **Leeds** 1956

Drypoint $4\frac{7}{8} \times 6\frac{5}{8}$ (125 × 167) on paper
$7\frac{1}{8} \times 8$ (181 × 205), printed by the artist at
Leeds College of Art, not editioned
Inscribed 'Terry Frost 56' b.r. and 'Leeds.
Cottage Rd never editioned possibly 4
printed'
Purchased from the artist (Grant-in-Aid)
1983

'Leeds' was made while Frost was Gregory Fellow at
Leeds University and refers specifically to the
landscape. It relates closely to a painting of the same
year entitled 'Winter Landscape' (British Council Collection, repr. *The British Council Collection 1938–1984*,
1984, p.61) which depicts similar spiral motifs. According to Frost, 'The spirals were to do with the movement
made in the sheep's wool by the wind in the Dales.'
Frost produced a number of paintings in this period
emphasising the contrast between black and white
which he had experienced in the snow-covered landscape. The use of drypoint in P 07985 emphasises the
blackness of the line. Frost had used this medium on a
number of previous occasions in St Ives.

This entry has been approved by the artist.

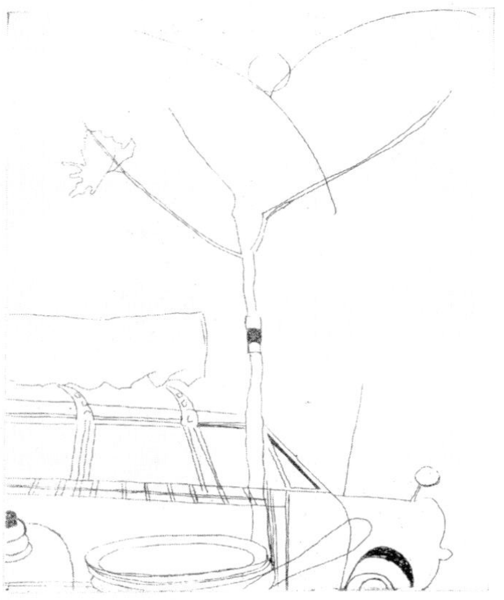

P 07986 **Camping, Anduze** 1979

Etching $10\frac{1}{8} \times 8\frac{1}{4}$ (257 × 209) on paper $15\frac{3}{8} \times 11\frac{3}{4}$ (391 × 300), printed at Reading University by the artist and Harry Redman, not editioned
Inscribed 'Terry Frost' b.r. and 'A/P Camping Anduze' and 'not editioned possibly 6 printed 1967 or 1968'
Purchased from the artist (Grant-in-Aid) 1983

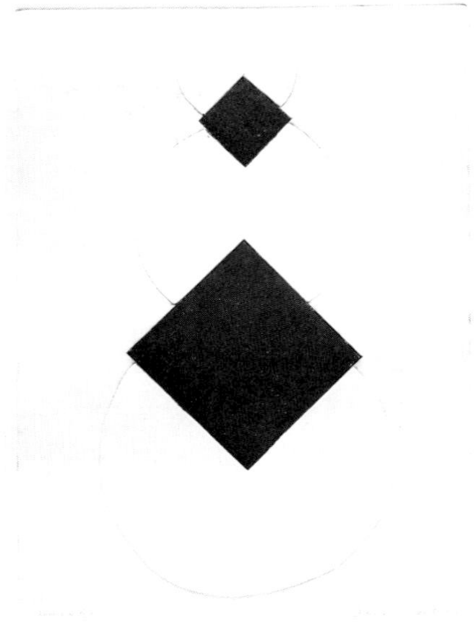

P 07987 **Umea, Sweden** 1979

Etching $13\frac{3}{4} \times 10\frac{1}{4}$ (348 × 256) on paper $16\frac{3}{4} \times 11\frac{3}{4}$ (399 × 299), printed by the artist at Umea Summer School, Sweden, not editioned
Inscribed 'Terry Frost 79' b.r. and 'Umea A/P'
Purchased from the artist (Grant-in-Aid) 1983

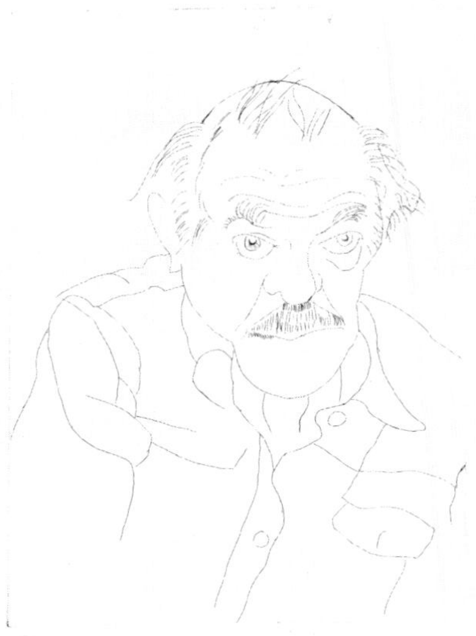

P 07988 **Self Portrait** 1980

Etching $10\frac{7}{8} \times 7\frac{7}{8}$ (277 × 200) on paper $17\frac{5}{8} \times 12\frac{3}{4}$ (445 × 324), printed by Jeff Clarke, Oxford, not editioned
Inscribed 'Terry Frost 80' b.r. and 'A/P'
Purchased from the artist (Grant-in-Aid) 1983

'Umea, Sweden' was made at Umea while Frost was directing the summer school there. It has generally been Frost's practice to make prints when the facilities have been easily available to him. This print depicts three circles in outline separated from each other by two roughly cut squares printed in dense black. The configuration is arranged vertically and 'is to do with the sun'.

'Camping Anduze' was made while Frost was visiting the sculptor, Elizabeth Frink, who lived nearby. It was preceded by a drawing executed at the camp site near Anduze where Frost and his family were staying. The print depicts a car parked beside a one-leaf tree which hangs over a saucepan and water bottle standing on a table. The sun is high in the sky. 'We were the only English in a totally French camp at that time, so we got the tree with only one leaf for shade.' Frost visited Anduze on three occasions between 1969 and 1979. Since inscribing the work he has recalled that he drew the image on his first visit to Anduze and printed it in *c.*1969–70.

This entry has been approved by the artist.

P 11046 The Martyrdom of St Saturus 1928

Wood engraving $3\frac{1}{4} \times 4\frac{1}{4}$ (83 × 108) on thin Japan paper $7\frac{1}{2} \times 6\frac{3}{4}$ (190 × 172), from *The Passion of Perpetua and Felicity* translated by Walter Shewring and published as an insert in *The Fleuron*, VII, 1928
Not inscribed
Bequeathed by Mrs E West 1982

Lit: John Physick, *The Engravings of Eric Gill*, London 1963, no.559; Malcolm Yorke, *Eric Gill, Man of Flesh and Spirit*, London 1981, ill.p.263 (on page with typography); *Eric Gill, Matter and Spirit*, exhibition catalogue, Gillian Jason Gallery, March–April 1982, no.266; Christopher Skelton, *The Engravings of Eric Gill*, Wellingborough 1983, ill.p.262

Eric Gill 1882–1940

P 11047 The Triumph of St Perpetua 1928

Wood engraving $3\frac{1}{2} \times 3\frac{1}{4}$ (90 × 83) on thin Japan paper $9\frac{1}{2} \times 5$ (242 × 127), from *The Passion of Perpetua and Felicity* translated by Walter Shewring and published as an insert in *The Fleuron*, VII, 1928
Not inscribed
Bequeathed by Mrs E West 1982

Lit: John Physick *The Engravings of Eric Gill*, London 1963, no.555; *Eric Gill, Matter and Spirit*, exhibition catalogue, Gillian Jason Gallery, March–April 1982, no.265; Christopher Skelton, *The Engravings of Eric Gill*, Wellingborough 1983, ill.p.261

Philip Guston 1913–1980

P 07999 Door 1980

Lithograph $19\frac{1}{2} \times 29\frac{1}{2}$ (495 × 749), printed and published by Gemini GEL, Los Angeles
Inscribed 'Philip Guston '80' b.r. and 'Door' and '42/50'; impressed with the printer's and publisher's stamp
Purchased from Gemini GEL (Grant-in-Aid) 1983

P 77009 Painter 1980

Lithograph $32 \times 42\frac{1}{2}$ (813 × 1079), printed and published by Gemini GEL, Los Angeles

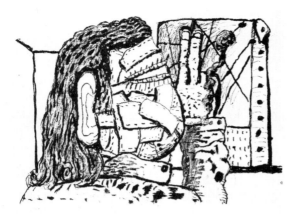

P 77009

Stamped 'Philip Guston' b.r. and
inscribed '34/50'; impressed with the
printer's and publisher's stamp
Purchased from Gemini GEL (Grant-in-
Aid) 1983

P 11078

P 11072–   **Room** 1980
11079   **East Side** 1980
            Rug 1980
            Summer 1980
            Sea 1980
            Car 1980
            Elements 1980
            Coat 1980

Eight lithographs in range 18 × 28
(457 × 711) – 30 × 39 (762 × 991), printed
and published by Gemini GEL, Los
Angeles
All inscribed 'Philip Guston '80' in various
places and numbered '22/50'. Each also
inscribed with the title and impressed with

the printer's and publisher's stamp
Presented by David and Renée McKee
through the American Federation of the
Arts 1984

P 11072–9 form the complete set of lithographs published by Gemini GEL as the first Guston portfolio in
1980. P 07999 and P 77009 are from the second and third
portfolio respectively. Guston began collaborating with
Gemini GEL in November 1979 working on transfer
paper and aluminium plates under the guidance of Serge
Lozingot. Within two weeks Guston had executed sixteen transfer drawings and plates which were subsequently processed at Gemini GEL and returned to
him in December. By this time Guston had completed
twenty more images, ten on transfer paper and ten on
plates. On 6 December he authorised the printing of
fourteen images from the first group and, on 8 February,
eleven images from the second group. Seventeen completed editions were signed at the beginning of April
1980. At the time of his death on 7 June 1980 seven
editions remained unsigned; these are numbered by
Gemini GEL and stamped with an estate stamp authorised by Guston's widow. P 77009 is one of these. The
three portfolios contain eight, seven and eight lithographs respectively. The first two portfolios were published during Guston's lifetime.

Guston's lithographs incorporate the vocabulary of
his late paintings which includes rusty railroad nails, old
shoes and shoe heels, bare light bulbs, old automobiles,
clothing and the smoking of cigarettes. In works made
after 1969 Guston renounced his previous interest in
abstraction in favour of 'a world of tangible things,
images, subjects, stories like the way art always was'
('Philip Guston Talking', *Philip Guston Paintings 1969–
80*, exhibition catalogue, Whitechapel Art Gallery,
October–December 1982, p.50). These lithographs contain a mixture of reality, fantasy, caricature and naturalistic observation which characterises all of Guston's
late work and which endows a biomorphic celebration
of life with both pathos and humour.

The composition of some of the lithographs reflects
Guston's earlier compositional concerns; 'Room' in particular can be directly compared with 'Design for
Queensbridge Housing Project' 1939 (repr. Whitechapel Art Gallery exhibition catalogue, p.69). A
number of the lithographs relate closely to late paintings
in terms of title and composition; 'Coat', for example,
relates to 'Back View' and 'The Coat' both of 1977 (both
repr. ibid. pp.34, 35). The sensuous and rich surface
of the late paintings has a direct correlative in the thick
and waxy surface of the lithograph.

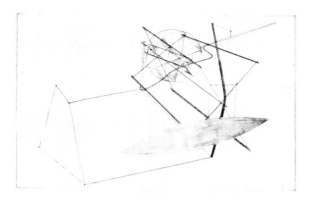

P 07648

P 07649

Richard Hamilton born 1922

P 07648–
07653

Reaper d, e, g, h, i and j 1949

Six etchings from a series of 16, printed by
the artist at the Slade School of Art in
small editions of varying trial proofs.
Purchased from the artist (Grant-in-Aid)
1982

Lit: Richard Hamilton *Richard Hamilton
Prints 1939–1983* 1984, nos.23, 24 and 26
to 29 respectively, all repr. pp.25–8

P 07648
Reaper d
Drypoint and roulette $6\frac{3}{4} \times 10\frac{5}{8}$ (173 × 270)
on paper 11 × $15\frac{1}{8}$ (280 × 385)
Inscribed '4/20' and on the back 'Reaper
(d)'

P 07649
Reaper e
Hard-ground etching with roulette $6\frac{7}{8} \times 8\frac{3}{4}$
(175 × 222) on paper 9 × $11\frac{3}{8}$ (230 × 290)
Inscribed 'RH' t.r. (partly erased) and
'2/10' and on the back 'Reaper (e)'

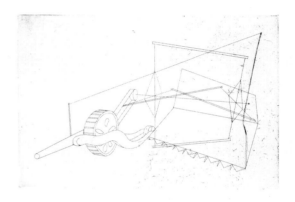

P 07650

P 07650
Reaper g
Hard-ground etching $8\frac{7}{8} \times 12\frac{3}{4}$ (225 × 325)
on unbleached Arnold paper $10\frac{5}{8} \times 14\frac{7}{8}$
(270 × 378)
Inscribed 'R Hamilton' b.r. and '3/25' and
on the back 'Reaper (g)' and 'REAPER 3gns'
and '(13)' (deleted)

P 07651
Reaper h
Drypoint and roulette $6\frac{3}{4} \times 9\frac{3}{4}$ (171 × 247)
on paper 11 × $15\frac{1}{8}$ (280 × 385)
Inscribed 'R Hamilton' b.r. and '8/20' and
on the back 'Reaper (h)' and 'REAPER 3gns'
and '(7)'

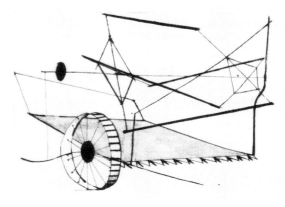

P 07651

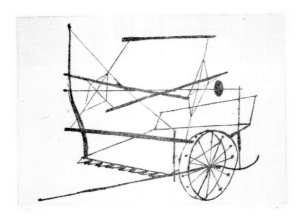

P 07652

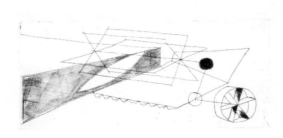

P 07653

This and the following entries have been approved by the artist.

P 07654   **Microcosmos (plant cycle)**
1950

Etching, drypoint, engraving and aquatint with punch impressions $7 \times 8\frac{3}{4}$ (177×225) on unbleached Arnold paper $9\frac{3}{4} \times 11\frac{1}{4}$ (250×287), printed by the artist at the Slade School of Art, not editioned
Inscribed 'R Hamilton' b.r. and '5/20' and on the back 'MICROCOSMOS (PLANT CYCLE) 3 gns'
Purchased from the artist (Grant-in-Aid) 1982

Lit: Hamilton no.39, repr. p.33; Richard Morphet, *Richard Hamilton*, exhibition catalogue, Tate Gallery, March–April 1970, p.18

P 07652
Reaper i
Aquatint $7\frac{7}{8} \times 10\frac{7}{8}$ (200×277) on paper $10\frac{1}{2} \times 13\frac{7}{8}$ (268×352)
Inscribed 'R Hamilton' b.r. and '5/25' and on the back 'Reaper (i)'

P 07653
Reaper j
Hard-ground etching and roulette $3\frac{7}{8} \times 8\frac{7}{8}$ (99×225) on unbleached Arnold paper $9\frac{1}{4} \times 11\frac{3}{8}$ (234×290)
Inscribed 'R Hamilton' b.r. and 'RH' b.r. and '1/20' and on the back 'Reaper (j)'

Hamilton had already made nearly 20 etchings when he began to experiment with the mechanical imagery provided by a reaping machine in order to test the depictive possibilities of the medium and the individual characters of the marks it would produce in a far more conscious way. 'The "Reaper" series was inspired by Giedeon's *Mechanization Takes Command*. Repetition of the simple contrasting forms of the agricultural machine provided material for investigating the tech-

This print, together with 'Structure', 'Heteromorphism' and 'Self-portrait' were made while Hamilton was working on the Institute of Contemporary Art's contribution to the Festival of Britain in 1951, an exhibition entitled 'Growth & Form'. Hamilton's display and the imagery he used were the central exposition of the new interest in biological-natural forms which expanded, in a style generally known as 'crystal structures', through fashionable textiles, ceramics and the new man-made materials. In terms of Hamilton's work, however, the significance of his work on 'Growth & Form' lay in his adoption of natural imagery from photographic sources and technical diagrams, and the way he used this now visual language to examine the problems of painting itself. Hamilton was interested in the principles of growth expressed in d'Arcy Thompson's book of the same title. By using images from microscopy and X-rays, as well as botanical or biological subjects, Hamilton created a new currency of forms recognisably natural yet distanced from traditional naturalism in painting. 'Microcosmos' is related to paintings of the same title;

'Hamilton first titled all [these works] 'Microcosmos', to affirm the analogy between the visual quality of works of this type and certain music of Bartok. Bartok's 'Mikrocosmos' are instructional pieces for the piano some of which are intended to be so simple as to be played by anyone; these works of Hamilton equally follow an open, step-by-step development... In these abstract works, as at all periods since, Hamilton is already consciously employing banal elements as the means to sophisticated ends' (Morphet, p.18).

P 07656 **Heteromorphism** 1951

Etching with aquatint and roulette $10 \times 7\frac{7}{8}$ (255×200) on paper $15\frac{1}{8} \times 10\frac{5}{8}$ (383×270), printed by the artist at the Slade School of Art, not editioned
Inscribed 'R Hamilton' b.r. and '8/20'
Purchased from the artist (Grant-in-Aid) 1982
Lit: Hamilton no.41, repr. p.34

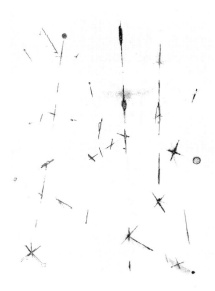

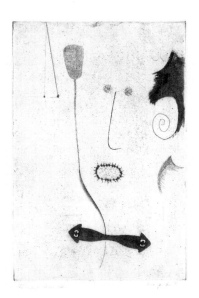

P 07655 **Structure** 1950

Etching, aquatint and roulette $15\frac{3}{4} \times 11\frac{7}{8}$ (400×303) on paper $19\frac{1}{4} \times 14\frac{1}{4}$ (490×362), printed by the artist at the Slade School of Art, not editioned
Inscribed 'R Hamilton' b.r. and '6/20'
Purchased from the artist (Grant-in-Aid) 1982
Lit: Hamilton no.40, repr. p.33; Morphet, no.6, p.18, repr. p.19

P 07657 **Self-portrait** 1951

Etching with aquatint and roulette $11\frac{3}{4} \times 7\frac{3}{4}$ (300×196) on paper $14\frac{3}{4} \times 10\frac{7}{8}$ (375×277), printed by the artist at the

Slade School of Art, not editioned
Inscribed 'Richard Hamilton' b.l. and
'Self-portrait'
Purchased from the artist (Grant-in-Aid)
1982
Lit: Hamilton no.42, repr. p.35

This print combines two aspects of Hamilton's work: his use of autonomous marks, the making of which in itself determines the form of the work, and his use of biological – i.e. natural – subject matter, drawn from Thompson's observation of the way things grow, as a visual language. Its third important aspect is described by Richard Morphet: 'Hamilton's mouth is a sea-urchin, his ear a shell, his tie a flat worm regenerating after section, and one side of his face is defined by a bull-sperm. The Arcimboldesque principle points up the fact that in all Hamilton's Self-portraits ... the artist becomes one with the substance of his current obsessions' (Morphet, p.23).

framework closely related to the traditional convention of drawn perspective. In these, natural forms were depicted in space. Morphet writes:

'The perspective paintings had populated Hamilton's conceptual pictorial world with forms of life, had examined the question of spectator movement, and had commented on the painter's own role in making a two-dimensional analogy for three-dimensional facts. In several works of 1954–5 [including 'Still Life?'], Hamilton brought his growing need for pictorial expression... to bear on all these problems simultaneously. These works... executed from life, mark Hamilton's return to figurative art at a moment when abstract painting in Britain was growing exceptionally in both scope and reputation (Morphet, pp.23–4).

'Still Life?' was the last of this group and the one in which Hamilton's interest in Futurist imagery is perhaps most evident.

P 07658   **Still Life?** 1955

Engraving $9\frac{5}{8} \times 6\frac{7}{8}$ (245 × 175) on paper $15\frac{3}{4} \times 11\frac{5}{8}$ (400 × 295), printed by the artist at the University of Newcastle upon Tyne, not editioned
Inscribed 'R Hamilton' b.r. and 'proof'; inscribed in the plate 'RH 55'
Purchased from the artist (Grant-in-Aid) 1982
Lit: Hamilton no.48, repr. p.38

Besides the works related to 'Growth & Form' Hamilton had, between 1950 and 1953, made paintings in which a multiple viewpoint was used as a kind of conceptual

P 07659   **Picasso's Meninas** 1973

Etching, aquatint, engraving, drypoint and burnishing $22\frac{1}{2} \times 19\frac{1}{4}$ (570 × 490) on Rives paper $29\frac{7}{8} \times 22\frac{1}{2}$ (760 × 570), printed by Pierro and Aldo Crommelynck, Paris, published by Propyläen Verlag, Berlin in an edition of 120
Inscribed 'Richard Hamilton' and 'Picasso's Meninas' and 'EA 3/15'
Purchased from Desmond Page (Grant-in-Aid) 1982
Lit: Hamilton no.88, repr. p.65; Richard S. Field, *Richard Hamilton Image and*

Process 1952–82, exhibition catalogue, Tate Gallery, December 1983–February 1984, no.38 pp.51–3, repr. p.53

This print was made for inclusion in Propyläen Verlag's mixed portfolio 'Hommage à Picasso', celebrating Picasso's 90th birthday.

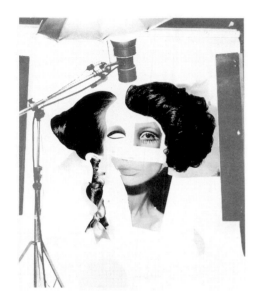

P 07937 **Fashion-plate** 1969–70

Screenprint with offset lithography, hand colouring and collage $29\frac{1}{2} \times 25\frac{5}{8}$ (749 × 650) on paper $39 \times 27\frac{1}{4}$ (990 × 692) watermarked 'FABRIANO', offset lithography printed by Sergio and Fausta Tosi, Milan, screenprinting by Chris Prater at Kelpra Studio, published by Petersburg Press in an edition of 70
Inscribed 'Tony's proof from Richard' b.r.
Purchased at Sotheby's (Grant-in-Aid) 1983

Lit: Hamilton, no.74, repr. p.55; Morphet, pp.86–7

'Fashion-plate' is related to a series of 'Cosmetic Studies' of the same title made in 1969, in which Hamilton put together fragments of photographs of models from fashion magazines. With a full-length painting on this subject in mind, three preliminary studies were made, then,

Determined to make a print as a further step towards a painting, Hamilton photographed, in collaboration with Tony Evans, a carefully-chosen grouping of studio equipment for fashion photography, to act as a frame for a head-and-shoulders image, and to emphasise the ritualistic character of the fashion photo-session. This was lithographed in Milan, soft tonality and luminous whiteness being accentuated. Hamilton began building up on the sheet... collage elements which should recur throughout the print's edition. As this proceeded, the difficulty of obtaining sufficient identical collage material for an edition combined with the developing physical interest of this and other studies to change the project to one of an interlinked series of collage-drawings (Morphet, p.86).

A further twelve collages were made (repr. Morphet, pp.88–9). In order to solve the problem of obtaining identical collage elements for the editioned print he still wanted to make using the same lithographed framework, Hamilton borrowed transparencies from David Bailey and had the fragments he required printed from them, also in Milan (the high technical quality of Bailey's original ektochromes permitted reproduction whereas printing from already-printed source material would not have been satisfactory). Areas of flat colour were screenprinted at Kelpra. Pochoir was done by the artist (with the assistance of Ernie Donagh) in his own studio; finally Hamilton added handmade marks in cosmetics.

Harry Holland born 1941

P 07805 **Door** 1982

Lithograph $7\frac{5}{8} \times 5\frac{1}{8}$ (195 × 130) on paper $15 \times 11\frac{1}{4}$ (380 × 285), printed by Nick Hunter and published by Garton & Cooke

Inscribed 'W H Holland' b.r. and '4/30'
Purchased from Robin Garton (Grant-in-Aid) 1983

The following entry is based on information supplied by the artist in a letter dated 21 April 1986. It has been approved by him.

Doors and social situations involving doors, in which a figure or figures are either standing in or walking through a doorway, are a recurrent theme in Holland's work. Holland has painted variations on this subject in 'Room' 1985 (repr. *Harry Holland*, exhibition catalogue, Artsite Gallery, Bath, August 1985, no.9) and 'Door' (repr. *Peter Archer Harry Holland Frank McKenna*, exhibition catalogue, Midland Group, Nottingham, April–May 1979, no.16). The artist has explained this interest as follows: 'Doors are flat objects and are therefore capable of asserting or denying the picture plane. They also have a symbolic significance. These two factors make for a fairly rich meaning/interpretation.' The figure in P07805 was drawn from memory and followed preliminary sketches now in the artist's collection. Although it is Holland's occasional practice to develop an idea from drawings via prints into paintings, this particular subject was not painted. Characteristically, the work resists any single literal interpretation. The figure occupies a doorway but it is unclear whether she is pausing in this space or is entering a room. The artist's treatment of detail is suggestive rather than descriptive. The viewer is invited to interact with the work by speculating on the actual appearance and meaning of the girl's facial expression, clothing and accessories for which only brief visual clues are supplied. By limiting literal information and consequently forcing the use of the observer's imagination, Holland is able to amplify the sense of an actual encounter with a real person, as opposed to a model, occupying real space. This is because the viewer, in being tempted to interpret the image, is compelled to draw upon memory which is the repository of his own real experiences.

P07805, together with P07806 and P07807 are part of a series of twenty lithographs which were executed as the result of a commission given to the artist by Robin Garton Gallery in 1980. The series was exhibited there in the exhibition *Harry Holland Twenty Lithographs*, November–December 1982. The artist has stated that lithography is his preferred printmaking technique because 'stone lithography can be reworked in a rich variety of ways'. It is particularly suited to Holland's interest in the effects of light as the artist is able to obtain highlights and dissolve hard edges by scratching into the stone after the image has been laid down in lithographic crayon.

P07806   Lovers 1982

Lithograph $5\frac{3}{8} \times 4\frac{1}{2}$ (136 × 115) on paper 15 × $11\frac{3}{8}$ (382 × 290) watermarked 'Somerset England', printed by Nick Hunter and published by Garton & Cooke
Inscribed 'W. H. Holland' b.r. and '6/30'
Purchased from Robin Garton (Grant-in-Aid) 1983

The following entry is based on information supplied by the artist in a letter dated 21 April 1986. It has been approved by the artist.

Holland has explained that 'The image originally derives from a subject which I reworked called "Roman Charity" a fairly common theme in the nineteenth century.' 'Roman Charity' refers to the story of Cimon and Pero which was extensively interpreted by artists of the 16th to 18th centuries, most notably by Rubens and Caravaggio. It appears to derive originally from Valerius Maximus who, in his *Factorum ac dictorum memorabilium libri* IX, under the heading 'De pietate in parentes' (5:4) tells how the aged Cimon, a prisoner awaiting execution and therefore being starved, was visited in his cell by Pero, his daughter, who nourished him by offering him her breast. Baroque examples often emphasised the sexual aspect of the subject and the title of the present work alludes to the fact that Holland also has developed the image beyond its original status as an icon of filial piety. Instead, the artist has used a situation deriving from the literature of antiquity as a framework in which to consider the complexity of human relations and the conviction expressed is that sensuality and sexuality are pre-eminent in this.

Although the artist made some preliminary studies for this work which are still in his possession, it was executed mainly from memory. Holland has not made any other prints on a similar theme but 'Lovers' is related to a painting of the same name and similar design which is now in Belgium.

P 07807 **TV** 1982

Lithograph 6 × 6⅛ (153 × 157) on paper
15 × 11⅛ (381 × 282) watermarked
'Fabriano 100/100 cotton', printed by Nick
Hunter and published by Garton & Cooke
Inscribed 'W H. Holland' b.r. and '1/30'
Purchased from Robin Garton (Grant-in-
Aid) 1983

The following entry is based on information supplied by the artist in a letter dated 21 April 1986. It has been approved by the artist.

In this work and in the six related 'Homage to Electricity' lithographs, in which the same title appears in different languages, Holland explores an image in which two naked girls are seen absorbed in a domestic task. In the first case, the girls seem to be switching on or tuning a television set. In the other prints they are involved in changing an electric light bulb. Both cases reflect Holland's interest in the depiction of light in electrically lit interiors. Although the scene appears commonplace there is an underlying eroticism which transcends the ordinariness of the moment. The artist has commented on the significance of the image that 'It is an extended visual joke e.g. as sculptures concerned with their own revelation.'

REJOICE! OUR TIMES ARE INTOLERABLE. TAKE COURAGE, FOR THE WORST IS A HARBINGER OF THE BEST. ONLY DIRE CIRCUMSTANCE CAN PRECIPITATE THE OVERTHROW OF OPPRESSORS. THE OLD AND CORRUPT MUST BE LAID TO WASTE BEFORE THE JUST CAN TRIUMPH. OPPOSITION IDENTIFIES AND ISOLATES THE ENEMY. CONFLICT OF INTEREST MUST BE SEEN FOR WHAT IT IS. DO NOT SUPPORT PALLIATIVE GESTURES; THEY CONFUSE THE PEOPLE AND DELAY THE INEVITABLE CONFRONTATION. DELAY IS NOT TOLERATED FOR IT JEOPARDIZES THE WELL-BEING OF THE MAJORITY. CONTRADICTION WILL BE HEIGHTENED. THE RECKONING WILL BE HASTENED BY THE STAGING OF SEED DISTURBANCES. THE APOCALYPSE WILL BLOSSOM.

Jenny Holzer born 1950

P 07847 **Inflammatory Essays** 1979–82
(i-xxix)

29 offset lithographs 17 × 17 (432 × 432)
on paper of various colours, printed at
Millner Bros., New York and published
by the artist in an unlimited edition
One inscribed 'Jenny Holzer' on the back
Purchased from Lisson Gallery (Grant-in-
Aid) 1983

Lit: Carter Ratcliffe, 'Jenny Holzer', *Print Collector's Newsletter*, XIII, November–December, 1982, pp.149–52; Allan Schwartzman, 'Bugs in the System', *Print Collector's Newsletter*, XV, March–April, 1984, pp.10–11; Jeanne Siegel, 'Jenny Holzer's Language Games', *Arts Magazine*, LX, December, pp.64–8

The following entry, which has been approved by the artist, is based on answers provided by the artist in a letter of 30 May 1986 to questions posed by the compiler.

A number of the 'Inflammatory Essays' were first published in book form by the artist as *Black Book Posters* in 1979. These took the form of paragraphs printed on green paper. In the 'Inflammatory Essays' street posters, Holzer offset the texts on as many different colours as the printer could supply.

In the 1970s Holzer abandoned her practice as an abstract painter in order to make more explicit statements and to establish more direct contact with a larger audience than would visit galleries. Her art began to appear in the form of texts on posters which were exposed on the streets like fly-posters. In Jeanne Siegel's article and interview with the artist Holzer stated: 'From the beginning, my work has been designed to be stumbled across in the course of a person's daily life. I think it has the most impact when someone is just walking along, not thinking about anything in particular, and then finds these unusual statements either on a poster or in a sign.'

The texts are provocative and their subjects range from the scientific to the political and interpersonal. According to Siegel almost any subject seemed suitable for exposition, with the exception of art which was deliberately avoided. Holzer explained to Siegel as follows:

What I tried to do, starting with the Truisms and then with the other series, was to hit on as many topics as possible. The truism format was good for this since you can concisely make observations on almost any topic. Increasingly I tried to pick hot topics. With the next series 'Inflammatory Essays', I wrote about things that were unmentionable or that were the burning question of the day.

In contrast to the 'Inflammatory Essays' which consist of paragraphs of text, 'Truisms' were statements confined to a length of one line which were either displayed together on a poster or broadcast as a continuous light display.

The tone of the 'Inflammatory Essays' is aggressive and challenging. The texts are the invention of the artist, although they do not necessarily reflect the artist's own views. From one Essay to another they 'display a spectrum of views, from far-left to far-right. I wanted to talk about things that are very important to people but in a non-didactic way (the series as a whole with its conflicting views is not didactic). I tried to show how dangerous and absurd it is to be a fanatic, but how important it is to get things done' (letter to the compiler). They often have the air of slogans found in graffiti form on walls in the city.

In preparation she read 'Mao, Lenin, Emma Goldman, various religious and right wing fanatics, miscellaneous American anarchists and some "folk" crackpot literature'. Her intention was to 'write things that were very hot – in tone and subject matter – to (hopefully) instill a sense of urgency in the reader. I wanted the reader to jump, at least, and maybe consider doing something useful.' To this end the posters were first 'wheat-pasted in the streets of Manhattan. They were placed wherever posters normally appear' but the choice of text was not always arbitrary. 'Sometimes I'd choose certain texts for certain neighbourhoods. It was fun to put particularly frightening ones uptown.' Each week Holzer pasted up a different poster. In order to make clear that a new poster was on display she had them printed on paper of different colours and 'to let the viewers know that the posters were part of a series,

I made each poster exactly 100 words long and 20 lines' (letter to the compiler).

When the posters are displayed in a gallery the artist likes 'them to be pasted directly on the wall, from floor to ceiling with their edges overlapping slightly so that no wall shows through. It's good to completely cover a wall 10' × 25' in vertical or diagonal stripes of posters' (letter to the compiler).

P 02561

Bill Jacklin born 1943

P 02559– **Anemones** 1977
02565   Seven etchings $11\frac{7}{8} \times 8\frac{1}{8}$ (302 × 206) on paper $25\frac{5}{8} \times 19\frac{5}{8}$ (651 × 499) watermarked 'BFK RIVES FRANCE', printed by Michael Rand and published by the artist in an edition of 40
Each inscribed 'Jacklin 77' b.r. and '19/40', and 'Anemones I to VII' respectively
Presented by the artist 1982

This portfolio marks a transition in Jacklin's imagery from regular abstract configurations to a more representational vein, while at the same time commenting on his visual language by showing an image of a vase of flowers evolving into an expressive pattern of line and tone. The first print shows anemones in a patterned vase on a window sill with a deep shadow to the front and right of the image. Numbers 'II' to 'V' show the flower heads dying and falling onto the sill and taking on a new formal role with the shadows and with fragments of the pattern from the vase. In 'VI' a regular pattern is forming at the top of the image and in 'VII' the pattern has become the complete image though it retains the identities of the original formal components.

Jasper Johns born 1930

P 07736 **Savarin** 1982

Monotype over lithograph $39\frac{3}{4} \times 29\frac{7}{8}$ (1010 × 759) on Rives BFK paper $50\frac{1}{4} \times 38$ (1275 × 965), printed by Bill Goldston with Thomas Cox and James V. Smith at Universal Limited Art Editions, Long Island, published by ULAE in an edition of 4 varying impressions
Inscribed 'J Johns '82' and '4/4' b.r.; impressed with the printer's and publisher's stamp
Purchased from Universal Limited Art Editions (Grant-in-Aid) 1983
Lit: Judith Goldman, *Jasper Johns: 17 Monotypes*, 1982 ('1/4' repr.)

In 1960 Johns made two sculptures, both entitled 'Painted Bronze'. One was a pair of Ballantine Ale cans and the other a Savarin coffee tin full of used brushes. In the painterly surfaces of these works reference and illusion were set up to embody and at the same time parody reality. The Savarin image recurs in the intervening years as a metaphor for Johns himself: taken from his studio, it is a surrogate for the persona of an artist and his working life, standing for his integrity and asserting itself as literal but with many, often para-doxical, connotations. Johns's '1st Etchings' 1967–8 include one in which Johns worked over a photo-etching of the sculpture, and the image appears again in a number of subsequent prints. There has been no painting on this theme (though a real Savarin can was attached to 'Field Painting' 1963–4) – it has remained a graphic image from the original sculpture.

In the present work the can of brushes stands against a background of brush-marks in a pattern of 'hatching' that has been a central theme in Johns's work since 1972. It has been said to derive from a pattern glimpsed on a passing car and from the bedspread on the right hand side of the painting 'Self Portrait Between the Clock and the Bed' 1940–2 by Edvard Munch. Two other references to Munch appear, in the initials 'E.M.' and the underlining of the image with the impression of Johns's arm like the skeletal arm across the bottom of Munch's 'Self Portrait' lithograph of 1895. The overt references to Munch reiterate the idea that in Johns' work Expressionism is displaced into a strict discipline, like the passions in traditional Japanese theatre. Using an extra plate from a lithograph of the 'Savarin' image used for the poster to his 1977 retrospective exhibition at the Whitney Museum, Johns had made a new lithograph which was editioned in 1981. Twenty-seven impressions had to be scrapped, however, when the tone of the paper on which they were printed turned out to be wrong. Preventing Bill Goldston from destroying these proofs, Johns set them aside and returned in January 1982 to use them as the basis for a series of monotypes. He painted onto plexiglas sheet and used ULAE's hand-fed proofing press to lay the paint over the printed image. An offset press was also used for some printings (but not for 'No.4'). In ten of the final seventeen they made between two and four impressions of the same painted image – though there is considerable variation between them – and these were numbered, so that the present example is 4/4, the fourth variant of the fourth monotype. Of the series of seventeen, eleven are over lithograph proofs (including 'No.4'), the rest being from painted images only. The variations on the theme through the series include the introduction of colour into the monochrome areas of the lithograph, alterations to the band containing the arm impression, coloured hand-impressions replacing the 'hatching' background, setting the image in an oval, darkening it and adding illusory nails, infusing it with red, radically changing the colour, replacing the arm with a date – '21 Jan. 1982' (the date '13 Jan. 1982' also appears: Johns is said to have made all seventeen monotypes in four working days), adding 'HALLELUJA', and finally making a soft, partly obliterated image by blotting from the penultimate print. In 'No.4' colour is added and the dark tones reinforced but the red arm impression and the initials are still visible across the bottom of the image.

This entry has been approved by the artist.

Allen Jones born 1937

P 07449   Box 1980

Lithograph on 4 sheets $41\frac{3}{4} \times 59\frac{7}{8}$ (1060 × 1520) overall on Velin Arches, printed by Ian Lawson and published by Waddington Graphics
Inscribed 'Allen Jones 80' to the right of bottom centre and '46/70'; impressed with the printer's and publisher's stamps
Purchased from Waddington Graphics (Grant-in-Aid) 1982

The following entry is based upon written answers by the artist to questions posed by the compiler in a letter of 18 April 1986 and has been approved by the artist.

P 07449 is a four part lithograph comprising one large rectangular sheet, predominantly in green, bordered on three sides by three narrower rectangular sheets, predominantly in red. The image depicts a stage as though seen from a box in a theatre. On either side of the box are two female figures, who are drawn as though glimpsed in the field of peripheral vision, and on the stage are depicted the legs of a ballerina who is leaping. Her torso is too high to be in vision and is therefore not depicted.

The figures are not fully described but only suggested and the artist has stated that when the 'focus is on the stage the nearer or surrounding elements become diffuse'. This idea, according to the artist, was also used by Jackson Pollock in 'The Guardians of the Secret' 1943 (repr. Francis O'Connor and Eugene Thaw (eds.), *Jackson Pollock*, Newhaven and London, 1978, I, pl.99) where 'figurative fragments guard or watch his performance within'.

Compositionally 'Box' relates to several of Jones's 'stage' paintings where the proscenium or orchestra pit is used to 'frame the action'. In P 07449 the action is literally framed by the three red sheets, which describe the box. Commenting on his reason for making the print in four parts Jones has written: 'The act of representation asserts an illusion of space in a painting that is avoided in non-figurative work. By sectioning the image, this is counteracted. Your eye is brought up onto the surface – the fact of the paper itself.'

The title of P 07449 refers not only to the box in a theatre but also to the notion of a boxed folio of prints.

P 07759   Take it from the Top 1982

Lithograph $28\frac{5}{8} \times 37$ (727 × 940) on Velin Arches, printed at Solo Press, New York and published by Waddington Graphics
Inscribed 'Allen Jones 82' b.r. and '25/50'; impressed with the printer's and publisher's stamps
Purchased from Waddington Graphics (Grant-in-Aid) 1982

The following entry is based upon written answers by the artist to questions posed by the compiler in a letter of 18 April 1986 and has been approved by the artist.

P 07759 is printed in black and depicts a conductor conducting in an orchestra pit who is observed by a female spectator seated in the front row of the stalls.

The conductor is a personification of 'the artist' or 'the creator'. He is concentrating on the performance or the art and is interposed between the spectator and the work itself. According to Jones in P 07759 'the theatre is an analogy for the acts of painting' in that the artist is a mediator whose presence is 'felt rather than seen'.

P 07759 is one of a number of prints and paintings which Jones has made concerning the stage and is based upon a painting entitled 'Rhapsody' 1982 (private collection, Manchester, repr. *Allen Jones Stages. Lithographs 1981–82*, exhibition catalogue, Waddington Galleries, 1982, month not known). Above the reproduction of this work the words 'reaction', 'control' and 'action' are printed which, according to the artist, 'define the significance of those divisions within the composition corresponding to the viewer, the artist (conductor) and the performance (picture/stage)'. These concepts are also embraced by P 07759.

Most of Jones's prints are in colour but he has explained that when finishing a period of intense production at a printer's it is difficult to 'wind down', so that whilst awaiting the last colour proofing he usually makes an image in black and white.

Peter Lanyon 1918–1964

P 07741 **The Returned Seaman** 1949

Linocut with hand colouring 21 × 29 (532 × 736), printed by the artist, not editioned
Inscribed 'Peter Lanyon /49' b.r. and 'The Returned Seaman'
Purchased from the New Art Centre (Grant-in-Aid) 1982
Lit: *Peter Lanyon: Drawings and Graphic Work*, exhibition catalogue, City Museum and Art Gallery, Stoke-on-Trent, April–May 1981, no.43

Sol LeWitt born 1928

P 07660– **The Location of Six Geometric**
07665   **Figures** 1975

Six etchings $15\frac{3}{4} \times 16$ (400 × 406) on paper $24 \times 19\frac{7}{8}$ (608 × 506), printed by Kathan Brown at Crown Point Press, Oakland, California and published by Parasol Press, New York

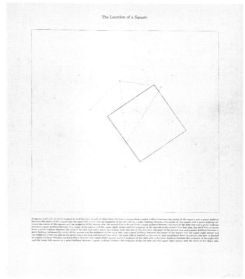

P 07661

Each inscribed 'LeWitt' b.r. and '2/25' and 'i/iv' – 'vi/vi'; each stamped on the back with the printer's name
Purchased from Lisson Gallery (Grant-in-Aid) 1982
Repr: *Sol LeWitt, Graphik 1970–1975*, Basel, 1975, pp.62–7

The following entry is based on a conversation between the compiler and the artist held on 27 November 1985 in London and has been approved by the artist. Each print consists of a text which provides details of the location within a square of a geometric figure. Each print concerns a different figure, the range being a circle, a square, a triangle, a rectangle, a parallelogram and a trapezoid. Above each text is an image which is a visual analogue of the text, for not only are the figures themselves portrayed but also the points which have been plotted and the lines drawn in order to locate the figures. The square in which each figure is located is defined by the borders of the plate mark.

In each case the writing of the text preceded the mapping out of the image. The image was worked out on paper before it was etched onto the plate, which the artist did himself. He chose etching as the medium because hard ground etching seemed an ideal way of making fine black and grey lines. The lines themselves are broken or solid, the solid variety defining only the figure, the broken lines signifying the constructional lines required to plot the outline of the figure but which do not form part of the figure itself. There are three different kinds of broken lines all with different functions.

The principle underlying the conception of the series is that the figures would be placed in a complex way and that the text would be complex to read. In achieving complexity only simple concepts were expressed in the most sparing but informative manner. All points are plotted relative to others and the only measurement employed is the half. Thus one point might be halfway between two others or a combination of others. The artist likens the system involved to that employed in plotting navigational routes and stated: 'As soon as you find one point you can find another by finding its relation to any other point.'

Since the image was drawn on paper first and etched afterwards it was necessary to reverse the instructions indicating right and left because the image would be reversed in the printing.

One other similar print exists which is apart from the series. It was published in German and entitled 'Die Plazierung eines Vierecks'. In this print the four sided figure does not have right-angled corners.

Richard Paul Lohse born 1902

P 07666– **Untitled** 1981
07671
Six screenprints each 26 × 26 (660 × 660) on paper 27½ × 27½ (698 × 698), printed and published by Editions Média, Neuchâtel
Each inscribed 'Lohse' b.r. and 'a' to 'f' respectively and '47/90'
Purchased from Editions Média (Grant-in-Aid) 1982

Robert Longo born 1953

P 07899 **Jules, Gretchen, Mark, State II 1982–3**

Lithograph and embossing 30 × 52¾ (762 × 1340) on Velin Arches paper 36½ × 68 (928 × 1728), printed by Maurice Sanchez and others at Derrière l'Etoile Studios, New York and published by Brooke Alexander Gallery, New York
Inscribed 'Robert Longo 83' b.r. and '19/30'
Purchased from Brooke Alexander Gallery, New York (Grant-in-Aid) 1983

P 07899 depicts three figures, two males and a female, in active poses and dressed in city clothes. The words 'State II' in the title refer to the fact that Longo made prints of each of these figures individually before combining them in one image. State I is in an edition of 45 each.

P 07899 is related to a drawing entitled 'Study for Final Life 1982/Untitled 1982' (repr. Carter Ratcliff, *Robert Longo,* Munich, 1985, pl.55) and to three untitled drawings, two of 1981 and one of 1982 (repr. ibid., pl.53). These last three drawings preceded the making of the prints.

Longo's images are deliberately ambiguous suggesting violence, drunkenness, dancing and dying. They are based on photographs which the artist takes but which he then works in such a way that the figures become anonymous. Ratcliff has identified that 'Longo's contorted men in suits have their origin in an image of assassination – a still from a Rainer Werner Fassbinder film, *The American Soldier*, which shows a man with his hand drawn to the bullet wound in his violently arching back' (Ratcliff, p.16). The series of drawings to which P 07889 relates is entitled 'Men in the Cities'.

Each image in P 07889 is embossed in such a way that the figures appear to be separately printed. The figures are drawn by hand.

This entry has been approved by the artist.

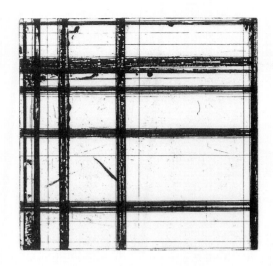

Brice Marden born 1938

P 07849– **Tiles** 1979
07852
    Four etchings with aquatint each approx.
8 × 8 (203 × 203) on Somerset paper
29¾ × 22⅜ (755 × 568), printed by Stephen
Thomas at Crown Point Press, Oakland,
California and published by Parasol Press,
New York
Each inscribed 'B Marden 79' b.r. and
'15/50'; impressed with the printer's and
publisher's stamp
Purchased from Parasol Press (Grant-in-
Aid) 1983

'Tiles' is a portfolio of prints from a series of drawings
and etchings in which Marden was working out ideas
for the design of ceramic tiles which, ultimately, were
not made. Unlike earlier works, which are more minimal
and explore the formal characteristics of the series,
'Tiles' is an expressive series in which the grid and
the notion of serial progression are both exploited and
subverted. They are subverted by the broad manner in
which the rosin is applied in the aquatint process and
by the general air of improvisation with which the prints
are endowed by the foul biting in the central black areas.
The use of large blotches of ink and the accidental (but
ultimately desired) appearance of foul biting reveal that
Marden's interests are not strictly speaking minimal
but are more expressive. Since 1972 his work has
reflected his interest in landscape and classical Greek
architecture and manifests a reaction 'against what have
become the excesses of Minimal painting' ('Brice

Marden Interviewed by Robin White', *View*, 111, June
1980). The grid is used not only to limit and define the
two dimensional surface but is also employed to create
an architectonic space.

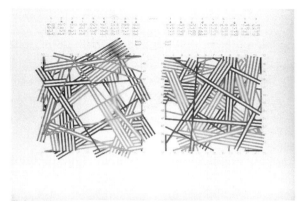

Kenneth Martin 1905–1984

P 07742 **Venice** 1980

    Screenprint 25⅛ × 35¼ (638 × 895) on two
sheets: white paper with tracing paper
overlay, printed at Editions Média,
Neuchâtel and published by Waddington
Graphics
Inscribed 'Kenneth Martin 80' b.r. and
'57/70'
Purchased from Waddington Graphics
(Grant-in-Aid) 1982

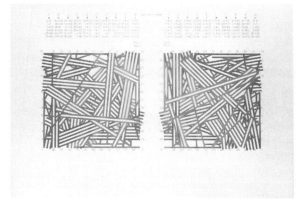

P 07743 **Pier and Ocean** 1980

    Screenprint 25⅛ × 35¼ (638 × 895) on two
sheets: white paper with tracing paper
overlay, printed at Editions Média,

Neuchâtel and published by Waddington Graphics
Inscribed 'Kenneth Martin 80' b.r. and '57/70'
Purchased from Waddington Graphics (Grant-in-Aid) 1982

The title 'Pier and Ocean' derives from the paintings by Mondrian of the same name but refers more directly to the *Pier and Ocean* exhibition, held at the Hayward Gallery, May–June 1980, which inspired Martin's print. 'Venice' was created at the same time and is closely related. The theme of the exhibition is, therefore, germane to the meaning of both these works. Originally intended as a history of Constructivism, the movement with which Martin was connected from the early fifties onwards, its aim was subsequently modified. Instead of presenting Constructivism as the unbroken evolution of a stylistic consensus, the exhibition postulated a break in continuity and a shift in the concept of space for which 1968 is seen as a turning point. Gerhard von Graevenitz selected the exhibition and explained the title as follows: 'The space of 70s art is an open space, to which the individual artwork relates as the pier does to the ocean. The ocean defines the pier and gives it its meaning: for the circumscribed always draws its meaning from the uncircumscribed' (*Pier and Ocean*, exhibition catalogue, Hayward Gallery, May–June 1980, p.6). The conceptual basis of Martin's work from 1970 onwards is founded on this concept of 'open space' which is developed here beyond the sense of physical space normally understood in relation to Constructivism to embrace also 'mental space' and 'the inner space of memory and imagination' (*Pier and Ocean* exhibition catalogue, p.6). For Martin, the most important constituent of this expanded concept of space is time. Martin recognised that change through movement is a universal law and therefore saw all art objects as kinetic, irrespective of whether they move or are framed, because their existence is generated by a sequence of events which are a function of time. Martin stated that he was 'fascinated by the ways in which movement can create form' (from 'The Development of the Mobile', unpublished, June 1955, quoted in *Kenneth Martin*, exhibition catalogue, Waddington and Tooth Galleries, June 1978, p.2) and in his own work this is manifested in an interest in process and progression in which chance is the main determining factor. This statement also alludes to the fact that for Martin, the meaning of the forms which constitute a work is inseparable from the nature of their origin in that the conceptual relationship between object and idea is itself given form. 'Pier and Ocean' and 'Venice' are related, in the way in which they were created, to the series of paintings, drawings and prints called 'Chance and Order' which Martin worked on from 1970 until his death and whose origin Martin described as follows:

Recently I have made works which combine chance and programming in the time sequence of activity ... Not only does chance define position, it gives sequence also. The points of intersection on a grid of squares are numbered and the numbers are written on small cards and then picked at random. A line is made between each successive pair of numbers as they are picked out. In early drawings, to show and use the fact that each direction was drawn in sequence, a system of parallel lines was invented. They were always on the same side of the direction throughout a work. Chance determined the sequence and also the number of parallel lines to each. 1 line would serve for the first drawn, 2 for the second, 3 for the third and so on. Each block of lines was drawn underneath the preceding ones and did not pass through them (*One*, October 1973, p.6).

Henri Matisse 1869–1954

P11048 **Small Aurore** 1923

Lithograph $5\frac{3}{8} \times 8\frac{1}{8}$ (136 × 206) on paper $11\frac{1}{2} \times 15\frac{1}{4}$ (292 × 387), printed by M. Duchâtel, Paris, published by the artist
Inscribed 'Henri Matisse' b.r. and '42/50'
Bequeathed by Mrs E. West 1982
Lit: Marguerite Duthuit-Matisse and Claude Duthuit, *Henri Matisse, l'Oeuvre Gravé*, Paris 1983, no.436

and 1953. Dupin describes the differences between the states as follows:

> Miró obtains effects of a negative impression by the modulation of tones and by differences in the pressure of the press: with slight pressure, the groove deeply hollowed out by acid and then inked leaves nothing but a white on the paper; with normal pressure, the same groove restores ink of the same colour to the paper that it itself bears. (p.18)

One such white passage exists in the centre of P 07900.

Joan Miró 1893–1983

P 07900 **Series II** 1952

Etching 14⅞ × 17⅞ (377 × 455) on Velin Arches paper 19¾ × 25⅞ (503 × 658), printed at Lacourière Imprimerie and published by Maeght Editeur, Paris
Inscribed 'Miró|1952' b.r. and '4/13'
Purchased from Isselbacher Gallery, New York (Grant-in-Aid) 1983

Lit: Jacques Dupin, *Miró Engraver*, I, Paris 1984, p.18, pl.86 (col)

This work belongs to the second of six series of etchings which Miró made in 1952 and 1953. The first and second series are more closely related in terms of imagery than the subsequent series. Both present boldly and broadly drawn figures reminiscent of some of the ceramics Miró was making with Artigas at the time, while retaining the sense of fluidity characteristic of Miró's biomorphic forms of this period. In particular, a number of motifs are to be found in an unpublished set of engravings of 1947 which surround the poems of Ruthven Todd (Dupin, pp.16–17, repr.). In P 07900 these have overtones of sexuality and reproduction.

'Series II' comprises a set of five etchings all from the same plate but inked as follows: (1) black; (2) black, green-brown with blue and brown; (3) black with blue, green, yellow and red; (4) black, green, yellow with blue and red; (5) black and red with blue and yellow. Miró does not appear to have indicated an order for the series. The numbering above follows the order established by Dupin. P 07900 is the fourth in the series. Apart from the edition of 13 there are several trial proofs touched up by the artist and several proofs *hors commerce*. According to Dupin (p.83) the plates were made at Hayter's studio, Atelier 17, New York in June 1947 but printed at Atelier Lacourière in Paris between 1952

Nicholas Monro born 1936

P 07672 **Estuary** 1982

Screenprint 27¾ × 38⅜ (705 × 975), printed at Kelpra Studio, published by Hélène Chetwynd
Inscribed 'Nicholas Monro 82' b.r. and '8/70'
Purchased from Hélène Chetwynd (Grant-in-Aid) 1982

Henry Moore OM CH b.1898

157 prints presented by the artist 1982 (numbers from the published catalogue raisonné of Henry Moore's prints are given in brackets and image sizes only are given)

P 02566– Sheep Walking 1974
02570 Sheep Resting 1974
Sheep Grazing 1974
Sheep Standing 1974
Sheep Climbing 1974

Five lithographs in range $5 \times 7\frac{1}{2} - 5 \times 9\frac{3}{4}$ ($127 \times 190 - 127 \times 248$) printed at Curwen Studio and published by the artist in an edition of 30 (HM 352, 350, 349, 351, 348 respectively)
Each inscribed 'Moore' b.r. and 'For the Tate'

P 02571 Earthquake in Harbour 1973

Lithograph $12\frac{1}{8} \times 5\frac{7}{8}$ (308×150) printed at Curwen Studio and published by Raymond Spencer for the Henry Moore Foundation in an edition of 75 (HM 371)
Inscribed 'Moore' b.r. and 'For the Tate Gallery'

P 02572 Ideas for Wood Sculpture 1973

Lithograph $12\frac{3}{8} \times 9$ (314×229) printed at J.E. Wolfensberger, Zurich, not editioned
Inscribed 'Moore' b.c. and 'v/x'

P 02573 Sculptures Dark Interior 1973

Lithograph $10 \times 13\frac{3}{8}$ (254×340) printed at Curwen Studio and published by Curwen Prints in an edition of 75 (HM 373)
Inscribed 'Moore' b.r. and 'For the Tate'

P 02574– Shipwreck I and II 1973
02575 Two lithographs each $10\frac{1}{8} \times 13\frac{1}{2}$ (257×345) printed at Curwen Studio, published by Raymond Spencer for the Henry Moore Foundation in an edition of 50 (HM 374)
Inscribed 'Moore' b.r. and 'For the Tate Gallery'

P 02576 Three Heads 1973

Lithograph $4\frac{1}{4} \times 6\frac{1}{4}$ (108×159), printed at Curwen Studio, published by Ediciones Poligrafa, Barcelona in an edition of 75 (HM 376)
Inscribed 'Moore' b.r. and 'HC 17/20'

P 02577– Black Reclining Figure
02580 I–II 1974

Four lithographs in range $8\frac{3}{4} \times 10\frac{5}{8} - 9\frac{7}{8} \times 12\frac{3}{4}$ ($222 \times 270 - 251 \times 324$), printed at Curwen Studio and published by Raymond Spencer for the Henry Moore Foundation in an edition of 20 (HM 378–81)
Each inscribed 'Moore' b.r. and 'IV/V'

P 02581– Girl Seated at Desk V–VII and
02584 IX 1974

Four lithographs in range $5\frac{1}{4} \times 5\frac{1}{4} - 10\frac{7}{8} \times 7\frac{1}{8}$ ($133 \times 133 - 277 \times 181$), printed at J.E. Wolfensberger, Zurich, published by the Henry Moore Foundation in an edition of 50 (HM 382–4, 386)
Each inscribed 'Moore' b.r. and 'For Tate Gallery'

P 02585 Reclining Figure 1974

Lithograph $6\frac{1}{4} \times 9\frac{3}{8}$ (160×238), printed at Curwen Studio, published by Ediciones Poligrafa, Barcelona in an edition of 75 (HM 387)
Inscribed 'Moore' b.r. and 'H C 17/20'

P 02586 Seated Figure Holding Glass 1974

Lithograph $4\frac{3}{8} \times 6$ (111×152), printed at Curwen Studio, published by Raymond Spencer for the Henry Moore Foundation in an edition of 50 (HM 388)
Inscribed 'Moore' b.r. and 'For the Tate'

P 02587– Four Grazing Sheep 1974
02593, Sheep and Lamb 1974
02698 Sheep Before Shearing 1974
Sheep in Field 1974
Sheep in Stormy Landscape 1974

Three Grazing Sheep 1974
Two Fat Lambs 1974
Sheep in Landscape 1974

Eight lithographs in range $5\frac{1}{4} \times 9\frac{1}{2}$–$7\frac{7}{8} \times 11\frac{1}{8}$ (133 × 242–200 × 282) printed at Curwen Studio, published by Raymond Spencer for the Henry Moore Foundation, P 02587–02593 in an edition of 30, P 02698 in an edition of 50 (HM 389–95 and 558 respectively)
Each inscribed 'Moore' b.r. and 'For the Tate Gallery'

P 02594–
02595

Circus Scenes 1975
High Wire Walkers 1975

Two etchings each approx. $9\frac{3}{4} \times 7\frac{3}{4}$ (248 × 200), printed by M. Basis, published by Ganymed in association with Fischer Fine Art in an edition of 75 (HM 414, 413 respectively)
Each inscribed 'Moore' b.r. and 'AP 9' and 'AP 10' respectively

P 02595

P 02596 Animal Heads 1975

Lithograph $8\frac{1}{2} \times 10\frac{3}{8}$ (216 × 264), printed at Curwen Studio, published by Raymond Spencer for the Henry Moore Foundation in an edition of 50 (HM 415)
Inscribed 'Moore' b.r. and 'For the Tate Gallery'

P 02597 Draped Reclining Figure 1975

Lithograph $13\frac{3}{8} \times 19\frac{7}{8}$ (340 × 505), printed by Roy Crossett, published by the Réunion des Musées Nationaux, Paris in an edition of 50 (HM 416)
Inscribed 'Moore' b.r. and 'For Tate Gallery'

P 02598 Friday Night Camden Town 1975

Lithograph $11\frac{1}{2} \times 11\frac{5}{8}$ (292 × 296), printed at Curwen Studio, published by Raymond Spencer for the Henry Moore Foundation in an edition of 50 (HM 417)
Inscribed 'Moore' b.r. and 'For the Tate Gallery'

P 02599 Group in Industrial Landscape 1975

Lithograph $6\frac{5}{8} \times 8\frac{3}{8}$ (168 × 213), printed at Curwen Studio, published by Ediciones Poligrafa, Barcelona in an edition of 75 (HM 418)
Inscribed 'Moore' b.r. and 'HC 17/20'

P 02600 Reclining Woman 1975

Lithograph $5\frac{1}{8} \times 7\frac{3}{8}$ (130 × 188), printed at Curwen Studio, published by Ediciones Poligrafa, Barcelona in an edition of 75 (HM 419)
Not inscribed

P 02601 Three Seated Figures in Setting 1975

Lithograph $8\frac{5}{8} \times 13\frac{7}{8}$ (220 × 353), printed at Curwen Studio, published by Ediciones Poligrafa, Barcelona in an edition of 75 (HM 421)
Inscribed 'Moore' b.r. and 'HC 17/20'

P 02602 Figures in a Forest 1976

Lithograph $11\frac{1}{2} \times 14$ (291 × 356), printed at Curwen Studio, published by Raymond Spencer for the Henry Moore Foundation in an edition of 50 (HM 427)
Inscribed 'Moore' b.r. and 'For the Tate Gallery'

P 02603– **Figures in Snow**
02604   1976
**Figures with Smoke
Background** 1976

Two lithographs each $13\frac{1}{2} \times 9\frac{7}{8}$ (343 × 251), printed at Curwen Studio, published by Ediciones Poligrafa, Barcelona in editions of 75 and 25 respectively (HM 428, 429) Each inscribed 'Moore' b.r. and 'HC 17/20' and 'HC 9/15' respectively

P 02605– **Mother and Child Shell** 1976
02608   **Mother and Child with Border
Design** 1976
**Mother and Child with Dark
Background** 1976
**Mother and Child with Light
Background** 1976

Four lithographs in range $12\frac{5}{8} \times 9\frac{7}{8}$ – $13\frac{1}{4} \times 13\frac{1}{2}$ (321 × 251–337 × 343), printed at Curwen Studio, P 02606, published by N. Helion, Paris in an edition of 75, the rest published by Raymond Spencer for the Henry Moore Foundation, P 02605 in an edition of 50 and P 02607 and P 02608 in editions of 30 (HM 432–435 respectively) Each inscribed 'Moore' b.r. and 'For the Tate Gallery'

P 02609   **Reclining Figure with Cliff
Background** 1976

Lithograph $9\frac{5}{8} \times 13\frac{1}{4}$ (244 × 338), printed by Curwen Studio, published by the Sonia Henie-Nils Onstad Foundation, Oslo in an edition of 75 (HM 436) Inscribed 'Moore' b.r. and 'For the Tate Gallery'

P 02610   **Seated Mother and Child** 1976

Lithograph $10\frac{1}{4} \times 8\frac{1}{2}$ (260 × 216), printed at Curwen Studio, published by Ediciones Poligrafa, Barcelona in an edition of 75 (HM 437) Inscribed 'Moore' b.r. and 'HC 17/20'

P 02611   **Three Reclining Figures on
Pedestals** 1976

Lithograph $22\frac{1}{2} \times 30\frac{5}{8}$ (570 × 777), printed at Curwen Studio, published by Galleria

Marino, Rome in an edition of 50 (HM 439) Inscribed 'Moore' b.r. and 'For the Tate'

P 02612   **Two Reclining Figures** 1976

Lithograph $9\frac{3}{8} \times 11\frac{3}{8}$ (240 × 290), printed at Curwen Studio, published by Ediciones Poligrafa, Barcelona in an edition of 75 (HM 440) Inscribed 'Moore' b.r. and 'HC 17/20'

P 02613   **Two Seated Figures with
Children** 1976

Lithograph $8\frac{5}{8} \times 10\frac{1}{2}$ (219 × 267), printed at Curwen Studio, published by the Clinique Neurochirurgicale of the Université Libre, Brussels in an edition of 50 (HM 441)

P 02614– **Mother and Child Studies and
02615   Reclining Figure** 1977
**Reclining Figure and Mother
and Child Studies** 1977

Two lithographs each $15 \times 12\frac{1}{4}$ (382 × 310), printed at Curwen Studio, P 02614 not editioned, P 02615 published by Christie's Contemporary Art in an edition of 75 (HM 452, 453 respectively) Each inscribed 'Moore' b.r., P 02615 inscribed 'For the Tate'

P 02616– **Reclining Figure
02619   Architectural Background**
I–IV 1977

Four lithographs in range $9\frac{3}{4} \times 12$–$19\frac{5}{8} \times 17$ (248 × 305–498 × 430), printed at Curwen Studio, P 02616 published by Raymond Spencer for the Henry Moore Foundation in an edition of 50, P 02617 published by Christie's Contemporary Art in an edition of 50, P 02618 published by Galerie Patrick Cramer, Geneva in an edition of 50 and P 02619 published by N. Hélion, Paris in an edition of 100 (HM 454–457 respectively) Each inscribed 'Moore' b.r. and 'For the Tate Gallery'

P 02620   **Reclining Figure Interior
Setting** I 1977

Lithograph $9\frac{5}{8} \times 12\frac{1}{2}$ (244 × 317), printed at Curwen Studio, published by the Société

Internationale d'Art XXe Siècle, Paris in an edition of 75 (HM 458)
Inscribed 'Moore' b.r. and 'For the Tate Gallery'

P 02621 **Stone Reclining Figure** 1977

Lithograph $19\frac{1}{4} \times 27\frac{3}{4}$ (490 × 705), printed at Curwen Studio, published by Raymond Spencer for the Henry Moore Foundation in an edition of 50 (HM 460)
Inscribed 'Moore' b.r. and 'For Tate'

P 02622–02626 **Dante Stones Album** 1977

Five etchings each $11\frac{1}{2} \times 7\frac{3}{4}$ (292 × 197), printed at JC Editions, published by Raymond Spencer for the Henry Moore Foundation in an edition of 50 (HM 461–465 respectively)
Each inscribed 'Moore' b.r. and 'HC 4/15'

P 02627 **Girl Reading at Window** 1977–8

Lithograph $7\frac{1}{4} \times 13\frac{1}{4}$ (184 × 337), printed at Curwen Studio, published by Raymond Spencer for the Henry Moore Foundation in an edition of 50 (HM 469)
Inscribed 'Moore' b.r. and 'For the Tate Gallery'

P 02628 **Male Figure in Landscape** 1977–8

Lithograph $9\frac{3}{8} \times 11\frac{1}{2}$ (237 × 292), printed at Curwen Studio, published by Raymond Spencer for the Henry Moore Foundation in an edition of 50 (HM 470)
Inscribed 'Moore' b.r. and 'For the Tate Gallery'

P 02629–02637 **The Reclining Figure Album** 1977–78

Nine etchings in range 6 × 8–9 × 12 (152 × 203–229 × 305), printed at Lacourière et Frelaut, Paris, published by Ganymed in association with the Louisiana Museum in an edition of 50 (HM 472–9)
Each inscribed 'Moore' b.r. and 'AP 6/15'

P 02640–02641 **Reclining Nude I and II** 1978

Two etchings each $5\frac{3}{4} \times 7\frac{7}{8}$ (147 × 200), printed at JC Editions, published by Raymond Spencer for the Henry Moore Foundation in an edition of 50 (HM 482, 483)
Each inscribed 'Moore' b.r. and 'For the Tate'

P 02642–02646 **Hands of Dorothy Crowfoot Hodgkin I–V** 1978

Five lithographs in range $5\frac{3}{8} \times 7\frac{7}{8}$–$5\frac{3}{4} \times 10$ (137 × 200–147 × 254), printed at Curwen Studio, not editioned (HM 484–488)
Each inscribed 'Moore' b.r. and 'IV/XXV'

P 02647 **Four Standing Figures** 1978

Lithograph $12\frac{1}{4} \times 15\frac{1}{8}$ (311 × 384), printed at Curwen Studio, published by Raymond Spencer for the Henry Moore Foundation in an edition of 50 (HM 489)
Inscribed 'Moore' b.r. and 'For the Tate Gallery'

P 02648 **Man and Woman Three Quarter Figures** 1978

Lithograph $10\frac{5}{8} \times 14\frac{1}{2}$ (270 × 368), printed at Curwen Studio, published by Raymond Spencer for the Henry Moore Foundation in an edition of 50 (HM 490)
Inscribed 'Moore' b.r. and 'For the Tate Gallery'

P 02649–02653 **Reclining Figure against Sea and Rocks** 1978
Reclining Figure Dawn 1978
Reclining Figure Sunset 1978
Standing Figure Storm Sky 1978

Four lithographs each approx. $9 \times 12\frac{1}{8}$ (229 × 308), printed by J.E. Wolfensberger, Zurich, published by J.M. Stenersens, Oslo in an edition of 50 (HM 491–494)
Each inscribed 'Moore' b.r. and 'HC 9/10'

P 02654 **Stone Reclining Figure II** 1978

Lithograph 23 × 30 (584 × 762), printed at Curwen Studio, published by Raymond

Spencer for the Henry Moore Foundation in an edition of 50 (HM 496)
Inscribed 'Moore' b.r. and 'For Tate Gallery'

P 02655 Two Reclining Figures 1978

Lithograph $10\frac{3}{8} \times 8\frac{5}{8}$ (264 × 219), printed at Curwen Studio, published by Pantheon Edition, Bruckman Verlag, Munich in an edition of 100 (HM 497)
Inscribed 'Moore' b.r. and 'For the Tate'

P 02656– Child Study 1979
02657 Sleeping Child 1979

Two etchings $9\frac{7}{8} \times 7\frac{3}{8}$ (251 × 188) and $7\frac{3}{8} \times 9\frac{7}{8}$ (188 × 251) respectively, printed at Lacourière et Frelaut, Paris, published by Raymond Spencer for the Henry Moore Foundation in an edition of 50 (HM 498, 499)
Each inscribed 'Moore' b.r. and 'For the Tate Gallery'

P 02658– Curved Reclining Figure in
02659 Landscape I–II 1979

Two etchings each $7\frac{3}{8} \times 10$ (188 × 254), printed by Michael Rand, published by Raymond Spencer for the Henry Moore Foundation in an edition of 50 (HM 500, 501)
Each inscribed 'Moore' b.r. and 'For the Tate Gallery'

P 02660 Elephants 1979

Etching $6 \times 7\frac{7}{8}$ (152 × 200), printed at Lacourière et Frelaut, Paris, published by Raymond Spencer for the Henry Moore Foundation in an edition of 50 (HM 502)
Inscribed 'Moore' b.r. and 'For the Tate Gallery'

P 02661 Half Figure 1979

Etching $5 \times 4\frac{7}{8}$ (127 × 124), printed by Michael Rand, published by Raymond Spencer for the Henry Moore Foundation in an edition of 50 (HM 503)
Inscribed 'Moore' b.r. and 'For the Tate'

P 02662– Head of a Girl I **and** II 1979
02663

Two etchings $9 \times 6\frac{1}{2}$ (229 × 165) and $10 \times 7\frac{3}{8}$ (254 × 188) respectively, printed at Lacourière et Frelaut, Paris, published by Raymond Spencer for the Henry Moore Foundation in an edition of 50 (HM 504, 505)
Each inscribed 'Moore' b.r. and 'For the Tate'

P 02664 Head of a Girl and Reclining
Figure 1979

Etching $9\frac{1}{8} \times 10\frac{7}{8}$ (232 × 277), printed at Lacourière et Frelaut, Paris, published by Raymond Spencer for the Henry Moore Foundation in an edition of 50 (HM 506)
Inscribed 'Moore' b.r. and 'For the Tate Gallery'

P 02665 Interpretation from Dürer's
Portrait of Conrad Verkell
with Landscape 1979

Etching $8\frac{3}{4} \times 6\frac{5}{8}$ (222 × 168), printed at Lacourière et Frelaut, Paris, published by Raymond Spencer for the Henry Moore Foundation in an edition of 50 (HM 507)
Inscribed 'Moore' b.r. and 'For the Tate Gallery'

P 02666 Mother and Child 1979

Etching $11 \times 8\frac{7}{8}$ (279 × 225), printed at Lacourière et Frelaut, Paris, published by Raymond Spencer for the Henry Moore Foundation in an edition of 50 (HM 508)
Inscribed 'Moore' b.r. and 'For the Tate Gallery'

P 02667 Reclining Figure Distorted
1979

Etching $8\frac{7}{8} \times 11\frac{1}{8}$ (225 × 283), printed by Michael Rand, published by Raymond Spencer for the Henry Moore Foundation in an edition of 50 (HM 509)
Inscribed 'Moore' b.r. and 'For the Tate Gallery'

P 02668– Reclining Figure Piranesi
02670 Background I–III 1979

Three etchings in range $6\frac{1}{4} \times 11$–$8\frac{7}{8} \times 11\frac{1}{8}$ (159 × 279–225 × 283), printed at

Lacourière et Frelaut, Paris, published by
Raymond Spencer for the Henry Moore
Foundation in an edition of 50 (HM 510–
512)
Each inscribed 'Moore' b.r. and 'For the
Tate Gallery'

P 02671– Reclining Mother and Child I
02673 and II 1979
Reclining Mother and Child I
Profile 1979

Three etchings each approx. $8\frac{7}{8} \times 11\frac{1}{8}$
(225 × 283), printed by Michael Rand,
published by Raymond Spencer for the
Henry Moore Foundation in an edition of
50 (HM 513, 515, 514)
Each inscribed 'Moore' b.r. and 'For the
Tate Gallery'

P 02674– Seated Figure 1979
02675 Seated Figure with
Architectural Background
1979

Two etchings $8\frac{7}{8} \times 6\frac{3}{4}$ (225 × 171) and
$6\frac{7}{8} \times 6\frac{3}{4}$ (175 × 171), printed at Lacourière
et Frelaut, Paris, published by Raymond
Spencer for the Henry Moore Foundation
in an edition of 50 (HM 516, 517)
Each inscribed 'Moore' b.r. and 'For the
Tate Gallery'

P 02676 Seated Mother and Child 1979

Etching $8\frac{5}{8} \times 6\frac{5}{8}$ (219 × 168), printed by
Michael Rand, published by Galerie
Patrick Cramer, Geneva with Raymond
Spencer for the Henry Moore Foundation
in an edition of 100 (HM 518)
Inscribed 'Moore' b.r. and 'IV/XXV'

P 02677– Seated Nude 1979
02678 Seated Woman 1979

Two etchings $10 \times 7\frac{3}{8}$ (254 × 188) and
$8\frac{7}{8} \times 6\frac{1}{2}$ (225 × 165) printed by Michael
Rand, published by Raymond Spencer for
the Henry Moore Foundation in an
edition of 50 (HM 519, 520)
Each inscribed 'Moore' b.r. and 'For the
Tate'

P 02679– Woman Putting on Stocking I
02680 and II 1979

Two etchings each approx. $10 \times 7\frac{1}{2}$
(254 × 190), printed by Michael Rand,
published by Raymond Spencer for the
Henry Moore Foundation in an edition of
50 (HM 521, 522)
Each inscribed 'Moore' b.r. and 'For the
Tate Gallery'

P 02681– Female Torso and Sculpture
02682 Ideas I and II 1979

Two lithographs each $11\frac{1}{8} \times 15\frac{7}{8}$
(283 × 403), printed at Curwen Studio,
published by Raymond Spencer for the
Henry Moore Foundation in an edition of
25 (HM 534, 535)
Each inscribed 'Moore' b.r. and 'For the
Tate'

P 02683 Homage to Sacheverell
Sitwell 1979

Lithograph over a reproduction of a
drawing $10\frac{3}{4} \times 7\frac{5}{8}$ (271 × 194), printed at
Skelton's Press, Wellingborough and
Curwen Studio, published by The Fairfax
Press, York with Raymond Spencer for the
Henry Moore Foundation in an edition of
40 (HM 537)
Inscribed 'Moore' b.r. and 'HC 16/30'

P 02684 Man and Woman 1979

Lithograph 9 × 13 (229 × 330), printed by
J.E. Wolfensberger, Zurich, published by
Raymond Spencer for the Henry Moore
Foundation in an edition of 50 (HM 538)
Inscribed 'Moore' b.r. and 'For Tate
Gallery'

P 02685 Opening Form I 1979

Lithograph $10\frac{5}{8} \times 13\frac{1}{2}$ (270 × 343), printed
at Curwen Studio, published by Raymond
Spencer for the Henry Moore Foundation
in an edition of 50 (HM 539)
Inscribed 'Moore' b.r. and 'For the Tate
Gallery'

P 02686– **Reclining Figure Arch Leg**
02688 1979
Reclining Figure Cave 1979
Reclining Figure Pointed 1979

Three lithographs in range $10\frac{3}{4} \times 16\frac{1}{8}$–
$13 \times 16\frac{1}{2}$ (273×409–330×419), printed at
Curwen Studio, published by Raymond
Spencer for the Henry Moore Foundation
in an edition of 50 (HM 541–543)
Each inscribed 'Moore' b.r. and 'For the
Tate Gallery'

P 02689– **Sisters with Children** 1979
02690 **Six Sculpture Ideas** 1979

Two lithographs $13\frac{1}{8} \times 19\frac{5}{8}$ (33×498) and
$12\frac{1}{2} \times 16\frac{3}{4}$ (317×425), printed at Curwen
Studio, published by Raymond Spencer
for the Henry Moore Foundation in an
edition of 50 (HM 544, 545)
Each inscribed 'Moore' b.r. and 'For the
Tate Gallery'

P 02691 **Two Reclining Mother and**
Child Studies 1979

Lithograph $7\frac{7}{8} \times 7\frac{7}{8}$ (200×200), printed at
Curwen Studio, published by Galerie
Patrick Cramer, Geneva with Raymond
Spencer for the Henry Moore Foundation
in an edition of 100 (HM 546)
Inscribed 'Moore' b.r. and 'IV/XXV'

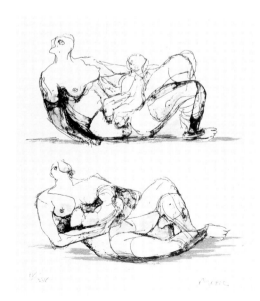

P 02691

P 02692– **Trees Album** 1979
02697 Six etchings in range $6\frac{5}{8} \times 8\frac{1}{8}$–$7\frac{1}{2} \times 10$
(168×206–190×254) printed at JC
Editions, published by Raymond Spencer
for the Henry Moore Foundation in an
edition of 50 (HM 547–552)
Each inscribed 'Moore' b.r. and 'Pl.I' to
'Pl.IV' respectively and 'HC 4/10'

P 02699– **Feet on Holiday** I and II 1979
02700 Two lithographs each approx. $8\frac{1}{4} \times 10$
(210×255), printed at Curwen Studio,
published by Raymond Spencer for the
Henry Moore Foundation in an edition of
50 (HM 562, 563)
Each inscribed 'Moore' b.r. and 'For the
Tate Gallery'

P 02701– **Reclining Figure** 1979
02703 **Idea for Relief Sculpture** 1980
Reclining Nude 1980

Three etchings in range $6\frac{5}{8} \times 8\frac{5}{8}$–$8\frac{3}{4} \times 11\frac{3}{4}$
(220×167–222×298), printed at JC
Editions, published by Raymond Spencer
for the Henry Moore Foundation with
Bernard Baer, P 02701 and 02702 in
editions of 25 and P 02703 in an edition of
75 (HM 571–573)
Each inscribed 'Moore' b.r. and 'IV/X'

P 02704 **Seated Mother and Child**
1979–80

Lithograph $16\frac{1}{2} \times 10\frac{7}{8}$ (420×278), printed
at Curwen Studio, published by Raymond
Spencer for the Henry Moore Foundation
in an edition of 50 (HM 570)
Inscribed 'Moore' b.r. and 'For the Tate
Gallery'

P 02705 **Female Figure with Grey**
Background 1980

Lithograph $9 \times 17\frac{1}{2}$ (230×445), printed by
J.E. Wolfensberger, Zurich, published by
Raymond Spencer for the Henry Moore
Foundation in an edition of 50 (HM 576)
Inscribed 'Moore' b.r. and 'For the Tate
Gallery'

P 02706– **Mother with Child on Lap** 1980
02707 **Seated Figure** 1980

Two lithographs $4\frac{5}{8} \times 3\frac{5}{8}$ (118 × 93) and $12\frac{5}{8} \times 14\frac{3}{4}$ (320 × 375), printed at Curwen Studio, published by Raymond Spencer in an edition of 50 (HM 577, 578)
Each inscribed 'Moore' b.r. and 'For the Tate Gallery'

P 02708 **Six Reclining Figures with Blue Background** 1980

Lithograph $9\frac{5}{8} \times 10\frac{1}{4}$ (245 × 262), printed at Curwen Studio, published by Raymond Spencer for the Henry Moore Foundation in association with Berggruen, Paris, in an edition of 50 (HM 579)
Inscribed 'Moore' b.r. and 'For the Tate Gallery'

P 02709– **Eight Sculpture Ideas** 1980–1
02712 **Seated Mother and Child** 1980–1
Seven Sculpture Ideas I and II 1980–1

Four etchings in range $13\frac{1}{2} \times 10\frac{1}{4}$–$14\frac{3}{4} \times 11\frac{1}{8}$ (344 × 260–376 × 283), printed at J C Editions, published by Raymond Spencer for the Henry Moore Foundation in association with Editions Albra, Turin in an edition of 50 (HM 587–590)
Each inscribed 'Moore' b.r. and 'HC 4/7'

P 02713– **Elephant's Head I and II** 1981
02714 Two lithographs $10\frac{3}{4} \times 9\frac{1}{4}$ (275 × 235) and 9×9 (230 × 230), printed by J.E. Wolfensberger, Zurich, published by Raymond Spencer for the Henry Moore Foundation in an edition of 50 (HM 606, 607)
Each inscribed 'Moore' b.r. and 'For the Tate Gallery'

P 02715– **Figures with Sky Background I and II** 1981
02716
Two lithographs $10\frac{1}{2} \times 10\frac{3}{4}$ (268 × 272) and $10\frac{1}{8} \times 13\frac{5}{8}$ (258 × 348), printed at Curwen Studio, published by Raymond Spencer for the Henry Moore Foundation in an edition of 50 (HM 608, 609)
Each inscribed 'Moore' b.r. and 'For the Tate Gallery'

P 02717 **Five Ideas for Sculpture** 1981

Lithograph $13\frac{3}{4} \times 9\frac{7}{8}$ (350 × 250), printed by J.E. Wolfensberger, Zurich, published by Raymond Spencer for the Henry Moore Foundation in an edition of 50 (HM 610)
Inscribed 'Moore' b.r. and 'For the Tate Gallery'

P 02718– **Six Reclining Figures** 1981
02719 **Six Reclining Figures with Red Background** 1981

Two lithographs each $8\frac{5}{8} \times 9\frac{3}{4}$ (220 × 248), printed at Curwen Studio, published by Raymond Spencer for the Henry Moore Foundation in editions of 20 and 50 respectively (HM 617, 618)
Each inscribed 'Moore' b.r. and 'For the Tate Gallery'

P 02720– **Three Sculpture Ideas** 1981
02722 **Three Seated Figures** 1981
Three Sisters 1981

Three lithographs in range $13\frac{3}{4} \times 9\frac{7}{8}$–$14\frac{3}{8} \times 10\frac{7}{8}$ (350 × 250–368 × 278), printed by J.E. Wolfensberger, Zurich, published by Raymond Spencer for the Henry Moore Foundation in an edition of 50 (HM 619–620)
P 02720 inscribed 'For the Tate Gallery', P 02721 and 02722 inscribed 'Moore' b.r. and 'For the Tate Gallery'

Bruce Nauman born 1941

P 07938 **NO (Black State)** 1981

> Lithograph $27\frac{1}{2} \times 54\frac{1}{4}$ (698 × 1038) on
> Arches Cover paper, printed by Chris
> Sukimoto and Richard Garst at Gemini
> G E L, Los Angeles, and published by
> them
> Inscribed 'B Nauman 81' b.r. and '9/25'
> Purchased from Castelli Graphics, New
> York (Grant-in-Aid) 1983

This lithograph is one of a pair, the other being titled
simply 'NO'. Nauman worked with Serge Lozingot
and Christine Fox at Gemini in the period between
December 1980 and June 1982. One aluminium plate
and one stone were used for both lithographs, the artist
drawing the image with rubbing ink and tusche. For
'NO' the stone was printed first in black and then the
plate in white, but for P 07938 the plate was printed first
in white and then the stone in black, the overlaid black
ink producing subtle grey tones. Nauman has used letters and words since making neon works in 1966–7
and continues to do so, often reversing, substituting or
overlaying the letters of a simple word or phrase.

Christopher Richard Wynne Nevinson 1889–1946

P 11049 **Survivors at Arras** 1917–18

> Etching and drypoint $11 \times 9\frac{1}{4}$ (280 × 232)
> on paper $20\frac{3}{4} \times 16\frac{1}{8}$ (527 × 413), printed by
> the artist
> Inscribed 'CRW Nevinson 1918' b.r. and
> 'I'
> Bequeathed by Mrs E. West 1982
> *Lit:* Kenneth Guichard, *British Etchers 1850–
> 1940*, London 1981, Appendix 4, p.79,
> no.13 (dated 1917)

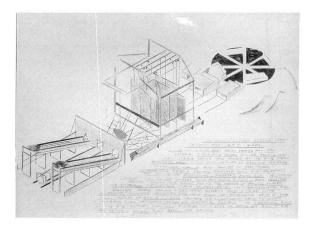

Dennis Oppenheim born 1938

P 07939 **The Diamond Cutter's Wedding** 1979–80

> Lithograph $38\frac{1}{8} \times 49\frac{7}{8}$ (968 × 1267)
> Inscribed 'Denis Oppenheim' bottom
> centre and '1980' and 'A P 17/46'; inscribed
> in the print 'THE DIAMOND CUTTERS
> WEDDING 1979 | PROJECT FOR A.R.C.
> PARIS' (and further text describing the
> construction)
> Purchased from Galerie Maria Malacorda,
> Geneva (Grant-in-Aid) 1983
> *Lit:* Steve Wood, 'An Interview with Dennis
> Oppenheim', *Arts Magazine*, L V, no.10,

June 1981, pp.133–7; Emily Braun,
'Dennis Oppenheim: The Factories', *Arts
Magazine*, LV, no.10, June 1981, pp.138–
41; Robert Ayres, 'Dennis Oppenheim',
Art Monthly, no.56, May 1982, pp.17–19;
Robert Ayres, unpublished interview with
the artist edited and circulated in
typescript at the Ikon Gallery,
Birmingham, April 1982; *Dennis
Oppenheim*, exhibition catalogue, ARC,
Musée d'Art Moderne de la Ville de Paris,
December 1980

Mimmo Paladino born 1948

P 07630 **Pool Water** 1980

Etching with aquatint, drypoint, spitbite
and sugarlift 22½ × 35¼ (572 × 895) on
paper watermarked 'ARCHES', printed by
Aeropress, New York and published by
Multiples Inc., New York
Inscribed 'Mimmo Paladino 1980' b.r. and
'10/35'; impressed with the printer's and
publisher's stamps
Purchased from Waddington Graphics
(Grant-in-Aid) 1982

P 07631 **Peter's Stone** 1980

Etching with drypoint and aquatint
15 × 14½ (380 × 370) on paper 18¾ × 17½
(475 × 445), printed at Aeropress, New
York and published by Multiples Inc.,
New York
Inscribed 'Mimmo Paladino 1980' b.r. and
'12/35'; impressed with the printer's and
publisher's stamps
Purchased from Waddington Graphics
(Grant-in-Aid) 1982

P 07854 **Menacing Caves** 1982

Etching with aquatint, drypoint and
linocut 15¾ × 9½ (400 × 242) on Velin
Arches 31 × 22½ (788 × 572), printed by
Aeropress, New York and published by
Multiples Inc., New York
Inscribed 'Mimmo Paladino 1982' b.r. and
'1/35'; impressed with the printer's stamp
Purchased from Waddington Graphics
(Grant-in-Aid) 1983

The following entry is based upon statements made by
the artist in a letter of 29 April 1986:

P 07631 depicts a man asleep while 'the shadow' of an animal 'passes away'. The title of the work in Italian is 'Pietra di Pietro' in which the similarity between the two principal words is intentional. The artist has written that 'in the Christian story Christ told Peter that [Peter] would be the rock [la pietra] upon which the Christian church would be founded. Therefore all of this is like a metaphor between what is involved in the act of becoming and the linguistic coincidences in the Italian language.' The shape of the plate is irregular and was deliberately cut to resemble the shape of a stone or rock. The red line at the right hand edge of the plate is 'a signal – an alarm'. Paladino states that he generally thinks of his titles after he has completed the work.

P 07630 depicts a head and a container of liquid set in a generalised landscape. The title of P 07630 in Italian is 'Acqua di Stagno' which is ambiguous, for 'stagno' means both pool and tin. The artist states that since both meanings may be inferred in Italian the interpretation of the image may be modified by 'the circumstances of things'. He suggests that the image of the head is a self-portrait and that the marks which were made outside of the plate mark – using sugarlift on a large copper plate – were 'a way of developing beyond the traditional confines of etching and at the same time [beyond the confines] of extraneous presences parallel to the principal subject of the work itself'. The head appears to be asleep but the image was not suggested by a dream or an experience. The artist states that he is 'never inspired by things that are not born from within the work itself. Inspiration is born while working.'

P 07854 also depicts a figure asleep surrounded by animals and demonic images. When asked whether the images surrounding the figure represented the figure's dreams the artist replied that 'There is not an atmosphere of dreams but something more subterranean, sleep at its most uncertain moment, something like death.' The cave mentioned in the title 'is a mystery and the darkness is always menacing'. The artist does not distinguish between dream and reality, stating that 'There are always two realities in reality.'

P 07854 is made from two plates, the smaller central plate, which depicts the figure of the sleeping man, being irregular in shape. The artist has explained that this smaller plate is 'like a unique shaft of light which if [the plate] had been too regular would have conformed too closely [in shape] with the central part of the work'.

P 07674

Guilio Paolini born 1940

P 07673– **Collection** 1974
07678

Six screenprints each approx $12\frac{5}{8} \times 12\frac{5}{8}$ (322 × 322) on paper approx. $19\frac{5}{8} \times 19\frac{5}{8}$ (499 × 499), printed and published by Jabik and Colophon, Milan
Each inscribed 'Giulio Paolini 1974' and '80/80'; P 07673 inscribed 'Isfahan', P 07674 inscribed 'Monitor', P 07675 inscribed 'Epiduaro', P 07676 inscribed 'Autologia', P 07677 inscribed 'Rebus', P 07678 inscribed 'Collezione'
Purchased from Lisson Gallery (Grant-in-Aid) 1982

Eduardo Paolozzi born 1924

P 07621 **Nettleton from Calcium Light Night** 1977

Screenprint with embossing $31\frac{1}{2} \times 21\frac{1}{2}$ (800 × 547) on paper 39 × $27\frac{1}{8}$ (990 × 690), printed by Chris Betambeau at Advanced Graphics and published by the artist in an edition of 200
Inscribed 'Eduardo Paolozzi 1977' b.r. and 'A/P 2/25'; impressed with the printer's stamp
Purchased from the artist (Grant-in-Aid) 1982

Lit: Rosemary Miles, *The Complete Prints of Eduardo Paolozzi*, exhibition catalogue, Victoria and Albert Museum, May–August 1977, no.185

When the portfolio 'Calcium Light Night' was given to the collection in 1980 it was found to contain only eight prints instead of nine. Consequently the missing print, 'Nettleton', was sought from the artist (the portfolio is also an artist's proof set, no.4/25, see P 01992–01999). The portfolio is dedicated to the American composer Charles Ives (it is often known as the 'Ives Suite') and contains texts taken from writings by or about Ives. Paolozzi started work on the prints while he was living in Berlin, working in a studio on Kottbüsserdam provided by the DAAD (German Academic Exchange) programme; Propyläen Verlag, Berlin, were to have published the set but in the event the artist was the sole publisher. Though it was based on an original collage in black and white, the technical data on the making of 'Nettleton' lists eight colour screens and embossing.

This entry and the following three have been approved by the artist.

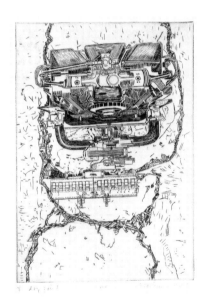

P 07679 **Head** 1977

Etching $11\frac{3}{16} \times 8\frac{7}{16}$ (284 × 214) on paper $20\frac{5}{8} \times 14$ (525 × 355), printed by the artist with Cliff White at White Ink Studio, not editioned
Inscribed 'Eduardo Paolozzi 1977' b.r. and 'AP'; impressed with the printer's stamp
Purchased from the artist (Grant-in-Aid) 1982

P 07680 **Head** 1979

Etching with drypoint $12\frac{1}{4} \times 8\frac{1}{8}$ (311 × 207) on cream paper $23 \times 15\frac{7}{8}$ (585 × 402), printed by the artist with Michael Rand at the Royal College of Art, not editioned
Inscribed 'E Paolozzi 1979' b.r. and 'A/P'
Purchased from the artist (Grant-in-Aid) 1982

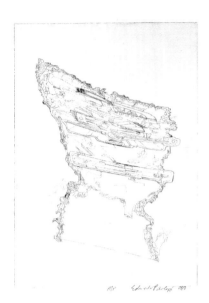

P 07681 **Head** 1980

Etching printed from another impression
$17\frac{5}{8} \times 11\frac{3}{4}$ (448 × 300) on Arches paper
$22\frac{1}{2} \times 15$ (572 × 380), printed by the artist
with Michael Rand at the Royal College
of Art, not editioned
Inscribed 'Eduardo Paolozzi 1980' b.r. and
'A/P'
Purchased from the artist (Grant-in-Aid)
1982

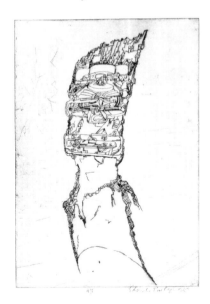

P 07682 **Head** 1980

Etching $17\frac{7}{8} \times 12$ (454 × 304) on paper
$22\frac{1}{2} \times 15$ (572 × 381) watermarked 'Arches

FRANCE' and '17', printed by the artist
with Michael Rand at the Royal College
of Art, not editioned
Inscribed 'Eduardo Paolozzi 1980' and
'A/P'
Purchased from the artist (Grant-in-Aid)
1982

These four prints are from a series of experimental
etchings made between 1977 and 1980; not more than
between five and ten copies of each have been printed.
The images were drawn with drypoint on aluminium
plates (which means they would not stand many printings without losing the burr and the quality of the
drypoint line). In some, such as P 07682 and P 07681,
Paolozzi was experimenting with pantographic distortion. He used a pantograph (a device usually used to
scale drawings up) assembled wrongly to distort his
original drawing by curving and elongating it. P 07681
is printed by placing a fresh sheet over a newly-printed
etching and running through the press again, i.e. by
printing offset from another print.

P 07683 **After Biagio di Antonio** 1980

Lithograph 6×10 (152 × 254) on paper
$13\frac{1}{8} \times 13\frac{1}{8}$ (334 × 334), printed by Hans
Kahler, Munich, not editioned
Not inscribed
Purchased from the artist (Grant-in-Aid)
1982

An image in the same format as this print appears in
the film 'The History of Nothing' which Paolozzi made
with Dennis Postle in 1960–2, but there the image seen
through the windscreen is the famous Greek sculpture
of Laocöon, the Trojan priest sentenced, with his sons,
to be crushed to death by serpents for warning the
Trojans against the wooden horse. In this print the
image is a detail from a cassone panel with three scenes
from the Trojan wars by Biagio di Antonio (in the
collection of the Fitzwilliam Museum, Cambridge).

P 07684 **Parkplatz** 1980

Etching $13\frac{1}{2} \times 19\frac{1}{4}$ (344 × 489) on paper $15\frac{1}{8} \times 22\frac{3}{4}$ (382 × 588) watermarked 'Arches FRANCE', printed by Cliff White at White Ink Studio, not editioned
Inscribed 'Eduardo Paolozzi 1980' b.r. and 'A/P'
Purchased from the artist (Grant-in-Aid) 1982

A photoetching was made from an enlargement of a photograph of a circuit with the grainy photographic images of cars collaged over it. The idea of the change in scale from a detail of a circuit to a piece of architecture is characteristic of Paolozzi's visual language. A drawing entitled 'Parkplatz' 1979 is illustrated in the catalogue for the exhibition 'Eduardo Paolozzi Work in Progress', Kölnischer Kunstverein, 1979 (p.92): it is a linear image of the same configuration. Paolozzi made a number of drawings and trial prints on this theme.

Tom Phillips born 1937

P 07482 –07989 **Dante's Inferno** 1979–83

Thirty-four Cantos each with text and either etchings, lithographs or screenprints, with title pages and colophon; the etchings were proofed and editioned by the artist and Nick Tite at Talfourd Press; the lithographs were proofed by Nick Hunter at Talfourd Press and editioned by Martin Davidson at the Dog's Ear Press; the screenprints were proofed and editioned by Chris Betambeau at Advanced Graphics (and in one instance, Brad Faine at Coriander).

All printed on a specially made tinted Inveresk Somerset paper $16\frac{1}{2} \times 12\frac{3}{8}$ (420 × 315) watermarked with the artist's signature, published by Talfourd Press in an edition of 100
All inscribed 'TP' b.r.
Purchased from the artist (Grant-in-Aid) in instalments 1981–3

P 07778
Title page
Screenprint $10\frac{3}{8} \times 8$ (263 × 203)

P 07777
Title page
Etching $5\frac{7}{8} \times 4$ (150 × 100)

Canto I

P 07685
Screenprint $11\frac{1}{2} \times 8$ (290 × 203)

P 07686
Lithograph $11\frac{3}{8} \times 7\frac{7}{8}$ (290 × 200)

P 07687
Lithograph $12\frac{1}{4} \times 8\frac{5}{8}$ (312 × 220)

P 07688
Screenprint $10\frac{3}{4} \times 8$ (275 × 203)

Canto II

P 07622
Screenprint $10\frac{1}{2} \times 8$ (265 × 203)

P 07623
Lithograph $11\frac{1}{2} \times 8$ (293 × 203)

P 07624
Screenprint $11\frac{3}{8} \times 8$ (290 × 203)

P 07625
Etching $11\frac{3}{8} \times 8$ (290 × 203)

Canto III

P 07561
Etching $12\frac{3}{8} \times 9$ (315 × 228)

P 07562
Screenprint $11\frac{1}{2} \times 8\frac{1}{8}$ (292 × 205)

P 07563
Screenprint $11\frac{5}{8} \times 8\frac{1}{8}$ (295 × 205)

P 07564
Screenprint $11\frac{1}{2} \times 8$ (290 × 204)

Canto IV

P 07761
Screenprint 13×8 (330 × 203)

P 07688

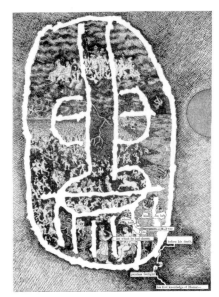

P 07692

P 07762

P 07778

P 07762
Etching $11\frac{3}{8} \times 7\frac{7}{8}$ (290 × 200)

P 07763
Screenprint $11\frac{3}{8} \times 8$ (290 × 203)

P 07764
Lithograph $11\frac{3}{8} \times 8$ (290 × 203)

Canto V

P 07565
Screenprint $11\frac{3}{8} \times 7\frac{7}{8}$ (290 × 200)

P 07566
Etching $12\frac{1}{4} \times 9$ (312 × 228)

P 07567
Screenprint $11 \times 7\frac{1}{2}$ (280 × 190)

P 07568
Etching, screenprint and lithograph
$12\frac{1}{4} \times 8\frac{3}{4}$ (312 × 222)

Canto VI

P 07765
Lithograph $11\frac{5}{8} \times 8$ (295 × 204)

P 07766
Screenprint with etching and aquatint
$11\frac{3}{8} \times 8$ (290 × 203)

P 07767
Lithograph $11\frac{3}{8} \times 8$ (290 × 203)

P 07768
Lithograph $11\frac{3}{8} \times 8$ (290 × 203)

Canto VII

P 07482
Screenprint 13×8 (330 × 203)

P 07483
Etching $12\frac{3}{8} \times 8\frac{7}{8}$ (314 × 225)

P 07484
Lithograph and screenprint $11\frac{3}{8} \times 7\frac{7}{8}$
(288 × 200)

P 07485
Etching $12\frac{1}{2} \times 8\frac{1}{4}$ (317 × 208)

Canto VIII

P 07689
Lithograph $11\frac{3}{8} \times 8$ (290 × 202)

07690
Etching $12\frac{3}{8} \times 8\frac{3}{4}$ (314 × 225)

P 07691
Screenprint $11\frac{3}{8} \times 8$ (290 × 203)

P 07692
Etching and aquatint $12\frac{3}{8} \times 8\frac{1}{4}$ (313 × 210)

Canto IX

P 07769
Lithograph $11\frac{3}{8} \times 8$ (290 × 203)

P 07770
Lithograph $11\frac{3}{8} \times 8$ (290 × 203)

P 07771
Etching and aquatint $11\frac{3}{8} \times 7\frac{7}{8}$ (290 × 200)

P 07772
Lithograph $11\frac{3}{8} \times 8$ (290 × 203)

Canto X

P 07693
Lithograph $11\frac{3}{8} \times 8$ (290 × 203)

P 07694
Lithograph $11\frac{1}{2} \times 8$ (293 × 204)

P 07695
Lithograph $11\frac{3}{8} \times 8$ (290 × 203)

P 07696
Lithograph $11\frac{3}{8} \times 8$ (290 × 203)

Canto XI

P 07773
Screenprint $11\frac{3}{8} \times 8$ (290 × 204)

P 07774
Screenprint $11\frac{3}{8} \times 8$ (290 × 203)

P 07775
Etching and aquatint $10\frac{7}{8} \times 7\frac{5}{8}$ (276 × 195)

P 07776
Screenprint $11\frac{1}{2} \times 8$ (293 × 203)

Canto XII

P 07626
Lithograph $11\frac{1}{4} \times 7\frac{7}{8}$ (300 × 200)

P 07627
Screenprint $11\frac{1}{2} \times 7\frac{7}{8}$ (290 × 200)

P 07628
Screenprint $11\frac{3}{8} \times 8$ (288 × 203)

P 07629
Lithograph $12 \times 8\frac{3}{8}$ (303 × 213)

Canto XIII

P 07486
Screenprint $11\frac{1}{2} \times 8$ (292 × 203)

P 07487
Screenprint $11\frac{1}{2} \times 8$ (292 × 203)

P 07488
Etching $12\frac{3}{8} \times 8\frac{3}{4}$ (315 × 222)

P 07489
Etching $12\frac{1}{2} \times 9$ (317 × 229)

Canto XIV

P 07784
Lithograph $11\frac{1}{2} \times 8$ (292 × 203)

P 07785
Screenprint $11\frac{3}{8} \times 8$ (290 × 203)

P 07786
Screenprint and etching $11\frac{3}{8} \times 8$
(290 × 203)

P 07787
Lithograph $11\frac{1}{2} \times 8\frac{1}{4}$ (292 × 207)

Canto XV

P 07490
Lithograph $10\frac{3}{8} \times 8$ (263 × 203)

P 07491
Screenprint $11\frac{1}{2} \times 8$ (292 × 203)

P 07492
Etching $12\frac{1}{2} \times 8\frac{7}{8}$ (317 × 225)

P 07493
Lithograph $11\frac{1}{2} \times 8$ (292 × 203)

Canto XVI

P 07788
Lithograph $11\frac{3}{4} \times 8\frac{1}{4}$ (300 × 210)

P 07789
Etching $12\frac{3}{8} \times 8\frac{7}{8}$ (315 × 225)

P 07790
Lithograph $11\frac{7}{8} \times 8\frac{1}{8}$ (302 × 208)

P 07791
Etching $11\frac{3}{8} \times 7\frac{7}{8}$ (290 × 200)

Canto XVII

P 07792
Screenprint $11\frac{3}{8} \times 8$ (288 × 204)

P 07793
Etching $11\frac{5}{8} \times 7\frac{7}{8}$ (294 × 200)

P 07794
Lithograph $11\frac{1}{2} \times 8$ (292 × 203)

P 07795
Lithograph $11\frac{3}{8} \times 8\frac{1}{8}$ (296 × 207)

Canto XVIII

P 07697
Etching and aquatint $11\frac{3}{4} \times 8$ (300 × 202)

P 07698
Etching $11\frac{3}{8} \times 7\frac{7}{8}$ (290 × 200)

P 07699
Etching $11\frac{1}{4} \times 7\frac{3}{4}$ (285 × 196)

P 07700
Etching $12 \times 8\frac{1}{2}$ (305 × 215)

Canto XIX

P 07494
Etching $12\frac{1}{2} \times 8\frac{7}{8}$ (317 × 225)

P 07495
Screenprint $9\frac{1}{2} \times 8$ (242 × 202)

P 07496
Etching $12\frac{1}{2} \times 8\frac{3}{4}$ (317 × 222)

P 07497
Screenprint $11\frac{3}{8} \times 8$ (288 × 202)

Canto XX

P 07701
Lithograph $11\frac{3}{8} \times 8$ (290 × 203)

P 07702
Lithograph $11\frac{5}{8} \times 8$ (295 × 203)

P 07703
Lithograph $11\frac{3}{8} \times 8$ (290 × 203)

P 07704
Screenprint $10\frac{3}{8} \times 8$ (263 × 203)

Canto XXI

P 07705
Lithograph $11\frac{1}{2} \times 8$ (293 × 203)

P 07706
Etching $12\frac{1}{8} \times 7\frac{5}{8}$ (310 × 195)

P 07707
Screenprint $11\frac{3}{8} \times 8$ (290 × 203)

P 07708
Etching $11\frac{3}{8} \times 8$ (290 × 203)

Canto XXII

P 07796
Lithograph $11\frac{7}{8} \times 7\frac{3}{4}$ (302 × 198)

P 07797
Screenprint $11\frac{3}{8} \times 8$ (290 × 203)

P 07798
Etching $10\frac{3}{4} \times 8\frac{5}{8}$ (275 × 222)

P 07799
Screenprint $11\frac{1}{2} \times 8$ (293 × 203)

Canto XXIII

P 07800
Lithograph $11\frac{5}{8} \times 8$ (296 × 203)

P 07801
Lithograph $11\frac{3}{4} \times 8$ (297 × 203)

P 07802
Screenprint $11\frac{5}{8} \times 8$ (296 × 203)

P 07803
Lithograph $12\frac{1}{4} \times 8\frac{1}{4}$ (312 × 210)

Canto XXIV

P 07855
Screenprint $10\frac{1}{2} \times 8$ (268 × 203)

P 07856
Lithograph $11\frac{1}{2} \times 8$ (292 × 203)

P 07857
Lithograph $11 \times 7\frac{3}{8}$ (280×187)

P 07858
Lithograph $11\frac{1}{2} \times 8$ (292×203)

Canto XXV

P 07883
Etching $12\frac{1}{4} \times 8\frac{3}{4}$ (312×222)

P 07884
Lithograph $11\frac{1}{2} \times 8$ (292×203)

P 07885
Lithograph $11\frac{1}{2} \times 8$ (292×203)

P 07886
Lithograph $11\frac{1}{2} \times 8$ (292×203)

Canto XXVI

P 07859
Lithograph $11\frac{1}{2} \times 8$ (292×203)

P 07860
Lithograph $11\frac{1}{2} \times 8$ (292×203)

P 07861
Etching $11\frac{1}{4} \times 7\frac{3}{4}$ (285×197)

P 07862
Lithograph $11\frac{1}{2} \times 8$ (292×203)

Canto XXVII

P 07863
Etching $11\frac{1}{4} \times 7\frac{3}{4}$ (285×197)

P 07864
Screenprint $11\frac{1}{2} \times 8$ (292×203)

P 07865
Etching $11\frac{7}{8} \times 8$ (302×203)

P 07866
Etching $11\frac{3}{4} \times 7\frac{7}{8}$ (298×200)

Canto XXVIII

P 07867
Screenprint $11\frac{1}{2} \times 8$ (292×203)

P 07868
Screenprint $11\frac{1}{2} \times 8$ (292×203)

P 07869
Screenprint $11\frac{1}{2} \times 8$ (292×203)

P 07870
Lithograph $11\frac{7}{8} \times 8\frac{1}{8}$ (302×207)

Canto XXIX

P 07871
Screenprint $11\frac{1}{2} \times 8$ (292×203)

P 07872
Etching $12\frac{1}{2} \times 8\frac{3}{4}$ (318×222)

P 07873
Lithograph $11\frac{1}{2} \times 8$ (292×203)

P 07874
Lithograph $11\frac{1}{2} \times 8$ (292×203)

Canto XXX

P 07875
Etching $12\frac{1}{4} \times 8\frac{3}{4}$ (312×222)

P 07876
Lithograph $11\frac{1}{2} \times 8$ (292×203)

P 07877
Etching $12\frac{1}{2} \times 8\frac{3}{4}$ (318×222)

P 07878
Lithograph $11\frac{1}{2} \times 8$ (292×203)

Canto XXXI

P 07879
Lithograph $11\frac{1}{2} \times 8$ (292×203)

P 07880
Lithograph $11\frac{1}{4} \times 8$ (286×203)

P 07881
Screenprint $11\frac{1}{2} \times 8$ (292×203)

P 07882
Lithograph $11\frac{1}{2} \times 8$ (292×203)

Canto XXXII

P 07887
Etching $12\frac{1}{4} \times 8\frac{3}{4}$ (312×222)

P 07888
Etching $12 \times 8\frac{1}{4}$ (305×210)

P 07889
Lithograph $11\frac{1}{2} \times 8$ (292×203)

P 07890
Lithograph and screenprint $11\frac{1}{2} \times 8$
(292×203)

Canto XXXIV

P 07891
Screenprint $11\frac{1}{2} \times 8$ (292×203)

P 07892I
Etching $11\frac{1}{2} \times 8$ (292×203)

P 07893
Lithograph $11\frac{1}{2} \times 8$ (292 × 203)

P 07894
Lithograph $8\frac{1}{4} \times 8$ (210 × 203)

Canto XXXIV

P 07895
Screenprint and lithograph $11\frac{1}{2} \times 8$
(292 × 203)

P 07896
Screenprint $11\frac{1}{2} \times 8$ (292 × 203)

P 07897
Etching $10 \times 5\frac{1}{2}$ (254 × 140)

P 07898
Lithograph $11\frac{1}{2} \times 8$ (292 × 203)

P 07989
Colophon
Etching $11\frac{1}{2} \times 8$ (292 × 204)
Inscribed 'Tom Phillips' centre and
'LXXXIII' and 'of the edition proper
consisting of one hundred copies this is
no.77'
Lit: Tom Phillips, *Dante's Inferno*, 1985
(bound edition of the complete work)

This work consists of Phillips's own translation of the *Inferno*, the first part of the *Divine Comedy* by Dante Alighieri. Each of the 34 Cantos is accompanied by an introductory image and then three illustrations opposite the text of the poem. In an introduction in a booklet published by Waddington Graphics in 1983, the artist writes:

The Inferno is Europe's harsh masterpiece of eschatology: magnificent descriptions alternate with bleak but moving confrontations with the range of Man's baser potentialities; through these we come to know Dante's own beliefs, trials and visionary hopes. We also acquaint ourselves through his narrative with the complete scope of mediaeval learning: we see the Renaissance, so to speak, at first light. However remote in epoch and name are the characters, time drops away and reveals to us real people: we recognise them and know their modern counterparts.

Phillips's illustrations are intended to provide a visual commentary on the text. He has employed a rich visual language which includes some text treated as in his long series of 'Humument' works. In these, text from the same Victorian novel is taken out of context and blanked out with paint and other media to produce new meanings in a way related to some concrete poetry in which words are strung out down a page. He has also translated

a wide variety of other kinds of printed imagery, particularly engravings and photographs, into these prints.

Phillips began work on the Dante project in 1976 but a fire at the Kelso Place studios of Editions Alecto destroyed most of the first year's work. He started again, setting up his own studio in Peckham to be both print workshop and publisher under the name Talfourd Press (after the name of the road). Much of the proofing and printing was done there although Phillips also used the screenprinting workshop Advanced Graphics and, in one instance, another screenprinting workshop, Coriander. The typography was done by Ian Mortimer and printed at IM Imprimit, using the typeface Walbaum. The work was printed in an edition of 185 copies in loose sheets; the edition was completed in 1983. Later, a bound facsimile edition was printed by Hansjorg Mayer, Stuttgart, in conjunction with the artist; this included Phillips's notes on each Canto and was published by Thames & Hudson.

This entry has been approved by the artist.

P 03301

John Piper born 1903

P 03297   **80th Anniversary**
–03304   **Porfolio** 1983

Eight prints on Velin Arches approx.
$21\frac{5}{8} \times 30$ (550 × 762), printed at Kelpra Studio, published by Orde Levinson in an edition of 75
Each inscribed 'John Piper' b.r. and 'For the Tate Gallery'; each impressed with the printer's stamp
Presented by Orde Levinson 1983

P 03297 **Foliate Head**
Etching with screenprinting $17\frac{1}{2} \times 25\frac{3}{8}$
(446 × 645)

P 03298 **Eye and Camera**
Etching $17\frac{7}{8} \times 26\frac{1}{4}$ (445 × 667)
P 03299 **Palazzo Pesaro**
Etching $17\frac{3}{4} \times 25\frac{1}{2}$ (450 × 645)
P 03300 **St Germain de l'Ivret**
Screenprint $18 \times 26\frac{1}{4}$ (457 × 668)
P 03301 **Blenheim Gates**
Etching $17\frac{7}{8} \times 26\frac{1}{8}$ (454 × 663)
P 03302 **Eastnor Castle**
Screenprint $18\frac{1}{8} \times 26\frac{5}{8}$ (460 × 677)
P 03303 **Saltash Bridge**
$17\frac{5}{8} \times 26\frac{7}{8}$ (448 × 683)
P 03304 **Lower Brockhampton**
Screenprint $18 \times 26\frac{1}{4}$ (457 × 668)

P 08208

Lucien Pissarro 1863–1944

P 08182– **Woodcuts from blocks at the**
08209 **Ashmolean Museum**

Twenty-eight woodcuts, printed by Iain
Bain and David Chambers, published by
the Ashmolean Museum with *Lucien
Pissarro, Notes on a Selection of Wood-
blocks held at the Ashmolean Museum,
Oxford* by David Chambers, in an edition
of 175, 1980
Not inscribed
Transferred from the Library 1982

P 08182 **The Parish Priest** *c.*1884
Woodcut $3\frac{3}{8} \times 3\frac{1}{8}$ (86 × 79) (Chambers,
p.17)
P 08183 **The Pastry Cook** *c.*1884
Woodcut $6\frac{1}{2} \times 2\frac{1}{4}$ (165 × 58) (Chambers,
p.18)
P 08184 **Young Girl** *c.*1884
Woodcut $6\frac{1}{8} \times 2\frac{1}{2}$ (155 × 64) (Chambers,
p.20)
P 08185 **April** 1890
Woodcut $3\frac{7}{8} \times 3\frac{1}{2}$ (98 × 89) (Chambers,
p.23)
P 08186 **Floreal** 1890
Woodcut $7 \times 2\frac{1}{2}$ (178 × 64) (Chambers,
p.24)
P 08187 **Contentment** 1890, **Tennis**
1890
Two woodcuts from one block $3\frac{7}{8} \times 7\frac{1}{2}$
(98 × 190) (Chambers, pp.26–7)
P 08188 **Portrait of Camille Pissarro**
1893
Woodcut $1 \times 1\frac{1}{8}$ (25 × 29) (Chambers,
p.22)
P 08189 **Boy and Pine Tree** 1894
Woodcut $1\frac{1}{8} \times 1\frac{3}{4}$ (29 × 45) (Chambers,
p.22)
P 08190 **A Simple Heart** 1900
Woodcut $2\frac{3}{4} \times 2\frac{5}{8}$ (70 × 67) (Chambers,
p.28)
P 08191 **Choice of Sonnets** 1902
Woodcut 3×3 (76 × 76) (Chambers, p.47)
P 08192 **Geese** *c.*1903
Woodcut $1\frac{1}{2} \times 2\frac{1}{8}$ (38 × 54) (Chambers,
p.31)
P 08193 **Boy Breaking a Stick** *c.*1905
Woodcut $2\frac{1}{2} \times 2\frac{1}{4}$ (64 × 58) (Chambers,
p.35)
P 08194–08196 **Consultation** *c.*1905
Three woodcuts in range 2×2–$3\frac{1}{4} \times 3\frac{3}{8}$
(51 × 51–83 × 86) (Chambers, pp.32–3)
P 08197 **Love Chained Down** *c.*1905
Woodcut $2\frac{7}{8} \times 2\frac{1}{2}$ (73 × 64) (Chambers,
p.36)
P 08198 **Bookplate and New Year
Card** 1905
Woodcut $2\frac{3}{8} \times 2\frac{1}{2}$ (64 × 64) (Chambers,
p.37)
P 08199 **Reading** *c.*1905
Woodcut $2\frac{1}{2} \times 1\frac{5}{8}$ (64 × 41) (Chambers,
p.36)
P 08200 **Women in Roundel** *c.*1908
Woodcut $1\frac{1}{2} \times 1\frac{1}{2}$ (38 × 38) (Chambers,
p.37)
P 08201 **New Year Card** 1909
Woodcut $1\frac{3}{4} \times 1\frac{3}{4}$ (44 × 44) (Chambers,
p.38)

P 08202 **The Shepherdess** *c*.1912
Woodcut $1\frac{3}{4} \times 1\frac{3}{8}$ (44 × 29) (Chambers, p.39)

P 08203 **Landscape: Blackpool, Devon** 1914
Woodcut $3\frac{8}{8} \times 3$ (79 × 76) (Chambers, p.39)

P 08204 **Rye** 1920
Woodcut $2\frac{1}{8} \times 1\frac{1}{2}$ (54 × 38) (Chambers, p.40)

P 08205 **New Year Card** 1923
Woodcut $1\frac{1}{2} \times 2\frac{1}{4}$ (38 × 57) (Chambers, p.41)

P 08206 **Christmas Card** 1925
Woodcut 2×2 (51 × 51) (Chambers, p.42)

P 08207 **New Year Card** 1925
Woodcut $1\frac{3}{4} \times 2\frac{1}{4}$ (44 × 57) (Chambers, p.43)

P 08208 **Shepherdess** 1929
Woodcut $3 \times 2\frac{7}{8}$ (76 × 73) (Chambers, p.45)

P 08209 **Ex Libris Isa Taylor**
Woodcut $2\frac{1}{4} \times 1\frac{1}{2}$ (57 × 38) (Chambers, p.45)

P 07709 **Backbone**
Drypoint $11\frac{5}{8} \times 16\frac{3}{8}$ (295 × 415)

P 07710 **Combed (Belly)**
Drypoint $9\frac{3}{8} \times 13\frac{1}{4}$ (240 × 335)

P 07711 **Red Field**
Drypoint $12\frac{3}{8} \times 17$ (316 × 432)

P 07712 **Head Behind**
Drypoint $9\frac{1}{2} \times 13\frac{5}{8}$ (241 × 347)

P 07713 **Violet Furrows**
Drypoint $13\frac{5}{8} \times 9\frac{7}{8}$ (347 × 251)

P 07714 **Cross I** 1977–80

Drypoint $45\frac{1}{4} \times 19\frac{1}{2}$ (1150 × 495) on paper $52\frac{3}{4} \times 24\frac{1}{8}$ (1340 × 613), printed by Karl Imhof, Munich, published by Edition Galerie Heiner Friedrich, Munich
Inscribed 'A Rainer' b.r. and '32/35'
Purchased from Galerie Heike Curtze, Vienna (Grant-in-Aid) 1982

P 07709

Arnulf Rainer born 1929

T 07709 **Five Reds** 1972–9
–07713
Five drypoints, on paper approx. $20\frac{7}{8} \times 30\frac{7}{8}$ (530 × 786), watermarked 'HAHNEMÜHLE' on P 07711, printed by Karl Imhof, Munich, published by Edition Galerie Heiner Friedrich, Munich
Each inscribed 'A. Rainer' b.r. and '3/35'
Purchased from Galerie Heike Curtze, Vienna (Grant-in-Aid) 1982

Robert Rauschenberg born 1925

P 07715 **Preview** 1974

From Hoarfrost Editions
Lithograph with newsprint, screenprint transfers and collage on silk chiffon and silk taffeta fabric $68\frac{7}{8} \times 80\frac{1}{2}$ (1750 × 2045) overall, printed by Ron McPherson, Charly Ritt, Anthony Zepeda, Ed

Hamilton, Robert Knisel and Jeffery Wasserman at Gemini GEL, Los Angeles and published by Gemini GEL in an edition of 32
Inscribed 'Rauschenberg 74' b.l. and 'AP 11'
Purchased from Delahunty Gallery, New York (Grant-in-Aid) 1982
Lit: Ruth E. Fine, *Gemini GEL Art and Collaboration*, exhibition catalogue, National Gallery of Art, Washington, D.C. November 1984–February 1985, pp.112–13 (repr. in col.)

Ruth Fine writes that the images employed in the Hoarfrost Editions, of which there were nine, were taken from newspaper and magazine photographs either transferred direct or from specially printed offset lithographs depicting similar material. She states that the difference in the source of the pictorial matter is crucial to the variations in scale. In *Preview*, large, powerful images – classical sculpture and classic cars – evoking memories of earlier centuries or decades, are in marked contrast to the small scale documentary newspaper events.

Fine describes how Rauschenberg, in the company of Rosamund Felsen, purchased the fabrics for the series in Los Angeles and how he also selected the printed matter there.

A group of magazine subjects, some as small as two by three inches, was enlarged many times to poster size, and then reprinted by offset. Approximately one hundred copies of the *Los Angeles Sunday Times* were separated into sections and organised into neat, discrete piles (a pile of one hundred magazine covers, for example, next to a pile of one hundred front sheets from the entertainment section). These piles

and the enlarged offset sheets were in effect Rauschenberg's palette.

For his master proofs, which preceded the printers' right-to-print proofs, Rauschenberg arranged the sheets of newspaper (some crumpled, some flat) and the offset images on the bed of the lithography press. Under pressure ... and with the use of special solvents, the ink from the images was transferred to the various fabrics lying on top of the newspaper-offset composition.

Each printer developed his own system for approaching the editions. Some assembled the necessary material for each impression piece by piece. Others made the equivalent of prefabricated print kits in advance, each one containing all of the necessary elements for a single impression: so many flat sheets of newspaper, so many crumpled sheets, and so many offset sheets.

In addition to the lithographs Rauschenberg also made a series of unique works with the same title which are broadly similar. Some of the source material is common to the unique and printed works. The title of the series is 'named for the frozen dew that forms a white coating of minute ice needles on surfaces exposed to temperatures below freezing point' (*Robert Rauschenberg*, exhibition catalogue, National Collection of Fine Arts, Smithsonian Institution, Washington, D.C., October 1976–January 1977, p.142).

P07715 is one of ten artist's proofs.

This entry has been approved by the artist.

P77010　**Yellow Body** 1971

Screenprint $48\frac{5}{8} \times 62\frac{1}{2}$ (1235 × 1588), on Aqua Bee 844 100% rag paper, printed by Adi Rischner at Styria Studio, New York and published by Untitled Press, Captiva Island, Florida

Inscribed 'Rauschenberg 71' b.l. and
'7/80'
Purchased at Christie's (Grant-in-Aid)
1984

In 1968 Rauschenberg made a transfer drawing in which the image is similar to P 77010 and which has the same title (repr. *Robert Rauschenberg*, exhibition catalogue, National Collection of Fine Arts, Smithsonian Institution, Washington, D.C., October 1976–January 1977, p.130). P 77010 is a photographic screenprint of this drawing. The drawing is just under half the size of the print.

P 77010 depicts an assemblage of photographs taken from magazines and newspapers, from editorial and advertising, placed together in a rectangle from which a certain number of additional images extend outwards. The image of the rock singer, Janis Joplin, occurs twice in the print, once alone (top right) and a second time with her band 'Big Brother and the Holding Company' (top centre). Joplin, like Rauschenberg, was born in Port Arthur, Texas, and later they met and became friends. One of the lithographic presses at Untitled Press (Rauschenberg's own print studio) is named 'Little Janis' after her. Rauschenberg used the single image of Joplin in another print, 'Signs' 1970, this time in reverse (repr. the Washington exhibition catalogue, p.160). Joplin died of an overdose of heroin in October 1970.

At the time of making the drawing 'Yellow Body' Rauschenberg made four other drawings with the following titles: 'Gray Body', 'Blue Body', 'Red Body' and 'Green Body'. He did not make prints from any of these drawings.

This entry has been approved by the artist.

Susan Rothenberg born 1945

P 07740 **Head and Bones** 1980

Woodcut 13 × 11¼ (330 × 286) on paper 26 × 18⅞ (659 × 480) watermarked 'RIVES'; printed by Gretchen Gelb at Aeropress, New York, published by Multiples Inc., New York, in an edition of 20
Inscribed 'S Rothenberg 80' b.r. and '12/20'; impressed with the printer's and publisher's stamps
Purchased from Multiples Inc. (Grant-in-Aid) 1982

Lit: *Susan Rothenberg Prints 1977–1984*, exhibition catalogue, Barbara Krakow Gallery, Boston, March 1984, no.7, repr.

This woodcut is from a group of four, Rothenberg's first editioned woodcuts, all made in 1980 with Gretchen Gelb at Patricia Branstead's Aeropress studio for the publisher Marion Goodman of Multiples. In the spring of that year Rothenberg had made four series, each of between three and six varying impressions, of unique woodcuts using pine blocks and she had previously made a set of fifteen variations on a single oak block. The image is closely related to Rothenberg's paintings, in which she had developed the use of a heavily outlined horse into the use of fragments of the same kind of figures – in this case a head and two vertical leg bones, with other less specific but equally resonant bone-like forms.

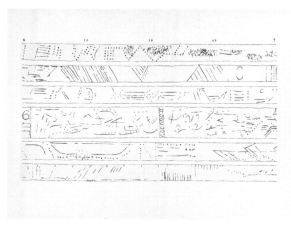

P 11059

Felix Rozen born 1938

P 11052– **Uncertain Opus** 1981
11061

Ten screenprints, nine $13\frac{3}{8} \times 23\frac{3}{8}$
(340×595), P 11052 $12\frac{7}{8} \times 23$ (327×584)
on paper $19\frac{3}{4} \times 25\frac{7}{8}$ (502×657)
watermarked 'ARCHES FRANCE', printed
by Yves Le Bas at Atelier 55, Paris,
published by the artist
P 11052 inscribed 'Rozen' b.r. and
'III/XXXIII'; the others not inscribed
Presented by Mrs Leslie Oliver through
the Friends of the Tate 1983

Edward Ruscha born 1937

P 07716 **Hollywood** 1969

Lithograph $4\frac{1}{8} \times 17$ (105×430) on paper
$6\frac{3}{4} \times 20$ (173×508), printed at Tamarind
Lithography Workshop, Los Angeles,
published by the artist and Tamarind in
an edition of 18
Inscribed 'E Ruscha 1969' b.r. and '2/18';
impressed with the printer's stamp

Purchased at Sotheby's, Los Angeles
(Grant-in-Aid) 1982

From the early 1960s to about 1970 Ruscha used words
as images and made drawings and paintings of West
Coast architecture and views. In this work these two
strands are combined in that the subject is the famous
sign on the hills above Hollywood composed of bill-
board size letters propped up on the horizon line. The
print is related to a series of drawings of the same subject
made in 1968–9. The extreme horizontal format is
characteristic of Ruscha's work and is related to certain
American styles of presentation such as cinemascope
and huge roadside poster boards as well as being natural
to the broad perspectives of West Coast landscape.
Ruscha was invited to work at Tamarind Lithography
Workshop in 1969; June Wayne, Tamarind's Director,
had established a scheme of Fellowships under which
artists were paid to work there for two months and the
introduction of new artists was a vital part of her training programme for printers.

This entry has been approved by the artist.

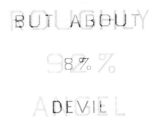

P 07940 **Roughly 92% Angel but about 8% Devil** 1982

Softground etching $14\frac{1}{2} \times 15\frac{1}{4}$ (368×388)
on Somerset paper $24\frac{3}{8} \times 22\frac{1}{2}$ (618×572),
printed by Peter Pettengill at Crown Point
Press Oakland, California and published
by them in an edition of 25
Inscribed 'Ed Ruscha 82' b.r. and '6/25';
impressed with the printer's stamp

[439]

Purchased from Crown Point Press, (Grant-in-Aid) 1983

From the early 1970s Ruscha was making drawings and paintings of single words or short phrases placed against soft unmodulated backgrounds, which took on paradoxical resonance in isolation from their mundane contexts. This etching is printed from two plates, the second half of the title text being superimposed on the first.

P 07718

Robert Ryman born 1930

P 07717– Seven Aquatints 1972
07723

Seven aquatints, six in range $11\frac{5}{8} \times 11\frac{3}{4}$–24 × 24 (297 × 300–610 × 610) and P 07723 $19\frac{1}{2}$ (490) in diameter, on Rives B.F.K. paper approx. 23 × 23 (605 × 605), printed by Crown Point Press, Oakland, California and published by Parasol Press, New York P 07719, 07721 and 07723 inscribed 'Ryman 72' b.r., P 07718 inscribed 'Ryman 72' bottom centre, P 07717 and 07720 inscribed 'Ryman 72' b.l., P 07722 inscribed 'Ryman 72' top right; all inscribed '23/50' and impressed with the printer's stamp
Purchased from Lisson Gallery (Grant-in-Aid) 1982

Lit: Naomi Spector, 'Robert Ryman: Suite of Seven Aquatints, 1972. Nine Unique Aquatints, 1972', *Art & Project, bulletin 70*, Amsterdam 1973, n.p.

'Seven aquatints' is Ryman's first group of etchings. He has subsequently produced other aquatints both singly and in series. 'Seven Aquatints' is consistent with many of the ideas and practices which Ryman has explored in his painting, notably in its emphasis on the medium as the subject about which he has stated: 'My aquatints are white not because I am interested in making white prints but because printing them in white is more to the point visually. If I printed in black, the printed areas would become shapes and the aquatint could not be seen as clearly' ('White in Art is White?', *Print Collector's Newsletter*, VIII, March–April 1977, p.3). By employing a white ink on a white paper Ryman plays down the importance of the geometric shape, the square, which he has consistently chosen in his work because it is 'the most perfect space ... I don't have to get involved with spatial compositions, as with rectangles and circles or whatever' (Phyllis Tuchman, 'An Interview with Robert Ryman', *Artforum*, IX, May 1971, p.46). 'Seven Aquatints' is unusual, however, because, although the printed motif is always square, in P 07723 a white square is printed on a circular sheet which is attached to a square backing sheet. All the other prints consist of white squares of various sizes printed on square white paper.

In all cases the ink is brighter than the paper but its strength is varied from print to print. This differentiation is enhanced by the different methods of aquatinting Ryman adopts. The distribution of rosin on the plates is achieved with a rosin box in some prints and by hand in others, giving rise to a smooth or rough texture respectively. In P 07721 Ryman has used sugar lift. This print is closely related to the 'Windsor' series of paintings Ryman made from 1965–6.

The treatment of the square motifs varies in each print as does the placing of the signature and numbering which become compositional elements. In addition P 07720 incorporates a blue line printed diagonally at the top of the sheet. According to Naomi Spector this is reminiscent of 'Impex', a painting of 1968, and of a silkscreen of 1969, Ryman's first edition of prints. The order of 'Seven Aquatints' is entirely flexible.

This entry has been approved by the artist.

Colin Self b.1941

P 07941 **Margaret in a Chair** 1963

Etching $7\frac{5}{8} \times 5\frac{3}{4}$ (193 × 147) on cream paper
$14 \times 11\frac{1}{2}$ (357 × 293), printed by the artist
at the Slade School of Art in an edition of
5
Inscribed 'Colin Self. 1963.' b.l. and
'Margaret in a Chair. No.1' and '1/5'
Purchased from the artist (Grant-in-Aid)
1983

The artist and Margaret were married in 1963 (but
separated in 1974); when this print was made, drawn
from life, he was living at 162 Ladbroke Grove. There
were two etchings of the same subject, this, made in the
winter of 1963, being the first, and the second, made in
the summer, being Self's 'Diploma of Love'; both were
etched and printed at the Slade where Anthony Gross
was teaching. 'Mr Gross used to make me print on a
little unused press which stood outside the etching
room, since my ideas were "way out" using machine
plates, which he (possibly correctly) thought might
damage the posh presses. He was a very good teacher'
(this and other quotations from correspondence with
the compiler, June 1986). Self made paintings of the
same subject which he describes as 'much broader'. 'So
... the pose, clothes, and style in the way the pattern
on the wallpaper is "drawn as it affects the minds eye".
Considered, whereas *later* works exist alone, on a
"psychological pedestal" in the middle of the paper.'

This entry and the following eight have been
approved by the artist.

P 07747 **Bomber No.1** 1963

Etching from found metal plates laid
together, with pencil, chalk and collage
$15\frac{5}{8} \times 22\frac{5}{8}$ (396 × 576), printed by the artist
at the Slade School of Art in an edition of
5
Inscribed 'Colin Self 1963' b.r. and
'(Bomber No.1)' and '1/1' and 'Edition of
5 or 6 varying prints No.2'
Purchased from the artist (Grant-in-Aid)
1983

'This was and is (remains) a *terribly important* little
etching and IS the world's first Multiple Plate etching.'
The insignia, from model-kit transfers, were added to
subvert orthodox printing practice and, as they were
different in each case, 'not to blame any one Nation for
the fearful state of the political world'. The plates were
found on a rubbish dump at University College; Self
sawed one in half to make the wings. Using popular art,
'people's art', such as transfers or found components
'waiting to be printed', was an important part of the
concept of this and other works of this date (and later).
This print is related to 'one or two "Rape" diptych
drawings where there were women on the right of the
drawing and where a nuclear bomber is flying into
the picture on the left. There were transfers on the
bombers.'

P 07942 **Monument** 1964

Etching from found metal plates laid
together, $30\frac{5}{8} \times 22\frac{5}{8}$ (778 × 575) on paper
watermarked 'T H SAUNDERS
ENGLAND', printed by the artist at
Norwich School of Art in an edition of 3
Inscribed 'Colin Self 1964' b.l. and '5th
Monument' and '1/3'; inscribed in the

plate 'MONUMENT II COLIN SELF'
Purchased from the artist (Grant-in-Aid)
1983

There were between four and eight 'Monuments' and
they followed on from the 'Bomber' works. 'Each one
was different. It was virtually impossible to "hold" all
those pieces in position as the print rolled through. A
slow process. Each one was like doing a painting. Each
had to be inked and wiped [and] positioned. So each
was original to counteract repetitive work.'

This print was made from torn papers inked and
printed. The image is from the universally loved character from Walt Disney, Mickey Mouse's dog Pluto. Self
made this monoprint and other drawings inscribed to
his children having been deeply affected by a postcard
sent to him by his uncle during the war. There is another
of Pluto with collaged photographs of the children and
another of Mickey Mouse.

P 07746   **Power and Beauty No.3** 1968

Etching $26\frac{5}{8} \times 40\frac{5}{8}$ (676 × 1032), printed by
Danyon Black and Maurice Payne at
Editions Alecto and published by them
Inscribed 'Colin Self' b.l. and 'Power &
Beauty No.3' and '72/75'
Purchased from the artist (Grant-in-Aid)
1983

P 07943   **Pluto** c.1964–5

Monoprint from torn paper $16\frac{3}{4} \times 23\frac{3}{4}$
(426 × 603), printed by the artist at
Norwich School of Art
Not inscribed
Purchased from the artist (Grant-in-Aid)
1983

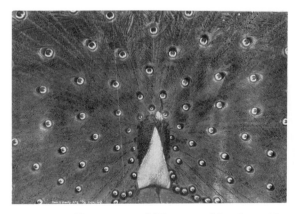

P 07745   **Power and Beauty No.6** 1968

Screenprint $27\frac{7}{8} \times 38\frac{3}{4}$ (707 × 985), printed
by Lynn Haywood at Editions Alecto and
published by them
Inscribed 'Colin Self' b.l. and 'Power &
Beauty No.6' and '68/75'
Purchased from the artist (Grant-in-Aid)
1983

P 07744 **Power and Beauty No.7** 1968

Screenprint $28\frac{5}{8} \times 39\frac{1}{8}$ (728 × 993), printed
by Lynn Haywood at Editions Alecto, not
editioned
Inscribed 'Colin Self' b.c. and 'Power &
Beauty No.7' and '2/2'
Purchased from the artist (Grant-in-Aid)
1983

There were six editioned 'Power and Beauty' prints,
P 07744 being a colour variant of the editioned version
of the image of a peacock (P 07745). The method for the
peacock was 'to screen a sheet of paper black. Screen
white through the screen with most holes in. [Then]
The blue one of the tri-chromatic separation. Then
print the three screens (colours) (blue-red-yellow) onto
this. This gave it the "darkness", the "edge" ... mystic.
Heavy. Sheen. But depth. Took a long time. On the
way I really liked the ghostly white on black one' – Self
therefore had two copies printed in this form.

The car image, of the first ever customised car by Joe
Baillon, 1948, came from a 1964 magazine and the whale
from an animal magazine belonging to Margaret's
grandmother. In his notes on the Alecto Gallery exhibition of prints and drawings, October–November
1968, Self wrote:

> The Power and Beauty prints are about images that
> have influenced my themes, drawings or sculpture,
> and about images which have haunted me ...
>
> The photo images I have presented in Power and
> Beauty have seemed complete, impregnable. All I
> have wanted to do with them so far is to foster them
> (a valid act) and to try to recreate those images and
> what they have made me feel. By using a standard
> size for all the prints (and other devices) the subjects
> are transformed, can be seen for appearance,
> aggressive or passive looks. This upsets the objects
> real physical size to a certain extent so that e.g. the
> cockerel looks deadlier and more massive than the
> charging elephant and Joe Baillon's classic
> customised car becomes elephantine, sinister and
> oppressive, more menacing than nuclear warheads.

P 07944 **Out of Focus Objects and
Flowers** 1968

Etching $11 \times 9\frac{7}{8}$ (280 × 251) on paper
$22\frac{3}{8} \times 10\frac{5}{8}$ (568 × 270), printed by the artist
at Editions Alecto, not editioned
Inscribed 'Colin Self 1968' b.r. and 'Out
of focus object and flowers' and 'trial proof
1/13'
Purchased from the artist (Grant-in-Aid)
1983

The first prints Self made at Editions Alecto were of
flowers pressed into soft or hard grounds; 'the out of
focus is the mind blurred by some event in one's infancy
which "clouds one's vision" but it happened so early
one doesn't "know" what it was. The flowers are nostalgia. The past, sweetness, new hope growing.'

P 07945 **Picasso's Guernica and the
Nazis** 1968

Lithograph with red biro $7\frac{3}{8} \times 12\frac{1}{4}$
(188 × 311), printed by the artist at

Editions Alecto, not editioned
Inscribed 'C.S. 1968' b.l. and 'Picasso's Guernica and the Nazis' and 'Lithotrial 2 1/3'
Purchased from the artist (Grant-in-Aid) 1983

The swastika badges were rubbings taken from a ring and transferred onto the stone. There are only two or three works on this theme, each with a different 'Picasso Forgery' drawn in ink, to 'bring out one of the "whys" of his art'.

P 07946 **A Letter to Christopher Logue** 1980

Xerox print with collage and blue ink $8\frac{1}{4} \times 11\frac{5}{8}$ (210 × 296), printed by the artist at the Circle Service Station, Norwich, published by the artist
Inscribed 'Colin Self' top left and 'A letter to Christopher Logue 1980' and '4/14'
Purchased from the artist (Grant-in-Aid) 1983

Self met Logue in 1964 and they became friends, maintaining an intermittent correspondence. The artist sent the original of this print to Logue, making some photocopies at the local garage beforehand:

it's 'down and out' art. Of (about) the creative activity still coming through in contemporary commercial commodity print media, even when the posh print houses of London dont want to know. . . . adding to each individually with postage stamps – linking them to my 'People's Art' theories, postage stamps being seen as 'People's Prints' with their own market value amongst the people – outside of 'Fine Art'.

The image is from a saying by Confucius ' "yes, all life flows on – like a river" '.

P 07748 **Lonewolf** 1981

Block-print $27\frac{3}{4} \times 19\frac{3}{4}$ (704 × 500) on black paper, printed by the artist
Inscribed 'Colin Self' bottom centre and 'August 1981' and '3/4' and 'The Lonewolf'
Purchased from the artist (Grant-in-Aid) 1983

Three prints were made using the same stencil, through which white, silver and yellow paint was sprayed; each was different. 'It was allegorical in a sense. It went like this. "Self" is from a Saxon name. Pre-Conquest Saewulf (ae) dipthong. Norman scribes got even this wrong (like today's bureaucracy). "Seolf" oe "Soelf". I thought of using this as a name for doing my own postcards, publications etc. . . . it sort of went over to "Lonewolf" – thinking it better.'

Cindy Sherman born 1954

P 07804 **Untitled** 1982

Four part photograph each 45 × 30 (1143 × 762) printed in an edition of 10
Not inscribed
Purchased from Metro Pictures, New York (Grant-in-Aid) 1983

Lit: Jack Cowart *Currents 20 Cindy Sherman*, exhibition catalogue, The St Louis Art Museum, March–April 1983 (n.p.)

Repr: *Cindy Sherman*, New York, 1984, pp.62–5 (col.)

i   ii

iii   iv

P 07804 consists of four colour photographs depicting the artist robed in a red towelling bathrobe. The works were initially conceived as four separate images but were subsequently put together to form one work.

Cindy Sherman came to photography as a means of recording her performance work in the mid–70s. Her first photographic works, beginning in 1977, each entitled 'Untitled Film Stills', evoke the atmosphere of B grade films of the fifties, Hollywood film magazines and urban street life. Using herself as the model, Sherman photographed herself in situations which implied a narrative, a before and after, inviting the spectator to construct his own scenario.

In 1980 Sherman began to use colour photography and closed in on the model to investigate more closely her persona. In an interview with Xavier Douroux and Frank Gautherot ('A Conversation with Cindy Sherman', *Succès du Bédac*, exhibition catalogue, Galerie Déjà Vu, Dijon, October–November 1982, n.p.) Sherman stated that she no longer used environments in her photographs 'because I've exhausted all the possibilities of using my living space as a background. That's why

it's closed in on the figure'. Although the environment was still used as an important prop it was implied with the barest means.

In 1981 she used a horizontal format in a series of photographs depicting women deep in reverie in apparently vulnerable positions within a very bare interior. To a certain extent they were parodies of titillating soft pornography but the situations were those of mundane life. The lack of contextualization, however, enhances the ambiguity of the poses.

After this horizontal series Sherman began working with a vertical format. The four photographs forming P 07804 came from this phase. Each section of the work depicts the artist who is seated and whose body fills the frame from top to bottom. Apart from the towelling robe, which appears in all four parts, the only recognizable prop is a chair in the fourth part. The photographs play on the contrast in texture and light between the artist's flesh and the material. The casual character of the poses is emphasised by the fact that the works are unexpectedly cropped. The very close range from which they were shot gives them an intimate air. Jack Cowart regards these photographs as 'a counterpart to draped nude photographs found in men's magazines' and as expressing 'pent-up sadness. It is as if Sherman does at times wonder what it would be like to be a magazine model, but as she lives out the fantasy she denies it the glamour.' Sherman herself has stated:

I was thinking of the idea of a centre-fold model. The pictures were meant to look like a model just after she'd been photographed for a centrefold. They aren't cropped, and I thought that I wouldn't bother with make-up and wigs and just change the lighting and experiment while using the same means in each' (Paul Taylor, 'Cindy Sherman', *Flash Art*, October–November 1985, pp.78–9).

More than any other previous photographs by Sherman this series of four expresses an intimacy and personal emotion. Sherman has written:

Pain or mental anguish is as important a feeling as ecstasy; they are mirror images of opposite emotions ... Mental agony can be appreciated for its beauty if it's an objective appreciation, if there is a distance. It's like listening to very, very sad music or watching a sad movie. You feel it's inside of you, your imagination could make you cry over it. That is the kind of sadness/beauty I try to express (*Succès du Bédac*)

Each photograph shows Sherman in a different pose and a different light and is focused differently. Sherman uses herself as the model and takes her own photographs because she wishes to retain maximum control. She uses mirrors to check on the set up. In the interview cited above she remarked that she does not think of her work 'as self portraits, as auto-portraits. I think of them as other people. When I'm working it's as if I have a model.' More than any previous works, however, these photographs are psychologically penetrating and less related to drama or cinema than to conventional portraiture.

Walter Richard Sickert 1860–1942

P 11050   **Ennui** c.1916–18

> Etching $8\frac{7}{8} \times 6\frac{3}{8}$ (226 × 162) on paper
> 14 × 10¼ (355 × 260) (watermark of a man's head with a halo not identified), published by Ernest Brown & Phillips at the Leicester Galleries
> Not inscribed; inscribed in the plate 'ENNUI' and 'published by Ernest Brown & Phillips at the Leicester Galleries'
> Bequeathed by Mrs E. West 1982

Sickert's first etching of this subject was made in 1914–15 (*Walter Sickert as Printmaker*, exhibition catalogue, Yale Center for British Art, New Haven, February–April 1979, no.72); he subsequently made two smaller versions, of which P 11050 is one.

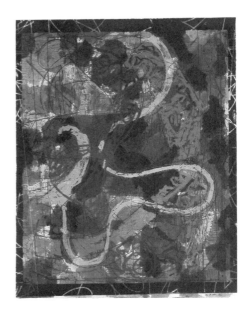

Frank Stella born 1936

P 07735   **Estoril Five II** 1982

> Etching and relief print $66\frac{3}{4} \times 51\frac{3}{4}$
> (1695 × 1315) on dyed paper handmade at Tyler Graphics, printed and published by Tyler Graphics, Bedford Village, New York
> Inscribed 'F. Stella '82' b.r. and '30/30'; impressed with the printer's stamp
> Purchased from Waddington Graphics (Grant-in-Aid) 1982
> *Lit:* Richard Axsom, *The Prints of Frank Stella*, New York, 1983, no.141

This print is one of a series collectively called 'Circuits' within which there are four 'Talledega', three 'Estoril' prints, one 'Imola' and one 'Pergusa' print: all are named after motor racing circuits. The imagery was developed from two earlier print series, the 'Polar Coordinates' 1980, made in memory of the racing driver Ronnie Peterson, and the 'Exotic Birds' 1976–9, for which the curving templates used to plot railway lines were used. Estoril, once a Grand Prix track, is on the Portuguese coast.

Wayne Thiebaud born 1920

P 07724 **Chocolate Cake** 1971

Lithograph $17\frac{1}{2} \times 13$ (445 × 330) on paper
watermarked 'Arches' $30\frac{1}{8} \times 22\frac{1}{2}$
(765 × 570), printed by Michael Knigin
and published by Parasol Press, New York
Inscribed 'Thiebaud 1971' b.r. and '13/50'
Purchased at Sotheby's, Los Angeles
(Grant-in-Aid) 1982

Wayne Thiebaud was well known in the sixties for his
depictions in rich and bright colours of consumer food
products, often in series. His images have always tended
towards the impersonal and the matter-of-fact. 'Chocolate Cake' is a monochrome print in brown but in other
respects is consistent with this approach. The work was
originally proofed in black and a single copy of this state
exists.

Valerie Thornton born 1931

P 02638 **Monterde** 1980

Etching with open bite $19\frac{1}{2} \times 27\frac{1}{4}$
(495 × 692) on paper $26\frac{1}{4} \times 33\frac{3}{4}$ (666 × 857)
watermarked 'BG 1978', printed by the
artist
Inscribed 'Valerie Thornton '80' b.r. and
'A.P.' and 'Monterde'
Presented by the artist 1983

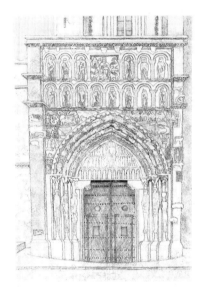

P 02639

P 02639 **Sangüesa** 1982

Etching with open bite $25\frac{1}{2} \times 16\frac{3}{8}$
(648 × 416) on handmade paper $30\frac{1}{2} \times 22\frac{1}{4}$
(775 × 565) watermarked 'BG hand made',
printed and published by the artist
Inscribed 'Valerie Thornton '82' b.r. and
'32/60' and 'Sangüesa'
Presented by the artist 1983

[447]

P 07749

Lit: *John Walker Prints 1976–84*, exhibition catalogue, Tate Gallery, January–March 1985, nos.14, 16 (ill.p.27), 18, 20 and 23 (ill.p.31) respectively

John Walker born 1939

P 07749– **Nos.3, 5, 8, 12 and 17 from The**
07753 **Prahran Etchings** 1981

Five etchings from a suite of 23, printed by John Neeson and Ian Parry at Prahran College of Advanced Education, Victoria, published by the artist
Each inscribed 'Walker 81' b.r.
Purchased from Nigel Greenwood (Grant-in-Aid) 1982

P 07749, etching with aquatint and open bite $17\frac{3}{4} \times 11\frac{3}{4}$ (450 × 298) on paper $27\frac{1}{4} \times 20\frac{3}{4}$ (695 × 527)
Inscribed 'Prahran 3' and '17/25'

P 07750 etching with aquatint and open bite $17\frac{1}{2} \times 23\frac{5}{8}$ (445 × 600) on paper $27\frac{1}{4} \times 31\frac{5}{8}$ (691 × 803)
Inscribed 'Prahran 5' and '14/25'

P 07751 etching with open bite $9\frac{7}{8} \times 7\frac{7}{8}$ (250 × 200) on paper $21\frac{1}{8} \times 20\frac{7}{8}$ (690 × 530)
Inscribed 'Prahran 8' and '1/25'

P 07752 etching with aquatint and open bite $4\frac{7}{8} \times 4\frac{1}{2}$ (125 × 115) on paper $20\frac{7}{8} \times 15\frac{7}{8}$ (530 × 403)
Inscribed 'Prahran 12' and '1/25'

P 07753 etching with open bite $4\frac{5}{8} \times 4\frac{3}{4}$ (118 × 120) on paper $21 \times 15\frac{7}{8}$ (533 × 403)
Inscribed 'Prahran 17' and '1/25'

P 11051 **Pacifica** 1982

Screenprint $61 \times 46\frac{7}{8}$ (1550 × 1190), printed by Chris Betambeau at Advanced Graphics and published by the artist
Inscribed 'Walker 82' b.r. and 'Pacifica' and '15/35'; impressed with the printer's stamp
Presented by the Contemporary Art Society to commemorate Nancy Balfour's retirement as Chairman, 1982

Lit: *John Walker Prints 1976–84*, exhibition catalogue, Tate Gallery, January–March 1985, no.28, ill.p.35

Andy Warhol born 1928

P 07725– **Electric Chair** 1971
07734

Ten screenprints each approx. $35\frac{3}{8} \times 47\frac{7}{8}$ (900 × 1216) on Velin Arches paper, printed by Silkprint Kettner, Zurich, published by Bruno Bischofberger, Zurich in an edition of 250
Each inscribed 'Andy Warhol 71' on the back and numbered on the back with a stamp

P 07728

P 07734

Purchased at Sotheby's, Los Angeles
(Grant-in-Aid) 1982
Repr: Hermann Wünsche, *Andy Warhol, Das Graphische Werk 1962–1980*, Bonn 1981, pls.59–68 (col.)

The image used for this portfolio of prints was derived from the 'Electric Chair' paintings Warhol made in 1967. It is also closely related to the 'Lavender Disaster' painting of 1964 (repr. *Warhol*, exhibition catalogue Tate Gallery, February–March 1971, p.47). According to the publisher, in a conversation with the compiler on 13 September 1985, he asked Warhol to do a publication and discussed with him which subject might be suitable. The publisher wanted something which would relate to Warhol's principal earlier work but cannot remember whether it was he or Warhol who proposed the eventual subject. It was intended to make a print of an image which Warhol had already made famous.

The actual image for the prints was taken from the earlier paintings the source for which was a newspaper photograph. According to Calvin Tomkins the particular eletric chair was at Sing-Sing prison ('Raggedy

Andy' in *Andy Warhol*, exhibition catalogue, Van Abbemuseum, Eindhoven, October–November 1970, p.13). The 'Electric Chair' paintings were part of a series on 'Death and Disaster'. According to Warhol it was Henry Geldzahler who gave him the idea to start the series. 'We were having lunch one day in the summer [of 1962] . . . and he laid the *Daily News* out on the table. The headline was "129 DIE IN JET". And that's what started me on the death series – the car crashes, the Disasters, the Electric Chairs . . .' (quoted in Carter Ratcliffe, *Andy Warhol*, New York, 1983, p.37). According to Rainer Crone (*Andy Warhol*, London, 1970, p.29) the 'Electric Chair' paintings are political statements, symbols of the misuse of government sovereignty, an open confession of a deficiency in cultural development. He claims that the paintings were made to insist on the message that the law of capital punishment be changed. There is little evidence from Warhol to substantiate such a specific claim.

Each print in the portfolio depicts the same basic image of an empty chair but they vary in colour. According to the publisher there is no particular order to the prints. He stated that Warhol made proofs with many different colours and together with the publisher chose those he liked best. The publisher has one hundred or more different proofs. The edition comprises ten prints the majority of which are printed in two colours. The image of the chair in eight of them is less distinct as though fading away or charged with electricity.

Warhol made one print with very gestural marks. According to the publisher the artist wanted to make the whole edition in this manner but the publisher dissuaded him because he felt it ran contrary to the spirit of the paintings from which they were derived. The artist persuaded the publisher to retain one image in this manner for the editioned set. Apart from the particular character of this print the portfolio differs from the screenprinted paintings in that the ground colour of the paintings was applied by hand with a roller, whereas each colour in the printed version required a separate screen.

Tom Wesselman born 1931

P 07760 **Seascape Dropout** 1982

Woodcut $21\frac{7}{8} \times 25$ (556 × 635), printed by Michael Berden, Boston and published by Multiples Inc., New York
Inscribed 'Wesselman '82' bottom centre and '4/50'; impressed with the publisher's stamp
Purchased from Waddington Graphics (Grant-in-Aid) 1982

'Seascape Dropout' relates to the series of paintings called 'Drop Outs' which Wesselman began in 1967. Writing under the pseudonym of Slim Stealingworth, Wesselman describes these works in *Tom Wesselman*, New York, 1980, as follows:

... the central image, a breast, was omitted from the shaped canvas, while the nipple and areola were retained ... These Seascapes are negative shapes. The shape is the shape one sees, for example, while lying alongside a woman who is seated on the beach. One can look up and see the opening formed by her breast, rib cage, and stomach on one side; by her descending arm on the other side; and by her thigh on the bottom. As can happen on a bright beach, the flesh drops away in this moment of awareness of the glimpse into the sunlit background, although the nipple stays a part of the scene because of its color, form, and importance as a focus (pp.52–6).

Of the paintings in the series, the Tate's print most closely resembles 'Study for Seascape 31', 1979, oil on canvas (repr. in col., *Wesselman*, p.279) and, apart from the additional detail in the paintings of tresses of the girl's hair falling across the clouds in the background, the composition of the two works is identical. The 'Drop Outs' works are themselves a development within the 'Seascapes' series which dates from 1965. The subject of the first works of this series was a foot or feet, which take the place of a full figure, set in a beach scene. Wesselman states that this particular setting was chosen because he 'had recently discovered vacations. A number of watercolour studies of the ocean and beach around Truro, Massachusetts, grew out of a two-week Cape Cod vacation. While these studies played only a small but direct part in the paintings, they did focus [my] attention and awareness on the sea' (*Wesselman*, p.45). The breast as a negative shape replaced the foot motif as the subject of the series from 1967 onwards,

notably in 'Seascape 19' 1967 (repr. in col., *Wesselman*, p.165). Wesselman's interest in the interplay of positive and negative shapes dates from the collages he was making in the early 60s in which there was a specific aesthetic goal which Wesselman describes as follows:

The ideal was competition rather than harmony – all parts of the painting competed throughout the painting, in many ways, in order to generate excitement and demand attention. One of the main tools besides colour was the use of positive and negative shapes or space. This is why [my] earliest nudes are often very curvy – to set up a strong positive – negative relationship between the positive shape – the body – and adjacent negative areas, so that both the adjacent area and the nude could break free and advance. If all positive and negative areas became as strong as possible, there would be no negative areas: the image could become one strong positive shape. What counted was that one final shape (*Wesselman*, pp.18–20).

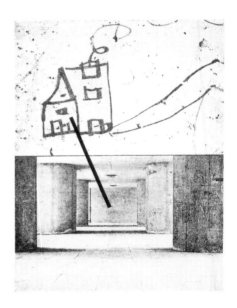

Stephen Willats born 1943

P 07947 **Wall Print** 1980

Offset lithograph 8 × 6 (203 × 152) on paper $11\frac{3}{4}$ × $10\frac{5}{8}$ (298 × 270), published by Jurgen Schweinebraden, East Berlin Inscribed 'Willats' on the back and 'Wall Print no.80' and '12' and 'edition specially made for Jurgen Schweinebraden in East

Berlin during June 1980. Edition
distributed throughout Eastern Europe'
Purchased from the artist (Grant-in-Aid)
1983

P 07968

Steve Willats is not a printmaker and this work is unique
in his oeuvre. It was produced at the request of the
Schweinebraden Gallery in East Berlin and followed a
successful exhibition of Willats's 'Lurky Place' project
held there in 1981.

The images on the print are a pair from a series
discovered and developed by Willats during his period
on a DAAD Scholarship in Berlin. He found that children in tower blocks had drawn on the concrete areas
around the base depictions of idealised homes and smil-
ing children. He contrasted one of these images with a
photograph of the tower block on which it was made.
Willats has published these pairs in 'Living in a concrete
house' (see *Leben in vorgegebenen Grenzen – 4 Inseln
in Berlin*, exhibition catalogue, Nationalgalerie, Berlin,
December 1980–January 1981; the graffiti house in
P 07947 ill.p.15, with the tower block in which it was
found). Willats prepared the print with two images
disposed on the sheet; the line that connects the images
was omitted since he anticipated that the completed
print would not be allowed into East Berlin. He
intended to carry the prints unfinished to the gallery
and add a line in letraset by hand to each of them. In
the event the border guards confiscated the unfinished
prints and Willats was left with only a few sheets that
he had decided not to take. As he wryly put it, 'the work
is about a wall and suffered at the hands of a wall'
(interview with the compiler, June 1986).

Wols 1913–1951

P 07948–   **Complete set of untitled**
07984   **etchings** *c.*1942–1951

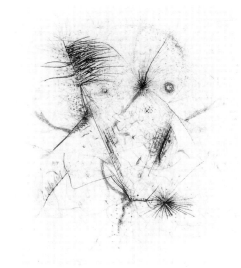

P 07969

Thirty-three etchings and drypoints in
range $2\frac{1}{2} \times 4$–$12\frac{1}{2} \times 9\frac{3}{4}$ (64 × 102–
324 × 248) on thin ivory Japan paper
approximately $15 \times 10\frac{1}{2}$ (381 × 267),
printed and published posthumously by
the artist's widow (edition size and printer
not known)
Not inscribed
Purchased from Reiss Cohen Inc., New
York (Grant-in-Aid) 1983

Lit: Will Grohmann, 'Das Graphische Werk
von Wols', *Quadrum*, 6, 1959, pp.95–118
(repr. with the exception of no.xxxv)

According to Grohmann, at the time of Wols's death
he left behind a number of copper plates which he had
been working on since *c.*1942. He states that the exact
number of these plates cannot be established since a
number were ruined or lost. In 1954 Wols's widow
commissioned the printing of thirty-five plates in an
edition of 6. At the time of Grohmann's article three of
these were in private collections and two belonged to
the widow and to the artist's brother. They were printed
on ivory coloured Velin Arches and stamped with the
stamp of the estate. In addition one set was made which
did not bear the stamp of the estate and was given to a
former schoolfriend of the artist. Some of these plates
had been printed during the artist's lifetime as illustrations to texts by Sartre, de Solier, Bryen and Artaud.
In 1955 the artist's widow commissioned the printing

[451]

of a further 10 sets on a thicker white paper. Three plates from the original set, according to Grohmann, were missing at the time of this printing, nos. X, XXIII and XXVII. These were printed by Georges Visat in Paris and numbered from 1 to 10. Each sheet was numbered in roman numerals and the set was numbered in arabic numerals. According to Dr Ewald Rathke (letter of 9 October 1985), a further edition was printed in 1962 by Lacourière et Frelaut, Paris in an edition of 50, each sheet stamped on the back with the stamp of the estate and numbered on the front out of 50. This edition contained impressions from the plates which Grohmann thought had been destroyed and included one plate which Grohmann had not recorded.

It is not possible to define exactly which edition P07948–07980 come from. They are printed on thin, ivory Japan paper and the set includes etching no.x. Therefore it cannot belong to the edition of 1955. The prints do not bear any inscriptions or stamps which suggests that they may be from the edition of 1953, and in particular be the set of prints given to a schoolfriend of Wols (see Grohmann, pp.95–6). However, Grohmann does not indicate that this set was printed on paper other than Velin Arches. The plates themselves are hard to date. According to Grohmann twenty were made before 1949.

The prints are in the manner of Wols's late works and are very finely and delicately etched. They depict images suggestive of botanical and biological forms as well as of faces, ships and landscapes.

Conservation of New Acquisitions

New acquisitions are examined by the Conservation Department to record their structure and condition and to carry out basic conservation treatment; including the mounting of works on paper, the provision or improvement of framing and the provision of storage/handling frames and cases for paintings and sculpture as necessary. Acquisitions which have received additional treatment are listed below.

GLOSSARY OF TREATMENTS

Support Treatments

BACKING: the reinforcement of an original paper support by lining with new tissue, paper or board.

BLEACHING: the chemical treatment of paper to remove stains and discolouration.

CONSOLIDATING: the reattachment of loose paint, delaminating boards or ruptured canvases usually with a suitable adhesive.

DE-ACIDIFYING: the chemical treatment of acidic paper, board or canvas to neutralise the acidity and provide an alkaline buffer against further deterioration.

FLATTENING: various treatments to remove serious distortions.

LINING: the attachment of a new fabric with an adhesive to the back of a deteriorated original canvas to reinforce and support it.

  LOOSE-LINING: the stretching of a new canvas behind the original to protect and support it; no adhesive being used to join the two.
  RE-LINING: the replacement of an existing lining with a new one.
  STRIP-LINING: the reinforcement/extension of the tacking edges of a canvas by lining with a suitable fabric and adhesive.

WASHING: the water treatment of paper to remove degradation products and imbibed dirt.

Surface Treatment

RESTORATION OF LOSSES: losses are filled and retouched with pigments bound in a medium chosen to be stable in appearance, removable and distinguishable from the original. Restoration is restricted to areas of loss and does not cover the remaining original.

SURFACE CLEANING: the removal of surface dirt and other accretions.

VARNISH/OLD RESTORATION REMOVAL: the removal of discoloured and deteriorated old varnishes and retouchings not applied by the artist.

VARNISH/REVARNISHING: the application of a surface coating to protect and enhance the surface selected for its stability, reversibility and appearance.

T03360 SICKERT
Surface cleaned

T03361 DELVAUX
Surface cleaned; paint consolidated

T03363 WYNTER
Restretched onto new stretcher

T03368 DERAIN
Varnish and old restorations removed; striplined; stretched onto new stretcher; losses restored; revarnished

T03373 KETTLE
Varnish and old restorations removed; relined; revarnished; losses restored

T03374 VAN DOESBURG
Surface cleaned

T03378 WAINWRIGHT
Surface cleaned; losses restored

T03379 JONES
Surface cleaned

T03383 RAYSSE
Structure repaired

T03395 LANDSEER
Surface cleaned; consolidated; losses restored; varnished

T03396 HART
Varnish removed; revarnished; losses restored

T03397 LIPCHITZ
Surface cleaned

T03398 WADSWORTH
Surface cleaned

T03399 HEPWORTH
Surface cleaned; split repaired

T03403 – T03405 KIEFER
Surface cleaned; striplined; stretched onto new
stretchers; losses restored

T03408 HAYTER
Striplined and restretched onto new stretcher; losses
restored

T03411 MCLEAN
Consolidated and tears repaired

T03419 BLAKE
Canvas reattached to board; old restoration removed
and damage restored

T03444 SALLE
Loose lined

T03447 WALTON
Varnish removed; revarnished; losses restored

T03454 LE BRUN
Restretched onto new stretcher

T03459 – T03463 BOSWELL
Surface cleaned; washed; bleached

T03466 GHEERAEDTS
Varnish, old restorations and overpaint removed;
revarnished; losses restored

T03537 ROY
Surface cleaned; losses restored

T03538 ANREP
Varnish removed; revarnished

T03543 ANDERTON
Varnish and old restorations removed; relined;
revarnished; losses restored

T03544 JONES
Surface cleaned; backed; losses restored

T03545 JONES
Surface cleaned; losses restored

T03546 JONES
Varnish removed

T03548 SICKERT
Varnish removed; revarnished

T03553 NOLAN
Surface cleaned; board consolidated

T03555 NOLAN
Consolidated; varnish removed; revarnished

T03556 NOLAN
Surface cleaned; board consolidated

T03557 NOLAN
Surface cleaned

T03558 NOLAN
Board consolidated; surface cleaned; losses restored

T03560 NOLAN
Surface cleaned; consolidated

T03561 GORE
Surface cleaned; stretching improved

T03564 DUFY
Paint consolidated; surface cleaned

T03568 MATISSE
Surface cleaned

T03569 MODIGLIANI
Varnish and old restorations removed; revarnished;
losses restored

T03572 PICASSO
Surface cleaned

T03574 RENOIR
Paint consolidated; old restorations and varnish
removed; revarnished; losses restored

T03592 MORRIS
Flattened; restretched onto new stretcher; varnished;
losses restored

T03593 DAUMIER
Varnish removed; revarnished; losses restored

T03595 KEMENY
Panel consolidated; surface cleaned; losses restored

T03597 CARLINE
Surface cleaned; stretching improved

T03600 BOMBERG and MICHELMORE
Consolidated; surface cleaned

T03602 MARLOW
Washed; bleached; de-acidified

T03607 CONSTABLE
Surface cleaned

T03611 AYRTON
Varnish removed; revarnished; losses restored

T03613 HOGARTH
Varnish and old restoration removed; revarnished;
losses restored

T03617 SOLOMON AFTER
Surface cleaned; backing removed; washed; bleached;
de-acidified

T03618 CHURCHYARD
Varnish removed; revarnished; losses restored

T03619 AND T03620 CHURCHYARD
Surface cleaned

T03621 CHURCHYARD
Surface cleaned; consolidated

T03626 MAITLAND
Surface cleaned

T03629 MAITLAND
Varnish and old restorations removed; revarnished;
losses restored

T03630 MAITLAND
Surface cleaned

T03631 MAITLAND
Varnish removed; revarnished; losses restored

T03632 MAITLAND
Varnish removed; revarnished; losses restored

T03635 MAITLAND
Varnish removed; revarnished; losses restored

T03636 MAITLAND
Retouching modified; varnished

T03637 MAITLAND
Surface cleaned; varnished

T03639 SCHUFFENECKER
Stains removed

T03642 SCHUFFENECKER
Backing removed

T03644–T03646 STUDD
Surface cleaned

T03647 MAITLAND
Surface cleaned

T03650 KELLY
Varnish removed; revarnished

T03651 KELLY
Surface cleaned

T03652 KELLY
Varnish removed; revarnished

T03653 KELLY
Surface cleaned

T03656 TIBBLE
Surface cleaned; consolidated; losses restored

T03660 HERON
Surface cleaned; consolidated; losses restored

T03661–T03663 PITCHFORTH
Surface cleaned

T03664 PITCHFORTH
Surface cleaned; stains removed

T03665 WILSON
Varnish and old restorations removed; revarnished;
losses restored

T03671 RAINER
Loose lined

T03677 JONES
Surface cleaned

T03678 MASON
Damage restored

T03683 GRIMSHAW
Varnish removed; consolidated and lined; revarnished;
losses restored

T03691 MIRO
Striplined and restretched onto new stretcher

T03693 LANYON
Loose lined onto new stretcher

T03695 BRUS
Surface cleaned

T03698 GILBERT
Paint consolidated; surface cleaned; losses restored

T03701 HOYLAND
Surface cleaned; flattened; loose lined

T03706 LATHAM
Construction reinforced

T03707 ERNST
Consolidated

T03713 CLARKE
Repaired

T03720 DOBSON
Surface cleaned

T03769 SOTO
Surface cleaned; repaired, losses restored

T03770 SOTO
Repaired; surface cleaned; losses restored

T03778–T03781 STUBBS
Surface cleaned; washed. bleached

T03784–T03788 BARRY
Surface cleaned; washed; bleached

T03789 LESLIE
Surface cleaned; losses restored

T03795 WILLATS
Surface cleaned

T03798 KOPPEL
Loose lined onto new stretcher

T03810 CLOUGH
Surface cleaned; consolidated

T03817 ROSSETTI
Surface cleaned

T03820 NASH
Surface cleaned

T03821 WILKIE
Surface cleaned; washed; de-acidified

T03823 TINGUELY
Repaired and losses restored

T03824 DE SAINT-PHALLE
Surface cleaned; consolidated

T03827 AND T03828 HOGARTH
Washed; bleached; de-acidified

T 03829 AND T 03830 KOKOSCHKA
Surface cleaned

T 03831 MORRIS
Surface cleaned; losses restored

T 03832 MONNINGTON
Backing removed; holes repaired

T 03833 MONNINGTON
Surface cleaned; restretched onto new stretcher

T 03834 KOKOSCHKA
Surface cleaned

T 03836 CRAXTON
Consolidated

T 03837 CRAXTON
Surface cleaned; consolidated; losses restored

T 03838 CRAXTON
Surface cleaned; consolidated; striplined; loose lined
onto new stretcher

T 03843 AND T 03844 STUBBS
Surface cleaned; washed; bleached